A History of Modern Psychology

A History of Modern Psychology provides students with an engaging, comprehensive, and global history of psychological science, from the birth of the field to the present. It examines the attempts to establish psychology as a science in several countries and epochs. The text expertly draws on a vast knowledge of the field in the United States, Britain, Germany, France, Russia, and Scandinavia, as well as on author Per Saugstad's keen study of neighboring sciences, including physiology, evolutionary biology, psychiatry, and neurology. Offering a unique global perspective on the development of psychology as an empirical science, this text is an ideal introduction to the field for students and other readers interested in the history of modern psychology.

Per Saugstad was a Norwegian psychologist. He served as professor of psychology at the University of Oslo from 1967 until 1990, when he retired.

A History of Modern Psychology

Per Saugstad
University of Oslo

CAMBRIDGE
UNIVERSITY PRESS

CAMBRIDGE
UNIVERSITY PRESS

University Printing House, Cambridge CB2 8BS, United Kingdom

One Liberty Plaza, 20th Floor, New York, NY 10006, USA

477 Williamstown Road, Port Melbourne, VIC 3207, Australia

314–321, 3rd Floor, Plot 3, Splendor Forum, Jasola District Centre, New Delhi - 110025, India

79 Anson Road, #06-04/06, Singapore 079906

Cambridge University Press is part of the University of Cambridge.

It furthers the University's mission by disseminating knowledge in the pursuit of
education, learning, and research at the highest international levels of excellence.

www.cambridge.org
Information on this title: www.cambridge.org/9781107109896
DOI: 10.1017/9781316272442

© Per Saugstad 2018

This publication is in copyright. Subject to statutory exception
and to the provisions of relevant collective licensing agreements,
no reproduction of any part may take place without the written
permission of Cambridge University Press.

First published 2018

Printed and bound in the United Kingdom by Clays Ltd, Elcograf S.p.A.

A catalogue record for this publication is available from the British Library

Library of Congress Cataloging-in-Publication data
Names: Saugstad, Per, author.
Title: A history of modern psychology / Per Saugstad.
Description: New York : Cambridge University Press, 2018. | Includes bibliographical references and index.
Identifiers: LCCN 2017058256 | ISBN 9781107109896 (hardback)
Subjects: LCSH: Psychology – History – 20th century. | Psychology – History – 19th century.
   | BISAC: PSYCHOLOGY / History.
Classification: LCC BF105 .S28 2018 | DDC 150.9–dc23
LC record available at https://lccn.loc.gov/2017058256

ISBN 978-1-107-10989-6 Hardback
ISBN 978-1-107-52546-7 Paperback

Additional resources for this publication at http://www.cambridge.org/9781107109896

Cambridge University Press has no responsibility for the persistence or accuracy
of URLs for external or third-party internet websites referred to in this publication,
and does not guarantee that any content on such websites is, or will remain,
accurate or appropriate.

Contents

Illustrations

Foreword

When my father, Per Saugstad, died at ninety years old, he left the manuscript for the present volume, the fruit of several decades of hard work. The book first appeared in Norwegian in 1998, and in 2009 in a second edition, which in fact was a completely revised text. During the revision he had prepared a parallel English manuscript, for which, however, he was unable to find a renowned international publisher before his demise in 2010.

A History of Modern Psychology is motivated by a concern to put psychology on a scientific footing. My father believed the schools of psychology have replaced one another without drawing sufficiently on what was good and useful, or mistaken, in the preceding school. His idea is that collaborators in the field should guide their work by greater familiarity with the attempts in modern time to establish psychology as a science. Lecturing on the history of psychology at the University of Oslo for twenty-five years, he studied these attempts in depth, and by seeking the experts in psychology and in adjacent fields, at home and abroad. The present publication reflects this broad and detailed scholarship in the treatment of the major schools of psychology in Germany, Britain, France, Russia, and the United States from about 1850 to the near present.

My father began his academic carrier in the humanities, achieving a master's degree in English, German, and Norwegian language and literature in 1945. He published a book on the Norwegian poets Henrik Wergeland and J. S. Welhaven, and an anthology of Norwegian poetry. In the late 1940s, the sociologists and social psychologists Paul F. Lazarsfeld and David Krech came to Norway to recruit students to study social science or psychology in the United States, and my father was encouraged to apply. Having become interested in psychological aspects of poetry, he applied to the psychology program at the University of Chicago, and went on to receive a PhD in psychology in 1952. Later, he often stressed how fortunate he was to have been taught and supervised at the University of Chicago by some of the leading figures in American psychology at the time – E. C. Toleman, L. L. Thurstone, W. Köhler, and A. A. Riesen.

In Chicago, my father had become interested in experimental psychology, and upon his return to the University of Oslo in 1952, he conducted experimental work on problem solving and perception. However, the contrast between the psychology in Chicago and in Oslo was notable, as the psychology department at the University of Oslo at that time was very much dominated by psychoanalysis. In this environment there was little interest in, and indeed little appreciation of, his American approach to psychology. He, on the other hand, found psychoanalysis unscientific as well as authoritarian, and soon he was embroiled in a disagreement with his psychoanalytic colleagues about the essence of the psychological discipline, which escalated into a fierce battle. To me and my siblings, Tone, Ola, Didrik, and Anne, this feud appeared as David's fight against Goliath. My father did become a senior lecturer in 1962, and in 1967 a full professor at the University of Oslo, where he supervised a large number of doctors of psychology during a long career.

The conviction that psychology was not yet a science turned my father's work from experimental psychology in the 1950s to a theoretical search for the foundation that would enable psychology to become a science. The search resulted in four monographs grappling with this problem: *An Inquiry into the Foundations of Psychology* (1965); *A Theory of Communication and Use of Language: Foundations for the Study of Psychology* (1977); *A Theory of Language and Understanding* (1980); and *Language: A Theory of its Structure and Use* (1989). These books express his enduring interest in human cognition, and the relation of language and thought in particular. They also mark a gradual development in his ideas on the appropriate foundation of the scientific study of psychology – from an attempt at reconciling phenomenology and behaviorism, via a phase much influenced by Ludwig Wittgenstein's later philosophy of language, and culminating in an approach to psychology adopting a Darwinian framework. I am under the impression that he developed his biological approach to psychology largely independently of what is now called evolutionary psychology, and he later stressed that it differs significantly from the way in which the latter approach applies evolutionary biology to psychological phenomena. Though he retained his belief in a Darwinian approach to psychology to his death, he clearly thought that such an approach should be informed by the history of psychology.

My father's main interest in life was always problems of an intellectual nature – in psychology, philosophy, biology and the natural sciences, and politics – and we, his children, became sparring partners from early on. Yet he was, of course, much more than an academic, and alongside the seriousness in intellectual matters he had a youthful playfulness that he retained as long as he lived. He loved swimming and hiking in the woods and the mountains. While he could at times be stern and edgy, especially in the difficult years of his battle at the University of Oslo, he was also gentle, kind, and generous, not caring much about accumulating personal wealth. He never obtained a driver's license, and traveled often by public transportation, taking the opportunity to engage his fellow travelers in spontaneous conversations, which is rather uncommon in Norway. My impression was that his fellow travelers appreciated these episodes just as much as he did.

Perhaps this blend of intellectual curiosity, playfulness, open-minded friendliness, honesty, and rigor in research and thought, is what made him a highly respected teacher at the University of Oslo. And amongst his colleagues, in Oslo and abroad, he was widely recognized as an uncompromising truth seeker, always measuring his own work by the highest academic standards.

A History of Modern Psychology reflects all the above: my father's broad academic background, his great delight in theoretical thinking, and his high academic standards and unrelenting questioning of widely accepted "truths." On behalf of the family, I want to express our gratitude to Cambridge University Press for making his life's work available to an international audience, and I hope his book will achieve for psychology what he aimed for.

Jens Saugstad

1

• •

Introduction

In this chapter, I shall first give a short description of psychology as an empirical science as it appears at the beginning of the twenty-first century. Then, I shall discuss how a study of the history of psychology can contribute to our understanding of present-day psychology. Further, I shall account for the way (I believe) psychology as an empirical science originated. Finally, before I present the plan for the book, I shall discuss reasons why empirical psychology over time has undergone changes. In this discussion, I shall be particularly concerned with the problem of assessing progress in psychology as an empirical science.

A Short Characterization of Present-Day Psychology

Here at the beginning of the twenty-first century, psychology as an empirical science has grown into a broad, diversified field of study. We can gain an impression of its breadth by noting that it borders on the biological sciences on the one hand and the social sciences on the other.

    Psychology is a theoretical as well as an applied science, and also a profession incorporating a number of specialties. In a wide variety of areas it has produced knowledge useful for the solution of theoretical problems as well as problems of practical and social life. However, so far, psychology has hardly produced comprehensive theories or scientifically acceptable principles of a general nature. Thus, the discipline appears highly fragmented.

The Present Approach to the Study of the History of Psychology

The attempt to establish psychology as an empirical science raised several questions that were not easily answered and that soon became controversial. Questions such as what is the relationship between mind and brain, between human and animal behavior, and between genetic endowment and environmental influence (nature and nurture) emerged at the inception of the discipline and have remained controversial to this day. At an early stage, disagreement arose about whether we should conceive of psychology as the study of mental experiences or the study of behavior. In what sense should we regard as mental experiences various types of nonconscious processes, such as the subconscious and the unconscious? How do society and culture influence human thinking and behavior? This last question emerged later in psychology's history and is of central importance for the advancement of psychology as an empirical science.

When controversial questions such as these have been satisfactorily answered, psychology will be considerably advanced. I believe a critical, historical examination of them can contribute to their conceptual clarification. For this reason, I give the study of its history a central place in the general study of psychology. Ernst Mayr (1982, p. 16), who called my attention to the prominent role played by the historical examination of long-standing controversies in a field of science, stated the point in his history of evolutionary biology as follows:

Even today's controversies have a root that usually goes far back in time. It is precisely the historical study of such controversies that often contributes materially to a conceptual clarification and thus makes the ultimate solution possible.

By clarifying the available concepts and creating new ones, scientists make their thinking and communication more efficient. As James Conant (1947/1951) and Mayr (1982) have argued, the best way to understand a science is to study how its main concepts are used. I agree with them on this point, and in this book I shall undertake a detailed examination of how some of the most influential psychological researchers have used their main concepts, including careful descriptions of their research.

My concentration on the scientific concepts does not suggest that I believe the invention of new techniques is not significant. Progress often comes with new techniques, but I believe that if new techniques do not result in new or improved concepts, their introduction does not represent important scientific progress.

How Did Empirical Psychology Originate?

A book on the history of psychology written by Harvard professor Edwin Boring in 1929 greatly influenced the ideas psychologists have had of the history of their discipline. To get an overview of the problems related to the question of how psychology originated, let us take Boring's book as our starting point.

Edwin Boring's Book on the History of Psychology

Boring (1929/1950) represented the origin of psychology as the convergence of two lines drawn through the scientific and intellectual history of the West: One through philosophy and the other through physiology. In his view, the lines converged in the study of perception started by German researchers around 1850 and eventually met in the psychological studies of Wilhelm Wundt. According to Boring, Wundt was the founder of experimental psychology, and, slightly altering Boring's account, several historians have dated the beginning of scientific psychology to Wundt's establishment of the world's first experimental psychological laboratory in Leipzig in 1879. According to Boring, we can regard experimental psychology as having been founded by Wundt in 1879 and as having spread first throughout Germany and subsequently to other European nations and to the United States. Boring's account of the origin of German experimental psychology, published fifty years after the establishment of the Leipzig laboratory, was comprehensive, yet at the same time outstanding in its simplicity. It remained unchallenged for nearly half a century.

To Boring, scientific psychology primarily meant experimental psychology, and his book was entitled *A History of Experimental Psychology* (1929/1950). Actually, it dealt with all areas regarded as belonging to scientific psychology during Boring's time. British comparative animal psychology, based on field studies, was included with the (doubtful) justification that animal psychology belongs to the laboratory; studies of individual differences and personality psychology were included because they are based on testing, and testing could be seen as a type of experimental psychology. Even stranger was the rationale for including clinical psychology: It might, said Boring in his foreword, become experimental.

History as University Politics

Boring had been appointed professor at Harvard a few years prior to writing his history. During the time he was working on the book, considerable controversy raged over the nature of psychology, both at Harvard and at other US universities. Behaviorism was about to become one of the dominant schools, and psychoanalysis was gaining ground in psychology and psychiatry. Boring himself represented the 1800s view of psychology, psychology as the study of consciousness; in his own empirical research he carried on the German tradition in experimental psychology. His teacher, Edward Titchener, to whom Boring's book was dedicated, was also a representative of this tradition.

Boring had additional goals. By highlighting German experimental psychology, he could, as John O'Donnell (1979) notes, claim that psychology first had to develop as an empirical theoretical discipline before it could become an applied discipline. Further, by claiming that Wundt had liberated psychology from philosophy, Boring could advocate his view of psychology as an independent discipline, a view the Harvard philosophers did not share. His book, therefore, had obvious university–political aims, as Mitchell Ash (1983) noted in a survey of the US study of the history of psychology.

Boring's account of the origin of psychology gave a useful perspective on the field. However, as later historians have shown, several of the questions he dealt with could be answered differently. The following three questions need a more careful consideration: How is psychology related to philosophy?; How is it related to other natural science disciplines?; and Where did it originate?

Philosophy and Scientific Empirical Psychology

In Western civilization, several problems of a psychological nature have been subjected to systematic examination, first by the Greek philosophers of antiquity, and then by the philosophers of the seventeenth, eighteenth, and nineteenth centuries. The latter debated, among other things, the relationship between body and mind, feelings and reason, sensation and perception, and perception and learning based upon associations, as well as remembering, innate and learned abilities, and the relationship between reflex-like (automatic) and voluntary movement. At the beginning of the 1800s, philosophers also focused on the problem of unconscious processes and studied psychological processes, and several works on psychology were written. Only occasionally, however, did philosophers' interest in psychology result in empirical investigations.

As early as the 1700s, there were thinkers interested in expanding science to include psychology. Towards the latter part of that century, Immanuel Kant (1724–1804) discussed in detail the question of whether psychology could be converted into a discipline similar to physics. Like most psychologists of the 1700s and 1800s, Kant understood a psychological study to be an investigation of mental processes. He concluded that a study of consciousness could not be similar to a study of physics because, among other reasons, mental processes could not be the subject of an experimental inquiry based on quantification and mathematics.

Kant's successor to the professorship in Königsberg, Johann Friedrich Herbart (1776–1841), was more open to the idea of a scientific psychology, although he agreed with Kant that psychology could not be converted into an experimental science. Herbart held that consciousness contains entities in fixed dynamic relationships to one another, and these relationships *could* be expressed mathematically. Consequently, mental processes could be subjected to mathematical treatment, and in this respect the study of psychology could be regarded as scientific. Herbart presented his thoughts about psychology in two widely read books, *Lehrbuch der Psychologie* (*Textbook of Psychology*) in 1816 and *Psychologie als Wissenschaft* (*Psychology as a Science*) in 1824–1825.

Some years after the publication of Herbart's book on psychology as a science, the French philosopher Auguste Comte (1798–1857) discussed the historical development of science in the Western world. Comte became the main representative of a broad intellectual movement known as positivism. I shall return to Comte in Chapter 2, but for now we can note that he rejected the idea that the introspective study of mental processes could be developed into an empirical science. On this point, he was opposed by John Stuart Mill (1806–1873), who argued that it *is* possible to undertake an experimental, scientific study of consciousness. Mill even claimed that by using experimental methods, the British philosophers of the empiricist tradition had arrived at scientific laws stating how associations between ideas were formed. In an influential work, *A System of Logic*, published in 1843, he further proposed that the psychological study of consciousness could be widened to include the study of human character, or what we today call personality.

Apart from Mill, none of the more influential philosophers in the first half of the 1800s wholeheartedly supported the idea of turning psychology into an empirical science. I think we can therefore conclude that the time was not yet ripe for an empirical scientific psychology.

During the latter half of the 1800s, however, the intellectual climate became more favorable to the idea. An increasing number of philosophers were then attracted to the notion that psychological problems could be investigated by empirical methods. Positivism arose as a strong movement within Western thinking, and a central belief in positivist thinking was that empirical scientific research could be expanded to include problems of philosophy.

Boring insisted that the establishment of Wundt's laboratory in 1879 was an expression of a new and more favorable attitude to the idea of developing psychology as an empirical science. However, more dubious was his claim that empirical psychology had thereby become independent of philosophy. Fifty years later, as we have seen, it was still important to champion this belief, and in fact the question of how empirical psychology is related to philosophy persisted to the end of the 1900s. In 1979, at the centenary of the establishment of the Leipzig laboratory in 1879, one of the most prominent methodologists of the day, Sigmund Koch, raised it again. Let us look at his view of empirical psychology.

Sigmund Koch's View of the History of Psychology

As the director of a large-scale project sponsored by the American Psychological Association and the National Science Foundation, and carried out in the 1950s and early 1960s, Sigmund Koch (1959–1963) held a central position in the discussion of methodological and historical problems in psychology. In this project, ninety leading psychologists of the time wrote reports describing their research and evaluating progress in their particular fields. Their detailed and thorough reports were published in six comprehensive volumes. As Daniel Robinson (1998) and Michael Wertheimer (1998) have noted, the project shed considerable light on the history of psychology as well as on present-day psychology. After examining the reports, Koch concluded that the concepts used by the theorists lacked clarity and precision, and that none of the theories discussed were acceptable.

Koch was particularly critical of the comprehensive theories from the first half of the 1900s, such as psychoanalysis, Gestalt psychology, and various versions of behaviorism. Unlike many earlier critics, he had soft spots for none of the theories, and he revealed fundamental weaknesses in all of them. Although he was far from alone, he probably contributed considerably to the maturing of psychology as a science by installing a more critical attitude to psychological work. After 1960, few attempts were made to construct comprehensive psychological theories for the rest of the century. The attitude seems to have been that psychology was not yet ripe for this task. Thus, we can see Koch's project of the mid-1960s as a manifestation of an important change in psychologists' attitude to their discipline.

Twenty-two years after Koch had finished his first large project, he and David Leary (Koch and Leary, 1985) edited a new collection of essays assessing contemporary psychology. For this collection, Koch (1985a,b) wrote an essay and an afterword in which he evaluated progress up to about 1980. As before, he was highly critical of the belief that psychology had made progress as a scientific, empirical endeavor. However, he felt psychology was ready to make some progress.

According to Koch (1985b), there were several reasons psychology had not progressed as an empirical science. One was a disdain for nonexperimental methods, and another was the idea that the experimental method is applicable only to certain areas of the field. The introduction of the experimental method had, therefore, not significantly advanced psychology as an empirical science. Nor had attempts at introducing the methods of the natural sciences resulted in a definite break with philosophy. In contrast to Boring, who wanted to show that empirical psychology should be considered independent of philosophy, Koch (1985b, p. 944) insisted that psychology had never been separated from it:

Our problems, concepts, terminology, questions have grown out of the history of philosophy; and any position, theory, model, procedural decision, research strategy, or lawlike statement that we assert presupposes philosophical commitments.

According to Koch, empirical psychology was not founded by the establishment of Wundt's laboratory in 1879. Nor could it be said to have been established at any other point during the 1800s or 1900s. I believe Koch was right, but in discussing the relationship between psychology and philosophy, he overlooked the fact that since the Renaissance, philosophy and conceptions of science had been intertwined. Thus, for example, Descartes contributed to the new directions in empirical science at the same time as he worked out his own philosophy, and we can see the philosophies of Hume, Kant, and other influential thinkers as responses to progress in natural science. Moreover, Koch overlooked that in the mid-1800s a change had taken place in philosophy, making it more open to the idea that philosophical problems might be investigated by the methods of empirical science.

Koch was right, however, in pointing out that in the universities the separation of psychology from philosophy was a far slower process than Boring suggests. Actually, in German and most other European universities, the study of psychology formed part of philosophy until the mid-1900s. On the other hand, prominent pioneers in German experimental psychology, such as Hermann Ebbinghaus and Georg Elias Müller, attempted to develop psychology independently of philosophy. Although many of the pioneer US psychologists had a close tie to philosophy, empirical psychology there was treated as a discipline independent of philosophy earlier than in Europe. Several early US psychologists were appointed professors of psychology without responsibility for the development of philosophy.

Expansion in Natural Science

In his account, I feel Koch gave too little weight to the effect of nineteenth-century progress in natural science that made the idea of empirical psychology more acceptable. Development in physiology was rapidly accelerating, and from 1860 on, surprising findings were being made about the functions of the brain. This stimulated interest in the empirical exploration of psychological problems, to which we shall return in Chapter 2. However, other important events also took place in natural science. In 1859, Charles Darwin presented documentation to convince a majority of biologists that biological evolution had occurred. This provided a new approach to the study of human nature, which led to a comparable psychological study of animals as well as to a study of heredity. Further, progress in neurology and psychiatry threw light on important psychological problems, and a clinical psychology emerged in France and Austria that originated in these advances. So much was new in the study of psychology in the latter half of the 1800s that I believe we may call it a new era in the field. Particularly new was the use of the procedures of natural science. In contrast to Koch, I believe these procedures have led to more or less continuous progress from the mid-1800s to the present, and I shall trace this progress through the history of psychology.

The idea of scientific psychology was not new with Wundt, and several researchers before him had undertaken experimental work on psychological problems. Moreover, Wundt had not consistently – and perhaps never – held that the study of psychology should be carried out independently of philosophy. As we will see in Chapter 3, it is an oversimplification to regard him as the founder of experimental psychology. I think Koch made an important correction of Boring's account of the role played by Wundt.

Where Did Psychology Originate?

We saw above that Boring described German experimental psychology as having one root in philosophy and one in physiology. This gave an adequate picture. But when he went on to describe the development of empirical scientific psychology as a branching out of German experimental psychology to European countries as well as to the United States, the picture became seriously distorted. When we examine matters more carefully, we see the differences in the types of problems studied by the early researchers, and how slight the influence of one country on another often was. Psychology in Great Britain, France, Austria, Russia, and the United States was widely different from German experimental psychology. Thus, scientific psychology was not the coherent discipline we meet in Boring's book, and Wundt played a far different role than that Boring ascribed to him.

We gain a better perspective on the origin and further development of empirical psychology by recognizing that it originated in several countries at almost the same time. The early psychologists had a common background of ideas; they believed in the importance of science and in the possibility of expanding it to include the study of psychology. However, they had different research interests, were linked to different research traditions, and on the whole worked independently of each other. These cultural and research differences led to substantial differences in their conceptions of psychology.

The Emergence of Scientific Psychology

Next I present a survey of the approaches to scientific psychology adopted in different countries and – to the extent that it is possible – describe them in chronological order.

Germany came first. Here, the study of sensory physiology and perception flourished about 1860, headed by Hermann von Helmholtz. In an extensive work published in 1874, Wundt described a number of problems that could be studied from the point of view of psychology as well as physiology, and he suggested that *physiological psychology* should be instituted as a study in the natural sciences. As we have already seen, he established the first laboratory in the world for experimental work in psychology some years later, in 1879. Conceiving of psychology as the study of consciousness, he extended the study of perception to include the study of attention and feeling. Some years later Ebbinghaus laid the foundation for an experimental study of verbal learning and memory.

In *Great Britain*, scientific psychology emerged in a completely different manner. There, the major inspiration was the theory of evolution, which gave an entirely new perspective to the study of the nature of human beings and laid the foundation for a comparative study of psychology. In 1872, Darwin published his highly influential studies on the expression of emotions and, in 1877, his notes taken thirty-seven years earlier on the development of his eldest son from birth to early childhood. These notes were an important contribution to modern infant and child psychology. They inspired Darwin's friend, the British–German physiologist William Preyer, who in 1882 published an influential book on developmental psychology based on extensive and careful studies of one of his sons. Moreover, inspired by the theory of evolution, Darwin's cousin Francis Galton laid the foundation for the psychological study of heredity. Galton constructed tests for measuring individual differences, thereby initiating the psychological study of individual differences and personality.

The development of psychology in *Russia* was entirely different again. Russian psychology was based on a view of the nervous system as the integration of different types of reflexes. As early as the beginning of the 1860s, this view had been elaborated by the Russian physiologist Ivan Setchenov, but not until the turn of the century did it form the basis for empirical investigations carried out by Ivan Pavlov and Vladimir Bekhterev. The Russians hoped to create what they believed to be an objective psychology, a psychology based on observations of an objective nature. This was a form of behaviorism.

In *France*, psychology emerged in the 1880s and 1890s as part of the neurological and psychiatric research that was then flourishing there. This was a clinical psychology, oriented towards practical life. Apart from pathological conditions, the early French psychologists took an interest in all forms of unusual mental conditions, and the study of hypnosis was a key interest of theirs. Two prominent names in early French psychology are Pierre Janet and Alfred Binet.

In *Austria*, inspired by the development of neurology and psychiatry, as well as by French clinical psychology, Sigmund Freud promoted a psychodynamic psychology. This psychology began not in consciousness but in ideas Freud claimed were unconscious. Psychoanalysis therefore conflicted with German experimental psychology and also with French clinical psychology. More or less independently of Freud, two other neurologists, Alfred Adler in Austria and Carl Jung in Switzerland, developed other versions of clinical and personality psychology. These were influenced by an entirely different philosophical tradition than the one that had inspired German experimental psychology.

These were the developments in Europe. But what of the United States? It seems to have been widely accepted that psychology was developed in the United States almost as early as in Europe. This conclusion needs some qualifications.

As we shall see in Chapter 11, early US psychologists produced a number of ideas that later influenced empirical psychology, and the American William James (1890) gave psychology a new and modern direction in an extensive, critical textbook. Only four years after Wundt established his laboratory in Leipzig, the first psychological laboratory was founded in the United States, and, as Ernest Hilgard (1987) notes in his *Psychology in America*, forty-two others had been set up by 1900. These performed studies in comparative animal psychology and child development.

Yet I believe an examination of the empirical research of the early US psychologists reveals that it was lacking in originality and in support from its neighboring disciplines: Physiology, evolutionary biology, neurology, and psychiatry. The experimental work is with few exceptions an elaboration of ideas of the early German experimentalists, and hardly any US study has comparable originality and quality. The same seems to be true for comparative animal psychology. The studies performed are mainly elaborations of work carried out in Great Britain, and the studies in child psychology in the early years are based on British and German ideas. Thus, while we may easily be led to believe that psychology in the United States developed in a similar way to that of the European countries, we must qualify the point.

When empirical psychology was being developed in Europe, the United States had just begun to build its scientific institutions. Its scientists and science administrators looked to Europe for models, and ideas were to a large extent imported from Europe, including German experimental psychology, British comparative psychology, and to some extent French clinical psychology. As a result, though it was lacking in originality, empirical psychology in the United States acquired a far broader foundation than it had in any of the European countries. But not until the 1920s and 1930s did it begin to flower.

All the research traditions I have listed above are incorporated in the modern, empirical study of psychology. While the diverse empirical research traditions originated in Europe, the organization of them into one field of study seems mainly to have been the achievement of the American psychologists, who in the 1920s also added to the field the study of social psychology. Further, they developed the study of personality into a quantitative pursuit and helped broaden the definition of psychology to include behavior.

As we shall see in the chapters to follow, not until several decades had passed was psychology organized into a coherent study. This is understandable when we consider that a number of highly different empirical research traditions had to be integrated into it, requiring far more than taking over the procedures worked out in the various research traditions. The ideas underlying the traditions were complex, and it took time to understand more concretely their implications for psychological theory.

Why Is Psychology Changing?

Historians have found a number of reasons why empirical psychology has changed from its inception at the latter half of the 1800s to the present. One is the changes taking place in the society in which psychology is studied and practiced.

For example, like all other scientific enterprises, psychology depends upon society's interest in recruiting students and obtaining salaries, laboratories, and financial support for research. As we shall see in Chapter 6, in Great Britain in the 1800s, many researchers financed their studies by private means, and in the United States, many larger research projects were financed through funds established by wealthy people. Today that support comes from universities and scientific institutions. However, these are not the only sources of funding. National governments, for example, are a significant source of funding.

As another example, from its early years, particularly in the United States but also in Europe, one of psychology's aims was to contribute to the planning of society and particularly to assist people in adjusting better to social life. As society changes, its need for the help of psychology also changes.

Finally, as Thomas Leahey (2004) said, "scientists are human beings socialized within a given culture." We can often see that in particular periods, despite individual differences, members of a society concentrate on specific values and views of ethics, religion, science, and so on. This is naturally true of psychologists too. Even if it is sometimes difficult to identify the influence of society and culture on psychologists' conceptions of their subject, this is what historians must try to do. For instance, many scholars have claimed that people in the United States place greater emphasis on individuality and have a more optimistic view of life than, say, Europeans. This applies equally to American psychologists. General historical accounts of the history of psychology should, therefore, include attempts at describing the relationship between society and culture on the one hand and psychology on the other. Leahey has pointed out many interesting relationships of this nature.

We have already seen that psychology is also influenced by progress in other natural science disciplines, primarily physiology, neurology, evolutionary biology, and genetics.

Further, philosophy has exerted – and still exerts – an influence on psychology. Other disciplines may influence subject matter as well as procedures. And closely related to these changes is progress in technology. For example, the development of computers has had a strong impact upon the thinking of psychologists in the latter half of the 1900s.

Research is a collective endeavor, and scholars develop their thinking and skills in interaction with others. They operate in a collective and a tradition. At the same time, it is reasonable to believe that a discipline changes as a result of the efforts of particular individuals. As John Benjafield (1996) has maintained, this view might also be pedagogically appropriate. By undertaking careful studies of the lives of historical figures who influenced our thinking about psychological phenomena, we can shed light on their work. I shall, however, concentrate on research carried out by the psychologists dealt with here and only occasionally go more deeply into their lives.

Progress in Empirical Psychology

Psychology has also undergone changes as a result of progress in research and practice; in other words, psychologists have learned from their activities. Because the aim of scientists *as* scientists is to advance their field of study, this is naturally the cause of change that interests them most.

For three main reasons, however, it is difficult to assess progress in psychology. First, progress is entangled with other causes of change, and it is difficult to separate the two. For this reason, I shall discuss progress in the wider context of the general history of psychology. Second, everyday life is based upon the extensive psychological knowledge we accumulate throughout our lives. To assess progress, we must be able to decide whether some idea or position is new, and this is often difficult because our everyday psychological knowledge is extensive as well as diffuse. Third, there are no simple criteria for assessment of progress in empirical research. I shall elaborate the second and third points; my concern is with ideas and empirical procedures, and not primarily with the creativity of the individual researchers.

Scientific Psychology Has a Basis in Everyday Knowledge

In his criticism of the belief that psychology had emerged at a particular time, Koch (1985a) started by pointing out that psychological knowledge is as old as mankind; being human implies having psychological knowledge. Like Koch, Daniel Robinson (1995) has maintained that our predecessors must have faced psychological problems similar to ours:

Our distant ancestors, no less than we, wrestled with the problems of social organization, child rearing, competition, authority, individual differences, and personal safety. Solving these problems required insights, no matter how untutored, into the psychological dimensions of life.

When we reflect a little on what is understood by psychological knowledge, we realize that all people who develop normally in interaction with their physical and social environments will acquire considerable knowledge of psychological states and reactions.

They will gain knowledge about the workings of the senses, about remembering, and thinking; they will have an understanding of emotions such as joy, love, sorrow, anger, fear, and jealousy; and they will learn about their own actions and those of other people. They will also acquire knowledge of what to expect from children at different ages and the changes people go through in old age. Moreover, they will have a vast knowledge of social relationships between human beings. They will know of ties between friends, married couples, and parents and children, and they will learn to respect or fear those with economic or political power. As members of a particular society and a specific culture, they will also share the knowledge accumulated in customs, moral rules, laws, religion, and art. Those in certain professions – for instance, teachers, priests, nurses, doctors, lawyers, and persons in the military and businesses – will accumulate a fund of knowledge of a psychological nature. Thus, from their personal experiences and as members of a particular society, all normally equipped people will possess an extensive psychological knowledge.

Clearly, we cannot attribute knowledge we have gained as a result of growing up in a given society to progress made in empirical psychology. For example, infants have ties of a psychological nature to their mother, which they manifest by smiling when she picks them up and holds them, or by clinging to her and crying when she leaves. Adults have known of these ties long before the establishment of scientific psychology. Therefore, to claim progress on behalf of scientific psychology, researchers must demonstrate that they have produced knowledge that goes beyond this everyday knowledge. As we shall see in Chapter 19, this has not turned out to be as simple as psychologists anticipated.

No Simple Criteria for the Assessment of Progress in Empirical Research

To advance knowledge, scientists carefully systematize the phenomena to be studied, extend and refine observations, undertake measurements, apply mathematics, state hypotheses relating phenomena to each other as explicitly and precisely as possible, note what can support or falsify their hypotheses, design experiments to determine causal relations, attempt to find relationships of a general nature between the phenomena studied, and search for adequate explanations of them.

Improvement in any of these procedures may represent scientific progress. However, improvements in procedure may also restrict the range of phenomena so that the use of the study is reduced. For example, by making observations more precise or by introducing measurements, we may narrow their range. Similarly, experiments may allow better control of relevant conditions but limit the number of phenomena studied. Moreover, to ascertain that one approach to a study of some problem is better than another, we cannot concentrate only on improvements in procedures. We must also consider that one approach may better agree with current knowledge at the time.

The fact that there is no simple way of assessing progress in psychology, and that assessments often call for subjective or arbitrary decisions, does not mean we cannot measure it. As a matter of fact, authors of textbooks and handbook chapters continually do so, and I shall do it here as I account for historical changes. I shall attempt to be as explicit as possible and to note where my beliefs seem to differ from current opinions.

Plan for the Book

Based on the views of the history of psychology outlined in this chapter, I have structured my presentation as follows.

In *Chapter 2*, I shall give a brief account of the progress made in physiology, and of the ideas of science that predominated in the mid-nineteenth century and constituted a common intellectual background for the early empirical psychologists. In *Chapter 3*, I shall present a description of the early German research in perception, emphasizing some features that became characteristic of the German psychological research tradition; and in *Chapters 4* and *5*, I shall continue the account of the German experimental psychology, first presenting Wundt and his contemporaries, and then phenomenology and Gestalt psychology. In *Chapter 6*, I shall discuss the theory of evolution and British psychological thinking in the mid-1800s; in *Chapter 7*, British comparative psychology with special emphasis on the concepts of instinct and motivation; and in *Chapter 8*, early Russian psychology.

In *Chapters 9* and *10*, I shall deal with European clinical and personality psychology, first French psychology, and then Austrian psychodynamic psychology. In *Chapter 11*, I shall turn to the psychology of the United States, first to the early empirical psychology and then in *Chapters 13, 14, and 15* to later developments: behaviorism, social psychology, and personality psychology. In *Chapter 16*, I shall review progress in the study of cognition in Europe and the United States in the first half of the 1900s, and in *Chapter 17*, progress in physiological psychology, particularly in neuropsychology in the 1900s. In *Chapter 18*, I shall report on some important changes taking place in American society, in the philosophy of science, and, more specifically, in psychology, and I shall review two approaches that emerged in the 1950s and 1960s: humanistic psychology and information processing. In a final chapter, *Chapter 19*, I shall review some important trends in the psychology of the twenty-first century.

2

The Scientific and Intellectual
Environment of the Mid-1800s

During the first half of the 1800s there was rapid growth in the natural sciences. In physics, scientists continued to build on the breakthrough of two hundred years earlier. Chemistry was transformed into a quantitative science and experienced an explosive expansion. Around the mid-century, physiologists began to apply principles from physics and chemistry to the study of bodily processes and provide it with a new and fruitful basis. It also became evident that scientific knowledge would be of great use in everyday life. The electric telegraph, electromagnets, electrical motors, and generators were constructed, and chemical products of practical value were produced. It became obvious to many that science would radically change society, and this naturally increased interest in it among politicians and leaders in industry and finance. At universities and research institutions, financial support for research increased, and schools gave more emphasis to the teaching of science.

A New View of Body and Soul

The progress in physiology was of special significance to psychology, which in Germany and Russia had originated as a physiological psychology. Pioneer psychologists, such as Fechner, Helmholtz, Wundt, James, Janet, Freud, and Pavlov, were trained as medical doctors. Of particular importance for psychology during the 1860s and 1870s were discoveries showing that a close relationship must exist between brain functions and mental phenomena. This relationship suggested that it might be possible to study aspects of consciousness through a study of the brain.

The new knowledge of the brain undermined the traditional view that humans consist of body and mind. It actualized the problem of determinism and free will and led to vigorous philosophical debates about the religious and legal institutions of society. At the end of the century, Western intellectuals seemed no less concerned with the relationship between body and mind than with the relationship between humans and animals made prominent by the theory of evolution.

Attempts to solve the mind–body problem raised not only intricate philosophical questions, but also complex methodological and philosophical questions, and contrasting views of the nature of consciousness soon arose among psychologists. Some of these problems remain unsolved. To gain an understanding of how earlier psychologists regarded the subject matter of their science, we must examine the way in which they looked at the relationship between mind and body.

Immediate Experience: The Soul Detached from the Body

Regardless of the position we take on the nature of consciousness, I think we must agree that, in a number of situations, we receive sensory impressions of objects outside ourselves *without being aware* that these impressions are determined by bodily processes. When we look at objects, listen to sounds, or feel surfaces touching our skin, we have an immediate impression of their presence, but no awareness of bodily functions. This is also the case when we recall events of the past, imagine a situation, or reason about some course of events. We perform the activities without an awareness that we need the body to perform them. In philosophy impressions of this kind are called *immediate experience.*

When it comes to emotions and expressions of will, the picture is more complicated. Under the influence of strong emotions – for instance, when we are angry or fearful – we can feel the body's reactions in the form of changes in heart rate and blood supply. But we can also experience emotions such as joy, satisfaction, wonder, and indifference, without being aware of our body. We sometimes feel that our voluntary actions require effort – for instance, when we need to move quickly, reach for something, concentrate, or stand up. When we are ill or tired, we have to pull ourselves together in order to carry out intentions and plans. At other times, however, we automatically hold a pencil to write, lift a coffee cup to our mouth, or sit down at a desk, and are not aware of any effort we make. Thus, we receive a number of impressions and have a number of experiences that do not seem to be related to bodily processes or functions.

From such considerations, it is natural to imagine that the impressions we receive are of a different nature from bodily processes and functions. Without knowledge of physiology, we can imagine a separation of mind and body. The distinction between the two was strongly emphasized in the Platonic–Christian philosophy that has characterized Western thinking for two thousand years. But this hardly implies that it has an origin in religion. In Western philosophy, René Descartes (1596–1650) drew a rather sharp distinction between body and mind. He claimed there are two different substances, a material one and a mental one, yet the two can interact. Descartes has played a major role in the history of philosophy, but to maintain that the distinction between mind and body originated in his thinking is to give him too much credit.

Progress in the Study of the Brain

In a comprehensive and lively account of the mind–body problem in the history of the Western world, Robert Boakes (1984) maintained that not until the 1860s were neurophysiological studies conducted to show that mental states and phenomena depend on the activity of the brain. Earlier researchers and thinkers had made similar claims. Already in the mid-1700s, the Frenchman Julien Offray de la Mettrie (1709–1751) and the Englishman David Hartley (1705–1757) declared that mental conditions and phenomena are a result of physiological processes. Approximately fifty years later, the German anatomist Franz Joseph Gall (1758–1828) proposed that there are in the brain a large number of centers corresponding to human mental abilities. These centers are developed differently in different persons. People possessing a high degree of a certain ability have a correspondingly large center, and those possessing low ability, a small center. Gall further held that the size of the centers determines the shape of the skull, so that by examining the skull we can determine a person's abilities. This type of physiological and psychological study was called *phrenology*. Gall's ideas became very popular, and phrenology was practiced until the beginning of the following century; in particular, it gained influence in the United States, where, as John O'Donnell (1985) noted, it prepared the ground for the application of psychological tests.

Gall could not support his speculations with facts from physiology, and most contemporary anatomists and physiologists rejected phrenology. A few decades later, one of the great neurophysiologists of the time, Pierre Flourens (1794–1867), claimed to have refuted Gall's assertion that diverse psychological functions are located in specific areas of the brain. Flourens introduced the *ablation technique*, in which he surgically removed various parts of the brain of an animal (usually a pigeon or hen) and compared its performance before and after. By this technique, he discovered the significance of the medulla oblongata for respiration, circulation of the blood, and body temperature. He also demonstrated that the cerebellum has an important function in coordinating muscular movements. However, Flourens held that mental functions are not located in specific areas of the brain; rather, the brain functions as a whole and is the seat of the mind. Even if his conclusions were rather rash, he was able to support them with findings of great importance for our understanding of the functions of the brain. He discovered that when animals had some of their brain tissue removed, over time they would often regain the ability to carry out certain functions they had been unable to perform immediately after the surgery.

Flourens's view of the functions of the brain was accepted by scientists until 1861, when the French physician Paul Broca (1824–1880) made a sensational discovery. He had thoroughly examined a patient who had lost the faculty of speech but otherwise seemed to function perfectly normally. The muscles which controlled the patient's vocal cords and tongue did not seem paralyzed. When the man died, Broca examined his brain and found a small, defined lesion in the left hemisphere. Based on this finding, he concluded that the faculty of speech depends on a specific area of the brain. Twelve years later, the German physician Carl Wernicke (1848–1905) found that another part of the brain also influences the faculty of speech. This area is likewise located in the left part of the brain, but further back than the area found by Broca. Based on the results of his own research and that of Broca, Wernicke formulated a theory of the role the diverse areas of the brain play in speech and thereby founded the study of *aphasia* (loss of the ability to express or understand speech and writing as a result of brain damage). From 1861 onwards, an increasing number of discoveries were made that showed mental activity to be dependent on the brain.

Although the brain research of the latter half of the 1800s showed that phenomena such as perceiving, imagining, remembering, thinking, feeling, and willing, traditionally regarded as mental, are indeed dependent upon the activity of the brain, no satisfactory solution was found for the mind–body problem. The pioneer psychologists took different positions on the issue. Some held that mental phenomena, like psychological processes, are physical in nature; some adopted Descartes's belief that mental phenomena represent events of another nature than physical events. Some took a double-aspect view, believing that mental and physical phenomena are aspects of the same underlying substance, and, finally, some regarded the mind–body issue as a pseudo-problem.

All these positions raised questions that could not be satisfactorily answered. As a consequence, at the time psychology was established as an empirical science, some were disappointed by the nature of its subject matter, and formulations of problems frequently became entangled with intricate philosophical questions. As we shall see in the chapters to follow, even if a number of problems in present-day research are studied without specific reference to the mind–body problem, it still represents a major challenge to empirical psychology.

The Concept of the Reflex in Philosophy and Early Physiology

The study of reflexes has a central place in the history of physiology and psychology. It led to a view of the nervous system that has had a profound influence on psychology. Russian physiologists and later American behaviorists made the concept of reflex a key element in their approach to psychology. I shall give a brief outline of the history of the concept until 1860.

Descartes drew a distinction between animals and humans and equipped only the latter with a soul. The soul is in contact with the body but has the freedom to act independently of bodily processes. Animals, on the other hand, do not possess such freedom and function as automata. Descartes gave an ingenious explanation of movement in animals. Apart from some of his speculations on the nature of the nervous system, his account was surprisingly modern. Roughly, it ran along the following lines. When the effect of the stimulation of a sense organ reaches the brain via a nerve leading from the sense organ, it produces a movement in the nerve that leads from the brain to a muscle, and this movement results in a muscle contraction that causes some part of the body to move. One hundred years after Descartes, de la Mettrie, and Hartley extended the concept of reflexes to movements in humans. We will see later in this chapter that Hartley also was able to give a plausible explanation of how voluntary movements result from the association between a particular reflex and specific types of stimulation affecting the sense organs.

Around the mid-1700s, the Scottish physiologist Robert Whytt conducted a number of experiments with frogs, demonstrating that specific types of stimulation to their legs result in specific movements. He also pointed out that in humans coughing, sneezing, reaction of the pupils, salivation, and erection of the penis are such reflexive reactions. Whytt further showed that other types of stimuli than those originally eliciting the reflexive reaction could acquire the ability to do so. For example, the idea of food, or thinking about food, causes increased salivation in a hungry person. However, on one point, his investigations resulted in a modification of Descartes's account of reflexes. Descartes proposed that nerves are designed much like blood vessels; that is, nerves are tubes through which "animal spirits" travel rather than blood. Reflexes occur as the fluid of animal spirits flows through the nerves. Like an earlier researcher, Whytt found that he could elicit reflexes in frogs in which he had severed the connection between the spine and the brain; this work demonstrated that Descartes's ideas about the nature and function of nerves were mistaken. In the early 1800s, the Scot Charles Bell and the Frenchman François Magendie discovered that the posterior (dorsal) roots of the spine contain one kind of nerves, while the anterior (ventral) roots contain another. This discovery made it possible to distinguish between sensory and motor nerves. In line with this finding, around 1830 Marshall Hall presented a view of the reflex as a movement dependent on a sensory and a motor nerve fiber connected by the nerve tissue of the spine.

Hall regarded reflexes as a specific kind of movement dependent only on the spinal cord and not on the brain, automatic and stereotyped, and independent of consciousness. As Boring (1929/1950) noted, Hall's view of the reflex prepared the way for the concept of the *reflex arc*.

Being automatic, stereotyped, and elicited by specific stimuli, reflexes could be regarded as kinds of movements different from complex, voluntary acts performed by humans. However, they could also be regarded as units making up more complex acts. As Boakes has made clear, this view of the reflexes met with difficulties. One was that, in order to account for complex acts, we would have to assume they represent integrations of a number of reflexes, and at Hall's time nothing was known of the nervous system that could explain how such integrations could take place. Another difficulty was that, in contrast to reflexes, complex movements are adjusted to changes in the environment. A third difficulty was that reflexes are involuntary and could not be instigated and governed by the will as other types of movement are.

In the mid-1800s, physiologists made discoveries suggesting how we could move from the idea of simple reflexes to a plausible account of complex, finely adjusted movements. It was found that the stimulation of certain nerves and certain areas of the brain has an inhibiting effect on muscle contraction. Researchers now began to focus on such inhibiting mechanisms. A pioneer in this research was the Russian Ivan Sechenov. He used the idea of inhibition to develop a view of reflexes that he thought would form a foundation for a study of psychology. His idea of reflexes and their inhibitions were subjected to empirical investigations around 1900 by Ivan Pavlov. In Chapter 8, I shall return to Sechenov and Pavlov.

British neurologists and physiologists developed a different view of inhibiting mechanisms from that of the Russian researchers. In the 1880s, Charles Sherrington (1857–1952) was able to provide a tenable explanation of how reflexes can be integrated into complex movements adjusted to the demands of the organism's surroundings. His account of the integration of reflexes gained him the Nobel Prize in Physiology or Medicine.

Finally, the assumption that our actions are a result of reflexes contains a view of motivation. If our actions are elicited and directed by external stimuli alone, we do not need a concept of motivation. The question of whether motivation also has an internal source was first raised within psychology at the beginning of the 1900s by Sigmund Freud and William McDougall, and it was clarified in the latter half of the 1900s.

Positivism and British Empiricist Philosophy

Science clearly produced more reliable and often more useful knowledge than everyday thinking. Therefore, the great expansion in the natural sciences in the first half of the 1800s gave support to the idea that scientific study could be extended to include humans and society, and the knowledge thus gained could be a foundation for the organization of human activity and social institutions. These ideas formed the basis for a broad philosophical movement called positivism. The philosophers launching positivism also put forward ideas on the nature of science that had a great impact on psychology. Familiarity with positivistic thinking, therefore, aids us in understanding how psychology as an empirical science arose, and the way in which scientific research was carried out. Early influential proponents of the positivist movement were the Frenchman Auguste Comte and the Englishman J. S. Mill – the latter belonging to the British empiricist tradition, with which positivism had much in common. In my account of Mill, I shall, therefore, also present some of the more important ideas of this philosophical tradition. (Surveys of early positivism have been given by Nicola Abbagnano, 1967, and Bruce Mazlish, 1967.)

Auguste Comte (1798–1857): A Society Governed by Science

Born at Montpellier, France, Comte studied at L'École Polytechnique between 1814 and 1816. This school, founded in 1794 with the objective of providing education for military engineers, had soon become a center for advanced education in the natural sciences and mathematics. Comte's studies there shaped his thinking of science and society. He became well acquainted with the mathematical treatment of scientific problems, understood that technology and science are closely related, and emphasized that science should be applied to the solving of problems in practical life.

In the 1820s, Comte embarked on a study of the way in which scientific thinking of the Western world had expanded to include new areas. In a comprehensive work published between 1830 and 1842, he gave a historical account of how he believed this development had taken place. According to Comte, the thinking of the West had developed in three stages. In the first stage, phenomena were explained by the postulation of supernatural and divine powers; in the second, the metaphysical stage, explanations were given in terms of abstract ideas; and, finally, in the third stage, the scientific or positive stage, scholars explained phenomena by identifying fixed relationships between them. In this last stage, thinking is firmly based on observation and scientific investigation. To reach this stage, it was necessary to replace philosophy with empirical science. Comte rejected philosophy not based on science. The idea that human thinking had developed through these three stages soon became widespread.

Comte did not limit his account to a consideration of the past; he also suggested that social organizations and institutions should be made the subject of empirical research. This made him one of the founders of modern sociology. For Comte, a major inspiration was the idea that science could be a means of controlling society. If we could discover the laws determining our social interactions, we would be able to govern society according to these laws. At the time he was writing his major work, technological progress had radically changed British society, and change was rampant. In France as well, the effects of the Industrial Revolution began to manifest themselves towards the end of the 1700s. These changes may have convinced Comte that it is important to plan and direct the development of society with the aid of knowledge acquired by research.

Comte devoted considerable attention to psychology as well. But because he believed that scientific observation should be objective and not of a private, subjective nature, he rejected the belief that a scientific psychology can be based on introspection. The introspective study of consciousness was a remnant of theology, he said, and raised the following objection. In order for us to make observations of our own thinking, we must divide our consciousness, and that, Comte thought, is not possible. This objection haunted scientific psychology from its earliest days.

According to Descartes, consciousness represents a domain of events and phenomena that clearly distinguishes it from physical events. Recall that he considered animals automata governed by mechanistic principles. Human consciousness, however, is not governed by such principles. Comte rejected the distinction between body and soul, and insisted that the difference between the higher animals and humans is a question of degree only. Less than one hundred years later, his ideas about the nature of science, the role of observation, and the fundamental similarity between humans and animals became the basis of American behaviorism.

Science and Society

For large proportions of the European population, industrialization resulted in social deprivation. This naturally caused considerable political instability in the 1800s. However, economic growth was continuing, and this fostered in many an optimistic belief in the future. Technology and science are instrumental in growth, so scientific progress became linked to that optimism. Further, if with the aid of science, we are able to eliminate disease, understand humans, and regulate their social relationships, conditions would be favorable for creating a society that would more adequately meet human needs. Hence, progress in science provided a fertile soil for visions of a new and better world. For many, these visions assumed a religious character. Among industrial workers, the vision of a society based on science, technology, and economic equality became a strong incentive for political activity. Karl Marx's ideas of economics and science became key elements in the European labor movements towards the late 1800s and spread outward to Russia and Asia. Even if middle-class people tended not to be interested in radical political change and did not share laborers' hopes for a future society based on science, they did share the hope that progress in science would produce economic growth, improved health, and better education. It is against this background of a strong belief in the value of science and technology that we must interpret the rapidly increasing interest in scientific psychology.

John Stuart Mill (1806–1873)

Comte's ideas of science and society appealed to J. S. Mill. He agreed with Comte that the study of society could be made an empirical science. However, unlike Comte, he believed mental phenomena could also be studied in this way. He even seems to have thought that, in the study of consciousness, laws of a scientific nature had been established based on experiments. The laws he was alluding to were the so-called *laws of association*, framed by earlier British empiricist philosophers. In addition to a scientific study of consciousness, Mill felt that it would be possible to extend science to include the study of human character – what we now term personality.

In *A System of Logic*, published in 1843, he added little to what his father, James Mill, and the earlier British empiricist philosophers had said about mental phenomena. However, he expanded and systematized this thinking and gave a comprehensive account of logic, language, and science. His book greatly influenced not only British but also German and American psychology; in particular, the British empiricist philosophers' view of perception and learning.

In his account of perception, Mill started by considering material objects such as stones, trees, and houses. Material objects, he said, may be ascribed physical characteristics such as size, shape, weight, and mass. These physical characteristics give rise to our sensory impressions of, respectively, the object's extension (size), shape, weight, firmness, and color, and are generally thought to be a result of a direct sensory stimulation. In contrast, the impression of an object as a whole is a thought, and not directly a result of stimulation. Rather, Mill held, it comes from our familiarity or experience with the object, through which our diverse sensory impressions combined, according to specific principles, to form our impression of the object. Mill – and before him some of the empiricist philosophers – referred to these principles as *laws of association*.

According to Mill, learning by association occurs under three conditions, the first having to do with similarities of the sensory impressions, the second with their temporal relationships – that they frequently occur simultaneously or in close temporal contiguity – and the third with the intensity of the impressions. Based on these three conditions, he formulated three principles of association: the principles of similarity, of temporal contiguity, and of intensity. In the later scientific psychological study of learning, researchers have concentrated on the second principle, and, in my account of the history of psychology, I shall discuss only this principle, which is usually referred to as *the principle of contiguity* or *learning by contiguity*. Mill believed sensory impressions leave images in the mind that he called ideas. The principles of association would hold also for ideas, so sensory impressions could be associated with ideas, and ideas with one another.

The associationist account of learning by temporal contiguity usually assumes that the situation in which learning is said to occur must be repeated, and the more frequently it is repeated, the more the association is strengthened. Further, the associations are assumed to form in a purely mechanistic manner. Thus, the elements are not equipped with specific characteristics or forces that cause them to be connected. On this point, thinkers in the associationist tradition of the eighteenth and nineteenth centuries were in agreement with the tendencies then current to explain phenomena by mechanistic principles.

The empiricist account also viewed perception as a process taking place without the organism's active participation. In *A System of Logic*, Mill illustrated (1843/1956, Book I, ch. 3) how he believed his perception of his writing desk arose:

My conception of the table at which I am writing is compounded of its visible form and size which are complex sensations of sight; its tangible form and size, which are complex sensations of our organs of touch and of our muscles; its weight, which is also a sensation of touch and of the muscles; its colour, which is a sensation of sight; its hardness, which is a sensation of the muscles; its composition, which is another word for all the varieties of sensation which we receive under various circumstances from the wood of which it is made, and so forth. All or most of these various sensations frequently are, and, as we learn by experience, always might be, experienced simultaneously, or in many different orders of succession at our own choice: and hence the thought of any one of them makes us think of the others, and the whole becomes mentally amalgamated into one mixed state of consciousness, which, in the language of the school of Locke and Hartley, is termed a *Complex Idea*.

Without discussing the complex epistemological problems relating to Mill's view of perception, I shall note that he emphasized the need to distinguish clearly between physical processes and what he regarded as mental ones. In this way, he contributed to strengthening the belief that psychology represents a domain of events that could be studied independently of physiology and behavior.

After the death of Mill, British philosophers strongly criticized his view of perception as resulting from combinations of sensory impressions. Apparently, Mill (Book VI, ch. 4) had a suspicion that it is perhaps not as easy to explain perception as he and the British empiricists believed, because he admitted that "When many impressions or ideas are operating in the mind together, there sometimes takes place a process of a similar kind to chemical combinations." The kind of chemical process he had in mind is the kind we observe when, for instance, hydrogen and oxygen combine to form a new compound, water. Hence, he seemed to think mental elements could at times combine in such a way that a content emerges that cannot immediately be broken down into elements. In these cases, it was more correct, he maintained, to say that single ideas *generate* more complex ones, than to say that they constitute them.

However, Mill never went beyond voicing a suspicion. He did not pursue the problem and never really rejected his father's view of elements and associations. If there is a purpose in speaking of generating ideas in the sense that something new emerges that we cannot explain by the parts alone, Mill would have needed to assume the elements possessed certain types of characteristics, and it is difficult to see what these characteristics might be. His view of perception raises the question of what we are to understand to be a mental element. If he had explored this problem further, perhaps he would not have maintained that the individual elements are associated with each other in perception, or that the laws of association had been established as a result of experiments. I call attention to this point because some historians still seem to ascribe to Mill a deeper and more modern view of the problems of perception.

Before we leave the concept of association, we should note that the idea of learning by association is so attractive because it seems so simple and so immediately obvious. Let me illustrate this with an example. Several times in succession I encounter a man with a dog. After some time, the sight of the man brings to mind the dog, and vice versa. What could be more understandable? Only after some reflection do I realize that, in order to combine the impressions of the man and the dog, I must assume that there can exist a relationship between them, and this relationship must in some way be of interest to me. Further, the man and the dog respectively form part of the two classes or categories, "man" and "dog." This reflection thus raises the question of what we are to understand by a mental element and by the association of ideas.

The idea of learning by association had been a major element in British empiricist philosophy since Locke's time. Because a study of its history before Mill scarcely makes us any wiser as to what we are to understand by mental elements and their associations, I shall draw attention only to David Hartley's attempt to give a physiological explanation of the formation of associations. Hartley proposed that stimulation of the sensory organs causes vibrations in the sensory nerves and the brain. When two external events occur close together in time (in temporal contiguity), the vibrations corresponding to them will be linked together so the vibrations corresponding to one event bring about the vibrations corresponding to the other. Hartley's explanation was speculative, though it suggested a possible way of explaining how activity in the nervous system could result in the formation of associations.

In Chapter 3 we shall see that Hermann Helmholtz further developed the idea that our perceptual representations can be seen as combinations of sensory elements and can be explained as a result of a kind of thinking he called *unconscious inference*. In Chapters 4, 8, and 12, we shall see that researchers in Germany, Russia, and the United States based their views of learning on principles of association.

Mill's View of Experimentation and Science

In his account of how we acquire knowledge, Mill placed little emphasis on thinking and intuition. He tried to show that from simple types of experience we can, by means of inductive reasoning, arrive at general and abstract conclusions. Even mathematics, he declared, is built on inductive reasoning. As John Losee (1980) points out, Mill understood that hypotheses and deductions have a place in science. Still, it is probably correct to say that, in his account, these aspects of scientific thinking were largely neglected. Hence, Mill contributed to the early positivist view, which one-sidedly emphasized that the scientific method is primarily concerned with how we can make accurate observations and, from these arrive by induction at general laws.

Mill was familiar with physics and chemistry and understood that experimentation had played a great role in the development of the natural sciences. He urged that psychology ought to be an experimental science; and in this way he came to influence scientific psychology in the latter half of the 1800s. For Mill, the experiment is primarily a means of clarifying causal relationships, and he restored the rules Francis Bacon (1561–1626) had formulated to achieve this goal. According to Bacon and Mill, the three most important rules are to discover whether the conditions under which a particular phenomenon occurs are the same, whether they are different in one definite respect, and whether two or more phenomena show concomitant variations. In psychology, relationships are usually extremely complex, and exercises in reaching experimental conclusions have become widespread in modern psychological teaching.

By concentrating on the experiment as a means of clarifying causal relationships, Mill tended to overlook its role as a means of testing hypotheses. This important aspect of scientific procedure was neglected in the early positivist philosophy, and little attention was paid to it in the early scientific psychology. Mill and the positivist thinkers of the 1800s also placed little emphasis on the experiment as a means of simply demonstrating that, by following a certain procedure, we can produce a particular phenomenon. As we shall see in later chapters, German Gestalt psychologists as well as B. F. Skinner relied heavily on experiments of this type.

Prior to J. S. Mill's publication of *A System of Logic*, John Herschel, one of Britain's leading scientists in the first half of the 1800s, had given an account of the nature of science in which he emphasized the role played by hypotheses and theories. At about the same time, the geologist and philosopher William Whewell wrote two extensive works on empirical science, in which he stressed the importance of creating new concepts that would make it possible to see facts in a new way. Whewell criticized Mill for placing too great an emphasis on the inductive method. However, it was Mill's view of science, and not Herschel's and Whewell's, that came to dominate the philosophy of science. Before I leave Whewell, I shall mention that – like Thomas Kuhn more than one hundred years later – he believed studies in the philosophy of science should be based on historical investigations of the development of science.

Scientific Thinking During the 1800s: Mechanism and Positivism

Scientific psychology emerged as the result of an attempt to apply scientific methods to psychological problems. Its development was shaped both by considerations of what constituted its problems and by conceptions of science. To understand the historical development of psychology, we should, therefore, be familiar with the ideas of science underlying psychological research in the different historical periods.

The Emergence of Mechanistic Views in Psychology

Nineteenth-century attempts to expand empirical science to include humans and society raised questions about the nature of scientific thinking. Many of those concerned with such questions believed the natural sciences should serve as a model, and from the very first efforts to establish psychology as an empirical science, classical physics has played that role.

The new physics of the 1600s emerged in an effort to account for the movement and equilibrium of objects. The pioneers in the field had discovered that this could be achieved without assuming – as Aristotle and other Greek thinkers had – that nature is governed by a purpose and a design. Instead, they endeavored to give purely mechanistic explanations in which movement and equilibrium were seen as the result of the effects objects exercise on each other. They had discovered they could do this by concentrating on the observable and measurable characteristics of objects, such as their weight and size, and by considering the relationships between them as a result of forces that could be defined quantitatively and thereby expressed mathematically. Based on the ideal of giving the simplest explanations possible, they had succeeded in accounting for their subject by means of a very small number of principles. The system developed by Newton in his work *Philosophiae Naturalis Principia Mathematica* (abbreviated *Principia*) in the late 1600s, possessed an exceptionally high degree of generality, logical coherence, consistency, and precision.

Newton's system was obviously based on very exact observations. However, not all concepts, including the key concept of gravitational force, could be determined by observation. Further, Newton operated with concepts such as "absolute space" and "absolute time." It was evident that experimentation had been of importance in the development of his system, but it was far from clear what role it had played. The system explained many aspects relating to movements of objects; still it was not obvious what he meant by *explained*. The model for scientific thinking used by psychologists thus provided certain guidelines, but fundamental points remained unclear.

Further, about 1800, chemists were able to give explanations without resorting to ideas of purpose and design. Hence, even here it seemed possible to base a study of science on mechanistic principles. This, in turn, raised the question of whether it was possible to do so for biological processes and phenomena too. Aristotle had provided descriptions of biological phenomena that appeared to be adequate even if he had made assumptions about purpose and design. Nevertheless, in the beginning of the 1800s, some physiologists began to ask whether it would be possible to base biology on principles employed in physics and chemistry, but throughout the first half of the 1800s, many held to the view – called *vitalism* – that biological processes are governed by special forces and that an explanation based only on physics and chemistry was not adequate. Around the mid-century, it was becoming obvious that the idea of a specific force was not needed, and this made it more likely that it would also be possible to explain mental processes and phenomena mechanistically. Could we, for instance, thus explain phenomena we describe by terms such as "intention," "attention," "expectation," "effort of will," and "decision"? This was not only a complex but also a sensitive question that deeply affected many people.

Thus, the historical development of science was also giving support to a mechanistic view of psychological processes and phenomena. To many psychologists, it became a central idea that psychological processes must be explained mechanistically, and throughout the history of psychology the question has been raised of whether this can be done. Russian reflexologists made such a view the basis of their approaches, and so did psychoanalysts and most American behaviorists. The question was a central one in the psychological debate when, in the 1950s and 1960s, the so-called *information-processing approach* emerged in the wake of computers.

Ernst Mach (1838–1916)

According to Frederick Suppe (1977), adherents of a mechanistic view of science paid little attention to epistemological problems in their attempts to provide objective descriptions of the phenomena they studied. In contrast to them, the Austrian physicist, mathematician, physiologist, and psychologist Ernst Mach (1886) was concerned with these problems. Inspired by the ideas of epistemology and science put forward by George Berkeley 150 years earlier, Mach formulated a philosophy of science that influenced not only philosophers but also many leading psychologists. Since Mach was an outstanding perception psychologist, we also discuss him in the next chapter.

Like Berkeley, Mach claimed we can have knowledge only of our sensory impressions. Our knowledge not only of material objects and the external world but also of our body, self, mind, and consciousness is based on sensory impressions, such as color, sound, heat, pressure, space, time, etc. Because all our knowledge was believed to be the result of combinations of sensory impressions, it is not possible to draw a fundamental distinction between an external and an internal world, or between material and mental processes. Further, no fundamental difference could exist between the different branches of science. Physics, physiology, and psychology all have a foundation in the same sensory impressions. The only way in which the various sciences differ is in respect to the objectives of the research. The idea that physics and psychology differ only in this respect influenced a number of psychologists towards the late 1800s and in the early 1900s.

The goal of science, as stated by Mach, is to find relationships between diverse types of sensory impressions. Sensory impressions form the foundation for science as well as for everyday thinking. But, in contrast to everyday thinking, science does not rest on hypotheses or metaphysical assumptions. It is primarily directed at describing sensory impressions accurately. According to Mach, all forms of speculation should be eliminated. Preferably, relationships between the diverse sensory impressions should be expressed mathematically.

The Scientific Ideal of Later Positivism: Accurate Observation and Description

Influenced by ideas from Comte, Mill, and Mach, a philosophy of science developed that held it is essential to avoid speculation. Scientists could achieve this in three ways: 1. by directly observing the events and phenomena studied; 2. by formulating general statements arrived at by inductive reasoning based on observation; 3. by describing the relationships between the diverse types of events without recourse to assumptions of underlying conditions or forces.

In early positivist philosophy, there was also a strong tendency to assume that progress in the natural sciences is due primarily to the use of specific methods. These methods, it was believed, could also be applied in investigations of problems outside the domain of natural science.

Early positivism put little weight on explanations, hypothesis testing, or theory construction. It was believed that, on the basis of observations, we could reach conclusions having a high degree of generality. Alan Francis Chalmers (1982, p. 5) has characterized this view of science as that of *the naive inductivist*:

According to the naive inductivist, then, the body of scientific knowledge is built by induction from the secure basis provided by observation. As the number of facts established by observation and experiment grows, and as the facts become more refined and esoteric due to improvements in our observational and experimental skills, so more and more laws and theories of ever more generality and scope are constructed by careful inductive reasoning. The growth of science is continuous, ever onward and upward, as the fund of observational data is increased.

As we shall see in later chapters, positivist philosophy had a strong impact on several approaches developed in psychology. But not all major figures in its history were influenced by it, and we must not – as some critics of scientific psychology seem to do – widen the term "positivism" so much that it covers all forms of empirical science. Neither Darwin, Helmholtz, William James, nor the Gestalt psychologists held views on science identical to those I have described here as positivist. Nor should we confuse early positivism with the later *logical positivism*, which emerged in the 1920s. In particular, even if positivism, especially since 1960, has been exposed to much deserved criticism, many of its adherents have made important contributions to psychology.

3

The Early Physiological Study of Perception

German Experimental Psychology (1850–1940): Introduction to Chapters 3, 4, and 5

German experimental psychology began as physiological psychology, and central in physiological psychology was the study of perception. When Wundt established his laboratory in 1879, this study had flourished for close to forty years. In his attempt at formally establishing psychology as a branch of empirical science, Wundt added studies of attention, feelings, and the will, and then, somewhat later, Hermann Ebbinghaus extended experimental psychology to include the study of remembering.

German experimental psychology thus remained a study of consciousness. A main trend in the physiological study of perception – as well as in the early studies of feeling, memory, and the will – had been to regard psychological processes as consisting of elements that combine in various ways. From the beginning of the 1900s, however, there was a growing reaction to this tendency, and new approaches were developed until German experimental psychology declined under the Nazi regime in the 1930s.

I shall begin my account of German experimental psychology with this chapter on the early sensory physiology. Then I shall treat the psychology of Wundt and his contemporaries in Chapter 4 and conclude with Chapter 5 on the new tendencies gaining force at the end of the nineteenth century. First we look at the society and culture in which German psychology originated.

German Society and Culture

Until 1871, Germany was divided into a number of independent states. While tariff frontiers restricted trade between these states, an open and extensive exchange of scientific ideas took place among all regions where the German language was spoken. German was also the administrative language of the Austro-Hungarian Empire, and in continental Europe there was therefore a large area of German culture. German-speaking scientists could obtain positions not only in the German states and Austria, but also in Zürich in German-speaking Switzerland, and in Prague in Bohemia.

The Industrial Revolution began later in Germany than in Great Britain and France, but it accelerated rapidly from the mid-1800s. One important reason for its expansion was that the Germans applied not only technology but also science in industry. This was far less the case in other Western countries and is presumably one of the major reasons why Germany so quickly became equal to Great Britain and France as an industrial and military power.

The German University System

Early German psychological research was carried out almost entirely in the universities. To understand the growth in German science, let us therefore take a look at the German university system as it developed from the beginning of the 1800s.

With the defeat of the Prussian army by Napoleon, the Prussian government was prompted to introduce changes in the educational system, including the universities. Napoleon had reformed the French educational system, and the Prussians initially thought of adopting the French system. However, they chose instead to work out their own plans to establish a new university in Berlin. A central person in this work was the German linguist and diplomat Wilhelm von Humboldt (1767–1835). His proposals and their implications for the German university system have been described by Rainer Müller (1990). Humboldt was a friend of Goethe and other prominent persons in the German humanistic movement, and several people besides him contributed to the innovations contained in his proposals. Some of the innovations had also been introduced in other German universities. Thus, Humboldt was far from alone in working out the plans.

Humboldt believed knowledge and scientific thinking have intrinsic value, and he emphasized that students should acquire a broad and extensive general education. At the same time, he urged that research centers of high standing be established within the individual disciplines, and that university teachers be of high caliber. He believed students should acquire knowledge by actively participating in discussions with their professors and their fellow students. In addition to lectures, therefore, seminars became an important aspect of student instruction. Humboldt's proposals formed the basis for the University of Berlin, which was established in 1811 and became a model for other German universities.

Professors were appointed by the government but had much freedom to develop their disciplines according to their own plans. In spite of the fact that Germany had an authoritarian government throughout the 1800s, debate within the universities was generally quite free – though with certain limitations. Later in the century, socialists did not easily obtain positions, and around the end of the nineteenth-century discrimination against Jews existed, though not to the same extent as in Vienna. Further, German women had no access to the universities or other higher education until the beginning of the 1900s.

In the early 1800s, German university professors played an active role in the formation of the German state, and they considered themselves national leaders. As civil servants, they depended on, and were loyal to, the German government after the establishment of the empire in 1871. As Fritz Ringer (1969) has pointed out, German civil servants represented a small group within a bureaucratic culture. This, I believe, is a significant factor in understanding the field of German psychology.

The state bureaucracy decided on the subjects to be taught at the universities and, as mentioned, also appointed the professors of the various disciplines. However, once appointed, professors had considerable freedom in administering their institutions, as well as in pursuing personal interests in their research. They were not dependent on grants from business or private institutions, or on the support of the general public. As long as they had support from colleagues and other university teachers, they could plan their activities without being concerned with what was happening in society at large. This contributed to the development of an elitist culture and tended to make the universities elitist institutions.

To gain entrance to a university, students needed a high-school education with emphasis on general education, classical languages, and philosophy. This created a unique kind of recruitment. The majority of the students were the children of civil servants and, as a consequence, the civil service and the universities were closely linked.

Those aspiring to be professors had to spend a number of years at a university after they had completed examinations in their subjects that gave them the title of doctor. They then had to write a dissertation, a so-called *Habilitationsschrift*. Normally, this was done under the supervision of the subject professor. When the dissertation had been approved, candidates obtained the right to teach at a university.

Usually, a professor was not appointed immediately but was allowed to establish himself as a private tutor instructing students for payment, or he could be attached to a university as a *Professor extraordinarius*. In the latter case, he assisted the professor in instructing the students, but without the authority to develop the subject. This system tied young scholars to the university and made them dependent on their professors.

Since the professors had sole responsibility for teaching and research, they might, if they chose, suppress opinions that deviated from their own. Younger scientists wanting to carry out their own plans for research and teaching would have to obtain a position at another university. As a result, there was frequently considerable variety in the way the same discipline was taught in the various universities.

Towards the mid-1800s, physiologists began to use the experimental method more extensively in their research and to apply principles of physics and chemistry in their explanations of physiological processes. The result was dramatic progress in understanding the processes taking place in the body. The German physiologists were the pioneers of the new study of physiology.

A subarea of the new physically oriented physiology was the study of sensory perception. This discipline aimed to account for the relationship between physical stimulation of the sensory organs and our sensory impressions. To achieve this, physiologists attempted to give accurate descriptions of the following: 1. the physical stimulation affecting the sensory organs; 2. the sensory organs and the parts of the nervous system assumed to be involved in the process leading to the sensory impressions; 3. the sensory impressions.

Research in the area required knowledge of physics, anatomy, and physiology and an ability to make accurate descriptions of the sensory impressions. The early German physicalist physiologists regarded sensory impressions as being of a mental nature. When empirical psychology arose, the study of sensory perception was incorporated as a part of the psychological study of consciousness.

As a subarea of physiology, sensory physiology has progressed more or less continuously to the present and has proven of great importance for the study of the brain. The neuropsychological study of color vision and movement in particular led to a new way of looking at the brain's workings. This work in turn influenced the study of cognition, as we shall see in a later chapter. It is clear that a better understanding of brain functions will lead us to a better understanding of psychological processes, and the study of sensory perception seems at present to be one important way of achieving this understanding. But the study of sensory perception is also important because sensory processes form an important basis for our acquisition of knowledge.

The study of sensory perception is complicated, and although physiologists have made numerous surprising discoveries over time, the theories of pioneer researchers such as Hermann von Helmholtz are still relevant. A study of the history of the discipline will help us better understand what is valuable in Helmholtz's work and that of others. It will also let us follow the development of German experimental psychology in the early twentieth century.

The concept of perception is not easily defined. The German physiologists limited their study to situations in which reactions are made to an ongoing stimulation. They did, however, believe that our perception of space and material objects is a result not only of ongoing stimulation, but also of remembering and imagining. To distinguish between what they assumed are the simpler and more fundamental processes and the process resulting from physical stimulation (as well as from remembering and imagining), they referred to the former as *sensations* and the latter as *perceptions*. The distinction may be unwarranted, as Zemir Zeki (1993) noted, and I shall use the term *perception* for both – but not for situations in which only memory and imaginary processes seem to be involved or in which we do not know whether reactions involve only memory and imaginary processes.

The changes taking place in the sensory impressions studied are subtle, and it requires ingenuity and patience to describe them adequately. One reason the study of perception was advanced almost exclusively by German researchers may be that they had developed a tradition of making accurate descriptions of sensory impressions. This tradition forms some of the background for the development of the study of perception, which I shall examine below. Then I shall turn to some early attempts to express relationships between stimulation and sensory impressions mathematically. This study, called *psychophysics*, attracted considerable attention in the mid-1800s and is still carried on today.

Finally, I shall turn to what we may term the physiological study of perception. Two researchers, Johannes Müller and his student Hermann Helmholtz, were central in establishing the discipline. I shall concentrate on Helmholtz, who is a towering figure in early physiological psychology. A study of Helmholtz's work will make it easier to understand more concretely what the discipline is about.

The issues Helmholtz dealt with were complex, and his treatment contained fundamental weaknesses. Some of these were revealed by his younger colleague Ewald Hering, and also by Ernst Mach. These two researchers therefore must have a place even in a short chapter on the early physiological study of perception.

Description of the Mental Experience

We may ask why German physiologists were so engaged in this problem area. One reason is their training and interest in philosophy and epistemological problems. Nearly all the prominent early sensory physiologists were fascinated by Kant's ideas of perception (for instance, David Leary, 1982). Arguing that the human mind contributes to the way the physical world appears to us, Kant had raised questions about perception. To many physiologists, it was natural to believe that at least some of these could be clarified by empirical investigations.

As Boring emphasized, another important reason was the interest many Germans took in the accurate description of perceptual phenomena. Here the poet and scientist Johann Wolfgang Goethe (1749–1832) was an important inspiration. Goethe was fascinated by the nature of light, and in 1810 he published a study of color that was widely read. Emphasis on the importance of accurately observing perceptual phenomena became a hallmark of the German study of perception.

I shall illustrate how interest in the accurate description of perceptual phenomena contributed to the development of the study of perception by reporting first on a well-known experiment ascribed to Goethe, the so-called colored shadows, and then on one of the most accurate observations ever made in the study of perception – namely, that of Johannes Purkinje on the brightness or whiteness of color.

In the colored shadows experiment, a sheet of white paper is positioned in such a way that it is illuminated by relatively weak white daylight from a window and also by yellowish-red light from a candle. The experimenter places a finger or a small stick on the paper so the daylight and the candlelight cast two different shadows on it. The part of the paper lying in the shadow of the candle is now illuminated only by the white light from the window. If our sensory impression of the shadow were determined by the white light reflected onto our eye, we would see the shadow as white. However, the impression we get is of a bluish shadow. Interested readers can perform this demonstration on their own. I shall return to the interpretation of it later in the chapter.

Goethe's color theory was admired by the Czech physiologist Johannes Purkinje (1787–1869), who published two volumes of descriptions of visual phenomena during the years 1824–1825. These contain some remarkable observations, the most important being about changes in the brightness of colors under different illuminations. Purkinje observed that the colors in his garden changed from dawn, when light was weak and bluish-green hues were most prominent, to mid-day, when light was strong and yellowish-red ones were more intense. This important phenomenon was later confirmed and further investigated in the laboratory. It was demonstrated that two clearly different curves are obtained when we examine the brightness of different colors during dark adaptation and light adaptation. Ewald Hering carried on Purkinje's method of approaching problems in visual perception.

Psychophysics

Ernst Heinrich Weber (1795–1878)

Ernst Heinrich Weber was one of the early research workers who attempted to combine knowledge of anatomy and physiology with accurate descriptions of sensory impressions. Weber was interested in the five senses (as they were thought to be at the time), but he concentrated on touch because he thought it was possible to carry out the most accurate investigations of this sense. In line with the thinking of his day, he believed the sense of touch included response to temperature and pain; his perspective was further limited by the fact that he did not know of kinesthesis, the muscle sense.

One of the problems Weber explored was the extent of the area of skin that, when touched at two distinct points, registers being touched at one point only. He used a modified version of a drawing compass that enabled him to touch the skin at two points located a measurable distance apart, and he found the extent of the relevant skin area varied from one part of the body to another. It was very small around the mouth and on the tongue and the fingertips, and much larger on the back and upper arms.

Weber believed we could explain this finding by assuming that, in order for us to experience the sensation of two distinct points, more than one nerve fiber must be present in the area, and he concluded that the smaller areas have more nerve fibers than the larger ones. This was later confirmed by anatomical studies. However, later research also revealed that the sensation arising from touching the skin derives not from pressure applied at a specific point, but from a deformation of an area of the skin as a result of the pressure. Altogether, the skin senses have proven to represent a very complex study. Still, Weber laid the foundation for their systematic and detailed exploration.

Weber was interested in all the senses and discovered another, more general, relationship. He found that the increase in the stimulus required to create a change in a sensory impression depends on the physical value of the stimulus. For instance, the increase needed to detect a difference between weights of approximately 1,000 grams is much greater than the increase needed to detect a difference between weights of 10 grams. Weber carried out measurements of both weight and length and used measurements obtained by others for sound. He found that the increase needed to produce an impression of change is approximately proportional to the physical value of the stimulus. Later researchers have referred to this finding as *Weber's law*.

Gustav Theodor Fechner (1802–1887)

Gustav Theodor Fechner was trained as a medical doctor at the University of Leipzig, where Weber was a teacher. Initially interested in physics, Fechner conducted studies of electricity that gained him a physics professorship. After some years, illness forced him to resign from his position, but after a decade in which he had not been able to do research, he returned with a very original project.

In addition to being a well-trained scientist, accustomed to the use of measurements and quantitative treatment of data, Fechner was a philosopher who, in the manner of the earlier generation of Romantics, was convinced that mind and nature are one. It occurred to him that he could prove there is an identity between mind and nature by demonstrating that changes in sensory processes (which he saw as the mental aspect) correspond to the physical stimulation producing the sensory impression.

He thus developed the concepts of differential threshold and absolute threshold. By *differential threshold* he meant the increase in physical stimulation needed to produce a change in the corresponding sensory impression; by *absolute threshold* he meant the smallest physical stimulation that could be detected. To accurately determine these thresholds, Fechner developed specific methods called *psychophysical methods*. The methods, which we need not describe here, aimed to arrive at reliable estimates by presenting the stimuli in prescribed ways and treating the responses in a quantitative manner. Fechner conducted his experiments with great thoroughness and was able to present a number of reliable threshold values.

In developing a mathematical expression for the relationship between the physical stimulation and the sensory impression, Fechner started from Weber's law, which, he believed, he had verified by his measurements. If we use the symbol R for the physical energy, the stimulus, and the symbol ΔR for the differential threshold, we can express Weber's law as follows:

$$\Delta R/R = K \text{ (where K is a constant)}$$

As he further developed his mathematical treatment, Fechner made a number of more or less reasonable assumptions. First, he believed the sensory impressions caused by a particular type of stimulation constitute a dimension. Further, he assumed that all threshold values he had identified are equal units. This meant he could state that one sense impression is, for instance, five units greater than another. Still further, he surmised that the absolute threshold represented a zero point on a scale of sensory impressions. Finally, he assumed that an infinitesimal increase in the physical stimulus corresponds to an infinitesimal increase in the corresponding sensory impression. Based on these assumptions, he was able to mathematically deduce the following equation, called *Fechner's law*, for the relationship between the sensory impression S and the stimulus R:

$$S = K \log R \text{ (where K is a constant for the specific type of sense}$$
$$\text{impression being examined)}$$

Fechner believed he had found a law expressing the relationship between various types of physical stimuli and the sensory impressions arising from these. By learning more about the sensory systems, he felt, we could arrive at a number of laws expressing relationships between body and mind.

His report of his investigations was published in 1860 and attracted considerable attention. Many believed Fechner had arrived at the first law of scientific psychology; others, however, were more skeptical. William James (1890) was not particularly impressed and wrote that all Fechner's law proved was that nothing can bore a German professor.

Like many other psychological findings, Fechner's law did not nearly fulfill initial expectations; it is in fact relevant, though not to the entire range of sensory impressions. Still, there is reason to believe it gives an approximate expression of an important biological relationship – namely, how the human organism reacts to changes in certain types of physical stimulations. The law also has a practical application: it allows us to identify deficits in hearing and vision, as well as differences in levels of light and sound stimulation. The study of perception psychology would be greatly advanced if it were possible to provide adequate quantitative and mathematical equations for the relationship between stimuli and sensory impressions. Fechner's finding is nonetheless of both theoretical and practical significance. Fechner is also known for his experimental studies of aesthetic impressions, and he presented ideas about how the feeling of pleasure originated; Freud made use of these ideas in his system.

Johannes Müller (1801–1858)

A major figure in physiology in the mid-1800s was Johannes Müller. Appointed professor of anatomy and physiology at the University of Berlin in 1833, he published an extensive handbook of physiology over the next several years, which was of great importance for the development of this field of research. Müller grew up at a time when physiologists were greatly influenced by the Romantics' view of nature, in which humans were seen as being one with nature, and mind and matter are two aspects of the same thing. However, Müller also urged that experimental procedures should be applied in investigations of physiological problems. Thereby he helped lay the foundations for the new experimental physiology that emerged in the mid-1800s. He was an extremely versatile scientist who also did extensive work on comparative physiological problems. In addition to being an outstanding scientist, Müller must have been a remarkable teacher. He trained an amazing number of students who contributed to progress in physiology from the mid-1800s.

In his handbook, Müller examined a number of problem areas relating to psychology, including perception, memory, imagination, thinking and emotions, sleep, and the basis for actions. Here we will look only at his ideas about perception.

Müller and Helmholtz on the Law of the So-called Specific Nerve Energies

Müller was particularly concerned with the fact that each sense gives sensory impressions of a specific quality or, as he said, a specific energy. He postulated that we could explain this by assuming that each of the sensory nerves has a specific state responsible for the quality, and so he formulated the *law of specific nerve energies (qualities)*. Researchers at that time had no means of determining the state of the nerve, and nothing was known about the structure of the brain or how the sensory nerves connected to it. It must, therefore, have been difficult for Müller's contemporaries to give the law a more concrete meaning, but they were greatly attracted to it. Helmholtz thought it was of the greatest importance.

Müller's law concerned the five senses recognized at the time. Helmholtz suggested that the sensory nerves contain different kinds of fibers, and that each kind has a specific state leading to a specific quality. Thus, he assumed the optic one contains different kinds of fibers giving sensory impressions of different chromatic colors. By careful experiments, Helmholtz had shown that all chromatic colors could be produced by mixing blue, green, and red. This finding could now be explained by the assumption that there are three different kinds of fibers in the optic nerve.

Helmholtz also suggested that there are different kinds of fibers in the acoustic nerve, each responsible for the impression of a certain pitch. By assuming that the fibers resonated to tones of different frequencies, Helmholtz claimed that it is possible to explain pitch discrimination.

The law of specific energies of nerves may have given Helmholtz inspiration to search for fibers of specific kinds in the sensory nerves, but it is also possible that in his enthusiasm for the law, he forgot that he may have obtained his ideas of the tri-chromatic color theory from the British physicist Thomas Young, who had formulated it nearly fifty years before him. The resonator theory of pitch discrimination had also been suggested by another researcher before Helmholtz's presentation of it.

Hermann von Helmholtz (1821–1894)

Hermann von Helmholtz was born in Potsdam. His father taught languages and philosophy at a high school, and Helmholtz was introduced to questions of philosophy at an early age, though his main interests while still at school were in the natural sciences. Because his father believed it would be difficult for his son to finance university study, Helmholtz was trained as a physician at a free military academy that educated surgeons for the Prussian state in exchange for serving a certain number of years in the army.

While at the military academy, Helmholtz visited the University of Berlin and became acquainted with Müller, forming friendships with several of his students and other scientists. As early as the late 1840s, he distinguished himself with a treatise in which he put forward a number of clear formulations of the principle of the conservation of energy.

The Speed of Conduction in Nerves

In 1850, Helmholtz published a remarkable experimental investigation of the speed of conduction in a sensory nerve. At that time, it was assumed, including by Müller, that the speed of conduction in nerves is immensely high, as high as that of light – approximately 300,000 kilometers per second. By a simple but ingenious means, Helmholtz measured the speed of conduction in a motor nerve in a frog's thigh and obtained a value of only 30 meters per second, which approximates the values obtained for certain types of nerves with modern measuring devices. The difference between the values obtained by Helmholtz and Müller's estimate indicates how important it is to perform experiments in science. Müller accepted Helmholtz's results, and after he had been convinced by his assistant that they had been arrived at accurately, he even helped with their publication.

Helmholtz did not restrict himself to studying the motor nerve of a frog; he also made direct measurements of the speed of conduction in a human sensory nerve. His procedure was as follows. He first trained his subjects to react with a particular movement to pressure applied to some part of the body. Then he measured the time it took for a person to react as quickly as possible to the pressure. In this way, he ascertained what we call *reaction time*. By measuring the reaction times for different points on the skin that activated the same sensory nerve – for instance, a toe and a point on the thigh – Helmholtz could estimate how long it took the impulse to move from toe to thigh by subtracting one reaction time from the other. After measuring the length of the sensory nerve, he could then calculate the speed.

Helmholtz arrived at values that correspond reasonably well to those obtained today with more refined measuring devices. He did not publish his research on the speed of nerve conduction in human beings, however, because he found such wide discrepancies in the times obtained for the measurements. Nevertheless, in the development of German experimental psychology, his procedure proved important and is still used in modern cognitive psychology; I shall return to it in Chapter 4.

Studies in Perception

From the beginning of the early 1850s until the mid-1860s, Helmholtz primarily concentrated on the study of perception. Between 1856 and 1866, he carried out extensive investigations in vision, included in a comprehensive work entitled *Handbuch der physiologischen Optik* (*Treatise on Physiological Optics*). In 1863, he published another work of fundamental importance on hearing, entitled *Die Lehre von den Tonempfindungen als physiologischer Grundlage für die Theorie der Musik* (*On the Sensations of Tone as a Physiological Basis for the Theory of Music*). Both works are still important sources for researchers wanting to acquire a thorough knowledge of perception.

After serving as a professor at two German universities, Helmholtz became professor of physiology at the University of Heidelberg in 1858. In 1871, he obtained the position he probably wanted most of all, the professorship in physics at the University of Berlin. In his later years, he was ennobled and consequently referred to as *von* Helmholtz ("von" indicating an order of nobility). After his death, a statue was erected in his memory.

Helmholtz's General View of Perception

In an extensive chapter in the final part of his *Handbuch der physiologischen Optik*, Helmholtz presented a general view of perception based on the concept of sensation. Sensations, he declared, have only the characteristics of *quality* and *intensity*. Hence, the only information about external objects we gain directly through our senses is that the sensation has a certain quality – for instance, a sensation of a specific color is present – and that the sensation has a certain intensity – for instance, light of a certain intensity is present. Helmholtz held that, in our sensory systems, there are no mechanisms giving us direct information that objects are located in a certain direction or at a certain distance from our body, or that they are of a specific size, shape, and form. These aspects of our perceptual representations emerged, Helmholtz said, as a result of a complex learning process. Through experience, through learning, we associate different sensations with each other.

Helmholtz termed his view "empiricist" and contrasted it with a nativist view that emphasizes mechanisms assumed to be innate. Like Descartes, he distinguished between physiological and mental processes. He believed the state of the sensory nerve to be somehow registered in the mind, in consciousness, and that the association of the sensations takes place in consciousness.

In his emphasis on experience and associative learning, Helmholtz is in agreement with British empiricist philosophy. However, contrary to J. S. Mill and the British empiricists, he emphasized that we are actively engaged in acquiring knowledge of the world surrounding us, and that associations are thus formed by our active participation. In this view, he was presumably influenced by Kant. Like Kant, he also believed we must take for granted that our mental representations are structured in time and space. Hence, our perception of space could not be explained only as a result of learning. I shall not go into these very difficult aspects of the study of perception but instead present enough to form a picture of his view.

Perception as Interpretation and Construction

Later research has revealed fundamental weaknesses in Helmholtz's theory of perception. But it had great value because Helmholtz supported it with great skill and maintained it with such consistency that its weaknesses became evident. He was a reflective scientist and knew perfectly well that he had undertaken an extremely difficult task. He said he had tried to create order from chaos and had worked from the point of view that a poor theory is better than no theory at all.

Helmholtz compared the use we make of our sensations with linguistic signs. In the same way we learn to interpret linguistic signs, we learn to interpret the information we receive from our sensations. Some interpretations occur frequently, and we can regard them as habitual. Interpretation, Helmholtz said, takes place according to two principles. The *first principle* states that we tend to interpret a sign, a sensation, so that it corresponds to the habitual interpretation. For instance, light striking the outer part of the eyeball most often comes from that part of the field of vision in the direction of the bridge of the nose. If, by applying pressure to this part of the eye, we produce an impression of light, we experience the light as coming from the bridge of the nose. Helmholtz believed the principle of the habitual interpretation covered all normal use of the eyes, in which we direct them towards the point on which we are focusing and, by focusing the lens, try to obtain the sharpest possible image of the object. In order to obtain as much information as possible, Helmholtz claimed, we would also move our eyes over the whole area in which we are interested, and here we would be inclined to follow contours. Helmholtz illustrated the use of his first principle in a number of concrete ways. Still, its application often became somewhat arbitrary.

Helmholtz's *second principle* was that we tend to be aware of our sensations only to the extent that we can make use of them for gaining knowledge of external objects; sensations that are of no relevance for our understanding of external objects are ignored. Helmholtz claimed this principle explained why phenomena such as afterimages, double images, and overtones ordinarily remain unnoticed. I shall expand a little more on his first principle.

The habitual interpretation, Helmholtz believed, was the result of an infinite number of stimulations of the same type. It could also be considered an inference. Since this meant it was *interpretation* that primarily determines our perceptions, perceptions had to be seen as a result of a judgment. In his attempt to clarify what he meant by inference, Helmholtz referred to Mill's view of the syllogism. Like Mill, he claimed that this type of inference most often takes place unconsciously. It is normally not the result of an act of will but instead forces itself upon us. Accordingly, our perceptions are, to a large degree, the result of unconscious inferences. By assuming unconscious inferences, Helmholtz thought he was able to explain why our perceptions appear to emerge spontaneously in spite of being a result of learning.

I shall illustrate Helmholtz's view of unconscious inferences by means of his interpretation of the phenomenon of colored shadows. When the shadow of the candle appears bluish, he maintained, the reason is that we assume the light from the candle falls on the entire white surface, and thus also that the shadow is illuminated by a yellowish-red light. He further assumed that experience has taught us that a bluish surface lighted by a yellowish-red light appears white or gray. From this we infer that the shadow must be of a bluish shade and experience the color of the shadow accordingly.

Some readers might find Helmholtz's explanation somewhat contrived. Actually, it has been shown to be incorrect because the phenomenon occurs as a result of a fundamental physiological mechanism in the nervous system – namely, *contrast*. For a number of other visual phenomena, however, the assumption of an unconscious inference appears more plausible. About one hundred years after Helmholtz presented his ideas on unconscious inferences, Adelbert Ames and his coworkers demonstrated that it is possible to influence visual perception by manipulating the viewer's assumptions about the nature of the situation actually seen. For this purpose, Ames and his coworkers constructed a room that, when seen through a peephole, appears ordinary even if it has quite different proportions. When a person is located at different places in this room, his or her size appears to change in a manner both spontaneous and surprising.

The Perception of Visual Space

To explain how we perceive the spatial characteristics of objects and the location of objects in space, Helmholtz assumed that we make use of a variety of *cues*. Some of these cues are, he argued, information we receive when the inner and outer muscles of the eye are activated. Focusing of the lens is such a cue; another is the convergence of the two eyes when they are directed at a particular point. Helmholtz also believed binocular disparity to be a cue, even if it is effective only after a period of learning. Other cues are the registering of retinal size, the covering of one object by another, and the positioning of one object between other objects (masking and interposition). To explain how our perceptions of space emerge, Helmholtz also relied on eye movements (such as the following of an outline) and movements of the head and body.

The cues Helmholtz used as a basis for the understanding of our perception of space were already known. But he contributed to our understanding of them by examining them critically and systematically, and often he gave his formulations a precise mathematical expression. As mentioned, he also contributed by developing the empiricist position so consistently that its weaknesses could more easily be detected. Ralph Haber (1985) insisted that Helmholtz's theory on spatial perception has been a challenge to researchers in perception until our time and still is. According to Haber, it was first challenged when James Gibson (1950) put forward his alternative theory, to which I shall turn in Chapter 13.

Helmholtz began his studies of perception before Darwin published his theory of evolution, and, unlike his teacher Müller and his critic Hering, Helmholtz was little inclined to explain perception by means of mechanisms resulting from the organism's adaptation to its environment. Apparently, he believed that visual stimulation results in activation of nerve fibers in small areas of the retina that are not connected to each other, so stimulation of one area is not influenced by stimulation of others. From the 1950s onwards, neurophysiologists have shown there *are* mechanisms that make possible various types of interaction between the receptors of the eye. The visual system, therefore, cannot be regarded as a system that brings limited, local information to the brain. These findings raise doubts that our spatial perceptions are based on learning in the way Helmholtz believed. Further, from the 1960s, research on infants has produced a number of findings that also cast doubt on Helmholtz's empiricist theory of spatial perception.

Müller and Helmholtz on Attention

Theories of attention played a major role in Müller's and Helmholtz's view of perception. Müller pointed out that when our attention is divided over several senses or several aspects within one single sensory modality, it appears to be reduced according to the number of senses or aspects engaged. He further noted that a constant stimulation that strongly engages our attention in some circumstances does not register under other circumstances, as, for example, when we are absorbed in some activity.

As we have seen, Helmholtz's second principle rested on assumptions of attention, and ideas about attention had a central place in his theory of perception. Some of the points he made concerning its nature deserve consideration. First, he maintained that at a specific point in time, we can be aware only of either a single impression or a group of impressions contained in single representation. Second, he believed attention has a tendency to wander. Only with effort are we able to concentrate on a specific object over a period of time, and it is possible to focus our attention on a specific object only as long as we can find new aspects of it (Helmholtz, 1856–1866/1924–1925, III, p. 498):

It is natural for the attention to be distracted from one thing to another. As soon as the interest in one object has been exhausted, and there is no longer anything new in it to be perceived, it is transferred to something else, even against our will. When we wish to rivet it on an object, we must constantly seek to find something novel about it, and this is especially true when other powerful impressions of the senses are tugging at it and trying to distract it.

The third point is that in certain situations we are able to train ourselves to use a particular stimulation so that we learn to notice objects, or aspects of them, of which we were not initially aware. For instance, we can train ourselves to notice objects in the periphery of our visual field that we did not notice before. Similarly, we can train ourselves to distinguish instruments in an orchestra or overtones in a tone. Helmholtz suggested that we learn this by anticipating what we expect to perceive.

Helmholtz on Science and Psychology

Helmholtz made major contributions to physics and mathematics as well as to physiology. Through his studies of vision and hearing, attention, and reaction times, he greatly influenced early psychology. His work on perception laid a foundation for the study of vision and hearing, and his investigation of reaction times formed the basis for *mental chronometry*, which I shall discuss in Chapter 4. His research on attention was continued by the early German psychologists, and William James (1890/1950) popularized his main ideas, but modern researchers have tended to overlook it.

Like most of his contemporaries, Helmholtz regarded mechanics as the model science and thought it the aim of science to explain events and phenomena as resulting from mechanical forces. Yet he was not a materialist who wanted to reduce all phenomena to statements about movements and forces. As we have seen, he believed that in attempts to increase scientific knowledge we must take a certain formal framework for granted, and he was not a positivist because he believed science has a firm foundation in observations. Further, he understood that an experimental approach has its limitations. He did not hold, for instance, that by empirical research we could prove a nativist point of view to be wrong. What we *could* hope to show is that a nativist view is less fruitful than an empiricist one.

Nor did Helmholtz believe, as the younger scholar Mach did, that theories should rest on sensations in the form of observations. Helmholtz was concerned with establishing *facts* on which theories could be built. Facts are not observations, but hypotheses for which the scientist had provided a solid foundation through empirical research. In his argument in favor of an empiricist theory of the perception of space, he sought to establish as facts what we have referred to above as cues.

Physicalism in Physiology

In the mid-nineteenth century, physiologists began to apply principles from physics and chemistry to the study of physiological processes, a movement known as *physicalism*. Helmholtz and his closer friends among Müller's students became avowed physicalists. (The story goes that they took an oath committing themselves to giving physiology a physicalistic orientation.) The physicalistic orientation contributed to the rapid acceleration of progress in physiology.

In addition to Helmholtz, others in the circle of German physicalists were Emil Du Bois-Reymond, who in 1848 published a major work on animal electricity and succeeded Müller at the University of Berlin; Carl Ludwig, perhaps the most outstanding physiologist in the latter half of the nineteenth century; and Ernst Brücke, who became a professor in Vienna. Among the many researchers who visited and worked in Ludwig's laboratory were Sechenov and Pavlov.

Proximate and Ultimate Explanations

By adopting a strictly physicalist approach to the study of physiological processes, German researchers contributed to a breakthrough in physiology. However, they overlooked that biological processes are the result of a long evolutionary development and of adjustments to a changing environment, and that they must be understood in a historical perspective. An explanation of biological processes should, therefore, include a historically biological aspect. In line with this way of thinking, biologists have made a distinction between two types of explanations. *Proximate explanations* are based on descriptions of the processes that take place in an organism at a given time. *Ultimate explanations* describe how the organism has adjusted to its environment through its phylogenesis over time.

For example, by studying changes in light and temperature, we are able to give a proximate explanation of why various species of birds migrate from one area to another at certain times of the year. But this does not provide an ultimate explanation of why or how migration originated in the species. Physicalism, as practiced by Helmholtz and his colleagues, led to a one-sided concentration on proximate explanations, which can often be successfully studied experimentally in a laboratory. Ultimate explanations, on the other hand, require comparative studies and detailed fieldwork.

By basing their thinking solely on physicalistic principles and an experimental approach, Helmholtz and his friends neglected comparative and field studies. Their teacher, Johannes Müller, who had been a pioneer in experimental physiology, was also an outstanding comparative anatomist and physiologist. However, he was a vitalist, and when his students rejected vitalism, they rejected comparative and historical methods as well. In his history of biology, Ernst Mayr (1982) has noted that Helmholtz and his physicalistic friends contributed to creating a schism in biology that persisted for a long time, to the detriment of the field.

From its very beginning, scientific psychology was strongly dependent on physiology, and the schism created by the German physicalists also had unfortunate consequences for the development of psychology. In Russian physiology, there was a strong element of physicalism in the research of Pavlov and Sechenov. They used animals in their laboratory experiments without making serious efforts to study empirically how the animals' behavior was the result of adjustments to a specific environment. After a short period in which they employed a broad biological approach, American comparative psychologists ended up with an animal psychology based almost exclusively on laboratory experiments with rats and pigeons.

Ewald Hering (1834–1918): An Alternative Approach to Perception

The idea that our perceptions are built up by association of sensations had a broad following among many German physiologists and psychologists in the 1800s, but not all. Ewald Hering adopted an alternate view.

In nearly all respects Hering was in opposition to Helmholtz. His research in vision was probably more original than that of his more famous contemporary, but, unlike Helmholtz, he was neither a great physicist, mathematician, nor philosopher of science, and therefore he came to live in Helmholtz's shadow. In his thinking about physiological mechanisms, Ewald was perhaps too far ahead of his time to be understood. The phenomenological approach to the study of perception was foreign to most English-speaking physiologists, and apart from the fact that Charles Sherrington studied with him, Hering's work did not receive much attention in the Anglo-Saxon world.

Hering was educated as a physician at the University of Leipzig, where Weber and Fechner had been his teachers, though he considered himself first and foremost a student of Johannes Müller, even if he did not actually study under him. Following a university position in Vienna, he succeeded Purkinje as professor in Prague, and then Ludwig as professor of physiology in Leipzig. In the 1860s, Hering published his most important works on spatial perception. Later he concentrated primarily on the study of light and color, and in the 1870s he published a major work on what he called the light sense. An extensive and revised version of this work was published in 1920, entitled *Grundzüge der Lehre vom Lichtsinne* (*Outlines of a Theory of the Light Sense*, translated in 1964 by the American researchers Leo Hurwich and Dorothea Jameson).

Emphasis on Phenomenological Description

Hering had learnt from Goethe and Purkinje to make accurate observations of perceptual phenomena, and he stressed that the point of departure for the study of visual perception should be experience, and not assumptions about the nature of light or the nervous system. He criticized Helmholtz for resting some of his conclusions on incomplete or inaccurate observations.

An important issue was to decide which colors should be considered primary. Helmholtz concluded that red, green, and blue must be the primary colors. Hering maintained that yellow should be also, and that red and green are one complementary pair and blue and yellow another. For one hundred years, scientists disagreed. Then in the late 1950s, two researchers were awarded the Nobel Prize for demonstrating that there are three, not four, different kinds of photoreceptors in the eye. Was Helmholtz right after all? A few years later, other scientists demonstrated that at a higher level in the visual system there are mechanisms linking our sensitivity to red and green and blue and yellow in pairs. This showed, as Hering had anticipated, that yellow has a place in the visual system similar to that of blue, red, and green.

Another important phenomenon Hering investigated was our experience of the color black. Helmholtz maintained that black originates as a result of the *absence* of light stimulation. Hering opposed this view by referring to the simple fact that when we close our eyes or sit in darkness, we experience gray rather than black. Black, he affirmed, is the result of a contrast effect. He showed that even fairly grayish hues give the impression of black if they are surrounded by a white surface. In his study of contrast effects, Hering drew attention to a fundamental aspect of the visual system, the color-opponent process theory. This theory states that the human visual system interprets information about color by processing signals from cones and rods in an antagonistic or contrasting manner.

Biological Mechanisms Behind Perception

In order to support his mechanistic explanations, Helmholtz had resorted to assumptions about various types of mental processes. Hering objected to the attempts to explain perception by resorting to judgments and unconscious inferences. Instead, he searched for specific biological mechanisms that could explain perceptual phenomena, and as a result he made a number of valuable contributions to the study of vision.

In his early studies of binocular vision, Hering postulated that the two eyes function as parts of a unified system. This system, he claimed, is governed by central processes in the nervous system. In this way, he could explain why the two slightly different images received by the eyes (through the phenomenon of binocular disparity) enable us to see objects in definite directions and at definite distances. He also postulated that two adjacent areas of the retina can interact and in this way produce a contrast effect. Hering insisted it was not correct, as Helmholtz and most of his contemporaries believed, that specific areas of the retina function as independent units integrated by mental processes. Hering's view of contrasts has also been accepted. Contrasts provided a better biological adjustment, he said, because they contribute to making the boundaries between different areas in the field of vision clearer; hence, we can more easily perceive material objects in our environment.

Helmholtz had explained the effect obtained in his demonstration of the colored shadows by postulating that we wrongly assume that the entire surface of the paper is illuminated by a homogeneous, yellowish-red light. Hering rejected this theory and explained the phenomenon as a result of interaction between two adjacent areas of the retina – in other words, a contrast effect.

Hering criticized Helmholtz's explanation based on unconscious inference as being circular. The basis for the judgment, he said, must simply be the light originating from the diverse parts of our field of vision. Based on the color of these areas, we cannot first deduce the presence of some sort of total illumination and then, on the basis of

this illumination, deduce the color of the areas. Even if this reasoning is not necessarily circular, Hering identified a problem with an explanation based on unconscious
inferences.

Hering's view that we should think of color as components appearing in pairs (red–
green, yellow–blue, black–white), was, as Hurwich and Jameson (1964) noted, often
misunderstood, because in Hering's time only a limited knowledge of the anatomy of
the visual system was available. When anatomical knowledge increased and new physiological techniques were developed, Hering's view was confirmed. But this was not to
occur until nearly one hundred years later.

Ernst Mach occupies an intermediate position in the history of the study of perception.
On the one hand, he was an advocate of the empiricist view that not only perception, but
also all knowledge, is built on sensations. In Chapter 12 we saw that he tried to formulate
an epistemology as well as a philosophy of science on this foundation. On the other hand,
he stressed that our perceptual impressions are determined by the relationships between
our sensations. In a number of simple demonstrations, he showed how relationships
determine perception. In one of these, Mach showed that the stimuli producing our
perceptions of the left and right halves of a figure are different. Nonetheless, we perceive
the two halves as similar.

In Figure 3.1, the visual impression is markedly altered when, instead of seeing the
black color as a pattern, we see the light color as a pattern. While Mach asserted that we
do not normally see color and shape, but rather objects in space, he does not seem to
have doubted that our perception consists of combinations of sensations. He therefore
did not believe that, through our sensory apparatus, we primarily receive information
about objects in space and from this information abstract attributes such as color, shape,
and size.

Figure 3.1 Perception of colors and shapes.

This way of looking at things first emerged with phenomenology and Gestalt psychology. Mach's interpretation of his experiments shows how deeply rooted he was in the assumption that our perceptual concepts are the result of sensations related to each other by association. In this, his thinking was in line with that of Müller and Helmholtz.

4

Expansion of German Experimental
Psychology

In his *Handbook of Physiology*, published in the 1830s, Johannes Müller covered various psychological problems. In the 1850s, several other research workers attempted to incorporate psychology into physiology as the study of consciousness. Therefore, when, in 1874, Wilhelm Wundt proposed that the study of the relationship between physiology and psychology should be established as a specific area of empirical science, the idea had already been maturing for a number of years. Wundt's proposal was presented in a book entitled *Grundzüge der physiologischen Psychologie* (*Principles of Physiological Psychology* (1873–1874). Wundt could rest his proposal on extensive empirical material. The book attracted great attention, and five years later, in 1879, he established his laboratory for experimental psychology. Students flocked to it, not only from Germany and Europe, but also from the United States.

Psychological research and teaching in Germany took place almost exclusively at the universities and formed part of the study of philosophy. Thus, students who wanted to receive training in psychology had to combine this with studies of philosophy.

Central Figures in Early German Experimental Psychology

Wundt was the central figure in early experimental psychology, but a number of other researchers who regarded themselves as psychologists made significant contributions to the establishment of scientific, empirical psychology. About the time Wundt established his laboratory, Hermann Ebbinghaus had independently begun research in learning and memory, apparently inspired by Gustav Fechner. He published his investigations in a book in 1885, which was considered a milestone in the new empirical study of consciousness. In 1887, the professor of philosophy at Göttingen, Georg Elias Müller, started a laboratory of psychological research. Like Ebbinghaus, Georg Müller was inspired by Fechner, and when Ebbinghaus's book appeared, he enthusiastically began research along similar lines. Towards the end of the nineteenth century, his laboratory was just as active and important as the one in Leipzig.

The same year Wundt's *Grundzüge* appeared, 1874, another German, Franz Brentano, published a book in which he discussed how psychology could be made an empirical science. His ideas fused with the ideas underlying the phenomenological approach to the study of perception, which had developed from the time of Goethe. Inspired by Brentano, a broad philosophical and psychological movement based upon the idea of a phenomenological description of mental events spread over the German-speaking intellectual world. This movement I shall deal with in Chapter 5. Here, I shall just mention that, in 1894, Carl Stumpf, a student and friend of Brentano, became the director of a laboratory for experimental psychology in Berlin. From the beginning of the twentieth century, this laboratory became the leading one in Germany.

In addition to the laboratories in Leipzig, Göttingen, and Berlin, a fourth laboratory in Würzburg carried out important research from the end of the nineteenth century. This laboratory was directed by Oswald Külpe, who had been a student of Georg Elias Müller and Wundt's laboratory assistant for many years. Over time, Külpe had uncovered some fundamental weaknesses in the approach on which research in Leipzig was founded. When he became the director of the laboratory in Würzburg, his students carried out research that contributed to undermining fundamental assumptions not only in the Wundtian approach, but also in the whole of German experimental psychology. Külpe can therefore be said to represent the end of an era.

Wilhelm Wundt (1832–1920)

In the first two decades of the twentieth century, Wundt was strongly criticized by both German and American psychologists. His way of thinking belongs to the past and is not easily accessible. However, because he played a great role in the establishment of empirical psychology, we must treat him more fully. It is also necessary to study him in some detail because, as Arthur Blumenthal (1975) and other scholars have pointed out, some of his important ideas may have been overlooked.

Wundt rarely discussed the epistemological questions underlying his approach, making it difficult to understand his thinking more precisely. Further, his ideas require interpretation in the light of a complex intellectual history. Finally, on important points he changed his opinions without telling us why. To be sure we are representing him correctly, we must sometimes go into detail about the ideas and circumstances forming the background of his psychological thinking.

A Short Biography

Wundt was born in Neckarau, a suburb of Mannheim in Baden, the son of a Calvinist minister. In his family there were several scientists and scholars, and – like Weber, Fechner, Helmholtz, and Hering – he belonged to what we can think of as a clan of civil servants. After the completion of his medical studies at the University of Heidelberg in 1855, Wundt practiced for a short time as a physician, but then he decided to become a physiologist and worked for a term with Johannes Müller and Emil Du Bois-Reymond. In 1856, he gained the title of *Dozent* and began giving courses in physiology. When he was twenty-five years old, he became seriously ill, and in later years he maintained that his philosophical and psychological convictions were formed during his illness. When Helmholtz was appointed professor of physiology at the University of Heidelberg in 1858, Wundt became his assistant and taught courses in physiology.

As Solomon Diamond (1980) has shown, there seems to have been little communication between Wundt and Helmholtz. In 1864, Wundt was appointed *Professor extraordinarius* (without a chair) of physiology. In this position, he received no salary and supported himself by private tutoring, which he continued until he published *Grundzüge der physiologischen Psychologie* (*Principles of Physiological Psychology*) in 1873–1874. This book, which appeared in six revised editions between 1874 and 1911, was an immediate success, and Wundt was appointed professor of philosophy first in Zürich and then, in 1876, in Leipzig, where he lived until his death. Here, he established his laboratory in 1879, and two years later an institute of psychology. Although his reputation declined after 1900, following the publication of *Grundzüge* he became an admired and important person in the intellectual life of Germany and received several marks of honor.

Wundt was a highly productive writer and produced more than 50,000 printed pages. *Grundzüge* was published in six revised editions, the last one in 1911. Before this work, he published *Beiträge zur Theorie der Sinneswahrnehmung* (*Contributions to the Theory of Sense Perception*) (1858–1862) and *Vorlesungen über die Menschen- und Tierseele*

(*Lectures on Human and Animal Psychology*) (1863). In 1881, he founded the journal *Philosophische Studien* (*Philosophical Studies*), which for a number of years was the journal for the new experimental psychology. In addition to editing this journal, he also contributed articles to it. In the 1880s, he published a book on logic in two volumes, a book on ethics in three volumes, and a book in which he presented his own philosophical system, also in three volumes. In 1896, he published an abridged edition of *Grundzüge*, entitled *Grundriss der Psychologie* (*Outline of Psychology*). Between 1900 and 1920, he wrote a work in ten volumes, in which he attempted to develop a social psychology based upon historical studies of language, myths, and customs. This extensive work he called *Völkerpsychologie* (*Social Psychology*). In the year he died, 1920, he completed his autobiography. Wundt was married, had children, and cultivated music and other artistic interests. In his youth he was, for a short period, also active in politics.

Idealist or Positivist? Wundt's Philosophical System

As I mentioned in Chapter 1, Boring's presentation of Wundt and the history of psychology dominated the views of psychologists for several decades. However, in the 1970s, Arthur Blumenthal (1975, 1980), Kurt Danziger (1980a, b), and other historians pointed out that Boring had overlooked important aspects of Wundt's approach to psychology. He had given a picture of Wundt that was in agreement with the conception of psychology of Boring's own teacher Edward Titchener, who was a student and follower of Wundt, and this conception was far from adequate. The historians reacting to Boring made some necessary corrections, but in the new presentation, they did not, in my opinion, distinguish between what Wundt said and what he actually did. They correctly underlined his idealistic, philosophical position but overlooked that he was also strongly influenced by positivist philosophy of science.

Wundt was inspired by the Romantic, idealistic German philosophy of the beginning of the nineteenth century. Like his Romantic models, he developed an extensive philosophical system, a *Weltanschauung*. Central to it was Leibniz's idea that consciousness reflects the world. In the first edition of *Grundzüge*, Wundt elaborated this idea, from which it followed that consciousness could not be explained by the help of physiological processes. Wundt did not have a dualistic view of the relationship between body and mind. He believed that matter, the physical, must be understood as fundamentally of a spiritual and idealistic nature. He regarded physiological and psychological processes as parallel, but he did not attempt to develop this view consistently. Because he did not try to show how physiological processes could be regarded as derivable from his idealist position, his view of the body–mind problem was very similar to a dualistic position. It is therefore not surprising that he has often been regarded as a dualist.

Wundt was influenced not only by Romantic, idealistic philosophy, but also by positivist thinking. Like the positivists, he wanted to base philosophy on science, and he believed psychology to be the science that could form this foundation. As I understand him, he had a vision of humans and the world based on what he thought was a scientific psychology. His attempt to lay the foundation for this scientific psychology was a link in his attempt to form an extensive, systematic philosophy. When we view his ideas in this way, it is easy to understand that, after he had written *Grundzüge* and established his laboratory, his work for the next two decades mainly concentrated on philosophical problems.

The psychological system Wundt developed was not an attempt to construct a theory based on physiological and psychological knowledge of his day, but rather an attempt to find a foundation *in psychology* for a philosophical system. Further, Wundt did not use his system to deduce hypotheses that could be investigated empirically; his system was a loose framework built around his psychological and philosophical thinking.

Thus, Wundt was not a scientific, empirical psychologist in the modern sense, as Boring tried to make him. First and foremost, he was a system or *Weltanschauung* builder in philosophy. It is not quite correct, as William James maintained, that Wundt's thinking lacked a central idea, though James was probably right in saying it lacked coherence. James himself struggled to keep philosophy and psychology apart, and Wundt's way of writing probably annoyed him. A little maliciously but not unfairly, he said first of Wundt that "he aims at being a Napoleon of the intellectual world," and then added, "Unfortunately he will never have a Waterloo, for he is a Napoleon without genius and with no central idea which, if defeated, brings down the whole fabric in ruin" (R. B. Perry, *The Thought and Character of William James*, II, 1935, p. 68).

Wundt's Scientific Psychology

Based on what I have said here about the philosophical framework of Wundt's scientific psychology, I shall first deal with his view of the subject matter and method of psychology, then with his psychological system, and finally with the empirical research undertaken in his laboratory.

The Subject Matter of Psychology

In the first edition of *Grundzüge*, the work Wundt thought might lay the foundation for a scientific psychology, he identified the subject matter of the new field: "In psychology man views himself in a sense from the inside and tries to explain the relationships between the events which reveal themselves by this view." This inner view he contrasted with what we perceive by our senses; he distinguished between an outer and an inner perception. According to him, physics, chemistry, physiology – in fact, all the natural sciences – are based on an outer perception; in contrast, psychology is based on an inner perception.

The inner perception gives us inner experiences in the form of perceptual representations, recollections, imaginary representations, thoughts, feelings, and utterances of the will. These inner experiences constitute the subject matter of psychology. Wundt held that inner experiences are contained in the idea of "soul," a concept of daily life necessary to psychology, pedagogically speaking. In other words, psychology is a study of "soul," or, to avoid religious overtones, *consciousness*.

Johannes Müller and Helmholtz regarded mental events as representing a specific domain. Wundt elaborated this idea and maintained that mental phenomena must be separated from bodily and material processes, that we cannot explain mental processes by means of physiological processes. Therefore, a scientific psychology cannot start from a study of physiological processes. Psychological processes and phenomena must be explained by reference to other psychological processes and phenomena. Wundt drew a line between physiology and psychology through the sensory processes; these are to be conceived of as partly physiological and partly psychological.

Wundt assumed a parallelism between physiological and psychological processes in the sense that certain psychological processes correspond to certain physiological processes. However, in an article from 1896, he stated that he did not think it possible to make extensive use of the principle of parallelism. To an increasing extent, therefore, his psychology became a study limited to mental events.

Earlier in the century, Johann Friedrich Herbart had argued that mental representations that disappear from consciousness might continue to exist as unconscious representations, from which state they could again enter consciousness. Wundt (1896a) rejected the idea of unconscious representations. What he believed was, as I understand him, that a mental representation results in a disposition to form a similar representation at a later time. Here Wundt emphasized that, as a result of practice, a change might take place in the nervous system, and this change results in the disposition to form representations similar to those previously present. In a discussion of Schopenhauer's conception of the will, he also rejected the idea that the will can be influenced by unconscious representations.

Without changing his view of the relationships between psychology and physiology and between psychology and behavior, Wundt later attempted to define the subject matter of psychology in a different way. Now he asserted, probably under the influence of Ernst Mach, that the natural sciences and psychology have a basis in the same mental processes and in the same type of mental experiences. The difference between psychology and natural science is that they consider mental experiences from different viewpoints. Mental experiences, he said, have two aspects, and we might distinguish between two factors: the content and our conception of the content. This distinction, he declared, corresponds to the object of the experiences and the experiencing subject. In the natural sciences, the object is regarded as being independent of the experiencing subjects. This conception of the object is an abstraction, and Wundt designated it as *mediated*. In contrast, in psychology, experiences are considered as they are present in the immediate subjective experience of the experiencing subject. In agreement with this view, the mental experiences as studied in psychology are considered immediate. Psychology is, therefore, to be regarded as the scientific study of immediate mental experiences.

Many psychologists of the generation after Wundt rejected his concept of psychology's subject matter. Apparently, it is possible to draw a distinction between an outer perception, a perception of the external world, and an inner perception taken as the registration of recollections, thoughts, feelings, and voluntary efforts. However, we run into difficulties when we attempt to account more concretely for what distinguishes an inner from an outer perception. In Chapter 2, I mentioned that J. S. Mill drew a sharp distinction between physical and mental events. This led him to distinguish between, on the one hand, the color of a material object as a physical attribute and, on the other hand, our experience of the object as a mental event. The distinction raises intricate epistemological problems, and it is apparently difficult to give a satisfactory argument for making it.

The new definition Wundt gave of psychology's subject matter in the mid-1890s allowed him to avoid drawing a distinction between an outer and an inner perception, but now he was faced with the problem of distinguishing between the object of a mental experience and an experiencing subject. What is meant by an experiencing subject? To my knowledge, Wundt did not deal with this question and did not give any guidelines about how he thought we could decide when to regard an experience as separated from the experiencing subject and when not. The next generation of psychologists were not fair in their criticism of Wundt, but I hope I have shown why they were dissatisfied with his definition of the subject matter of their discipline.

Wundt's View of Method

As we saw in Chapter 2, a central point in the early positivist philosophy of science was that the object of study must be observed directly. This represented a crucial point in Wundt's psychology, in line with which he maintained that mental experiences must be observed directly by the person in whom the experiences take place. This led Wundt to state that scientific psychology must be based on a study of persons capable of registering and reporting on what took place in their consciousness. This meant that the study must be limited to normal adults.

Wundt thought, however, that on the basis of an introspective study of normal, adult persons, we can extrapolate about processes taking place in children, in persons suffering from mental disturbances, and also in animals. It is, therefore, not quite correct to say that Wundt limited psychological study to normal adults. However, his *direct* study of consciousness was limited to normal adults.

It may be noted that the procedure on which Wundt based psychological study deviates from the procedure we use in everyday life when we obtain knowledge of mental events and phenomena. In everyday life, we limit introspection not only to events that we seem to register immediately, but also to events and phenomena we register by way of retrospection. Further, we seem to take for granted that we can infer mental processes and states in other persons by registering their behavior. On the basis of facial and bodily expressions, we infer joy, anger, ill will, and sorrow, as well as purposes and intentions, thoughts and recollections. We may wonder whether our social life would be possible if we were not able to make inferences of this kind. (But as we shall see in Chapter 5, Brentano did not accept Wundt's specific procedure in the study of consciousness.)

While Wundt based his study of consciousness on the introspective method, he held that this method, as it had so far been used, could have no place in scientific psychology. In his book on logic (1880–1883), he gave an account of what he held to be the methods of science. Here he emphasized that introspection, as used in everyday life, is too unreliable to be used in scientific studies. He gave several reasons. Among other things, mental experience changes extremely rapidly over time and is also affected by the attitude of the person who undertakes the introspection. To be able to perform reliable observations of consciousness, Wundt asserted that the observer first has to be prepared, to direct attention towards the events to be observed, and, further, to know when the event to be observed is to take place. However, the method could be made acceptable for scientific research by arranging the situation in such a way that the observations can be undertaken under experimental conditions. Wundt had a number of conditions in mind. In the first place, by means of an experimental procedure, the experimenter could inform the person when the event to be observed would occur and control the time of the occurrence. Second, the experimenter could repeat the event and, third, vary the conditions so as to study the event in a systematic manner. Wundt's requirement for introspection was thus that it should be undertaken under experimental conditions. He called his form of introspection *self-observation*.

Undoubtedly, Wundt's requirements for experimental control would improve the reliability of the introspective reports. However, by requiring that the study be based on the subjects' reports of their own mental experiences, he left it to them to undertake certain important controls. They would have to decide whether or not some mental experience is present. The question arises, do the subjects possess a knowledge of mental processes that enables them to make this decision? The procedure also lets subjects decide whether or not they have controlled their attention as required by the experimenter. Again we may ask whether subjects are capable of doing this. It is not as easy as Wundt seems to have imagined to undertake controlled experiments of mental events and phenomena.

In addition to restricting the use of the method to experimental situations, Wundt also held that it could be applied only to processes he regarded as simple, fundamental psychological processes. Processes that involve thinking could not, therefore, be made the object of experimental investigations. These processes, Wundt affirmed, are decisively determined by the culture to which the person belongs, and therefore they assume knowledge and skills produced in the culture. These are the result of a variety of historical circumstances and cannot be controlled experimentally.

Still it was possible, he thought, to undertake accurate observations of cultural products, and these products could then be made the subject of a historical study and indirectly shed light on the more complicated psychological processes. In his *Völkerpsychologie*, he suggested making a study of the cultural products of a particular people or nation. In this study, language, myths, and customs have a central place. Two of the ten volumes on *Völkerpsychologie* were devoted to a thorough study of language. To contrast it with the *Völkerpsychologie*, which was a kind of social psychology, Wundt called the experimental study *individual psychology*, though it is not easy to draw a clear line of division between them. His *Völkerpsychologie* inspired later psychologists interested in the relationship between the individual and society, but it was his individual psychology that attracted the interest of his contemporaries.

Wundt's Psychological System

Wundt based his treatment of mental phenomena on a comprehensive and very complicated system. The system rested on the assumption that consciousness contains elements that make connections of different types. For some time, Wundt had worked with the famous German chemist, Robert Bunsen, and he believed that the great progress made by chemistry was due to undertaking first an analysis showing the composition of the various compounds and then a synthesis showing how the compounds emerge as a result of connections between atoms. Wundt wanted to show that mental events and phenomena could be broken down into elements and then to show that the elements are connected to each other so that different forms of mental content arise. Like Johannes Müller and Helmholtz, he believed sensations represent elements of consciousness. This assumption gave his approach an essential feature in common with the thinking of Helmholtz and the British empiricist philosophers.

In contrast to the British philosophers, however, Wundt accorded the will a central place in his thinking. The will is connected with feelings, and he aimed to create a system where he could account not only for cognition, but also for feelings and voluntary action. To mark the difference between his and the British empiricist philosophers' approach, he called his system *voluntaristic*, as it aimed at understanding voluntary human actions. By combining ideas of cognition, feelings, and motivation, he wanted to give a picture of the dynamics of mental life. Thus, if we merely consider his programmatic declarations, it is misleading to call his system *structuralist*, if by "structuralist" we mean a static system. However, when we examine his expositions more carefully, we discover that Wundt hardly ever gave a satisfactory account of what he meant by a mental process. The presentation is, as far as I can see, always based on what he believed to be definite forms of mental content. Although he insisted that we must not confuse mental processes and mental content, his conceptions became highly static. When this is taken into account, it is legitimate to call his system structuralist.

Sensations and Feelings

Helmholtz had attributed two properties to his sensations, quality and intensity, and Wundt added feeling as a third. According to this way of looking at matters, an impression of the color red, for example, has three properties: 1. the quality red in contrast to other colored qualities; 2. a definite intensity; 3. a definite feeling. In the 1890s, Wundt regarded the feeling component as a specific element and accordingly asserted that there are two different types of elements: *sensations* and *feelings*.

In his account of the elements, Wundt presented a theory of feelings that attracted the interest of psychologists. Until the mid-1890s, he thought feelings could be arranged along a dimension extending from pleasantness through a neutral point to unpleasantness. To this dimension he now added another two. The first extended from excitation to inhibition or calm, and the other from strain to relaxation. As an example of feelings that could be arranged along the dimension pleasantness–unpleasantness, he mentioned impressions of odor and taste. Examples illustrating the second dimension were feelings he believed to be connected with impressions of color. In agreement with a widespread earlier belief, he thought, for example, that impressions of the color red are exciting, and those of the color blue are depressing or soothing. An example illustrating the third dimension was the feeling of expectation, or of an event about to happen, and the relaxation that occurs when the anticipation is fulfilled.

Johannes Müller and Helmholtz had underlined that elements always form parts of compounds; an element is not found in isolation. Therefore, we can identify elements only by analysis; an element represents an abstraction. This view of the nature of elements Wundt also accepted. Yet he insisted that when elements form a connection, the connection has other properties than the elements have by themselves. However, he did not specify when and how the new properties arise. Therefore, his principle that the whole is more than the sum of the parts, is close to being empty of empirical content.

The elements can form many types of connections, which are unities or wholes. At first, Wundt called these unitary connections *representations*. Later, in *Grundriss*, which appeared in 1896, he called them "psychische Gebilde," which I have translated as *mental structures*. These mental structures are formed by associations. Like the British empiricists, Wundt gave the idea of association a central place in his system. Associations are formed in a passive and automatic manner, but only between elements. In contrast, connections between mental structures have to be accounted for by another type of process – namely, by the process of *apperception*, the willful direction of one's attention and the basis of the creative synthesis that leads to a construction of knowledge.

Wundt insisted that mental structures always contain elements of the types of sensations as well as elements of the types of feelings; in other words, there are no perceptual or conceptual representations that do not have an aspect of feeling. Nor are there feelings or emotions that do not have a cognitive aspect. What distinguishes perceptual representations and memories of these from feelings, emotions, and voluntary acts is that they consist mainly of sensations, whereas emotions and voluntary acts consist mainly of elements of feeling.

Perception and Apperception

Because the will is so central in Wundt's psychology, I shall make a few remarks on his ideas of voluntary actions. Wundt thought that voluntary actions are closely associated with feelings. However, they also have a component associated with cognitive representations of various types. The first might perhaps be translated as *incentive* and the latter as *motive*. An example of the first type is the appropriation of another person's property or the elimination of an enemy, and an example of the second is a feeling of lacking something, a feeling of hatred, revenge, envy, etc. Wundt left it to the reader to specify more concretely what elements might be present in what he called, respectively, "incentive" and "motive." Here I will only point out that his use of concepts is abstract and diffuse.

The mental structures form numerous types of connections, on a higher level than the connections between the elements. In his treatment of the connections between the mental structures, Wundt gave an account of how he conceived of consciousness. Unfortunately, this account differed from one work to another. I shall only mention that, in addition to resting his account of consciousness on the idea of mental elements, he thought it a characteristic of mental life that it undergoes continuous change.

To make clear what he believed to be an important aspect of consciousness, Wundt drew an analogy with the concept of visual field used by ophthalmologists. He proposed that consciousness represents a field having a center and a periphery, and that a content of consciousness (such as a specific thought, feeling, idea, impression, etc.) might be present either in the periphery or at the center. However, the field of consciousness has at its center not a point but a central, limited area. A content of consciousness would, under certain conditions, move from the periphery into the central area. In the first case, he said that the content is *perceived*. (Note that the word "perceive" here is used in a way different from the usual one.) In the latter case, the content is *apperceived*.

"Apperception" is a term introduced by Leibniz and later by Kant and Herbart with somewhat different meanings. Wundt, too, changed the meaning. According to him, when content is apperceived, attention is actively directed towards it. The concept of "apperception," therefore, is closely connected with the concept of "attention." Wundt attributed to the central area the capacity to direct itself towards different aspects of the content, and towards different parts of the field in succession. We must therefore understand apperception as a force acting in consciousness.

From the examination he had given earlier of the concept of will, Wundt believed he could conclude that apperception is an act of will and a creative process. By means of this process, mental structures are combined into more complex entities and complex entities analyzed into components. Thus, Wundt gave more complex processes, such as those involved in memory, imagining, and thinking, the status of creative processes of an apperceptive nature. He believed his speculations about apperception as a force in consciousness are supported by the results of some experiments in reaction time that I will describe below. Here, I shall just point out that Wundt made no attempt to explain how this force arises in consciousness, or how it is directed to and unites mental contents. It is thus difficult to understand how the idea of apperception can be used in empirical work.

Empirical Research in the Leipzig Laboratory

Over a number of years, a comprehensive research program was carried out in the Leipzig laboratory, primarily directed towards problems in perception, memory, attention, feeling, voluntary actions, and the speed of different types of reactions (reaction time). Most of the experiments were studies of perception. Since neither Wundt nor any of his students made substantial contributions to this area, which had already been advanced so productively by Weber, Fechner, Helmholtz, Hering, and Mach, I shall not review this work. For similar reasons, I shall not consider the research on memory and feeling, but instead concentrate on the research on attention and reaction time.

Span of Apprehension

The question of the nature of attention has a central place in Wundt's psychology and, on the whole, in the psychology of the 1800s. In the Leipzig laboratory, great efforts were made to determine the size of the so-called *span of apprehension* (span of attention) – that is, how many discrete units a subject could immediately apprehend. Laboratory research confirmed previous findings that about six discrete units could be apprehended. In his model of attention, Wundt had held that we can register a content of consciousness without having our attention directed towards it. There was a *field of consciousness*, and this is wider than the span of apprehension. In accordance with this idea, attempts were made to determine the total number of entities that could be present in consciousness at the same time. The conclusion was that this number is four times as great as the span of apprehension. As we shall see in Chapter 5, the view that a melody is perceived as a whole had recently been raised by one of Brentano's students; another of Brentano's students, Carl Stumpf, used the part–whole problem differently from Wundt.

The problem of whether we can register more in content to which we are attending was revived about 1960 in modern research on cognition. We are still striving to understand what is meant by attention, consciousness, and unconscious processes.

Experiments in Reaction Time

Experiments in reaction time were inspired by Helmholtz's attempt to measure the speed of the human nervous impulse. As we noted in the previous chapter, Helmholtz measured differences in subjects' reaction time to the touching of different points on the skin, and this work was continued by the Dutch physiologist Franz Donders (1868/1969). Donders assumed that the reaction to a complex stimulation could be divided into components, and that the total reaction time could be seen as the sum of the times taken by each component. In one famous experiment, he used five different syllables: Ka, Ke, Ki, Ko, Ku. In one part of the experiment, the a-reaction, subjects were always presented with the syllable Ki and were to react by pronouncing this syllable. In another type of experiment, the b-reaction, they were also presented with one syllable, but now it could be one randomly selected from the five, and the subject was to react by pronouncing the same syllable as the one presented. In a third type, the c-reaction, the syllables were presented in the same way as in the second part, but the subject was now to react by always pronouncing Ki. Donders assumed that the time of the c-reactions was the result of the time it took to perform the a-reaction plus the time it took to discriminate between the different syllables. Hence, by subtracting the a-reaction time from the c-reaction time, he would obtain the time spent on discriminating between the syllables. In the same way, he thought he could find the time it took to choose the response by subtracting the c-reaction from the b-reaction. This form of investigation is called *mental chronometry*.

Wundt and his students continued the studies in mental chronometry. Robert Wood-worth (1938) has reviewed the work. I shall mention only the experiment that Wundt maintained gave support to his idea of apperception. To the three types of reactions mentioned above, he added a d-reaction. Instead of just reacting to the syllable in the c-reaction type experiment, the subject was to identify it. After some time, the research workers found – and this was hardly surprising – that it was difficult for the subjects to determine exactly when they had identified the syllable, and, as one of the research workers in the laboratory pointed out, there was no reason to believe the subjects would begin by giving the response at the same time as they identified the syllable. Hence, this was apparently not a good test of Wundt's hypothesis of apperceptive processes.

One finding in the work on reaction times was that they were longer when subjects were instructed to concentrate on the stimulus than when they were asked to focus on the response. The difference was first explained by assuming that in the first instance the subjects must apperceive the stimulus, whereas in the other instance they had only to perceive the stimulus. The finding resulted in extensive experimentation. Woodworth concluded that the most reasonable interpretation of the difference was to assume that under the first type of instruction the subjects were not so well prepared to carry out the response. It also frequently proved difficult to reproduce the results of the experiment. Therefore, this experiment did not support Wundt's idea of an apperceptive process either.

A more significant criticism of mental chronometry was raised by Oswald Külpe. He pointed out that by far the greatest portion of the mental activity seemed to take place while the subjects prepared for the reaction, and not after the stimulus had been presented. Ordinarily, during a *foreperiod*, the subjects received a signal that they should prepare to react 2 seconds before the stimulus was presented. When the stimulus was presented, the processes seemed to take place rapidly and to be accompanied by only a small amount of mental activity. This, Külpe thought, suggested that the course of events of the part components was already determined in the foreperiod. If so, it was difficult to believe that the time for a complex reaction could be conceived of as a sum of the times of the part processes. This argument contributed strongly to discrediting the idea of a mental chronometry.

Wundt believed the reaction-time experiment could also be used in a study of voluntary action. He assumed the reaction to the stimulus could be considered as the performance of a voluntary act and that, by varying the conditions under which the stimulus is presented and the response is given, experimenters could study voluntary actions. However, as the American James McKeen Cattell and other experimenters in the laboratory found, no manifestations of the will seemed to be present in the consciousness of the subjects. In their work on voluntary action, Wundt and his students apparently overlooked that the studies were undertaken under specific social conditions. As Horst Gundlach (1987) has remarked, in consenting to participate in the experiment, the subjects had agreed to cooperate with the experimenter, who told them what to react to and when. Owing to the difficulty of finding clear evidence of the will, the studies were discredited. In Chapter 5, we shall see how Kurt Lewin studied the will in a wider context and in a more objective way.

While the studies of reaction times failed to shed light on voluntary actions, they disclosed an important phenomenon – namely, that when reactions are frequently repeated they become automatic and gradually disappear from consciousness. In Great Britain, J. S. Mill and Alexander Bain had been concerned with the automatization of certain types of actions. In the reaction-time experiments, experimenters could, under controlled conditions, demonstrate that this automatization takes place. The study of automatization has a central place in modern research on conscious, as well as unconscious, processes.

Wundt's View of Language

Wundt was very interested in language and was an able linguist. In his study of language, he was inspired by ideas that Alexander von Humboldt had developed earlier in the century (and that were revived about 1960 in Noam Chomsky's theory of language, to which I shall return in Chapter 18). Like von Humboldt, Wundt emphasized that the use of language is a creative process, which cannot be explained only by assumptions about the formation of associative connections between words. Wundt (1896a) based his account of language on the idea that, by an apperceptive process, a unitary representation (*Gesamtvorstellung*) is created. By an apperceptive process, we can also divide this representation into two components. If, for example, the unitary representation of "a big house" has been formed, this representation can be broken down into the representations "big" and "house." Wundt believed the speaker starts with the unitary representation "big house" and then breaks this representation down into "big" and "house." This breaking down of the unitary representation is then given linguistic expression in the sentence, "The house is big." The verbal expression would awaken "big" and "house" in the listener, who would then, by an apperceptive synthetic process, combine the two representations in the unitary representation "big house." Because this sentence corresponds to a unitary representation, Wundt regarded the sentence as the linguistic unit. As Blumenthal (1985) has shown, Wundt also proposed that sentences seeming to have the same meaning but different grammatical structures are transformations of the same underlying mental structure.

Concluding Remarks About Wundt

Since Wundt established his laboratory in 1879, numerous psychologists have aimed to extend the use of the experimental method to new problem areas, and most present-day psychologists agree that experiment has decisively contributed to the progress made in empirical psychology. Wundt's main contribution was to convince students interested in the study of psychological problems that the experimental method could be used productively. This gives him a central position in the history of psychology.

The idea of using the experimental method in the study of psychology was, as we noted in Chapter 1, not new to Wundt. J. S. Mill had eloquently argued for its use thirty-six years before Wundt's laboratory was established, and the German physiologists had productively used the method on problems at the border between physiology and psychology.

Unlike Weber, Fechner, Helmholtz, Hering, and Mach, Wundt was not an experimentalist. Nor did he contribute to experimental psychology by suggesting ideas that proved productive in experimental research. Instead he assembled from research already started a variety of problems appropriate for experimental work. From the German physiologists, he appropriated problems in sensory perception; from Helmholtz and Donders, the reaction-time studies; from Galton, the study of associations; and, as noted by Woodworth (1938), from British philosophers, the study of the span of attention. He had original ideas concerning the study of emotions as made up of elementary feelings and ideas of apperception. But none of these ideas proved to be productive. Moreover, few of the problems he and his coworkers took over in the laboratory were elaborated in a productive manner. Wundt's contribution was in gathering a variety of problems that promised to open a new field of experimental inquiry.

In the first edition of the *Grundzüge der physiologischen Psychologie*, Wundt suggested that physiological psychology should be treated as a specific field of empirical science. This proposal probably helped to draw the study of psychology closer to the study of physiology, even if, towards the end of the 1800s, Wundt increasingly tended to study psychological problems that are isolated from physiology. We can see his proposal as an elaboration of Johannes Müller's view of physiology as including problems of psychology, such as perception, remembering, and emotions.

At the beginning of the 1900s, Wundt's belief that psychology could be advanced as an experimental field of science was widely accepted. However, few of his more specific ideas about subject matter and procedure survived. As we saw earlier in the chapter, Wundt attempted to counteract the weaknesses in the introspective method by using it in combination with the experimental method. This procedure eliminated some weaknesses but left him unable to perform rigorously controlled experiments. Whereas the study of sensory perception as undertaken by the physiologists progressed continuously, little progress was made in Wundt's experimental work. A comparison between Wundt's procedure and that of the sensory physiologists reveals the weakness of his procedure.

In the experiments of the sensory physiologists, reactions were sought to one of several aspects of a sensory impression. For example, the subject was to react to the hue and not to the brightness, form, or size of a patch of color. Thus, the subject had to direct attention to one of several possible aspects of the impression. In this sense, the experiment could be said to have a basis in introspection. The subjects were given verbal instructions, but the experimenter was able to control their attention by noting that their reports agreed with changes in the physical stimulation. Thus, when a definite change was made in wavelength, the experimenter could note whether this resulted in an expected change in the report on hue. If it had not been possible to control the attention of the subjects, sensory physiology would hardly have progressed as an experimental science.

When Wundt extended the use of the method to other problems than those treated in sensory physiology, he was not able to control attention. For example, in the experiment on apperception in which he instructed the subjects to identify the syllable in the d-type reaction, he had no means of controlling whether the subjects followed instructions as he intended. I think it is fair to conclude that when Wundt applied the experimental method to problems outside sensory perception, he was unable to control attention.

Wundt may also have misdirected the course of psychology by insisting that the subjects' reports should be treated as direct observations of psychology's subject matter. In other words, he insisted that the events studied represent immediate and not mediated experience, and in line with this position, he regarded the content of the report not as inferred, but as directly observed. Thus, Wundt developed a specific version of introspection.

As I noted earlier in the chapter, Wundt's way of using introspection deviated from the way we use it in everyday life and from the way it was traditionally used in philosophy. Wundt's British student Edward Titchener, who led an active laboratory in the United States, adopted Wundt's version of the method, as we shall see in Chapter 11. Like Wundt, Titchener believed that by the use of the experiment he could control the attention of his subjects. Wundt and Titchener's particular use of the introspective method may have led to an overly negative attitude towards the use of introspection. Even if it is hardly possible to reach safe conclusions by this method, it may be an indispensable means of obtaining hypotheses about our mental life that can later be subjected to controlled experimentation.

Hermann Ebbinghaus (1850–1909)

From the beginning of the 1890s until his death nearly twenty years later, Hermann Ebbinghaus was a major figure in the new German experimental psychology, in spite of the fact that he did not direct a famous laboratory. He apparently formed his view of psychology mainly by reading J. S. Mill. He seems to have received inspiration from Fechner to carry out empirical research. In cooperation with one of Helmholtz's students, he established *Zeitschrift für Psychologie und Physiologie der Sinnesorgane* (*Journal of the Psychology and Physiology of the Sense Organs*) in 1890. Psychologists and physiologists who did not belong to Wundt's circle published in this journal. Wundt, as you will recall, had taken the initiative with the publication of the journal *Philosophische Studien* (*Philosophical Studies*).

In Germany, psychology formed part of the study of philosophy up to World War II. Ebbinghaus had written his doctoral thesis on the treatment of the unconscious in Eduard von Hartmann's philosophy, and when he was appointed professor, the designation of his chair was philosophy, as for the other German professors of psychology. He combined the study of psychology and philosophy to only a minor extent, however, and attempted to develop psychology as a branch of natural science.

In contrast to most of the other pioneers in psychology, Ebbinghaus did not belong to a family of state officials. His father was a merchant, and this may explain why his academic career did not follow the usual pattern. Ebbinghaus was born in Barmen, near Bonn. After finishing school, he studied history, philology, and philosophy at several universities and received his doctorate in Bonn in 1873. Instead of then studying with an established professor as was customary, Ebbinghaus carried out independent studies at the University of Berlin and then traveled to Britain and France. In these countries, he earned his living as a private tutor and started empirical investigations of learning and memory on his own initiative. He continued these investigations when he returned to Berlin. In 1883, he was appointed senior lecturer (*Dozent*), and three years later he was attached to this university as a *Professor extraordinarius*. Later he was appointed professor in Breslau and then in Halle. He published his research on learning and memory in the book *Über das Gedächtnis* (*On Memory: A Contribution to Experimental Psychology*), the publication of which in 1885 made him famous. His *Grundzüge der Psychologie* (*Fundamentals of Psychology*, 1897, 1902) was a much-used handbook, even if Ebbinghaus did not have time to complete the second of the two planned volumes. A short textbook of psychology, *Abriss der Psychologie*, published in 1908, became a classic. In 1897, Ebbinghaus devised a sentence-completion test to measure the mental ability of schoolchildren. On the centenary of the publication of *Über das Gedächtniss*, two symposia were arranged about him and his research (Traxel and Gundlach, 1986; Gorfein and Hoffman, 1987.)

Verbal Learning and Memory: A Quantitative Approach

In attempting to construct a scale to measure the intensity of sensory impressions, Fechner had found he could use the threshold as the unit. Probably inspired by him, Ebbinghaus attempted to find an element that could be used as a unit in quantitative measurements of learning and memory. Since he was trained as a philologist and interested in language, it was natural for him to assume that words could make up such units. However, upon reflection, he concluded that too many associations were attached to words, and a more appropriate unit would be syllables of a special type – namely, a vowel between two consonants. By making up lists of such syllables, he thought he might obtain fairly homogeneous material. Although the syllables could be ascribed meaning in varying degrees, he thought the differences in meanings between different lists would balance out. In later research on verbal learning, these syllables have been called *meaningless syllables*. When Ebbinghaus referred to them as meaningless, according to Werner Traxel (1986), he hardly thought they were actually meaningless. What he had in mind was probably that it is difficult to ascribe a definite meaning to a list consisting of a number of such syllables. Thus, he probably did not hold that an experimenter could find material without meaning.

As a criterion for learning, Ebbinghaus chose the number of times he had to read through a list of syllables in order to be able to recite it without error. To find a quantitative expression for memory of the material, he reasoned in the following manner: if learning a list has an effect on memory, it is reasonable to think that to learn it without error at a later point in time will require fewer readings. In line with this reasoning, he thought he might arrive at a method of measuring memory by subtracting the number of readings necessary to learn the list the second time from the number of times required to learn it the first time. This method for determining the degree or quantity of memory he called *the saving method*.

By means of the lists of syllables, Ebbinghaus could now study the effect on learning of such conditions as the length of time between the first and second learning, the length of the list, and overlearning – that is, reading the list a number of times *after* it could be recited without error. Further, Ebbinghaus performed comprehensive investigations to find out whether associations had been formed between syllables that did not follow each other in immediate succession. If A, B, C, D, E are taken to designate different syllables, he studied whether associations had been established not only between A and B, but also between A and C, A and D, A and E, etc.

Ebbinghaus's most famous finding was the course of the *curve of forgetting*. The curve (Figure 4.1) shows a very rapid fall during the first few minutes, and a smaller but still rapid fall during the following hours. Then the fall is fairly continuous until the curve flattens out. Ebbinghaus could also show that associations had been formed between all the syllables in the list, both forward and backward, that overlearning plays a role in memory, and naturally that the length of the lists is important.

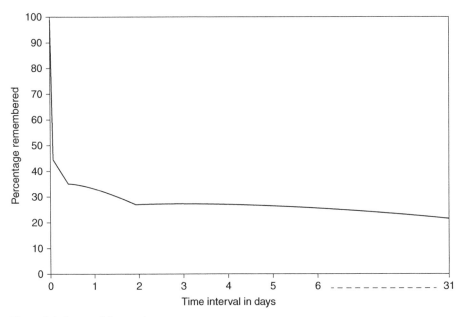

Figure 4.1 Curve of forgetting.

Evaluation of Ebbinghaus

Ebbinghaus's procedure made it possible to study a number of conditions affecting verbal learning and memory. He thought learning is primarily a result of the formation of associations in a mechanical process that depends on the number of times repetitions have been carried out. The idea that learning takes place in the same way in different types of situations was adopted by American behaviorists when, almost fifty years later, they made the study of learning their main area of psychology. This oversimplified view of learning was dominant up to the end of the 1950s. Like the British empiricist philosophers, Ebbinghaus regarded learning as a passive process. However, already a few years after he had published his results, Georg Elias Müller showed that when subjects are learning lists of syllables, they actively try to find meaning in the material. We also know that, with regard to memory, meaning is often a decisive factor. According to Ralph Haber (1985, p. 271), the role of meaning has only slowly been accepted: "He [Ebbinghaus] invented the nonsense syllable, and we struggled for a half-century before we realized that memory implied meaning and the whole enterprise of nonsense memory was nonsense." Even if Ebbinghaus did not believe his material was without meaning, Haber may have put his finger on a weakness in the research tradition Ebbinghaus began. Yet, I think Haber overlooked that Müller made important discoveries in using Ebbinghaus's syllables.

Around 1900, Ebbinghaus was a highly admired research worker, and the tradition in verbal learning he began was, as we shall see later, carried further by very active groups of American psychologists in the years 1920–1960. The results of this research were significant, though strong criticism of it was raised when the new cognitive psychology became dominant in the 1960s.

Georg Elias Müller (1850–1934)

Müller was perhaps the most active of the German research workers in psychology towards the end of the nineteenth century and at the beginning of the twentieth. He was appointed professor at Göttingen in 1881 and established a laboratory in 1887. Müller started with the work of Fechner and Ebbinghaus and, like them, tried to introduce objective methods into psychology.

Müller was born in Grimma in Sachsen, the same year as Ebbinghaus; like him, he began his university studies with an interest in philosophy and the humanities. After serving in the Franco-Prussian War, he went to Göttingen in 1871 to study with Rudolph Hermann Lotze (1817–1891). Lotze had taken his medical degree in Leipzig and had been the student of both Weber and Fechner. He had performed work on sensory perception, which had inspired Helmholtz as well as Hering. Lotze wrote a much-studied book on medical psychology in 1852 and was regarded as a central figure in German intellectual life about the mid-nineteenth century. Müller was his close friend and was trained by him in science as well as philosophy.

Müller's doctoral thesis, published in 1873, was a theoretical study of attention. Even if some points are not clearly stated, this thesis was an outstanding piece of work. After having taken his degree, Müller fell seriously ill. During his convalescence, he came to know Fechner and began a critical investigation of Fechner's psychophysical studies. This research resulted in a comprehensive work on psychophysics that appeared in 1878. Müller was appointed senior lecturer (*Dozent*) in Göttingen, and in 1881 he succeeded Lotze as professor of philosophy. In the nearly forty years he was in charge of the laboratory in Göttingen, Müller worked on perception and, as mentioned, did considerable research in psychophysics. When Ebbinghaus's investigations on memory appeared, he was fascinated by them and began extensive studies in learning and memory. Like Ebbinghaus, Müller believed learning occurs by association, but, as we shall see, his studies led him to modify this view. Like many of his contemporaries, he was much concerned with the part–whole problem, and in 1923 he wrote a book in which he criticized Gestalt psychology and presented an alternative to it: *Komplextheorie und Gestalttheorie* (*Complex Theory and Gestalt Theory*).

Müller's Research

In his doctoral thesis, Müller started from Helmholtz's work on attention in his attempts to register double images, afterimages, fusion of two pictures in stereoscopic vision, training of peripheral vision, and practice in discerning specific tones in harmonics. Müller agreed with Helmholtz that we try to anticipate properties in the objects towards which we direct attention. In addition, Müller believed, as I understand him, that during attention sensitivity in parts of the sensory system increases. This is a view that now seems to be confirmed by research. Further, Müller apparently meant that, when we are attentive to an object, we suppress aspects of what we perceive that are not important. Later Wundt as well as Oswald Külpe emphasized this aspect of attention.

Within psychophysics, Müller conducted extensive research to provide data for determining psychophysical relationships in different sensory modalities. He also contributed to psychophysics by devising a new method of determining thresholds.

His main contribution to psychology was probably his studies of memory. Here he introduced an important new method in which subjects are presented with the items to be remembered in pairs. Later they are presented with only the first element of the pair, and their task is to say what the other element was. Like Ebbinghaus, Müller was strongly influenced by the British empiricist philosophers' view of learning as a result of the formation of associations. He did, however, come to realize that learning does not take place as mechanically as Ebbinghaus assumed. The subjects' attitude to the task seems to be an important factor in learning. For example, Müller found that reading through a list of syllables without the intention of learning it only slightly improved learning. Further, he discovered that subjects used a number of techniques to create relationships between the items, such as rhythm, rhyme, and alliteration. They also tried to find meanings that allowed them to see relationships between the syllables. In other words, his research showed that during learning the subjects would actively attempt to organize the material. Associations are, therefore, not formed in a simple, mechanical way, as Ebbinghaus and empiricist philosophers had believed. However, his findings did not lead Müller to abandon his reliance on association, but only to modify it.

Along with Alfons Pilzecker, Müller showed that learning new material has a negative effect on the memory of already learned material (*Experimentelle Beiträge zur Lehre vom Gedächtnis, Experimental Contributions to the Theory of Memory*). A *retroactive inhibition* takes place, as well as a *proactive inhibition*. Earlier thinkers had believed forgetting is the result of a form of decay that takes place in the memory processes. But the demonstration of retroactive and proactive inhibition made possible a new explanation of forgetting, – namely, that mental activity before and after the learning of material *interferes* with the learning of a specific task. Müller and Pilzecker also proposed that after material has been learned, a process of *perseverance* starts in the nervous system that continues for a period after the task has been completed, and during this period a *consolidation* of the processes in the nervous system is necessary for remembering to take place.

The hypothesis of consolidation has been the subject of much research in the latter half of the twentieth century, and several well-controlled experiments performed on both humans and animals show that a consolidation process is necessary for what we call long-term memory to form. Further, evidence strongly suggests that a specific area of the brain, the *hippocampus*, has a central function during consolidation (see Larry Squire, 1992). In Chapter 18, I shall return to the concept of long-term memory.

Müller was concerned with the problem of finding procedures to control introspective reports, and thus make them more objective. In psychophysical experiments that ask subjects to compare two stimuli presented in succession, we cannot control how the subjects undertake this comparison. In this sense, the procedure is subjective. Still, by repeating the procedure, by varying the conditions of the presentations, and by comparing the results of different forms of presentation, we can control the subjective element. The experimenter can also observe the subjects' behavior – for example, their eye movements, body movements, pronunciation, and verbal expressions they use in the report – and compare their introspective reports with their performance. Müller discussed in detail how we might better control the statements given in the subjects' reports. As Ib Kristian Moustgaard (1990) pointed out, Müller thought the main question to be answered about the introspective method was whether the experimenter had obtained satisfactory experimental control of the subjects' reactions. Even if a procedure based on introspection may have low reliability at the initial stage, it is often possible to improve the procedure in such a way that objectivity is increased. It is not a question of either accepting or rejecting introspection as a method. This is a position with which a great number of modern psychologists will concur.

The views Müller presented on the part–whole problem in his criticism of Gestalt psychology are still relevant today. Müller realized that, to account for perception and learning, we must explain how we can divide the material into groups or organizations of various types; he was concerned about the problem of how various types of wholes arose. Perceived objects that have a closer spatial and temporal relationship to each other he called a *complex*, which, he held, could arise as a result of simultaneous or successive organization. The concept of "complex" covered a number of different types of organization. For example, the number 10 he regarded as a complex consisting of the digits 1 and 0. Similarly, words could be regarded as complexes consisting of letters.

Müller pointed to different factors that would affect the organization of complexes. Elements spatially near to each other would be organized together; another factor is the similarity between the elements; and in visual perception, the shape is also important.

Müller attributed a major role in the organization of complexes to attention and seems here to have taken a position close to Wundt's idea of apperception. Like Wundt, Müller did not deal with the question of *how* the elements could be organized by means of attention.

Even if it was far from clear what Müller meant by a *complex*, and how attention and learning contribute to the formation of wholes, he helped to clarify problems by pointing to the fact that there are many different types of wholes. Further, he showed that an element forming part of a group or a whole, like the digit 1 in the number 10, sometimes could also be conceived of as an isolated unit.

In my opinion, Müller had a far better understanding than Wundt, Titchener, and Ebbinghaus that there must be an interplay between theory and observation in productive scientific research. He seems to have been liberating himself from the view of early positivism that the researcher must start with a set of observations and then inductively arrive at laws and more comprehensive theories. Having a more productive view of the relationship between theory and observations, Müller was more inclined than the other three psychologists to modify his position.

Oswald Külpe (1862–1915) and the Würzburg School

Oswald Külpe represented a link between the first and second generations of German experimental psychologists. A study of the historical development from Wundt to the later Külpe reveals internal development in German psychology; psychologists learned from their research activity. Müller and Külpe prepared the ground for the psychology taking shape in the years before World War I.

Külpe's father was a notary public from a German family that had settled in Latvia. After finishing school in Latvia, Külpe went to Leipzig in 1881 to study history. Like Müller and Ebbinghaus, he began his university studies with an interest in history and philosophy, and for a number of years he was unable to decide whether he should make history or psychology his specialty. In Leipzig, he became acquainted with Wundt and experimental psychology, but after a year he went to Berlin to study history. In 1883, he moved to Göttingen to study with Müller. Here Külpe started working on a philosophical thesis on feelings. After another year of study with Wundt, he received his doctorate in 1887. To qualify as a senior lecturer, he wrote a philosophical thesis on the discussion of the will in modern philosophy. In 1888, he became Wundt's assistant, and together with Wundt he directed the laboratory until he became professor in Würzburg in 1894. Here Külpe remained until 1908. His best-known psychological works are *Grundriss der Psychologie* (*Introduction to Psychology*, 1893) and *Vorlesungen über Psychologie* (*Lectures on Psychology*), which appeared after his death. While Ebbinghaus and Müller devoted most of their efforts to experimental psychology, Külpe seemed to have been more occupied with philosophy and wrote several books on the subject; his introduction to philosophy was much read.

Külpe's name as a teacher and laboratory leader is associated with the University of Würzburg. He developed the laboratory there into a leading center for psychological research, so that apart from several smaller facilities, there were now active German laboratories in Leipzig, Göttingen, Würzburg, and Berlin. This shows the breadth of German experimental psychology towards the end of the 1800s and the beginning of the 1900s. Through his introductory textbook on psychology and his management of the laboratory, Külpe had a great influence on psychology. His work in the laboratory was first and foremost directed towards investigations of thinking. Several of his students made independent contributions, but it is easy to see that ideas presented by Külpe in his *Introduction to Psychology* influenced their treatment of problems.

Oswald Külpe

Külpe's *Introduction to Psychology*

Külpe had been Wundt's assistant for five years when he published *Grundriss der Psychologie* in 1893. The book was dedicated to Wundt, who was also cited in several places. In its main features, Külpe's presentation is identical to Wundt's, but on some points he deviated from his teacher, and to this Wundt must have reacted strongly. Two years later, as Gundlach (1987) discovered, Wundt published a book with exactly the same title as Külpe's, and with the same publisher.

Külpe maintained that psychology was the study of facts about mental life, and not the study of immediate experience as Wundt had held. Indeed, he added that the psychologist must try to see connections between the facts and the subject registering them. Concerning the introspective method, he stated that this could also be used even if the report was not produced in an experimental situation. Wundt must also have strongly disliked Külpe's giving only a summary treatment of the studies of the will. Külpe had systematically attempted to remove all unnecessary speculations about the phenomena studied and had a critical attitude to much of the research undertaken in the Leipzig laboratory.

Külpe did not break with Wundt's conception of psychology as the study of consciousness in the adult human being. However, he cast doubt on the idea that mental life could be understood as chains of simple processes, and held that most of the mental activity in the reaction-time experiments took place while the subject prepared for the reaction. Külpe arrived at this conclusion by using introspection in a way that did not meet Wundt's requirements in respect to method. Külpe's emphasis on the importance of the preparation period not only suggested an alternate interpretation of the reaction-time experiments but also contained the beginning of a more unitary conception of psychological processes than Wundt had advocated. Based on Külpe's idea of the importance of the preparation period, intensive research activity was carried out in the Würzburg laboratory at the beginning of the twentieth century, which we discuss next.

In *Grundriss* Külpe reviewed much of the research conducted so far on problems relating to attention. He discussed Müller's and Wundt's theories in relationship to experimental findings and reported on techniques devised to investigate how attention is created and under what conditions it is maintained. Given what was known about the importance of preparation, it was natural to investigate how, with the help of different forms of stimuli, the experimenter could make a person attentive to a succeeding stimulus. Here, Külpe probably anticipated what we call the *priming technique*. I have reported on this early German research because it seems to have been almost completely overlooked by the British and American researchers who revived the study of attention around 1960.

The Research of the Würzburg School

The psychologists in Würzburg argued that several of the central beliefs in the experimental psychology of the nineteenth century had to be modified. They questioned the role attributed to elements in learning and the explanation of learning as chains of associative connections. Nevertheless, they never doubted that it is possible to base a study of cognitive activities on mental processes because these processes are accessible through introspection. Further, they were convinced that learning, memory, and thinking have a foundation in the formation of associations. Their position was that we could not give a *complete* explanation based on the laws of association.

Unfortunately, neither Külpe nor his students undertook a comprehensive review of the research carried out in the Würzburg laboratory, and the presentation in several of the reports is unclear and incoherent. It is, therefore, not easy to obtain an overview of their research, even if good help has been given by Robert Woodworth (1938) and George Humphrey (1951).

Imageless Thought

A view of thinking we can trace back to Aristotle is that it is mediated by mental images. Some philosophers disputed this view, but at the beginning of the twentieth century it was widely accepted. The French psychologist Alfred Binet had questioned it, but it was the Würzburg research workers who placed the problem on the psychological agenda. One of the first investigations dealing with the question was performed by Karl Marbe in 1901.

Marbe studied the way we make judgments and found it difficult to identify conscious content to explain the process. He presented his subjects with the task of comparing pairs of several different types of material – for example, two weights, musical tones, colors, geometric forms, arithmetic problems, or verbal translations. A traditional way of comparing the impression of the weights of two objects is to compare the impression of the second weight with the mental image left by the impression of the first weight. In making this comparison, however, Marbe's subject did not seem able to register a concrete impression that could form the basis for the judgment. In spite of the fact that the subjects made quite correct judgments, they were unable to report on a mental content that could be traced to sensations in one form or another. Nevertheless, they insisted they registered something, even if no images were present. The Würzburg psychologists referred to the contents of the report as *Bewusstseinslage* (*consciousness*).

Marbe's finding stirred up controversy among psychologists, and researchers in and outside the Würzburg laboratory turned to the question he had raised. In Würzburg, the psychologists insisted they had made several findings supporting the belief that thinking could occur without being dependent upon images. However, at Cornell, Titchener protested strongly and undertook a long series of experiments to disprove this conclusion. Note that the term "mental image" was restricted to images of a visual nature or images that originate in other sensory modalities. Titchener regarded kinesthetic images as especially important.

The struggle between psychologists at Würzburg and Cornell became so heated that Titchener accused Külpe and his students of being poor observers and inadequately trained. (Külpe had been the assistant in Wundt's laboratory when Titchener received his training in the Wundtian form of introspection.) Wundt (1907) himself launched what he regarded as devastating criticism of the research of the Würzburg school. He pointed out that their use of introspection meant they could not be said to perform controlled experiments. Recall that Wundt had argued that thinking cannot be studied by means of experiments. The Würzburg researchers' results raised doubt about whether mental images are necessary for thinking to take place. As Woodworth (1938) pointed out, however, it was hardly possible to draw a decisive conclusion. In the first place it is difficult to decide whether mental images are present, and in the second place, if they are, it is difficult to say whether they are actually necessary for thinking to occur.

Since the psychologists did not agree about whether thinking can take place without mental images, it was natural to conclude that their methods were inadequate. A result of the disagreement was, therefore, increased doubt about whether introspection is an appropriate method for scientific psychological study. Hence, it is reasonable to believe the struggle paved the way for behaviorism.

After the debate at the beginning of the twentieth century, psychologists seem to have lost interest in the study of the role of imagery in thinking for more than fifty years. In the 1970s, this study was revived, and an intensive new discussion began of what we can understand a mental image to be, as well as whether mental imagery has a function in our cognitive activities. I shall return to this research in Chapter 16.

Thinking as a Result of the Task

As we have seen, Wundt and G. E. Müller had concluded that the principles of association are not sufficient to account for learning. Two Würzburg psychologists, the Scot Henry Watt (1905) and Naziss Ach (1905), started from Külpe's idea of the role of preparation in the reaction-time experiment and conducted experiments to examine the effect the task has on thinking. They arrived at the conclusion that associations alone cannot explain thinking.

Watt's and Ach's Experiments

Watt designed his experiment on the model of the reaction-time experiment. The subjects had to react to a stimulus word, but instead of simply reporting the associations elicited by the word, they had to solve various tasks involving the meaning of the word. Altogether, six different tasks were used, three of which were finding words designating concepts that were superordinate, subordinate, or coordinate to the concept designated by the stimulus word. If the word "dog" is the stimulus, for instance, the correct response to the first task was the word "animal"; to the next task the name of any breed of dog, for example, "golden retriever" or "setter"; and to the third task the words "cat" or "wolf," or any other name designating a coordinate to dog. The subjects were told to report retrospectively on everything occurring in their consciousness from the moment they received the instruction until they had given their response.

In line with what Külpe had pointed out, the reports showed that most mental representations were given in a foreperiod, a period when the subjects prepared their reports. The results also revealed another interesting aspect of the thought process. When the same type of task was repeated several times, the subjects reported that the richness of the content of consciousness decreased, and that after some repetitions, the processes appeared to occur almost automatically without any mental content being present. Further, Watt could show that the mental content varied from task to task, and also that reaction times sometimes differed from task to task. On the basis of this finding, he maintained that it was possible to distinguish between the effects of the stimulus word and the effects of the task. As he saw it, the stimulus word would produce a definite number of associations, and the task would have an effect on the associations produced. To explain the thought process, it was necessary to take account of both the associations elicited and the effect of the task.

Watt was unclear on two main points. First, he did not specify what he meant by an association, or how it could be identified. Second, he could not specify the effect of the task. As a consequence, it is difficult to understand how the effect of the stimulus word and the effect of the task can be distinguished, and, further, how the thought process was a result of both the stimulus word and the task. But Watt used tasks involving the meaning of words, and this raised intricate linguistic and philosophical problems.

Ach (1905) used a procedure similar to Watt's, but he formulated the aim somewhat differently. Instead of speaking of the task as affecting the thought processes, he preferred to say that the thought processes were determined by a voluntary effort; they were governed by a *determining tendency*. During thinking, this tendency worked together with the association principle. Ach's experiments can be criticized on the same basis as Watt's. In one experiment, he instructed his subjects when they were under hypnosis and found that in the posthypnotic state they followed the procedure.

Woodworth (1938) and several contemporary researchers believed that Watt and Ach contributed to our understanding of cognition by showing that the instructions (the tasks) created a *set* in the subjects. This resulted in connections between certain cognitive patterns and tendencies to actions that then proceeded more rapidly and effectively. Under the influence of the set, in other words, the subjects were more efficient at finding the appropriate form of reaction in the situation. A great number of experimental investigations of set were performed during the first decades of the 1900s, and the designation *set* is often used in psychology. However, James Gibson (1941) questioned whether the set is a fruitful concept, pointing out that it was used in descriptions of situations that were highly dissimilar. We may also ask whether the concept of set is distinguishable from the concept of attention.

Otto Selz (1881–1944)

In a later chapter, I shall discuss *act psychology*, which became prominent at the beginning of the 1900s. Külpe's emphasis on the role played by the preparation and the task was in line with the ideas of this movement. Otto Selz, who worked with Külpe in the first years of his research career, developed a position in line with the new movement, but, unlike Külpe, Watt, and Ach, he completely rejected the view that associations have a place in accounts of thinking.

On the basis of detailed introspective reports on the same types of problems Watt had used, Selz concluded that the solution to a problem arose as a whole when the task was closely connected with the stimulus word. He explained this by hypothesizing that, before being presented with the problem, the subjects possessed knowledge of the relationship between the task and the stimulus word. For example, when the subjects were presented with the task of finding the superordinate concept for dog, they already knew the concept "dog" had a definite relationship to the concept "animal." This knowledge was actualized when the stimulus word was presented. In other words, if I have understood him correctly, Selz felt the relationship between the task and the stimulus word was not established during the experiment but had been formed earlier and was only actualized when the stimulus word was presented. I think Selz here raised a fundamental question for the study of thinking. However, in order to answer it, he would have had to go into the age-old discussion of the origin of universals (see Saugstad, 1989b).

Selz came to live in the shadow of Gestalt psychology. In the 1950s, some of his ideas were revived by promoters of the information-processing approach. In my opinion, Selz's work, like that of the Wützburgers, suffers from too great a reliance on introspective data. Useful reviews of parts of his work have been given by Woodworth (1938), Humphrey (1951), and Jane and George Mandler (1964).

Concluding Remarks on the Würzburg School

The Würzburg psychologists based their research on the hypothesis that we can arrive at a satisfactory description of psychological processes by having a person report the content of his or her consciousness during the solution of a task. Many modern researchers in cognition apparently agree that retrospective reports are useful in their studies, but they do not believe we can achieve a satisfactory description of cognitive processes by means of introspective reports alone. For this reason, not only are they unwilling to accept statements based on the type of research done by the psychologists of the Würzburg school; they are also unwilling to examine more thoroughly the way in which those psychologists formulated their problems.

Historians frequently finish their report of the Würzburg school by saying that these psychologists proved wrong Wundt's contention that it is not possible to study thought processes by an experimental approach. Even if Wundt's (1907) criticism was based on too strict criteria for defining something as an experimental procedure, I think we must say that the experiments conducted by the Würzburg school hardly helped to clarify fundamental aspects of thinking. Perhaps Wundt's ideas about thinking, as well as those of the Würzburg school, were too unclear to allow productive formulations of problems or experimental work.

William Preyer (1842–1897) and the Absence of Ontogenesis in German Experimental Psychology

Preyer was a British–German physiologist and embryologist who wrote a pioneer work on child psychology based on observation of one of his sons. It was thus not an experimental work, and Preyer does not strictly belong in a chapter on German experimental psychology. However, like most German physiologists of his time, he was interested in the senses and wrote at length on the development of perception in the child he studied.

Preyer was born and grew up in Great Britain but finished high school in Germany and settled there. He was fascinated by *On the Origin of Species* (1859/1979), and became a friend of Darwin. After having taught at the University of Bonn, he was appointed professor at Jena, where he worked until 1888 when illness forced him to resign his position.

In Chapter 6, I shall report on Darwin's observations on the development of one of his sons; other research workers have also published similar observations. However, Preyer's book, *Die Seele des Kindes* (*The Mind of the Child*) (1882/1923) was innovative in important respects. In the first place, his observations were very thorough and systematic. Second, Preyer tried to find a physiological basis for the psychological development of the child, and, third, he viewed his subject from an evolutionary perspective. For this reason, he seems a modern child psychologist. In his presentation, he started by describing the development of the senses, perception, and feeling, and then of movement and the will, and finally of thinking and language.

All these aspects of development Preyer treated thoroughly and with interest and love for the child. Especially impressive, in my opinion, is his comparison of his son's linguistic development with the defects in the speech and language of adults suffering from brain damage of different types. As I see it, he argued convincingly for the view that language development is based on cognitive development. In other words, he did *not*, like many philosophers of language at the beginning of the 1900s, regard language as a precondition for the development of thinking.

Siegfried Jaeger (1982) has pointed out that Preyer tended to emphasize the role of heredity to the detriment of the influence of the social environment, and that he considered the development of the child as primarily the result of a process of maturation. In my opinion, Preyer struck a good balance between the role played by heredity and that of the environment.

Recall that Helmholtz had emphasized that perception develops in a complicated interaction between the child and its environment. Ebbinghaus, G. E. Müller, and Wundt stressed the importance of associative learning in the development of perception. We might, therefore, expect the German experimental psychologists to have attempted to explore problems of perception by a study of ontogenesis. However, they did not. Hilgard (1987) has suggested that one reason for this lack of interest in ontogenesis was that Wundt had not given the study of the child a central place in his psychology. Another reason may have been that the German psychologists did not think the psychological development of the infant and the child could be studied by experimental methods, and being bent on advancing psychology as an experimental science, they may not have taken an interest in ontogenetic studies.

In their study of memory, Ebbinghaus, Müller, Watt, Ach, and Selz all used verbal material, and it might have been natural for them to consider the ontogenetic development of language. But it was not until after World War II that a productive study of the development of perception in children began. As a result of the lack of understanding of the importance of learning, German psychology came into opposition with American psychology, in which, as we shall see, learning was made central.

5

Phenomenology and Gestalt Psychology

A New Generation's View of Perception: Focus on Wholes

Like their precursors, the new generation of German experimental psychologists who started their university careers immediately before and after World War I regarded mental processes as their subject matter. Perception was the central area, as it had been for the previous generation, and, like the previous generation, they neither included behavior in their thinking nor based their treatment of psychological questions on biological evolution.

With these features in common, the psychologists of the first and second generations may appear to modern psychologists as rather similar. The new generation believed, however, that their approach was entirely different from the approach they attributed to the psychologists of the 1800s. The new generation's criticism was primarily directed against the way the earlier generation had tried to describe mental events, and the tendency to break psychological processes down into elements.

The early German students of perception emphasized, as we have seen, that great care had to be taken to describe perceptual experiences accurately and without preconceived ideas, in attempts that have been called *phenomenology*. Outstanding representatives of early phenomenology were Goethe, Purkinje, and Hering. Towards the end of the nineteenth century, the tendency to emphasize accurate descriptions was strengthened when a broad philosophical movement arose that tried to clarify problems of epistemology and the philosophy of science by starting from accurate descriptions. The originator of this movement was Franz Brentano, who first taught in Würzburg and then in Vienna. His ideas spread throughout the Austro-Hungarian Empire and Germany.

In probably all empirical sciences, researchers are faced with the problem of understanding the relationship between some kind of wholeness and some kind of partness. One generation of scientists may be more occupied with problems concerning the wholes in contrast to another generation concentrating more on the parts. The German experimental psychologists of the 1800s were markedly concerned with the parts. At the beginning of the 1900s, interest was directed more towards the wholes. The Brentano school strongly contributed to this change of interest. An important event in this development was the realization by one of Brentano's students, Christian von Ehrenfels (1890), that certain perceptual impressions should be regarded as new types of elements in addition to those traditionally conceived of as elements. A melody is an impression of this kind. Von Ehrenfels called this impression a *Gestalt quality*, to which we shall return later in this chapter.

Phenomenology: A Historical Outline

In this chapter, we shall discuss the phenomenological tradition as it was manifested by the Brentano school. Barry Smith (1994) has given a comprehensive presentation of many of the intricate philosophical questions treated by the adherents of this movement. I shall consider only a few questions that seem directly relevant to psychology. To provide an overview, I shall give a brief historical outline showing how the school branched out across the Austro-Hungarian and German empires.

Brentano first taught at the University of Würzburg, where Carl Stumpf became his student and lifelong friend. Later Stumpf was appointed professor of philosophy and psychology at Berlin and was a central figure in philosophical and psychological circles around 1900. As Mitchell Ash (1995) has documented, Stumpf was the teacher of a group of psychologists later called *Gestalt psychologists*. They reacted critically to some of the teachings of Stumpf and Brentano but agreed with them that phenomenological descriptions must form the foundation of a scientific psychology. Stumpf also had other students who became influential, such as Kurt Lewin. Like the Gestalt psychologists, Lewin had a phenomenological orientation, but he had other interests and scarcely regarded himself as a Gestalt psychologist. For this reason, I shall treat him separately, later in this chapter.

In addition to Stumpf, Brentano had students who worked in Prague, such as Christian von Ehrenfels, who, as I have already mentioned, was the first to draw attention to Gestalt qualities. A center for Brentano's ideas also arose in Austria, and the so-called Graz school still has active researchers in Italy.

Stumpf had a student, Edmund Husserl, who shared his interest in mathematics, logic, and philosophy, and who also became a student of Brentano. Husserl's development of Stumpf's and Brentano's ideas made him one of the most influential philosophers of the first half of the 1900s. His philosophy is not easily accessible, but it is not necessary to have a deeper understanding of his ideas in order to grasp the main features of the phenomenological tradition, which did not begin with him. I believe some historians have overestimated his importance for psychology; in fact Stumpf repudiated Husserl's later view of psychology.

The German phenomenological tradition includes a number of different approaches, which have in common only a belief in the importance of undertaking accurate descriptions of mental experience. The designation *phenomenology*, therefore, covers a wide variety of approaches. However, it is also used in a narrower sense as the name of a philosophical movement that arose at the beginning of the twentieth century, with Husserl as its central figure. Husserl inspired Martin Heidegger and other so-called *existential philosophers*. In turn, these philosophers inspired clinical psychology and the psychology of personality, emphasizing questions of a metaphysical nature, such as the way we look at death, suffering, loneliness, feeling of community, and the meaning of life. In psychology, existential philosophy exerted an influence, particularly in the period around 1960.

Through Gestalt psychology, phenomenology had an impact on American psychology of perception, learning, memory, and thinking, and through Kurt Lewin, Solomon Asch, and Fritz Heider, many influential American social psychologists of the latter half of the 1900s may be said to be Stumpf's spiritual grandchildren. Next we shall discuss Franz Brentano, the problem of relationships and Gestalt qualities, Carl Stumpf, Gestalt psychology, and, finally, Kurt Lewin.

Franz Clemens Brentano (1838–1917)

Franz Brentano, who belonged to a well-known Italian-German family, was born in Marienburg on the Rhine. After experiencing a religious crisis at the age of seventeen, he decided to become a Roman Catholic priest and studied theology and philosophy at several German universities. In 1862, he received his doctorate and two years later was ordained as priest. In 1866, he obtained a position at the University of Würzburg, and some years later he was appointed professor. This appointment was dependent upon his being a priest in the Catholic Church, and some years later when he disagreed with church leaders on some questions of faith, Brentano felt obliged to resign his professorship. In 1873, he left the church and the following year was appointed professor at the University of Vienna. In order to marry, he had to relinquish his Austrian citizenship. He then lost his professorship at the university but continued to lecture there until 1895. After the death of his wife, he lived in Italy and Switzerland.

In 1874, Brentano published *Psychologie vom empirischen Standpunkt* (*Psychology from an Empirical Standpoint*). This book was of great importance for psychology at the end of the nineteenth and the beginning of the twentieth century. Brentano was a very popular lecturer and an outstanding teacher, inspiring many students who were later influential at several universities in the German-speaking world. Among his psychology students were Carl Stumpf, Edmund Husserl, Christian von Ehrenfels, and Sigmund Freud, who audited his lectures for several terms.

Brentano's View of Empirical Psychology

Brentano's main work *Psychologie vom empirischen Standpunkt* appeared in the same year as Wundt's physiological psychology. Brentano's views differed from those of Wundt on fundamental points. Whereas Wundt based his psychology on what he thought to be direct observations of mental processes, Brentano, like Comte, rejected the idea that a scientific psychology can be based on introspective *observations*. Still, in contrast to Comte, he did not think this meant we could not make inner experience an object of scientific study. Inner experience could be studied retrospectively, as a recollection of a course of mental events. Further, Brentano held that inner experience could be studied indirectly through the verbal descriptions made of it by other persons. It was also possible, he asserted, to study inner experience as it is indirectly expressed in the behavior of animals, children, and adult human beings.

Like J. S. Mill and Wundt, Brentano attempted to draw a distinction between natural science and physiology on the one hand and psychology on the other hand. Inspired by Aristotle and Scholastic philosophy, Brentano drew a distinction between physical and mental events, maintaining that, in contrast to physical events, mental events form part of a mental act intentionally directed at the object. Physical objects are not included in an act in the same way, because they do not engage with intentional experience in the same way as mental events.

Brentano's idea of mental acts as intentional raised an important but complex question. It is not easy to understand what is meant by a *mental act*. When we search for a definite object and look in a definite direction, it appears clear to say that, when the object appears for us, it is the result of an act. Similarly, when we listen to a definite sound, it is also easy to believe that we have committed an act. However, if we are walking and suddenly discover a stone in our path, it is perhaps less natural to say the object we are seeing is included in an act. Brentano's distinction raises the question of whether we should conceive of perception as a passive or as an active process. His distinction is very subtle, and he seems to have given priority to mental life at the expense of physiological processes.

Brentano's view of consciousness seems to contain a point Wundt overlooked. On the other hand, his view led him to distinguish between, for instance, a color as a mental object and a color as a physical object. Here, it is perhaps not so easy to follow him. Wundt, like Mach, maintained that mental experience is the foundation of psychology as well as of physics. The difference is that in psychology we do not abstract the experience from the subject. As we saw in the preceding chapter, Wundt's view presents difficulties, but it is perhaps in closer agreement with our experience to say that the experience we have of color when we observe an object belongs to the object, and not to try to distinguish between the color of an object as both a physical and a mental entity.

Because mental acts are not easily subjected to experimental investigation, Brentano held that empirical psychology must be advanced primarily as a descriptive science based upon a classification system. This made his psychology different from that of Wundt. Brentano divided mental acts into three classes: sensations and mental representations; judgments; and wishes, love, dislike, and hatred.

Husserl's Pure Phenomenology

While Brentano and Stumpf considered the study of mental life as an empirical study, their student, Edmund Husserl (1859–1938), attempted to develop it as a *formal* science. Originally, Husserl agreed with Brentano that psychology must be studied as a descriptive science. Later, he came to believe that, in order to clarify psychological problems, we must first create a science that makes clear the nature of consciousness. This science should form the foundation not only of a scientific psychology, but also of all sciences. Like mathematics and logic, it must be of a formal and not of an empirical nature. To create this formal science, researchers needed a method that made it possible to conceive of mental phenomena as independent of the external world and preconceptions about it. An effort of this type naturally meets with a number of complex problems that I shall not go into.

Phenomenology and Introspection

Rubin's Studies of Figure–Ground

The phenomenological orientation resulted in the discovery of new aspects of our mental experiences. Let us illustrate this by means of the *figure–ground phenomenon*. Many research workers have given this phenomenon a central place in the study of psychology, and it has often been used to emphasize changes that may also take place in phenomena of a more abstract, cognitive nature.

Mach had drawn attention to the difference it makes to our perception whether we perceive a pattern as the figure or as the ground (background). Based on some simple experimental demonstrations, the Danish researcher Edgar Rubin (1915/1921) presented a more systematic description of the figure–ground relationship. In the years just before World War I, Rubin studied with G. E. Müller, and in Göttingen, where Husserl was teaching at this time, he became acquainted with Husserl's philosophy. Like the other phenomenologically oriented psychologists, Rubin directed the psychological study towards experiences of daily life. He stressed that we must try to describe mental experiences without any preconceptions, or as he himself expressed it, we must describe what we experience when we adopt a simple, straightforward attitude.

The figure–ground phenomenon, well known to artists before the time of Mach and Rubin, can be demonstrated by presenting a light-colored, two-dimensional figure on a darker, two-dimensional surface. For instance, we can cut an irregular figure from a white sheet of paper and glue it to a dark gray paper (Figure 5.1).

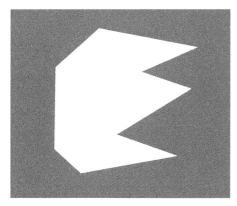

Figure 5.1 Example of the figure–ground phenomenon.

When Rubin asked his subjects to describe their impressions, most reported that they perceived the light-colored part of the material as the figure, and the dark part as the ground. Rubin characterized this response by stating that the figure has shape, whereas the ground seems to make up a more or less diffuse background; that the contour separating the figure and the ground seems to belong to the figure and not to the ground; that the ground seems to extend continuously behind the figure; that the figure seems to give an impression of being thing-like; that the figure seems to protrude a little, to be a little closer to the viewer than the ground; and, finally, that the figure seems to be more impressive, better remembered, and more apt to be associated with meaning.

We might, perhaps, ask whether Rubin's investigation was not an elaboration of the trivial. But after we have looked at the image for some time, we see that what was previously the ground suddenly appears as the figure, and what was the figure is now the ground, and this time the impression is quite different from the one in which we saw the light part as the figure. To illustrate the strength of this difference in perception, Rubin cut out the white part like a vase, but in such a way that when the black part appeared as the figure, the viewer saw two profiles of a face. What we see as the figure and what as the ground can be of decisive importance. Rubin concluded that a relationship must exist between the figure and the ground that determines our perceptual experience. Rubin designated the figure–ground phenomenon a Gestalt.

Before we leave Rubin, I shall just mention a provocative address he gave to the International Congress of Psychology in 1926 on attention, in which he argued that, when we carefully describe phenomena we refer to by the word "attention," we find they share so few features that we cannot regard them as representing a specific type or class of phenomena. Therefore, said Rubin, there can be no such thing as a study of attention. His view was extreme, but he may have been right in thinking that attention is not the simple, unitary phenomenon the earlier German psychologists – and many modern cognitive psychologists – assumed.

Apparently, Rubin's attitude towards the phenomenon he described differed from that of Wundt and his students. This raises the question, does a phenomenological description represent a different method from introspection? Wundt and Titchener attempted to describe mental events as consisting of discrete, constitutive elements. The phenomenologically oriented psychologists insisted that descriptions of mental experience should be made without assumptions or expectations as to the nature of the experience; descriptions should, as they said, be made without prejudice. Unfortunately, it is not easy to decide when a description of a mental phenomenon is made in an unprejudiced manner. We need criteria that can help us decide what is meant by prejudice in descriptions of mental phenomena. Rubin and later phenomenologically oriented psychologists did not provide psychology with such criteria.

In my judgment, it is always possible to describe our mental experience in a situation in more than one way. If so, phenomenological descriptions alone cannot form the basis for psychological study.

Actually, it is not easy to say what we mean by an introspective or phenomenological method. In the first place, we may ask whether these are methods or just ways we use language when we describe our mental experiences in everyday life. I shall not attempt to answer this question, but whether we make what we regard as an introspective or a phenomenological description, I believe the description must in some way be verified.

The Idea of Gestalt Qualities: Christian von Ehrenfels (1859–1932)

As I mentioned in Chapter 3, Helmholtz thought all the sensory cells are connected to fibers leading directly to the brain, without any connections to other fibers in the path from the retina to the brain. He thus seems to have assumed there is a one-to-one connection between the stimulation of a small area of the retina and the sensory impression that arises in the brain.

Mach realized this view presented difficulties; for example, how could our experience of a definite figure gave the impression of unity when this experience is the result of the stimulation of a number of different points? Mach believed the impression of unity could be explained if we assume the stimulation of the individual points to be combined into a unitary impression as a result of the fact that the eye is moved in definite ways. His explanation was not convincing. Still, he raised an important question.

Mach's question was answered by a discovery made by one of Brentano's students, Christian von Ehrenfels (1890). Von Ehrenfels was a professor with many interests, one of which was music, and he drew upon his understanding of music in his study of perception. When a melody is transposed into another key, listeners still perceive it as the same melody even if the tones are different. This, von Ehrenfels declared, must mean that the impression of a melody cannot be based upon properties of the tones taken individually; we must regard it as a property that exists in addition to the properties of the individual tones, and this characteristic must be the result of a definite relationship between the tones. In other words, in addition to the impression of the individual tones, we have an impression of some sort of whole.

We also find an impression of a whole of this kind within other sensory modalities, said von Ehrenfels. If, for example, we put our finger lightly down on a rough surface, we do not experience that it is rough. The impression of roughness first arises when we move our finger over the surface. Here, a series of successive impressions combine to give the impression of a definite property – namely, roughness. With regard to visually perceived figures, the impression of wholeness may also come in addition to the properties of the sensations taken individually. Von Ehrenfels termed properties he thought to be the result of specific relationships between sensations *Gestalt qualities*. (The German word *Gestalt* is a difficult one to capture in English but means something akin to form, whole, relational organization, meaningful structure, etc.)

Carl Stumpf (1848–1936): Perception of Relationships

Under Stumpf's leadership, a special procedure for performing experimental work in psychology was created. The starting point for psychological research was to be an accurate description of the mental experiences to be studied; not until an accurate description had been given of the phenomenon to be studied could experimental work begin. Further, still in agreement with Brentano's view, researchers should choose simple, everyday experiences as the subject of their studies. This view of psychological research became characteristic of the work of the Gestalt psychologists and of Lewin; later in the century, it also, as I have already mentioned, strongly influenced American social psychology. Stumpf is, therefore, a central figure in the history of psychology.

At the age of seventeen, Stumpf was fascinated by Brentano's lectures at Würzburg. He was a passionate lover of music and a gifted mathematician, with interests in philosophy and psychology. After receiving his doctorate under Hermann Lotze in Göttingen in 1868 and moving from university to university for many years, he was appointed professor at the University of Berlin, Germany's leading university, in 1894, and became the first official director of its psychological laboratory. We may wonder why Stumpf and not Wundt was given this prestigious position. Stumpf was primarily known for his studies in hearing and music theory, and here he supplemented and corrected the work Helmholtz had previously done. As Smith (1994) has emphasized, Stumpf was an original philosopher and a skillful psychological methodologist. Ash (1995) has shown that, under Stumpf's leadership, the psychological institute at the University of Berlin became a center of German psychological research, on a level with the institutes at Leipzig, Göttingen, and Würzburg.

Stumpf's most important works were his *Tonpsychologie* (*Psychology of Sound*), which appeared in two volumes in 1883 and 1890, and his *Erkenntnisstheorie* (*Theory of Knowledge*), published posthumously in 1939 and 1940. Smith and Ash have treated him in detail, and I shall describe only his view of the role of relationships in perception.

Part–Whole

Recall that G. E. Müller pointed out that in impressions of wholes, we can identify independent units. For example, in the number *10*, we find the figures *1* and *0*. Stumpf went into the problem of part–whole in detail, not only within auditory perception, but also within visual perception. In his examination of impressions of music, he elaborated von Ehrenfels's view of the melody as a relationship between different tones. Our impression of the relationship, he declared, does not occur spontaneously but appears gradually as we hear the tones, and a cognitive element is involved in our perception of it. A melody makes up what he called an *articulated whole*. We can also find articulated wholes in visual impressions – for example, in our perception of shapes. However, in our perception of the whole, the impression of the parts does not disappear, the impressions of the separate tones still being present in our perception of the melody. When a particular tone enters into another musical context, we recognize it as the same tone, but it could have another function. Stumpf distinguished between articulated wholes, such as a melody or a definite visual shape, on the one hand, and, on the other hand, amorphous wholes for which we cannot discern specific parts, such as the perception of an individual tone or of a homogeneously colored spot.

Like Mach, Stumpf was concerned with the phenomenon that we seem to perceive relationships spontaneously, directly, without reflection. In addition to pointing out that we spontaneously perceive similarities between two objects, he emphasized that, when objects decrease or increase continuously with respect to size, we sometimes have the impression that size forms a gradient (a series with increasing or decreasing values). The same sometimes happens when we perceive tones of gray in objects; we perceive gradients in which grayness decreases or increases.

German Psychology from World War I to World War II

The rest of this chapter deals with the years from just before the outbreak of World War I to the outbreak of World War II. World War I led to the collapse of the German Empire and a deep economic depression, increased unemployment, and great social unrest. In spite of this, German experimental psychology flourished in the 1920s, but it ended abruptly when the Nazis seized power. After World War I, there was great interest in applying psychological research to social problems, within both education and industry, and also within society. At the universities, psychology continued as a pursuit carried on by academics interested in the empirical study of theoretical problems.

When the Nazis came to power, almost all the leading German and Austrian psychologists emigrated, and even if the number of psychologists later increased, and there were some productive psychological researchers under the Nazi regime, the creative intellectual debate characteristic of the first three decades of the 1900s was brought to a halt. It is important to note that some researchers were members of the Nazi Party, but many were not; all, however, had to work under the structure of the Nazi regime. For this reason, I shall end my presentation in the mid-1930s.

Gestalt Psychology

There is a broad consensus among psychologists today that the Gestalt psychologists made important contributions to psychology. I believe it is also widely accepted, however, that they were not able to clarify their main concept, "Gestalt," in a satisfactory manner. In a history of Gestalt psychology, therefore, we must attempt to make clear the contributions as well as the weaknesses of the approach.

The Study of Whole and Form

The Gestalt psychologists aimed to create a new approach to the scientific study of psychology. They wanted to bring about a revolution and rejected almost all the psychology of the previous generation. Their main interest was in the study of perception, and their criticism was first and foremost directed against Helmholtz's view of perception as arising from an association between sensations. Other, but – in their opinion – less important, targets of criticism were the psychologies of Wundt and Titchener. When the Gestalt psychologists became acquainted with behaviorism in the 1920s, this approach became their main target. First and foremost, they objected to the behaviorists' use of the concepts "stimulus" and "response." (We shall return to this point in Chapters 12 and 13.) The reflexology of the Russians was also a stimulus–response psychology, as we shall see in Chapter 8, and the Gestalt psychologists opposed the idea of a conditioned reflex as well. On the whole, the Gestalt psychologists criticized all formulations of psychological problems involving what they regarded as elements of some kind. Their criticism was supported by a variety of clever experimental demonstrations.

Wundt had declared that the whole is more than the sum of its parts. The Gestalt psychologists believed this statement was nearly meaningless because the notion of a whole was so unclear. They radically changed the idea of a whole, viewing it not as built up by means of parts but as spontaneously created as the result of stimulation of the brain, and said it must be understood in terms of the principles determining the activity of the brain. The parts were abstracted from the whole. Therefore, the examination of a phenomenon had to start from the whole and proceed to the parts.

The Gestalt psychologists were deeply impressed by the changes that had taken place in physics at the end of the 1800s and the beginning of the 1900s, and they tried to apply the concepts of field theory to the functioning of the brain. As Ash showed, they were also occupied with formulating a philosophy that could form a bridge between the natural sciences and the humanities.

An interpretation of the German word *Gestalt*, as already mentioned, is form. The Gestalt psychologists wanted to explain how our mental experiences obtain form – that is, are organized. At first they were interested in the problem of form as it arises in visual perception, but they extended the concept to include phenomena in auditory and tactile perception as well. Further, they thought their principles could be applied to the study of memory, learning, and thinking, and they also tried to formulate a view of human personality and values.

By carrying out accurate phenomenological descriptions and performing experiments, they tried to clarify what they meant by "Gestalt." To explain how the experience of form originated, they went into neurophysiology and developed a radically new view of how the brain functions. The three leading Gestalt psychologists, Max Wertheimer, Kurt Koffka, and Wolfgang Köhler, worked together and were friends throughout their lives. Before I discuss their research, I shall present some biographical information about them.

The Triumvirate: Wertheimer, Koffka, and Köhler

Max Wertheimer (1880–1941)

Wertheimer grew up in Prague in a Jewish family. He went to Catholic schools but was also instructed in Hebrew and Judaism, and learned to play both the piano and the violin; like Stumpf and von Ehrenfels, he was a passionate lover of music. In 1898, Werthehimer began his studies at the German-speaking university in Prague. Here, he was fascinated by von Ehrenfels, who was one of his teachers. From 1902 to 1904, he worked in Stumpf's laboratory, but he received his doctorate under Külpe in Würzburg in 1904. Wertheimer taught at the universities of Frankfurt and Berlin before he emigrated to the United States in 1933. He worked as a teacher at the New School for Social Research in New York, and wrote a monograph on stroboscopic movement in 1912, and an article formulating what he thought were laws for the formation of a Gestalt in 1923. A book on thinking (*Productive Thinking*, published posthumously in 1945), was widely admired.

Kurt Koffka (1886–1943)

Kurt Koffka was born in Berlin and grew up a cosmopolite in a well-to-do family. His mother was of Jewish heritage but registered as a Protestant; his father was a lawyer. Koffka entered the University of Berlin in 1903 and attended classes in philosophy, as well as classes in psychology led by Stumpf. Two years later, after studying in Edinburgh for a year, he began work in Stumpf's laboratory. Inspired by discussions of rhythm in one of Stumpf's seminars, he wrote a thesis on that topic and received his doctorate in 1908. After having taught at several German universities during the 1920s, he emigrated to the United States, where he obtained a position at Smith College, which gave him good opportunities for doing scientific research. In his book *The Growth of the Mind* (1924), he attempted to extend the Gestalt view to child psychology, and in his comprehensive work *Principles of Gestalt Psychology* (1935), he gave a systematic and detailed presentation of the ideas of Gestalt psychology and the empirical research carried out to clarify and support them.

Wolfgang Köhler (1887–1967)

Wolfgang Köhler was born in Reval (now Tallinn), Estonia. In 1893, the family moved to a little town near Braunschweig, where his father became the headmaster of a *Gymnasium* (higher secondary school). Köhler graduated from this *Gymnasium* in 1905. In 1907, he began studying for his doctorate under Stumpf, after having taken mathematics, natural science, psychology, physics, and philosophy at two other universities and studying with Max Planck at one of them. Köhler received his doctorate in 1909, having worked on a problem in auditory psychology. From 1913 to 1920, he led an animal laboratory established by the Prussian Academy of Sciences at Tenerife. In 1922, he succeeded Stumpf as professor at the University of Berlin. Köhler had the courage to resist the Nazis, but in 1935 he felt he should resign his position. He then settled in the United States and held a position as a teacher at Swarthmore College. In 1959, he was elected president of the APA, and during the last decade of his life he received many marks of honor. Notable among his many books and articles were his comprehensive investigations of problem solving by chimpanzees, which appeared in 1915, a book introducing Gestalt psychology to the United States in 1929, and his studies of brain fields, made in cooperation with

American researchers. A collection of Köhler's articles was published posthumously in 1971.

The Empirical Research of the Gestalt Psychologists

The origin of Gestalt psychology is often traced to Wertheimer's experiments on stroboscopic movement, which led to the demonstration of the *phi-phenomenon*. In 1911, Koffka and Köhler, who had been his fellow students in Berlin, were subjects of Wertheimer's experiments. When Wertheimer explained to his two friends the ideas underlying the experiments, they were so fascinated that from then on they joined him in developing Gestalt psychology.

Stroboscopic Movement and the phi-Phenomenon

Stroboscopic movement allows us to see filmed images as if they were moving. We also experience it when, under certain conditions, two different areas of the retina are successively illuminated.

Wertheimer's laboratory equipment made it possible to control conditions and introduce a number of variations. By means of a projector, he successively showed two figures, usually two lines, but sometimes also two points, on a screen. The phenomenon depends on a number of conditions, including the size and form of the successively illuminated areas, the distance between them, and the color and intensity of the light. The critical variable, however, is the time interval between the stimulations. If it is too short, two simultaneously illuminated areas are seen. If it is too long, two areas successively illuminated are seen.

The study of stroboscopic movement interested not only people working in the production of films, but also physiologists and psychologists. When Wertheimer undertook his study, several psychologists had already carried out research with the aim of explaining the phenomenon. Wertheimer performed very careful investigations and excluded eye movements, afterimages, imagination, and attention as explanations. He was particularly interested in investigating what he called *pure movement*.

The characteristic of this experience is that we seem to see movement in spite of the fact that there is no object moving from one position to another. Thus, the experience of movement seems to be attached neither to a definite object nor to definite positions in the field of vision. We could, therefore, regard it as a phenomenon in line with the experience of color and form, and Wertheimer thought it should have a specific name, the phi- phenomenon. Because the experience of movement arises despite the fact that a stationary stimulation of two separate areas of the retina is present, Wertheimer argued that it was difficult to explain it as the result of the formation of a simple connection between elements. The experience could not, he held, be broken down into elements but is the result of a unitary process; it makes up a Gestalt.

It is easy to see how this research helped explain the neurophysiological mechanism that allows human beings to register movement visually. Wertheimer did not limit his interpretation to visually experienced movements, however. He held that, like the phi-phenomenon, most of our mental experiences cannot be explained by assuming connections between elements. Instead we must see them as the result of the total stimulation affecting a sensory organ at a given moment in time. These ideas, which Wertheimer only outlined in his monograph, were elaborated by him and his two friends from 1912 onwards. According to the three psychologists, instead of attempting to break down the impression of a whole with the aim of finding the parts, we should attempt to understand how a definite form of stimulation is organized into a whole and find the structure pertaining to the whole. The concepts of "organization" and "structure" were, therefore, important in their attempt to express what they meant by "Gestalt."

The Brain as a Field of Force

In the monograph in which Wertheimer reported on his research, he briefly indicated what he believed could be a neurophysiological explanation of our experience of the phi-phenomenon. According to this belief, stimulation of an area of the retina results in an excitation of a point in the cortex. From this point, a wave-formed excitation spreads to other parts of the brain. When two areas of the brain are stimulated successively in such a way that the phi-phenomenon is produced, a form of electrical short circuit arises between the excitations of the two areas of the cortex, and it is this short circuit that results in the experience of movement; in other words, the experience is caused by dynamic processes in the brain.

Wertheimer and his two friends gradually worked out a view of the brain according to which it functions like an electric field. In an electrical field, the voltage at every point is determined by the field taken as a totality; that is, a change within one area of the field results in a change in the whole field, and, conversely, a change in the whole field results in a change in every point in the field. The changes occurring in the brain, the Gestalt psychologists thought, are the result of the stimulation taken as a totality. They were believed to occur spontaneously as a result of the fact that the brain functions as a system regulated under the principle of equilibrium. At the end of the 1800s, Maxwell's description of electrical and magnetic phenomena by means of a field model had been widely accepted. The three Gestalt psychologists declared that their view was in agreement with this description and thus with the latest advances in physics. The new and crucial point in their explanation was that the phi-phenomenon arises not as a result of the fact that excitation spreads through a network of nerve cells by way of definite nerve fibers, but as a result of changes in the state of the medium.

Relationships Between Consciousness and Physiology

The triumvirate attempted to formulate a new view not only of the nature of wholes and of brain functions, but also of the relationship between consciousness and physiological processes. As already mentioned, at the end of the 1800s, many physiologists and psychologists regarded psychological and physiological processes as being parallel; they thought the processes correspond to each other and occur simultaneously. The

Gestalt psychologists added to this view of parallelism the idea that the two types of processes are similar in form; there is what they called an *isomorphy* between mental and neurophysiological processes. We may illustrate this view as follows. To two separately illuminated points in the visual field, there correspond processes in the nervous system that are also separate, and, in the experience of a movement from one area in the visual field to another, a movement occurs in the electro-physiological field. The idea of isomorphy still fascinates some philosophers and psychologists. However, for the idea to be of use, we must be able to give a description of it which clearly shows a structure in the mental experiences. While that may be possible in the future, it is difficult today to have sufficiently clear ideas about this structure to make use of the idea of isomorphy.

Like all German professors of psychology, the Gestalt psychologists were both psychologists and philosophers, and in outlining their philosophy, they emphasized a correspondence not only between mental processes and brain processes, but also between mental processes and physical processes.

The Gestalt Laws

In 1922, Wertheimer formulated several principles that could explain how wholes of different types arise. These principles are known as *the Gestalt laws*, laws for the formation of Gestalts. Wertheimer thought he could demonstrate the laws by presenting different constellations of points and lines on a sheet of paper. His first law, the law of proximity, was demonstrated by an arrangement of points, as in Figure 5.2.

Figure 5.2 The law of proximity I.

In this instance, he held that we perceive the points A and D, C and D, E and F, etc. spontaneously as groups. We do not form the groups B and C, D and E, and F and G. We group together points that are situated nearest to one another.

Some readers will probably protest that the two points we are inclined to group together do not make up a whole, a Gestalt. Perhaps they will find the perception of the points in Figure 5.3 more convincing. Here the points appear to be organized spontaneously as vertical lines.

Figure 5.3 The law of proximity II.

By means of another arrangement, Figure 5.4, Wertheimer thought he could demonstrate *the law of similarity* – namely, that points which are similar are organized as lines that we perceive as vertical.

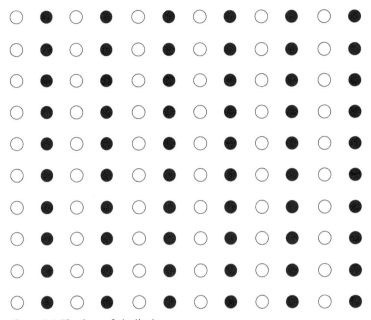

Figure 5.4 The law of similarity.

Our perception is also organized according to three other principles. The first two are *the law of good continuation* and *the law of closure*. The third principle, *the law of common fate*, states that the parts of the visual field that move in the same direction are perceived as belonging together.

Wertheimer also formulated a law he called *the law of good figure* (*the law of Pragnanz*). According to this law, our perceptual representations tend to become as simple as possible, and as a result we perceive forms as being as simple and symmetrical as possible. Koffka (1935) regarded this as a superordinate principle. Many modern researchers in perception are still concerned with this principle, which is often called *the minimum principle*.

An Evaluation of the Gestalt Laws

G. E. Müller had proposed factors of perceptual organization similar to those of Wertheimer. In contrast to Wertheimer, he claimed that attention is involved and explained the organization as resulting from an association of the different parts. Wertheimer agreed that attention in the form of a set can influence perception, but only as a tendency to continue an ongoing process. If, for example, we have begun to perceive something as a figure against a definite background, there is a tendency to continue to organize the stimulation in this way. Wertheimer did not deny that previous experience could influence the organization, but previous experience would then operate only with the principles he had formulated. Several psychologists, among them Jean Piaget (whom we will discuss in Chapter 16), have criticized the Gestalt psychologists for not giving sufficient weight to learning. Although the Gestalt psychologists stressed that learning plays a role, they did not attempt to specify how it and the Gestalt principles could interact. The criticism may, therefore, be justified.

Against the Gestalt laws as demonstrated by Wertheimer, we can argue that our perception is more in accordance with von Ehrenfels's view of Gestalt qualities than with Wertheimer's view that we spontaneously see the whole and then, from this whole, abstract parts. When we examine the arrangements of points and lines used in the demonstrations, I think it is natural to say that the tendencies he postulated are present, but, as von Ehrenfels and Stumpf emphasized with regard to the melody, they are present together with a perception of the elements. For example, we clearly perceive *the points* in the demonstration of the first two laws. Therefore, we might think we perceive a whole, a Gestalt, simultaneously with our perception of the points; in other words, we perceive separate points and a Gestalt quality.

In connection with the point made above, we should mention the research of the Italian-Austrian psychologist Vittorio Benussi (1914). Benussi showed that, in various instances, visual perception is unstable in the sense that we can perceive material in more than one way; perception can be ambiguous. When unstable material is organized in one definite way, it is, therefore, natural to think that perception involves a cognitive element which is a result of previous learning. This was what Stumpf had emphasized as well.

Benussi belonged to a group of philosophers and psychologists who, like Wertheimer, Koffka, and Köhler, were concerned with Gestalt problems. This group is often referred to as the Graz school (after the city of Graz, Austria). There are still psychologists who continue to work along their lines, such as the Italian Gaetano Kanisza (1994). Kanisza has called attention to the fact that the principle of Pragnanz, the minimal principle, is unclear, because it can refer either to the fact that something appears to be specific, or to the fact that a perceptual structure tends to be perceived as simple. With regard to the tendency towards simplicity, Kanisza and one of his coworkers showed that this principle is not always valid. Look, for example, at Figure 5.5. We do not see the three figures as respectively a circle, a triangle, and a square; we see an interrupted circle, a maimed triangle, and a misshapen square. It is necessary, Kanisza said, to distinguish between our visual perception and our interpretation, our conceptualization of it. This point was overlooked, he claimed, by the Gestalt psychologists, and by many modern researchers in perception.

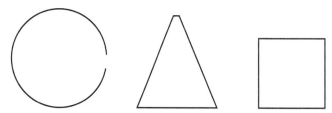

Figure 5.5 Example of perceptual statement.

Wertheimer used two-dimensional figures to demonstrate his laws. In our perceived environment, space extends in three dimensions, objects form parts of a wider perceptual field, and we usually see them as three-dimensional. Haber (1985), as I understand him, argues that perception of shape forms part of our perception of a visual field extending in three dimensions. This may mean it is not possible to understand how form (shape) arises in visual perception unless we have accounted for our perception of three-dimensional space. If this is correct, Wertheimer's way of demonstrating the laws may suffer from a fundamental weakness.

The Gestalt psychologists claimed that our perceptual representations are formed spontaneously. With respect to the laws of similarity, closure, and good continuation, it is not easy to decide whether the formation of the representations is dependent on the fact that we direct attention towards certain aspects of the figures presented. The Gestalt psychologists did not discuss in detail how attention might be an important factor in the perception of form.

Wertheimer's demonstrations of the postulated laws have an intuitive appeal, but I think it is fair to conclude that many questions must be answered before we can say that form is a result of the factors he pointed to as decisive.

The Perceptual Constancies

One type of phenomenon of particular interest to the Gestalt psychologists are the *perceptual constancies*. It was already known that the perceived size of an object is approximately constant, even if the distance between the observer and the object varies. If, for example, a person moves until he is approximately 50–60 meters from us, we perceive his size as being about the same. When we take into consideration that the projection of the object on the retina is inversely proportional to the distance of the object, it is strange that the perceived size does not vary in a similar manner. It was also known that the visual impression of the form of an object appears approximately the same even if the object turns relative to the plane in which we see it. A door, for example, appears rectangular even if it swings towards or away from us, in spite of the fact that the projection on the retina now has the form of a trapezoid. Further, we experience brightness as an attribute of material objects in the same way, even if the light reflected from an object undergoes great variations. A piece of charcoal is perceived as black even in strong sunlight, and a piece of white paper looks white even in a relatively dark room. There is also a constancy in our perception of chromatic colors. These phenomena must mean that different forms of stimulation can give rise to the same perceptual experience. In other words, there is a kind of invariability in respect to the impressions we obtain from the ongoing stimulation.

Relationships as Explanation of the Constancies

Helmholtz had explained this invariability by his theory of unconscious inference. Hering had focused on the role of contrast in his account of color constancies; he had also pointed out that the impression of an object's chromatic color is a result of our recollection of the color. The Gestalt psychologists attempted to explain the perceptual constancies by pointing to various types of relationships present in the situations where constancy arises. Regarding the amount of light reflected from an object, we can show that it makes up a constant fraction of the amount of light falling on the object. Thus, there is a constant relationship between reflected and incident light. Different objects reflect different fractions of the incident light, but the *relationship* between these fractions is constant, even if the intensity of the illumination changes. This constant relationship can explain brightness constancy.

A simple experiment performed by Adamer Gelb (reported in Koffka, 1935) convincingly reveals the role played by the pattern of stimulation. With a minimum of equipment, readers can perform this experiment themselves. We illuminate a black disk in a dark room in such a way that no light falls outside the disk; under a relatively strong illumination, the disk will appear white. If, however, part of the disk is covered with a small piece of white paper, the disk will spontaneously appear black. The introduction of the white paper changes the frame of reference by which we evaluate the brightness of the black disk. The relative amount of light reflected from it is far less than from the white paper, and for this reason, the impression is now quite a different one. As long as light is reflected from several objects, it is of no importance whether the intensity of illumination increases or decreases, because the relationship between the amounts of light reflected from the objects remains the same. Koffka argued that size and form constancy could be explained in a similar fashion.

In this experiment it is difficult to believe that the sudden change in the appearance of the disk is a result of a contrast effect. It is, however, conceivable that our visual system contains a mechanism allowing us to register the relationship between incident and reflected light. Size and form constancy can also be explained if we assume the existence of mechanisms that allow us to register similar relationships.

Empirical research on perception constancies has revealed that relationships are important in explaining them, but experience and expectation may also play a role. Hence, the results of research do not unambiguously support a Gestalt psychological interpretation.

The Study of Thinking

Conway Lloyd Morgan, whom we will meet in Chapter 7, wondered whether animals could perceive causal and meaningful relationships. He had discovered that it was difficult for a dog to enter his garden gate with a stick in its mouth and concluded the dog was not capable of perceiving relationships. Some years later, the American Edward Lee Thorndike, to be discussed in Chapter 12, performed investigations of problem solving by animals, particularly cats. On the basis of his investigations, he held that animals learn by mechanical trial and error, associating accidental responses with aspects of the situation in which animals operate. Leonard Hobhouse, covered in Chapter 7, concluded on the basis of his investigations that monkeys and apes probably possess what he called *articulate ideas*; they are capable of understanding certain relationships. Köhler wanted to show that chimpanzees can understand complex relationships, and his experiments have become classics.

Köhler's Studies of Thinking in Chimpanzees

Köhler undertook his experiments in Tenerife, where, beginning in 1913. he directed the Prussian Academy of Sciences' research station. At the onset of World War I, he was isolated on the island and was forced to stay there until 1920. Hence, he had plenty of time for experiments, and, compared to the experiments of Morgan, Hobhouse, and Thorndike, his research on problem solving in animals was of very high quality. The situations were carefully arranged, and the animals, five or six adult chimpanzees from the African mainland, were systematically observed over an extended period of time.

Köhler took over several of Hobhouse's problem situations, but he also constructed new ones. His experiments on the ability of chimpanzees to use sticks are perhaps the best known. The animals were placed before a grating, and a fruit, preferably a banana, was placed behind the grating beyond their reach. To get the fruit, the animal had to use a stick. The problem could be varied by having the animal first use a shorter stick to obtain a longer stick that could reach the fruit, or connect two sticks to obtain a sufficiently long one. In one problem the banana was placed in a case with grating in one of the walls that allowed the chimpanzee to put its hand inside, but not far enough to reach the banana. Gratings in another wall had openings sufficient to allow the passage of the stick but not the chimpanzee's hand. When a banana was placed close to this grating, the chimpanzee had to use the stick to push the banana to the other wall, where it could reach it with its hand. Apparently, this is a very difficult problem. In another type of problem, a banana was hung from the ceiling; to reach it, the chimpanzee had to place a box under it and then stand on top of the box. A third type of problem used different arrangements of strings. For example, by untying a string from a hook fastened to the wall, the animal could lower the fruit that was hanging from the ceiling by the other end of the string.

Learning by Insight

All the problems mentioned were solved by one or more of the chimpanzees. According to Köhler, therefore, chimpanzees are capable of conceiving complex relationships, and in this sense they displayed a capacity for thinking. On the basis of his observations, Köhler asserted that the animals did not solve the problems by a trial-and-error procedure. The solution often occurred as an abrupt change in their behavior, and sometimes the animals would even sit quite still for some time and then suddenly make movements leading to the solution of the problem. In Köhler's opinion, learning, therefore, did not occur gradually, as Thorndike had claimed. Instead, the animals solved the problems by conceiving of relationships, a form of solution Köhler called *insight*. Animals, he declared, have the capacity for insight.

By "insight," Köhler meant the animals had found the solution to the problem more or less suddenly and without trial and error. Another criterion of insight was that once the animal had found a solution to a problem, it would subsequently solve this problem immediately. A third criterion was that the animal would transfer the procedure it had used to solve a problem to other problems of a similar nature. By means of these criteria of insight, Köhler succeeded in giving a more precise meaning to the expression "perception of relationships."

Thorndike and many other psychologists and physiologists had attempted to show that higher, abstract forms of intelligence could be explained as simple reactions of a mechanistic nature. Köhler's experiments cast doubt on this view and raised the question of whether the more developed primates should be ascribed a high degree of intelligence, a high capacity for thinking. Field studies of chimpanzees and gorillas undertaken by later researchers support this view. Chimpanzees throw stones and sticks at their enemies, break nuts with branches and stones, use small branches and straws to capture termites and ants, and obtain water from holes with small sticks and dry leaves. Further, a wealth of observations of their social lives suggests they have a capacity for abstract thinking.

Köhler argued that, to test whether an animal possesses insight, the situation must be so arranged that the animal can overview it. On the basis of this requirement, he criticized the investigations performed by Thorndike. Nevertheless, Köhler's experiments do not conclusively show that the concept of "insight" is a fruitful one. It is frequently difficult to decide whether a movement is a link in a goal-directed attempt to solve a problem, or a movement the animal accidentally makes in the situation. It is also frequently difficult to decide when a solution occurs suddenly, or gradually, as a result of trial-and-error. Further, it is conceivable that animals, like human beings, are capable of anticipating solutions without making movements. A weakness of Köhler's experiments is that he had insufficient knowledge of the animals' previous experience, since he had received them from Africa when they were already nearly mature. Consequently, he could not control their ontogenetic development. Later research by Herbert Birch (1945) has shown that, if chimpanzees have not had experience with sticks, they will not solve stick problems, even in their simplest form. The tendency to overlook previous experience and thus the role learning plays in the development of psychological abilities is, as I have emphasized, a weakness in the Gestalt psychologists' approach to almost all the psychological problems they examined.

Animal Studies of Perceptual Constancy

In addition to his experiments on problem solving, Köhler performed experiments to answer questions about perceptual constancy in chimpanzees. The German psychologist David Katz (1911) had undertaken comprehensive experimental research on the perception of colors in human beings. He had concluded that color constancy is partly a result of an interaction between different areas of color in the visual field, and partly a result of the fact that the subjects are capable of estimating the intensity of the illumination falling on the object. The latter point was in line with the explanation Helmholtz had given of the colored shadows. Köhler opposed Helmholtz's and Katz's view, and declared that the animals react to relationships and not to estimates of absolute light intensities.

To demonstrate this, he conducted a very clever experiment. He trained a chimpanzee to choose a definite shade of gray and then placed the animal in a situation where it had to choose between two pieces of paper of different shades. When the animal had learned to make this discrimination, Köhler replaced the piece of paper the animal had *not* learned to prefer with a piece of paper darker than the one it had learned to prefer. If the animal had learned to react to the absolute brightness of the pieces of paper, it should continue to choose the same piece of paper as before. However, Köhler found that the animal now preferred the substitute shade. His conclusion was that the animal had learned to react to the relationship *darker than*. Köhler also performed experiments in which he rewarded the choice of the brightest piece of paper and obtained the same result. He did, of course, control for the so-called position effect by placing the rewarded piece of paper randomly, sometimes to the right and sometimes to the left.

In the 1930s, the results of these experiments were regarded as an important objection to Clark Hull's theory of learning. As we shall see in Chapter 13, Hull's coworker Kenneth Spence then performed some clever experiments showing that Köhler's results could be explained as a consequence of learning.

Wertheimer's View of Problem Solving and Teaching

Wertheimer was concerned with logic and thinking throughout his scientific career. In his book *Productive Thinking*, which appeared posthumously in 1945, he argued that to be fruitful teaching must not be based on memorization and learning by heart but must aim at improving children's understanding. Children must attempt to understand processes as wholes and not as parts. The book was directed against a view of learning emphasizing associative principles. In line with the principle of Pragnanz, Wertheimer attempted to show that a solution to a problem frequently arises because the structure of the problem creates vectors, or tensions, that are dynamically related to the stated requirements and that lead to a good Gestalt.

The concepts he used are poorly defined, and it is not easy to follow his presentation. For example, he distinguished between productive and reproductive thinking without discussing how the distinction could be made. He was primarily interested in the study of problem solving, but he neglected to discuss differences and similarities between various types of problems. It is also difficult to understand what he meant by "whole" and "structure" in the situations he examined. The reader is left with few clues to follow Wertheimer's thinking when he concluded that a "good Gestalt" is present, and hardly any guidance in understanding what he meant by vectors in thought processes.

Before Wertheimer undertook his studies of thinking in children, a number of studies had suggested, as Woodworth (1938, ch. 29) points out, that previous learning plays a major role in children's thinking. Wertheimer did not acknowledge that the results of his studies could be explained as being due to previous experience. This seems to have been a serious weakness in his research on thinking.

Problem Solving as a Successive Reformulation of the Problem

Wertheimer emphasized that the solution to a problem emerges as a result of a perception or comprehension of the problem situation taken as a totality. One of his students, Karl Duncker (1935/1945), broke away from his teacher and presented a view of problem solving according to which the problem solver finds the solution by successively trying out hypotheses expected to lead to the correct solution. Duncker illustrated his view of the process by presenting protocols of the words of the subjects, who were asked to think aloud. One of the problems he used in his studies was the following: "Remove an inoperable tumor in the stomach of a patient by X-ray without damaging the healthy tissue." The subjects would report hypotheses of the following type: find a way of shielding the healthy tissue, vary the intensity of the radiation in such a way that the intensity is greatest on the tumor, rotate the patient while the radiation is focused on the tumor, or rotate the source of radiation while it is focused on the tumor.

Duncker conceived of the hypotheses presented as successive attempts to solve the problem, and the solution as a result of successive reformulations of the problem. He stressed that at the same time that the problem solver was cognizant of the requirements for finding a solution, he or she would try out various hypotheses.

While Wertheimer held that the solution is the result of conceiving of the problem as a totality, Duncker attributed greater importance to the examination of the material, which would generate hypotheses of various types. Of particular importance for the generation of the hypotheses is the understanding that the object under study could have a functional value. As Woodworth and Schlossberg (1954, p. 821) noted, we can see Duncker's view of problem solving as "the testing of hypotheses as a form of trial and error." According to Duncker, the hypotheses are the result of partial insight and not of blind trial and error.

In Chapter 12, I shall report on the account the American philosopher and psychologist John Dewey (1910a) made of problem solving. Here I shall anticipate by saying he thought of problem solving as a trying out of various hypotheses. The difference between Duncker and Dewey is that Duncker believed the hypotheses represented insights and that they could be seen as being successively reformulated. Although he emphasized that the hypotheses represent partial insights and that the problem solver had to view the situation as a totality, he clearly deviated from Wertheimer by attributing a greater role to the material as forming parts of the problem. In contrast to his teacher, he also drew attention to the role played by the functional value of the material for the solution of the problem. With Köhler as one of my teachers at the University of Chicago in 1950, I (Saugstad, 1955, 1958) elaborated Duncker's emphasis on the functional value. In discussing Duncker's work, Köhler told me Wertheimer had rejected Duncker's view and that therefore he and not Wertheimer had written the preface to

Duncker's monograph on problem solving. I mention this to underline that even if Duncker was inspired by Wertheimer and was his student, he was hardly a Gestalt psychologist.

Before Duncker, in a reproduction of a classic experiment by Thorndike (to be reviewed in Chapter 12), D. K. Adams (1929) had described the problem-solving behavior of cats as a successive trying out of hypotheses. Some years later, I. Krechevsky (who later changed his name to 'David Krech') (1932) had demonstrated that maze learning in rats could be seen as a successive trying out of definite hypotheses. Hence, the idea of problem solving as a successive trying out of hypotheses was supported by several psychologists in the first half of the 1900s. I shall return to this idea in my review of the information-processing approach in Chapter 18.

Functional Fixedness

In studies of the role played by objects in problem solving, Duncker performed a series of experiments demonstrating that it might be difficult to use an object in a definite way when it was being used in another way. For example, he presented his subjects with the problem of making a board stay in position across an open doorway. To do this, the subjects had to use a piece of cork as a wedge between the end of the board and the door jamb. The problem was more difficult when the piece of cork was in use as the stopper of an inkwell than when it was lying with other materials on a table. Duncker called this negative effect *functional fixedness*.

It has also been shown that when an object has recently been used in a certain way it may be more difficult to use it in another way even if this latter way is a familiar one. This shows that previous experience can also have a *negative* effect on our thinking.

A dramatic demonstration of the negative effect of previous experience was made by Abraham Luchins (1942). Luchins gave his subjects the task of figuring out how they could obtain a specified amount of water by pouring it from one jar into another. The subjects had an unlimited amount of water at their disposal.

The subjects were shown how they could obtain 20 quarts of water, having at their disposal a jar containing 29 quarts and one containing 3 quarts, by pouring water from the first container three times into the other. Then they were shown how they could solve a problem by pouring from jar A once into jar B and twice into jar C. Thus, they could solve this task according to the formula A–B–2C. Then the subjects had to work out the solutions to five problems that could all be solved by using the formula. Having practiced using the formula, they were given the simple problem of obtaining 25 quarts given jars containing 28, 76, and 3 quarts (A–C). The majority could not solve this problem in 2½ minutes, evidently unable to abandon the formula A–B–2C.

While the Gestalt psychologists provided inspiration to much work on thinking in the years 1920–1960, not all of it was planned to test Gestalt theory. The work demonstrating the negative effects of previous learning and experience on problem solving continued throughout the latter half of the twentieth century.

Evaluation of Gestalt Psychology

The Gestalt psychologists' idea that wholes arise as the result of the effects of stimulation of the brain was radically new and would have revolutionized psychological thinking if it had been true. As we have seen, however, they produced little or no evidence to demonstrate its truth. As Smith (1994) has emphasized, the Gestalt psychologists never succeeded in giving a satisfactory account of what constitutes a whole, nor did they explain how the parts are abstracted from the wholes. In Wertheimer's demonstrations of the Gestalt laws, the starting point is constellations of points and lines. In the demonstration of the laws of proximity and similarity, the points are clearly present, even if there is a strong tendency to perceive them as lines, as Wertheimer pointed out. Evidently, Julian Hochberg (1979, p. 114) was justified in his conclusion:

Without a physiological basis, the theory rests only on the "laws of organization." For the most part, these remain subjective demonstrations of questionable reliability and of unknown quantitative strengths. But because they are compelling, as far as they go, and because they do carry the promise of having some explanatory power, various objective and quantitative treatments of the *minimum principle* have been attempted. Some of these have continued into recent years, but they have been essentially dissociated from the Gestalt theories about brain fields.

If the beliefs underlying Gestalt psychology are not tenable, why has this approach had such a profound and widespread effect on psychology? In my opinion, the answer must be that the Gestalt psychologists extended knowledge and gave a new perspective by pointing to a variety of situations in which the relationships between the various parts of the stimulation determine perception. Thus, they shifted attention from a concern with elements to one with patterns of stimulation. This was extremely fruitful in many instances. Their insistence that we must take into account the relationships between parts influenced not only the study of perception, but also the studies of learning, memory, and motivation.

The focus on relationships was not new to Gestalt psychologists. Even Helmholtz and Wundt had been concerned with them, and, as I noted in Chapters 3 and 4, Hering, Mach, and G. E. Müller had repeatedly pointed to their effects. When the Gestalt psychologists received their training, students of Brentano, such as Stumpf, von Ehrenfels, Husserl, and psychologists of the Graz school were intensely occupied with the problem of the role relationships play in perception. The contribution of Wertheimer, Koffka, and Köhler was primarily the realization that this problem is central in the study of psychology.

Gestalt psychology rests on the idea that the brain functions as an electrical field. Most modern physiologists would probably agree with Semir Zeki (1993) that this idea is not very plausible; it was also regarded as empty speculation by most physiologists active at the time the idea was launched. Hence, Hochberg's assertion that Gestalt theory has no physiological foundation was justified. If it is difficult to find support for the idea that the brain functions as an electrical field, it is also difficult to define concepts such as "structure," "organization," "tension," and "vector."

Even if we must discard the Gestalt psychologists' model of the brain, it did propose that perception is the result of a specific organization of the brain. As Hilgard (1987) has remarked, this may have contributed to the view that our general manner of perception is genetically determined. Attempts at finding support for this belief have resulted in some very surprising and important findings in the study of perception in infants, as we shall see in Chapter 19.

In science it is of course important to answer questions, but as Köhler often remarked, it is just as important to ask them. As we shall see in Chapter 13, the questions raised by the Gestalt psychologists helped James J. Gibson and Edward Chase Tolman reorient the studies of perception and learning, respectively. In Chapter 17, we shall see that Karl Lashley and members of the group around him derived much inspiration from Gestalt psychology. Finally, one of the central figures in social psychology at the mid-twentieth century, Solomon Asch, was strongly influenced by Wertheimer, as we will see in Chapter 14. Altogether, Gestalt psychology has had an important and lasting influence on psychology.

Kurt Lewin (1890–1947)

Kurt Lewin worked in close contact with the Gestalt triumvirate at the Institute of Psychology in Berlin. Still, for reasons made clear below, I think it distorts the picture of the far wider phenomenological movement to regard him as a Gestalt psychologist. While living in Germany, Lewin primarily studied personality, and later, after he had emigrated to the United States, he studied it within social psychology.

A Short Biography

Lewin was born in Mogilno, a small town in Germany near the Polish border. He belonged to a Jewish family that does not seem to have been accepted by either its German or its Polish neighbors and obtained its income from a shop and a small farm. Thus, unlike Wertheimer, Koffka, and Köhler, Lewin did not grow up in the wealthier German upper-middle class, even if he graduated from one of Berlin's most respected high schools. In 1910, he entered the University of Berlin as a student of philosophy, with a particular interest in the philosophy of science and psychology. He came under the influence of Stumpf, and in 1914, just before the outbreak of World War I, he finished his doctoral thesis under Stumpf's guidance. During his years of study, he was active in the student socialist association, but he does not seem to have had any reservations about fighting in World War I, in which he distinguished himself as a soldier. In 1921, Lewin was attached to the Psychological Institute at the University of Berlin, but when the Nazis seized power, he emigrated to the United States. In Chapter 14, I shall report on his research activities there.

Lewin and Gestalt Psychology

Lewin was deeply influenced by the broad phenomenological movement. Like his German contemporaries, he emphasized the necessity of describing our immediate experiences, and in line with Brentano's and Stumpf's view of psychology, he directed his studies towards the experiences of everyday life. Wertheimer, Koffka, and Köhler wished to extend Gestalt psychology into all aspects of psychology; however, they focused on problems of perception, thinking, and memory. In contrast, Lewin concentrated primarily on motivation and human social relationships. Like his three colleagues, he rejected the earlier atomistic psychology; however, he was not greatly concerned with the central problems of Gestalt psychology – that is, how forms arise in our mental experiences. Even if he, like Köhler, attempted to develop the idea of a psychological field, his psychology does not share the features characteristic of the Berlin Gestalt school. Therefore, if we classify Lewin as a Gestalt psychologist, it must be with important reservations.

Lewin was interested in the theoretical problems of psychology as well as in the application of psychology to social problems. He wanted to use psychology to create a more humane society and gradually directed his research towards social and political problems. As a researcher, he had a remarkable aptitude for devising experiments that could throw light on psychological problems. Even though his experiments derived from his reflections on practical life, they also provided a general theoretical perspective.

Lewin's Field Theory

His great interest in the philosophy of science led Lewin into close cooperation with influential philosophers of science. Based upon his ideas on the nature of science, he created his own particular approach to empirical studies in psychology. The philosopher Ernst Cassirer (1874–1945) aroused his interest in the scientific ideas of the Renaissance, which had resulted in a decisive break from the Aristotelian mode of thinking. In a 1931 article entitled "The Conflict Between Aristotelian and Galilean Modes of Thought in Contemporary Psychology," Lewin pointed out that, in contrast to Aristotle, Galileo regarded physical events as the result of the effects of definite causes, and not the result of inherent fundamental processes in objects. Like Galileo, psychologists should (said Lewin) treat psychological processes as manifestations of forces operating within what Lewin later called a *psychological field*. Psychologists should also try to formulate general laws in which behavior emerges as a result of the total effect of psychological forces at a given point in time; psychological thinking should not be based on characteristics thought of as inherent in the organism, such as drives, instincts, or abilities. Nor must we classify human beings into types or classes such as normal or abnormal, or based on features shared by different classes or individuals – for example, features common to children at the age of two to three years.

In line with this orientation, Lewin (1935, 1951) regarded the person and his or her environment as a field, which he referred to as the person's *life space*. The environment, the person, and thus the life space are divided into different regions. Between the regions in the environment and in the person, various types of forces arise. Lewin expressed this view by a general formula in which he regarded behavior (B) as a function (f) of the person (P) and the environment (E): $B = f(P, E)$.

Lewin also attempted to introduce a specific area of mathematics, topology, in the hope of attaining a better overview of and greater precision in identifying the forces he believed to be operative in the psychological field.

An Evaluation of Lewin's Field Theory

The main premise of Lewin's field theory is that behavior must be understood as the result of an interaction between the person and the situation in which the person finds him or herself; our description of behavior must be based on the idea that the person and the situation make up a sort of totality. This raises the question: What are we to understand by "person" and "situation"?

Apparently, in order to say what we mean by *person*, we must provide him or her with properties of various kinds, and the same is true of *situation*. Lewin's conception of "person" and "situation" rested on descriptions he and others could give based on everyday thinking and everyday language. In my opinion, his theoretical field approach is fruitful to the extent that we can have confidence in phenomenological descriptions of our relationship with our environment. If such a description does not satisfy a scientific psychology, then Lewin's idea of a field hardly qualifies as a scientific theory. At least during a certain period of his life, Lewin seems to have thought his concept of "psychological field" corresponded to the concept of "field" in contemporary physics. As William Estes (1954) noted, it is difficult to see more concretely how the two concepts correspond to each other. Dorwin Cartwright (1959) has made a careful and critical review of Lewin's field theory and research.

Lewin's field theory is perhaps best regarded as a reminder that in psychological studies we must recognize that the person and the environment interact with each other. Lewin's approach represented a corrective to both the one-sided emphasis psychoanalysis placed on properties inherent in the person and the behaviorists' one-sided emphasis on the environment and belief that the environment of humans and animals can be described in physicalist terms.

It is difficult to understand how we can make more precise deductions from Lewin's conception of the person and the environment as making up a field; the hypotheses he investigated hardly qualify as deductions or predictions. His field theory may have given him a certain inspiration, but it seems most likely that his empirical investigations were a result of his aptitude for making observations and of his understanding of social phenomena.

Lewin on Conflicts and Motivation

Lewin conceived of motivation as tension arising between regions in the person and regions in the environment, and this tension might result in conflict. He presented a model of the different types of conflicts. In short, a person might have to choose one of three options, two attractive and one repulsive, or two alternatives of which one was attractive and the other repulsive.

Noncompleted Tasks

In the preceding chapter we noted that Watt and Ach studied the effect the task had on thought processes. Ach regarded this effect, the determining tendency, as an expression of the will. Lewin and his coworkers pursued Ach's approach and carried out several interesting experiments on the importance of the will in solving a task. Lewin's student Bluma Zeigarnik (1927) gave her subjects a number of simple tasks and interrupted them while they performed some of them. It turned out that the subjects tended to remember better the tasks they had *not* completed. The effect, named after Zeigarnik, has proved to be reproducible.

In line with the thinking of Ach and Lewin, we can expect to find subjects more inclined to remember tasks not completed than those completed. Lewin and one of his coworkers also subjected this hypothesis to a simple experimental test and found it tenable. This result also seems to be reproducible. In contrast to Ach, Lewin tried to understand the role played by the task without making assumptions about associations. Further, he gave more weight to the properties of the situation than Ach had done. Still, we can regard his investigations as a continuation of the work of the Würzburg school.

Desires and Self-Esteem: Level of Aspiration

William James (1950, I, p. 310) had pointed out that our self-esteem is dependent not only on what we have achieved or are capable of achieving, but also on what we wish and hope to achieve. Further, our fear of failure may determine the types of tasks we engage in, and the way we perform them. A study of our aspirations may then give information about our personality. On certain types of tasks, some persons will set high goals for their performance, whereas others are satisfied with achieving less. Lewin and his coworkers devised simple tasks that allowed them to measure and then compare what the subjects planned to achieve, their *level of aspiration*, and what they actually achieved. The game of quoits was one such task.

Psychologists have intensively studied the conditions determining people's level of aspiration. As we might expect, the results show great individual differences in these levels, as well as in reaction to failure. Further, our level of aspiration depends on the levels set by other people and naturally varies from one sphere of life to another. For this reason, it is difficult to find tasks that are representative of a person's level of aspiration. Still, the work of Lewin and his students probably started important research in the study of personality.

Dembo's Study of Anger

Of some twenty experiments Lewin and his coworkers performed at the Institute in Berlin, one on anger undertaken by Tamara Dembo (1931) is noteworthy. After having performed a variety of preliminary investigations by asking people whether they had recently been angry, why they were angry, and what had happened when they became angry, Dembo constructed the following situation. The subjects were given two very simple tasks in which it was not possible to satisfy the requirements of the experimenter.

One task was to throw a wooden ring around the neck of a bottle placed 5 meters away ten times in succession. In the second task, the subjects were told that, without moving outside a marked area, they must reach a flower in three different ways, although this was possible in only two ways. If the subjects gave up in their attempts, the experimenter insisted that the requirements must be met. Although it must have been of relatively little importance to the subjects whether they succeeded or not, their attempts to meet the experimenter's requirements led to reactions of anger that gradually increased in strength. Dembo interpreted her results in line with Lewin's idea of a field. According to this view, behavior, in this case the reaction of anger, is dependent upon the person as well as upon the person's environment. Dembo had identified an important aspect of anger – namely, that it frequently builds up over time when, despite persistent attempts, we are not able to master the situation in which we find ourselves, even if it is a trivial one.

Dembo was right in pointing out that in a study of anger we must always realize that an interaction between the person and the situation takes place. Yet, as far as I can understand, it is not possible to make more precise statements about that interaction unless we also specify certain characteristics of the person. For instance, will strong and unusual expressions of anger arise only when people's self-esteem is involved? Such questions of individual differences and personality characteristics were what Lewin wanted to avoid by means of his field approach.

An Evaluation of Lewin's View of the Person and the Situation

As Kurt Danziger (1990) has made clear, Lewin's focus on the interaction between the individual and the situation was new in the study of personality. By taking this approach, Lewin avoided using the type of introspective reports on which Ach had based his studies and thereby contributed to making research more objective. In studying the interaction between the person and the situation, Lewin could also focus on social factors affecting personality. On the other hand, it is scarcely possible to understand the interaction between the person and the situation without assuming a number of personal characteristics, which Lewin's Galilean approach prevented him from doing. This was, in my opinion, a serious limitation in his work on thinking.

6

Early British Psychology

Intellectual and scientific life in Great Britain differed in important respects from that of Germany, and the psychology emerging in the two countries had little in common. German psychology arose, as we have seen in the preceding three chapters, in close contact with experimental physiology. In contrast, early British psychology grew along with the study of biological evolution and was not based on experiments. Whereas German psychology was organized and carried out at the country's many universities, psychological research in Great Britain was undertaken mainly by private researchers outside the universities. Cooperation between Britain and Germany in the study of psychology was hindered not only by the great differences between their schools of thought but also by intense political rivaly. Efforts to integrate the psychology of the two countries were made by US psychologists, as we shall see in Chapter 11.

    The study of evolution led to an entirely new persepctive on human nature, and the formulation of the Darwinian theory of evolution was a milestone in the history of empirical psychology. In addition to starting the comparative biological study of psychology, Charles Darwin can also be credited with laying the foundation of the modern study of emotions and initiating the study of child development. However, while Darwin is undoubtedly the great name in the study of evolution, the idea did not originate with him but was the result of some broad general trends in European science. Familiarity with these trends helps us understand Darwin's thinking as well as the reception of his ideas by contemporary and later biologists.

Familiarity with the study of evolution before Darwin also helps us understand the role played by Herbert Spencer in the early study of empirical psychology. As Mayr emphasized (1982, p. 385), Spencer was not a great biologist. But this must not prevent us from examining his ideas about psychology. As we shall see in the chapter on US psychology, they are of decisive importance for the development of empirical psychology. Before I turn to Darwin, I shall therefore sketch the general historical background of British psychology and say a few words about the early study of evolution. Following that and a discussion of Spencer, we turn to Francis Galton's studies of the role of inheritance in the development of mental abilities, along with his studies of individual differences. We conclude with Alexander Bain of Scotland, who had a strong effect on early American psychology. We can draw a clear line from Bain's work to that of Edward Thorndike and B. F. Skinner, although his influence on the American psychology of learning has tended to be overlooked.

British Social Life and Culture

Great changes took place in Great Britain in the nineteenth century. In the one hundred years from 1801 to 1901, the population increased from 10 million to 37 million. Greatly improved agriculture, industrialization, and trade with the remaining colonies and other countries spurred enormous growth in the wealth of the nation. This wealth, however, was not evenly distributed. Landed proprietors, industrialists, and financiers accumulated great wealth, while, in contrast, the great mass of agricultural, mining, and factory workers lived in miserable conditions. Their diet was poor, and many died of epidemic diseases due to poor sanitary conditions. Working hours were long, and even women and children frequently labored in dirty and dangerous situations. There was great social and political unrest, particularly until the 1860s. Towards the end of the nineteenth century, economic and social conditions improved, including those of the masses.

Advances in technology and science and the increase in the wealth of the nation laid the foundation for the British belief in progress that prevailed throughout the century in spite of distress and poverty. The country's extensive colonial empire produced a strong national pride; imperialist attitudes developed, and also racism, particularly towards the end of the century.

In the first half of the nineteenth century, Great Britain was the world's leading nation in science and technology, with France second. Scientific research took place largely outside the universities. There were many good scientists at the universities, but there was no requirement, as in Germany, that university teachers be distinguished scientists responsible for the training of future scientists. The universities were responsible for giving young people a general education and preparing them for positions in administration;

the rules for admission to Oxford and Cambridge greatly favored the youth of well-to-do families. In Scotland, in contrast, even young men without means could obtain a university education. Women were not admitted to the universities in the nineteenth century. Religion had a strong position in Great Britain throughout the century, and university teachers were frequently ministers in the Anglican Church as well.

The Study of Evolution

When the scholars of the Renaissance revived the study of antiquity, it became apparent that European civilization had undergone considerable change during the last millennium. The revival of interest in Greece and Rome contributed to an increased understanding of history, the study of change over time. For biology, it was of special impotance that around the mid-1700s physicists such as Laplace and Kant began to ask questions about the origin of the solar system, and that philosophers about the same time raised the question of the age of the Earth. Towards the end of the 1700s and beginning of the 1800s, it became evident that the Earth did indeed have a long history. Geology was establised as a branch of empirical science, and Charles Lyell of Scotland became an inspiration for Darwin and his close friend.

Also at the beginning of the 1800s, a breakthrough was made in the study of fossils, *paleontology*. Descriptions of fossiles had been made in the 1600s, as George Simpson reports (1983), but only slowly was it understood that fossils are the remains of plants and animals deposited in rocks at different times and at different places. Decisive progress in this area was made by the Frenchman Georges Cuvier (1769–1832). Studying vertebrate fossils in the Paris basin, he realized that whereas some fossils are similar to living species, others clearly differ from any such. According to Simpson, Cuvier proposed three hypotheses to explain the differences from exisitng species: 1. the fossils could be of animals that were still living but had not yet been described; 2. the fossils might be remains of animals that had undergone metamorphoses into living counterparts; 3. the fossils might be remains of animals that had become extinct. All three hypotheses are correct. Cuvier did, however, concentrate on the third, and, as we will see, Darwin gave conclusive support to the second hypothesis.

Through his studies of fossils, Cuvier made clear that animals could not be arranged in a hierarchy from the simplest to the most complex, as in the much earlier *scala naturae* or "great chain of being." However, although his ideas may have influenced Darwin, Cuvier himself did not come to think of existing animal life as the result of evolution, as did his older compatriot Jean-Baptiste Lamarck.

Jean-Baptiste Lamarck (1744–1829)

Lamarck was not only an outstanding naturalist; he was also a skilled geologist. He understood that the Earth is several million years old, that it undergoes continuous change, and that animals also must change in order to adjust to their environment. In other words, Lamarck was concerned with the problem of animals' adaptation to their environment. As Mayr (1982) has noted, perhaps his greatest contribution to the understanding of evolution was his grasp of the role time had played in the development of animals.

Lamarck believed biological evolution is driven forward by changes in the environment. He assumed that all forms of life have a tendency to develop from the simple to the more complex, from the less perfect to the more perfect. For Lamarck, this was a major principle of evolution. However, in order to explain the great diversity in existing species, he also formulated the principle of the inheritance of acquired properties. This principle had a central place in biology until the 1930s, and many psychologists applied it. Let us see how Lamarck thought it could be applied.

Lamarck believed changes in the environment that are significant for an organism create needs that lead to a greater use of some organs, which in turn lead to the development of specific properties or traits in the individual over the course of its life. These traits can also be transmitted to descendants by inheritance and might undergo changes over time; in this way, differences between individuals arise. Typical examples are the exceptional running ability of certain mammals and the long necks of giraffes. The principle also operates, Lamarck thought, in the nonuse of an organ; then, certain traits might become less distinctive and might even completely disappear. For example, the visual sense might deteriorate in animals living in dark caves. Thus, Lamarck's principle of use and disuse was based on the assumption that properties acquired during an individual's life could be inherited by its descendants.

In the nineteenth century, the principle of the inheritance of acquired traits appeared highly plausible, and Darwin and most contemporary biologists accepted it. As Mayr has made clear, to demonstrate that the principle is false was a complicated process. Not until the 1880s, when the German biologist August Weismann was able to shed light on some of the fundamental mechanisms of genetics, did scientists begin to realize that the principle is false, but they did not universally reject it until the 1930s after decisive progress in genetics had been made.

Lamarck believed the simplest species of animals emerge by what he called spontaneous creation. He also contended that humans are a result of evolution and not of a specific act of creation. His ideas were in opposition to traditional thinking and ran counter to fundamental religious dogma. The major French naturalists ridiculed his ideas of evolution, and leading naturalists of the first half of the nineteenth century did not accept them either. Still, Lamarck had some adherents, and his ideas influenced psychologists for more than one hundred years.

Charles Darwin (1809–1882)

The problems confronting Darwin in his attempt to account for evolution were extremely complex. To understand his role in the study of evolution, we should note, as did Mayr (2002, p. 94), that what is frequently referred to as the *Darwinian theory of evolution* actually consists of several views. When Darwin published *On the Origin of Species* in 1859, an overwhelming majority of naturalists accepted his arguments for the hypothesis that evolution had taken place. But some of his ideas, such as the principle of natural selection, were accepted only by a few biologists until the 1930s and 1940s.

The discussion of evolution that took place in the eighty years following the publication of *On the Origin of Species* sheds important light on Darwin's views, and on the attempts empirical psychologists have made from the end of the 1800s to the present to relate psychology to evolutionary biology. I shall therefore report on some of that discussion, but first I shall make some remarks on Darwin's life and his background in British science and social life. These will show some of the context in which he carried out his research.

Some Remarks on Darwin's Life

Darwin has a place in the history of science that has been compared to Newton's, and his life has naturally been the subject of many studies. I have mainly used three sources for my sketch of Darwin's life and ideas: the biographies by Adrian Desmond and James Moore (1991) and by Janet Browne (1995, 2002), and Mayr's (1982) history of biology. Based on his works, notebooks, and extensive correspondence, the biographers Desmond and Moore have traced the development of Darwin's ideas from his early youth to his death and have made great efforts to relate his ideas to the political, economic, and intellectual events taking place in Darwin's lifetime. In his account of Darwin, Mayr (1982) concentrated on the relationship of his ideas to those of his precursors as well as to those of his successors. Mayr (2002) also wrote a book on evolution that I have used.

Darwin was born and grew up in Shrewsbury, in Shropshire, England. His father was a well-to-do medical doctor, as was his grandfather Erasmus Darwin. The latter was also a natural scientist and philosopher concerned with the idea that biological evolution had taken place. Darwin grew up in the country and from his early days was interested in plants, animals, and hunting. He did not excel as a student in school. When he was sixteen, his father sent him to Edinburgh to study medicine, where he was introduced to zoological fieldwork and comparative anatomy by a trained biologist, an ardent follower of Lamarck. The young Charles did not like medical study, and, in 1828, he instead began to study theology at Cambridge, with a view to becoming a minister in the Church of England and settling in the countryside. At Cambridge, he also continued his naturalist studies.

Immediately after he had completed his theological examinations in 1831, Darwin sailed with an expedition to South America, Haiti, the Galápagos Islands, Australia, Tasmania, and South Africa. The voyage on HMS *Beagle* lasted five years. It allowed him to study geological formations, fossils, life in the Brazilian jungle, and, last but not least, differences in the fauna of the Galápagos Islands. He collected a large amount of material and described various species of plants and animals. Once back in England, Darwin lived in London for six years studying his collection, and meeting many of the leading scientists in Great Britain. He had inherited a fortune, and this made it possible for him to live as an independent scientist. During this period, he also began to suffer from migraine, stomach pain, dizziness, heart palpitations, and depression. While the nature of his illness is unknown, it remained with him for the rest of his life. In 1839 he married, and in 1842 he moved to Downe in Kent, where he lived quietly on his estate, corresponding with other scientists, some of whom visited him.

Darwin had begun to formulate his ideas of evolution after his return to England, and in 1844 he wrote them out in a manuscript, which he instructed his wife to publish after his death. Biographers have documented that he had a fear of offending official religion. I shall not contest this, but I also believe he did not feel the scientific community was ready for his ideas. Darwin associated with a number of Great Britain's most prominent scientists, most of whom did not believe in evolution, including Lyell and John Herschel. His views ran counter to prevailing views of religion, but morality must not overshadow the fact that his ideas of evolution represented – and still represent – a conceptual challenge.

Having withheld publication of his manuscript, Darwin was shocked when in 1858 he received a letter and manuscript from the naturalist Alfred Russel Wallace (1823–1915), in which Wallace outlined an account of evolution based on the principle of natural selection. Two of Darwin's friends then arranged a meeting of a scientific society in which they read Wallace's manuscript and an abstract of Darwin's. Wallace, who was an outstanding naturalist, had great respect for Darwin's knowledge and judgment, and the incident led to no controversy over the claim to priority of the principle of natural selection. Darwin afterwards extended and elaborated upon his manuscript, and the following year he published *On the Origin of Species*. He did not include in it his ideas of the origin of humans; these appeared later in the 1871 book entitled *The Descent of Man and Selection in Relation to Sex*. Taken together, the two books contain Darwin's main ideas on evolution.

Darwin, who had been afraid of offending religion and established opinion, was the subject of great admiration when he died in 1882 and was buried in Westminster Abbey.

Darwin as a Product of British Science and Social Life

Darwin had a university degree in theology and no formal training in the study of natural history. But when he left Cambridge for his voyage on the *Beagle*, he had for his age and his era a very solid training in naturalist fieldwork. He lived in a time when many British intellectuals took an interest in natural history, in the cultivation of plants, in animal breeding, in fossil finds, and in the reports of explorers of the biota of distant parts of the world. Before he was offered the chance to join the *Beagle* expedition, he had planned a private naturalist expedition of his own to the Canary Islands, a testament to the young theologian's great interest in natural history. Taking this into account, it is reasonable to believe Darwin learned a great deal from the fieldwork he did in natural history during his student days. While in Edinburgh, he apparently did extensive work on invertebrate animals under the guidance of an able naturalist. At Cambridge, he became a close friend of one of his teachers who was an outstanding botanist and eager to train him. Further, before he left university, he had participated in fieldwork in geology and paleontology.

Thus, when he left on his voyage, he was well prepared for naturalist fieldwork, having been trained in zoology, botany, geology, and paleontology.

At Cambridge Darwin also had an outstanding teacher in the philosophy of science, William Whewell, J. S. Mill's opponent. And he studied work on the same topic by the prominent British physicist John Herschel, who later became his friend. These studies probably prevented him from following Mill's extreme views of inductivism, which were fashionable at that time. Instead Darwin learned to alternate between inductive and deductive reasoning. During his five years on board the *Beagle*, he had a remarkable opportunity to widen his knowledge and learn to rely on his obeservations. When he returned to England, he was probably one of the best trained naturalists of his day.

Views of Evolution

Biologists consider biological evolution to be an accepted theory that is a general form of explanation. As we have noted, the idea of evolution attracted the attention of a number of naturalists before Darwin and independently of him; Wallace formulated a theory highly similar to the one Darwin had worked out. Darwin is usually credited with having proposed the theory of evolution by natural selection because he was able to argue convincingly that a large amount of biological knowledge could be seen as compatible with a belief in evolution, and that the main objections against the belief could be eliminated.

Principle of Common Descent

Central in Darwin's argument was *the theory of descent with modification*, or, as it was later called, *the theory of common descent*. Darwin conceived the idea for this theory when he was studying the biota of the Galápagos Islands. He had observed three species of mockingbird, one at each of three different islands. He knew only one mockingbird had been found in South America. Assuming the Galápagos Islands had been colonized from South America, he concluded that the South American species of mockingbird was the ancestor of the three species he had found in the Galápagos Islands. According to Mayr (2002, p. 23), who is my main source on Darwin's development and use of the theory of common descent, this theory solved a long-standing puzzle of natural history: Why did groups of animals, such as frogs, snakes, birds, and mammals, have the same anatomical structure yet differ in a number of characteristics, and why were they totally different from insects? By assuming that animals with certain characteristics in common descended from a common ancestor, Darwin could show that it was highly probable all forms of life had a common ancestor and could be traced back to a single origin.

By means of the idea of evolution, Darwin could thus account satisfactorily for a large number of biological phenomena. Particularly impressive was his account of fossil finds. He showed that the fossils of the oldest strata are more dissimilar to existing forms of animals than fossils of later strata. Another important finding he explained was that the fauna and flora of different continents differ. Finally, he dealt satisfactorily with the knowledge accumulated in embryology.

Evolution gives a historical account of how life has evolved on Earth. History, however, has given us limited means of determining causality, and Darwin could not use the procedures of physics to demonstrate his point. As Mayr explains (2002), since the publication of *On the Origin of Species* in 1859, biologists have made thorough investigations of numerous points in Darwin's account, and these investigations have given results that clearly support belief in evolution.

Principle of Natural Selection

In *On the Origin of Species*, Darwin did not want only to describe how life had evolved on Earth. He also wanted to explain how evolution had taken place. This part of his task proved to be difficult, and even if later researchers have retained his principle of natural selection, they have had to modify his account on important points. To obtain a deeper understanding of the principle of natural selection, it is necessary, I believe, to be familiar with some of the difficulties Darwin met with in his attempt at explaining evolution. As Mayr (1982, p. 405) reports, Darwin's mentor and friend Lyell had pointed out that organic life could be seen as consisting of species, and he had asked a number of questions about the concept of "species." He first asked whether species are constant or mutable. This question may have led Darwin to concentrate on the concept of species (consider the title of his book).

Darwin, however, had noted that variation can exist between groups or populations of individuals within a species. In his search for an explanation of evolution, he concentrated, as Mayr (2002) emphasizes, on the population. With regard to the individuals within the population, Darwin observed that there is also variation among them, and he assumed each individual was different from all the other individuals – in other words, unique. Darwin made this variation the basis of his explanation of evolution.

In *On the Origin of Species*, he devoted the first two chapters to the problem of variation. In the third chapter, he pointed out that more individuals are born than can survive; consequently, there is a struggle for existence. This means a struggle between all forms of life, but it would be most severe between individuals of the same species. It could also be a struggle against the physical conditions of life. Darwin (1859/1979, p. 63) emphasized that the expression "struggle for existence" was to be taken in a large and metaphorical sense. Included in the concept was "dependence of one being on another" and, what he regarded as more important, a struggle for "not only the life of the individual, but success in leaving progeny."

Having accounted for the idea of variation and the struggle for existence, in the fourth chapter Darwin introduced the idea that possessing a certain variation that gives an individual an advantage would increase the individual's chance of survival and procreation, while possessing an injurious variation would destroy the individual. In line with his three ideas, he formulated the principle of natural selection by stating (1859/1979, p. 81): "This preservation of favorable variations and rejection of injurious variations, I call natural selection." By assuming that most of an individual's traits are heritable, he concluded that the population would continuously undergo changes, and over time this would produce new species.

In his chapter on natural selection, Darwin included a section on *sexual selection.* "This," he said, "depends not on a struggle for existence, but on a struggle between the males for possession of the females; the result is not death to the unsuccessful competitor, but few or no offspring" (1859/1981, p. 88). In *The Descent of Man and Selection in Relation to Sex* (1871/1981) Darwin expanded upon the topic. He accounted for the way sexual selection contributes to sexual dimorphism in animal species, such as antlers in deers and the tail of the peacock. There is, he pointed out, a competition among males for the females, and this competition frequently results in fights between the males, as is usually the case in mammals. There are also other ways in which males attempt to achieve access to the females – for example, by their coloring, the ability to obtain territory, and parental investment. Thus, sexual selection worked in a number of ways, and Mayr (2002) has suggested that a more appropriate expression might be *selection for sexual reproduction.*

Darwin apparently thought sexual selection is a case of natural selection. The principle of natural selection would, therefore, cover a wide variety of factors favoring the possibility that an individual would produce descendants. Thus, while it is relatively easy to understand in broad outline how the principle of natural selection works, to apply it in an adequate manner we must know a great deal about a population of animals or plants.

The principle of natural selection has a central position in present-day biology, but it took a long time before it was generally accepted by biologists. There were several reasons for this delay. As we have noted, the idea of variation among the individuals of the population represented an important component of the principle. Darwin had inadequate conceptions of inheritance and could not satisfactorily account for variation. The Czech scientist and monk Gregor Mendel had given an account of inheritance that could have set Darwin right, but because Darwin either did not understand Mendel or did not read him, he did not break away from the more traditional thinking of the day as far as genetics is concerned. Mendel's account was overlooked by his contemporaries, and when, in the 1900s, geneticists were able to account more satisfactorily for what happens in the population, they were at first not able to reconcile it with Darwin's principle of natural selection. The experimental geneticists and the naturalists thus became divided on the interpretation of evolution.

The Descent of Man

Darwin did not discuss humans in *On the Origin of Species*, but for a biologist who accepted the theory of common descent it would be clear that humans have a primate ancestor. Already, in 1863, T. H. Huxley had argued convincingly that this ancestor was probably a species of great ape. In *The Descent of Man*, published in 1871, Darwin gave a systematic presentation of humans' relationship to the animal kingdom. His view was almost immediately accepted by biologists, but, as we know, it came as a shock to the general public.

Darwin could show that human anatomy, physiology, and embryological development have so many points in common with those of the other mammalian species that humans clearly descended from one of these. A comparison with the primates allowed him to conclude that our primate ancestor must have been an extinct ape closely related to the chimpanzee and gorilla.

When Darwin wrote *The Descent of Man*, there were no fossil finds of hominids that could have allowed him to construct a record bridging the gap between the ape-like ancestor and *Homo sapiens*. He did, however, make great efforts to give an account of humans' mental evolution. While he thought the difference in mental powers between humans and the "most organized ape" to be enormous, he insisted that the quantitative difference between humans and animals is only one of degree. We and the higher animals, he held, had the same senses and many emotions in common. Further, the higher animals possessed the faculties of "imitation, attention, memory, imagination, and reasoning."

Darwin believed human physical characteristics and mental powers had evolved either through natural selection or as byproducts of traits that had so evolved. He did, however, find it difficult to account satisfactorily for human social life as a result of natural selection. Social traits, such as sympathy, fidelity to comrades, and courage in helping members of the group in attack and defense, could to a certain degree evolve through natural selection (1871/1981, ch. 5). But Darwin doubted that within the same tribe a large number of members could be endowed with such traits, and that they could be perfected within the group.

He did, however, suggest two steps in the evolution of such traits. The first was that members of the group learn from experience that if they help another member on one occasion, that member would tend to return the favor at another occasion. The second step was that such traits are strengthened by praise and shame. When a social trait had evolved to a certain degree, the possession of it in members of the tribe would favor that tribe. In other words, Darwin thought that when a social trait had evolved to a certain degree, it could evolve further by group selection.

As we shall see in Chapter 19, one hundred years after the publication of *The Descent of Man*, the question of the evolution of human social straits was still hotly debated, and so was the idea of group selection.

Darwin and Social Darwinism

In the fifth chapter of *The Descent of Man*, under "natural selection as affecting civilized nations," Darwin discussed factors that could influence competition and counteract tendencies leading to the elimination of the weak. But he did not discuss how the organization of society and the transmission of culture might affect the individual. Thus, it is not easy to understand from the text whether he intended his views on evolution to describe not only animal life but also contemporary human society, and historians disagree on this point.

Spencer, who developed a view of evolution based upon ideas from Darwin as well as from earlier evolutionists, became a chief spokesperson for the (now mostly discredited) theory called *social Darwinism*. According to social Darwinism, politicians should not interfere with economic competition, which was thought to be analogous to natural selection, and should not attempt to increase welfare and social equality.

Darwin himself cited a clue to his idea of natural selection in the work of the English economist and philosopher Robert Malthus (1766–1834). Malthus argued that human populations increase faster than they can produce the means of subsistence, and he discussed factors such as disease, famine, and war that keep down the increase in population. Some historians have thought Malthus's influence indicates that Darwin intended his views as a description not only of animal life, but also of human societies. Evolutionary biologists, as Mayr (1982) reports, have tended to dismiss this claim. Desmond and Moore (1991, p. xix), however, came to a different conclusion:

Did he see society, like nature, progress by culling its unfit members? "Social Darwinism" is often taken to be something extraneous, an ugly concretion added to the pure Darwinian corpus after the event, tarnishing Darwin's image. But his notebooks make plain that competition, free trade, imperialism, racial extermination, and sexual inequality were written into the equation from the start – "Darwinism" was always intended to explain human society.

Browne (1995, p. 390) has also made clear that Darwin thought his views gave a description of contemporary British society. On the other hand, in his discussion of human evolution in *The Descent of Man*, Darwin emphasized factors such as sympathy, reasoning power, and sensitivity to praise and blame in our ancestors.

If Darwin had not intended his views as an explanation of contemporary society, in my opinion it is reasonable to believe he would have said he disagreed with Spencer on this issue. In *The Descent of Man*, he referred to Spencer in several places, once calling him "our great philosopher," but he did not explicitly oppose Spencer's view on the question of evolution and human society.

Evolution and Psychology

The theory of evolution provided a new foundation for the study of biology. As Darwin pointed out, it was natural to believe human psychological characteristics are also a result of biological evolution. This idea has profoundly influenced psychological thinking. In the later decades of the nineteenth century, psychological thinkers were already trying to apply the theory of evolution to psychological problems. While interest in evolutionary psychology declined during the first half of the twentieth century, it exploded in the second half, mainly as a result of progress in genetics and the reformulation of the theory of evolution.

In addition to giving psychology a new orientation, Darwin performed studies of various psychological phenomena. His book *The Expression of the Emotions in Man and Animals*, which he originally thought should form part of *The Descent of Man* and which he published in 1872, has been a source of inspiration to several later students of the emotions. In 1877, he published in the recently established journal *Mind* some systematic observations he had made some decades earlier of the development of one of his children. During his later years, he undertook studies of earthworms in his garden and published his observations in *The Formation of Vegetable Mould, Through the Action of Worms, with Observation of Their Habits* (1881). Here, he asked whether a relatively simple animal possessed the capacity to profit from earlier experiences. I shall return to this research in Chapter 7.

Darwin on emotions and learning

In his book on the expression of emotions, Darwin viewed this subject from an evolutionary perspective and formulated three principles for the purpose. Two were based on the assumption that, in human phylogenesis, learning has created certain habits or patterns of reaction that, in accordance with Lamarck's principle, have been transmitted through successive generations. The third principle, which Darwin admitted was obscure, stated that, when the brain is strongly excited, an excess of nervous energy arises, and this energy follows certain nervous pathways and affects certain muscles or groups of muscles, resulting in, for example, increased heart rate. The principles were probably too vague to enable Darwin to build a convincing argument on them. Still, they allowed him to draw attention to fundamental aspects of our emotional life. Thus, he pointed out that emotional expressions probably have their origin partly in the muscular movements that accompany vital forms of behavior, such as attack and flight, and partly in muscular movements involved in fundamental physiological processes, such as respiration and blood circulation. Here, he suggested a possible phylogenetic origin for emotional expressions. Further, he proposed a close connection between our emotions and fundamental forms of behavior, on the one hand, and fundamental physiological processes, on the other hand.

Darwin's book is a treatment of the *expression* of emotions, not a general treatment of emotions. He did, however, emphasize that emotions, as states of mind, are strongly dependent on the fact that we express them. This, he thought, was also an essential point in understanding them.

In contrast to Wundt, Darwin described emotions not only from his own mental experience, but also from the behavior of animals and humans. Being an experienced observer, he noted that it was frequently easier to make observations of emotions in children, persons suffering from mental disturbances, and animals, than in adult human beings, and, further, that the student of emotions can learn from the way artists express these.

Finally, Darwin conducted a cross-cultural study of emotions by obtaining reports from Europeans living in different parts of the world. On the basis of the descriptions he received, he concluded that the most fundamental expressions of emotions are the same all over the world. Darwin also noted that emotions play a role in social interaction and in this sense have an adaptive function, but he did not explore this aspect. In the twentieth century, material was collected that enabled us to understand more concretely the communicative significance of the emotions (see John Sabini, 1995). Darwin's view was limited in another essential point – namely, in respect to the adaptive significance of changes taking place in the physiological processes that form part of the emotions. Not until the American physiologist Walter Cannon (1915) presented his theory of what he called *emergency reactions* was a better understanding of this aspect of the emotions attained.

Darwin's description of the ontogenetic development

Long before Darwin, educators had, of course, been interested in children's development. By performing a careful study of the growth of one of his sons from birth to early childhood, Darwin contributed to making this field more systematic and more directed towards finding continuity in development. His brief study is characterized by good sense and a remarkable capacity for making accurate observations. He began by stating that great differences are probably present in children's development and then proceeded to describe reflexes, the development of the senses, movements, emotions, thinking, morality, communication, and language. All the questions he attempted to answer later became important areas of child psychology.

Herbert Spencer (1820–1903)

Herbert Spencer was the son of a schoolmaster in Derby. After erratic school attendance, he worked for some time as an engineer and then as a journalist. In 1848, he became one of the editors of the periodical *The Economist*, and through his work as an editor, he became acquainted with a large number of influential writers and thinkers in Great Britain.

At an early age, Spencer was inspired by Lamarck's idea that life is steadily evolving towards greater perfection. He believed the same progression to be found in biological evolution is present also in social and cultural development. Inspired by the publication of Darwin's work on the origin of species, Spencer decided he would show that the same progression is present in biological, psychological, and sociological phenomena. In a work of ten volumes, his *Synthetic Philosophy*, he gave an account of what he considered to be the progressive development within these fields. Two of the ten volumes were devoted to psychology. By 1855, Spencer had also published a comprehensive work entitled *The Principles of Psychology*. He extended and revised this work in the two psychology volumes in *The Synthetic Philosophy*, which appeared in 1870 and 1872.

Spencer's philosophy represented new and interesting ideas. He had faith in progress and stressed that development towards greater perfection takes place as a struggle in which the fittest survive. This idea appealed to members of the British middle class, who, after hard political struggles, had become the leading social class and had accumulated great wealth, whereas industrial and agricultural workers lived in poverty and the landed gentry were in decline. Spencer became a champion of a liberalist economy. He also claimed the political and economic leadership of Great Britain and the West are the result of progressive development. Hence, there were prominent features in his philosophy that made it particularly attractive to many intellectuals of the nineteenth century, not least in the United States, where his ideas were frequently confused with Darwin's.

Spencer possessed a wide perspective and frequently formulated generalized statements without attempting to resolve contradictions or meet objections. His formulations were frequently so abstract and vague that it requires patience to discover what he meant. We have seen that Darwin took over his expressions *struggle for life* and *survival of the fittest*. However, as Mayr (1982) has noted, Spencer contributed very little to the development of the theory of evolution. On the other hand, as we shall see later in this chapter, he contributed to the advancement of modern neurology and had a decisive influence on psychology.

A Functional View of Consciousness

Spencer (1855) held that mental processes had developed gradually from physiological processes. Therefore, no one stage in evolution could be found at which consciousness or mental life had evolved. Psychology and physiology, Spencer said, are different aspects of the same fundamental truth. Most modern psychologists would probably agree that it is not possible to draw a clear boundary between physiological and psychological processes, but in the mid-nineteenth century this was far from the accepted point of view.

The central idea in Spencer's psychology (1855, p. 374) was that what he called *inner relations* must be adapted to *outer relations*. This generalized and vague formulation was even his definition of life ("the continuous adjustment of internal relations to external relations"). In agreement with this definition, Spencer insisted that there is a correspondence between the physiological and psychological functions of an organism, on the one hand, and the outer environment, on the other hand.

Emphasizing the correspondence between outer and inner relationships, he called attention to the fact that psychological processes must be understood as a result of adaptation to the environment. This point was far from trivial in 1855 but was overlooked by many psychologists in the latter half of the nineteenth century. William James (by 1890) understood its significance and made it central in his discussion of psychological problems. James (1950, p. 6) introduced what he called Spencer's formula in the following way:

On the whole, few recent formulas have done more real service of a rough sort in psychology than the Spencerian one, that the essence of mental life and of bodily life are one, namely, "the adjustment of inner to outer relations." Such a formula is vagueness incarnate; but because it takes into account the fact that minds inhabit environments, which act on them, and on which they in turn react; because, in short, it takes mind in the midst of all its concrete relations, it is immensely more fertile than the old-fashioned "rational psychology," which treated the soul as a detached existent, sufficient unto itself, and assumed to consider only its nature and properties.

Inspired by Spencer, James declared that consciousness has a function in adaptation.

Evolution of the Intellect

Spencer's view (1870–1872) of the development of the intellect became highly influential. He thought simple reflexes are the first manifestations of mental life. In the further development of consciousness, reflexes of different types become associated with each other to form more complex reaction patterns (habits), and, as Lamarck did in his own view of inheritance, Spencer claimed these patterns become inherited when they have been functional through successive generations. He thus regarded instincts as acquired by use, and their development as succeeded by the development of memory and higher mental processes. Spencer also thought intelligence could be seen as hierarchically structured. The hierarchical structure, he held, is reflected in the structure of the nervous system.

This view, which in a certain sense must, of course, be correct, inspired the English neurologist John Hughlings Jackson (1835–1911), who was regarded by many as the most influential neurologist in the latter half of the nineteenth century. Jackson proposed that the nervous system has a hierarchical structure in which several levels can be distinguished, and that when the brain is damaged, the highest centers stop being functional first. At this point the functions of the lower centers become more apparent. Also inspired by Spencer, Jackson claimed at the beginning of the 1860s that all centers in the brain are of a sensory-motor nature. Jackson used his ideas of the nervous system and its functions to describe epileptic and aphasic disturbances. His ideas influenced later French psychologists (see Chapter 9).

The positive effect Spencer's vague and general speculations had on such an outstanding neurologist as Jackson is a reminder that making reliable observations that can form the foundation for inductive inferences is only one aspect of science. Hearnshaw (1964) wrote of Jackson that he had a rare capacity for combining philosophical ideas and clinical observations. Jackson himself regarded as an illusion the idea that discoveries can be made by means of Francis Bacon's inductive method.

Francis Galton (1822–1911)

One aim of empirical scientific psychology is to account for our thinking and behavior as a result of the interplay between heredity and environment. To the extent it achieves this goal, we can perhaps call psychology a natural science discipline. By the end of the twentieth century, research on the roles of heredity and environment had made considerable progress. Francis Galton was the researcher who first began the study of these problems in psychology. Galton also contributed indirectly by developing techniques for the quantitative, statistical, and mathematical treatment of psychological problems.

In Chapter 1, I stressed the importance of understanding how society and culture affect the scientific and professional opinions of psychologists. Galton was an independent, creative researcher who possessed considerable insight into many problems, but he was also a typical representative of the well-to-do citizens of the British Empire. The values of the middle classes influenced his research, and we should see him not only as a scientist open to new knowledge, but also as a product of his time.

When *On the Origin of Species* appeared in 1859, Galton became an enthusiastic adherent of the theory of evolution. First and foremost, he was captivated by the role individual differences and heredity had played in evolution. He understood that forces operating in evolution were also operating in modern society, and he was absorbed by the thought that it might be possible to control human evolutionary development by adopting specific strategies that either increased or decreased the possibility of spreading a favorable or unfavorable genetic endowment. He believed this control should be undertaken in a humane manner, and drastic measures should not be carried out before opinion was ripe for them. One strategy Galton suggested was to encourage people who had what he believed to be a favorable hereditary endowment to marry early with the aim of producing many children, and to encourage persons having an unfortunate hereditary endowment, such as those suffering from genetically determined diseases, not to have children. He proposed that the study of ways to improve the genetic endowment of humankind should be made a special science, which he hoped to establish – he called it *eugenics*.

Galton (1883, p. 473) regarded the study of individual differences and their hereditary foundation to be of religious significance, and he saw working for eugenic principles as a moral duty. After becoming strongly attracted to the theory of evolution, he devoted his considerable working capacity to the study of eugenics. From this scientific and metaphysical perspective he carried out diverse types of investigations, which contributed to scientific psychology.

Galton's Life

Galton, who shared a grandfather with Charles Darwin, belonged to a family that had produced outstanding political, religious, and military leaders. His father was a rich banker in Birmingham, and at twenty-three Galton inherited a fortune that allowed him to live as an independent English gentleman. When he was sixteen, Galton had begun studying medicine in deference to his father's wishes, but he broke off this study after two years and instead undertook a study of mathematics at Cambridge. He had a nervous breakdown during his university years but completed his examinations. After the death of his father in 1844, he spent his time on hunting, sport, traveling, and, among other things, an expedition to Africa. For a report of this trip, the Royal Geographical Society awarded him a gold medal. In the 1850s, Galton also published important works on meteorology. Reading *On the Origin of Species* aroused his interest in the study of heredity and environment. In addition to a number of articles, he published four influential books on this subject: *Hereditary Genius* (1869), *English Men of Science: Their Nature and Nurture* (1874), *Inquiries into Human Faculty* (1883), and *Natural Inheritance* (1889).

Galton understood that, in the study of heredity and environment, it is important to carry out measurements that can be treated statistically and mathematically. He himself contributed to statistics by devising a method for computing correlations between two variables. In his work on statistics, he cooperated with the mathematician Karl Pearson. To advance the study of eugenics, he provided the money to establish an Institute for

National Eugenics, of which Pearson was the first leader. Pearson was succeeded by Ronald Fisher, who, in addition to being regarded as the founder of modern statistics, was also an excellent biologist and in the 1930s contributed to the reformulation of the theory of evolution so that it could be reconciled with progress in genetics. A third person working within the biological and psychological tradition started by Galton was Charles Spearman (1904), who laid the foundation for factor analysis and later was known for his *two-factor theory of intelligence*, which proposed that intelligence can be seen as the operation of a general factor (the g factor) on a variety of specific factors. Galton was knighted in 1909.

Galton on Heredity and Environment

We can often see a striking similarity between children and their parents, and the idea that human beings inherit traits from their parents did not, of course, emerge with Darwin. Long before him, others had been interested in the question of heredity and environment, and people had been breeding plants and animals for centuries. The theory of evolution made heredity a key issue in biology, as Galton realized. He also recognized the great importance the interaction of heredity and the environment have for psychology and developed methods to study it.

From the principle of natural selection, Galton reasoned, it follows that the properties giving certain people a prominent position in society are determined by heredity. Claiming that great intellectual capacity – genius – was such a property, he began a comprehensive investigation of the family relationships of gifted persons and collected extensive biographical material on those who had revealed one or another form of intellectual gift. These were regarded by their contemporaries as outstanding politicians, religious leaders, scientists, poets, or artists. Galton presented the results of his investigations in the book *Hereditary Genius*. Here, he first showed that the 1,000 persons meeting his criteria for genius belonged to only 300 families, and thus that the number of gifted persons in each of these families was far greater than might have been expected from a comparison with the rest of the population.

As Kurt Schlesinger (1985) has emphasized, Galton's conclusion that genius is determined by heredity was actually based on a more refined reasoning. When a family contained several outstanding members, Galton examined the closeness of the family relationships among them. He found that, where there was a gifted person in a family, other gifted people would be found in close rather than more distant relationships with that person. For example, gifted fathers would have more gifted sons than gifted grandchildren.

Of course, Galton realized his findings could be interpreted to mean that children of famous persons have greater opportunities than children of nonfamous persons. He presented different types of evidence that he felt countered this objection, but they are not convincing.

Galton's study of family relationships and genius was followed by a number of psychological investigations of properties that seemed to accompany members of certain families. Yet it was even more important for the study of heredity and environment that Galton began a comparison of the performance of twins growing up together and those raised apart. He found that identical twins are highly similar even if they have grown up in different environments, and that fraternal twins are dissimilar even if they have grown up in the same environment. (Significant advances in the study of the inheritance of psychological characteristics were first made when larger samples of twins were obtained and the methods for measuring psychological traits were refined.)

In *Hereditary Genius*, Galton stressed the role of heredity over that of the environment, and, as Schlesinger (1985) has noted, he also tended to do this in his treatment of intellectual capacities. In his one-sided emphasis on the role played by heredity, Galton tended to overlook that heredity and environment always work together. According to Plomin et al. (1997), he thereby started a needless battle over *nature versus nurture*. Yet, as Hergenhahn (2009) has pointed out, Galton modified his view in his next book, *English Men of Science*, and emphasized there that human personality is the result of an interaction between heredity and environment – of, he said, "*nature and nurture.*"

A long time was to pass before psychologists understood that heredity and environment always work together. Instead of trying to understand the interplay between the two, they engaged in a discussion of which was the more important. The nature of intelligence was a particularly hot issue; this discussion was very emotional and correspondingly unprofitable. In Great Britain, the debate was about whether intelligence as a property is evenly distributed among the members of the different classes of society, and thus it affected educational policy. In the United States, the disagreement hinged on whether blacks are as intelligent as whites. Another question was the role played by instincts as opposed to acquired behavior. Here again, the debate polarized in an unfruitful manner. Not until the 1970s and 1980s did a decisive breakthrough take place in the psychological study of heredity and environment. To this, I shall return in a later chapter.

The Program of Eugenics

Galton's program of eugenics was in line with the positivists' wish to exercise control over the development of society by means of science. It gave a new perspective on the role played by heredity, but by being almost exclusively concerned with the importance of heredity, Galton underestimated the role played by culture. He understood that political, economic, and social conditions influence the population at large. However, like his cousin Charles Darwin, he believed the forces underlying biological evolution affect society relatively independently of culture. In fact when Karl Marx wrote to Darwin asking whether he could dedicate *Das Kapital* to him, Darwin declined. An important point in Marx's philosophy is that our political, religious, and moral ideas are determined by the economic interests of the class to which we belong. Neither Darwin nor Galton seems to have understood this view.

Galton represents the values endorsed by members of the upper-middle class in Great Britain at the end of the nineteenth and the beginning of the twentieth centuries. He was convinced that the peoples of the world vary considerably in their endowments of desirable and less desirable properties, and that Europeans – or perhaps particularly the British – are superior to other people. He also interspersed his writings with remarks suggesting women are inferior to men in intelligence as well as in other respects. Further, he paid little attention to the fact that persons of the lower economic strata of the population have limited opportunity to realize their potential to develop their intelligence and assert themselves in society.

Galton's program for improving the genetic endowment of humankind never had a great following in Great Britain. In the United States, in contrast, it was influential. At the beginning of the twentieth century, it strongly influenced immigration policy and also led to concrete initiatives to prevent persons with certain properties from reproducing. The eugenics movement in the United States was brought to a halt when the Nazis began to carry out their own particular eugenics program. Today, progress in genetics and the ability to diagnose disabilities *in utero* have revived discussion of Galton's ideas.

In addition to its clearly ethical aspect, Galton's eugenics program suffered from two fundamental weaknesses. First, he did not systematically discuss what he meant by favorable and unfavorable properties. Second, he did not seem to realize that a genetic endowment favorable at a certain stage of social development is not necessarily so after society has undergone change.

Galton on Individual Differences and Intelligence

The theory of evolution is based on the premise that individuals in a population exhibit variations in their possession of the traits essential for biological adaptation. It therefore actualizes the question of individual differences. Galton understood this and began an extensive study of individual differences, making him a pioneer in the area.

He was much concerned with the problem of finding measurable expressions of individual differences and constructed tests to quantify them. In the book *Inquiries into Human Faculty* (1883), he reported on these tests. Galton claimed that, because our senses are the doors through which our experience must pass, our capacity for sensory discrimination must be an expression of our intellectual capacities. Acting on this view, he started measuring individual differences in visual acuity, color discrimination, and discrimination of pitch. He did not discuss whether there is a correlation between performances on the different tests – for example, between performance on visual tests and tests of pitch discrimination. On the whole, he did not go into a systematic examination of the concepts of "intellectual capacity" and "intelligence." In constructing the tests, Galton seems to have uncritically taken as his premise the Lockian view that knowledge has a basis in sensory impressions, and this (though he is regarded as a pioneer in intelligence research) seriously limited the value of his investigations. The Frenchman Alfred Binet, who was the first to construct a useful intelligence test, rejected Galton's assumption that the capacity for sensory discrimination is a measure of intelligence, as we shall see in Chapter 9.

British researchers who contributed to the study of personality in the 1940s and 1950s were inspired by the tradition Galton had begun in his research of individual differences. I shall return to this point in Chapter 15.

Associative Connections and Mental Representations

Galton insisted that scientific studies should be based on measurement and the mathematical treatment of problems. In some experiments on associative connections and mental representations, he showed how useful even simple measurements can be in the study of psychological problems.

In his experiments with associative connections, he devised the following procedure: He selected a fixed number of words (seventy-five) that he read to himself one at a time, and then, after about four seconds, he wrote down the associations each word had elicited. He repeated this procedure four times at different time intervals. His examination of the data revealed that, in a great number of instances, he had given the same associations on all four occasions. From this finding, he concluded that our store of associations is not as great as we are frequently inclined to believe. Galton also tried to identify the period of his life in which the associations had been formed and found that about 40 percent originated in his boyhood or youth. These early associations accounted for a great many of those he repeated on all four occasions, while associations from later periods did not have the same consistency. He further observed that he sometimes gave the same associations without being aware of it and suggested that his procedure could be a means of uncovering concealed mental processes. On the whole, by this approach Galton was able to shed light on memory. His procedure was later elaborated by psychologists in Wundt's laboratory and by Carl Jung.

Galton's ingenuity was also revealed in his research on *mental representations*. His procedure consisted of having the subjects describe a familiar situation from their recollections of it. The situation he chose was the person's breakfast table. Galton made up a questionnaire in which the subjects were asked whether the objects on the table appeared dim or clear, colored or not, and detailed or not. He found great individual differences. At one extreme were persons who had difficulty in producing images, and at the other were those who could describe the imaged situations with almost photographic accuracy. The results suggested that individual differences in imaging ability are normally distributed. A surprising finding was that scientists seemed to have a very poor capacity for imaging. Another was that some persons associated visual forms with numbers, and some linked colors with sounds.

Summary and Evaluation

In Chapter 19, I shall report on what seems to have been a breakthrough in the psychological study of heredity and environment, *behavioral genetics*. Galton not only performed the first family study of a psychological trait; he also provided the study with a methodology that evaluated twins and siblings reared apart. Further, he invented a technique for computing correlations, which was later refined into an efficient instrument for correlational studies. Still further, he contributed to psychology by his investigations of associations and imagery, and by his studies of individual differences.

Galton was strongly influenced by the positivist philosophy that had begun to manifest itself around the mid-nineteenth century. To him, scientific procedure was first and foremost a question of finding quantitative expressions for observed relationships, and then subjecting the quantitative expressions to a statistical and mathematical treatment. In contrast to Darwin, he attached little importance to developing scientific concepts that promoted fruitful thinking about the phenomena studied. His view of intelligence, as well as of associative learning, seems to have been based on a rather uncritical reading of the British empiricist philosophers. Further, unlike Darwin, he failed to develop the ability to seriously consider objections to his ideas.

Alexander Bain (1818–1903): New Ideas of Learning by Association

Bain's Life

Alexander Bain was the son of a weaver in Aberdeen. After a poor schooling with very limited access to books, he was admitted to a university in Aberdeen at the age of eighteen. He completed his studies with top marks, and after having assisted the professor of philosophy at the University of Aberdeen for some years, he went to London, where he joined the circle around J. S. Mill. Here he lived as a journalist until, in 1860, he was appointed professor of logic and rhetoric at the university in his hometown. In 1855 he published the first part, *The Senses and the Intellect*, and in 1859 the second part, *The Emotions and the Will*, of a comprehensive psychological work. In 1876, Bain founded the journal *Mind*, which in its first years contained articles on psychology. Later, the journal was devoted exclusively to philosophy.

Bain was a friend of Mill, and, like him, he worked within the framework of British empiricist philosophy. He did, however, extend the scope of psychological study. In addition to the introspective study of mental processes, he included observations the researcher could make of other adult persons, children, and animals. Further, he regarded knowledge of the processes going on in the nervous system as relevant to psychological study, and already in the 1850s he had oriented this study towards physiology. Thus, Bain's conception of the study of psychology differed from Wundt's, which was mainly restricted to an introspective study of the psychologist's own consciousness.

Reflexes and Voluntary Actions

In his study of physiology, Bain focused on a claim made by Johannes Müller that certain types of movements must be seen as spontaneous; that is, they cannot be seen as elicited by external stimulation and are not reflexes as Descartes meant the term. Bain grasped the distinction between spontaneous movements and reflexes, and he began a research tradition in psychology that led to Edward Thorndike's *law of effect* and B. F. Skinner's *theory of operant conditioning.*

Bain was primarily concerned with the problem of free will – as Skinner would be seventy-five years later. Starting from what he believed to be spontaneous movements, Bain thought he could explain the development of voluntary actions by combining ideas of association with ideas about hedonism. He held that movements leading to pleasure would be repeated, whereas movements leading to pain or displeasure would be avoided. He described several examples of how spontaneous movements are governed by their hedonistic consequences. It was of particular importance to Bain to show how voluntary acts could have arisen ontogenetically. He discussed in detail an example from everyday life. An infant lies in bed at the side of its caregiver. As a result of having wet itself, the infant feels cold, which is unpleasant (gives pain). The impression of pain would, Bain said, lead to an increase in spontaneous movements. Some of these movements would bring the infant closer to its caregiver. As a consequence, the feeling of pain would be relieved. Eventually, the process would be repeated.

Bain seems to have believed the infant had in some way formed a mental representation of the favorable result of its movements, an idea that was very like Thorndike's account, as we shall see in Chapter 12. As Robert Boakes (1984) showed, in at least one place in the second edition of his *Principles of Psychology*, Spencer (1870–1872, I) did give an account of learning as resulting from hedonistic objectives without making assumptions of mentalism of some sort. Thus, he anticipated Skinner's view that learning can take place without the use of mental representations. I mention this because it gives a perspective on American behaviorism, which we discuss later.

Returning now to Spencer, we note that in the first edition of *The Principles of Psychology* (1855), he based his thinking almost exclusively on associative principles. In the second edition, he seems to have followed Bain. Like Bain, he tried to explain how hedonistic states might change spontaneous movements into purposeful ones. As Boakes (1984) has pointed out, Spencer was hardly consistent in accounting for the way in which this kind of learning might take place, but he seems, at least in one place, to have believed it need not require us to assume the existence of a mental state. According to Boakes, the view of spontaneous movements being governed by their consequences was known as the *Spencer–Bain Principle* until Thorndike presented the same idea in 1898, in his formulation called *the law of effect.*

An important element in Bain's thinking was the idea that the will is closely associated with action; it is the preparation for action. This idea was of decisive importance in the development of the philosophies of the two Americans Charles Peirce and William James. They were both concerned with the consequences of actions. Bain also emphasized the role habits play in human life, which James elaborated in his psychology.

7

British Comparative Psychology

As we have seen in Chapters 3, 4, and 5, German psychologists concentrated on the experimental study of human behavior and thought processes and gave little attention to comparative psychology. Nineteenth-century British psychologists, in contrast, concentrated on comparative study and were little concerned with experimental studies of human psychology. The combination of the two approaches, which forms the basis for present-day psychology, was the achievement of American psychologists.

Comparative psychology had a promising beginning after Darwin's and Wallace's formulation of the theory of evolution, but by around 1900 interest in it had evaporated in Great Britain. Still, the comparative study of psychology continued in Continental Europe and the United States. In Europe, it was carried on by zoologists as a study of behavior, which they named *ethology*. Their research remained largely unknown to psychologists until about 1950. In the United States, during the first half of the twentieth century, psychologists approached the study of behavior differently. Whereas the Europeans concentrated on perception and genetic factors, the Americans studied ontogenetic development and emphasized the importance of learning. A confrontation arose, leading to an open academic debate that Robert Hinde (1995) has described as being productive for the development of psychology. I shall return to this confrontation in Chapter 19 and link ethology more closely to psychology; here, I shall merely note the connection between them.

The British comparative psychologists were particularly concerned with the following two problems: the relationship between the intellectual capacities of animals and humans, and the question of whether animals and humans possess instincts. With regard to the latter problem, the discussion revolved primarily around whether any forms of behavior could be regarded as innate. However, at the beginning of the twentieth century, researchers also asked whether behavior is elicited not only by direct outer stimulation but also by an inner state. This question became central in the study of motivation and personality. To gain a perspective on the study of motivation, we will view it in the context of the debate on instincts. These two problems that interested the early British comparative psychologists are related, but at the same time so different that I think it is appropriate to give each of them a separate treatment.

The Intellectual Capacities of Humans and Animals

As Darwin made clear, humans have so many anatomical and physiological traits in common with the primates that it is highly plausible we evolved from a primate species and hence must be regarded as a primate species ourselves. Unwillingness to accept our close relationship to the primates is probably due mainly to religious convictions. However, it may also be due to the fact that our intellectual capacities are so superior to what we find in the chimpanzee and gorilla that it is difficult to believe in a close relationship. As we noted, Wallace differed from Darwin on this point. Even today some prominent philosophers are unwilling to accept that the chimpanzee's capacity for thinking is of the same kind as humans. Many would insist that the sophistication of the human facility for using language is what marks human experience as profoundly different than that in other primates. In his defense of the thesis that humans descended from a primate species, Darwin devoted much attention to the difference in intelligence between humans and animals and showed that many of the same patterns of reactions are found in both. He also turned the problem around and showed that intellect and intelligence are also present in animals, even if to a lesser degree. In his investigation of the expression of emotions, he took the first approach, and in his study of the earthworm the second. In the latter, he wanted to show that the earthworms he studied in his garden were able to benefit from experience.

Almost any phenomenon in nature was of interest to Darwin, and hardly any problem was too insignificant for investigation. He had also a remarkable capacity for asking questions, giving him a perspective on even apparently trivial phenomena. Darwin had observed that earthworms pull leaves into their subterranean passages, apparently in order to prop up the passages; this raised the question of whether they benefited from their experience with these leaves. If so, it was natural to believe they would pull the leaves into the passages in the most appropriate manner, with the narrowest part of the leaf first. To test this assumption, Darwin studied the way the worms handled pieces of paper folded into triangles of various shapes. With some hesitation, he concluded that earthworms do seem to be able to benefit from experience.

Whether an organism can learn from experience was the criterion Darwin used to identify the presence of intelligence or intellect. It was a reasonable point of departure. Psychologists still frequently use this criterion to distinguish between physiological and psychological processes, regarding psychological processes as modifiable by experience, by learning.

The point Darwin wanted to demonstrate was that even the simplest forms of organisms have intellect. Psychologists have elaborated the point he made about learning. Reasoning that learning is more or less the same process in all animal organisms, and that it is more effectively studied in simpler organisms, they have made the study of simpler organisms central to the study of learning. I shall return to the historical development of this research in Chapters 12, 13, and 14, and in Chapter 19, I shall discuss objections to the idea that learning takes place in more or less the same way in all animal species.

Georges Romanes (1848–1894)

At the time Darwin did his research on the earthworm, he and his friend Georges Romanes were planning a comparative psychological study. Romanes had studied the natural sciences at Cambridge, and after his examinations, he had worked in a physiological laboratory there. Like Darwin, he had inherited a fortune, and this enabled him to carry out his research as an independent English gentleman.

In agreement with the early positivist view of science, Romanes published a book called *Animal Intelligence* (1882) in which he presented what he believed to be the facts on the mental life of animals. In *Mental Evolution in Animals* (1883) and *Mental Evolution in Man* (1887), he systematically ordered his findings and gave them a theoretical interpretation.

In the choice of species to be included in the material, Romanes followed a zoological classification system. He held that it was more expedient to follow such a system even if there were only a rough correspondence between the mental and the zoological characteristics of animals. He thus presented material about insects, mollusks, fish, amphibians, reptiles, birds, and a broad range of mammals. To decide whether animals have intelligence, he used the same criterion as Darwin: the ability to benefit from experience and from learning. Romanes realized that this criterion had limitations, and, like Darwin, he also did not systematically discuss what he meant by "experience" and "learning." He used words and expressions from everyday language, such as "sensation," "perception," "memory," and "will." To indicate differences in the levels of complexity of the function, he followed Spencer in distinguishing between reflexes and instincts, and between instincts and reason. The difference between instincts and reflexes was that the former contained a mental element. Reason differed from instinct by having what Romanes regarded as an intentional adaptation of the means to reach a goal. He did not clarify how we could decide when a mental element is present in an instinct, or when a mental process is an expression of an intentional adaptation of the means to reach a goal.

Romanes's Method

Romanes insisted that we must infer mental phenomena from a description of behavior. This inference, he said, should be based on an analogy with the way we infer states of consciousness in other people. Although he admitted that it was difficult to infer intellect in animals in a way analogous to our understanding of our own mental life, he held that inference by analogy is the only possible procedure and followed it to the extreme. He believed, for example, that he could observe anger in ants and bees.

The distinctions Romanes hypothesized between reflexes and instincts, and between instincts and reason, made his procedures highly subjective. It is difficult to decide what in his material are facts and what are mere speculations.

The observations he reported were not only his own but had also been made by others who, at his request, had observed species of which he believed they had particularly good knowledge. It turned out that many of the observations his contacts reported were made in an uncritical manner, as were some of his own. In spite of the fact that Romanes criticized what he called the anecdotal procedure, he gained a reputation for being a representative of this approach.

Romanes classified mental processes primarily according to concepts used in everyday life, which are only loosely related to one another and not anchored in behavior. As a result, his descriptions of the animals' behavior were vague and arbitrary. Romanes shared the positivist conviction that it is possible to draw a clear line between observation and theory. This contributed to his poor understanding of the problems he met with in his attempts to develop principles that could serve as a classification system for a comparative psychological study.

Conway Lloyd Morgan (1852–1936)

Conway Lloyd Morgan, who continued Darwin's and Romanes's comparative psychological studies, was interested in the study of birds and the theory of evolution from his youth. With the natural sciences as his main interest, he entered the London School of Mines, where students received a broad introduction to this subject. There he could attend the lectures of Darwin's friend T. H. Huxley, who was professor of biology and comparative anatomy. Like Darwin, Huxley had participated in a scientific expedition extending over a number of years. In the process, he had carried out some very good investigations of a group of marine animals and had obtained a reputation for being an outstanding comparative anatomist.

After having spent some years as a teacher in South Africa, where he had also carried out biological studies, Morgan was appointed professor of biology and geology at the recently established university in Bristol. His main work is *An Introduction to Comparative Psychology*, which appeared in 1894. In 1890, he had written *Animal Life and Intelligence*, and in 1896 he published lectures he had given the same year in Boston, New York, and Chicago. This book was entitled *Habit and Instinct*.

Morgan was a far more profound biological thinker than Romanes. He was also a keen observer and a good experimenter. In my opinion, he does not have the place he deserves in the history of psychology. While historians have rightly emphasized that he was more discriminating than Romanes, they have overlooked the fact that, in contrast to Romanes, he separated the comparative study of psychology from the comparative study of anatomy and physiology of animals. This may have been unfortunate because it suggested a split in which psychology only addressed matters of cognition rather than understanding cognition in the context of physiology. Like Romanes, Morgan claimed that a study of animal psychology must begin with considerations of human mental life, and he created a framework for the comparative study of psychology based on this belief. Although his observations were accurate, the framework he developed had a limited foundation in actual knowledge. This point may explain why American and later European comparative psychology were so little influenced by him.

Consciousness: Perceiving Relationships

Morgan undoubtedly reflected deeply on a number of problems concerning the structure of consciousness. However, by and large, he seems to have adopted the ideas of J. S. Mill and the British empiricist philosophers. Accordingly, he thought mental phenomena have a basis in sensations and are linked together by associative principles of learning. He limited his studies to vertebrates, and, at the lowest levels, he ascribed to them only the capacity for forming associations between sensations. He claimed that animals have gradually evolved the ability to form associations between a number of diverse sensations, and between sensations and specific acts. Evolution had also led to an increase in memory, which had resulted in what Morgan called a *capacity for perceiving relationships*.

The concept of "capacity to perceive relationships" is unclear, and it is difficult to find appropriate criteria for determining when it is present. Apparently, when Morgan introduced the concept, he had in mind a few definite examples, to which I shall later return. Only humans, he said, have the capacity to form concepts, such as those of concrete objects of different kinds. This capacity is closely related to the capacity to perceive relationships. Verbal communication depends on the capacity to form concepts, but use of language has also contributed to its development.

Critical to the development of intelligence is the capacity to perceive, as opposed to the capacity for sensation. Morgan's position here was in agreement with the central ideas of British as well as German psychology. The distinction between sensation and perception is problematic, and so is his assumption of associative connections between sensations.

Observations on a Fox Terrier

Morgan held that few animal species possess the capacity to perceive relationships. He illustrated this with observations of his own fox terrier. Attempting to enter a gate in the garden fence while holding in its mouth a stick longer than the opening was wide, the dog repeatedly failed. Apparently, it had difficulty in learning to grasp the stick at one end so that it could carry it through the gate in a position parallel to its body.

Morgan did not doubt that the dog was able to learn this, but repeated attempts at teaching it to do so led him to conclude that the animal had great difficulty in mastering the task.

In accounting for the fox terrier's failure to solve the problem, Morgan, in my opinion, overlooked an important point. For the animal, it is not only a question of perceiving the relationship between the length of the stick and the opening of the gate; it is also a question of being able to manipulate the stick. To get it through the gate, it must grasp the stick at one of the ends so it could be carried parallel to the body. To solve the problem, the dog must therefore not only visually perceive the relationship but at the same time have an understanding that it must manipulate the stick by grasping it in a particular way. It is not valid to conclude from the dog's failure to solve this problem that it lacks the capacity to perceive relationships.

A little reflection will, I think, show that Morgan's conclusion concerning the perception of relationships is dubious. To take a very simple example: given the choice between a big and a small lump of meat, a hungry dog will choose the larger. Obviously, it perceives relationships. To take another example, a dog placed on the other side of a garden fence some distance from a gate will experiment a little before finding the gate to join its master. If it has previously entered the gate a couple of times, it will instantly run along the fence until it reaches the gate. Animals repeatedly confront and solve this kind of relationship problem. Turning to monkeys, we know they move with great ease from branch to branch, evidently judging whether the branches are sufficiently strong to carry them, and make their jumps based on an evaluation of a number of relationships. Again, they select the fruits they like best according to diverse perceptual criteria. The capacity to perceive relationships can, therefore, hardly be attributed only to humans. Nor can it depend only on linguistic communication, as many psychologists and philosophers claim. Thus, the concepts Morgan used to account for the development of mentality or intelligence in animals suffer from significant weaknesses.

Morgan's Canon

With the aim of sustaining a more critical and objective attitude to problems of comparative psychology, Morgan (1894, p. 5) formulated a rule based upon the assumption that psychological capacities could be ordered on a scale from lower to higher, and that researchers should not interpret an act as a result of a higher psychological capacity if it is possible to interpret it as a result of a lower one. Morgan claimed this rule was in line with the theory of evolution because it followed that psychological processes must have become increasingly complex as a result of the evolutionary changes taking place.

Unfortunately, Morgan's canon, which has become famous, leaves so many conditions unspecified that it is of very limited use. To apply it, we must know when an act found in one animal species is the same as an act found in another species. Consider an extreme example. Bees have remarkably good spatial orientation. They fly long distances from the hive to find nectar, discriminate between a variety of different flowers, and then return to the hive in a surprisingly straight line. Human beings can hardly perform better in a similar journey or task. To all appearances, the behavior patterns of bees and human beings are identical in many important respects. Applying Morgan's canon, we should therefore interpret humans' spatial behavior at the lowest level. Naturally, this would be entirely misleading since Morgan's scale does not give us a way to assign meaning to the terms "higher" and "lower." This in turn raises the question: when can a behavior manifested in one species and a behavior manifested in another species be legitimately ordered along the *same* scale?

Morgan's canon does not answer this question of how appropriately evolutionary biologists are able to order biological organisms in a taxonomic system. As Todd Preuss (1995) recently pointed out, modern evolutionary biologists tend to think the history of evolution is more appropriately described as a tree than as a unitary scale. Of course, in some sense, evolutionary development may be a unitary process, but, as Todd emphasized, so far evolutionary biologists have not been able to say what this process is like.

Leonard Hobhouse (1864–1928)

At the end of the nineteenth century, the British took a great interest in the question of how human consciousness is related to that of animals. In addition to Romanes and Morgan, Leonard Hobhouse undertook several studies to answer this question.

Hearnshaw (1964) and Boakes (1984) have given fascinating accounts of Hobhouse's unusual career. Here, I shall simply mention that he ended up as a professor of sociology at the London School of Economics after having been a fellow in philosophy at Cambridge University, and that he carried out his investigations in the zoo in Manchester while he was a member of the editorial staff of the *Manchester Guardian*. As Hearnshaw has pointed out, Hobhouse wanted to find support for his philosophy by undertaking a comparative study of intelligence in animals and presented a report on his research, together with his thoughts on animal intelligence, in a comprehensive book called *Mind in Evolution* (1901). Hobhouse was very ingenious in constructing problems appropriate for investigating the intellectual capacities of animals (as mentioned earlier, Köhler used several of them). I shall concentrate on some of his views that have been significant for the later development of psychology.

Three Intellectual Levels

Hobhouse measured the intellectual level of animals in a manner similar to Morgan's. On the first level the animal is capable of forming *simple associations;* it does not discriminate between the individual elements in the associations. On the next level, the animal is capable of discriminating relatively clearly between the elements; Hobhouse referred to this capacity as *practical intelligence.* On the third level, the animal is capable of discriminating not only between the elements in a relationship but also between relationships. At this level, the animal has what Hobhouse called *articulated ideas.*

Hobhouse believed his observations justified the conclusion that monkeys and apes are capable of perceiving relationships at a level of articulated ideas. Here, he anticipated the conclusion Köhler made on the basis of his studies of the intelligence of chimpanzees.

On the whole, as Hearnshaw (1964) notes, Hobhouse anticipated a problem that became central in German psychology at the beginning of the twentieth century – the role played by relationships.

Imitation

Hobhouse devoted much of his work to finding out whether animals can learn by imitation. Unfortunately, he did not control the experimental conditions sufficiently well to justify the conclusion that animals can learn from imitation, but he raised a well-founded criticism of an experiment Edward Thorndike had done to show that animals could *not* do so. Thorndike's procedure was to place a cat in a cage so that it could observe another cat attempting to solve the problem of how to get out of the cage. Hobhouse pointed out that, although the cat was able to observe its fellow, Thorndike had not ensured that it had actually done so. Further, in contrast to primates and human beings, cats seem to develop complex social relationships to only a minor extent. For this reason, in most situations a cat would probably not be interested in what another cat is doing.

In conjunction with his report on his research, Hobhouse made an interesting critical examination of whether the behavior of animals is goal-directed. He saw no reason to assume a purpose was involved as far as reflexes and instincts were concerned, but when an animal applied what it had earlier learned to a new and different situation, it was natural to regard the new behavior as goal-directed.

Instincts: Innate or Learned?

Darwin had insisted that most instincts are formed according to the principle of natural selection. He did, however, hold that some had evolved as a result of the inheritance of acquired traits. The view of instincts as having evolved in accordance with Lamarck's principle was kept alive until the 1930s and contributed to obscuring the discussion. Another issue in the study of instincts was whether they were innate or a result of learning. Morgan and Douglas Spalding examined this problem.

Douglas Spalding (1840–1877)

Bain (1859) had studied the behavior of newborn lambs during the first hours of their lives. He described their first movements as accidental and claimed that it was not until 6–7 hours had passed that the sight of their mother had meaning for them, and not until after about 24 hours that they moved up to her when they saw her. Douglas Spalding, who at that time worked as a roofer, attended Bain's lectures in Aberdeen at the beginning of the 1860s. He had doubts about Bain's attempt at explaining instinctive behavior as resulting from learning, and at the end of the decade he performed some simple but well-planned experiments to demonstrate that Bain was wrong.

Spalding's experiments were known to psychologists towards the end of the nineteenth century, but it was not until the 1950s that his work again attracted attention.

Both Hearnshaw and Boakes have given interesting presentations of his work, and I shall draw upon these.

Spalding hatched chickens and, as soon as they came out of the eggs, he put covers over their heads or filled their ears with wax. When, after a couple of days, they had developed coordinated movements, he removed the covers or the wax. He now found they were capable of orienting themselves in their environment, of reacting to the clucking of their mother, and of pecking at and eating insects, just as well as chickens that had lived under normal conditions. Spalding performed a similar experiment on swallows and other small birds to study the development of their capacity for flying and their vision. Immediately after they hatched, he placed them in hollow cylinders that prevented them from using their wings. It turned out that the swallows were later capable of flying about as well as the birds that had developed under normal conditions. Spalding also observed that one-week-old chickens would hide when a sparrow hawk flew above them.

In addition he discovered that when he removed the covers from chickens and ducklings after two days, they would follow him if he stood close to them. If the covers were not removed until after three or four days, the birds showed fear of him and did not follow him. Spalding had discovered what was later called *imprinting* and *critical periods*.

Spalding was primarily interested in showing that certain types of behavior are dependent upon the organization and materialization of the nervous system. Yet, he recognized that the behavior he studied could be modified by previous experience. He noted, for example, that at an early age chickens peck at their own excrement but soon stop doing this. He further noted that chickens and ducklings do not visibly react to water until, in some way or other, they come in physical contact with it. Spalding's research shows that even simple experiments can give important information if they are well planned.

Spalding later trained as a lawyer in London, became a friend of J. S. Mill, and obtained a position tutoring the elder brother of the young Bertrand Russell. On the estate where he then lived, he continued his investigations of the behavior of young animals, with Lady Russell as his scientific assistant. He died of tuberculosis while only in his thirties.

Morgan on Instincts and Behavior

In his *An introduction to Comparative Psychology*, Morgan discussed in depth what was understood by instinct and behavior, anticipating questions that were not fully answered until the 1960s and 1970s. Unfortunately, he did not relate his position explicitly to those of Bain and Spalding. In experiments similar to Spalding's, he limited himself to saying his results in certain respects did not correspond to those of his predecessor. Nor did he discuss the position taken by Bain. Morgan (1894, pp. 211–212) expressed the central point in his view of instincts and learning in the following way:

[A]nimals and men come into the world alike with an innate capacity for active response to certain stimuli. This is part of their organic inheritance. The response may be from the first an accurate and adequate response: in such cases we term it instinctive. But more frequently the responses have a variable amount of inaccuracy and inadequacy; in such cases the animal, as a matter of observed fact, has a power of selective control over the responses; and this power of selective control over the activities which are essential to daily life, is the first stage of intelligence.

Apparently, Morgan thought the movements and responses of an organism are at first all of an instinctive nature, in the sense that they are genetically determined. However, very few of the movements could be regarded as accurately and adequately directed towards the stimuli that elicit them. To be able to give such responses to specific stimuli, animals and humans must go through a process of learning. Further, Morgan held that this learning is to some extent accidental, a result of trial and error. Thus, he agreed with Spalding that organisms' responses in the earliest stages of their development are of an instinctive nature but needing to be improved by learning. Spalding believed improvement took place in the development of animals' movements but did not attach the same importance to these as Morgan did.

Morgan's view differed from Bain's in that Morgan emphasized the instinctive nature of the early movements, but he agreed with Bain that trial-and-error learning is necessary. In contrast to Bain, Morgan did not regard any responses as spontaneous. All earlier responses are of an instinctive nature, directed towards objects. According to Morgan, in order to understand what is meant by a movement, a response, we must be able to identify the stimuli eliciting it; we must make clear the instinctive nature of the response. Therefore, we cannot simply divide responses into those elicited by definite stimuli and those not so elicited.

Morgan's Observational Basis

Morgan based his view on a number of observations of, and experiments performed on, chickens and ducklings, which he studied with the aim of understanding how their behavior developed after they had been hatched. One behavior he studied was chickens' pecking at objects lying on the ground. He found that at first the chickens pecked not only at insects and worms but also at small stones, pieces of paper and cloth, and cigarette butts. They also pecked at their own excrement but ceased to do this after a couple of times. Soon they limited their pecking to edible objects, and after a brief period, the precision of their pecking became extremely high.

In a famous experiment, Morgan presented two of his chickens with a worm and a cinnabar caterpillar. This caterpillar has a characteristic color, and animals seem unwilling to eat it. After some hesitation, the chickens began pecking at the caterpillar as well as at the worm. However, after pecking at the caterpillar a few times, they stopped doing so and then hardly seemed to notice it.

In another experiment, in which he clearly anticipated a procedure later used by Thorndike, Morgan observed chickens in an enclosure, the walls of which were constructed of newspapers. A seven-day-old chicken began to peck at a newspaper in a corner of the enclosure and happened to pull it so that an opening was formed through which it escaped. Morgan wondered whether it would again be capable of escaping from the enclosure if it were put back in it after he had replaced the newspaper. He set the chicken down close to the corner where it had escaped and found that it again pulled at the newspaper and escaped from the enclosure. Next, he placed the chicken as far away as possible from the corner where it had escaped and noted that after three to four minutes the chicken moved over to the corner, repeated its earlier procedure, and escaped.

In 1894, Morgan seems to have taken the position that the learning required to make an adequate response could be more or less complex, but there was no major difference between, for example, the learning involved in distinguishing between the worm and the cinnebar caterpillar, and the learning involved in the chicken's escape from the enclosure. Morgan (1894, p. 216) stressed that both instances may be explained in the same way: Through experience, the act had been associated with favorable and pleasurable consequences. Thus, by his simple experiment he had found support for the Spencer–Bain principle (see Chapter 6).

Imitation and the Role of Learning in Development

Morgan realized that imitation and learning play a great role in the ontogenetic development of animals. In *Introduction to Comparative Psychology*, he claimed that imitation and training have a particularly great importance for animals living in colonies. Here again, he noted something of fundamental importance. Unless an animal pays attention to its fellows, it will not imitate them. This indicates that an animal is endowed with definite social tendencies; for example, primates are social to a marked degree.

Morgan was an excellent observer, but in repeating some of Spalding's experiments, he overlooked how careful Spalding had been in reporting that the development of certain types of behavior occurs at particular stages in animals' lives. In other words, he lost sight of the critical periods. Morgan simply reported that his chickens did not react to the clucking of the mother; he neglected to note their age. Similarly, he apparently did not understand the significance of maturation or of the development of the birds' ability to fly. Further, he overlooked what Spalding had said about imprinting. Konrad Lorenz rediscovered this form of behavior more than fifty years after Spalding first described it.

The Role of Imitation in Phylogenetic and Ontogenetic Development

In *Introduction to Comparative Psychology*, Morgan emphasized the role played by imitation in animal life and pointed out that learning by imitation plays a major role for animals living in colonies. Boakes (1984) has called attention to two points in Morgan's ideas about imitation that reveal the sophistication of his thinking. Noting that instinctive behavior shows little variation from individual to individual and is often stereotyped, Morgan suggested that we might partially account for this by assuming the animals imitate each other. In this way he explained, among other things, the great similarity in the songs of individual birds in the same species.

Morgan also suggested that we might reconcile Darwin's and Wallace's views of human evolution by emphasizing the role played by imitation among human beings. Recall that Wallace argued that the principle of natural selection could not explain human evolution. Morgan pointed out that, in addition to the principle of natural selection, culture could explain human development, and he objected to Darwin and Galton's view that the evolution of humans could be understood exclusively as a result of biological evolution. Like his teacher Huxley, he opposed social Darwinism.

Morgan was a reflective thinker, with deep insight into the problems of evolution. By the 1890s, he realized that August Weismann had cast doubt on Lamarck's principle of the inheritance of acquired traits. As Mayr (1982) remarks, Morgan also contributed to making the idea of *emergent evolution* acceptable to biologists. According to this idea, at certain stages in evolution, systems have emerged that have properties not fully explainable in terms of the properties of their components. Many biologists think multicellular organisms, nervous systems with particular structures, consciousness, and language may have arisen as a result of emergent evolution.

The Problem of Motivation

Spencer asserted that instincts could be seen as a chain of reflexes, each of which is elicited by a definite stimulus. Instincts could thus be explained as stimulus–response connections. If this view were tenable, there would be no need to explain how instincts are activated, or how they direct behavior towards a goal; in other words, no theory of motivation would be needed. However, consider that instinctive reactions, such as nest-building in birds, do not occur throughout the year. Birds build their nests at particular times, and when they have built them, they do not immediately begin building new ones. In addition to nest-building, they must perform several other types of activities – find food, defend their territory, reproduce, and take care of their progeny. This means the same stimuli do not always elicit the same responses. There must be something in the animal that makes it vary its behavior. When we study human beings, we likewise find them alternating between different activities at more or less regular intervals. They eat and drink, rest and sleep, engage in sexual activity, work and play sports, enjoy art, and engage in games and other types of hobbies. The alternation in their activities must somehow be governed by processes in the organism. To account for this, we need a concept of motivation.

As Dalbir Bindra (1985) made clear, we need a concept of motivation for two other important reasons. First, the same activity is elicited by different types of stimuli. For example, a hen can be prompted to eat by the sight of food, and also by the sight of another hen eating. In humans, several different types of conditions can activate eating. Second, instinctive reactions in animals are often performed by means of different muscular movements, or different responses. For example, in building their nests, birds use movements that vary according to a variety of circumstances. The same is evidently true about the way an animal procures food. Particularly in mammals, we find great variations in muscular movements to reach what can be regarded as the same goal.

William McDougall (1871–1938)

If we cannot explain instincts as the formation of stimulus–response connections, we may conclude they are governed by inner processes of some kind, by a form of energy in the organism that activates the movements and directs the organism towards definite goals. The German philosophers Schopenhauer and Nietzsche had proposed a view of human thinking and actions as driven by inner, unconscious forces. In the chapter on psychoanalysis, I shall return to these two German thinkers. At this point, I shall simply mention that William McDougall was probably inspired by them when he attempted to combine the idea of inner forces with the idea of biological evolution in a doctrine of instincts.

As I emphasized, Morgan claimed that responses elicited early in ontogenesis must be directed towards specific aspects of the environment. He held that the more complex and varied the behavior is, the less clearly it would be directed towards definite stimuli, towards definite objects. For this reason, only a few clearly defined instinctive tendencies are found in humans; instead we have a great number of inborn capacities for motor responses that form when we are children.

Darwin had taken a somewhat different view, maintaining that humans possess instincts like self-preservation, sexuality, maternal love, and food-seeking. In his *Principles of Psychology* (1890/1950), William James had argued that humans possess a variety of instincts. McDougall was strongly influenced by James and put forward the idea that humans are born with several forms of behavior directed towards definite goals. In 1908, he published *An Introduction to Social Psychology*, in which he hoped to lay the foundation for the study of social psychology. He did not, however, devote much space to human social environment and society. For this reason, the title is somewhat misleading. The book is more appropriately regarded as a work on personality psychology. If we substitute the term "motive" for "instinct," we have the beginning of a modern psychology of personality. There were more than twenty editions of *Introduction to Social Psychology*.

McDougall's Life

Like Darwin, Galton, and Romanes, William McDougall belonged to a prosperous family, allowing him the opportunity to study and do research without having to earn a living. He obtained an unusually good education. At only fifteen, he began studying natural science at Cambridge University; at nineteen, he passed his first examination with top marks. Then he studied physiology at Cambridge, and after passing his second examination, also with top marks, he received his medical degree. In 1898, he joined an anthropological expedition to the Dutch East Indies and studied a tribe in Borneo. William James's *Principles of Psychology* awakened his interest in psychology, and on his return from the expedition, he studied with G. E. Müller in Göttingen for a year. At the turn of the century, he also performed some highly rated experiments in the study of vision. There was no position in Great Britain that would have allowed him to use his excellent training and capabilities, however. Not until he went to the United States in 1920 did he obtain a professorship, first at Harvard and then at Duke University. Before that he lectured at Oxford, and during World War I, he served as a doctor and studied what was then called shell shock (post-traumatic stress disorder). This study led to an interest in psychoanalysis and a visit to Carl Jung, who analyzed him.

McDougall was a champion of the view that intelligence is mainly a result of heredity; his views were considered racist and made him unpopular in the United States. Further, he declared himself an adherent of animism, supported with psychical research, and, as late as the 1920s, carried out experiments to show the validity of Lamarck's principle that acquired traits could be inherited. He was one of the first to express the opinion that psychology should be regarded as a study of behavior. However, his view of behavior differed from that of American psychologists at the time, and as a consequence he remained outside the behaviorist movement. His unpopularity in the United States may be the reason he has scarcely received the recognition in the history of psychology he deserves. Along with Freud, he made an important contribution to the study of motivation.

In addition to *Introduction to Social Psychology*, he wrote several books, including *Psychology: The Study of Behavior* (1912) and *An Outline of Abnormal Psychology* (1926). I shall next discuss his theory of instincts.

McDougall's View of Instincts and Motivation

An *instinct*, McDougall said, is an inborn psychophysical disposition containing an afferent, a central, and a motor component. To this psychophysical disposition there corresponds a cognitive, an emotional, and an expressive component. An instinct represents an impulse to activity that is directed towards a goal. Hence, the instinct may be regarded as a motivating force, a force giving energy and direction to behavior; it is elicited by a definite stimulation and contains a motor component. Still, the stimulation as well as the motor component may be modified through experience and learning. Further, a definite feeling or emotion is characteristic of each instinct. For example, a feeling of fear is characteristic of the instinct of *flight*. Finally, instincts are assumed to be accompanied by mental processes.

In accordance with these criteria, McDougall (1931, p. 25) defined an instinct in the following way:

We may, then, define an instinct as an inherited or innate psycho-physical disposition which determines its possessor to perceive, and to pay attention to, objects of a certain class, to experience an emotional excitement of a particular quality upon perceiving such an object, and to act in regard to it in a particular manner, or, at least, to experience an impulse to such action.

He insisted that it is possible to identify specific instincts in humans and made up a long list of these, which he revised over the years. I shall mention only a few to illustrate how he conceived of them: the instinct of flight, with the corresponding emotion of fear; of fight (aggression, hostility), with the corresponding emotion of anger; of parental love, with the corresponding feeling of love and tenderness; of sexuality (wish for mating), with the corresponding feeling of lust, of desire; of submission, with the corresponding feeling of inferiority, of humility; of dominance (asserting oneself), with the corresponding feeling of superiority; of companionship (wish for belonging to a group), with the corresponding feeling of loneliness.

Inspired by an earlier British thinker, McDougall developed the view that instincts are organized in systems around the objects eliciting them. He used the expression *sentiment* of such a system. Expressions of sentiments are love, hate, admiration, gratitude, contempt, attraction, envy, and shame. McDougall conceived of personality as a combination of sentiments and held that they are organized in a hierarchy. In the development of personality, he regarded the instincts of dominance and self-abasement as particularly important.

The Organism Striving Towards a Goal

Central to McDougall's thinking (1931, pp. 460 ff.) was the idea that the organism strives towards a goal. Its activity is characterized as follows: an internal energy is led into channels, which direct the organism to approach goals of different types; the directing of this energy into definite channels is carried out by cognitive activity; the activity continues until the goal is reached. To approach the goal is a satisfying experience, whereas it is a painful or unpleasant experience to be prevented from, or not to succeed in, reaching the goal. McDougall regarded both pleasure and pain as resulting from attempts to reach a goal, yet he was strongly opposed to the idea that the activity of the organism is governed by pleasure and pain. On this point, he was in opposition to Freud, to many behaviorists, and, as we noted above, to Morgan, Bain, and Spencer. McDougall regarded joy as a feeling different from pleasure.

An Evaluation of McDougall's View of Instincts

McDougall paid little attention to the research on instincts carried out by Darwin, Spalding, and Morgan. Morgan demonstrated by his observations and experiments that instinctive acts are most frequently dependent on experience, on learning. In dealing with the problem of human instincts, he had concluded that the earliest human responses are probably directed towards definite aspects of the environment, but not towards clearly delimited stimuli. Human activities are therefore the result of a very complicated process of learning. McDougall did not go into the earlier discussion of instincts as being mainly determined by either heredity or learning. The types of behavior covered by his concept of instincts are complex, and many psychologists have realized that it is difficult to support the notion that instincts are inborn.

In the 1920s, psychologists began increasingly to emphasize the role played by learning in behavior, as opposed to the role of genetic endowment. As a result of this new orientation, McDougall's approach to the study of psychology came into disrepute. Actually, as Robert Woodworth and Mary Sheehan (1965) made clear, the question of whether instincts are genetically determined or a result of learning was not an essential aspect of McDougall's theory, and in his last work, he dropped the use of the term "instinct." Instead of regarding behavior as determined by a number of instincts, he now regarded it as determined by a number of motives.

While it is reasonable to regard behavior as so determined, we here run into two problems. In the first place, it is difficult to find clear criteria for dividing motives into groups. Psychologists had criticized McDougall for being arbitrary in his division of instincts into categories, and for failing to specify criteria for making the division. Still, there is no compelling reason why it should not be possible to divide human motives into different categories. Indeed, a description of human personality in terms of motives along the lines suggested by McDougall was elaborated by Henry Murray (1938) and, as we shall see in Chapter 15, by Raymond Cattell (1965) some years later. Many modern researchers still prefer to describe personality in terms of motives.

The second problem in conceiving of instincts as motives arises from the attempt to specify how the internal source of energy originates, as well as how it activates and directs behavior towards a goal. McDougall failed to discuss these problems. Of course, the concept of motive can be used only descriptively, as was done by the researchers on personality mentioned above. However, if we use motive as part of the explanation, the question of how the internal source of energy originates, and how it activates and directs behavior, must be answered. Ten years after the publication of McDougall's *Social Psychology*, Woodworth (1918) pointed to the difficulty in conceiving of an internal source of energy. As we shall see in Chapter 17, he gave some valuable suggestions about how the problem of motivation could be formulated in a more profitable way than McDougall did. Unfortunately, few psychologists understood the seriousness of Woodworth's criticism and simply substituted the terms "drive" and "need" for instinct. Not until about 1960 did the majority of psychological researchers realize that it is scarcely practical to operate with the concepts of *drive* and *need* as unspecified internal forces.

Even if McDougall failed to see that it is problematic to conceive of instincts as inborn and to postulate an internal source of energy as the causal factor of behavior, he made an important contribution to psychology by showing that motivation must be regarded as also caused by internal processes, by internal states. Further, he inspired Edward Chase Tolman, as discussed in Chapter 13, to conceive of behavior as goal-directed.

European Ethology

While interest in comparative psychological had almost vanished in Great Britain by the beginning of the twentieth century, it flowered in Continental Europe. The two best-known representatives of this study were the German Konrad Lorenz (1903–1989) and the Dutch Niklass Tinbergen (1907–1988). Together with Karl von Frisch, they received the Nobel Prize for Medicine in 1973. The research they started in the 1930s and 1940s gave an important impetus to the study of learning in the 1960s, as well as to child psychology. Further, it led clinical psychologists to seek more systematically for genetic factors to explain mental disorders.

About 1900, the American Charles Wrightman had proposed that characteristics of animal behavior, in addition to anatomical and physiological characteristics, be used as criteria of biological classification. This idea was further elaborated by the German Oscar Heinroth, who at the beginning of the century began a systematic descriptive study of animal behavior that he called *ethology*. Heinroth was the teacher of Lorenz and Tinbergen; Robert Hinde (1991, 1995) has given a critical review of their work.

Ethology was promoted as a broadly comparative study of animal behavior, and Lorenz and Tinbergen studied various animal species. In their opinion, it was important to study animal behavior in the animals' natural environment. They insisted that laboratory experimental work on animal behavior was not of value until the animals have been studied in their natural habitats. This insistence was analogous to the phenomenologists' basing their psychological study on descriptions of everyday experience. The parallel between the two movements may be no mere coincidence, since ethology arose at a time when phenomenology as a philosophical and psychological movement was spreading over Continental Europe. As noted by Tinbergen (1951), the ethologists were influenced by the Gestalt psychologists' emphasis on the role played by patterns in perception.

The comparative study of animals aims to account for both similarities and differences between species. Whereas most earlier students of behavior had tended to emphasize similarities, Lorenz and Tinbergen noted that individuals of different species also have *species-specific characteristics*. The emphasis on species-specific characteristics in animal and humans had a great impact on psychology around 1970.

As successors of Darwin, the ethologists insisted that behavior is genetically determined, and they took an interest in phylogenetic development, but they tended to ignore ontogenetic development and the effects of learning on behavior. They appear not to have been interested in Morgan's studies of the ontogenetic development of animal behavior, and they tended to explain the fully developed behavior of animals exclusively as a result of heredity. Darwin believed most instincts are the result of natural selection. Lorentz and Tinbergen did not attempt to study the origin of instincts. Tinbergen did believe, however, that ethology was not yet ripe for this study but should be extended to include it.

Lorenz and Tinbergen made the study of instincts central in ethology. They conceived of instincts as made up of a complex series of acts characterized by a high degree of repetition. The movements involved were elicited by specific stimuli and governed by specific mechanisms. Lorenz and Tinbergen were preoccupied with reproduction and aggression in animals and humans. Here I shall give a brief description of Tinbergen's famous study of these behaviors in a fish, the three-spined stickleback.

In spring, the male stickleback leaves the school, migrates to warm, shallow waters, establishes a territory, and builds a nest into which it attempts to attract a female. It defends its territory against other male sticklebacks. The female stickleback approaching the territory is courted by the male, who performs a zigzag dance; this may lead to her following him to the nest. Here she spawns, and he fertilizes the eggs.

Tinbergen found that the male is attracted to the female mainly by two stimuli: her swollen abdomen and a specific posturing movement. What attracts the female are principally two distinct stimuli: the male's red belly and the zigzag dance. Aggressive behavior in the male stickleback is evoked when another male stickleback intrudes into his territory and displays two types of stimuli: a red belly and a posturing movement. To demonstrate that these stimuli form the basis of the sticklebacks' reactions, Tinbergen constructed dummies whose characteristics he could vary, thus identifying the stimuli that elicited the different types of reactions.

In his discussion of the nature of the stimuli eliciting instinctive behavior in animals, Tinbergen pointed out that the stimuli must be regarded as *patterns of stimulation*. Hence, the stimuli affecting the animal cannot be described simply in terms of the physical energy impinging upon the sensory organs of the animals. He claimed that animals are capable of reacting to far more aspects of physical stimulation than those making up the stimuli that elicit their instinctive acts.

Later research has shown, however, that instinctive behavior is not so rigorously determined by specific stimuli as Lorenz and Tinbergen assumed. In a summary of the research on this aspect of instinctive behavior, Felicity Huntingford (1991) has shown that it is not as easy as Tinbergen reported to have the female stickleback react to models, and further that red models are less frequently attacked than gray ones. Several conditions also determine whether a male stickleback, having established its territory, attacks an intruding male – how large the intruder is, whether the two have been in contact previously, whether it has a nest in the territory, whether the nest contains fertilized eggs, and whether a predator is present (see also Hinde, 1991, 1995).

The Inner Source of Energy

Lorenz and Tinbergen had a view of motivation very similar to McDougall's. They thought the stimuli eliciting different acts liberate energy in a nerve center, which in turn triggers the act. The energy is progressively built up and has to be released. Observations that appeared to support this view were that animals would sometimes also perform instinctive acts when the appropriate stimuli were not present and when a long time had passed since the instinct had been elicited. In a monograph (1935) on the instincts of birds, Lorenz had collected a wealth of observations that he claimed supported this view. However, his idea of an inner source of energy was strongly criticized and has not been supported by later research.

Lorenz and Tinbergen were – like Darwin, Romanes, McDougall, and James – convinced that humans have instincts. In line with their belief that instincts have a basis in built-up energy, Lorenz and Tinbergen attempted to account for aggression in humans, giving somewhat different accounts. They even attempted to specify conditions relating to war and peace between nations. Lorenz's (1966) book *On Aggression* stirred up a heated debate. The two ethologists had a political message. Lorenz was an outstanding observer who repeatedly insisted he made his observations without prejudice. Still, we may wonder whether his idea of an inner source of nergy did not derive from a reading of Freud and McDougall, and not from his research.

In 1948, Tinbergen accepted the offer of a professorship at Oxford University. Here, he became a key person in the training of animal psychologists who had a strong impact on comparative psychology. In a book entitled *The Tinbergen Legacy* (Dawkins et al., 1991), which appeared the year after his death, several of his students expressed their indebtedness to him, as well as a critical assessment of his main ideas. When European ethology became known in the United States, there was a dispute between the ethologists and the American behavioristically oriented animal psychologists. To this important event, I shall return in Chapter 19.

8

Russian Reflexology

Johannes Müller's students had laid a new foundation for the study of physiology by insisting on the application of the experimental method and physicalist principles in explaining physiological phenomena. They were consistent in their rejection of vitalism and in their application of physical and chemical principles to the explanation of bodily processes. However, they were unwilling to apply physicalist principles to mental phenomena. Helmholtz seems to have regarded mental phenomena as a specific realm of events separate from that of physiology, and his friend Du Bois-Reymond declared in a famous address that science would never be able to explain consciousness.

The new German physiology attracted Russian physiologists, but, in contrast to their German colleagues, the Russians attempted to base the study of mental phenomena on physiology. Starting from Descartes's view that reactions in animals and bodily reactions in humans are reflexes, they held that the brain acts as a machine producing definite movements (definite responses) when definite forms of stimulations (definite stimuli) affect it. The Russian physiologists believed such great advances had been made in the understanding of the nervous system that it was now possible to account for the reflexes which, they believed, form the foundation of mental phenomena. They took notable inspiration from Germany, but they deviated radically from most of their German colleagues in their view of consciousness.

Boakes (1984) has given a fascinating presentation of the political, intellectual, and scientific background of the Russian reflexologists. He has made clear how their approach combined earlier European and new Russian ideas, and he has given a central place to Ivan Sechenov, who, fifty years before John Watson, presented a detailed plan for an objective, behavioristic psychology. In retrospect, the most important contribution of reflexology was probably that it produced an experimental technique for the study of associative learning. The innovators were two outstanding physiologists, Ivan Pavlov and Vladimir Bekhterev, the first of whom has had the most lasting influence on psychology.

Political and Cultural Setting

Compared to Germany and other Western European countries, Russia was industrialized slowly; before the revolution in 1917, it had been predominantly an agrarian country. Even though serfdom had been abolished in 1861, farmers continued to be economically dependent on their landlords, and across the country a large part of the population lived in poverty. The slow growth of the economy also limited the ability to fund science. Moreover, the development of schools and universities was greatly inhibited by the authoritarian Czarist government, which closely controlled the educational system and public debate. Nevertheless, during this period, Russia fostered several outstanding scientists, and poetry and art flourished. Novelists including Tolstoy and Dostoyevsky created descriptions of human life that are still read throughout the world. As in earlier and later periods of Russian history, intellectuals lived in an atmosphere of constant conflict between traditional Russian values and Western influences. This conflict probably helped increase interest in psychological problems and the growth of distinctive and independent thinkers. At the same time, it and the constant struggle of intellectuals against a repressive political regime may have helped produce a tendency to dogmatism.

Ivan Sechenov (1829–1905)

A Short Biography

The life of the physiologist and psychological thinker Ivan Sechenov is fascinating. His father belonged to the lesser nobility in Sibirsk, and Sechenov grew up on the family's country estate. He received excellent instruction in German and French but had no opportunity to pursue university studies because his father died when he was ten years old. At the age of fourteen, he was sent to a high school for the education of military engineers in St Petersburg. After four years of study, he began to work for the military in Kiev. However, this work did not interest him, and, in 1850, he undertook the study of medicine in Moscow, receiving his medical degree in 1856. He then went to Western Europe to study, spending the small fortune he had inherited from his father.

First, Sechenov went to Berlin to study under Johannes Müller. While he was auditing Müller's lectures, he conducted empirical research under the guidance of Du Bois-Reymond, who was Müller's assistant. Before he returned to Russia, Sechenov also studied for some time with Helmholtz and Carl Ludwig, forming a lifelong friendship with Ludwig. After having spent some years in Russia, he went again to Western Europe for a longer period of study, this time with the famous French physiologist Claude Bernard. In Bernard's laboratory, Sechenov performed experiments on reflexes, which revealed that specific forms of stimulation of a frog's brain cause reflexes to be inhibited. These experiments shed light on a problem that had greatly occupied the minds of contemporary physiologists, as well as of Russian and British scientists in the later nineteenth and early twentieth centuries.

After two years, Sechenov was appointed professor at the Medical Military Academy associated with the University of St Petersburg. He opposed the authoritarian political regime, fought for women's right to university studies, and openly discussed sexuality. Although he was watched by the authorities, he was never arrested or dismissed from his university positions. Besides working in St Petersburg, he was also attached to the University of Odessa for several years, and later to the University of Moscow.

After having written a report of his experiments on inhibition, Sechenov published in 1863 a comprehensive work meant to demonstrate how to give psychology a physiological foundation without the use of introspection. The manuscript passed the censor, but the authorities demanded that the title be changed, and it appeared under a title that was translated as *The Reflexes of the Brain*. The book was much read and discussed by the Russian intelligentsia and was a major source of inspiration for Pavlov and Bekhterev. It was not translated into English, however, until 1935.

The Nervous System as a Machine

Sechenov's view of the brain was not new. In the mid-eighteenth century, Julien Offray de la Mettrie had championed the idea that the brain functions as a machine, and a number of later writers and thinkers elaborated the idea. Sechenov argued that not only muscular movements but also mental events are produced by specific stimuli. He regarded all connections between stimuli and responses as reflexes. By assuming that reflexes could be formed as a result of mechanical associations, he attempted to explain perception, memory, abstract thinking, feeling, and even self-awareness. To the two concepts "sensation" and "association," taken from the British empiricist philosophers, he added a third: "movement" ("response"). He assumed certain reflexes are inborn and proposed that diverse, more complex reflexes could be formed by associative learning. Thinking, Sechenov declared, represents reflexes in which the movement, the response, has been inhibited. Here, he referred to his own finding that reflexes could be inhibited.

With the exception of this latter hypothesis, his account of consciousness did not seem to add anything new to the thinking of the British empiricist philosophers. Apart from the reference to his experiments with frogs, he was not able to support his account with experimental results. Sechenov had, however, a successor in his compatriot Ivan Pavlov, who made a systematic attempt to provide an empirical foundation for his view of the relationship between the brain and psychological processes.

Ivan P. Pavlov (1849–1936)

When Ivan Pavlov began his studies of conditioned reflexes at the end of the 1890s, he had already carried out work on the digestive processes, for which he received the Nobel Prize in 1904. The starting point for his study of reflexes was observations he and his coworkers had made during their research on digestion in animals. They had noted that, when the animals were to be fed, they produced saliva simply at the sight of the food, and that stimuli present while the animals were eating would also produce saliva. As I noted in Chapter 2, these observations had already been made 150 years earlier by Robert Whytt. Still, they had not been empirically investigated, and Pavlov decided to undertake a systematic study of them, devoting the rest of his life to this work.

To begin with, he accounted for conditioned reflexes in mentalistic, subjective terms. Gradually, however, he grew convinced that it was more useful to account for the phenomenon in terms of objective observations and of knowledge of the nervous system. He took his starting point in Descartes's concept of the reflex, and he recorded those stimuli that elicited definite forms of responses. This made Pavlov a pioneer in objective psychology. His primary aim was to throw light on the functions of the cortex, but he also made it clear that his research was directed at laying the foundation for a scientific psychology. For these reasons, it is fair to say he anticipated American behaviorism.

A Short Biography

Pavlov, the son of a priest, was born in Ryaz, a small village southeast of Moscow. He did not receive regular education until he began to attend first the high school in Ryaz, and later its theological seminary. In this seminary, education was very liberal, so Pavlov had the opportunity to read books on natural science, and became interested in medicine and biology at an early age. As noted by Alexander Vucinich (1963/1970) in his book on science and culture in Russia, the Russian intelligentsia took great interest in physiology at the time Pavlov was receiving his education. Pavlov soon became familiar with German experimental physiology by reading a translation of an English book on modern physiology.

In 1870, Pavlov began the study of natural science at the University of St Petersburg, specializing in physiology. On the completion of his study in 1879, he obtained a position as a scientific assistant and, while studying medicine, became the director of a small laboratory. He worked in this laboratory until, in 1890, he was appointed professor of pharmacology at the military medical academy associated with the university. The following year he was appointed director of the department of physiology at a large, private, experimental medical institute. It was at this institute that Pavlov conducted his research and spent most of his time.

In 1883, he completed his medical studies and then obtained a fellowship for two years, which allowed him to live in Germany for that period. During this time, he worked in the laboratory of Carl Ludwig and also in the laboratory of one of Du Bois-Reymond's earlier students. As I have mentioned, even as a very young man he was attracted to the new German physiology and gained important ideas from it. Influenced not only by German physiological psychology but also by Spencer and Darwin, Pavlov viewed the functioning of the brain from an evolutionary perspective. He abandoned the religious faith in which he had been brought up, but he did not become as radical as Sechenov and continued to identify with many Russian national values. This was probably one of the reasons he had the freedom to carry out his work in Czarist Russia, and after the revolution of 1917 as well. His mechanistic views of scientific problems were in line with the official decrees of the communist regime.

Behavior and Thinking as Reflexes

As Vucinich (1963/1970) made clear, Pavlov was no extreme materialist. While he rejected vitalism, he did not attempt to base his physiological research on physical and chemical principles. Still, he avoided using psychological concepts with a subjective basis and did not use concepts such as "perception," "attention," "thinking," "goal-directedness," "expectation," and "will" in his accounts of the phenomena he studied.

Like Sechenov, Pavlov began with Descartes's idea of a reflex, believing it could be seen as a result of the activity of the brain. Hence, we could understand the activity of the brain by making an empirical study of the way the different types of reflexes are formed. This understanding of brain function would in turn bring us to an understanding of human and animal behavior. An objective study of the brain's function in humans would also provide a scientific understanding of our mental functions. In accordance with this view of the brain, all types of behavior and mental functions could be understood as reflexes of different types.

Pavlov (1927, 1928, 1932) based his system on the knowledge physiologists had already gained about the so-called inborn reflexes, the physiological reflexes, which, as I noted in Chapter 2, were studied throughout the nineteenth century, and, at the beginning of the twentieth century, were thought to be of vital significance for the study of the nervous system. The reflexes were known to be stereotyped, consistent, and automatic reactions to specific stimuli, such as the sucking reflex in the infant, the stretch reflex, and the salivary, pupillary, and blinking reflexes. Pavlov emphasized that, to lay a solid foundation for the building of the system he had in mind, a thorough study was needed to identify the physiological reflexes, and he claimed to have discovered two specific ones of great importance: one was the reaction when movements are restrained, the so-called *reflex of freedom*, and the other was the reaction in humans and animals to changes in the environment, the so-called *exploratory reflex*. Inspired by Spencer, Pavlov regarded instincts as chains of reflexes and, as a consequence, also included in his concept of the reflex several types of instinctive acts. According to Pavlov, the physiological reflexes are the foundation on which the whole of the nervous system is built.

Conditioned Reflexes

Having made clear that his system had a basis in physiological reflexes, Pavlov emphasized that these reflexes develop as a means of biological adaptation. However, to adapt to a more complex environment, animals need an additional type of reflex, formed on the basis of the physiological ones. Whereas the physiological reflexes depend on activity in the spinal cord and the lower brain centers, the conditioned reflexes presuppose activity in the cortex. Hence, a study of them would shed light on the activity in this part of the nervous system. The focus of Pavlov's study, therefore, was reflexes conditional on other reflexes, and for this reason he called them *conditional reflexes*, usually translated as *conditioned reflex*. I shall use the latter term, even if it is a little inaccurate.

Procedures: Pavlov's Dogs

The concept of conditioned reflex has a central place in the study of learning, and, as we shall see in Chapter 19, intensive research is still carried out to clarify its meaning. For this reason, I shall deal with Pavlov's procedures in some detail.

Starting from the observation that stimuli other than food in the mouth of an animal elicit salivation, Pavlov devised a procedure to present two stimuli to an animal simultaneously, one that automatically elicits a reflexive reaction and one that does not. Pavlov took advantage of his earlier research on digestive processes and concentrated on salivation in his animal subjects, mainly dogs. By means of a simple operation, he was able to collect a measurable quantity of saliva secreted in the mouth of the animal. In this way, he could register when the animal began secreting saliva, as well as the quantity. Having performed this operation, he placed the animal in a laboratory, where he strapped the animal so firmly that it could not move. This allowed him to control when the animal could perceive the two stimuli he presented to it, as well as the length of time the stimulus was presented and the time between the presentation of the indifferent stimulus and the placing of food in the animal's mouth. Using this procedure, Pavlov then performed the following experiment. At the same time that he gave food to the animal, he would present what he called an *indifferent* stimulus that would not ordinarily elicit the secretion of saliva, such as the ringing of a bell. This he would do within a definite time period, giving the animal a definite quantity of food and having the bell ring for a definite length of time. After a few minutes, the procedure was repeated, for a fixed number of times in an objectively describable manner.

Pavlov showed that the indifferent stimulus would elicit a reflexive reaction when he presented it for a number of trials at the same time the dog received the food. He termed the physiological reflex an *unconditioned reflex*, and the connection he had established between the indifferent stimulus and the elicited reaction a *conditioned reflex*. The stimulus and response in the physiological reflex he called, respectively, the *unconditioned stimulus* and *unconditioned response*, and the stimulus and response in the conditioned reflex he called, respectively, the *conditioned stimulus* and *conditioned response*. Further, he termed the presentation of the unconditioned stimulus *reinforcement*.

Main Results

By means of his procedure Pavlov could systematically vary several conditions that might conceivably affect the connection between the conditioned stimulus and the conditioned response. Using various measures to determine the strength of the conditioned response, such as the quantity of saliva, he showed that an increase in the number of trials resulted in an increase in the strength of the response. Further, with regard to the time interval between the presentation of the conditioned and the unconditioned stimulus, he concluded that the two stimuli must be presented simultaneously, though he added that the conditioned stimulus must be presented immediately before the unconditioned. On the basis of these findings, Pavlov concluded that a conditioned response is formed when an indifferent stimulus is repeatedly presented simultaneously with an unconditioned stimulus. Hence, the critical variables were the temporal relationship between the conditioned and unconditioned stimuli, and the number of trials.

Pavlov also made other important findings. One was that, when he presented the conditioned stimulus without reinforcement, the strength of the conditioned response decreased for each trial. For example, the quantity of saliva decreased for each trial when he presented the ringing of the bell without giving the animal food. After the conditioned stimulus was presented without reinforcement for a definite number of times, the conditioned response would disappear. Pavlov called this phenomenon *extinction* and found that when the conditioned response had been extinguished for some time, it could return spontaneously. It might also return when he introduced a new indifferent stimulus. Hence, extinction was apparently different from forgetting.

Further, Pavlov showed that a stimulus similar to the conditioned stimulus would elicit the conditioned response. By selecting stimuli that could be measured objectively, such as tones differing in frequency, he could identify similarity in an objective way; the closer two tones were in frequency, the more similar they were believed to be. He showed that if, for example, he conditioned an animal to a tone with a frequency of 1,000 hertz, the quantity of saliva would decrease the further a tone was from the tone of 1,000 hertz. He called this phenomenon *generalization.* By giving reinforcement to a stimulus possessing a specific characteristic, such as a tone of 1,000 hertz, and not to tones of other frequencies, Pavlov showed he could make the animal discriminate between stimuli differing in this specific characteristic. This he called *differentiation.* By means of differentiation, it is possible to measure sensory discrimination in animals very accurately.

Among Pavlov's findings, the following have attracted considerable attention. Under certain conditions, the animal became sleepy and could even fall asleep. Under other conditions, it exhibited a behavior similar to that of hypnotized persons. When the animal was required to make successively finer discriminations until it seemed unable to improve its performance, as in discriminating between a circle and an ellipse as it approaches the shape of a circle, the animal would stop reacting to the stimulation and exhibit a behavior indicating that it was strongly stressed. This phenomenon Pavlov called *experimental neurosis.*

In most of his experiments, Pavlov used dogs as his subjects, but he also applied the procedure to a number of animal species and studied other types of reflexes than the salivary reflex. This enabled him to compare the performances of different animal species and different types of reflexes.

Interpretation of Pavlov's Results

Many psychologists and physiologists received Pavlov's ideas of conditioning with enthusiasm, while many, such as the Gestalt psychologists and the ethologists, were critical. Since Pavlov conducted his experiments, *Pavlovian* or *classical conditioning* has been extensively studied. While progress has been made in understanding the phenomenon of conditioning, it has become clear that it is far more complex than Pavlov and his enthusiastic adherents believed at the beginning of the twentieth century.

Although Pavlov readily admitted his debt to Descartes, he was reluctant to relate his research to the British associationistic tradition. However, to understand him, we must view him from its perspective. The British philosophers had studied associations between mental representations and assumed they were made in a mechanistic manner. One important condition they saw for the formation of an association is that the two mental representations to be associated must occur in temporal contiguity. Pavlov rejected all studies of association based on assumptions of mental phenomena and insisted that it must be accounted for in terms of an objectively defined stimulus and response. He further modified the view that association is formed in a purely mechanistic fashion by assuming that the new reflexes must be formed on the basis of the physiological reflexes; an unconditioned reflex must be present – a form of reinforcement is necessary. Hence, Pavlov's account of the formation of conditioned reflexes is built on the belief that as long as the conditioned stimulus is followed by the unconditioned stimulus, the formation of the conditioned reflex will take place. In other words, as long as reinforcement takes place, temporal contiguity is sufficient to explain the formation of the reflex.

Pavlov thought the conditioned reflexes are formed in the cortex, and he postulated a number of cortical processes to explain them. Other experiments suggest that the cortex is not necessary for the formation of conditioned reflexes. As far as I know, there is no evidence supporting his speculations concerning the cortex.

Pavlov's account of conditioning has long been debated, and numerous experiments have been performed to clarify the nature of the phenomenon. In retrospect, the criticism of Pavlov by the Gestalt psychologists and the ethologists seems to have been particularly important for research on the processes in classical conditioning, as well as on the role of conditioning in animals' adaptation to their environments.

The Gestalt psychologists found Pavlov's view too mechanistic. They argued that it is wrong to think that the conditioned and unconditioned stimuli are two distinct, unrelated events until after association by Pavlov's procedure. For an adequate account of the processes in conditioning, we must consider the dog's perception, meaning that the relationship between the two types of stimuli is of central importance. Apart from stating that the stimulus to be conditioned must not elicit the unconditioned reflex, Pavlov (1927) had not gone into the problem of the possible existence of a pre-experimental connection between the two types of stimuli. (As we shall see in Chapter 19, experiments in the 1960s and 1970s showed that the relationship between the conditioned and unconditioned stimuli must form part of an account of the phenomenon, and that it is of great importance what types of stimuli are chosen as the conditioned stimuli.)

Some decades later, the ethologists also objected that Pavlov had failed to take into account the relationship between the conditioned and unconditioned stimuli, although their argument was different from that of the Gestalt psychologists. They argued that animals in their natural environment tend to react to specific stimuli, even if they have the capacity to react to a wide range of stimuli; stimuli are species-specific. Therefore, to adequately account for classical conditioning, we must consider the genetically determined tendencies in different species of animals to react to species-specific stimuli.

The objections of the Gestalt psychologists and the ethologists raised doubts about whether classical conditioning is as widespread a phenomenon as Pavlov had assumed. As the critics pointed out, the fact that many species of animals could be conditioned did not prove animals learn reactions that cause them to become more adapted to their environments in the way Pavlov proposed.

Despite the debate, there appears to be a growing consensus that the forming of emotional reactions to objects can be regarded as an example of Pavlovian conditioning. Techniques widely used in treatments of phobia and anxiety disorders are based upon principles of classical conditioning.

Pavlov believed the brain functions as a machine for producing reflexes. But unless we are able to define what we mean by a conditioned reflex, this is scarcely a profitable way of looking at the brain. As the above discussion has revealed, it is not easy to give a clear and precise definition of a conditioned reflex. A further difficulty is that the conditioned reflex is never identical to the unconditioned reflex; for example, as Pavlov reported, the amount of saliva produced when the conditioned reflex has been established is always less than that produced by the unconditioned reflex. How similar must the conditioned reflex be to the unconditioned reflex to count as a reflex?

Overall Evaluation

As Pavlov admitted, other researchers before him had noted the phenomenon of conditioned reflexes. Therefore, his demonstration that it is possible to establish them was hardly new. Still, he must be credited with recognizing that a study of conditioning might give us a perspective on learning, and with devising a procedure to make such a study possible. Furthermore, he contributed to psychology by showing that a complex psychological problem could be studied by objective methods. Yet we can also say his strict insistence on objective methods limited his perspective, because it prevented him from exploring problems of perception and attention in cognitive processes. Most likely he would have benefited from using concepts of a more subjective nature, such as "perception," "expectation," and "attention," along with his objective concepts. Pavlov adopted an evolutionary, biological orientation, but, like many of his contemporaries, he placed too little emphasis on the fact that animals have species-specific characteristics.

Vladimir M. Bekhterev (1857–1927)

Bekhterev began his studies of conditioned reflexes about the same time as his colleague Pavlov, and independently of him. As I have mentioned, the reason Pavlov is regarded as the central figure in the history of the study of conditioned reflexes is that he laid a better and more systematic foundation for the investigation of the phenomenon. I shall call attention only to some differences between the two that may have some theoretical importance.

Bekhterev's Life

Bekhterev studied at the University of St Petersburg at the same time as Pavlov. He obtained excellent training as a physiologist and a medical doctor. After having gained his medical degree, he studied in Leipzig with Wundt and in Paris with Charcot, contributing to several areas of medicine. His main interest was in neurology and psychiatry, and at an early age he was appointed professor of psychiatry in Kazan. Here, he began experimental studies on several psychiatric and psychological disorders. In 1893, he was appointed professor at the military medical academy in St Petersburg, to which Pavlov was also attached, and the two were colleagues until Bekhterev's death in 1927. They were both inspired by Sechenov and based their studies on the assumption that all connections in the nervous system are of a reflexive nature; both insisted that the study of psychology must be made objective. As Vucinich (1963/1970) has remarked, however, Bekhterev maintained that introspection could also be useful in the study of conditioned reflexes. In the years 1907–1912, Bekhterev wrote a comprehensive work on objective psychology, *La psychologie objective*, which was translated into French and German in 1913. A later book was also translated into English in 1932 under the title *General Principles of Human Reflexology*.

Disagreements Between Bekhterev and Pavlov

Bekhterev and Pavlov were in sharp disagreement. Boakes (1984) has given a vivid account of how they acted out their differences. I shall simply mention that Pavlov criticized Bekhterev for lacking both depth in his thinking and care in his experimenting. In turn, Bekhterev criticized Pavlov for being superficial in his attempts at applying the results of his animal experiments to complex human phenomena.

In respect to their different views, Bekhterev thought it mistaken to base a study of reflexes on salivary secretion. A better starting point, he held, would be reflexes involving skeletal muscles – in other words, striated muscles, not smooth muscles as in Pavlov's experiments. Accordingly, he developed a procedure for the study of the reflexive withdrawal of a foot or a hand. The foot or paw of an animal, or the hand or foot of a human being, was placed on a metal plate. At the same time that an electric shock was administered via the plate, the subject was presented with a stimulus to be connected to the physiological reflex.

On the one hand, a study of reflexes of striated muscles may provide a more useful approach to understanding the behavior of humans and animals. On the other hand, it has proved difficult to control conditions in the study of these types of muscles, because animals and people can control their movements in accord with their expectation of what is going to happen, and it is difficult to distinguish this reaction from the one involved in the physiological reflex. Still, the experimental procedure developed in Bekhterev's laboratory has been extensively used, and a number of procedures have been proposed to ensure that the movement is reflexive and not voluntary.

Russian psychology continued to progress after the revolution of 1917, and several other approaches to psychological problems were developed. In a later chapter I shall review some of the work produced in the years following the Russian Revolution.

9

The Study of Clinical Psychology and
Unusual Mental States in France

A Sketch of the History of Psychiatry in the Nineteenth Century: Introduction to Chapters 9 and 10

As made clear in the American Psychiatric Association's *Diagnostic and Statistical Manual of Mental Disorders* (*DSM–V–TR*) (2013, see p. 164), the subject matter of psychiatry is pathological thinking and behavior. Psychology is frequently divided roughly into the study of thinking and the study of behavior, two disciplines that are closely related to each other. As we shall see in Chapters 9 and 10, some interactions have occurred between the two disciplines, but on the whole they have developed independently of each other. I shall therefore not go into a detailed study of the history of psychiatry. To understand the development of clinical psychology, however, and as a background for Chapters 9 and 10, I shall present a sketch of the history of psychiatry in the 1800s.

Mental illness is universal among the peoples of the world, as shown in *Kaplan and Sadock's Synopsis of Psychiatry* (Sadock and Sadock, 2007). Although the prevalence and manifestations of mental disorders vary with culture and history, mental illness is not a myth created by psychiatrists, or explicable as deviations from social norms or as stigmatization of specific groups of people. Therefore, as Brendan and Winnifred Maher (1985a, b) point out, while the names of mental disorders have changed through Western history, our ancestors were plagued by many of the same types of mental disorders as afflict us today. Thus, when psychiatry was being established as a specialty of modern medicine at the beginning of the 1800s, its pioneers were confronted with many of the same mental disorders as are treated in modern healthcare: intellectual and developmental disabilities, senile dementia, the effects of alcohol abuse, schizophrenia, bipolar disorder, personality disorders, and obsessive-compulsive disorders as well as other anxiety disorders.

The development of psychiatry as a scientific discipline probably owes much to the general progress made in medicine. But as Henri Ellenberger (1970, p. 197) shows, the ideas of the Enlightenment may also have contributed to its advance, by dispelling the medieval view of mental disorders as caused by evil spirits and encouraging a more respectful view of the mentally ill.

The Era of Asylums

According to Edward Shorter (1997), at the beginning of the 1800s, most of the persons afflicted with mental disorders were in private care, living with their families, or in the custody of other private citizens. In the cities, some were also in large general hospitals, some in poorhouses, some in prisons, and some in institutions or asylums specifically established for the mentally ill. According to many contemporary reports, the mentally ill were treated inhumanely, being poorly fed, left in filth, and isolated in separate rooms, basements, or stables. In the asylums they were confined in unsanitary conditions in overcrowded rooms. Whether in private or public care, they were frequently chained.

In France, Germany, Great Britain, Italy, and the United States, some physicians and philanthropists tried to reform the care of the mentally ill. From the end of the 1700s, changes were made in the old institutions, and new institutions were established with a view to improving their welfare. In the first decades of the 1800s, many people came to believe institutions could be established that would have a therapeutic effect on persons suffering from mental disorders. Some widely accepted ideas at the time were that the mentally ill should be separated from their families, protected from the stress of ordinary social life, and permitted to live a healthy life occupied with work that would discipline them.

A central idea in several reformers' views was that the mentally ill would benefit from *moral treatment*; that is, they should be treated with respect, and doctors should attempt to understand and correct their irrational and inappropriate ideas. The philosophy of moral treatment can be seen as the beginning of modern psychotherapy. During the first half of the 1800s, the idea of asylums as therapeutic institutions for the mentally ill gained ground in Europe as well as in the United States, and numerous asylums were built. However, in spite of the many good intentions of the reformers and the acceptance of the view that the mentally ill should be treated humanely, life in the asylums tended to be miserable. Edward Shorter (1997, p. 33), who has been my main source on the history of psychiatry, summed up the history of asylums from the beginning of the 1800s to World War I as follows:

The rise of the asylums is the story of good intentions gone bad. That the dreams of the early psychiatrists failed, is unquestionable. By World War I, asylums had become vast warehouses for the chronically insane and demented.

Many reasons have been suggested for the failure of the asylums. First, it is extremely demanding to take good care of the mentally ill. Prior to the discovery of psychoactive drugs, such care was much more difficult than it is today. Second, the spread of syphilitic infections and increased alcohol consumption made the asylums overcrowded. Third, the expectations of improvement and cure were unrealistic, and, when this was realized, pessimism may have taken the place of early optimism. And we cannot overlook that one important reason for establishing the asylums was simply to have a place where the mentally ill could be confined, as Michel Foucault (1961/1966) has argued.

When supernatural explanations of mental illness were dismissed, it was logical to think the cause could instead be found in either a malfunctioning of the brain or the personal and social experiences of the afflicted. The two explanations were not mutually exclusive, and most early as well as later psychiatrists probably did believe both were needed. However, throughout the history of psychiatry, there has been a tendency to a polarization of the two views of the causes of mental disorders.

In the mid-1800s, great progress was made in the study of the brain, and this directed the attention of the psychiatrists towards brain malfunction as a cause of mental disorders. The German Wilhelm Griesinger (1817–1869) contributed greatly to this reorientation in psychiatry. His textbook of psychiatry, published in 1845, was revised and expanded and became highly influential in its second edition in 1867. As Ellenberger (1970) has said, Griesinger conceived of psychiatric problems broadly as being concerned with associations of ideas, emotions, and the functions of the self. The important message of the book, however, was that mental illness is an illness of the nerves and the brain. Griesinger was a professor of psychiatry at the University of Berlin and organized and directed a psychiatric clinic there from 1865 until his early death in 1869. His textbook and clinic made him central in German psychiatry. Besides Griesinger, Theodor Meynert in Vienna and Henry Maudsley in London were influential in promoting the view that mental illness is an illness of the nerves and the brain.

The discovery of psychoactive drugs in the 1950s has given strong support to Griesinger's claim that mental illness is a brain disorder. Even if drugs do not cure the illness, the fact that they can restore many afflicted persons to a condition whereby they can again participate in ordinary social life shows that one important cause must be some malfunctioning of the brain. Of course, this does not exclude the fact that environmental factors can cause these disorders as well.

The idea that mental illness is a brain disease was a productive one. However, in the latter half of the 1800s, mental disorders were poorly described and little was known about the brain. Hence, the relationship between mental disorders, as they were manifested in thinking and behavior, and the changes taking place in the anatomy and chemistry of the brain were too poorly understood to allow for productive research.

The search for a basis of mental illness in brain pathology led to much empty speculation, and towards the end of the 1800s, there was a reaction against the search for biological causes. The German Emil Kraepelin (1856–1926) insisted that at the present state of knowledge, psychiatrists should concentrate on describing and categorizing the diverse mental disorders. Not until adequate descriptions had been given could psychiatrists search for general laws and explanations. Kraepelin worked out a categorization that had a great impact on psychiatry from the beginning of the 1900s.

Born in Neustrelitz in northern Germany, Kraepelin passed his medical examination at the University of Tübingen in 1878. After working for four years as a medical doctor at the psychiatric clinic in Munich, he went to study with Wundt in Leipzig and became Wundt's assistant. But on Wundt's recommendation he continued his work in psychiatry, becoming director of the psychiatric clinic at the University of Heidelberg in 1891. In 1902, he returned to Munich as the director of the university clinic. Under his direction, the clinics at Heidelberg and then at Munich became international centers of psychiatric research.

Kraepelin based his descriptions and categorizations on a large number of patients, using the course of the illness over time as an important criterion. But he also relied on the patients' symptoms. His most famous categorizations were of the mental disorders called *psychoses*. These were disorders that strongly affect thinking and behavior with no obvious cause. In contrast to Griesinger, who had conceived of them as representing one group, Kraepelin split the psychoses into three groups: dementia precox, manic-depressive (bipolar) disorder, and paranoid disorders, the first two being the most common.

Kraepelin believed the onset of disorders of the first group (precox) is early, and that the illness results in dementia. The Swiss psychiatrist Eugen Bleuler (1857–1939) became famous for elaborating on Kraepelin's first group. He regarded himself as a follower of Kraepelin but insisted that the onset of the illness is not always early and that it does not usually lead to dementia. He emphasized that the disorder is characterized by a split between thinking, emotions, and behavior, and he renamed the group schizophrenia. As Sadock and Sadock (2007) have shown, the split is not in personality.

Kraepelin had already published a small textbook of psychiatry in 1883; its eighth and last edition occupied four volumes (1909–1915). The system of categories he worked out had two apparent weaknesses: The categories were more or less unrelated to each other, and the boundaries between them were blurred. We have seen that Kraepelin thought the search for laws and explanations should be postponed until the categories had been more precisely defined. This turned out to be a strength because it made his system readily applicable. But it may also have directed psychiatric work to description at the expense of theory and explanation.

Kraepelin did extensive experimental studies of attention, memory, associations, emotions, fatigue, and motivation in his patients to shed light on their psychological functioning. In this way he contributed to the experimental study of psychopathology, as Maher and Maher (1985a, b) and Hilgard (1987) recount. However, to understand Kraepelin's great influence on present-day psychology, we must trace the influence throughout the 1900s of his attempts to categorize mental disorders.

As Shorter (1997) shows, at the beginning of the 1900s, Kraepelin's ideas exerted considerable influence on American psychiatry, but from the 1930s to the 1970s other influences, particularly psychoanalysis, became dominant. When the American Psychiatric Association in 1952 published the first edition of the *Diagnostic and Statistical Manual of Mental Disorders* (*DSM–I*), Kraepelin's ideas played no significant role. The same was true of the second edition of the manual. But in the third edition in 1980, efforts were made, in line with Kraepelin's ideas, to base categorizations on clinical features and avoid relying on theories of the origin of disorders. The fourth edition in 1994 (*DSM–IV*) and fifth edition in 2013 (*DSM–V*), widely recognized all over the world as a useful means of communicating about mental disorders in daily clinical work as well as in research, were elaborated along the same lines. Principles highly similar to those underlying *DSM–IV* guided the tenth edition of the *International Classification of Mental and Behavioral Disorders* (*ICD–10*) issued in 1992 by the World Health Organization. Thus, Kraepelin's ideas still play a role in psychiatry at the beginning of the twenty-first century.

Like psychiatrists, clinical psychologists of the twenty-first century use the system of classification worked out by the American Psychiatric Association in their communication about mental disorders. Moreover, since the end of the 1900s, psychologists have increasingly engaged in empirical research aiming at clarifying the nature of the disorders described in the categories of *DSM–V*. Thus, Kraepelin's ideas are also of great importance to present-day psychology.

In preceding chapters we noted that German and Russian empirical psychology grew out of physiology and that British empirical psychology grew out of the theory of evolution. Deriving their inspirations from different branches of empirical science, the psychologies of the different countries became different. The inspiration for French psychology came mainly from psychiatry, and it was primarily a clinical psychology. Influenced by British and also German psychology, it became different from both these.

As Régine Plas (1994) shows, however, we would have an incomplete picture of early French psychology if we narrowed our attention only to problems of clinical psychology. Early French empirical psychologists were interested in a wide range of problems: hypnosis, suggestion, behavior in crowds, hallucinations, dreams, trances, ecstasies, automatic writing, and accomplishments of great artists. Theirs was a study of mental disorders, but also of *unusual mental states*.

The study of hypnosis had a central place in early French psychology. Its history gives a good introduction to the history of psychotherapy and is of topical interest in psychology today. I shall, therefore, deal with it in some detail. Jean-Martin Charcot is an important figure in this history, and I shall give an account of his use and view of hypnosis. Then I shall review some of the work of two early champions of empirical psychology in France: Théodule Ribot and Hippolyte Taine. Finally, I shall treat in some detail the empirical studies of two psychologists who contributed important ideas to the development of psychology in the 1900s: Pierre Janet and Alfred Binet.

Historical and Social Background

While industrialization did not take place as rapidly in France as in Great Britain, nor lead to such dramatic change or acute social crisis, France was still one of the leading nations in the Industrial Revolution. A rich middle class and a poor working class emerged, and after France's defeat in the Franco-Prussian War of 1870–1871, a right and a left formed in French politics. Since both groups consisted of many factions, however, there was little stability. From the 1830s, France had embarked on an expansive and aggressive colonial policy and was also engaged in wars in Europe. Rivalry arose between France and Germany, and between France and Great Britain. These fostered a strong nationalism and, as happened in Great Britain, racism emerged.

The French University and Educational System

The organization of French science can also shed some light on the development of French psychology. In the seventeenth and eighteenth centuries, the European universities functioned mainly as educational institutions for the privileged. They were not centers of intellectual life, as they had been in the Middle Ages. Scientific research and intellectual discussions frequently took place at particular institutions and academies.

Besides the French Academy of Science, the Collège de France, established in 1530, was also an important institution. Here, the most outstanding scientists in France lectured, but they usually carried out their research at other institutions. Another important institution was the École Normale Supérieure, established in 1794. This was an institution for the education of university teachers, politicians, bureaucrats, and intellectuals, which continues to train a great number of French scientists and prominent intellectuals. The École Normale Supérieure did not give training in empirical research. Therefore, students interested in this pursuit needed to go to the University of Paris or other institutions.

The universities were done away with during the French Revolution, and, under Napoleon, the higher educational system was reorganized. Universities were administered centrally from Paris by the University of France, which was in charge of the entire French educational system. This system, which lasted until the end of the nineteenth century, left the staff with less freedom and the students with fewer opportunities to choose their fields of study than in the German and American universities.

Politics, Philosophy, and Psychology

The conflicts in France's internal politics are, as Jacqueline Carroy and Régine Plas (1993) have said, reflected in its philosophy and psychology. The leaders of the French Revolution were inspired by the ideas of the Enlightenment and also often by materialist philosophy as it had been shaped by British empiricism. Many regarded materialistically oriented philosophy as a threat to the social order established after the Napoleonic Wars, and this probably contributed to the strongly idealistic character of the dominant philosophy. Body–mind dualism was accentuated, and the idea of a unitary self that was responsible for its actions by virtue of the will was stressed. When Auguste Comte denied that the introspective study of psychology could be made an empirical science, he probably had in mind the spiritualist philosophy dominating French intellectual life in the period after the Napoleonic Wars.

The Study of Hypnosis

Even as modern psychological researchers struggle to gain a deeper understanding of the nature of hypnosis, its study has produced knowledge that may be of fundamental importance in understanding basic psychological processes. The history of this endeavor reveals how difficult it often is to conceive of psychological problems so that they can be made the subject of fruitful empirical research.

Until the end of the eighteenth century, religious beliefs were a hindrance to understanding the nature of hypnosis. However, the greatest obstacle to progress after that seems to have been the patterns of thought dominant in science and the intellectual world. Consider how hypnosis may have appeared to those without knowledge of the relationship between body and mind. Should they consider it physical or mental? It had points in common with mental disorders, but very little was known about the latter. Was it like minor epileptic seizures, or neurotic phenomena? We can better understand the difficulty confronting researchers by looking at the healing efforts of Johannes Gassner, a minister who worked in Switzerland and Germany (Ellenberger, 1970).

Johannes Gassner (1729–1779)

People sought out Johannes Gassner for help in curing various ailments, including bodily pains, seizures, paralyses, and trembling. Gassner believed some of these ailments had their origin in physical conditions, whereas others were the result of possession by evil spirits. The idea that people could be possessed by the devil was still widespread in large parts of the population at this time. The last execution of a woman accused of being a witch in Europe took place in Switzerland as late as 1782.

According to a contemporary report, Gassner treated a woman suffering from strong convulsions in the following manner. He instructed her to kneel before him, inquired about her disease, and asked whether she would agree that everything he commanded should take place. Gassner then solemnly declared that if there were something supernatural in this disease, it should manifest itself in the name of Jesus. When the woman then had convulsions, Gassner regarded this as a manifestation of the operation of an evil spirit, of the woman's being possessed. He then demonstrated his power over the evil spirit by asking it to produce convulsions in different parts of the woman's body. Further, he produced in her manifestations of mental states, such as sorrow, stupidity, guilt, anger, and death. When he had ascertained that he had power over the evil spirit, he ordered it to leave her body. Many people Gassner treated reported feeling better afterwards.

Obviously, this condition resembles a hypnotic trance. By asking the person to agree to all he ordered to happen, Gassner established a mutual relationship, a *rapport*, between himself and the person. A long time was to pass before the importance of this relationship was understood, and it is still regarded as an essential element in all psychotherapy. Gassner also revealed an insight into the illness of his patients by first ascertaining that the symptoms manifested themselves in different parts of the body. If he did not succeed in this, he sent the person to a physician. In other words, he understood that the same symptoms could have different causes, either a bodily disease or an evil spirit that had entered the mind and exerted an effect upon it. One hundred years later, the distinction between these two types of causes was important in diagnosing what was then termed *hysteria* and is now called neurosis (as we see below).

Franz Anton Mesmer (1734–1815)

Gassner achieved great success with his treatment. However, the end of the eighteenth century was dominated by the ideas of the Enlightenment. Many doubted the mind could be possessed by the devil and wished to reject this idea. A committee appointed to investigate Gassner's activities gave Franz Anton Mesmer the opportunity to present his explanation of the ailments Gassner had treated.

Mesmer's explanation fit the prevailing patterns of thinking. The gravitational theory of a force acting at a distance was regarded as a decisive scientific advance, and progress had also been made in the study of electricity and magnetism. Mesmer explained Gassner's results by assuming the existence of a definite force, which he called *animal magnetism*. Everyone possesses this force, but in some people disturbances in it could occur, with unfortunate consequences. Other people could exert an effect on the animal magnetism of persons in whom disturbances had arisen. In accordance with his assumption that hypnosis represents a form of magnetism, Mesmer touched the persons he was treating with an iron bar. He believed he had discovered one of nature's deepest secrets, and a principle that would make it possible to heal all forms of disease. At the end of the eighteenth century, he traveled to Paris where he began a treatment based on his theory of animal magnetism.

Beliefs Concerning Hypnosis Within Science

Like Gassner, Mesmer initially had great success. His theory of animal magnetism spread rapidly, and many began practicing as "magnetizers." Yet, after some time, skepticism grew concerning his practice, called Mesmerism, and a committee was appointed to examine it.

The committee rejected the idea of animal magnetism as empty speculation. Its evaluation of Mesmer's idea discredited not only his procedures for healing mental disorders, but also the study of the phenomena involved. Now it was no longer acceptable within established science to be interested in hypnosis. Scientists could even ruin their careers if they practiced and studied it. Still, outside established science, many demonstrated hypnotic phenomena and used hypnosis in the treatment of various types of ailments, and some made progress in understanding the phenomenon. One of Mesmer's adherents believed the hypnotic state had features in common with somnambulism (sleepwalking). The opinion spread that hypnosis was a form of sleep. (The word "hypnosis," Greek for *sleep*, was used for the first time by an English physician in the 1840s.) This added knowledge of hypnotic phenomena did not enter the scientific world, however, and it had largely been forgotten when science accepted the study of hypnosis in the 1880s.

An address on hypnosis given by Jean-Martin Charcot in the French Academy of Science in 1882 attracted great attention and led to its acceptance for scientific study. Charcot's views, however, were wrong on certain essential points. He believed hysterical disturbances to be the result of a specific disease of the nervous system and thought it followed that only persons having this disease could be hypnotized. In the latter half of the nineteenth century, there was a strong tendency within psychiatry to regard mental disorders as a result of damage to, or diseases of, the nervous system, and this was probably the reason hypnosis was found worthy of scientific study at this time.

Thus, over the course of one hundred years, hypnosis had successively been explained as a result of possession by the devil, a disorder of animal magnetism, and a disease of the nervous system. These diverse explanations, all incorrect, demonstrate the role that prevailing patterns of thought can play in attempts to explain a phenomenon subjected to scientific study.

Interest in Abnormal Mental States

Early French psychiatrists took a great interest in the different mental states found in their patients and gave descriptions of them. According to Ellenberger (1970), the following four were frequently referred to: *somnambulism, lethargy, catalepsy*, and *multiple personality*. Incidents of somnambulism had been described earlier; in Shakespeare's well-known depiction, Lady Macbeth, sleepwalking, reveals her guilt in the murder of the king. In the nineteenth century, many writers described unusual acts that revealed deep and sometimes unconscious wishes in the sleepwalker. Sleepwalkers seem unaware of what they are doing, and French psychiatrists called attention to the fact that the movements performed seem to be mechanical and automatic.

In the state called lethargy, the patient appears to be in a deep sleep not accompanied by physical movements. During catalepsy the patient appears out of touch with the surrounding world, stiffened in a fixed posture like a wax figure. Like sleepwalkers, such patients seem to function as automatons.

In the fourth disorder, multiple personality, patients behave as if they possess two or even several different personalities, each of which manifests itself through specific forms of behavior. While inhabiting the separate personalities, such patients exhibit different memories, values, and names, and might even speak different languages, without being aware of one or more of their other personalities. Of course, it is difficult to define the concept "personality" in such a way that we can identify two or more in the same person. Nevertheless, many modern psychiatrists and clinical psychologists hold that multiple personalities do exist. We can easily understand that this problem occupied French psychiatrists; its study led directly to the question of whether our self constitutes a unit.

Hysteria and Neurosis

A psychiatric disorder attracting much attention at the end of the nineteenth century was hysteria. Fits of hysteria had been known from antiquity, when they were believed to occur only in women as the womb moved in the body, "hysteria" being derived from the Greek word for *womb*. Towards the end of the nineteenth century, disagreement arose as to whether hysteria could also occur in men, but it continued to be seen as mainly a disorder of women.

Hysteria could manifest itself in one or more ways: as convulsions, trembling, paralysis, and insensitivity to pain in particular parts of the body. Observations suggested it to be accompanied by lethargy, catalepsy, somnambulism, hallucinations, and ecstasy. Sometimes multiple personalities could also appear.

As early as 1859, the French medical doctor Paul Briquet published a systematic treatment of hysteria. He had studied a great number of patients over a period of ten years and had described symptoms as well as different forms of treatment. Further, he had examined conditions he believed might cause hysteria and claimed it had a basis in a disturbance of the central nervous system; for this reason, he called it *neurosis* (a term used earlier for disorders believed to originate in neurophysiological dysfunction).

To explain how the disorder arose, Briquet also called attention to psychological conditions, such as strong emotions, deep sorrow, family conflict, and disappointment in love. He opposed the widespread opinion that the roots of family and romantic conflicts are to be found in sexual disorders, and noted that neurosis appears to be more common among prostitutes than among nuns.

Gradually, the term *neurosis* came to be used by clinicians, who believed it could originate exclusively in psychological relationships. In the *ICD-10* and *DSM-V*, what used to be called hysteria is now designated partly as somatoform disorders and partly as conversion disorders.

Jean-Martin Charcot (1835–1893)

When Jean-Martin Charcot gave his speech on hypnosis to the French Academy of Science in 1882, he was breaking new ground in neurology and was regarded as one of the greatest scientists in France. In 1862, he had been appointed chief physician of one of the wards of La Salpêtrière. He reorganized his ward and divided it into units for treatment, research, and instruction, and he also found space for rooms and laboratories where different types of medical examinations could be undertaken. Charcot's lectures were famous. They were audited not only by his coworkers, assistants, and students but also by prominent guests such as distinguished writers. Privately, he also associated with artists, politicians, and heads of state. Charcot had the power and prestige to have hypnosis accepted as a scientific study, and an intense interest in the topic emerged in the 1880s and 1890s.

As an intern at La Salpêtrière, Charcot had realized that the hospital offered an unusual opportunity to study rare and unknown diseases, and, returning to it as director of a ward, he carried out research that gave him a reputation as the leading neurologist in the world. He was trained as an anatomy pathologist and maintained that the psychiatric disorders he studied had a basis in the nervous system. However, he gradually came to emphasize the role played by psychological factors in neurological and psychiatric abnormalities. This emphasis seems mainly to have been the result of his speculations on the nature of hysteria, which increasingly concerned him during his scientific career.

We saw above that Charcot used hypnosis in his studies of hysteria and had come to believe, incorrectly, that only hysterical individuals could be hypnotized. He also believed that a hypnotized person passes successively through the states of lethargy, catalepsy, and somnambulism. This has also been proved incorrect.

Below, I shall turn to criticisms raised by Hippolyte Bernheim, but first I shall deal with Charcot's attempt at distinguishing between symptoms found in hysteria and symptoms resulting from definite damage to the brain. According to Ellenberger, he had previously shown that a distinction could be made between epileptic and hysterical convulsions, and between paralysis due to brain damage and paralysis found in hysteria. Charcot believed paralysis could be caused by a psychological factor. To demonstrate this, he showed that by means of hypnosis he could produce paralysis in a subject, and further that the paralysis produced could be removed by instructions given during the hypnotic trance. He also used the same procedure to show that other symptoms found in hysteria could be due to psychological factors.

An important point in Charcot's account of paralysis was that he believed a strong psychological shock, a *traumatic experience*, could produce a state analogous to that produced by hypnosis. In this state, people could give themselves an instruction that had the same effect as the hypnotist's. This point became central in Pierre Janet's thinking, and I shall return to it.

Apparently, Charcot strongly believed that ideas produced by thinking and the imagination play a major role in the formation of mental disorders and even bodily changes. The idea that subjective representations could produce mental disorders became central in Freud's view of neurosis in the mid-1890s, and, in a somewhat different version, they are central to modern cognitive therapy.

Hippolyte Bernheim (1849–1919): Criticism of Charcot

In the countryside surrounding Nancy, the village physician Auguste Liébeault practiced the art of the old magnetizers and had great success with the hypnotic technique. After visiting him, an intern at the university clinic at Nancy, Hippolyte Bernheim, was convinced many of the effects were real, and he began practicing hypnosis as part of the treatment for many of his own patients. He wrote a book on hypnosis in 1884, and a comprehensive textbook in 1886 on the therapy he had gradually developed. The latter was translated into English in 1897.

Bernheim disagreed with Charcot that only persons suffering from hysteria could be hypnotized. The hypnotic state was a result of *suggestion*, he believed, and all people were to a greater or a lesser degree suggestible. He also challenged the description Charcot had given of the course of hypnosis. Bernheim gradually began to use suggestion without having first hypnotized his patients and referred to his method as psychotherapy. Around the turn of the century, he was considered Europe's leading psychotherapist, with adherents in many countries, including Bekhterev in Russia (Chapter 8).

From the 1880s until Charcot's death, a bitter struggle was fought between the centers in Paris and Nancy. Gradually, it was realized that Bernheim was correct on almost all points. We can only wonder how Charcot, who was such an excellent observer and so accurate in his descriptions of diseases, could give such a fallacious description of hypnosis. Several reasons have been given. The most important one was that perhaps Charcot did not understand that a complicated interaction takes place between the person hypnotized and the hypnotist, and that in this situation the hypnotized will comply with the wishes of the hypnotist and behave in agreement with the latter's expectations. Charcot also discussed his patients' diseases in their presence, and this, of course, could have contributed to making the patients even more attentive to what he expected from them. They may have learned to play a particular role because the hypnotic session was repeated a number of times; some of his assistants may even have rehearsed with some of the patients Charcot used for his demonstrations the behavior he described as typical of the course of hypnosis. It also has been claimed that at least in his later years he did not visit his ward.

As Charcot's errors became known, his standing greatly declined. He was a man with many enemies, and at the time of his death his reputation had been ruined. It was forgotten that he had accomplished groundbreaking work in neurology and set a standard for the organization of hospital wards. Even though his studies of hysteria and hypnosis were defective, they called attention to the fact that behavior and cognitive impairments resulting from damage to specific parts of the brain could also be produced by hysteria. While his claims about the usefulness of hypnosis in exploring and treating hysteria were highly exaggerated, he called attention to the usefulness of the method in psychology and psychiatry.

Positivist Attitudes to Psychology

Around the mid-nineteenth century, several authors began to react strongly to the idealist philosophy of the early 1800s. In 1870, two books appeared that advocated pronounced positivist ideas. *La psychologie anglaise contemporaine: l'école expérimentale* was written by Théodule-Armand Ribot, and *De l'intelligence* by Hippolyte Taine. The two authors were educated at the École Normale Supérieure, and both greatly influenced French psychology.

Théodule-Armand Ribot (1839–1916)

Ribot was a great admirer of Herbert Spencer's philosophy and gave an account of this as well as of the psychological thinking of J. S. Mill. His book was published before Darwin's monograph on the expression of emotions and before the beginning of British comparative psychology. Hence, it did not report on British empiricist psychology, which appeared at the end of the nineteenth century.

Spencer's thinking and John Hughlings Jackson's neurological investigations could, Ribot thought, provide a foundation for scientific psychology. A study of psychological disorders could illuminate normal human psychological functions. In other words, the normal must be understood through a study of the abnormal. In the 1880s, Ribot wrote three widely read books based on this view. The first dealt with what he called diseases affecting memory, the second with diseases of the personality, and the third with diseases relating to the will.

In his *Origins of Neuroscience*, Stanley Finger (1994) called attention to Ribot's contributions to the study of dementia. Jackson had argued that the psychological functions acquired latest are the first to degenerate. Inspired by him, Ribot pointed out that when memory declines in dementia, the latest acquired memories are lost first, more complex memories disappear before simpler ones, experiences having a basis in the will are lost before reflexive and automatic acts, and more organized acts are lost before least organized acts. Whereas biological evolution progresses from the simple to the more complex, the decline in memory progresses from the more complex to the simple. Finger (1994, pp. 365–366) shows that in 1881 Ribot had already distinguished between what we now call declarative and procedural memory – that is, between memory of factual knowledge and memory of skills and behavior.

In line with his evolutionary perspective, Ribot held that scientific psychology must be based on the study of the development of children, and on a comparison of individuals in European societies with individuals in what he regarded as more primitive societies. The view that individuals in cultures other than European functioned on a simpler, more primitive level was widespread in psychological thinking at the end of the nineteenth century and the beginning of the twentieth. Galton believed this too (Chapter 6).

Hippolyte Taine (1828–1893)

When Hippolyte Taine wrote *De l'intelligence*, he was already famous for a book on English poetry that had a great impact on the development of French naturalistic poetry. Taine took an extreme positivist view of science, emphasizing that psychology first and foremost requires accurate descriptions of psychological phenomena. He contributed to scientific psychology by describing the linguistic development of one of his children, inspiring Darwin to publish his observations on the development of his young son (Chapter 6).

Like Ribot, Taine thought the normal could be understood through a study of the pathological. However, as Carroy and Plas have argued, Taine's orientation to psychology differed substantially from Ribot's. Taine wanted to illuminate everyday psychological activities by a study of unusual psychological phenomena and mental states, which, he claimed, could be regarded as magnifications of everyday psychological phenomena; a knowledge of these provided the psychologist with an instrument comparable to a microscope or a telescope. In addition to investigations of the linguistic development of children, and of dreams, hallucinations, achievements of poets and artists, mental disturbances, somnambulism, hypnosis, and mediums used in séances, Taine thought psychological study also ought to be included.

In connection with séances, I shall note that spiritualism seems to have arisen in the United States at the end of the 1840s and spread rapidly to Europe. Apart from the supernatural aspect, it raised several interesting psychological questions, as Taine remarked. Mediums – those supposed to have the capacity of mediating between spirits of the deceased and the participants in the séance – frequently produced reports that appeared extraordinary from a psychological viewpoint, including experiences to which they had no access when they were not in the trance. As Taine noted, a split or doubling of consciousness appeared to occur. The study of phenomena related to spiritualism led to several investigations, and, by 1882, an association for so-called *psychical research* was established in Great Britain. Study was gradually extended to include extrasensory perception and clairvoyance. Several outstanding psychologists, among them Pierre Janet,

William James, and Carl Jung, were fascinated by *psychical phenomena*, known today as *parapsychology*.

Taine's book *De l'intelligence* was a great success; between 1870 and 1940, it appeared in 13 editions. In 1875, Taine began the publication of another book that also influenced psychology. He had been shocked by the cruel acts of the crowds during the Paris Commune in 1870 and during the French Revolution. In a comprehensive work on the origin of modern France (*Origines de la France contemporaine*), Taine claimed that when certain conditions are present in crowds whose members have common interest and aims, human judgment declines and reactions become more primitive.

At the end of the nineteenth century, researchers speculated that members of a crowd behave as if hypnotized, with the leader acting as the hypnotizer. Hypnotic phenomena, as we shall see later in this chapter, were thought to be related to unconscious thoughts and impulses, and it was thought that the leader appealed to these unconscious processes. Hypnosis had also been related to ideas on suggestibility, and members of a crowd were thought to be more suggestible than active people under everyday conditions. Interest in the thinking and behavior of members of a crowd arose out of the great mass movements stemming from the organization of labor unions at the end of the nineteenth century, and was further strengthened by the growth of fascist and communist movements, in which the leader was given almost unlimited power.

In 1895, a book by Gustave Le Bon on the psychology of crowds, *Psychologie des foules*, appeared and was widely read. The book raised questions about the formation of attitudes, the way different types of leadership affect the individuals in a group, and what made members of a large group suggestible, obedient, and conforming. These questions interested the German psychologists who emigrated to the United States to escape Nazism, and who carried out extensive empirical, social psychological investigations. At the end of the 1960s, comprehensive social psychological studies were undertaken about the way in which individuals are affected when they enter a group and lose their awareness of themselves as individuals. The effect is frequently referred to as *deindividuation*.

Pierre Janet (1859–1947)

Charcot's work on hysteria and neurosis was continued by Pierre Janet, who, from the mid-1880s, began systematic studies of cases of hysteria by means of hypnosis. The results of Janet's studies were published in a doctoral thesis in 1889 that instantly became famous and appeared in ten editions during the next forty years. However, after World War I, interest in his ideas decreased dramatically, and at his death in 1947, few psychologists regarded him as a central figure in the history of psychology. Even in France, his work was overshadowed by Freud's. Yet, in the 1960s and 1970s, interest in Janet's idea of a *divided consciousness* was revived, and when his work is more thoroughly studied by modern psychologists, other important insights may yet be revealed. Ellenberger has given a detailed exposition of Janet's life and work, and Régine Plas (1994) has placed his work in a historical context.

A Brief Biography

Janet, who was born in Paris, excelled as a student in high school and was admitted to the École Normale Supérieure, where he passed his examinations in philosophy in 1882, at the same time as Émile Durkheim (1858–1917). At this elitist school, Janet established a lifelong friendship with Henri Bergson (1858–1941), who some years later was regarded as one of the most prominent philosophers in France. Having passed his examinations at the École Normale Supérieure, Janet worked as a high-school teacher of philosophy in Le Havre and carried out the work required for his doctoral thesis referred to above. When he had finished his study of philosophy, he began the study of medicine and obtained a laboratory in Charcot's ward at La Salpêtrière. Three years later, he passed his medical examinations and won the right to practice psychotherapy.

In 1902, Janet succeeded Ribot in the prestigious position of professor of psychology at the Collège de France. In his *Principles of Psychology* (1890/1950), William James had already discussed Janet's ideas, and Janet was twice invited to universities and research institutions in the United States. Throughout his life he was a hard worker, wrote numerous articles and books, and had an extensive private practice as a psychotherapist. In 1894, he married and settled in one of the most fashionable parts of Paris. At an international medical conference in 1913, he clashed with Jung on some questions about psychoanalysis and later tried in vain to meet Freud when he visited Vienna.

Among Janet's extensive writings, the following are notable: *L'automatisme psychologique: Essai de psychologie expérimentale sur les formes intérieures de l'activité humaine* (his doctoral thesis, 1889); *Les névroses* (1909); *Les médications psychologiques* (1919); and *De l'angoisse à l'extase* (1926). Janet presented the main features of his psychology in an article, "La psychologie de la conduite" in the *Encyclopédie française* (VII, 1938). His autobiography was published in English in 1930.

A Link Between Wundt and Freud

Many nineteenth-century psychiatrists and authors were fascinated by the idea that we are sometimes unaware of the motives for our actions, even if those actions are directed towards specific goals; unconscious processes sometimes seem to direct us. Janet was one of the first to explore such processes and was thus a forerunner of Freud and the psychoanalysts. However, whereas Freud made a break with the earlier conception of psychology as the study of consciousness and started with assumptions about unconscious processes, Janet was strongly anchored in the earlier psychology of consciousness. He forms a link between Wundt and Freud. This may sound a little strange because Wundt regarded all unconscious processes as being of a physiological nature. However, like Wundt, Janet thought consciousness is organized in a given moment through apperception. That may give us a better understanding of the thinking of Wundt, Janet, and Freud, and for this reason, I shall deal a little more specifically with this point in respect to Wundt and Janet. They both regarded mental and physiological processes as parallel and believed mental events constitute a separate area, existing independently of physiology. Janet attached great importance to the behavioral component of our actions and even developed a behavioristically oriented psychology. Still, I think it is correct to say that he did not succeed in accounting for psychological processes as resulting from behavioral adjustment. Therefore, his thinking was almost exclusively restricted to what he regarded as the domain of mental events. In his famous thesis, he wanted to give an account of mental life, starting from simple forms of actions.

Automatism as Element, and Hypnosis as Method

I have mentioned French psychiatry's interest in somnambulism and activities that seem to take place automatically without awareness and conscious control. Janet believed these activities represent simpler forms of human behavior, which he called *automatisms*, and that a study of them would illuminate normal behavior. He felt that in carrying out such activities we are aware of them to some degree, but that they are little influenced by consciousness. He characterized them as *subconscious*, a term he introduced. Janet regarded automatisms as making up elements of consciousness. They occur spontaneously; that is, they are not stereotyped by repetition or produced by external stimuli, though they are in some way governed by consciousness.

In the normal human being, automatisms are organized into a unitary mental state. This organization occurs more or less spontaneously, but in order for the individual to function normally, consciousness must continuously be organized into a unit, to be adaptive to the situations and tasks confronting the individual. Directly referring to Wundt's concept of apperception, Janet held that consciousness could be regarded as a field in which the parts, the automatisms, are organized into a unity. In a sense, then, his psychology of consciousness has the same origin as Wundt's.

Janet considered himself not only a psychiatrist, but also a psychologist who wanted to shed light on normal mental life by means of the study of mental disorders. This, he thought, he could accomplish by means of hypnosis. Charcot had attempted to produce hysterical symptoms in his hysterical patients. Janet followed this procedure.

He assumed different types of automatisms are involved in mental disorders and believed he could study these mechanisms in his patients when hypnotized and instructed to exhibit the symptoms associated with their mental disorders. It is easy to understand that many contemporary psychiatrists, psychologists, and philosophers were fascinated by Janet's project. However, it is also easy to see why many were skeptical of a project of this nature. It was difficult to ascertain that his observations and descriptions of the patients' disorders were accurate, and to know more concretely what happened during the hypnotic session. Janet had made a thorough study of the history of hypnosis and used the technique more critically than Charcot. Still, like his predecessor, he believed that unless people suffer from hysteria, they cannot be brought into a hypnotic trance. He rejected Bernheim's view of hypnosis as resulting from suggestibility, and thus he was vulnerable to the same criticism as Charcot.

Automatisms, Mental Disorders, and the Unconscious

As I have mentioned, Janet based his account of mental disorders on a model, according to which consciousness represents a field that is more or less spontaneously organized. To explain the operations of the automatisms in a person, he assumed the person is unable to organize the field as a totality. As a consequence, some automatisms are left outside the mental field, and thus outside the person's control. They are split off from the field of consciousness; a dissociation has taken place. Being dissociated, the automatisms could manifest themselves unconsciously as different types of pathological symptoms; they might even cause a split of the personality.

In his further account of dissociation, Janet introduced the idea that mental life demands *mental energy*. For various reasons, he believed mental energy is sometimes not present in sufficient quantities, and this results in an incomplete organization of the field of consciousness. Janet used the expression "psychological poverty." Helmholtz's formulations of the concept of energy came to occupy a central position in natural science in the latter half of the nineteenth century, and many psychological thinkers used it in their explanations. In Chapter 7, we noted that McDougall made use of the concept in his view of instincts, and in the next chapter, we shall see that Freud made it central in his ideas of the psyche.

Admittedly, it is not easy to see what is meant by a field of consciousness and by control of remembered material. Nevertheless, Janet may have been able to draw attention to clinical phenomena modern psychologists still try to understand. In his account of mental disorders, he also made use of Charcot's proposal that, as a result of having had strong traumatic experiences, his patients developed ideas that affected their adaptation to reality. Janet called these *idées fixes*. Ideas of this kind might manifest themselves in phobias and compulsions, as well as in other ways. They could be changed or removed only with difficulty, and Janet devoted much effort to finding out how. Here he may have found a way to understand the mechanisms underlying certain types of mental disorders. Based on the ideas of a mental field, mental energy, and *idées fixes*, Janet undertook a classification and explanation of neuroses. Here, I shall simply mention that he believed neuroses are caused by genetic as well as psychological factors.

Starting from his ideas on the nature of neuroses, Janet gradually developed a comprehensive view of therapy. Even if he followed different procedures in his treatment of neuroses, the use of hypnosis remained an important tool. The idea of mental energy led him to emphasize the patient's need for sleep, rest, and recreation. Further, he thought many forms of social relationships could require disproportionately more energy or could lock up energy in a person. He constructed an extensive psychological system in which, like Ribot, Spencer, and Jackson, he regarded consciousness as being built up hierarchically. He postulated five levels in the hierarchy. Jackson may also have convinced him that conscious processes are always accompanied by bodily movements. In accordance with this belief, Janet developed a behavioristically oriented psychology.

In contrast to Charcot, Janet believed the hypnotist and the hypnotized mutually affect each other. Like magnetizers before him, he had noted that when a person is repeatedly hypnotized by the same hypnotist, unusual relationships might arise, sometimes characterized by intense love, supernatural fear, admiration, or jealousy. While some accepted the hypnotist's power, others would rebel. Janet believed similar relationships arise between the psychotherapist and his patients and devoted much attention to clarifying these.

An Evaluation of Janet's Contributions

Janet had wide interests in philosophy, medicine, and psychology, and discussed a variety of problems in his long career. Of his many ideas, only dissociation seems to have currency in modern psychology. Ernest Hilgard (1977) revived it, and John Kihlstrom (1999) stated that it offers a different perspective on the views of modern cognitive psychologists studying what is perhaps best referred to as "nonconscious processes." As we saw, Janet coined the term "subconscious." The concept of mental energy occupied a central position in his treatment of psychological problems. As he used it, it was probably too diffuse to be of value in scientific empirical research. However, given a more precise meaning, it may again be of interest to psychologists.

Ellenberger has offered several reasons why Janet's reputation declined so dramatically at the beginning of the twentieth century. Janet was identified with Charcot and was damaged by the criticism of the latter's work on hysteria and hypnosis. Further, his work was overshadowed by Freud's. As we shall see, Freud placed more emphasis on the emotions, and many clinical psychologists would probably agree with McDougall (1926) that Janet gave too little weight to the role played by emotional conflicts in his account of mental disorders. On the other hand, Janet attributed great importance to traumatic experiences. Further, he called attention to the fact that stress and conflicts arise in human life when decisions have to be made in the choice of education, employment, partner, or marriage. The role played by decision making in the development of personality was later brought into focus in both existential philosophy and humanistic psychology, during and after World War II.

In the next chapter, we shall see that Joseph Breuer developed a view of certain types of neuroses highly similar to Janet's, and this seems to have been the starting point for psychoanalysis.

Alfred Binet (1857–1911)

Alfred Binet became known for the intelligence test he constructed in cooperation with a colleague, but, as Plas has emphasized, he was a clinical and developmental psychologist, with a keen interest in problems of thinking. When Binet – and not Galton – succeeded in constructing a useful intelligence test, his experience as a student of thinking in children and adults had probably given him a better understanding than Galton's of the nature of cognitive processes.

Binet was born and grew up in Nice. After finishing high school in Paris, he studied various subjects at the Sorbonne without passing the final examination. This may have been unfortunate for his university career. Janet, not Binet, was appointed a professor at the Collège de France, and Binet also failed to obtain the chair in psychology established at the Sorbonne. In 1894, he became the director of the psychological laboratory established at the Sorbonne five years earlier. In collaboration with a colleague, he founded the journal *L'Année psychologique*.

The Psychology of Thinking

Binet had broad interests and was a versatile researcher, doing work on problems of multiple personalities and sexual deviations. The psychology of thinking was one of his main interests, and in the later part of his career, he was particularly interested in thinking and intelligence in children. Binet profited from his empirical research. To begin with, as Plas has remarked, he based his study of thinking on the traditional view that it is carried out by means of images, but gradually he noticed that images are not always present, and he began to doubt the role attributed to them. Thus, his work anticipated that of the Würzburg school.

Binet based his studies of thinking on introspection but did not limit its use to simple reports. Like Oswald Külpe, he thought the subjects of his research should be allowed to give a more complete description of their experiences. Still, a decisive point in his procedure was that the subjects should give their reports as answers to questions or as attempts to solve definite tasks. This procedure he applied in his studies of thinking in his two daughters. He regarded his procedure as an experimental method and termed the studies of his daughters experimental studies. When Piaget later made use of this method, he was probably influenced by Binet.

Individual Differences

Binet believed the more fundamental individual differences in thinking would not manifest themselves unless he used rather complex tasks, and not the simple ones used by Galton and his American student James Cattell. In 1895, Binet and his coworker Victor Henri presented in detail their ideas on how individual differences could be most profitably studied. The two Frenchmen criticized the tests constructed by Emil Kraepelin for taking too much time and for boring the subjects. A useful test should not exceed an hour. Binet's opinion of how tests, and particularly intelligence tests, should be constructed was a result of extensive studies that had led him to break with traditional practice and also with his own earlier thinking.

Binet and Henri made efforts to identify more complicated faculties and skills that would reveal individual differences. They proposed and examined the following types: memory, the ability to form mental images, imagination, attention, comprehension, suggestibility, aesthetic feeling, moral evaluation, muscular and voluntary strength, motor skills, and visual estimates. In their discussion of the study of memory, they pointed out that memory should not be conceived of as a single faculty; there were many types of memory. They criticized Kraepelin for having overlooked this. In their studies of the formation of images, they elaborated the tests Galton had developed. Binet and

Henri regarded suggestibility as a tendency manifesting itself, on the one hand, in the effect a person has on other individuals and, on the other hand, in the tendency a person has to obey others. In line with this view, they discussed important relationships of a social psychological nature. They also proposed to assess moral evaluations by having children react to pictures, including photos, that would produce strong emotions such as an image of a beheading. On this point, they anticipated the later Thematic Apperception Test (TAT). Their proposal for the measurement of muscular strength did not attempt what Galton had done when he measured the strength of hand pressure. Instead, they tried to develop a test measuring voluntary strength in muscular exertion.

Many of Binet's and Henri's proposals were purely speculative, but several proposals were based on empirical research. Familiarity with empirical, scientific, psychological studies had, in certain respects, undoubtedly matured their views. Psychology had begun to obtain a professional, inner development.

The Development of Intelligence Tests

In 1899, Binet had joined an association to promote the scientific study of children. Having been the director of this association for some years, he was well prepared when, in 1904, he and his coworker Theodore Simon were appointed to a committee to examine problems in the instruction of children with intellectual and developmental disabilities. In conjunction with the views Binet had presented in the article he wrote with Henri in 1896, he and Simon constructed their first intelligence test, meant to distinguish between children functioning normally and children displaying disabilities. In 1908, they published a modified form of this test as a general test of children's intelligence, which eventually became the model for most later types of intelligence tests.

The construction of the test was based on the idea that the average number of tasks children of a given age between three and thirteen could solve, forms steps or levels on a scale that indicates the child's degree of intelligence. The level was usually determined by presenting five tasks of the same type, of which 75 percent would be solved by children of a given age. The level at which a child succeeds in solving all the tasks, or all the tasks with one exception, fixed the child's position on the scale, later referred to as *mental age*. Some years later, another psychologist proposed that an appropriate expression of a child's performance could be obtained by dividing mental age by chronological age and then multiplying the result by 100. The figure obtained was called the *intelligence quotient*, or *IQ*.

The most important and difficult challenge was to find tasks appropriate for the test. Binet and Simon constructed a number of tasks but also employed tasks used in earlier tests or as part of clinical examinations. Several were verbal and aimed at testing children's understanding of words, their capacity for naming things, and their ability to repeat and define words. The verbal part could be made more or less difficult, and in this way the test constructors could use tasks that resemble each other regardless of the child's age. Other types of tasks that made it possible to increase the degree of difficulty were to ask the child to repeat series of numbers, to count, and to name the days of the week, the months of the year, and the different parts of the day (morning and evening). Binet and Simon also made use of pictures to be described in different ways, figures to be copied, objects to be arranged in order of weight, and puzzles.

What is Intelligence?

It was an extraordinary achievement to construct a test that could be administered in less than an hour to assess the intellectual level of a child. Binet and Simon's test became very popular and was translated into many languages. In the West, extensive as well as intensive testing of children's intelligence was undertaken during a period of almost fifty years. However, it was gradually shown that the usefulness of the test is limited; many instances were found when the test results of the individual child correlated poorly with his or her other intellectual performances. More importantly, it proved difficult to determine the meaning of the concept "intelligence." As we shall see in Chapter 11, the tests were refined by US and British psychologists, but in spite of much investigation, it has not proved possible to arrive at a relatively simple and acceptable definition of intelligence. Hence, it seems fair to say the attempt at quantifying intelligence had a fate similar to Fechner's effort to quantify perceptual experience; neither fulfilled initial expectations. This does not mean intelligence tests are without value, however. They often represent a useful supplement to clinical evaluation, and when a not-too-refined objective measure of intellectual function is needed, they are useful.

Claude Bernard (1813–1870)

Claude Bernard introduced ideas into physiology that, along with those of Johannes Müller and his students, contributed to the major breakthrough in physiology and medical research around the mid-nineteenth century. Bernard did not carry out psychological research, but one of his main ideas, that of an internal physiological environment, was introduced into psychology in the first half of the twentieth century. Bernard made clear that physiological processes could be seen as occurring in an internal environment, separated from the external world. A characteristic of this environment was equilibrium; for example, the temperature and the quantity of liquids and gases in the body are approximately constant. In the first half of the twentieth century, this idea led to a view of motivation as resulting from a deviation from equilibrium – that is, from a normal level called *homeostasis*. The American physiologist Walter Cannon used Bernard's thinking in his account of motivation, to which I shall return in Chapter 17.

Bernard (1865) also wrote a book about experiments that has become a classic. He had considerable experience as an experimentalist and had developed a far more thoughtful and considered attitude than J. S. Mill, who had presented his highly influential view twenty-two years before. In contrast to Mill, Bernard emphasized that the experiment is a means of testing hypotheses, and that hypotheses originate in attempts at systematizing existing knowledge within a definite scientific problem area. Hence, experiments have other important uses beyond providing reliable observations.

The Later Development of French Psychology

Unlike the case in Germany and the United States, empirical psychology in France did not achieve a strong position in the scientific life of the country. It is difficult to say why. A partial answer may be that psychology in France, as in Great Britain, was not introduced as an empirical research discipline at a greater number of universities. In contrast to Germany and the United States, science in France was strongly centralized, with Paris as the main center. This may have made it difficult for those with an interest in a new field to obtain a position in the scientific world. Psychology, as a study separate from philosophy, was first introduced in France in 1949.

10

Psychodynamic Psychology

Advances in the study of the brain at the end of the 1900s led to a new medical specialty, *neurology*, the study of diseases of, and damage to, the nervous system. This new specialty was closely associated with psychiatry, and the relationship between the functions of the brain and mental life was central in it.

Neurologists were doctors of the mind, and they gradually earned a reputation as scientists having the knowledge to treat mental disorders. Science, and not least medicine, had great prestige around 1900, and this contributed to great expectations of and confidence in neurologists. We should see the considerable fame attained first by Janet and Freud, and then by Jung and Adler, against this background. Until now, ideas about psychological problems had been governed by religious and moral traditions, but in the first half of the twentieth century, many sought a foundation in scientific knowledge. The new doctors of the mind filled a vacuum created by the weakening of religious and moral traditions. Thus, they not only solved people's specific problems; they also provided guidance for everyday living.

The new specialty was based to only a limited extent on firmly documented medical knowledge. Still, neurologists were more competent to treat and express opinions about mental disorders than people without their training. Through their practice, they also obtained information about the social background of their patients. In addition to their knowledge of the nervous system, therefore, they could claim to have clinical psychological experience. By systematizing this knowledge, they worked within a scientific tradition and were regarded as scientists.

The problems dealt with in the new medical specialty were largely psychological in nature, and many neurologists practiced what we would today regard as clinical psychology. Having only a slender basis in physiology and neurology, neurology was strongly influenced by cultural traditions and for this reason was practiced differently in different countries. It was also heavily influenced by the particular interests and personalities of the people giving it shape. We have seen how Pavlov and Bekhterev developed a Russian branch of neurology, and how Charcot, Ribot, and Janet formed another version in France. The most influential clinical psychology, based on his neurological practice, was that of Sigmund Freud.

In Vienna, there was another neurologist, Alfred Adler, and in nearby German-speaking Switzerland, a third, Carl Gustav Jung, who developed influential clinical psychologies. Along with their medical interests, Freud, Adler, and Jung also shared an interest in philosophy and a fascination with the ideas of human nature launched by the German philosophers Arthur Schopenhauer and Friedrich Nietzsche. These two philosophers gave a picture of humans as torn by conflicts resulting from unconscious, irrational forces. As Henri Ellenberger (1970) and Frank Sulloway (1979/1983) show, the similarities are so great between their ideas, which were widely discussed in the German-speaking world, and those of the three neurologists that it is reasonable to believe Freud, Adler, and Jung may have been influenced by their work. I therefore think it possible to regard Schopenhauer and Nietzsche as forerunners of dynamic clinical psychology, and after briefly describing life in Vienna (where Freud and Adler lived), I will present some of their ideas as an introduction to this chapter.

Adler and Jung cooperated for some years with Freud, but after having disagreed with him on certain issues, they left his group. Freud was the oldest of the three and probably influenced his younger colleagues more than they influenced him; historians have tended to regard Adler and Jung as followers who later opposed Freud and revised his work. As Ellenberger has argued, however, Adler and Jung were independent thinkers and established neurologists who had developed the beginning of their clinical psychologies before meeting Freud. By presenting Adler and Jung in that light, I hope to give a more nuanced picture of the clinical psychology arising in German-speaking countries at the beginning of the 1900s. Further, by relating the ideas of Freud, Adler, and Jung to those of Schopenhauer and Nietzsche, I hope to emphasize the close relationship dynamic psychology has to philosophy and culture.

Vienna During the Austro-Hungarian Empire

At the time of Freud, Vienna was the capital of a large and old empire. It had already been a center of trade for several hundred years when the rapid industrialization of the late

1800s increased its economic importance for central Europe. The city had a rich upper-middle class and a happy and relaxed atmosphere; it was renowned for its architecture, music, and theaters and was one of the world's leading medical centers. However, like the other European cities that became centers of rapid industrialization, Vienna also had a large, poor working class suffering from a scarcity of housing and a poorly developed public health service. The period leading up to World War I was characterized by deep political conflicts and much social unrest.

The Austro-Hungarian Empire contained several ethnic groups, and as nationalism increased during the 1800s, it grew difficult to keep the empire together. Emperor Franz Joseph, who governed from 1848 to 1916, was ultra-conservative and unwilling to carry out political and social reforms, and this reluctance ensured great instability. During his reign, the empire was engaged in several wars. These wars, the ethnic conflicts, and the poor progress in improving the general welfare led to despair and pessimism. After World War I, Vienna was a large capital in a small territory, peopled by German-speaking Austrians.

Allan Janik and Stephen Toulmin (1973) have noted, in the introduction to a book on Wittgenstein, that several of the intellectual movements arising in Vienna had in common a revolt against conventional and traditional points of view. This resistance is found in art, music, and literature; in philosophy; and not least in psychoanalysis. Janik and Toulmin regard the revolt of the intellectuals as a reaction against the authorities' tendency to cover up tensions and conflicts, and to cultivate traditional and conventional values. The intellectual climate of Vienna provided a fertile ground for Schopenhauer's and Nietzsche's picture of humans as incapable of adapting to reality and constantly misrepresenting it.

Freud, as well as Adler, brought the family structure into focus, so it is of interest to note that the family structure in contemporary Vienna was strongly patriarchal. As in the rest of Europe, conventions forbade women to have sexual relations before marriage or to work outside the home unless economic conditions necessitated this, and it was a widely accepted view that women need no higher education. While social conventions also demanded that men have no sexual activity outside marriage, it was not unusual for them to visit prostitutes. The social structure and conventional morality probably favored a preoccupation with problems relating to the effects of sexual temperance, and to speculations concerning psychological differences between women and men. Certainly, the Viennese debated sexual problems extensively.

Arthur Schopenhauer (1788–1860)

Arthur Schopenhauer's main work, *Die Welt as Wille und Vorstellung* (*The World as Will and Idea*), was published in 1819, but few took an interest in his thinking until the 1850s. In the decades following his death, his ideas became very popular, not least in Vienna.

Schopenhauer introduced new ideas on human motivation. Independently of, but in agreement with, the theory of evolution, he claimed that human thinking and actions are largely determined by instincts and drives. In line with Romantic philosophy from the beginning of the nineteenth century, he also denied the role attributed to rational thinking by the philosophers of the Enlightenment, and the mechanistic explanations that had been so central in Descartes's philosophy and in British empiricism. For him, the world is the result of a force having no other purpose than to uphold physical structures and biological forms of life. Because the force has no purpose, no deeper meaning can be attributed to existence. The force manifests itself in humans as a striving to preserve life and to reproduce. It finds expression in the will, but it is not a result of rational thinking and cannot be understood by introspective study of mental life. According to this metaphysical orientation, humans are governed by an irrational force. Schopenhauer emphasized that biological processes, particularly the sexual drive, affect thinking and actions. In this way of looking at matters, human motivation has important features in common with instinctive acts in animals.

The purposeless force underlying existence and upholding life leads, in Schopenhauer's opinion, to numerous conflicts in the individual's thinking and actions as well as in social life. Schopenhauer stressed that unconscious tendencies are frequently opposed to conscious thinking. The means of solving the conflicts that thus arise are, he believed, highly limited. In line with this conclusion, he had a pessimistic view of life. Further, Schopenhauer emphasized that the drives governing human mental life can lead to a repression of experiences associated with shame and humiliation. Thus, he postulated mental mechanisms that may lead to various forms of repression.

Friedrich Nietzsche (1844–1906)

Friedrich Nietzsche pursued Schopenhauer's idea that humans do not understand the forces underlying thinking and actions. He took as his starting point the idea that civilization has prevented human beings from thinking and acting according to their nature. As a consequence, sexuality and aggressive tendencies have been repressed or are expressed in a distorted manner, and human beings deceive not only others but also themselves. Nietzsche wanted to uncover what he regarded as humans' *real* motives. Contemporary authors, such as Dostoyevsky, Ibsen, and Strindberg, had explored motives they regarded as either hidden or given a distorted expression. The latter half of the 1800s was a period in which thinkers examined traditional human values in depth – and often rejected them. Nietzsche went beyond most of his contemporaries in this regard. Not only did he reject the Jewish and Christian religions and Western morality, but he also denied that it was possible to establish an objective science.

Seven years after Wundt had established his laboratory, Nietzsche (1886, 1967, p. 27) declared that "the whole of psychology has up to the present been stuck in moral prejudice and anxiety: it has not ventured to go in depth." To produce a valuable psychology, the researcher must struggle against an unconscious resistance in his or her own mind. We can regard this declaration as the guiding principle in Freudian psychoanalysis.

Nietzsche tried to trace the origin of the mentality of modern humans through cultural history. He believed individuals of the lower classes have developed a tendency not only to express their aggression against the ruling classes in a distorted manner, but also to direct their destructive reactions against themselves. As a consequence, self-contempt, self-hatred, helplessness, and a lack of self-confidence have developed. Further, as a result of being forced to suppress their true nature, human beings have stopped expressing their natural inclinations. This in turn has necessitated that they rely heavily on their thinking and on their ability to anticipate events and plan for the future. Hence, mental life has attained a disproportionately great significance. According to this view, rational thinking must be regarded as the result of weakness.

Nietzsche expressed himself in a brief but suggestive way, frequently in the form of aphorisms. His idea of repression was stated in a famous aphorism: "'I have done it,' says my memory. 'I cannot have done it,' says my pride and remains unyielding. Finally, my memory gives way" (*Jenseits von Gut und Böse* (*Beyond Good and Evil*, Aphorism 68)).

He was also interested in the nature of sleep and dreams and held that our dreams reveal our true nature. Further, he believed that earlier periods in human cultural history are revived in our dreams. Thus, a study of dreams could assist us in achieving a better understanding of earlier cultures. A modification of the idea that dreams express our true nature is found in Freud's interpretation of dreams, and the belief that early human history is preserved in our dreams was an important part of Jung's view of the unconscious.

Regarding the role childhood experiences could have for the development of personality, Nietzsche stressed that unresolved conflicts in relationships to parents lead to permanent inner suffering. A child could have its hardest fight with a bad and hypocritical father or a childish and angry mother and would never overcome the effects of these experiences (*Menschliches, Allzumenschliches* (*Human, All Too Human*)).

Nietzsche not only wanted to reveal how we conceal our true nature; he also appealed to his readers to bring their natural inclinations to expression in their thinking and actions. Humans should manifest a *will to power*. To act according to this guideline, we must not only express our natural strivings and emotions but also develop all our human abilities. For Nietzsche, God is dead, and we must find out for ourselves what can give life meaning. This message made him, along with Søren Kierkegaard (1813–1855) and Feodor Dostoyevsky (1821–1881), a forerunner of *existential philosophy*.

Schopenhauer had elaborated the idea that we can relieve our sufferings by cultivating art and the beautiful. Nietzsche urged that, in order to liberate themselves, human beings must fight against conventions and traditions suppressing their true nature. A heroic fight of this kind would produce what he called a *superman*. It is not easy to understand more concretely what he meant by this term. The Nazis appropriated his ideas for their ideology, though later research has shown they overlooked important aspects of his thinking. On the other hand, later interpreters have perhaps not given sufficient weight to the fact that Nietzsche failed to clearly state that his aim was not to encourage a brutal suppression of other people and a rejection of all previously accepted humanist ideas.

Sigmund Freud (1856–1939)

From the mid-1890s, Sigmund Freud began developing an approach to the study of psychology based on his clinical experience. He claimed to have worked out a procedure that was not only effective in treating mental disorders but also led him to discover a number of fundamental psychological mechanisms. His procedure, which he called *psychoanalysis*, was thus a means for treating people suffering from mental disorders as well as for carrying out scientific psychological investigations. Referring to the procedure and the discoveries he believed to have made, Freud claimed to have laid the foundation for a scientific psychology.

From the end of the 1800s until his death, Freud worked out a comprehensive psychological system in which he brought together ideas of mental disorders, unconscious processes, motivation, sexuality, child development, personality, evolutionary biology, and the history of civilization. Major ideas in his system were that our thinking and actions are the result of conflicts between unconscious irrational forces, that sexuality and aggression are prime motives, that sexual impulses and desires influence all of human mental life, that sexuality – which develops from infancy to adulthood – is at the root of all mental disorders, and that affects (the feelings of pleasure and pain) direct and regulate human life.

In the first two decades, psychoanalysis was strongly opposed by many European psychiatrists, according to Shorter (1997), mainly because it shifted the emphasis from the psychoses to the less grave mental disorders. After World War I, psychoanalysis exerted an increasing influence until German psychiatry was halted in its development by the Nazis' rise to power. US psychiatrists responded favorably to psychoanalysis at the beginning of the 1900s, and, according to Shorter (1997), it dominated their psychiatry in the years 1940–70. In the latter decades of the 1900s, its influence strongly declined.

Believing that human thinking and action are governed mainly by forces of which we are not aware, Freud concentrated on the study of what he regarded as unconscious processes and developed his psychology in opposition to the German psychology of consciousness. Further, because he did not believe his approach could benefit from the use of experiments and tests, his psychology evolved independently of the experimental psychology that had obtained a footing in many European and US universities at the beginning of the 1900s.

While experimental psychologists tended to be skeptical of the psychoanalytic approach because it was based on clinical procedures, some psychologists were eager to explore Freud's ideas through experiment. Already at the beginning of the 1900s, developmental psychologists were interested in psychoanalytic ideas, and as American personality psychology began to grow in the 1920s and 1930s, psychoanalysis had an impact on this emerging discipline. Further, when clinical psychology became a psychological discipline during and after World War II, many psychologists began practicing psychoanalysis. Interest in psychoanalytic ideas seems to have declined within psychology and psychiatry at about the same time.

In line with the plan of this book, I shall review Freud's work with the primary view of assessing his contributions to scientific, empirical psychology. I shall examine his concepts of the unconscious, drive (instinct), sexuality and sexual development, affects, the origin of mental disorders, anxiety, and the structure of mental life (id, ego, and superego). I shall also examine his procedure and review the framework in which he formulated his problems, but first I shall present a sketch of his life to help the reader understand the origin of his ideas.

A Sketch of Freud's Life

Freud was born in Freiburg in Moravia, which at the time was part of the Austro-Hungarian Empire. In 1860 his family moved to Vienna, where he grew up, went to school, and lived until he emigrated to Great Britain in 1938 to escape from the Nazis. His mother and his father, a merchant, were Jews who, according to Ellenberger (1970), adopted the way of life of the Viennese middle class.

Freud received excellent scientific training. In 1873, he left high school with top grades and entered the University of Vienna as a medical student. For five years during his studies, he was assistant to the professor of physiology, Ernst Brücke, and he was one of Johannes Müller's prominent students (Chapter 3). Freud received his medical degree, somewhat belatedly, in 1881. The reason he passed his medical examinations so late was probably that he engaged in many extracurricular studies. Among other things, he audited Brentano's lectures in philosophy for five terms.

After having obtained his medical degree, he held a poorly paid position as Brücke's teaching assistant for a year while he performed his own scientific studies in histology. Although he apparently wanted to continue his scientific studies at the university, he changed his plans and became an intern in the Viennese General Hospital, qualifying as *Privatdozent* (unsalaried private teacher) with a specialty in neurology in 1885. Brücke had a high opinion of the scientific work of his assistant, and Freud admired Brücke. Therefore, Freud probably changed his career plans because there was no vacant position in physiology coming up for a number of years. In 1885, on Brücke's recommendation, he received a traveling fellowship and went to Paris to visit Charcot's clinic for five months. After returning to Vienna in 1886, he married and began private practice as a neurologist.

While Freud was working in Brucke's laboratory, he formed a friendship with Josef Breuer, a distinguished Viennese neurologist who had developed a procedure, the *cathartic method*, for treating some of his patients suffering from hysteria. When Freud began his private practice, he used the method in the treatment of some of his own patients, and, in 1895, he joined Breuer in reporting on their use of the procedure in the book *Studien über Hysterie* (*Studies on Hysteria*). Among the cases they reported was that of

Anna O., which was to be widely cited in the neurological literature. In later years, Freud regarded the cathartic method as a forerunner of psychoanalysis, and I shall return to it in my review of Freud's therapeutic and scientific procedure.

Freud scholars have drawn attention to two events in his life that may have decisively affected his career as a psychological researcher. From the mid-1890s to about 1900, according to Jones (1953–1957, pp. 334 ff), Freud suffered a mental crisis characterized by great shifts in mood and fear of death, of open places, and of traveling. He also felt depressed after the death of his father in 1896. Probably in the hope of understanding his sufferings better, he began to analyze his dreams and apply to himself a method he had developed in the treatment of his patients. It was during the analysis of his own dreams that Freud claimed to have discovered the Oedipus complex, and his analysis of himself is now regarded as a seminal event in the history of psychoanalysis. At this time, a decisive shift occurred in his views on the cause of hysteria and neurotic disorders.

In 1896, Freud gave a lecture on the origin of hysteria to the Society of Psychiatrists and Neurologists in Vienna. He declared that his patients had been sexually abused as children, and this was the cause of their neuroses. The audience doubted the hypothesis, and the highly respected psychiatrist Richard von Krafft-Ebing called it a scientific fairy tale. About a year later, Freud abandoned this hypothesis, the so-called *seduction theory of hysteria*, and now held that the children had not been abused but had imagined the sexual events. Jones maintains that the shifts in Freud's opinion were a result of his self-analysis. This contention has been opposed by another psychoanalyst, Jeffrey Masson (1984), who, on the basis of comprehensive archival material, believed he could show that the cause of the shift should be sought in the very unfortunate treatment Freud and his friend Wilhelm Fliess had given to a young woman. However, both views are disputed by Malcolm Macmillan (1991). I shall not deal with this point but only emphasize that it is an essential feature of psychoanalysis to ascribe a decisive role in the development of abnormal personalities to fantasies, and only a minor role to material conditions such as poverty, disease, harsh punishment, failing care, sexual abuse, and lack of schooling.

Apart from the negative reactions of European psychiatrists early in the 1900s, Freud's work immediately gained recognition. He was appointed professor (*Professor extraordinarius*) in 1902. The same year, he began gathering around him a group of persons, mostly medical doctors, to discuss his ideas. This was the beginning of the organization of the psychoanalytic movement. In 1908, the Psychoanalytic Society in Vienna was established, and, in 1910, the International Psychoanalytic Association was founded. In 1909, Freud was invited to the celebration of the twentieth anniversary of the founding of Clark University in Massachusetts. After his participation in this event, psychoanalysis spread rapidly in the United States. Freud led the psychoanalytic movement in an authoritarian manner; those who disagreed with him on essential points had to leave it.

In addition to numerous articles, Freud wrote many books. I have already mentioned the one on hysteria written with Breuer in 1895. He regarded *The Interpretation of Dreams* (1900) as his main work. His other widely read books include *The Psychopathology of Everyday Life* (1904); *Three Essays on the Theory of Sexuality* (1905); *Totem and Taboo* (1912–1913); *Introductory Lectures on Psycho-Analysis* (1916–1917); *Beyond the Pleasure Principle* (1920); *The Ego and the Id* (1923); *The Future of an Illusion* (1927); *Civilization and Its Discontents* (1930); *New Introductory Lectures on Psycho-Analysis* (1933); and *Moses and Monotheism* (1939). An English-language edition of Freud's collected works has been published in twenty-three volumes.

Freud's Ideas of a Scientific Psychology and Procedure

Idea of a Scientific Psychology

When Freud began his psychological studies in the mid-1890s, he had been engaged in work in physiology and zoology, with a special interest in neurophysiology, for twenty years. Like Brücke and others of his teachers, he was profoundly influenced by the physicalist ideas that had been introduced into physiology about 1850. Freud wanted to extend these ideas to mental life and for some time worked intensely to find a foundation for psychology in neurophysiology. Being dissatisfied with the model he constructed, he never published the manuscript in which he had worked it out. Two of the manuscripts have been published posthumously, however, under the title *Project for a Scientific Psychology* (Freud, 1950).

As shown by Jean Laplanche and J.-B. Pontalis (1967) and accounted for in more detail by Sulloway (1979), although Freud gave up his attempt to find a foundation for psychology in neurophysiology, he continued to carry out his psychological thinking in terms of his physicalist ideas. Thus, he conceived of mental life as strictly determined by physical forces interacting dynamically with each other in a physical system. This view, which he named the *dynamic point of view*, was supplemented by the *economic point of view*. According to the latter, the processes making up mental life are regulated by an underlying mental energy. The distribution of this energy determines what happens within what Freud assumed to constitute a psychic system. The two points of view, as well as a third, the *topographic point of view*, which referred to the division of his postulated psychic system into an unconscious, a preconscious, and a conscious sphere, made up the framework of his psychological thinking.

It is difficult to determine the empirical status of Freud's physicalist premises. For example, he conceived of motives such as hunger, sex, and aggression as forces. It is difficult to deny that we can think of them in this way. On the other hand, it is also difficult to understand how these motives can be represented as forces in a physical system. Freud and his followers have insisted that his system must be treated as some sort of totality. Again, it is difficult to reject and also to accept this belief. While I believe a systematic evaluation of Freud's concepts requires that they be examined separately,

I shall have in mind the relationships they seem to have to each other. Before I turn to this examination, I shall review his procedure.

Therapeutic and Scientific Procedure

As already mentioned, Breuer had developed the cathartic method of treating patients displaying certain forms of hysteria. He believed they suffered from the effects of a mental trauma that continued to trouble them because they had not been able to express their emotions in the traumatic situation. In line with this belief, he had his patients recall the events that caused the trauma and then try to relive them as faithfully as possible while describing them to him and trying to give vent to the emotions they had felt at the time. Breuer usually carried out this procedure after hypnotizing the patients and found that when he succeeded in having them act according to his instructions, they were relieved of their symptoms. He borrowed the word "catharsis" from Aristotle to name his method.

Freud seized upon the finding that his own patients seemed opposed to bringing to mind events that were embarrassing, shameful, or in some way distressing to them. He and Breuer referred to this tendency as *resistance*. Freud further thought he could register in his patients a wish to forget, to repress thoughts that seemed distressing to them or incompatible with their self-image. He referred to this phenomenon as *repression* and made it the cornerstone of his system.

At the time Freud was working with Breuer, he began modifying the cathartic method. Finding that hypnosis did not give lasting results and that some patients were not hypnotizable, he stopped using it. Further, instead of instructing the patients to try to remember the traumatic event, he asked them simply to report on anything coming into their minds. With the patients lying on a couch to relax while he sat behind them, Freud asked them to tell him everything coming into their minds, even if it seemed irrelevant, silly, futile, shameful, embarrassing, or distressing. When the patients reported an unusual or bizarre thought, hesitated, or made an unusually long pause, Freud believed this could indicate resistance. The new procedure, which Freud named the *method of free association*, was thought to be a better way of detecting resistance than the cathartic method. Freud further believed it gave more lasting results. In the therapy, Freud also had patients relate their dreams and react to parts of their dreams by the "rule" of free association. Further, he would have them react to errors of the type (primarily slips of the tongue) he had discussed in his *The Psychopathology of Everyday Life*.

In *Studies on Hysteria*, Breuer and Freud emphasized that patients seemed to resist reporting certain memories. Freud elaborated upon the idea of resistance, believing its emergence indicated that the reported material was somehow associated with the patient's conflict. By overcoming resistance, Freud believed he might gradually help patients understand the nature of these conflicts. The way to achieve this was to have the patients react to his interpretations of the meaning of their reports. Apart from giving some general remarks on this point of the procedure, Freud stated no rules as to when and how the therapist should give interpretations.

Another important point in the procedure was the handling of the so-called *transfer*. On the basis of the patient's reports and reactions, Freud concluded that they reacted to him as they had reacted to their father, mother, or other important persons in their childhood. The patients seemed to transfer their earlier experiences to him as therapist. Gradually, he came to attribute a central role to transference in psychotherapy.

Freud's aim was to bring to consciousness ideas that were repressed but still operating in the unconscious and therefore causing the conflict. He emphasized that the patients must achieve a rational understanding of the cause of their mental disorder. Like Breuer, he also stressed that the patient must work on the emotions arising during the treatment. A successful therapy, then, should result in a better understanding, a deeper insight into the causes underlying the mental disorder. Freud thought the treatment liberated psychic energy that had been bound to conflicts in the psyche in an unfortunate way. The therapy should establish a better balance in the distribution of energy.

Psychoanalytic therapy was time-consuming; it could often extend over several years, with sessions several times a week. Moreover, it was very complicated and difficult to carry out, and gradually the circle around Freud came to believe that aspiring therapists should go through a *learning therapy*. This, they believed, would also give them a better insight into their own mental life.

Freud's Concept of the Unconscious

At the end of the nineteenth century, many thinkers took a great interest in phenomena suggesting that perceptions, memories, and feelings of which we are not aware can affect our thinking and actions. Wundt had opposed this view and argued that the question of what happens to a mental content when it leaves consciousness belongs to physiology. In contrast, Freud (1912) asserted that mental representations that have been in consciousness might continue to exist as unconscious representations. It is a fact, he said, that a mental representation can be present in consciousness, then disappear, and then re-emerge in consciousness without stimulation. In agreement with this view, he thought it reasonable to assume the existence of representations that are unconscious.

Further, Freud claimed that representations, even if unconscious, can influence our thinking and actions. This he believed to be documented in *post-hypnotic suggestion*. That is, when a person in a hypnotic state receives an instruction to carry out an act after the hypnotic state is suspended, such as to open a window at a signal from the hypnotist, the person will carry out the act without being aware that the instruction causes this to happen. Freud interpreted this finding to mean that mental representations excited by the instruction are active in the psyche of the hypnotized person in spite of the fact that the person is not aware of it. Only a dynamic view, he claimed, could explain how an unconscious representation could be active in the psyche.

Consciousness, the Preconscious, and the Unconscious

Of course, unconscious processes cannot be observed, and Freud made it clear that they must be inferred from descriptions of conscious phenomena. In a theoretical article on the unconscious in 1915, he wrote that unconscious processes could be described with the help of categories commonly used to describe conscious processes. Thus, it is possible, he said, to describe them in terms of categories such as representation, impulse (*Strebung*), and decision. In other words, the processes in the unconscious have essential properties in common with conscious processes and can, therefore, be referred to as mental representations.

Freud seems to have thought that no clear dividing line could be drawn between preconscious and conscious representations; the difference between them is one of degree. In contrast, there is a distinct boundary between unconscious representations, on the one hand, and preconscious and conscious representations, on the other hand. Hence, he thought of the unconscious as an area clearly delimited from the rest of the psyche. It was this area he wanted to explore by scientific methods; this was the domain of psychoanalysis.

Central Ideas in the Description of the Unconscious

In the next section on motivation, I shall in some detail go into Freud's concept of drive. Here, I shall just mention that the unconscious representations are connected with different drives, and this in some way provides them with energy. Thus, the representations are representatives of the drives, and this means the unconscious representations strive towards a drive *satisfaction*; they are impulses to wish fulfillments of various types. Freud further postulated that unconscious representations are directed towards becoming conscious. He did not go into the problem of how they acquire this property, but he noted, as we saw above, that attempts to enter consciousness meet with resistance. Further, he believed unconscious representations can interact with each other, making diverse types of connections and transferring energy to each other.

In the article "Instincts and Their Vicissitudes," Freud (1915a) set out how he thought drive energy could be transformed from one representation to another. A characteristic of representations in the unconscious is that, in contrast to representations in consciousness, they strive for satisfaction without a consideration of reality. Further, they are completely governed by the desire to obtain pleasure. The processes of the unconscious are often called *primary processes*, in contrast to the processes in consciousness and the preconscious, which are called *secondary processes*.

In the first decade of the century, Freud primarily concentrated on the relationship between the unconscious and the conscious. He postulated that one part of the psyche has the faculty of deciding which of the unconscious representations may enter into consciousness. This part exerts a form of censorship and is accordingly designated the *censor*. The censor prevents unconscious representations unacceptable to the person's *I* (see below) from entering into consciousness, unacceptable meaning of a sexual and aggressive nature. The censor was further accorded the function of repression, keeping representations that are unacceptable to the ego in the unconscious. Thus, resistance and repression are both a result of censorship. Freud claimed to have arrived at the central ideas in his conception of the unconscious through his self-analysis and the interpretation he had undertaken of his dreams during this analysis. He called the study of dreams *the royal road to the unconscious*.

The Study of Dreams: The Royal Road to the Unconscious

Freud held that dreams contain material from many different sources: recollections from childhood, bodily sensations felt during sleep, experiences from the previous day, and ideas from earlier stages in human phylogenesis and cultural history. In what he called the *dream-work*, the material is organized around one or more wishes. Dreams, he said, are always expressions of wishes; they are wish fulfillments. The total material making up a dream is the *latent content*. The dream as it appears to and is reported by the dreamer he called the *manifest content*. In other words, dreams, as they appear to the dreamer, are regarded as constructions, and in these constructions unconscious processes are active. Freud believed a study of how the dream-work tskes place could provide the analyst with knowledge of the mechanisms operating in the unconscious.

He also thought it possible, by studying dreams, to discover that the dreamer makes use of a number of symbols. In *Introductory Lectures on Psycho-Analysis*, Freud (1916–1917) listed the following (among others) as representing the male genitalia: extended objects such as sticks, knives, and snakes. Representing the female genitalia are holes, cloaks, and bowls. Freud declared that the censor guarding the entrance to consciousness is less severe during sleep, and representations that are not allowed entry into consciousness under other conditions might then enter it. However, they would still have to be transformed, distorted, to do so. In other words, dreams are symbolic and distorted expressions of wish fulfillments unacceptable to the conscious.

Many modern psychologists probably agree with Freud that dreams can reflect psychological conflicts, but it does not follow from this that dreams are unconscious representations organized according to Freud's view. The conflicts manifesting themselves in dreams can, of course, be well known to the dreamer, or they can have been conscious but so frequently thought of that they have become automatized and *in this sense* can be regarded as unconscious.

Research has shown that the brain is active during sleep but has so far given no evidence supporting Freud's idea of unconscious representations. At present, it seems most probable that dreams are created as a result of some spontaneous activity of certain groups of nerve cells in the brain. There is thus in neurophysiology no basis for the belief that the study of dreams is a royal road to knowledge of the unconscious.

The Interpretation of Dreams was followed by a book on the psychopathology of everyday life, which appeared in 1904. In this book, Freud argued that the so-called *parapraxes*, the errors we sometimes make in the pronunciation and spelling of words, our misuse of words, our forgetting of names, and the performance of different types of inadequate acts, can be explained as expressions of unconscious wishes. This book, like the one on the interpretation of dreams, reveals Freud's unusual mastery of the art of writing, but it gives no convincing evidence that his interpretation of the phenomena described is more than one possibility among a number of others.

Status of Freud's Idea of the Unconscious in the Debate in Modern Psychology

Studies of dreams and parapraxes seem to have given little support to Freud's view of the unconscious. Psychodynamically oriented psychologists have tried to procure evidence for it by a variety of different types of studies, however, and today there is an extensive literature. In assessing this literature, we should bear in mind that other psychologists developed alternate views of unconscious processes. The question, therefore, is not simply whether there are unconscious processes, but whether there are unconscious processes of the type postulated by Freud. What characterizes his view is that mental representations are pushed out of consciousness, repressed, and prevented from entering consciousness, and further that, though unconscious, they exert an influence on thinking and action. Another important characteristic of Freud's view is that our unconscious representations are primarily of a sexual and aggressive nature, and that they constitute an isolated part of the psyche.

In their account of psychoanalytic approaches to personality, Westen and Gabbard (1999) have drawn together results of research on unconscious processes and provided interesting perspectives on these. Unfortunately, they do not distinguish between evidence supporting the belief in the existence of unconscious processes and Freud's specific view. This is probably one reason why Kihlstrom (1999), after reviewing the same material, concluded that the Freudian view of the unconscious "to date has found little or no support in empirical research."

One important reason opinions are divided on Freud's view of the unconscious is that, unless a number of controls are put in place during attempts to obtain evidence for the psychoanalytic view, it is not possible to decide whether the results are relevant. At present, so many objections can be made against the conclusions of those researchers who favor Freud's view that it seems justifiable to say that *up to the present* there is no clear evidence in favor of his view of the unconscious.

The situation may change. Like Nietzsche, Freud believed that in attempts to defend their self-image, human beings constantly distort reality. A large majority of clinical psychologists believe that, at least in certain situations, we do use *defense mechanisms*. If this is true, research aimed to lay bare the mechanisms used in such defenses may give support to Freud's dynamic view of unconscious processes. I shall return to this question later in the chapter.

Freud's View of Motivation and Sexuality

Central to Freud's view of motivation was the concept of an inheritable instinctive force. He called this force *Trieb* in German, often rendered as "instinct" in English, though a better word may be "drive," as Laplanche and Pontalis suggest.

Freud's Concept of Drive

A fundamental point in Freud's (1915a) view is that the drive has its origin exclusively in internal bodily processes. Freud did not specify its biological origin, however, limiting himself to stating that it is a need (*Bedürfnis*). The idea of the drive was introduced by analogy to physiological reflexes; Freud conceived of it as the stimulus for the psychic, for mental life; because it operates internally, it can not be avoided but must be satisfied. Another important point in his speculations about the drive was that the goal of the drive is satisfaction, and not necessarily an external object. A third point was that Freud related the drive to the affects, the feelings of pleasure and pain, holding that pleasure arises when a drive decreases in intensity, and pain when it increases in intensity. This way of looking at pleasure and pain he referred to as the *pleasure principle*. Taking a hedonistic view of motivation, he insisted that our whole mental life is directed towards obtaining pleasure and avoiding pain, and he made the principle central in his psychology. As Laplanche and Pontalis (1967) and Sulloway (1979) report, Freud was aware of the difficulty of conceiving of pain as resulting from an increase in intensity of the drive, but he did not give a more precise definition of the concept.

Freud assumed the existence of many different types of drives. Until 1920, he divided them into two types: drives that have to do with the preservation of life, called *ego drives*, and *sexual drives*. Note the plural form in the last type of drive: Freud believed there are several different sexual drives. Underlying these drives is a specific form of energy called *libido*.

Ideas of aggression had a place in Freud's earlier works, but it was not until his famous book *Beyond the Pleasure Principle* in 1920 that he ascribed a central role to it. He then postulated a death drive. This was a drive that could be directed not only towards others in aggression but also against oneself. As Sulloway (1979) has noted, Freud introduced a drive of this nature in order to make his biological and clinical thinking more consistent. The brutality of World War I probably also led him to place a stronger emphasis on aggression in humans.

Libido and the Psychosexual Development

Freud named the energy underlying the sexual drive libido and accorded it a central role in the distribution of mental energy, and thus in mental life. In his monograph *Three Essays on the Theory of Sexuality*, he (1905) explained how he believed his hypotheses about libido could help us understand human sexuality.

When Freud began his studies of sexuality, Darwin (1871/1981) had already described, in the *Descent of Man and Selection in Relation to Sex*, the great variety found in animal sexual behavior. In 1881, the prominent Viennese psychiatrist and forensic physician, Richard von Krafft-Ebing, had described a number of deviant forms of human sexual behavior. One of Freud's aims in his *Three Essays on the Theory of Sexuality* was to show that varieties in human sexual practice could be explained as manifestations of the same underlying mechanisms. What they had in common, he said, was the aim of receiving pleasure from stimulation of the skin. This pleasure, he held, could be derived from any part of the skin.

Freud then went on to suggest that during definite stages of development, which he called *psychosexual stages*, stimulation of some specific area of the skin produces a particularly strong feeling of pleasure in the child. Thus, to each stage belongs an area, a so-called *erogenous* (*erotogenic*) *zone*, giving this particular pleasure. To each erogenous zone, Freud also ascribed a specific sexual drive. His concept of sexuality thus differs from the traditional view. Next I shall describe the psychosexual stages.

The *oral stage* lasts from birth to about two years. At this stage, the child derives a feeling of pleasure by being stimulated in the region around the mouth. The sucking of milk from the mother's breast provides the child with pleasure of a sexual nature, a libidinous feeling of pleasure. The child also achieves this feeling by sucking its thumb, touching objects with its lips, and putting these into its mouth.

The *anal stage* extends from about two to about four years. During this stage, the child obtains the libidinous feeling of pleasure by stimulation of the region around the anus. The feeling of pleasure Freud believed to result from defecation and also from the retention of excrement, as well as from touching the region. The child was also thought to manifest aggressive tendencies at this stage, and it has therefore often been referred to in psychoanalysis as the *anal-sadistic stage*.

In the *phallic stage*, extending from about four to six years, certain events occur that Freud referred to as the *Oedipus complex*. He believed these events to be of the greatest importance, and we must deal with this stage in some detail. The child now achieves a feeling of pleasure by stimulation of the genitalia, and masturbation gives children of both sexes a feeling of pleasure. The course of the stage is, however, different for the two genders. The boy goes through the following development. First, he is sexually attracted to his mother. This attraction makes him feel that he is a rival of his father. At this time, the boy discovers that a girl does not have a penis, and he imagines that her penis has been removed, and that he could be punished by his father, who might cut off his penis. This belief makes the boy experience *castration anxiety*. The conflict is overcome in that the boy gradually identifies with his father. Castration anxiety contributes to the development of the child's conscience, however, and by identifying with his father, the child acquires moral ideas, and the moral ideas of the society of which the father is a member.

The girl, like the boy, is at this age initially attracted to her mother. (Freud assumed that all human beings are constitutionally bisexual.) However, as a result of the discovery that she has no penis, the girl feels animosity against her mother, blaming her for the defect. Now the girl turns towards her father, wanting him to provide her with a penis. She imagines that giving birth to a child would be equal to having a penis and wishes to have a child by her father. Gradually, however, she identifies with her mother. Because the girl has no penis, she does not experience castration anxiety in the same way as the boy and does not develop an equally strong sense of morality. Moreover, she envies the boy his penis. Freud called this feeling *penis envy* (he gave a more detailed account of the girl's sexual development in *New Introductory Lectures on Psycho-Analysis* (1932).

From six to puberty, there is a new organization of sexuality, and for this reason Freud spoke of this period not as a stage but as a *period of latency*. The child's sexual energies are now primarily directed towards activities other than sexual ones, particularly artistic production and intellectual exploration. Further, in this period the child reacts against its earlier sexual fantasies with a feeling of shame and disgust and represses them. This reaction is strengthened by the predominant attitude of society to sexuality.

Next we have the *genital stage*. At this stage, beginning at puberty, the diverse sexual drives attached to the earlier stages are integrated under the dominance of the genital organs. Thus, the sexuality of the adult contains the earlier manifested sexual drives.

Evaluation of Freud's View of Motivation and Sexuality

Freud's view of motivation, as made clear by Dalbir Bindra (1985), suffers from the same weakness as that of McDougall. It sees motivation one-sidedly as arising from processes originating within the body, and not as a joint effect of properties of the organism and aspects of the environment. To make Freud's idea of a drive a useful concept in empirical research, it is necessary to specify the following:

1. What is the biological origin of the postulated mental energy underlying the drive?
2. How does the drive stimulate the organism?
3. How does it direct human thinking and action?

With regard to the sexual drive, the lack of specification of the libido makes it difficult to understand what Freud meant by claiming that the mental energy attributed to the libido affects all mental life, and that disturbances in its distribution are at the root of all mental disorders.

Freud opposed the traditional view of sexuality, which assumes a close connection between the sexual drive and an individual of the opposite sex as the object of the drive and the possessor of some definite attributes eliciting inherited reactions. Instead of assuming that reactions to attributes of the object are inherited, Freud assumed, as we saw, that reactions to stimulation of definite areas of the skin are inherited. Thus, during evolution, according to Freud, human beings have adapted not to the attributes of individuals of the opposite sex, but to stimulation of some areas of the skin providing particularly strong feelings of pleasure.

If we assume the sexual behavior of human beings has developed from the sexual behavior of primates, we would expect it basically to conform to that of primates. Among primates, attributes of the opposite sex seem to play a fundamental part. For example, the swollen genitals of the female chimpanzee in heat apparently have a decisive role in copulation. It seems highly reasonable to believe the male's reactions to this attribute are inherited. If inherited reactions to attributes in individuals of the opposite sex are a main determinant of sexuality in primates, it is natural to believe sexuality in human beings is determined in a similar way.

Freud was evidently right in pointing out that a theory of human sexuality must account for infantile sexuality as well as for sexual deviations, and he was probably also right in insisting that experience plays a role in human sexuality. Finally, he was correct that stimulation of areas of the skin other than around the genital organs plays an important role in human sexuality. But, as far as I understand, accepting these points does not imply that inherited reactions to attributes in an individual of the opposite sex do not play a fundamental role in human sexuality.

With regard to the psychosexual stages, it is difficult to decide whether we should view the feelings of the child provided by stimulation of the postulated erogenous zones as being of a sexual nature. On the whole, there seems to be little – if any – evidence for Freud's thesis of the psychosexual stages (cf. Westen and Gabbard, 1999).

The Origin of Sexual Deviations and Neuroses

The explanation Freud gave of abnormal sexuality was that children do not always go through all the stages of psychosexual development in a normal manner. Due to constitutional factors or unfortunate environmental circumstances, a part of the libido might be permanently tied to the sexual activities characteristic of a particular stage, and development would in some sense be arrested at that stage. Freud referred to this as *fixation*. He also hypothesized that when satisfaction of the libido is blocked in adults, they turn their libido towards the activities characteristic of the arrested stage, in what he termed *regression*. Freud's account of sexual deviations is very complex. I shall limit my attention to a few points.

As we have noted, Freud hypothesized several sexual drives. All were biologically determined and could be included in the sexual activity of the normal adult. However, in normal development, these sexual drives must be integrated in such a way that the drive satisfied by stimulation of the genital organ becomes the dominant drive. Freud distinguished between normal and abnormal sexuality, but normal sexuality could be given many expressions. Without going more deeply into his account, I shall note that he believed all human beings are constitutionally bisexual, as mentioned earlier, and that sexual deviations are primarily a result of fixations at earlier stages in psycho-sexual development. Like his contemporaries, he regarded homosexuality as a mental disorder.

All neuroses, according to Freud, have their origin in sexual disturbances of some kind. However, he did not regard all neuroses as being caused by abnormal psychosexual development; he distinguished between the so-called *actual neuroses* caused by bodily or external circumstances preventing sexual satisfaction, and the *psychoneuroses*, which have their roots in psychosexual development. Most of his work is directed towards understanding the latter group of neuroses.

Freud's account of psychoneuroses has important points in common with his account of sexual deviations. When persons who are fixated at an earlier stage in their psychosexual development are prevented from satisfying their sexual drives, they regress to this stage; that is, they attempt to satisfy their sexual desires by activities characteristic of this stage. However, in some persons a direct expression of these desires is repressed from consciousness because they conflict with the conceptions the persons have of themselves. As a result of that repression, a conflict arises between forces striving for entry into consciousness, and forces preventing this entry. Because thoughts and impulses from the unconscious enter consciousness in a disguised, distorted, form,

Freud believed neurotic symptoms are distorted expressions of conflicts, representing a compromise between opposing forces in the psyche. In Freud's view of neurosis, there are two principal causes of psychoneuroses. First, the person must be prevented from satisfying his or her libido, and, second, the person must have been fixated at a specific stage in his or her psychosexual development. Further, Freud regarded the symptoms not as causes of the neurosis, but as effects caused by an unconscious conflict.

Structure and Mode of Operation of the Psyche

After World War I, Freud changed first his view of drives and then, a little later, his view of the way the psyche is structured. In 1923, he wrote an article in which he attempted to give a systematic presentation of his new ideas. Up to that time he had based his description of the psyche on the assumption of a polarity between unconscious and conscious processes. Further, he had proposed an *I*, which he introduced by saying it is in control of the perceptual and motor apparatus. This model Freud now regarded as inadequate to illustrate the relationship between the unconscious and the conscious. Whereas he had earlier conceived of censorship as a selective barrier between the unconscious, on the one hand, and the conscious and preconscious processes, on the other hand, he now stressed that repression is undertaken by the *I*. Because repression is an unconscious process, one part of the *I* must be unconscious. Still, in the main, he did not change his view of the unconscious, even if he changed its name and now used the German gender-neutral pronoun *das Es* for it (a term he had taken from Nietzsche). In English, the terms *ego* and *id* are used, respectively, for the postulated *I* and for what Freud called *das Es*.

What Freud found particularly unsatisfactory in his old model was first and foremost his view of the *I*. He now believed human moral and ethical ideas must be ascribed a more central role in the psyche; the model had to incorporate what he called *ego ideals*. Nor did the early model allow him to understand how self-contempt and self-hatred could develop. To improve the model on these points, he postulated that a third psychic instance, a *superego*, had been differentiated from the ego during the individual's ontogenetic development and represented the person's moral and ethical norms. It could turn against the ego and in this way create self-contempt and self-hatred. In the years following the publication of *Three Essays on the Theory of Sexuality*, Freud had attributed a growing importance to the Oedipus complex. Now he declared that the superego is primarily formed during the child's attempts to master this complex. Thus, through children's interactions with their parents at this stage, the moral and ethical norms of the parents and society are incorporated into the superego.

To summarize, the id corresponds to what Freud had earlier called the unconscious; it contains repressed representations, infantile representations, and representations inherited from earlier generations. This part develops first and gives energy to mental life. As in Freud's earlier thinking, the ego is ascribed control of the perceptual and motor apparatus and also mediates between the unrealistic id impulses and the person's conceptions of reality. In addition to its earlier functions, the ego is now a structure that decides whether the impulses are reconcilable with the demands of the superego, which represents the person's moral and ethical norms. In the new model, not only the functions of the id but also some of the functions of the ego and the superego are unconscious. The model gave a more central place and function to the ego, in defending itself against the anxiety of the superego, anxiety caused by exceptionally strong drive impulses, and anxiety originating in the external world.

The model is abstract, and it is difficult to specify the three instances in such a way that they can be made the object of empirical investigation.

Summary and General Conclusions

One reason many pioneers of scientific empirical psychology insisted psychology ought to be advanced as an experimental science was that they realized it was difficult to make reliable observations without experiments. They also saw that experimentation is of major importance in making causal analysis. Freud did not share their beliefs and held that his clinical procedure gave an adequate basis for a scientific psychology. In view of what we now know of the problems of observation and causal analysis in psychology, it is difficult to believe Freud's clinical observations warrant his claims.

Although research (to which I shall return in later chapters) demonstrates that going through psychoanalytic therapy has a favorable effect on persons suffering from diverse mental disorders, this effect may be due not to the specific procedure used by psychoanalysts, but simply to general psychological factors that psychoanalysis shares with other therapies. (On this point, see Michael Lambert and Benjamin Ogles, 2004.)

Freud attempted to support his theoretical system with knowledge from biology, anthropology, and cultural history, as we have seen. Still, the foundation for his statements was primarily the knowledge he thought he had gained through his clinical practice. This raises the question of whether the clinical practice, as he described it, could in fact enable him to be sure his assertions were correct.

To reach a conclusion on this point, we would need to precisely record the patients' initial utterances and the sequence of utterances up to the point when the therapist gives his first comment, his first interpretation of the patient's report. Next, we would need a detailed and exact description of how the patient and the therapist interact. Freud did not follow this procedure and did not even put down his observations during the therapy session; instead he postponed reporting until after the session. This, of course, makes us doubt that his observations were adequate.

Towards the end of the twentieth century, an increasing number of clinical psychologists who were initially supportive of psychoanalysis had begun to doubt that Freud's procedure was adequate. Lawrence Pervin (2003, p. 5), a clinical psychologist and a prominent researcher on personality, expressed the changing attitude to psychoanalysis in the following way: "What is particularly troubling is that it is not just the theoretical formulations that are being challenged, but the very nature of the observations themselves." As Pervin made clear, a crucial point in the discussion of psychoanalysis as a scientific endeavor is this question: Where are the data?

We should also note that while Freud and his followers attached great importance to some of the cases he described, historians have shown that several of the descriptions are in important respects incomplete, and perhaps even incorrect (see Ellenberger, 1970; Macmillan, 1991). This further strengthens the belief that Freud's observations do not warrant his conclusions. While historians have frequently based their reviews of psychoanalysis on Freud's case histories, I have deviated from this practice because I believe it may easily give a distorted picture.

In addition to questioning whether Freud adequately described the events taking place in the therapy sessions, psychologists have begun to doubt whether the patients reported their thoughts and impulses as freely as Freud supposed. Critics have pointed to the fact that patients may be led by the therapist to react in specific ways and may even be indoctrinated by continuous suggestions. (On this point, see Macmillan, 1991.) Experiments have shown that subjects may report with great certainty suggestions implanted by the experimenter that are not true. It has also been convincingly shown that we recall emotional events better than unemotional ones. Both these findings throw doubt on whether repression plays the role attributed to it by psychoanalysts. (For a summary of research on repression, see Delroy Paulhus et al., 1997.)

Further, examination of Freud's theoretical concepts reveal so little specificity that it is difficult to understand how they can be productively used in empirical research. We cannot say, of course, whether future researchers will define the concepts of psychoanalysis so they can be used productively in scientific, empirical research. What we can conclude with some certainty, however, is that, so far, Freud's core concepts of the "unconscious," "drive," "affect" (feeling of pleasure and pain), "resistance," "repression," "transfer," "anxiety," "psychosexual stage, "fixation," "regression," "anxiety," "id," "ego," and "superego" have not been so defined.

Up to about the 1970s, Freud was probably the most admired and most cited of all psychologists, and there can be no doubt that in formulating their research problems many psychologists were inspired by him. In the chapters to follow, we shall have occasion to note his influence, particularly in the chapter on American personality and clinical psychology. Even if he was not the only one to begin psychological studies of unconscious processes, mental disorders, sexuality, and aggression, Freud did contribute to a broadening of psychology with his work. However, of his many hypotheses, only the one that stimulation of skin areas other than around the genital organs plays a role in sexuality seems supported by clear evidence so far. As we produce more knowledge about the processes occurring in psychotherapy, we may find support for at least some of his other ideas, as well as for his claim that the therapeutic technique he invented works according to his theory.

Emil Kraepelin and Freud

Emil Kraepelin and Freud were born the same year and shared a background in the neurology of the later 1800s. However, they took entirely different approaches to the study of mental disorders. Kraepelin worked in psychiatric hospitals with patients afflicted with severe mental disorders, whereas in his private practice Freud concentrated mainly on patients suffering from neuroses. Kraepelin made efforts to avoid theoretical speculations and concentrated on descriptions and categorizations of mental disorders, while Freud developed a comprehensive theory. Kraepelin attempted to distinguish carefully between the normal and the pathological, and to define the categories as distinctively as possible. Freud attempted to see the pathological and normal as different degrees of the same tendencies.

Kraepelin and Freud dominated the psychiatry of the 1900s, with Kraepelin more prominent until about the 1930s. From then to 1970, when the United States became the center of psychiatry, Freud was more influential. Then again, after 1970, Kraepelin's view of how to study mental disorders again took hold.

Ego Psychology

Many psychiatrists and psychologists were convinced that Freud's ideas about motivation, the unconscious, psychosexual development, the origin of neuroses, and the best way to conduct therapy had a basis in scientific research, and they carried out their work in agreement with these ideas. Within the psychoanalytic movement, as it had been shaped by Freud, acceptance of these ideas was a condition of membership. Freud, however, had introduced certain modifications into his system when he launched his new model of the human psyche in 1923, according the ego a more central and even increasingly significant place. In the 1930s and 1940s, the revision of this aspect of his system was continued by his daughter Anna Freud and other psychoanalysts, especially Heinz Hartmann (1939) and David Rapaport (1959).

Anna Freud (1895–1982) worked for some time as an elementary schoolteacher before she started her training as a psychoanalyst. She was psychoanalyzed by her father and in 1936 published a book on the ego and defense mechanisms. After emigrating to Great Britain in 1938, she worked with children and attempted to adjust psychoanalytic treatment to their needs. Attributing a greater role to the ego, Anna Freud emphasized its role as a solver of conflicts. In this capacity, the ego was accorded a number of defense mechanisms. Many psychologists – as well as psychologists critical of psychoanalysis – consider these mechanisms important in understanding human thinking and behavior.

Anxiety and Defense Mechanisms

Anna Freud and her father both saw defense mechanisms as closely related to his view of anxiety, which in turn is linked to his ideas on psychosexual development and the libido. In *Introductory Lectures on Psycho-Analysis*, Freud began his account of anxiety by drawing a distinction between fear and *real anxiety*, that is, between anxiety about external situations that usually excite anxiety in human beings, and a free-floating anxiety that has no definite external object. He did not go into how he would draw the boundary more concretely between the two forms of anxiety. Having made this distinction, he related anxiety to his ideas of libido, holding that the ego would react to a heavy building up of libido in the same way as it would react to an external danger; in other words, a build-up of libido would excite anxiety. In his later speculations, Freud held that anxiety would signal to the ego that there is danger of an accumulation of libido. Anxiety could thus have its origin in an external as well as an internal danger.

A central point in Freud's speculations about anxiety was that anxiety in the young child is different from real anxiety. It is more like the free-floating kind. Further, he supposed strong anxiety emerges for the first time at birth, which he regarded as a trauma for the child. After birth, anxiety would be expressed according to culturally inherited forms; in other words, a child could have the same kind of anxiety that primitive humans had. They experienced anxiety primarily when confronted with something unknown, and it would come to express itself as helplessness. Anxiety could be aroused in the child when it is separated from the mother, and this would represent a continuation of the birth trauma. Later, anxiety could be tied to the different psychosexual stages. As we have seen, Freud attributed significant importance to what he believed to be castration anxiety. Finally, he presumed that when anxiety operates in the unconscious, it may be associated with all types of representations and complexes of representation, and its effects may not be counteracted by rational reflections. When the ego is threatened by a build-up of libido, anxiety operates in the unconscious and there exerts its effect. In this way, anxiety is associated with repression, inhibition, and distortion.

Anna Freud divided the reactions to anxiety into ten different types. These different forms of defense merged into each other, and psychoanalysts have categorized them somewhat differently. Here, I shall mention only those that are frequently referred to.

Repression had a central place in Freud's theory. Closely related was *denial*, which differed in being more dependent upon events taking place in the environment. An often-cited example is a person denying he or she has been diagnosed with an incurable disease. In *reaction formation* a person with a particular motive gives expression to the opposite motive. For example, a parent who does not want his or her child makes extreme sacrifices to satisfy what he or she considers the wishes of the child. In *projection* we attribute to another person a motive unacceptable to ourselves; we may, for example, attribute to someone else a sexual desire for us when we actually have an unacceptable desire for the other person. In *displacement* we transfer our feelings and emotions about someone to another person, such as by directing our anger towards our partner or spouse after receiving criticism from our superior. *Rationalizations* are partly true, or perhaps untrue, reasons we give for actions and opinions of our own that we find unacceptable. Closely related is *intellectualization*, in which we speak of emotionally tinged problems in an abstract, intellectual manner. In *identification* a person identifies with, and assumes the values of, a person attacking or repressing him. Finally, in *sublimation* we channel mental energy of a sexual nature into other activities, such as intellectual, artistic, and scientific pursuits.

Evaluation of the Idea of Defense Mechanisms

Schopenhauer, Nietzsche, and writers before them noted that we distort reality in our attempts to defend our self-esteem in threatening situations. Sigmund and Anna Freud may have contributed to psychology by formulating ideas on psychological defenses in such a way that psychologists became willing to accept their potential importance. Still, as documented by the extensive review of the literature by Delroy Paulhus, Bram Fridhandler, and Sean Hayes (Paulhus et al., 1997), there is no consensus on how to describe or explain the possible mechanisms. We can think of them as often-repeated strategies for dealing with threatening situations that may have become automatic, and in this sense unconscious. Recently, the idea of repression has been much discussed. I believe that since it has been difficult to perform controlled investigations of repression, we must admit that the traditional distinction between repression and suppression may not be valid.

By giving the ego an important role in her explanation of defense mechanisms, Anna Freud drew greater attention to ego functions in psychoanalysis. A revision of the system along these lines was carried out by Heinz Hartmann and David Rapaport, among others. Freud held that the id is the part of the psyche developing first in ontogenesis, and he attributed to it the administration of psychic energy. The ego, in obtaining its energy from the id, emerged as a result of conflicts between impulses from the id and reality. Hartmann revised Freud's view on this and proposed that the ego emerged independently of the id, and, further, that this part of the psyche is not dependent on energy from the id. Hence, the ego also represents functions unrelated to the id's conflict with reality. According to Hartmann (1939), the psyche contains what he called a *conflict-free ego sphere*.

By believing the ego has a more independent function in the psyche, psychoanalysts thought they could more easily understand their clients' psychological conflicts. The new orientation led some psychoanalysts to emphasize that a person's lack of autonomy, or, as they expressed it, lack of *ego strength*, might be the cause of conflict. In everyday thinking, people seem to assume their actions are governed by what they conceive of as an *I*, a self. Thus, they apparently assign a more central place in thinking and action to the self than Freud did in his model of the psyche. We may consider that the new psychoanalytic orientation to ego psychology contributed to bringing psychoanalysis more in line with everyday .thinking.

Object Relations Theory

In his account of the Oedipus complex, Freud argued that the bonds children establish with their parents determine their later relationships with other people. In line with this view, conflicts that adults have with other persons may be due to the fact that as children they were bound to one of their parents or to some other important person in an unfortunate manner. In the years following Freud's death, psychoanalysts, particularly British, began concentrating more strongly on the possible effects of unpleasant social relationships during early childhood. They developed theories about the way children later establish relationships with other people, and they were particularly interested in how early relationships could explain *personality disorders*. These attempts have been named *object relations theory*.

The child is dependent upon caregivers for a long period, and it would be strange indeed if this had no effect on later development. Towards the end of the twentieth century, there was increasing interest in explaining certain types of personality disorders in terms of the effects of the child's early relationships. The object relations theories have drawn attention to individual differences between people in the way they react to criticism, unfriendliness, and failure, calling the tendency to react poorly *vulnerability*. Differences in vulnerability are explained as being due to unpleasant social relationships in childhood.

Object relations theory originated in psychoanalysis, but it need not be linked to Freud's ideas of the Oedipus complex. As noted by Westen and Gabbard (1999), the theory modified Freud's view that drives are primarily directed towards pleasure and not towards objects in the external world. Although this modification is more in line with modern psychological accounts of motivation, it seems rather esoteric to refer to relationships between human beings as object relations. It may obscure the difference between the relationships human beings and other mammals have to their fellow creatures and the relationships they have to physical objects.

Moreover, the object relations theorists placed more weight on the role of upbringing in the development of children than Freud did and emphasized the effects of deprivation in infancy and early childhood. As we shall see later in this chapter, unlike Freud, Adler focused on the effect of deprivations as well as social relationships. In the 1950s, interest in object relations theory fused with the increasing interest in an evolutionary perspective on the development of children, resulting in attachment theory. I shall return to this point in Chapter 19.

Erik Erikson (1902–1992)

Freud's idea that personality passes through definite stages was continued by Erik Erikson (1950). Erikson had been psychoanalyzed by Anna Freud and regarded himself as a psychoanalyst; his ideas are often considered a continuation and elaboration of Freud's thinking. As Ellenberger has remarked, however, it is more accurate to see Erikson's ideas about development as a combination of ideas from Freud, Adler, and Jung.

Erikson followed Freud's chronological order for the first five stages, but he gave them quite another content. Like Adler, he viewed development not as psychosexual, but as *psychosocial*. Further, he postulated that what happens at the oral stage is characterized not only by the child's wish to obtain satisfaction by stimulation of the mouth region, but also by the fact that the child develops either a trustful or distrustful relationship with its caregivers. Erikson held that in order to pass through this stage in a satisfactory manner, the child must develop a trusting relationship with its caregivers. If this does not happen, the development of the child at later stages is impaired. Thus, the important point at this first stage is the development of *trust versus distrust*.

At the second stage, the anal stage in Freud, Erikson postulated that the child develops autonomy by gaining satisfaction through exercising self-control, making decisions, and exercising will. A child restrained in these activities experiences shame. Thus, at this stage, the child develops a *sense* either *of autonomy or of shame*. At the third stage, the phallic stage in Freud, the child begins to feel satisfaction by directing activities towards goals, mastering tasks, and achieving results. If this does not occur, the child feels guilt. Thus, at this stage, the child develops a *sense either of initiative or of guilt*. At the fourth stage, Freud's latency stage, the child is engaged in diverse types of tasks and develops persistence and industry. If restrained in this effort, the child develops a sense of inferiority. Thus, at this stage, the child develops *a sense either of industry or of inferiority*.

At the fifth stage, which includes adolescence, a major concern is to compare what we feel we are with how we appear in the eyes of others, and to connect the roles and skills cultivated earlier in life with those required at this stage. Some of the concrete problems we meet with are sexual identity and career choice. According to Erikson, satisfactory solving of these problems leads to *an ego identity as contrasted with role confusion*.

The sixth stage, *early adulthood*, is characterized by a need to share thoughts and feelings, and to work with others. If this stage is not passed through in a satisfactory manner, a person will try to avoid intimacy and form only superficial relationships with other people. In the seventh stage, *middle age*, there is a tendency to engage in professional work and to form relationships with others. If development is inadequate, a lack of interest in work and a lack of depth in personal relationships occur. Successful development at the eighth stage, *old age*, results in a feeling that life has been continuous and meaningful, and satisfaction with ourselves and what we have achieved. If development does not follow a natural course, a person has a fear of death and a feeling of bitterness and frustration because expectations have not been fulfilled. As Ellenberger (1970) noted, the tendencies ascribed to persons in the three last stages resemble the strivings Jung regarded as characteristic of middle and old age, a striving towards developing a harmonious personality.

Remarks on Erikson and Stage Theories

A great deal of research has been carried out to find support for Erikson's hypotheses about adolescence, ego identity, and diffusion. Ego identity means there is identity between a person's conceptions of himself or herself as a person (the self) and the expectations the social environment have for his or her behavior. In modern Western societies, many adolescents probably experience conflicts concerning their ego identity, but the phenomenon may not be universal. As Roy Baumeister (1997) has argued, identity crisis is a modern phenomenon reflecting ideas of the self emerging late in the nineteenth century.

Erikson's stage theory had strong appeal to many psychologists in the 1950s, and, as shown by Dan McAdams (1999), it is still a subject of interest. As a stage theory, however, it must overcome the difficulty of determining the succession of the stages. In my judgment, it is problematic to claim, for example, that trust develops prior to autonomy or autonomy prior to initiative. Like all psychological stage theories, this theory also raises the question of whether development proceeds in stages or is continuous.

Carl Gustav Jung (1875–1963)

Today, Carl Jung probably exerts the greatest influence on people who are primarily interested in the history of religion and culture, and fascinated by the creative aspect of art and the use of symbols. Although he is now a more peripheral figure in modern scientific psychology, he did contribute to mainstream academic personality research.

A Biographical Sketch

Born in Kesswil in Thurgau, Switzerland, Jung spent most of his childhood and youth in a village that is now a suburb of Basel. His father was a minister in the Swiss Reformed Church, and from early youth Jung held ideas in opposition to those of his father. He searched for answers to his religious queries outside the Christian tradition, but he apparently considered himself a Christian throughout his life. While Freud had a young and beautiful mother who admired him, Jung's mother has been described as not particularly beautiful, and her son seems to have regarded her as a little capricious. As Ellenberger notes, Freud made the Oedipus complex central to his system, while Jung rejected the idea.

On finishing high school, Jung embarked on his medical studies, which he completed in 1900. Even in his early adolescence, he began reading extensively and was fascinated by Schopenhauer, among others. In his student years, Nietzsche's *Also sprach Zarathustra* (*Thus Spoke Zarathustra*) (1891) also made a strong impression on him, and he occupied himself with Nietzsche's ideas for the rest of his life. After completing his medical studies, he specialized in psychiatry at Burghölzli Mental Hospital. His doctoral thesis was an examination of a spiritualist medium, and Jung was engaged in parapsychology throughout his life. In 1902, he spent some time in Paris, where he studied with Pierre Janet. The following year he married and returned to Burghölzli, where, in 1905, he was appointed chief physician and *Privatdozent* at the University of Zürich.

In 1898, Eugen Bleuler (1857–1939), who along with Kraepelin was a pioneer in research and treatment of schizophrenia, was appointed director of Burghölzli Mental Hospital. He encouraged Jung to study word association with a view to constructing a test. Along with coworkers at the hospital, Jung carried out extensive studies of word association. This research and a book he wrote on schizophrenia made him internationally renowned, and, with Freud, he was invited to Massachusetts for the twentieth anniversary of the founding of Clark University in 1909.

Jung started corresponding with Freud in 1906 and visited him the following year. The two formed a close friendship. Bleuler and the staff at Burghölzli were also interested in psychoanalysis. Nevertheless, a conflict arose between Jung and Bleuler. Jung resigned from his position at the hospital, began a private practice, and devoted himself to the psychoanalytic movement. He was the first president of the International Psychoanalytic Association and was appointed editor of the first psychoanalytic journal. In 1913,

Jung broke with Freud and the psychoanalytic movement, calling his own approach to psychology *analytic psychology.*

Jung published an extraordinarily large number of articles and books. His collected works have been translated into English and published in twenty volumes. A fascinating autobiography was published in 1961. I shall deal only with those parts of his work that fall within what most psychologists regard as scientific empirical psychology. Moreover, I shall also briefly comment on his ideas of unconscious processes.

In 1914, Jung also resigned from the University of Zürich and devoted himself to an intensive study over several years of what he regarded as his own unconscious, a task similar to the one Freud had undertaken earlier. In 1921, he published an influential and much-read book on personality types. From his youth, Jung had been absorbed in theological, philosophical, and parapsychological questions, in the history of religion and art as well as in the use of symbols and mysticism. The material he had collected in these studies was used to support views he presented in his book on personality types as well as in his later writings.

After World War II, Jung was accused of having taken a pro-Nazi and anti-Semitic attitude. So far, it seems not to have been convincingly documented that these accusations were correct. However, he seems to have taken a surprisingly long time to acknowledge the aggression and brutality of the Nazi regime. Nevertheless, in the 1930s, Jung became known not only as a great psychological researcher, but also as a sage. Many regarded him as a defender of spiritual values, which in their opinion had been left out of scientific psychology. Jung received a number of honors for his contributions to psychiatry and psychology – for instance, an honorary degree from Harvard in 1936 and from Oxford in 1938.

Freud and Jung: Similarities and Differences

Like Fechner and Wundt, Jung was strongly influenced by the Romantic idea of a union between humans and nature. His thinking was also deeply rooted in the intellectual movements represented by Schopenhauer and Nietzsche; Jung combined ideas from these movements with ideas from biological evolution. He was influenced by Janet and French psychiatry and clinical psychology.

Jung attributed great importance to sexuality, but he did not conceive of libido as a general force underlying all phenomena of mental life. He also rejected Freud's view of psychosexual development. In contrast to Freud, he emphasized that personality develops throughout life and is not determined only by childhood events. In his therapy, Jung stressed that humans must use their potential, achieve a realistic attitude to life, and direct thinking towards the future. He thus had a view of human personality and human life that differed from Freud's in essential respects.

The study of dreams is, according to Jung, an important means of understanding the unconscious and the whole of a person's mental life, though he did not accept Freud's distinction between a manifest and a latent content of dreams. Further, Jung held that dreams could be understood without making assumptions about repression. In the interpretation of dreams, knowledge of the way symbols are used in mythology and religion is important. Finally, Jung and Freud differed in their views of the relationship between therapist and patient. Jung claimed the two must cooperate.

Experimental Studies in Psychopathology

In reporting on his research on word association, Galton had suggested these studies might be a means of disclosing hidden, unconscious mental processes, and Kraepelin had also attempted to shed light on mental disorders by means of word association. Jung undertook most of his studies of word association between 1902 and 1910. To begin with, he continued the tradition started by Kraepelin, but then he found he could use experiments on word association as a means of disclosing the presence of ideas associated with strong feelings and mental conflicts. He called the ideas bound together by a strong emotion a *complex*. We may infer the presence of a complex, Jung thought, by noting whether the subject's reaction to a word was in some way unusual. For instance, did the subject respond after an unusually long time, give an unusual association, or fail to answer? In 1920, the American psychologists Grace Kent and Aaron Rosanoff extended and refined Jung's procedure, constructing a test bearing their names that has been much used. On the basis of research from 1,000 subjects, they worked out tables of the frequency with which the associations were given for 100 words selected for the test.

The idea of a complex is similar to Janet's ideas that certain mental representations could be dissociated from the memories usually available to a person. Janet had also argued that traumatic experiences might lead to disturbances of the memory processes. In an article written in 1911, Jung presented an interpretation of his findings that seems to be in line with Janet's ideas, though we can also interpret them as similar to Freud's ideas of repression.

In his studies of emotions associated with mental representations, Jung also used measurements of changes in the electrical conductivity of the skin, the *galvanic skin reflex* (GSR), and combined these with a word association test. Altogether, he was a pioneer in the study of relationships between mental representations and emotions.

Divisions of Personalities into Types

His attempts at describing personality also make Jung a pioneer. In his book on personality types, he described personality as having three dimensions. One dimension had feeling as opposed to thinking; another, intuition as opposed to sensation; and a third, extroversion as opposed to introversion. Later researchers have been particularly interested in the last dimension because it has turned up in so many descriptions of personality. To Jung, extroversion–introversion represented an attitude or orientation towards the world. He did not think some persons were extroverted and others introverted; the difference referred to the degree to which a person was extroverted or introverted. Whereas the extroverted were more oriented towards events and objects in the external world and towards action, the introverted were preoccupied with events and phenomena of their own mental life. Jung supported his belief in a three-dimensional personality with biographical descriptions of historical figures as well as with descriptions he had made of cases in psychopathology.

The Collective Unconscious

Jung thought there are two types of unconscious phenomena. The first, called the *personal unconscious*, consists of mental experiences once conscious but forgotten or repressed. The second, called the *collective unconscious*, consists of instincts or predispositions of different kinds that are inherited from preceding generations and common to all human beings. The collective unconscious also included what Jung called *archetypes*. He claimed to have found the archetypes in myths and fairy tales and in the fantasies, dreams, deliriums, and obsessions of persons he had studied; the archetypes are accompanied by definite feelings.

The Archetypes

The archetypes represent forces in the psyche to which we must adjust to achieve a healthy, rich, and normal mental life. In Jung's descriptions, they appear almost as mythical beings. This, of course, makes modern researchers reluctant to engage in a study of them. Still, many down-to-earth psychologists are fascinated by the idea of the archetypes because they seem to touch upon some important aspects of human personality. Jung claimed to have found a large number of different archetypes. I shall consider only those thought to be particularly important.

Jung conceived of personality as having two different parts: one oriented towards the external and the other towards the internal world. On the border between these two, he postulated the presence of an ego. He thought the archetypes surround the ego and interact with it. One important archetype is the *persona*, representing the attitudes we take to the diverse groups with whom we associate, such as persons of the same age, class, political party, profession, or nationality. The persona may be compared to a mask behind which are thoughts, feelings, and human features we are reluctant to reveal to others. Thus, we can think of it as the conventional part of a person. If we identify too strongly with our persona, we could lose contact with our internal life or develop social or ethnic prejudices.

Another archetype is the *shadow*. The shadow personifies features of our personality we are unwilling to accept because we regard them as inferior and associated with feelings of guilt, but that nevertheless intrude upon us. The shadow could, Jung thought, be traced back to our animal predecessors. However, it represents not only negative and destructive tendencies, but also normal instincts and purposeful reactions – realistic perceptions as well as creative impulses. Ellenberger gives the following example: A man who regards himself as a good husband and father, and as liked and respected by his subordinates and his fellow citizens, ignores the fact that he is an egoistic husband and a tyrannical father, is hated by his subordinates, and is more feared than respected by his fellow citizens. The shadow is made up of the negative features of which the man is not cognizant.

Like Freud and other contemporary thinkers, Jung assumed bisexuality in both sexes. He believed the psyche of the woman contains a component representing characteristic features of the male psyche, and man's psyche contains a component representing characteristic features of the female psyche. The male component of the woman's psyche and the female component of the man's represent the archetypes *animus* and *anima*, respectively. Jung held that owing to the presence of these archetypes we might see persons of the opposite sex in an idealized and distorted manner.

The most important archetype is the *self*. Like Schopenhauer, Nietzsche, and Freud, Jung stressed the conflicting tendencies found in the human personality. There were conflicts, for example, between the persona and the shadow, between tendencies towards extroversion and introversion, and between tendencies to act according to male or female characteristics. Jung did, however, claim the psyche contains a force striving towards reconciliation of conflicting tendencies, towards a state of balance and harmony in mental life that he called *individuation*. This force, the *self*, represents potential in humans. The idea of individuation comes close to what the later humanistic psychologists called *self-actualization*.

One objection to Jung's archetypes is that he seems to have believed they represent characteristics acquired by individuals of earlier generations; in other words, he seems to have relied on the Lamarckian principle of the inheritance of acquired traits. However, it seems possible to explain at least some of the archetypes by assuming they represent genetically determined dispositions to react in certain ways. For example, we may have a genetically determined unwillingness to admit what we regard as inferior features in our personalities. Then again, the concept of the archetypes is not necessary because we can explain such tendencies in simpler ways.

Alfred Adler (1870–1937)

In his presentation of the history of dynamic psychology, or as he called it, dynamic psychiatry, Ellenberger gave a detailed and lengthy treatment of Adler. He noted that several psychological thinkers who were credited with modifying psychoanalysis by pointing to the importance of social relationships in the development of personality had obtained their ideas from Adler without mentioning this.

A Biographical Sketch

Alfred Adler was born in a suburb of Vienna and belonged, as Freud did, to a Jewish family. After a good education, he gained his medical degree in 1895. In childhood, he felt he was not accepted by his mother but was protected by his father. He maintained that he experienced rivalry with his older brother and characterized his childhood as unhappy. In 1899, he began a private practice in Vienna, and in 1902, after becoming interested in Freud's book on the interpretation of dreams, he contacted him and began to collaborate with him. Adler was elected President of the Society of Psychoanalysis in Vienna in 1910, but the next year he and Freud broke with each other, having disagreed on some of the central ideas of psychoanalysis. Adler converted to Protestantism in 1904. Of his publications, the following four should be mentioned: *Study of Organ Inferiority and Psychical Compensation* (1907), *The Neurotic Constitution* (1912), *The Practice and Theory of Individual Psychology* (1920), and *Understanding Human Nature* (1927). All have been translated into English.

In his youth, Adler was active in the Social Democratic Party in Vienna, and throughout his life he was in sympathy with social democratic ideas. He was influenced by Marx, and in 1897 he married a Russian student dedicated to socialism.

Adler never obtained a position at the University of Vienna. In 1912, he had applied for a position as *Privatdozent* but was not accepted. In fact Janet, Freud, Jung, and Adler all worked privately as psychotherapists and were not directors of university clinics. This may help to explain why early clinical psychology had so little contact with academic psychology.

After World War I, Austria was reduced to a small state. The disintegration of the Austro-Hungarian Empire and the destruction caused by the war led to a recession, social unrest, and distress in the 1920s and 1930s. The Social Democrats came to power and introduced a number of social reforms, recommending, among other things, that education be made available to all groups of the population. Being sympathetic to social democracy, Adler sought to bring his ideas into the new educational program by giving courses to teachers in schools and kindergartens as well as by acting as a consultant to the staffs of educational institutions. He was appointed professor at the Pedagogical Institute of Vienna in 1924. Adler advocated less authoritarian upbringing of children and spoke in favor of equal rights for women. During the 1920s, he frequently visited the United States to give speeches and lectures, and in 1934 he and his family emigrated there. When Hitler's popularity increased, Adler realized the evil nature of his ideas and that the Nazis would come to power – thus, perhaps, he revealed a psychological insight missed by Jung and probably also by Freud. Adler also foresaw early that an oppressive regime would arise in the Soviet Union. He died in 1937 during a visit to Great Britain.

As I have emphasized, Adler's psychology differs significantly from Freud's. Adler rejected the libido theory, the idea of psychosexual development, and the Oedipus complex. Although he regarded many psychological processes as unconscious, he had quite different ideas about their nature from those held by Freud. He attributed great importance to childhood experiences but stressed other types of experience as more important in development, and he also held that human behavior is fashioned by future goals. Further, he maintained that human beings have the freedom to make decisions and are responsible for their actions.

Adler's Theory of Neurosis

In *The Neurotic Constitution*, Adler set forth a theory of neurosis and psychological disorders and gave an account of how he believed they should be treated. Whereas Freud based his explanation of neurosis on his idea of sexuality, Adler started from the fact that the infant is dependent upon others to satisfy its needs and to master its environment. He claimed this creates a *feeling of inferiority* in the child. The child attempts to overcome its feeling of inferiority and, as Adler put it, tries to compensate for its inadequacies. Under unfavorable conditions, the child also *overcompensates* for these. Adler believed the feeling of inferiority is characteristic of all children and is a dominant factor in the development of personality. Persons manifesting it to an extreme degree suffer from what he called an *inferiority complex*.

Extreme symptoms of feeling helpless could have different causes. In his first book Adler had argued that children with defective body organs might sometimes develop a feeling of inferiority and concentrate on the defect in a harmful manner. In *The Neurotic Constitution*, he broadened his view of the causes of maladjustment to include defects in childcare, poverty, and poor external social conditions, as well as a deprived upbringing. In respect to the latter, Adler held that the child's training might be detrimental not only if it is strict and cruel, but also if it is overprotective.

Starting from the thesis of inferiority, Adler formulated a view of the child's onto-genetic development. Like Freud, he concentrated on the fantasy life of the child. He thought the child sets goals for its social adjustment and forms a plan to master its surroundings, achieve recognition, become a unique personality, and attain influence and power. The strivings of the child are directed towards future goals. Thus, expectations of the future contribute to forming personality, not only experiences in the past. The child gradually generates what Adler called a *lifestyle*. Because lifestyle originates in early childhood, it is marked by oversimplified and infantile thoughts. Under unfavorable circumstances, these thoughts might further develop and become entrenched with increasing age. The end result might then be a complete maladjustment to society.

Because the plans made by the child are so strongly dominated by its fantasy life, they are frequently unrealistic; they may be fictitious. Adler did, however, underscore that the child has creative power and ability to realize its plans. He maintained, as we saw, that humans are capable of making choices and are responsible for their own lives. In acknowledging their debt to Adler, later humanistic psychologists also emphasized this point.

Making use of an expression taken from Nietzsche, Adler called the child's strivings to achieve superiority over its surroundings the *will to power*. The will to power might reveal itself in extreme expressions of ambition, miserliness, distrust, envy, disparagement of others, and malice and brutality. Adler admitted his debt to Nietzsche and brought to the fore human inclination to think and act aggressively.

Our Feeling of Community

In contrast to Nietzsche, Adler claimed that a *feeling of community* is a fundamental characteristic of humans. Human beings strive not only for self-realization and power, but also for entrance into a social community. Ideas from Marx and socialist ideology formed a part of Adler's *Weltanschauung* (worldview) and psychology. He believed that if human beings remain outside the social community, it leads to suffering for the mal-adjusted persons as well as for society.

The idea of a feeling of community is present in the book on the neurotic constitution, but more prominent in *Understanding Human Nature*. Adler held that parents signifi-cantly affect the child's lifestyle and ascribed a decisive role to the mother in developing the community feeling in the child. He is also known for pointing out that the develop-ment of a child may be influenced by its birth order. For example, the firstborn is treated differently from the second born, and the two children have a different relationship to each other, all of which could affect their development. Adler pointed out the impor-tance of the social environment for the child's development before psychoanalytically oriented psychologists, such as Anna Freud, Erik Erikson, Harry Stack Sullivan, Karen Horney, and the object relations theorists, began to draw upon the social aspect in their thinking about the way mental disorders arise.

Adler criticized Freud for underestimating the role played by social and cultural factors in human development. His opposition to Freud is well illustrated by his rejection of the idea that penis envy is a force in the development of girls. For women, Adler maintained, that force is frequently a demand for equality with men. Disagreement on this issue was the specific reason Alder left the group surrounding Freud.

According to Adler, maladjustment may be the result of several different types of unfa-vorable conditions. Those deriving from poverty and disease must, he held, be eliminated by social policies and improvements in health services. Conditions resulting from unsat-isfactory childcare must be remedied by advanced educational science. After World War I, Adler was deeply engaged in educational problems as well as in efforts to improve the upbringing of children in all groups of society. He became a spokesperson for a social democratic educational policy.

Adler's Therapy

From what we have said of Adler's thoughts on human development, it is clear that his therapy aimed to impress on his clients that their wishes, desires, and plans are not in agreement with social reality, and that the strategies and lifestyle a maladjusted individual chooses have unfortunate consequences. Adler did not base his psychotherapy on definite procedures, as Freud had done. He had no particular method that might lead the therapist to a better understanding of the conflicts causing the maladjustment. The therapist should form a picture of the client's situation by means of conversations in which the client tells the history of his or her life and accounts for problems, and the therapist asks questions about the client's recollections of early childhood, of difficulties met with at that age, of dreams, and of wishes and plans. The task of the therapist is to present to clients his view of the nature of their problems. The clients are then asked whether they want to change their lifestyle.

Some Concluding Remarks on Alder

Adler's books, particularly *Understanding Human Nature*, bear witness to his exten-sive psychological knowledge and emphasis on the importance of social factors in the development of personality. Adler contributed to a more balanced view of this development. Further, as already mentioned, he inspired later humanistic psychologists and probably made clinical psychologists more attentive to the role played by feelings of shortcomings and inferiority in human thinking and actions. However, he scarcely formulated the problems relating to these phenomena clearly enough for them to be empirically investigated in a fruitful manner, and this is probably why relatively little empirical research has been undertaken to shed light on them.

11

Early American Psychology (1890–1920)

Psychology in the United States had its origin in the same set of ideas that inspired the psychologies of Germany, Great Britain, Russia, France, and Austria, but, like those, it also had a unique development. To understand this development, we need some knowledge of US society in the latter half of the 1800s.

Some Features of Nineteenth-Century American Society

While much of the nineteenth-century United States had once been a British colony, independence in 1776 had severed the political-administrative but not the cultural connections between the two states. The new nation was dominated by people who spoke English as their native language and whose roots were in British culture and thinking. The social order was based on British traditions, and all this remained so far into the 1900s.

The United States underwent great changes in the period after the Civil War (1861–65). Before the war, the greater part of the population had lived and worked on farms of relatively modest size. Afterward, in the years following 1865, rapid technological development took place in agriculture. The use of new machinery created a revolution, and the production of food increased enormously. At the same time, great changes also took place in ownership; large agricultural areas came to be owned by relatively few people, and the number of agricultural workers increased. Industry experienced explosive growth, and people poured into the new industrial areas, which rapidly became large cities. At the same time, streams of immigrants began arriving in the new Promised Land, needing food, housing, education, hospitals, and churches and bringing with them rapid changes in US society.

People emigrated to North America for different reasons. Most probably hoped to find a means of subsistence for themselves and their families. Some sought wealth, some political freedom, and some sought to practice their religion according to their convictions. Common to all was that they left countries in which they did not feel they had sufficient opportunities. A desire for self-realization and freedom came to mark Americans, for whom individualism became a central value. The craving for individual freedom and the possibility of amassing substantial capital helped make the United States a society characterized by capitalist ideas.

For most people in the United States of the 1900s, it was a hard struggle just to exist. Still, many felt the country offered the possibility of a richer life, and it seemed the land of opportunities and optimism. The belief that human beings have the capacity to realize their potential as social, constructive beings has deeply influenced American psychology.

Science Directed Towards Practical Life

Although individualism is an important factor in American social life, the United States has also produced great organizers. The millions streaming into the country after the Civil War frequently lived in very poor conditions. Nevertheless, Americans were able to establish enduring institutions and create a standard of living that was very high compared to the rest of the world, an achievement that clearly demanded great organizational ability. While Americans gave religion a central place in their social life, they also valued knowledge and science. In the course of just a few decades, beginning in the 1880s, they succeeded in establishing modern universities on a par with the best in Europe, with independent administrations and distinctive characters. Nonetheless, US scientists cooperated across the nation.

Science in the United States started and expanded at a time when it was evident that it would have great consequences for society. The US view of science was also strongly affected by the practical problems confronting the nation as it conquered and colonized the vast North American continent. This endeavor gave US society a more pronounced orientation towards application than was the case in Europe. Many historians have noted that in a society where the citizens met with so many problems requiring immediate solution, the theoretical aspect of scientific activity tended to be pushed into the background. Problems with no quick solution were regarded as problems of less importance.

Foundations of Early American Psychology

The idea of making psychology an empirical science rapidly gained a footing in American scientific life. The first psychological laboratory was established in 1883, and forty-two laboratories had been started at universities and colleges by 1900 (Hilgard 1987). Two journals for the publication of research were started, *The American Journal of Psychology* in 1887, and *The Psychological Review* in 1894. In 1892, an association for the promotion of psychology, the American Psychological Association (APA), was founded. Finally, scientists of other disciplines acknowledged the existence of empirical psychology; several of its pioneers were elected to the National Academy of Sciences (Hilgard 1987).

The pioneers approached their subject in different ways and treated a great number of diverse topics. Thus, as Eliot Hearst (1979), D. Alfred Owens, Mark Wagner (1992), and most later historians note, it is not easy to point to distinctive features in the early psychology developed in the United States. At the end of the 1800s, the pioneers had introduced the main German and British research traditions and were energetically building up their own. These all formed the foundation of early US psychology. As an introduction to the work of the individual US research workers, I shall briefly account for the way the foreign and national research traditions were represented.

German experimental psychology was amply represented in the psychological laboratories. It was thoroughly treated in three widely used textbooks: William James's *Principles of Psychology* (1890/1950), George Ladd's *Elements of Physiological Psychology* (1887), and Edward Titchener's *Experimental Psychology: A Manual of Laboratory Practice* (1901–1905), in four volumes. As for British psychology, James opposed Wundt's psychology by elaborating Spencer's views. Strongly influenced by the theory of evolution, James viewed the mind as the result of adaptation to the environment through biological evolution; accordingly, he stressed its biological functions. His student at Harvard, Edward Thorndike, began extensive studies in comparative psychology in 1896, a direction in which several researchers later continued. Further, Thorndike elaborated Spencer's view of psychology into a version of behaviorism and founded the behaviorist tradition in animal learning. At Columbia University, James McKean Cattell began research on individual differences in 1891, based on tests in the Galton tradition. Test construction and psychometrics became an American specialty. At the beginning of the 1900s, studies of heredity in the Galton tradition were also undertaken. Thus, the main British psychological research traditions were being incorporated along with the German research traditions.

The psychology of the New World was from the onset more strongly oriented towards the solution of practical and social problems than was European psychology. Psychology followed the general pattern of US science and was soon used in hiring and advertising. However, the great interest of most of the pioneers was in education and child development. Granville Stanley Hall was a leader here. Inspired by early educational research in Germany, he undertook extensive studies of children's knowledge at the time they begin school. He attracted a great number of researchers to educational and developmental psychology when he was teaching at Johns Hopkins University and later at Clark University. Among his first students was John Dewey, later to be the most influential US philosopher in the first half of the 1900s, a famous educator, and a persistent advocate of the importance of applying psychological research in education as well as in other aspects of social life. Dewey was appointed chairman of the department of philosophy, education, and psychology at the University of Chicago in 1894. Educational psychology was also the main interest of Thorndike, who taught the subject at Columbia University from 1902. A fourth influential developmental psychologist was James Baldwin, who took over as the chairman at Johns Hopkins after Hall had gone to Clark. As early as 1896, Ligtner Witmer established a clinic at the University of Pennsylvania for children suffering from psychological disability.

The study of educational and developmental psychology attracted the interest of a broad group of intellectuals. Their work provided an important background for US empirical psychology, the central theme of which became the study of learning (comparable to the focus on perception in Germany). As a result of this interest in applying psychology to problems of social life, psychology in the United States was organized as a profession on a par with teaching, medicine, and law. As John O'Donnell (1985) shows, the creation of psychology as a profession had a significant effect on the development of the field in the United States.

US psychology did not start as a single endeavor that then branch off in different directions; from the outset, it included diverse approaches that were not easily integrated. Wundt undoubtedly had a strong impact on the early psychology of the New World. He inspired the study of physiological psychology and convinced many students that psychology could be advanced as an experimental science. Many of the most prominent US pioneers in empirical psychology took their doctorates with him or studied for some time with him at Leipzig. When we consider their number, and the number of laboratories established for the promotion of experimental psychology, we might think Wundtian experimental psychology completely dominated the early psychology of the United States, but this was not at all the case.

Some of those originally attracted to Wundt's psychology returned home from studying with him to carry out research along other lines. Some, such as James and Hall, became critical of his psychology, and at the beginning of the 1900s a conflict arose between his followers and his critics. Edward Titchener, who became the director of the psychological laboratory at Cornell University in 1892, was regarded as the chief representative of Wundt's psychology. In opposition, James Angell developed a program representative of the psychology of the University of Chicago. That conflict was soon overshadowed, however, by the conflict between psychologists conceiving of psychology as the study of mind and those who saw it as the study of behavior.

In this chapter, I shall review the work of James, Hall, Dewey, Dewey's coworker George Mead, Baldwin, Titchener, Cattell, some work in test and applied psychology, and Thorndike's behaviorally oriented studies of learning. I shall end the chapter with a review of the ideas of Titchener and Angell. The next chapter, the first on behaviorism, will cover Thorndike, and Robert Woodworth, a central figure in US psychology, appears in Chapter 17 on physiological psychology. Before I turn to these reviews, I shall say a few words about *pragmatism*, an influential philosophical movement with a great impact on American psychology.

Pragmatism

In the years closely following the end of the Civil War, a small group of young Americans formed a club for the discussion of philosophical problems. This resulted in the emergence of original ideas, which two of the participants – Charles Peirce (1839–1914) and William James (1842–1910) – gradually developed into systematic attempts to answer fundamental philosophical questions. The two formulated their thoughts somewhat differently, but their ideas have so much in common that it is natural to regard them as a specific movement within philosophy, *pragmatism*.

The eldest in the group, Chauncey Wright (1830–1875), was already a relatively well-known philosopher. He was familiar with evolutionary biological thinking and may have given Peirce and James a thorough introduction to this. The group must have had remarkable intellectual potential, because a fourth member, Oliver Wendell Holmes, Jr., later became a famous professor of law and a Supreme Court justice. In his recollections of these meetings, Peirce has underlined that the group was first and foremost concerned with the British philosophers Mill, Bain, and Spencer. At the end of the nineteenth century and the beginning of the twentieth, pragmatism dominated US philosophy and psychology.

In Chapter 6, we noted the importance Bain attributed to pleasure and pain in the acquisition of new actions. Bain also insisted that the meaning of our beliefs is determined by the actions to which they lead. Peirce and James carried on the ideas of Bain and the utilitarianists that our beliefs are determined by their consequences. In an article published in 1878, Peirce outlined a procedure for determining the meaning of concepts. He was particularly concerned with scientific concepts, but also with the meaning of words and sentences. One of the examples he used to illustrate his procedure was the concept of force in physics, the meaning of which, he believed, we could determine by examining the *effects* of the force. In agreement with Bain, Peirce maintained there was a close connection between our beliefs and our actions. Actions, he said, always have concrete consequences. We could clarify our beliefs by examining the consequences of actions that could be seen as the result of those beliefs. He underlined that the consequences are always concrete and practical. The procedure he proposed for clarifying our beliefs was an original contribution to philosophy.

While Peirce was principally concerned with the philosophy of science and logic, James's thinking was directed towards the relationship between science, religion, and morality, and he applied the pragmatic procedure to assessing the value of religious and moral ideas. In a series of lectures given in Edinburgh in 1902 and published under the title *Varieties of Religious Experience: A Study of Human Nature* (1902, p. 444), he gave his assent to what he believed to be the essence of Peirce's thinking:

Beliefs, in short, are rules of action; and the whole function of thinking is but one step in the production of active habits. If there were any part of a thought that made no difference in the thought's practical consequences, then that part would be no proper element of the thought's significance.

By stressing the concrete and practical consequences of thinking, Peirce and James gave expression to what was probably the central point in the worldview of the North Americans, whose practical philosophy appealed strongly to contemporary as well as to later Americans. In the first half of the twentieth century, John Dewey (1859–1952) was regarded as the most important representative of pragmatic philosophy. He attempted to combine Peirce's ideas of how we can elucidate philosophical problems with James's ideas of religious and moral values.

William James (1842–1910)

James did not carry out any important empirical research project. Nor did he lead an active research laboratory. Still, he had a profound impact on empirical psychology. For many contemporary US psychologists, it was he, not Wundt, who had explained what empirical psychology is about, and to many later psychologists he was a chief inspiration. However, as Barbara Ross (1991) reports, some regarded him as the spoiled child of US psychology, and at a committee meeting in the 1930s, Karl Lashley, a distinguished Harvard professor, even proclaimed that James was "the biggest mistake that had ever befallen scientific psychology, especially psychology at Harvard" (Taylor, 1992). Evidently, the conceptions psychologists have of their study strongly affect their assessments of James's contributions.

A Biographical Sketch

The literature on William James is extensive. For my biographical sketch and as an aid in interpreting his main psychological work, I have primarily relied on Ralph Perry's (1935) and Gerald Meyers's (1986) biographies, as well as the collection of essays entitled *Reinterpreting the Legacy of William James*, published by the APA under the editorship of Margaret Donnelly (1992). William's father, the philosopher and theologian Henry James, was a notable person, and William's brother Henry is regarded as an eminent American novelist. As we might expect, the James family has been studied extensively.

William James was born in New York in 1842 and was nineteen when the Civil War broke out. Hence, he became an adult before US society underwent the radical changes brought about by technological advances and capitalism. From the old society, he retained a contemplative attitude to life based on the religious, moral, and political ideas represented by the dominant and enlightened middle classes of New England. His thinking can be seen as an attempt to reconcile his view of life with the new ideas created by the advancement of science and technology.

James was critical of several of his father's opinions and arguments, but he seems on the whole to have accepted the same principal values. Both men believed humans have moral and religious obligations and that society should be organized with a view to securing the rights of the individual and to bringing about social solidarity. Like his father, he believed American democracy represented a unique opportunity to create a good society. His father wanted his children to go to US schools but at the same time to benefit from instruction in the best European schools. To attain this goal, the family lived for long periods in Great Britain, France, Germany, and Switzerland while the children were growing up. William became a cosmopolite and a moderate US patriot. He had close contact with many distinguished scientists and thinkers in the United States as well as in Europe. This upbringing, and his mastery of language, may in part explain his supreme ability to examine intellectual problems. In an elegant and humorous manner, he could both express intimate personal confessions and mount heavy attacks on the opinions of others.

James seems to have had difficulty in choosing a profession. First, he studied for a year at an academy of art with a view to becoming a painter. He gave this up and began medical studies at Harvard. In 1865, he took a year off and joined a biological expedition to Brazil. In 1867 and 1868, he lived in Europe in the hope of improving his health and did not pass his final medical examinations until 1869. Throughout his life, James was plagued by insomnia, indigestion, and eyestrain. After he finished his medical studies, he went into a deep depression in which he seems to have had serious thoughts of suicide. Apart from the periods in which he was traveling in Europe, he lived in the house of his parents until he married in 1878. He suffered from depression throughout his life.

Following his medical studies and in a prolonged state of depression, James was strongly influenced by the French philosopher Charles Renouvier (1815–1903), whose work convinced him that the will is free. After having read an essay by Renouvier in 1870, James wrote in his diary: "My first act of free will shall be to believe in free will"

(Perry, 1935, I, p. 322). Meyers (1986) has accounted for James's view of the will and the influence of Renouvier in a detailed and judicious presentation of his life and thought. In brief, James's psychology and philosophy can be said to center on the question of free will. While this was apparently a result of his personal experience, in Western thinking and philosophy throughout the nineteenth century there was great interest in problems associated with the will.

James claimed that executing what he regarded as his free will relieved his depression. In 1873, he felt he was able to take a position as lecturer in physiology and anatomy at Harvard. In 1876, he was appointed professor at this university, first in philosophy and then in psychology; in 1897, the title of his chair was changed back to philosophy. James engaged in a number of questions in which he took sides against well-established and widespread beliefs – for example, he upheld the right of women to study. In the latter half of the nineteenth century, there was great interest in telepathy, clairvoyance, and spiritualism in the United States, Great Britain, and France. James took an interest in these phenomena too and, in 1884, founded the American Society for Psychical Research.

By then James was already famous for an article in which he presented a theory of emotions. His *Principles of Psychology*, on which he had worked for twelve years, appeared in two large volumes in 1890 and in a shorter version two years later. He continued to lecture on topics in psychology after he had finished his *Principles*, including abnormal psychology, personality, and educational psychology. His lectures on education were printed as *Talks to Teachers on Psychology* (1899). Further, in *The Varieties of Religious Experience* (1902), James described the experiences of mystics and converts, drew attention to abnormal and pathological religious states, and also discussed the role of religion in the life of the normal human being. In these lectures, he also spoke of his own depression at the beginning of the 1870s, and the way in which it had led him to understand morbid and abnormal states in other people.

James on Subject Matter and Methods in the Study of Psychology

James was ten years younger than Wundt and finished *Principles of Psychology*, his main psychological work, sixteen years after Wundt had published his *Grundzüge*. He seems to have been thoroughly familiar with Wundt's contributions but probably developed his ideas independently. James and Wundt had many points in common, as Danziger (1980c) and Hilgard (1987) noted. Both were trained as medical doctors and had taken a particular interest in psychology. Both conceived of psychology as the study of mind and believed the will is central in mental life. Moreover, they both regarded introspection as the main method, though their views of the use of the method were different. As a result, in my opinion, their psychologies became different in important respects.

According to Wundt, to be a reliable procedure, introspection had to be used in the study of simple mental experience and only under experimental conditions. Thinking and more complex mental processes had to be studied differently, via *Völkerpsychologie* (see Wundt, 1900–1920). James restricted introspection neither to simpler types of mental experience nor to experimentally controlled situations. Further, whereas Wundt attempted to account for the nature of different types of mental experience by show-ing how they were built up by elements forming different structures, James made no assumptions about elements and described mental experience with everyday language, as it appeared to him. Thus, his approach had some similarity to phenomenology, as developed by Brentano and Stumpf. James was familiar with Brentano's work and was a friend of Stumpf and may have been influenced by them.

The greatest influence on James's thinking about consciousness, however, came from Darwin and Spencer. As James explicitly made clear, he was inspired by Spencer's def-inition of life, by what he referred to as Spencer's formula: "the adjustment of inner to outer relations." Spencer, he said, had helped him realize that the mind could not be seen as isolated from the environment. Our mental life also seems to be directed towards some end, some goal, and our mental activity is a means to reach this goal. James (1890/1950, p. 8) made this view central in his psychology: "The pursuance of future ends and the choice of means for their attainment are thus the mark and cri-terion of the presence of mentality in a phenomenon." According to this view, mind has a function, and James's approach has been called *functionalism*. In his *Principles of Psychology*, he tried to account for human attainment of goals by drawing on ideas of reflexes, instincts, and interests determined by biological needs. In his treatment of the concept of self, he pointed out that it has a basis in what he called the instincts and interests of self-preservation, and in his treatment of attention he showed how it is governed by our interests.

The idea that mind is a means of attaining a goal agrees with Darwin's views of evolution. According to the theory of evolution, it is logical to assume that mind has evolved as a means of survival. James (1890/1950, pp. 146 ff) was a declared adher-ent of evolution, even if, like most of his biologically oriented contemporaries, he did not understand the central role played by natural selection. We can see his attempt at orienting psychology towards the study of the functions of consciousness as a result of his reflections on evolution. Still, however, it was problematic to develop a view of consciousness in line with that theory.

James was critical of the use of the experimental method in psychology. He admitted it had proven to be of some value and might one day produce useful knowledge of more substantial psychological problems, but so far the results were trivial. He was, however, aware of the fact that psychology needed procedures for controlling reports on mental processes. Introspective reports, James (1890/1950, p. 194) insisted, could be supplemented by material obtained by *comparative methods*, by which he meant studies that produced material which could supplement introspection, including studies of animals, children, persons suffering from mental disturbances, and tribal people.

Apparently, Wundt and James wanted to include in their studies both animals and human beings who could not introspect. Wundt wanted to use introspective reports as premises for the study of animals, children, and persons suffering from mental distur-bances. James, on the other hand, wanted to supplement introspective study by a study of subjects who could not introspect. At first we may think the difference is merely a choice of words. But on reflection we see that a consequence of Wundt's approach was that the method determined the topics selected for research. Wundt may be said to sacrifice range of topics for method. James, on the other hand, was free to choose topics for study but had no adequate method for describing mental experience. He might be said to sacrifice method for range of topics.

Next I shall deal with James's view of instincts and habits, consciousness, the self, attention, the will, and his theory of emotions.

James on Instincts and Habits

James (1890/1950, p. 6) believed a broad conception of psychology's subject matter was more fertile than a narrow one and that "at a certain stage in the development of every science a degree of vagueness is what best consists with fertility." Thus, he treated psychological problems from a physiological, an evolutionary biological, and a human ontogenetic perspective. Sometimes he also brought in psychiatric and cultural perspectives, in agreement with a view of psychology widely accepted by present-day empirical psychologists. The breadth of his approach is well illustrated by his treatment of instincts and his remarkable willingness to consider ideas opposed to his own, as well as his careful consideration of alternatives to his preferred way of looking at matters.

James (1887, p. 355) accepted what he regarded as the usual definition of an instinct – "the faculty of acting in such a way as to produce certain ends, without foresight of the ends, and without previous education of the performance." Like Spencer, he believed instincts represent connections of reflexes, and he included in his definition physiological reflexes as well as emotions. A characteristic of instincts was, James pointed out, that they are elicited by a definite sensory stimulus. He conceived of the stimulus as a key to a lock. This was a characteristic later attributed to instincts by Lorenz and Tinbergen. Darwin had suggested that humans have a few instincts. James took the original position that we have numerous instincts, more than any other animal. On this point he anticipated a view that prevailed at the end of the twentieth century.

James emphasized that instincts may be modified by experience and habit. The role played by most human instincts is to provide a basis for the development of habits, and once a habit is formed, the instinct fades away, though James did not say how. Instincts are not opposed to reason, he believed. Initially, they are blind, but they might be modified as a result of experience of their consequences. Further, an instinct could be neutralized by another instinct opposed to it. Reason could not inhibit an instinct, said James (1890/1950, p. 343), but it could determine which of two opposed instinctive reactions is favored.

In contrast to McDougall, James (1890/1950, ch. 28) understood that Weismann had undermined Lamarck's view of the inheritance of acquired traits. Like Darwin, James attempted to understand how an instinct in an animal is the result of an interaction between the environment and an organism having a specific genetic endowment. Further, also in contrast to McDougall, he emphasized that instincts are modified by experience and learning, particularly in humans. Thus, he viewed human instincts as more or less genetically determined reactions. This view was not subject to the criticism raised against the idea of instincts in the years following the publication of McDougall's *An Introduction to Social Psychology* in 1908.

However, the human instincts James regarded as most important were so vaguely defined they hardly allowed of a more rigorous discussion. I shall not go into this but just mention that he regarded agoraphobia – excessive fear of open places – as instinctive and observed that phobias of spiders and snakes are unusually hard to overcome. This has become a widely accepted view in present-day psychology.

Habit

James thought habit played a central role in human life and eloquently described this in a passage (1890/1950, ch. 4) that has become famous:

Habit is thus the enormous fly-wheel of society, its most precious conservative agent. It alone is what keeps us within the bounds of ordinance, and saves the children of fortune from the envious uprising of the poor.

While instincts fade away when the habits based upon them are formed, habits– once established – are preserved for a long time, frequently the whole of life. Habits form an important part of a person's character, and James held that "by the age of thirty, the character has set like plaster, and will never soften again."

The chapter on habit (1890/1950, ch. 4) was the first chapter in his *Principles* in which James dealt with a specific problem area in psychology. The reason he treated this subject so early in the book was evidently that he thought habits had a central place in human life. But it probably also allowed him to introduce a physiological model on which he based much of his discussion. Central to it was an idea of the nervous system as consisting of paths corresponding to *reflex arcs*. Simple habits, such as sniffing, putting hands in pockets, and biting nails, are the results of what he called a reflex discharge. More complete habits are built up as a chain of discharges in the nervous system. Whereas the first discharge is the result of a sensory stimulation or an idea, the discharges setting off the next reflex, as well as the following reflex discharges, are muscular contractions.

James's model was illustrated by an example of a baby learning to attach pain to the grasping of the flame of a candle. James regarded this learning as a result of the coupling of two reflexes: the assumed reflex of reaching for the flame upon seeing it and the reflex of withdrawing the hand upon being burned. The chain, the connecting of the two reflexes, is accomplished, he held, by the establishment of connections in the brain of impressions between sensations and movements. In this process, the muscular impression of grasping was thought to be associated with the impression of the pain that is the stimulus for withdrawing the hand.

James agreed the model could be elaborated to include a number of reflexes, all of which could be elicited by any one of them. The cortex would thus function as "the great communicating switch-board at a central telephone station." This image had a profound effect. In the mid-1900s, James's idea of habits as consisting of chains of reflexes was, however, subject to a serious criticism by Karl Lashley, as we shall see in Chapter 17.

In his account of sensory perception, Helmholtz had placed great weight on the role played by eye movements and movements of the head. But on the whole the German experimental psychologists were little concerned with the role movements play in the interaction of the organism with its environment. James's view of the role played by muscular movements in the chaining of reflexes can be seen as the beginning of a shift of emphasis in US psychology from perceiving and thinking to movement.

Attempt at Describing Consciousness

James treated problems of consciousness in his *Principles* as well as in his later philosophical works. The description he gave of consciousness in *Principles* has been admired by psychologists since the book was first published. I shall limit my treatment to the ideas he introduced in this book. In his attempts at stating what he meant by *consciousness*, he made use of the term "thinking" or "thought." This term referred to every possible form of consciousness. James listed five points that characterized consciousness.

1 Every thought tends to be part of a personal consciousness.
2 Within each personal consciousness, thought is always changing.
3 Within each personal consciousness, thought is sensibly continuous.
4 Consciousness always appears to deal with objects independent of itself.
5 Consciousness is interested in some parts of these objects to the exclusion of others, and it welcomes or rejects – *chooses* from among them.

The beliefs stated in the five points are all plausible, and they may direct our attention to some important aspects of mental life. However, when we examine them more closely, it is difficult to understand more concretely what they mean. In the first point, we meet with the difficulty of understanding how we can distinguish between what James termed a "thought" and a "personal consciousness." In points 2 and 3, in order to determine whether a thought is changing or permanent, we must have criteria that allow us to decide when a thought is present. In points 4 and 5, what is meant by personal consciousness? In our discussion of Wundt's conception of the subject matter of psychology, we noted the difficulty of distinguishing between the content of consciousness and the experiencing subject. We also noted the difficulties of understanding what he meant by a field of consciousness, and by apperception as a force in consciousness. Apparently, James ran more or less into the same difficulties as Wundt.

In the last quarter of the 1900s, British philosophers began seriously criticizing the British empiricists' concept of sensation. James joined in this criticism. Beyond the fact that we seem never to directly observe sensations and abstract them from complex impressions, he felt sensations would always enter into new contexts, changing so radically that they would not be the same from one situation to another. As a consequence, consciousness would constantly be changing. James proposed that consciousness could be thought of as a stream, and the expression *stream of consciousness* has become famous. In my judgment, however, James failed to present criteria by which we could decide what should count as a change. As he himself remarked, Bain had used the expression before him, but Bain had insisted that what was at stake was a series of discrete thoughts. As long as we lack clear criteria to determine what is meant by continuity, it is hardly possible to decide who was correct, Bain or James. Hilgard (1987) has pointed out that the expression "stream of consciousness" is a metaphor that might be useful to poets but is hardly helpful to empirical psychologists.

Thoughts About a Self

In his discussion of consciousness James (1950, p. 226) concluded that "no psychology, at any rate, can question the *existence* of personal selves," and he made the concept of self central in his thinking on mental life. In his further treatment of the concept, he made a distinction between a knower and something known, between an *I* and a *Me*. In his *Psychology – Briefer Course* (1892), he introduced it in this way:

Whatever I may be thinking of, I am always at the same time more or less aware of *myself*, of my *personal existence*. At the same time it is *I* who am aware; so that the total self of me, being as it were duplex, *partly known and partly knower*, partly object and partly subject, must have *two aspects discriminated* in it, of which for shortness we may call one the *Me* and the other the *I*. (James, 1892, p. 189)

James tried to clarify the distinction by pointing out more concretely what he had in mind by a *Me*. He divided the *Me* into a material, a social, and a spiritual *Me*. Our material *Me* incorporates our bodies, our clothes, our possessions, everything we can say belongs to us. Our social *Me*, our social self, is the recognition we get from the persons we associate with, our friends. He argued that we have many social selves. Our spiritual self is our conception of our intellectual abilities, our inclinations, and our form of spiritual activity. In the spiritual *Me*, the most enduring and intimate part of the self manifested itself.

In reviewing Lewin in Chapter 5, I reported on his and his coworkers' ideas on the concept of level of aspiration. James (1950, p. 310) anticipated these by pointing out that our self-esteem is dependent not only on what we have achieved and are capable of achieving, but also on what we wish and hope to achieve. This was an important clinical insight.

Although some thinkers have doubted that we have a self-image, most people do probably believe they have a self-image in the sense that we can think about ourselves. We have what we can call a *reflexive self*. On the other hand, difficulties arise when we attempt to mark off this reflexive self from an *I*. The American psychologist M. Brewster Smith (1992) has pointed out that James seems to have ended up describing the *Me* as the active part, which is strange when we consider that he began by saying the *Me* is an object of our thinking. What is it that thinks this *Me*? James seems to have thought he could answer this difficult question by maintaining that we do not need to make any assumption about a thinker except in the sense that we assume a thought is occurring at a given moment. As Hilgard (1987) has emphasized, this is a strange standpoint. It is also strange, Hilgard thought, that James seems to have concluded that the foundation of his own spiritual self, as he conceived of this, is certain muscular movements in the larynx and the forehead. Gordon Allport (1943), who revived James's ideas of the self, referred to the contradictions and unclear points as "James's paradoxes."

The Nature of Attention

The power of James's functionalist approach is revealed in his treatment of attention. He found important ideas in Helmholtz, G. E. Müller, Janet, and other contemporary researchers that he integrated into a unitary functionalist view. He began by drawing attention to the great role we attach to attention in animal and human life: "The practical and theoretical life of whole species, as well as of individual beings, results from the selection which the habitual direction of their attention involves" (James, 1950, p. 424).

In his account of the effect attention has on the ability to perceive, distinguish between objects, remember, and think, James claimed that, when we have been attentive to an object, we will retain it in memory, while impressions of objects to which we have not been attentive will not leave a trace. Moreover, he emphasized that, as a result of attention, the sensory organs become adapted to the situation. This adaptation finds expression in different forms of behavior; for example, we adjust our eye muscles and turn our head or body when we examine something by looking or listening. When we taste or smell something, we adjust the tongue and lips to the objects, and when we want to obtain an impression of the surface of an object by means of touch, we move our hands. During attention, we also suppress behavior that can distract us. We shut our eyes when we want to taste something and hold our breath when we listen. By performing these movements, we prepare the organism. Another important characteristic of the attention processes is that, as Helmholtz had underlined, we try to anticipate what we will sense; we try to form a representation of it. James expressed this idea by saying that attention is a *preperception*. When preperception is at its peak, it can be difficult to decide what we should attribute to the stimulation and what to our imagination.

Like Helmholtz, James was convinced that it is not possible to direct attention to an object for more than a very short time, at most a couple of seconds, unless the object is undergoing a change of some sort. (This point apparently anticipated the idea of short-term memory.) In order to succeed in maintaining attention over a longer interval of time, we must find new aspects of the object and relate it to other objects. James also underlined that when we instruct children, we must first attract their attention, and then we must develop their ability to attend to an object for a longer period of time.

The Gestalt psychologists, as I reported in Chapter 5, attempted to explain perception and thinking without invoking the concept of attention. We shall see in the next two chapters that the behaviorists thought they could dispense with it. Although interest in attention was kept alive all through the first half of the 1900s, Helmholtz's and James's contributions were largely overlooked until the end of the century. We can see from works such as that of Gazzaniga et al. (2009) that they are now once again appreciated.

Of Emotions

James had some highly provocative ideas about emotions, claiming that the emotional experience is the result of our bodily reactions to the situation that arouses our emotion. In other words, he turned upside down what we usually believe to be the causal chain of events when we experience emotions. While we tend to think we experience something in a situation that elicits an emotion in us and then react to the emotion, James claimed that we first experience something in the situation, react to this with bodily movements, and then react to our own motor reaction. He gave the following as examples: We see a bear, run, and then react emotionally to the fact that we ran; we lose our fortune, weep, and feel sorrow; we receive an insult, strike, and feel anger. In his first formulation of the theory, James mainly had in mind reactions in skeletal muscles. Later, influenced by the Danish physiologist Carl Lange, who had presented a similar theory, he also included vascular-motor reactions. James's and Lange's views of emotions are jointly referred to as the *James–Lange theory*.

Darwin (1872/1965) had called attention to the fact that emotions in humans and animals have evolved in close connection with fundamental bodily functions – breathing, the beating of the heart, fighting, and reproduction. We can see James's studies of emotions as an elaboration of this point. James made the bodily reactions accompanying what he referred to as our *coarser emotions* the basis for our emotional feelings. When we concentrate on this point and not on his view of the sequence of events in emotions, we can understand why researchers have been attracted to his views of emotions to this day. When we start with the bodily reactions we can link the study of emotions to physiology, and this starting point allows us to base our research on reliable observations as well as on measurement. Further, this approach allows us to view emotions in an evolutionary biological perspective.

James admitted that it was difficult to test his and Lange's theory. The evidence he could adduce for his view was almost exclusively of an introspective nature. His main argument in favor of his view was the following thought-experiment (1950, p. 451):

If we fancy some strong emotion, and then try to abstract from our consciousness of it all the feelings of its bodily symptoms, we find we have nothing left behind, no "mind-stuff" out of which the emotions can be constituted, and that a cold and neutral perception is all that remains.

To perform the thought-experiment James urged us to undertake, we must first be able to abstract the emotion from the context in which it occurs and then from this abstraction abstract what appears to be the bodily reactions accompanying it. We have no criteria, however, by which we can determine whether James, or anyone else, has performed this thought-experiment in the proper way.

James did point to an indirect way of testing the theory. A corollary of his view was that it ought to be possible to produce emotions by exciting skeletal muscles and viscera involved in the diverse emotions. He did think it would be difficult to carry out an experiment along these lines, partly because so many bodily reactions are involved in a single emotion and partly because we have so little voluntary control of internal organs. However, Darwin had called attention to the great role played by facial muscles in expressions of emotions, and in the late twentieth century researchers found ways of activating specific facial muscles and producing changes in emotions. An instructive critical review of this research is given by Carlson (2007).

When James and Lange formulated their views, the functions of the autonomic nervous system were not known. Nor was it known how the brain is informed of changes taking place in skeletal muscles and viscera. As Stanley Finger (1994) reports, in the first three decades of the 1900s considerable progress was made in the study of these problems. One of the pioneers in this study, the Harvard professor Walter Cannon, gave what was then considered a trenchant criticism of the James–Lange theory, and interest in it declined.

But then, towards the end of the century, interest in the theory was revived. One reason was the success researchers had in producing changes in emotional feelings by activating facial muscles. Another reason was that knowledge had accumulated revealing that some of Cannon's main objections did not have the support he believed they had. A critical review of Cannon's criticism of the James–Lange theory is given by Carlson (2007).

James held that it was unproductive to classify or categorize emotions. He did, however, distinguish between emotions that had and did not have a distinct bodily expression. The former were referred to as the *coarser emotions* and the latter as the *subtler emotions*. His theory was formulated, he stated, to account only for the coarser emotions.

While Wundt (1896a) held that emotions are composed of feelings and centered his view on the concepts of pleasantness and unpleasantness (*Lust* and *Unlust*), James paid little attention to the problem of accounting for the relationship between feelings and emotions. He admitted that pleasure and pain, central to Bain's view of psychology, played a great role as instigating and regulating factors in human behavior, but he did not regard these feelings as forming part of emotions. He treated them in his chapter on the will. He also regarded the coarser emotions as instincts and discussed them as such: anger, fear, resentment, sympathy, curiosity, sociability, shyness, shame, and love. Finally, James was not concerned with the functions of feelings and emotions. In view of the fact that he made great efforts to orient the study of mind towards the functions of mental life, this is surprising. By starting with the bodily expressions of the emotions, James called attention to a central aspect of our emotions, but it seems justified to say that a satisfactory theory of emotions must account for feelings as well as for the functions of emotions.

Of the Will

I have mentioned that the will had a central position in James's psychology. Like Wundt, James treated the will and motivation as mental phenomena. This gave him a narrow basis for accounting for human motivation. However, as pointed out by James Deese (1990) and earlier in this chapter, James thought humans had many different types of instincts that motivate behavior. Thus, he did not treat motivation one-sidedly as a mental phenomenon; however, he did not succeed in expressing a more unified view of it. Discussions of the will disappeared from psychology in the first decades of the twentieth century.

Nevertheless, even if James did not have a particularly interesting theory of motivation, it is perhaps natural to ask today, when cognitive processes again hold a central place in psychology, whether his view of voluntary acts can give useful insights into what may take place when we make mental effort. In his treatment of voluntary acts, James took as a starting point the idea that consciousness contains representations that attract our attention in varying degrees. Voluntary acts emerge, he claimed, when we try to direct attention towards representations that seem to attract it to only a small degree. He admitted it was difficult to give a scientific explanation of how we could undertake such acts. Even if it sounds somewhat mystical, it is easier than it used to be to think we can influence attention by making different types of voluntary choices. Neurophysiologists discuss *parallel processes* in the nervous system, and in everyday psychology we have expressions such as, "putting an idea out of our heads," "trying to forget," and "directing attention towards other aspects of a subject."

Evaluation of James's Contributions

James would probably have had a name in the history of psychology even if he had only published the paper on emotions (James, 1884). His influence on empirical psychology is, however, far more profound. His *Principles of Psychology* gave new directions to the study of scientific psychology. The book provided a better understanding of what could be regarded as the subject matter of psychology, even if James did not elaborate his ideas into concrete research projects.

James held that at an initial stage in the study of a problem area, it is more productive to start out with a broad than with a narrow conception of subject matter. He broadened psychology by assembling in one study earlier as well as contemporary research in psychology and created a field of study that included German experimental psychology, British comparative psychology, French clinical psychology, and studies of unusual mental states. Thus, to repeat, he provided psychology with a much broader foundation in the United States than it had in Europe.

Further, James deepened conceptions of psychology's subject matter by elaborating Darwin's idea that the mind has evolved as a means of survival and thus must have a function. In line with Darwin's idea, he believed humans have instincts. Unlike Darwin, he held we have numerous instincts and viewed the self as a means for what he referred to as material and social self-seeking. He also viewed attention in an evolutionary perspective. But, as I noted, James seems to have overlooked that we must also see emotions in this perspective.

Granville Stanley Hall (1844–1922)

G. Stanley Hall was about the same age as James but had a different background and took an entirely different approach to the new psychology. He wanted empirical psychology to be a means of influencing society in directions he thought would be worthwhile, and he distinguished himself as an organizer.

Hall's Background

Hall grew up in the same period as James, in which great economic, social, and political changes took place. Like James, he had a background in Protestant religion and morality, and strove to accommodate his religious and moral values in the knowledge produced by the science of his time. The two men differed in some important respects, however. James grew up in a well-to-do urban family and from childhood was familiar with a number of European countries and acquainted with influential intellectuals. In contrast, Hall grew up on a middle-sized farm in Massachusetts and went to a country school. At the age of nineteen, he went to college, graduating in 1867. After some years of study at the Union Theological Seminary in New York City, he borrowed money to study theology and philosophy in Germany. On returning to the United States, he finished his examinations at the institution where he had begun his studies. He then taught language, literature, and philosophy at a college in Ohio. He had to struggle harder than James to achieve results and to make a place for himself in contemporary intellectual and scientific life.

His reading of Wundt's *Grundzüge* in 1876 aroused Hall's interest in physiological psychology, and he began studying physiology at Harvard. Here, he also studied psychology under James, and in 1878 he received a doctorate in psychology, the first granted in the United States. Having finished his doctoral studies, he once more went to Europe, staying there for two years. He audited Wundt's lectures, and also lectures on zoology and physiology given by Ludwig and other outstanding physiologists. Hall characterized his relationship to Wundt in a letter to James in 1879 (Perry, 1935. II, p. 17), remarking that even if he was greatly indebted to Wundt, he was disappointed in him. Thus, apparently, he could not quite identify himself with Wundtian experimental psychology.

Of greater importance for Hall's later career as a researcher and practical psychologist was probably the fact that he was acquainted with William Thierry Preyer's research in child psychology. Before he went back to the United States in 1880, he audited a lecture in which Preyer gave an outline of his book on child psychology, which appeared in 1882. Hall followed up Preyer's studies, and when he had returned home, he gave lectures on child psychology at a forum attached to Harvard. In 1881, he obtained a position at the newly established Johns Hopkins University. Here he was appointed professor of psychology and education in 1884. In 1888 he became president of Clark University, which opened the following year. He served as the president of this university and as chair of the psychological and educational institute until his death. In 1887, Hall established the first scientific journal of psychology in the United States, *The American Journal of Psychology*, and, in 1892 he took the initiative to found the American Psychological Association (APA). At the twentieth anniversary of Clark University in 1909, Hall arranged a conference on psychology attended by some of the most prominent psychologists of the day, and to which Freud and Jung were invited. This helped create an interest in psychoanalysis in the United States.

When Hall was appointed lecturer at Johns Hopkins, he established a psychological laboratory there in 1883, only four years after Wundt's in Leipzig. While this laboratory was one of the first psychological laboratories in the world, and the first in the United States, during the time Hall was directing it, neither the quality nor the quantity of the research was comparable to that of Wundt's laboratory.

At Johns Hopkins, Hall also gave a course on experimental psychology based on his own doctoral thesis, on experiences from his time in Germany, and on the interests of his students. The scientific projects being discussed do not seem to have been of particular significance. Still, the establishment of the experimental psychological laboratories and the emphasis on experimentation in the instruction of many early American

G. Stanley Hall

psychologists contributed to giving psychology in the United States a strong orientation towards experimental research. However, this emphasis also led to what Stephen Toulmin and David Leary (1985) have characterized as a cult of empiricism.

Studies of Childhood and Adolescence

At the end of the nineteenth century, there was great interest in the scientific study of children's development. Hall wanted teaching in schools to be based on empirical psychological research and hoped to improve society by reforming the school system. He had close contacts with schoolteachers and became one of the leaders of the child study movement, aimed to carry out school reforms.

Preyer had concentrated his studies on the child's first three years. Hall (1883) carried out investigations of children who had just started school. Believing schoolteachers were not sufficiently well informed about children's knowledge, thinking, interests, and activities, he undertook a systematic study to procure information. To survey children's knowledge of animals, plants, parts of the body, geometrical figures, numbers, and professions, as well as their fantasies and conceptions of morality, he worked out comprehensive questionnaires and asked teachers to fill them out for the children in their classes. Hall tabulated the responses and compared groups: boys and girls, children growing up in the countryside and in the cities, and children who had and had not been to kindergarten. The study was informative and suggested questions for further research. Although Hall did not intend to evaluate the intelligence of the children, many of the categories in the questionnaires had points of similarity with those Binet and Simon later used in their construction of their intelligence test. Hall's investigations of children's fantasies anticipated some studies Piaget undertook forty to fifty years later. Unfortunately, however, Hall discussed his results within a broad, rather vague and unsystematic framework and did not formulate precise hypotheses in his attempt to explain the results.

Hall's main work was an extensive book in two volumes on adolescence. The full title reveals his broad interests and strong social engagement: *Adolescence: Its Psychology and Its Relations to Physiology, Anthropology, Sociology, Sex, Crime, Religion, and Education* (1904). There can be no doubt that the author of the book possessed comprehensive knowledge of adolescence, but the descriptions of psychological development were unsystematic and uncritically based on what he regarded as fundamental moral values. As was the case in his previous work, Hall failed to construct a fruitful theoretical framework and to present clearly formulated hypotheses. Moreover, he claimed that in adolescence the individual recapitulates earlier phases of human cultural development. This combined a Lamarckian view of evolution and Haeckel's recapitulation theory, which states that ontogenetic development repeats phylogenetic development. (On the recapitulation theory, see Mayr, 2002.) Even if only a few contemporary psychologists understood that Lamarck's view of evolution was not tenable, it could perhaps have been expected that Hall would discuss whether it is reasonable to believe human cultural history is reflected in adolescent development. It is understandable that Thorndike, who also was concerned with problems in ontogenetic development, was critical when he reviewed the book.

Hall's Contributions

Hall's contributions were to give US psychology an empirical orientation, establish a psychological profession, and create an interest in developmental psychology. His studies aimed to assess the knowledge, skills, and activities of children at different ages. One of his students, Arnold Gesell (1880–1961), became famous for his extensive and careful descriptions of the development of normal children from birth to school age. Gesell worked out norms indicating when a child could be expected to master diverse forms of behavior, such as crawling, sitting, standing, walking, speaking, and gaining control of the bladder and bowel movements.

Gesell and some of Hall's other students emphasized, as their teacher had done, that the child ought to develop as freely as possible. A major point in Gesell's view of development was that it is mainly a result of the *maturation* of the child. The emphasis on maturation as opposed to learning had a great influence on American and also European, child upbringing. Another of Hall's students who became an influential test psychologist as well as developmental psychologist was Lewis Terman. I shall return to him later in this chapter.

Hall began his career as a theologian, but he seems gradually to have substituted his religious faith for a faith in science. While acceptance of the theory of biological evolution by British intellectuals frequently seems to have led to deep personal conflicts, this does not seem to have been the case among most US psychologists. If so, it is strange since almost all were brought up in Christian homes. As Daniel Boorstein (1974) has remarked, Hall, during his study in Germany, noted the great importance of school reforms in the building of the new German state, and had a vision of creating a new and better society based on scientific child psychology. This made him a champion not only of scientific psychology, but also of a society based on a scientific child psychology. D. K. Ross (1972) subtitled her biography of Hall *The Psychologist as a Prophet.*

John Dewey (1859–1952)

John Dewey was probably the most influential American thinker in the first half of the twentieth century. In his younger years, he was strongly influenced by Kant and Hegel, and the latter's influence was present in his thinking throughout his long, productive life. Yet, Dewey probably received his strongest inspiration from Peirce and James.

Dewey's (1896) examination of the reflex concept attracted much attention. He also gave a reasonable description of thinking and problem solving and urged psychologists to develop a social psychology. In 1899, he was elected President of the APA. His impact on US psychology was due not only to his work in psychology, however. He also influenced it indirectly through his philosophy, and by attributing a central role to psychology in education, he contributed to the great interest in educational psychology in the United States.

A Biographical Sketch

Dewey was born in Burlington, Vermont. His father was a grocer, and the family seems to have been solidly anchored in Christian, middle-class values. After four years at the University of Vermont, Dewey taught high school for three years. In 1882, he began studies for his doctorate at Johns Hopkins University, where he took courses under Hall and Peirce. After teaching for nine years at the University of Wisconsin and for one year at the University of Minnesota, in 1894 he was appointed chair of the philosophy department at the University of Chicago, which had been established two years earlier. This philosophy department also included psychology and education.

Along with research and instruction, Dewey was engaged in many of the social and political struggles occurring in the 1890s. Although he was neither a Marxist nor a revolutionary, his view of many social problems was related to the ideas of social democracy. Among other things, he was active in the management of Hull House, a settlement for immigrant workers. Throughout his life, he actively supported a great number of causes in favor of minorities and the weaker groups in society and was admired as a champion of women's suffrage. At the University of Chicago, he established a laboratory school for exploring and practicing his educational ideas. The management of this school brought him into conflict with the university administration, and in 1904 he accepted a position at Teachers' College, which was attached to Columbia University. Dewey taught in this institution until he was eighty and continued to publish books until his death. He enjoyed a worldwide reputation as an educator and is regarded as one of the most outstanding US philosophers. At the same time he was known for his straightforward and modest manner.

Dewey's Philosophy

While the North Americans founded their society on European culture and searched for inspiration in European science and thinking, many hoped to create a new and better society that was not dependent upon what they regarded as certain unfortunate European traditions. Dewey's philosophy can be seen as an attempt to create a philosophy that would contribute to a society based upon democratic ideas, scientific thinking, and tolerance of new ideas and change. In contrast to several central European thinkers, Dewey believed it was not possible to find a foundation for knowledge that was absolutely certain. Therefore, the aim of his philosophy was to develop methods that could create knowledge as certain as possible. In this attempt, he made his most important philosophical contribution.

Human knowledge, Dewey claimed, originates in a situation that is unsatisfactory because it contains conflicting cognitive elements. When this state of affairs is acknowledged, the next step is to formulate the problem. In the third step, guesses are made about how the problem could be solved and hypotheses formulated. Fourth, the hypotheses are examined until a plausible solution is found. Finally, at the fifth step, attempts are made to find support for the hypotheses, and, if that seems possible, to carry out an experiment that could demonstrate it is tenable. The procedure Dewey suggested for undertaking epistemological investigations has validity, he claimed, for all forms of thinking, and in 1910 he published a book under the title *How We Think*, in which he gave a psychological account of thought processes without going into epistemological problems. The book, as Hilgard (1987) remarked, is both understandable and reasonable.

To Dewey, thinking is an instrument humans use to adapt to their environment. By emphasizing the instrumental aspect of thinking, Dewey contributed to leading US psychology away from Wundt's and Titchener's focus on consciousness as an object of introspection. The view of thinking he presented is flexible and practical. Unfortunately, his description of how thinking begins, and what its cause is, is seriously lacking in precision and concreteness. He did not undertake empirical psychological investigations himself, and the use of concepts in his psychological works is vague and diffuse.

Dewey had an optimistic faith, believing that human beings have the potential to develop thinking in a community without being hampered by conventions and taboos. He was convinced humans have great abilities for self-realization. Moreover, he was confident that science would bring progress, and he emphasized that as far as possible philosophers should follow scientific procedures in their thinking.

Dewey's ideas of child upbringing and teaching were central to his philosophy. By reforms of the educational system, he hoped, as did many of his contemporaries, that society could be improved. He wanted school to be a democratic society in miniature, a society where students and teachers worked together. Instruction should encourage interests and initiative in the students. Further, children should learn by doing things themselves, not just by passively absorbing knowledge.

Like Hall, Dewey insisted that psychology is an important means of improving teaching. This belief naturally helped create an interest in educational psychology and orient US psychology towards the study of learning, which, as I have already mentioned, became a main area in the latter half of the twentieth century.

Dewey on the Reflex Arc

In his article on the reflex arc, Dewey (1896) elaborated James's idea that instincts and habits may be seen as chains of reflexes. As reported by Leahey (1999), the article had a great impact on contemporary and later US psychology.

While James had argued that sensations do not appear as discrete entities but instead form part of the stream of consciousness, he had not abandoned the view that the reflex arc could be regarded as a coupling between a discrete sensation and a discrete response. Dewey insisted that reflex arcs form part of more comprehensive acts aimed at definite goals. According to this view, the role of the sensations and responses contained in the act depends upon the act taken as a whole, and thus they vary from one act to another. Dewey pointed out a deficiency in attempts to account for acts in terms of the stimulus–response paradigm.

However, he claimed more for his view of the reflex arc. He argued that perception must be seen as starting in responses and not in sensations. Thus, in the child-candlelight example given by James, Dewey held that the act did not start in the sensory stimulation emanating from the candle flame, but in movements of muscles in the eye and the neck. Sensations – if I understand him correctly – are always dependent upon the ongoing activity. In support of this view, Dewey pointed out that our reactions to the same stimulation are different when the ongoing activity is different. Thus, a person reading might react differently to a loud sound than a person hunting, a person on watch at night, or a person performing a chemical experiment.

Dewey was right in insisting that our reactions to a definite stimulation in many instances depend upon the ongoing activity. But this is not always so. For example, suppose a man is hunting birds and suddenly hears the growling of a bear. His perceiving of the sound would then probably not be affected by his ongoing activity, and the sensation would start an entirely new sequence of reactions. Indeed, if our reactions to sensory stimulation always depend on the ongoing activity, we would not have survived. Perceiving can form part of an ongoing activity, but it can also start an entirely new activity.

In his discussion of the child-candlelight example, Dewey held that the child's reaching for the flame did not originate in a sensory stimulus, but, as I understand him, in movements of eye, neck, and body muscles. It is, of course, correct that these movements form part of an act of vision. Dewey did, however, overlook that the movements of these muscles are controlled by the stimulation of the eye.

A third point about Dewey's treatment of the reflex arc is that while the child's withdrawing of its hand upon being burned is part of a physiological reflex, the grasping of the flame upon seeing it is not; it is a voluntary act probably dependent upon complicated learning of a sensory motor reaction. This naturally makes it difficult to conceive of the act of reaching for the light and withdrawing the hand as a combination of two reflexes, as James and Dewey did.

In this connection, recall that Pavlov insisted that in conditioning the starting point must be taken in psychological reflexes and not in voluntary movements. Evidently, he understood that difficulty would arise if he started with responses not forming part of physiological reflexes. He would then not know what stimulation was eliciting them. James and Dewey do not seem to have been aware of this difficulty.

Dewey pointed out that as long as a complicated act is performed smoothly, we have no experience of mental processes, and it is not necessary to resort to such processes in descriptions of it. Here he apparently anticipated a point that, as we have seen, the psychologists in Würzburg made some years later. According to Dewey, mental processes do not enter into an act unless conflicts of some sort arise in the performance of it.

Earlier and contemporary German experimental psychology paid little attention to the role played by the activity of the organism in its attempts to adjust to the environment. Dewey's article was important because it called attention to this role and thereby gave a place to the responses, the movements involved in the organism's reactions to the environment. Thus, his view of the reflex arc oriented the study of psychology towards behavior as its subject matter. However, Dewey did not give sufficient weight to perceptual processes. As Woodworth and Sheehan (1965, p. 118) pointed out, behaviorism neglected the study of perception, and, in my opinion, Dewey contributed to this neglect by under-evaluating the role played by perception in human thinking and action.

James Mark Baldwin (1861–1934)

Like Hall and Dewey, James Mark Baldwin took a special interest in the development of the child. He believed an empirical study of this development could explain how the human individual becomes part of the social community. To Baldwin, the ontogenetic development of the human being was also a key to understanding logic, epistemology, and morality. Still further, he believed a study of ontogenetic development could shed light on phylogenetic development.

A Biographical Sketch

James Mark Baldwin was born in Columbia, South Carolina. He belonged to a prominent family and began his university studies at Princeton with an interest in theology. During a stay in Germany in 1884–1885, he studied for one term with Wundt and became an enthusiastic follower of the new scientific psychology. In 1889, he received his PhD in philosophy at Princeton, and by 1891, he had published a handbook in psychology in two thick volumes. After working as a teacher at a small US university, in 1889 he was appointed professor in Toronto, where he established a psychological laboratory. With Darwin and Preyer as his models, Baldwin described the psychological development of his two daughters. In 1893, he returned to Princeton. Ten years later he became a professor at Johns Hopkins. In 1894, he cofounded the journal *Psychological Review* with Cattell, and two years later he was elected chairman of the APA. At the beginning of the 1900s, he was considered a highly respected US psychologist. In 1908, however, he disappeared from the scene, leaving almost no trace in American psychology. This was because he had been caught by the police in a brothel employing black women, and he was obliged to resign from his position at the university.

After spending some years in Mexico, Baldwin moved to Paris, teaching at L'École des Hautes Études Sociales. He lived in Paris until his death in 1934. Here, he was in contact with Janet and several other distinguished philosophers and scientists. When US psychologists became interested in Piaget's psychology in the 1960s, Baldwin's work was rediscovered as the antecedent of his psychology. US psychologists began to study Baldwin, and he is now considered a pioneer in the field of developmental psychology as well as in social psychology. (See John Broughton and D. John Freeman Fi Moir, 1982; Robert Cairns, 1992.)

Baldwin was a prolific writer. Of his many books, I shall list the following: *Handbook of Psychology* (two volumes, 1889–1891); *Mental Development in the Child and the Race*

(1895); *Social and Ethical Interpretations in Mental Development* (1897); and *Thoughts and Things, or Genetic Logic* (three volumes, 1906–1911).

The Study of Socialization as a Bridge Between Sociology and Psychology

Baldwin was familiar with the French sociology that flourished in the 1880s and 1890s and was engaged in the dispute between Émile Durkheim and Gabriel Tarde. He suggested that the study of how children are integrated into society through their ontogenetic development could shed light on the issue. In *Social and Ethical Interpretations in Mental Development*, he accounted for this view. The subtitle of the book was *A Study in Social Psychology*.

Baldwin's ideas about the development of the self were central to his perspective. Preyer had begun to study the development of the self in children, and James allotted a central place to the idea of the self in psychology. Baldwin's point of departure was, on the one hand, Preyer's views of the development of the self, and, on the other hand, James's views of the social self. Baldwin attempted to fuse the two together by assuming that at an early age the child forms an impression of an ego based on the perception of body, emotions, and efforts of will. The ego engages in an interaction between the child's perception of other persons, an *alter*. Ego and alter influence each other in such a way that the child perceives others on the basis of his experience of his own self, and his experience of others also influences his perception of self. The child's perception of ego and alter has a mutually dialectic relationship leading to a continuous development of his or her perception of self.

Baldwin did not substantiate Preyer's views of a self with new and more reliable observations. It is therefore difficult to understand more concretely what he meant by a dialectic relationship between an ego and an alter. Nevertheless, this hypothesis of our self-perception as being based on such interaction is highly plausible. Baldwin further claimed that the interaction between the ego and the alter occurs when the child attempts to imitate others. In imitation, the child learns to understand both himself and others. Again, although it is difficult to understand more precisely what he meant by imitation, it is reasonable to believe that imitation plays a major role in the development of the child. Further, Baldwin, unlike Piaget, included the development of the self in his account of how knowledge comes into being, as Kohlberg (1982) has emphasized.

Baldwin's Idea of a Genetic Epistemology and Contributions to Biology

Based on his idea that the development of the child could explain the functioning of the adult, Baldwin believed that problems in epistemology and morality could be elucidated by a study of human ontogenetic development. He started what Piaget (without referring to him) called *genetic epistemology* and wrote massively on this subject. Problems of epistemology are complex and we will not go into this part of Baldwin's work. With a view to Piaget's stage theory, to be discussed in Chapter 16, I shall just mention that

Baldwin proposed that the intellectual development of the child passes through three discrete stages.

I must also mention that he contributed to biology. Like many of his US colleagues, he was interested in the theory of evolution. His interest led to comprehensive studies. Baldwin was in contact with Lloyd Morgan, and, already in the 1880s, they realized that Lamarck's principle of the heredity of acquired traits was untenable. Based on astute reflections on issues in biological evolution, they pointed out that ontogenetic development could influence phylogenesis. Thus, it was not only the case that phylogenesis determined ontogenesis, as the recapitulation theory claimed. Under certain conditions, ontogenesis could also determine phylogenetic development. This view was eventually accepted, and it is now referred to as the *Baldwin effect*. Baldwin and Morgan were far ahead of their contemporaries in understanding biological and psychological development, while some psychologists, such as Freud, Jung, and McDougall, employed Lamarck's principle even into the 1920s, thirty years after others had understood it was untenable.

George Herbert Mead (1863–1931)

Like most of his contemporary psychological thinkers, George Herbert Mead grew up in a religious home. He was born in South Hadley, Massachusetts, where his father was a Protestant clergyman and later became a professor at Oberlin Theological Seminary. His mother became president of Mt Holyoke College in 1881 when her husband died. Like Dewey, Mead appears to have liberated himself from a strict religious upbringing by studying Hegel. He received a BA at Oberlin College in 1883, but he did not continue his university studies. Instead, he taught primary school for some time and worked on the roads. From 1887 to 1888, he studied at Harvard with James and others. During this year, he lived with James's family working as a private tutor.

From 1888 to 1891, Mead studied physiology, psychology, and philosophy at the University of Berlin. In 1891, he married and was employed as a teacher at the University of Michigan, where he was a colleague of Dewey, and a lasting friendship formed between them. When Dewey was appointed head of the new department of philosophy, psychology, and pedagogy at the University of Chicago in 1894, he demanded to have his friend with him, and Mead worked there as a teacher for the rest of his life. An esteemed teacher, he exerted a great deal of influence on many social researchers through his lectures. Unfortunately, he never wrote his own thoughts down in a systematic form, and the books that recount his ideas are for the most part derived from his students' notes of his lectures. I will here focus on his *Mind, Self and Society from the Standpoint of a Social Behaviorist*, a book that has become a classic. It was published by one of his former students, the philosopher Charles Morris, in 1934.

The Relationship Between the Individual and Society
Whereas Baldwin was primarily inspired by contemporary French social psychological thinking, Mead was oriented towards German cultural life and appears in important

ways to have been inspired by Hegel and Wundt. Farr (1996) claimed that Mead's social psychological thinking can be viewed as an attempt to combine Wundt's experimental psychology and *Völkerpsychologie*.

Like Baldwin, Mead thought he could explain the relationship between the individual and society by way of an evolutionary perspective. From this, he claimed, we could also explain the progression from simple to higher psychological processes. By this reasoning, he also concentrated on assumptions about the self, and he stressed the crucial importance of language.

Inspired by Darwin's ideas of emotions, Wundt had hypothesized that gestures acquired a communicative meaning, thus forming the basis for language development. Mead developed this idea by including the reaction of the other person to such gestures, claiming the individual who has produced the gesture in turn apprehends the other's reaction. This experience is the basis for the development of the individual's consciousness, language, and sense of self. Through interaction with others, the individual learns to put himself or herself in the other person's place. By consistently reacting in this way, the individual with time becomes one with his or her group. Some gestures that receive the same interpretation by the person producing them as the one responding to them come to acquire a symbolic meaning in time, thus functioning as linguistic signs.

An Evaluation of Mead

According to Mead, consciousness and the sense of self come into being as a result of behavior, and Morris, in his edition of Mead (1934) characterized Mead's approach to social psychology as *social behaviorism*. Mead tried to give consciousness a place in his account of behavior, and in this he differed from Watson, who was one of his students. We may ask, however, how the individual is capable of apprehending how others respond to him or her. To understand another person's response to his or her movements, the individual must have developed complex cognitive capacities. Mead did not discuss this point, which in my opinion (Saugstad, 1989a) renders his thinking inconsistent. Nor did he account for the effect of the physical environment on child development. The child must overcome resistance in order to move the body and limbs, and he or she reacts to pressure on the skin and to innumerable forms of inner stimulation. It is difficult to imagine how the child's experience of the self as a person could develop independently of interaction with the physical energy affecting the body. But even if Baldwin was unable to account concretely for the role of interaction between the physical and the social in the development of a sense of self, he at least raised the issue. In Mead's work, the entire question seems to be missing, though Mead did highlight something important when he directed attention to the value for the development of the self of understanding others' reactions to us. It was also helpful that he discussed communication and the role of language in the development of mental conceptions and social interaction. In discussing pragmatism, I noted the emphasis it placed on the consequences of our actions. When Mead used the reaction of others as his point of departure, he helped develop the principal idea of pragmatic philosophy.

To Mead, the sense of self is a result of social interaction. In this interaction he gave logical priority to society. This means society is a prerequisite for the development of a sense of self and consciousness in the individual. The psyche of the individual is therefore determined by his or her social belonging to or inclusion in a group. In this, as we shall see later, Mead's view is similar to Durkheim's, and it was primarily sociologists who developed what has been termed *symbolic interactionism*. Mead's social psychology became a part of sociology and had little impact on psychology.

Researchers' understanding of the relationship between the individual and society is easily colored by their political persuasions. Socialism emphasizes the effect of society on the life of the individual, whereas capitalism places more emphasis on the role of the individual in the development of society. Although Mead can hardly be called a social democrat, he placed much greater emphasis on the impact of social institutions on the development of the individual than most US psychologists. The reason he came to have negligible influence on psychology in the first half of the 1900s is perhaps that he published very little. Another reason may have been that he fell outside the scope of US social psychology, conceived of as a subdiscipline of psychology with its emphasis on the role of the individual in the structure of society.

Baldwin's and Mead's attempts at bridging the gap between psychology and sociology were not followed up, and, as mentioned, two forms of social psychology came into being, one with a basis in sociology and the other with a basis in the psychological study of the individual.

Applied Psychology and Professionalization of Psychology

The extensive use of technology in agriculture and industry, and in the building of large cities, made the North Americans particularly open to the positivist idea of founding a society on a science of humans. In addition to Hall and Dewey, US psychology had in James Cattell an enthusiastic champion of this idea.

James McKeen Cattell (1860–1944)

James Cattell was born in Easton, Pennsylvania, where his father was president of a college. After finishing his studies at this college, Cattell studied literature and philosophy in Germany for a time. In 1881, he enrolled at Johns Hopkins as a philosophy student. Here he attended Hall's course in experimental psychology, and two years later he went to Wundt in Leipzig, where he carried out experiments on association and voluntary actions, then a popular theme. In Chapter 4, I mentioned that Cattell was critical of Wundt's interpretation of the results of his experiments on the will.

After receiving his doctorate in Leipzig in 1886, Cattell taught for some time at Cambridge University. Here he was acquainted with Galton and became interested in his studies of individual differences, his tests, and his statistical treatment of empirical results. Cattell also became an adherent of eugenics. In 1889, he obtained a professorship in philosophy at the University of Pennsylvania, and two years later a professorship in psychology at Columbia, where he worked until 1917. Cattell attracted many students and was an effective sponsor and administrator. As already mentioned, Thorndike wanted him as a sponsor because he was more strongly oriented towards empirical psychology than James. Together with Dewey, Cattell made Columbia University and the associated Teachers' College a center for the training of educational psychologists and educators. In 1894, he founded the journal *Psychological Review* with James Baldwin. In 1901, he was elected president of the American Academy of Sciences, and in 1929 he was president of the International Conference in Psychology, which was held that year in the United States for the first time.

The Study of Individual Differences and Ability Tests

When Cattell came to Columbia in 1891, he concentrated his empirical work on studies of individual differences, the construction and use of ability tests, and the application of statistics to empirical data. He invented a method of ranking as a means of scaling attributes. Unfortunately, the tests he constructed during his first decade at Columbia had a very low correlation with each other and with school performance. This was shown by one of Cattell's students in an investigation published in 1901. Cattell constructed his tests according to the same principles as Galton, basing them on simple types of abilities, such as sensory discrimination, reaction time, and simple measures of muscular strength. In other words, the tests he and Galton had worked out were unsuitable for use as tests of scholastic skills and intelligence. As I mentioned in Chapter 9, Binet conceived of the task of constructing an intelligence test in a more reflective manner.

Cattell's enthusiasm for science and psychology helped raise interest in the study of psychology and in laying a more solid foundation for the training of psychologists. However, his uncritical view of the positivist philosophy of science may have contributed to a one-sided emphasis on the collection of observations and facts, to the detriment of integration and theory construction. As Michael Sokal (1982) notes, from his youth Cattell was a staunch adherent of Bacon's inductivism (of which J. S. Mill was representative in the nineteenth century, as Chapter 2 notes).

Educational Psychology and Professionalization

The country's large investment in the educational system and widespread interest in the upbringing of children led many US psychologists to work in the service of schools. This effort in turn contributed to the professionalization of US psychology. Thorough accounts of early applied psychology and this professionalization have been given by Hilgard (1987), Leahey (1999), and O'Donnell (1985). An important event in the development of educational psychology was the establishment of clinics for the diagnosis and treatment of children with learning disabilities.

The pioneer in this type of clinical work was Lightner Witmer (1867–1956). He was one of Cattell's students, and on Cattell's recommendation he had finished his studies under Wundt, receiving his doctorate in Leipzig in 1892. Witmer then succeeded Cattell as head of the Psychological Institute at the University of Pennsylvania, and for some years he did research on individual differences. In 1896, he was asked to help a child struggling with reading disability. The request inspired Witmer to establish a clinic to help other children with learning disability. In his clinical work, he developed diagnostic procedures as well as forms of treatment for various types of disabilities. While he insisted that clinical work should have a foundation in scientific psychology, he took care to establish a close cooperation between physicians, physiologists, and social workers. In the course of a few years, several other clinics of the type Witmer had established were started, and before World War I there were close to twenty of them. Gradually, their work was extended to include vocational guidance and psychotherapy.

Intelligence Tests

When Binet made a breakthrough in the construction of intelligence tests, American psychologists threw themselves into the task of refining the test. Along with his coworkers, Lewis Terman (1877–1956) at Stanford University undertook extensive work on the standardization of Binet's test. The result of this standardization, completed in 1916, was known as the Stanford–Binet Test. Later intelligence tests were also modeled on Binet's principles.

Terman proceeded with great thoroughness in his standardization of intelligence tests. The appropriateness and degree of difficulty of the individual tasks were carefully estimated, and great efforts were made to have the tests agree with the performance of the children in school. Further, Terman and his coworkers applied statistical methods in their work. The resulting test was therefore constructed in a far more systematic manner than Binet and Simon's. Terman contributed to setting a high standard for the construction of tests, and US psychologists gradually developed test construction as one of their specialties.

The work of scoring and measurements, psychometry, became a separate area in psychology, and US psychologists became the leaders in it, along with the British. Particularly creative among the American researchers was Louis Thurstone (1887–1955). He refined factor analysis, a mathematical technique Spearman had invented to determine the degree of correlation between performances on different types of tests (Thurstone, 1947). On the basis of extensive studies, Thurstone concluded that intelligence must be seen as several abilities. Each covered parts of the subject's performance on intelligence tests, but no single ability was involved in all types of performance. In his research, Spearman had found a general ability, a so-called general intelligence factor. Thurstone also became known for the construction of a scale for the measurement of attitudes.

When the United States entered World War I in 1917, a team led by Robert Yerkes worked out a group test to test a large number of recruits. The test proved useful, but as Sokal (1984) has noted, its value was restricted to choosing men to be trained as officers and eliminating those unfit for military service. Yet, the results were so good that this work created an interest in tests in civilian life as well.

L. L. Thurstone

When Yerkes and his coworkers published the results of their extensive testing of recruits after the war, a controversy arose over their interpretation. The results revealed differences between the white and African-American populations, between African-Americans in the South and in the North, and between immigrants from countries in northern Europe and countries in eastern Europe. The results were clear, but Yerkes and his group interpreted them as genetic differences in intelligence. Like Cattell, Terman, McDougall, and many of the other pioneers in psychology, Yerkes was an adherent of the eugenics movement. The report was criticized by other psychologists and also by persons outside the psychology profession, and for a time this reaction contributed to the discrediting of psychological testing. An issue had emerged that was to surface again and again in American psychological research – namely, whether there was a genetic difference in intelligence among the various groups of the US population. This issue, as well as the disagreement between Spearman and Thurstone, raised the question: what do we mean by the concept of intelligence?

Applied Psychology in Public and Private Administration

During World War I, another group of psychologists also worked on the problem of selecting military personnel. This group was led by Walter Dill Scott (1869–1955). The group constructed eighty-three different tests and tested three million men. The work proved useful and was praised outside the military, helping to make psychology known and give it status in administration and business. At the beginning of the twentieth century, Scott, who had received his doctorate under Wundt, had already begun applying psychology in the advertising of various types of goods. He had written several articles and a book, *The Theory of Advertising*, in 1903, and in 1916 he was appointed professor of applied psychology at Carnegie Institute of Technology in Pittsburgh. After the war, he established his own consulting firm for administrative management, joined by several of his colleagues from the military including some of the most prominent US psychologists. According to Sokal (1984), his firm assisted more than forty industrial and commercial organizations.

The person who perhaps contributed most to making psychology known in the United States before World War I was Hugo Münsterberg (1863–1916). Münsterberg was born in Germany and received his doctorate under Wundt in 1885. James had persuaded him to come to Harvard in 1892 to direct the psychological experimental laboratory. When he arrived, Münsterberg was opposed to the application of psychology to everyday life, but from the beginning of the twentieth century he engaged himself in applied research and wrote several books and articles for a wider audience. His most important book was perhaps the one he wrote on criminology and witness psychology, *Forensic Psychology* (1908). The book ran through many editions and was reprinted in 1976 when renewed interest emerged in the questions its author had raised. In 1909, the year Freud visited Clark University, Münsterberg published a book entitled *Psychotherapy*, and in 1913 he wrote a bestseller, *Psychology and Industrial Efficiency*, in which he described his experiences and research in what has come to be called *industrial psychology*. J. Spillmann and L. Spillmann (1993) have reviewed the life and work of this versatile psychologist.

US Comparative Psychology

A great spur to US comparative psychology was the work carried out by Thorndike at the end of the nineteenth and beginning of the twentieth centuries. I shall report on this work in the next chapter. Here I shall briefly mention two other comparative psychologists who also had an impact on this area in the United States.

Interest in comparative psychology had almost died out in Great Britain at the turn of the twentieth century but then picked up in the United States. In 1908, Margaret Floy Washburn (1871–1939) published a book on comparative psychology. It contained a critical review of comparative studies of sensory discrimination, space perception, and attention. Washburn was a student of Titchener and, like Darwin, Romanes, and Morgan, she conceived of comparative psychology as a study of mentality in animals; she called her book *The Animal Mind*. However, she was independent of and critical of Titchener, James, and contemporary psychologists, and she tried to avoid unnecessary speculations based on assumptions about the nature of consciousness.

Margaret Floy Washburn

Washburn was highly respected and was the second woman to be elected to the National Academy of Sciences, and she also served as president of the APA.

Robert Yerkes (1876–1956) carried out comprehensive investigations of sensory discrimination in different species and tried to construct an apparatus with a view to comparing animals of different species. Further, he carried out research on problem solving in apes of the type earlier performed by Hobhouse and Köhler. In 1930, Yerkes took the initiative in establishing a laboratory for the study of primate biology in Orange Park, Florida, and this laboratory, first attached to Yale and later transferred to Harvard, had a great influence on psychological research.

Edward Bradford Titchener (1867–1927)

Edward Titchener was born in Chichester, England. From 1885 to 1900, he studied at Oxford University, taking philosophy for four years and physiology for one. During his studies, he became interested in Wundt's psychology and went to Leipzig in 1890. He received his doctorate there after two years and taught for some months at Oxford, but he realized there was no interest there in the new experimental psychology, so, in 1892, he accepted a post as director of the laboratory at the newly established Cornell

University in the United States. Here he stayed for the rest of his life, associating mainly with his own students and usually not with his US colleagues. Titchener wrote many books, including *An Outline of Psychology* (1896); *Experimental Psychology: A Manual of Laboratory Practice* (1901–1905); and *A Textbook of Psychology* (1909–1910).

Titchener led a very active laboratory at Cornell and attracted many students, several of whom – in addition to Boring and Washburn – became influential in American psychology. Later psychologists have not taken much interest in the experiments performed in Titchener's laboratory, but one by C. W. Perky (1910), on the relationship between perceiving and imagining, should not be forgotten. Perky showed that under certain conditions it is not possible to distinguish between our perceptual and imaginary processes. According to Allan Paivio (1971), her findings have been reproduced by modern researchers.

Many of his contemporaries regarded Titchener as the chief representative of Wundt's experimental psychology, and it is mainly in this role that he takes a place in the history of psychology. When US psychologists became increasingly critical of Wundt in the early 1900s, however, Titchener became a main target of the criticism. I shall present his ideas and then the criticism, given mainly by Angell in his project of *functionalism*. Boring (1929/1950) has been criticized for identifying Titchener's psychology with Wundt's. I shall briefly review Titchener's ideas while noting the differences between him and Wundt.

Like Wundt, Titchener believed mental processes could be studied independently of physiological processes and independently of the body's interactions with the environment. Also like Wundt, he believed we could study mental states by directly observing them introspectively. However, to make the observations objective and precise, we should study them in an experimental setting as Wundt described. In the Preface to *Experimental Psychology*, Titchener emphasized that what he had learnt from Wundt was the proper method of undertaking systematic introspection.

Because only normal adults can make adequate observations of their mental experience, Titchener, like Wundt, believed a direct study of the minds of children, animals, and individuals suffering from mental disorders is not possible. The mental life of these individuals can be studied only by extrapolation from the study of normal human adults. The subjects in the experiments should also be trained. Agreeing with Wundt on this point, Titchener made great efforts to find out how he could train his subjects in introspection. They must particularly learn to avoid committing what he called the *object error* or the *stimulus error*. That is, the subjects must discount the meaning they could attach to the physical stimulation; they had to avoid being influenced by the context in which the elements to be identified appeared. Underlying this view was the belief that mental elements have no meaning, and that meaning does not arise until elements are combined.

Finally, like Wundt, Titchener believed mental experience is composed of combinations of elements, and that the study of psychology should be directed towards identifying the elements and showing how they are combined into more complex

E. B. Titchener

entities. An apparently minor difference between him and Wundt was that in addition to sensations and feelings, Titchener regarded images as a third kind of element.

In contrast to Wundt, Titchener attributed no role to the will as an organizing force in mental life and did not conceive of attention as a force in consciousness manifesting itself in apperceptive processes. He regarded attention as an attribute of sensation. Finally, Titchener found a place only for the dimension of pleasantness–unpleasantness in his study of feeling and thus left out the other two dimensions Wundt had introduced.

In a much-debated article, Titchener (1898), claimed a distinction had to be made between a study of the mental elements and their combinations, and the study of the functions mind has when seen in a wider biological context. He referred to the former study as *structuralism* and to the latter as *functionalism*. Both studies were needed to achieve an adequate understanding of mind. However, not until structuralism was undertaken could functionalism be productive.

James Rowland Angell (1869–1949) and Functionalism

James Angell was Dewey's student at the University of Michigan and became his coworker at the University of Chicago in 1894. Before that he had also studied with

James at Harvard for one year, and had studied for another year at German universities. In 1904 Angell published a much-read textbook entitled *Psychology: An Introduction to the Study of the Structure and Function of Consciousness*. In his presidential address to the APA in 1906 (published in *Psychological Review* the next year), he delineated his own program for functionalism. Angell formulated his program as a protest and an alternative to Wundt's and Titchener's approach to the study of psychology. He did not refer specifically to the article in which Titchener drew the distinction between structuralism and functionalism. But he seems to have taken the distinction as the starting point for his discussion.

Angell's program had three points that he claimed converged in his view of *functionalism*. First, functionalism was concerned with the functions as contrasted with the contents of consciousness. Second, functionalism studied consciousness in the wider context of biological evolution and included the study of animals and children, and also treated problems of social utility. Third, the study of consciousness should be closely related to bodily processes, to physiology, and should also include the study of psychopathological states.

Structuralism, Gestalt psychology, psychoanalysis, and – as we shall see in the next two chapters – behaviorism can be regarded as schools of psychology in the sense that psychologists said to belong to any of them claimed to have specific conceptions of subject matter as well as procedures. Historians have debated whether functionalism as described by Angell represented a school of psychology. The issue is not easily resolved.

In the first half of the 1900s, there apparently were many psychologists who conceived of psychology as the study of the mind but did not accept Titchener's view. However, they probably did not believe structuralist studies should *not* be included. Further, despite accepting the theory of evolution, few – if any – made sustained efforts to show that the phenomena they studied in human beings had originated and developed in biological evolution. Charles Tolman (1993) was right, I think, in insisting that there was no tradition in psychology "marked by a devotion to evolutionary principles stretching from James and Dewey to Carr and Woodworth." Thus, Robert Woodworth's work reveals little influence from evolutionary biology. Evidently, the conceptions of subject matter by psychologists who believed psychology was the study of the mind but rejected Titchener's claims were not sufficiently uniform for us to regard them as representing a school of psychology.

Under the leadership of Dewey and Angell, psychology became known as *Chicago functionalism*. Harvey Carr (1930), who took over as head of psychology at the University of Chicago, insisted that there was not one but many functional psychologies. Columbia University has been designated another center of functionalism. Here Woodworth was regarded as a chief representative of functionalism.

12

Behaviorism

Innovations in Psychology in the United States: Introduction to Chapters 12–15

At the beginning of the twentieth century, its prodigious expansion in agriculture, industry, and commerce had made the United States an economic superpower. Its involvement in World War I was crucial to the war's outcome and also demonstrated the country's military superiority. Heavy investment in the school system and universities led to a blossoming of US science during the first decades of the twentieth century, making the North Americans independent of European culture and science.

Technological development continued its rapid growth, greatly influencing US society. The latter half of the 1800s was a period in which a number of new technological inventions appeared. The United States had already begun contributing at the time of the Civil War, and at the end of the nineteenth century, it had created technological products to revolutionize life at a rate that surprised the rest of the world. Electric lights and the telephone were mass-produced at the end of the 1800s, and the beginning of the 1900s saw the arrival of cars, refrigerators, and radios. Europe and eventually Japan were developing innovations as well, but the Americans were way ahead, as they continued to be throughout the twentieth century. Interest in technology became widespread in the United States and probably contributed to an emphasis on control over understanding in science, and perhaps strengthened the desire to account for psychological phenomena in mechanistic terms.

Empirical psychology was still at an initial stage at the beginning of the 1900s. It had little to offer in the way of new psychological insight, and perhaps more importantly, it had proved to be of little practical use. Feeling more independent of European science and thinking and believing in their own strength, US psychologists began developing their own versions of psychology. In the 1920s, they began laying the foundation for social psychology as a new subarea of psychology. In the next two decades it expanded into a broad field, and I shall treat its development in a separate chapter, Chapter 14.

The clinical and personality psychology of European neurologists was introduced to the United States in the first decades of the 1900s. Inspired by the success of measurements in the study of intelligence, US psychologists in the 1920s began to construct tests for the assessment of personality characteristics. This work led to important innovations in the study of personality, and in the next decade original approaches to this study were set out. The development of original approaches to psychotherapy took more time. The better-known types of psychotherapy worked out by American psychologists first appeared in the 1940s and 1950s. In Chapter 15, I shall review the progress taking place in personality and clinical psychology in the United States. The most important innovation undertaken by US psychologists was probably the attempt to make behaviorism a complete and consistent approach to psychology. This attempt is the subject of Chapters 12 and 13.

Testifying to the vigor of US psychology are the many longitudinal studies of development. Preyer had made a systematic study of his son up the age of three. In the 1920s, research was begun in which individuals were followed from childhood to adulthood. I shall here say a few words about these studies.

Human beings differ considerably in the ease with which they acquire psychological abilities and functions and the age at which they do so. For these reasons, *cross-sectional studies* miss important information necessary to form a coherent account of development. In cross-sectional studies, samples of subjects of different ages are studied more or less simultaneously and differences between the samples are taken as an indication of development, though they may not reflect difference in the development of individuals. To register the development of the individual, we need longitudinal studies, which study the same subjects over time.

To indicate the scope of the early longitudinal studies, I shall briefly report on three. In the Berkeley Growth Study begun in 1928, an original sample of seventy-four children was tested every month for fifteen months, every three months until the age of three, and every six months from the age of three to the age of five. The children were followed until they were thirty-six. In the Fels study begun in 1929, some eighty-nine children were followed from birth to from fifteen to twenty-five years of age. They were given intelligence tests but also observed in natural settings with a view to assessing personality characteristics. In the first and probably most successful of the early longitudinal studies, the Stanford Gifted Child Study initiated by Lewis Terman in 1921, about 1,500 children in their early school years were selected on the basis of scoring above 135 on intelligence tests and were retested every twelve years. A follow-up study was undertaken as late as 1973. The educational and occupational success of the subjects, as well as their social adjustment, was studied.

As these examples from the 1920s show, longitudinal studies are large-scale projects requiring the participation of several researchers and the cooperation of children and parents over a number of years. Further, they require considerable financial support, and the researchers starting the project run the risk of not reaping the harvest of their investment. Thus, the many longitudinal studies started in the 1920s are testaments to the faith psychologists had in scientific psychology.

To achieve a deeper understanding of development, research must uncover the causes of change. Longitudinal as well as cross-sectional studies are based on correlations, and while correlational studies can indicate relationships, they are rarely effective in uncovering *causal* ones. To identify causal relationship, we need theories of development and hypothesis testing. As noted by Hilgard (1987), the early longitudinal studies were carried out with only the most general hypotheses. The outcome of the studies was rather modest, but gradually many of their weaknesses have been overcome. The early longitudinal studies thus represented an important event in developmental psychology.

It is difficult to divide US psychology into periods, but so many innovations took place in the 1920s that it is perhaps sensible to regard those years as the beginning of a new period, even if some innovations started earlier and some results became manifest in the 1930s and 1940s. The 1960s are also years in which great changes occurred, and we can regard them as the end of one period and the beginning of another.

Behaviorism grew into a broad intellectual movement with a great impact on American life. I agree with Leonard Krasner (1996), that it "has a highly complex history within the broader context of development in psychology, science, and American society." Still, since it was a movement within empirical psychology, I believe we can understand behaviorism's main ideas as a critical reaction against prevailing tendencies in US psychology at the beginning of the 1900s.

We saw in Chapter 11 that several influential US psychologists criticized Wundt's experimental psychology for being too narrow, and after about 1920, it ceased to exert an influence. Psychology conceived of as the study mainly of functions of consciousness did, however, continue as a broad movement through the first half of the 1900s.

A few years after Angell presented his program of functionalism, his student John Watson formulated a program for behaviorism in a 1913 article in *Psychological Review*. Although Watson had already achieved a prominent position in psychology upon being elected president of the APA in 1916, it took time, as Franz Samuelson (1981) has shown, for behaviorist ideas to become more widely recognized. But in the 1930s, several of the most influential psychologists declared themselves behaviorists, and the years between 1930 and 1960 were the heyday of behaviorism. Behaviorism had still to vie for supremacy with functionalism, however, and psychoanalysis and Gestalt psychology also exerted considerable influence. This was the era Koch called *the era of theories*. Then, in the 1960s, interest in behaviorism began to rapidly decline.

To understand behaviorism, it is useful to begin by considering the fact that in our daily association with other people we seem frequently to infer their thoughts and feelings from their behavior. Thus, we can begin a study of psychology by describing certain kinds of behavior. Actually, Edward Thorndike stated in the first paragraph of his doctoral dissertation, published in 1898, that psychologists make two sorts of statements about human nature: statements about consciousness and statements about behavior. Thinking along the same lines, McDougall argued in 1908 that psychology could be conceived of more appropriately as the study of behavior than as the study of the mind (see Chapter 7). Further, we saw in Chapter 8 that Pavlov and Bekhterev developed versions of behaviorist psychology independently of what happened in the United States. Thus, perhaps it is not more natural to think empirical psychology can start as a study of consciousness than as a study of behavior.

Spencer's view of psychology seems to have been rather close to behaviorism. As noted in our review of James, Spencer seems to have thought of psychology as the study of interactions between an organism and its environment. James seized upon this idea, naming it *Spencer's formula*. It seems a small step to elaborate this position into a study of the organism's behavior under diverse types of stimulation. Hughlings Jackson, as we saw in Chapter 6, was strongly influenced by Spencer and thought all pathways in the brain are stimulus–response connections. James did not develop a Spencerian position into a kind of behaviorism. But, as I shall argue later in the chapter, his student Thorndike did.

As these remarks about Spencer, Jackson, McDougall, and Thorndike reveal, when Watson launched a manifesto for behaviorism in his 1913 article, behaviorism already existed as an alternative to the study of the mind. However, none of those researchers attempted to develop it into a systematic study of consciousness, as Watson did.

Behaviorism resulted in a broadening of psychology. Watson wanted to include the study of animals and extend psychology to problems of social importance. Angell's program of functionalism already gave a place to these problems, however. Watson's critical reaction to the prevailing psychology was, therefore, probably not primarily motivated by a desire to broaden the scope of psychology's subject matter. His main reason was probably methodological. He wanted to bring the procedures of psychology into agreement with the procedures of natural science. This, he thought, he could do only by basing psychology on observations that are objective in the sense that they could be made public. Choosing behavior as the subject matter instead of mental experience would allow him to do so. Thus, while James, Dewey, and Angell primarily were concerned with broadening the scope of psychology's subject matter, Watson was primarily concerned with improving its methodology.

The idea of making psychology a study of behavior was elaborated in different ways, and different versions of behaviorism were presented. Thorndike was the first to work out a complex psychological problem experimentally from a behaviorist perspective. Further, his theory of learning became an important inspiration to many of the behaviorists, who thought understanding learning was the key to explaining psychological processes. I shall begin my review of behaviorism with a review of Thorndike's work. Watson gave inspiration to all the prominent later behaviorists, as well as to Thorndike, and it is logical to treat them together.

In 1927, the American physicist Percy Bridgment argued in a book that scientific concepts may be defined by reference to the procedures used in the study of a problem. This view, named *operationalism*, had a strong impact on behaviorists of the 1930s and still exerts considerable influence. I shall, therefore, insert a section on operationalism before I turn to the later behaviorists.

B. F. Skinner became the most famous behaviorist. He was strongly influenced by Thorndike as well as by Watson, and he should, in my opinion, be seen as closely associated with them. Watson and Skinner seem to have believed that psychology's subject matter could be directly observed. In this respect, their views of science are highly similar to those of Wundt and Titchener. An important line in the history of psychology can be drawn from Wundt to Watson and Skinner via Titchener. In contrast to Watson and Skinner, Clark Hull and Edward Tolman, the most influential behaviorists of the 1930s and 1940s, seem to have taken another view of the question of the role of observations in science. I have therefore treated them in a separate chapter. Behaviorism, particularly that of Skinner, had a strong effect on clinical psychology, and I shall finish the present chapter by a review of this effect. But before I turn to the reviews listed above, I shall discuss what seem to have been the core ideas in behaviorism.

Core Ideas in US Behaviorism

The different versions of US behaviorism had some central beliefs in common. Chief among these was that psychology must have a basis in objectively observable events. The actions performed by the organism in its interaction with its environment are events of this type. Thus, in contrast to the study of consciousness, the study of behavior is directed towards the actions of the organism.

The Stimulus–Response Paradigm

Another core idea in behaviorism is that the thinking and actions of humans and animals can be accounted for in terms of connections established between a specific physical stimulation and definite movements elicited by the stimulation. Characteristically, behaviorist accounts of psychological phenomena were made in terms of stimulus–response connections.

In the study of the brain, many neurologists had conceived of the nervous system as consisting of stimulus–response connections, and they made the physiological reflex central in their study. As I noted in the preceding chapter, James had attempted to account for the establishment of associations by means of the concept of a reflex arc, and in his famous article Dewey had warned that the reflex arc must be placed in a proper context. Further, Thorndike had outlined how learning could be accounted for as stimulus–response connections. Independently of them, Pavlov and Bekhterev had developed psychologies based on a stimulus–response paradigm. Thus, by adopting this paradigm, the behaviorists aligned themselves with a central tendency in American as well as European thinking.

Concentration on the Study of Learning

A third idea, which the US behaviorists also shared with their Russian counterparts, was that the study of learning constitutes the central area of psychological study. As I pointed out in Chapter 11, education and child development were topics of central interest to the early US psychologists, and out of this interest grew the modern American study of learning. Thorndike was a great inspiration, but Pavlov also exerted considerable influence. Like Thorndike and Pavlov, the American learning theorists of 1920–60 tended to think of learning as the same sort of process whether it occurs in human beings or in animals capable only of simple reactions to the environment, or whether it occurs in the infant or the adult human being. Doubts about this belief in the 1950s and 1960s contributed to a decline in interest in behaviorism.

The emphasis on learning as opposed to perception made US psychology different from that of Germany, and when German psychologists immigrated to the United States in the 1930s, there was a confrontation between German psychology focusing on perception and t North American psychology focusing on learning. As we shall see in Chapter 17, integration of the two orientations was begun in the 1930s by Karl Lashley and the group around him, and also by Tolman.

Emphasis on Environmental Factors

A fourth core idea in American behaviorism was that ontogenetic development is determined mainly by environmental and not by genetic factors. This was an idea US psychologists did not share with the Russian reflexologists or Continental European ethologists. Nor did they share it with Thorndike. Actually, a change took place in US psychology concerning the role heredity plays in ontogenetic development. Whereas many US pioneer psychologists had been strongly influenced by Galton and his eugenics program, in the 1920s many began to focus strictly on environmental factors. In his earlier work, for instance, Watson took a balanced view of the issue, but in the 1920s, he became an ardent advocate of the environment as playing a dominant role in the development of the child. This belief naturally helped strengthen the interest in learning.

With few exceptions, the leading behaviorists did the major part of their work with animals, but they took only a minor interest in comparative psychology. As we shall see in Chapter 19, the evolutionary perspective is almost missing from 1920 to 1960. It is not easy to give a good reason for this neglect. One guess is that the attribution of only minor importance to genetic factors may have led to a neglect of evolutionary biology. Another guess is that the behaviorists concentrated so strongly on the experimental method that they neglected the comparative method, and along with it the comparative study of psychology.

In behaviorism, as in psychology in general, few efforts were made in the period 1920–1960 to find a basis for psychology in neurophysiology. I shall return in Chapter 18 to this characteristic of the period.

Edward Lee Thorndike (1874–1949)

The great interest in education in the United States brought the study of problems of learning to the forefront of US psychology. One of the most active and influential researchers in learning and educational psychology was Edward Thorndike. He became famous for his experiments on animal learning, published in 1898 as part of his doctoral thesis. His impact on later researchers has been aptly characterized by Edward Tolman (1938, p. 11):

The psychology of animal learning – not to mention that of child learning – has been and still is primarily a matter of agreeing or disagreeing with Thorndike, or trying in minor ways to improve upon him. Gestalt psychologists, conditioned-reflex psychologists, sign-gestalt psychologists – all of us here in America seem to have taken Thorndike, overtly, or covertly, as our starting point.

As is usual in histories of psychology, I shall concentrate my review of Thorndike on his animal studies of learning. In line with what I said about British influence on American psychology earlier in this chapter, however, I shall begin by accounting for Spencer's influence on Thorndike. A study of the development of Thorndike's thinking is helpful in understanding the strength and weaknesses of behaviorism. I shall therefore go into some detail.

A Biographical Sketch

Edward Thorndike was born in Williamsburg, Massachusetts, where his father was a minister in a Methodist community. He finished his college studies at Wesleyan College in 1895. In college, he had read James's *Principles* and decided to study psychology under James at Harvard. He received his master's degree in psychology at Harvard in 1897 and then began studies of animal learning for his thesis in the basement of James's house. Although he respected James throughout his life, he felt his teacher was too weakly oriented towards empirical psychology. Thorndike wanted to create a psychology based on observation and experiment.

In the hope of getting more attention for his ideas about empirical research, therefore, he moved to Cattell at Columbia University. Here, in 1898, Thorndike finished his doctoral thesis, entitled *Animal Intelligence*. A revised edition of the thesis, which had made him famous, was published in 1911. After having taught for one year at a college in Cleveland, Thorndike returned to Columbia where he remained until 1940. In addition to studying problems in the psychology of learning, he carried out extensive studies of intelligence, language, and practical educational problems. Like his teacher Cattell, Thorndike was convinced that science has produced concrete methods that can give speedy and effective solutions to psychological and educational problems. Starting from what he believed was scientific thinking, he tried to work out concrete plans for schoolteaching. Of his many books, I shall just mention one in three volumes on educational psychology that appeared in 1913–1914. His most important contribution to scientific psychology was the studies of animal learning reported in *Animal Intelligence*. I shall report only briefly on other parts of his work. An extensive biography and reviews of his main works have been given by Geraldine Joncich (1968). My account will deviate somewhat from hers.

Thorndike's Move from a Spencerian to a Behaviorist Position

Thorndike (1898/2000) noted that psychologists tend to make two kinds of statements about human nature, about consciousness, and about behavior, and he tried to combine the two. Thus, at this stage, he accepted that psychology is not only about behavior but also about consciousness.

In his attempt to combine the two kinds of statements, Thorndike emphasized that a study of the mind must include a study of the movements of animals and their connections with other features of the animal's life. He (1898/2000, p. 16) then went on to state: "The truth of the matter is, of course, that an animal's mind is by any definition, something intimately associated with his connection-system or means of binding various physical activities to various physical expressions." Here he took a Spencerian position. Thirteen years later, in the revised edition of *Animal Intelligence*, Thorndike (1911) added a chapter in which he expressed his ideas of learning in a more formally elaborated theory. A premise for the thinking underlying the theory was the following expression of Spencer's position: "Every response or change in response of an animal is then the result of the interaction of its original knowable nature and the environment" (Thorndike, 1911, p. 242).

According to this premise, psychology should be studied as an interaction between an organism having specific characteristics and the organism's environment. Instrumental in this interaction are movements directed towards specific aspects of the organism's environment.

In his doctoral thesis, Thorndike used the term "impulse" to designate the type of movement he had in mind. The impulse is an instinctive, hereditarily determined movement. Thorndike (1911, p. 37), however, also defined the impulse with respect to the consciousness he assumed accompanied movements. In the revised version of *Animal Intelligence*, he substituted "response" for "impulse." He insisted the response has a hereditary, a genetic, basis, but dropped all references to consciousness. Apparently, Thorndike had moved to a behaviorist position. The point I want to make is that this move was just an elaboration of a Spencerian position, and not an elaboration of a conception of consciousness as a specific realm of inner events, as supposed by Wundt and his German contemporaries. Thorndike's move from a Spencerian to a behaviorist position was not motivated by the results of new experiments he had performed after he had formulated his initial position. It was primarily a change in terminology.

The emphasis on movements as instrumental in the interaction of organisms with their environments promised to free the study of psychology from reliance on more or less dubious postulations of conscious processes. But, as we shall see in this and the two succeeding chapters, it raised the problem of finding psychological processes that would link the movements of the organism to the environment.

Thorndike's Experimental Studies

Like the British empiricist philosophers, Thorndike thought learning consists of the formation of associations. However, he believed associations are formed not between two mental experiences, two ideas in the mind, but between movements and sensory impressions. I shall begin by describing his experiments.

Thorndike used chickens, dogs, and cats in his studies of animal learning. The experiments performed with the cats are best described. The cats were placed in a cage known as Thorndike's puzzle-box. The walls and the top of the box were made of wooden bars that allowed the animal to see and be seen. In order to escape from the cage, the animal had to manipulate a mechanical device that kept the door closed. In one instance, it had to pull a string, one end of which was fastened to a latch holding the door closed, and the other end of which was hung from the top of the box. Outside the door, Thorndike placed a piece of fish the cat was allowed to eat on escaping from the cage. By repeatedly placing it back in the cage after it had escaped, he was able to divide the cat's performances into a number of successive trials. Thorndike noted the time the animal spent at each trial. Thus, the criterion for learning was the time spent in each trial in escaping from the cage. Thorndike also recorded the movements the cat performed.

The time on each trial was found to gradually decrease, and Thorndike was able to draw a curve showing a more or less gradual decrease in time from one trial to the next. He also noted that movements that did not seem to be directed towards the string or the device keeping the door closed were gradually eliminated. Thorndike (1898/2000) called the movements performed by the animals *impulses*, as mentioned, and he claimed on the basis of his findings that impulses that did not have a successful result were eliminated – as he put it, stamped out – whereas impulses leading to the opening of the door were retained, stamped in, as a result of the pleasure the animal attained in escaping from the cage and obtaining the fish.

Later Thorndike substituted the term "response" for "impulse," formulating his view of learning in two laws. Of these, the so-called law of effect has received most attention. Thorndike wrote:

The Law of Effect is that: Of several responses made to the same situation, those which are accompanied or closely followed by satisfaction to the animal will, other things being equal, be more firmly connected with the situation, so that, when it recurs, they will be more likely to recur; those which are accompanied or closely followed by discomfort to the animal will, other things being equal, have their connections with that situation weakened, so that, when it recurs, they will be less likely to occur. The greater the satisfaction or discomfort, the greater the strengthening or weakening of the bond. (1911, p. 244)

The law of exercise stated that the more frequently a response was given in a situation, the more strongly it was associated with the situation.

An Evaluation of Thorndike's Experiments

Thorndike concluded that since the time the animal needed to escape from the box decreased from trial to trial, a successive improvement in learning to escape from the box took place. This conclusion seems warranted. However, difficulties arise when we try to understand more specifically what the animal learns in its attempts to escape. Thorndike asserted that associations are established between specific responses and definite sensory impressions.

The term "response" Thorndike had taken from physiology, where it denotes the movement elicited by a specific stimulation, such as the movement involved in the physiological reflex. According to this way of using the term, a response must be specified relative to a specific type of stimulation. Thorndike (1911) insisted that responses have specific causes, but he did not explain how researchers might identify the specific stimulation eliciting the movement of his animals. He also proposed that responses had an instinctive hereditary basis even if they were modified by experience. However, while he understood that responses have a genetic basis, Thorndike did not explain how this basis could be determined as a cause of the response. Thus, it is difficult to attach a more precise meaning to the term "response."

Thorndike used the term "situation" to refer to the environment the animal reacted to in the experiment. The situation provided the animal with the sensory impressions assumed to be connected with the responses; the meaning of the term, therefore, must closely depend upon the sensory impressions the animal received through its perception of the cage. But the animal's perception of the cage would naturally vary as it changed location in the cage or moved parts of its body or eyes. In other words, the situation would change not only from trial to trial, but also from moment to moment. According to this way of looking at matters, the term "situation," like the term "response," is so lacking in precision that we may doubt it is useful for describing the learning taking place in the experiments. What Thorndike demonstrated was hardly more than that the cat learned to escape from the box.

Thorndike thought an effect – in the form of a state of satisfaction or discomfort – is a necessary condition for learning to take place. From what we know of our own behavior and that of others, behavior seems in many instances to be determined by the satisfaction or discomfort derived from it. I think we may also concede that a state of satisfaction or discomfort is in some way an important means used by the organism to register adaptively favorable or unfavorable behavior. It is possible, however, that learning is determined by other mechanisms; in other words, that there is no such thing as the law of effect. As we shall see in this as well as in the next chapter, the relationship between satisfaction and discomfort became heatedly debated in the following period – and still is at the beginning of the twenty-first century.

As the above evaluation makes clear, there were a number of essential controls Thorndike did not undertake, and Koch (1985b) was shocked to note that an experiment so poorly controlled could have had such a great impact on the development of psychology.

Almost thirty years later, Donald Adams (1929), inspired by Köhler's studies of problem solving in chimpanzees, repeated Thorndike's experiment. He introduced a variation in the type of food placed outside the cage and found that the behavior of the animals escaping did not seem to be influenced by changes in this variable. More important, perhaps, was that the cats' behavior was different in important respects from what Thorndike described. The animals did not perform as many movements as Thorndike had reported, and the manipulations they employed in opening the door seemed to be different from one attempt to the next. This, Adams concluded, must mean that no specific associative connections had been established between specific aspects of the situation and specific responses.

Thorndike and His British Precursors

As noted in Chapter 6, Bain had combined principles of association with ideas of hedonism and had suggested that what he regarded as random, spontaneous movements are governed by their hedonistic consequences. Spencer had adopted a similar view that became known as the Spencer–Bain principle. Morgan, as we saw in Chapter 7, had rejected the idea of random, spontaneous movements, insisting that all movements have a hereditary, genetic basis, even if most of them are perfected by experience. He had also explicitly asserted that in perfecting the act, the animal proceeds by trial and error.

Finally, Morgan had stressed that the learning of an act is a result of the fact that movements are associated with favorable or pleasurable consequences. Thorndike's idea of learning as taking place by trial and error, as well as his idea that a favorable effect is necessary for learning, was apparently anticipated by the British researchers. Hence, it is difficult to understand what is new in his law of effect.

Morgan had also performed experiments with the cinnebar caterpillar and his chicken who escaped from its enclosure. Thus, Thorndike was not the first to demonstrate the ideas underlying the Spencer–Bain principle. His contributions seem mainly to consist of designing experiments in which certain aspects of an animal's behavior could be better controlled.

Whereas Morgan conceived of the study of psychology as the study of consciousness and made his formulations in terms of postulations of consciousness in his animals, Thorndike eventually dropped all reference to consciousness. Even if this led to oversimplifications, it resulted in a clearer focus on the problem and made it easier to manipulate conditions presumably affecting the learning processes. Thorndike's formulations, therefore, challenged researchers in quite another way than Morgan's did.

Unfortunately, however, Thorndike did not relate his position to those of his British precursors. He referred to Morgan in his discussions of the role of consciousness in thinking and intelligence, but not to him as his precursor in the study of learning. As a result, later researchers traced the law of effect back only to Thorndike and not to the British researchers.

Thorndike's Later Research

Thorndike had originally planned to undertake research on children for his doctoral studies, but when it turned out to be difficult to carry out these plans, he chose to perform animal experiments. He was not particularly interested in animals (cf. Joncich, 1968). When he obtained his position at Columbia University, he started broad and intensive studies of educational questions and of children's learning. Among other things, he tried to find support for his "laws" of learning by using verbal material. For example, he presented his subjects with the task of learning Spanish words. For each Spanish word in a series, the subjects had to choose among five English words, one of which was the correct equivalent. When the subjects guessed correctly, the experimenter confirmed the choice by saying "correct," and in the opposite case by saying "wrong." Thorndike's proposed "law of effect" suggested that by being rewarded for their guess and for whatever strategy they used to make the guess, the subjects were more likely to guess in the same way in the future and thereby, presumably, learn the correct meaning of certain words. Thorndike carried out further research to find out under what conditions children would learn skills such as reading and computing, and, in general, under what conditions instruction in school should be given to be most effective.

Thorndike on Comparative Psychology

Thorndike's experiments on learning formed part of his studies in comparative psychology. As Darryl Bruce noted, for six years from 1896 to 1901, Thorndike was very active in comparative research, reporting experiments with fish, chickens, cats, dogs, and monkeys. In individuals of all these species, he claimed to have found that learning occurs in the same way, according to the laws of effect and exercise. Thorndike (1911, p. 279) even wondered whether these laws are manifested in an organism as simple as the protozoan, and he claimed that learning by these laws was the main form of learning in the animal kingdom. Later US theorists adopted this belief that learning is mainly of one form. As we shall see in Chapter 19, it was challenged by ethologists at the mid-century.

Naturally, Thorndike realized that animals of different species have different capacities for learning. But he thought these differences could be explained by the assumption that species differ in the degree to which they can form associations. Thus, he conceived of the difference in intelligence between individuals of different animal species as a quantitative one. He believed the capacity for forming associations reflects differences in the number of brain cells in the animals; the more brain cells, the more associations could be formed. Thorndike's view of the evolution of the brain and the intellect has presented a challenge, as we shall see, and still does.

John Broadus Watson (1878–1958)

John Watson's life reflected the great changes American society underwent in the years 1870–1920. A brief biography will therefore help us understand how psychology was affected by these changes.

A Biography

John Watson was a charismatic leader who influenced both psychology and society. According to Buckley (1989), his life is a story of social mobility. Watson grew up on a small farm near Greenville in South Carolina. His father was an alcoholic and a vagabond who left the running of the farm and the care of the family to his wife. The neighbors looked down on the family and avoided contact with them. In 1890, Watson's mother sold the farm and moved to Greenville. Here Watson went to school, and from 1894 he attended college, receiving a master of arts degree after five years of study. He appears to have had difficulty in adapting to his school environment; he was much teased and often ended up fighting. He was once arrested after a fight with black people; as Buckley has suggested, it took some doing to get arrested for fighting blacks in a Southern state rife with violence and racism. Watson's devout mother hoped that John, her eldest son, would become a preacher, and she gave him as middle name the last name of a well-known Baptist preacher. In later years, Watson strongly rejected all religion and theology. After having been a schoolteacher in another small town in South Carolina, he was admitted as a student at the University of Chicago in 1900.

He had not excelled in his studies so far, but at the University of Chicago he had a lightning career. He took his PhD as early as 1903, and the same year he was hired as a teacher in psychology there. During his time as a student, he had developed an interest in physiology and animal psychology. Philosophy held no fascination for him, and he later said he could not understand Dewey. Angell, the head of the department of psychology at the university, was one of Watson's supervisors and appears to have been a social support for him. However, Watson was little influenced by the psychology practiced at Chicago. I believe the influence of the physiologist Jacques Loeb (1859–1924) had a crucial effect on Watson's development. Loeb's work also left its indelible mark on Skinner's psychology. I will therefore give a short account of him.

Loeb: A Source of Inspiration to Watson and Skinner

Jacques Loeb grew up in Germany, where he received his education and was influenced by the physicalistic orientation then dominating German physiological thinking. He was soon recognized for his studies of what was once called *trophism* and is now called *taxis* (Loeb, 1889, 1918). A taxis is the locomotory movement elicited in individuals of some animal species in response to specific forms of stimulation, such as light, gravity, or certain chemicals. An example of a taxis is the moth's attraction to a strong light. Taxes can be understood as the effects of specific forms of energy influencing physical and chemical processes in the organism.

According to Loeb, evolutionary biological viewpoints are superfluous; a physicalistic approach would meet all requirements. To begin with, Loeb attempted to explain behavior in terms of physiological processes. He later adopted a view of science in line with the approach advanced by Ernst Mach. As mentioned in Chapter 2, Mach thought the researcher should not indulge in speculations about underlying processes. Instead the job was to find the functional relationships between different types of observations. Loeb therefore tried to present animal behavior as a function of specific forms of physical influence and would not hypothesize about inner processes or mechanisms in the organism, which he viewed as an empty *black box*. Whereas Watson was greatly influenced by Loeb's early reductionist viewpoints, his successor Skinner was influenced by Loeb's view of the organism as a black box and the view that behavior must be studied as functions of given forms of physical stimulation.

Watson's Academic Career

A person with a childhood and youth such as Watson's must have been exceptionally gifted to advance so rapidly in one of the United States's leading universities. He was also hired as a teacher so soon, however, because Angell wished to develop research in animal psychology, and because Watson felt at home in the animal psychological laboratory. Like his friend and contemporary Robert Yerkes, who shared his strong interest in animal psychology, Watson had grown up on a farm in close contact with animals. Neither he nor Yerkes felt comfortable with philosophically oriented psychology, and, as John O'Donnell (1985) has emphasized, Watson's subsequent insistence that psychology must be the study of behavior may have been motivated by a wish that the study of animals not fall outside the field of psychology. It is plausible to think the study of animal psychology drew the study of psychology towards behaviorism, but, as Samuelson (1981) pointed out, neither Yerkes nor Washburn was willing to take a behaviorist position in his animal work. Thus, there seems to be no clear causal link between taking a behaviorist position and having an interest in work with animals.

James Baldwin, head of the psychology department at Johns Hopkins, was instrumental in the appointment of Watson as professor there in 1908. Baldwin had to resign his position the following year, and Watson replaced him. At Johns Hopkins, he acquired three colleagues of great distinction: Adolph Meyer, Herbert Jennings, and Karl Lashley. Meyer, considered one of the most significant psychiatrists of the first half of the twentieth century, established the famous Phipps Psychiatric Clinic in Baltimore. Jennings was known for his studies of one-celled organisms and had written a book titled *The Behavior of the Lower Organisms*, published in 1906. Jennings was strongly opposed to Loeb's view of taxes and held that they are determined by inner processes as well as external stimuli. Lashley received his PhD with Jennings. During his study of biology, he began to work with Watson, a collaboration that lasted six years.

Watson worked at Johns Hopkins until 1920. In 1913, he delivered a series of lectures on comparative psychology at Columbia University. In them, he presented his program for a behaviorist psychology. The entire series was published in 1914 as a textbook, *Behavior: An Introduction to Comparative Psychology*. During and after World War I, Watson directed his research interests more towards the study of human beings and society. After World War I, he began studies of emotions in infants and expanded his behaviorist studies to encompass human beings. In the book, *Psychology from the Standpoint of a Behaviorist* (1919), he presented a more complete version of behaviorism, accounting for his ideas on perception, learning, emotions, language, and thinking, and he also described the formation of conditioned reflexes as a fundamental type of process in the development of animals and human beings. Watson's time at Johns Hopkins ended abruptly in 1920. After a divorce resulting in a public scandal, he was obliged to resign his position. He had difficulty in obtaining a new university position and took a job as a consultant in an advertising agency. Here again he advanced rapidly and became a highly paid advertising executive.

Although Watson had left university circles, he continued to exert considerable influence on psychology during the 1920s. In 1920, he and his second wife Rosalie published an article reporting on their experiments in the conditioning of emotions in infants. In 1924, he published the book *Behaviorism*, which became a bestseller, and in 1928, he published *Psychological Care of Infant and Child* together with his wife. He also wrote a series of popular articles in newspapers and journals.

In the 1920s, his viewpoints became more extreme. He denied that human beings possess instincts and became the spokesperson for a uniform emphasis on the role of the environment in the development of the human personality. In his discussions of child-rearing practice, he warned parents not to display emotions because this could lead their children to bond emotionally with them. Watson himself appears to have been rather insensitive to emotions in children, and his two sons from his second marriage lamented that he had been unable to express emotions towards them.

In his book on comparative psychology, Watson showed that he had the knowledge and ability for a comprehensive discussion of issues. In this book he reported on, among other things, field studies he had conducted with Lashley on two types of terns during the summers of 1907, 1910, and 1913. These studies contain good observations but hardly any noteworthy new viewpoints. He also reported on his own experimental studies on maze-learning in rats, but he appears not to have contributed notably here either. He argued that learning is primarily a question of the formation of associations by repetition. Without contributing significantly to the study of perception, in his earlier research he had conducted several studies on sensory discrimination in animals.

His only research that can be said to constitute a lasting contribution to psychology was, in my judgment, the studies he conducted with his wife Rosalie on conditioning of emotions in children. I will return to these later. Watson's contribution to psychology thus appears primarily to have been his attempt to evolve a consistent behaviorist approach, and it is on this attempt that I will concentrate here, discussing primarily his views of science and psychology.

Watson on Science and Psychology

In the article in which Watson (1913) presented his program for behaviorism for the first time, he claimed the behaviorist study of psychology could be "a purely objective branch of experimental science." He criticized the use of the introspective method and complained that psychology as the study of consciousness had neither clarified any significant theoretical issue nor been of use in solving the problems of practical life. Most of the article was devoted to championing the view that comparative psychology forms part of psychology even in instances when it does not shed light on problems of consciousness. He also argued, however, that psychological phenomena could be accounted for as stimulus--response connections, though he did not deal with this question in any detail.

Six years later, in *Psychology from the Standpoint of a Behaviorist*, Watson (1919) emphasized more strongly the methodological weaknesses in the study of consciousness. Now he insisted that observations in all natural sciences are objectively verifiable; that is, the observations can be reproduced and controlled by trained observers. To meet this requirement, Watson (1919, p. 5) insisted that the subject matter of psychology must be behavior:

For the behaviorist, psychology is that division of natural science which takes human behavior – the doings and sayings, both learned and unlearned, of people as its subject matter. It is the study of what people do from even before birth until death.

Without denying the existence of mental states, Watson declared that the study of consciousness did not meet the requirement of reproduction and control. Consequently, the study of perception, attention, feeling, and thinking taken as mental processes had to be rejected, and so had the introspective method.

The reason he chose this position seems to have been his belief that to achieve objectivity we must directly observe the subject matter of psychology and not just infer it. He held that, in contrast to mental states, behavior, is directly observable. Thus, in *Psychology from the Standpoint of a Behaviorist*, Watson (1919, p. 13) asked, "What is it the psychologist can observe?" His answer was, "Behavior, of course."

Five years later in his book *Behaviorism* (1924, p. 6), Watson again expressed his belief that behavior is observable:

The behaviorist asks: Why don't we make what we can observe the real field of psychology? Let us limit ourselves to the things that can be observed and formulate laws concerning only these things. Now, what can we observe? We can observe *behavior – what the organism does or says*.

Insisting that the subject matter of psychology should be observable, Watson could rule out mental states as the subject matter of psychology. Taking this position, however, seems to narrow the range of phenomena to be included in the study of psychology. Watson thought he could include the study of perception by conceiving of it as discrimination. It was more difficult to extend the study of behavior to the study of thinking. Watson believed he could circumvent this difficulty by regarding thinking as implicit speech. This was an important point, because it would severely restrict the field of study if he had to exclude speaking and other forms of verbal communication. The study of emotions also raised problems. These Watson attempted to solve by making feelings dependent upon physiological reactions, such as changes in blood circulation and secretions from glands. According to this way of looking at matters, behavior need not only be overt and observable; it could also be implicit.

Attempts to account for the role of observations in scientific thinking raise several questions that are not easily answered. It does seem warranted to believe, however, as Ernest Nagal (1961) argued, that in the advancement of the natural sciences researchers have often postulated entities that are not observable. Thus, resorting to the idea of implicit behavior is probably unnecessary to ensure sound scientific thinking. The reason Watson insisted that the subject matter of psychology should be observable was probably that he wanted to have a criterion for excluding entities assumed to represent mental states.

In his insistence that scientific psychology must have a basis in direct observation of the events to be studied, Watson took the same position as Wundt and Titchener. While Titchener and Watson disagreed on questions of subject matter, they agreed on this important point in procedure.

The only part of the earlier experimental psychology with which Watson appears to have been familiar was Wundt's psychology, as represented by Titchener. Prior to the establishment of Wundt's laboratory in Leipzig, Helmholtz and Hering had advanced the study of sensory perception by basing it on a careful description of sensory impressions. We may even doubt this study could have been advanced if no one had taken this starting point. Helmholtz, Hering, and the other sensory psychologists took great care to make their study objective and therefore succeeded in laying a solid foundation for the study of sensory perception. However, all of them seemed to have believed that they did describe sensory impressions as forming part of a physiological as well as a psychological reality. Thus, if we regard sensory impressions as manifestations of consciousness, we cannot draw a clear line of division between psychology studied as behavior and psychology studied as mental experience.

Defining the concept of behavior in such a way that it can be used productively in empirical research raises intricate problems. Watson (1919) conceived of behavior as being accompanied by muscular or glandular activity and apparently thought he could define it without accounting for the fact that not only animal but also human behavior is in some way genetically determined. Heredity can be inferred from behavior, but it cannot be directly observed.

If we assume that as a result of some hereditary mechanism behavior is goal-directed, the behaviorist who holds that behavior is directly observable must explain why, whereas we can observe the movements of an organism, we can hardly observe that they are directed towards a goal. We can only infer the goal. To this problem, I shall return in the discussion of Tolman's work in the next chapter.

In a wide variety of human activities, it is frequently difficult to get an idea of what is going on unless we ask the persons acting to tell us. The range of phenomena studied in psychology would be seriously narrowed if we could not include speaking in our concept of behavior. Of course, we can directly observe the movements made by the tongue, mouth, and lips of the person speaking and register that sounds are made, but we cannot directly observe the meaning of the utterances. As I have argued elsewhere (Saugstad, 1989b), speaking can in one sense be regarded as behavior, but in another sense we must regard it as thinking. Therefore, Watson's declaration that speaking is behavior is problematic.

Having argued that speaking is behavior, Watson proposed that thinking could be regarded as subvocal speech. I shall return to this after I have reviewed his idea of how behavior could be accounted for in terms of stimulus–response connections, and his view of the goal of a scientific psychology.

Stimulus and Response

Like Spencer, Pavlov, and many physiologists in the nineteenth century, Watson saw behavior as chains of stimulus–response associations. In *Psychology from the Standpoint of a Behaviorist*, he introduced these concepts with reference to the physiological reflex. In this context, a stimulus is a specific, determinable physical energy. To render this concept generally applicable to psychology, Watson conceded that it must be expanded to encompass more complex groups of stimuli. He termed this expanded concept of the stimulus a *situation*. The point of departure for him was that a stimulus must be describable in terms of physical energy. Complex stimuli could be analyzed down to groups of simpler, physically describable stimuli. Watson did not think the definition of stimulus raised perceptual problems.

The concept of response could also be understood in terms of its use in physiology, where the term stood for the motor component in the physiological reflex, such as the movement of the leg caused by a tap on the tendon under the knee in what is called the knee reflex. But the term "response" also had to be expanded, because several complex responses are often evoked simultaneously. Watson's suggested term for this expanded type of response was an *act* or an *adjustment*. As examples, he mentioned the following: a person eats, builds a house, swims, writes a letter, or speaks.

Watson introduced his stimulus–response psychology at about the same time the Gestalt psychologists commenced their attacks on the concept of the stimulus. Thus, it was perhaps not to be expected that he was oriented towards the new research in perception psychology. However, his teacher Dewey had argued convincingly for two points of relevance for his stimulus concept. First, Dewey had made it clear that the effect of physical energy on the sense organs depends on the responses the organism is already involved in at the time of stimulation. An ongoing interaction between stimuli and responses makes it difficult to separate the individual components to determine what the stimulus is. Second, Dewey stated that the effect of physical energy on the sense organ depends on the state of the organism. Watson ignored both these points and insisted that stimulus–response connections could be analyzed down to simple, physicalist components.

With a basis in these thoughts about behavior as stimulus–response connections, Watson formulated the goal of psychology thus: first, to find the response when the stimulus is given. In other words, he thought that it is possible to differentiate stimuli and responses. For example, we could initiate a psychological analysis of behavior by starting from a given response. Watson did not address the problem that then arises. In the case of responses that are clearly physiological reflexes, it is reasonable, as Morgan pointed out, to view such responses as being directed towards specific objects at an early stage, and they must therefore be apprehended as sensory–motor connections. An adequate description of behavior therefore implies that it is directed towards different types of objects. This orientation is a result of the phylogenetic development of the organism and thus cannot be accounted for in mechanistic terms without first setting it in an evolutionary biological context.

In his inauguration speech as president of the American Psychological Association in 1915, Watson claimed that the development of many types of stimulus–response connections could be seen as the result of conditioning. In *Psychology from the Standpoint of a Behaviorist*, he allowed this thought a central place in his account of ontogenetic development.

The Goal of Scientific Psychology: Prediction and Control

The first lines of Watson's most famous paper (1913) have become classic: "Psychology as the behaviorist views it is a purely objective experimental branch of natural science. Its theoretical goal is the prediction and control of behavior." Traditionally, the overarching goal of science is regarded as achieving understanding, and prediction and control are thought to be the result of an increase in understanding. Samuelson (1981) notes that in insisting the goal of psychology is prediction and control, Watson broke with a traditional view of science.

After a careful study of the passages in which Watson stated the goal of psychology in his unusual way, Samuelson concluded that what Watson had in mind was social control of the individual and groups through the use of psychological knowledge. Buckley (1989) and Leahey (2004) have elaborated this point and aligned Watson's view with the political strivings of many members of the professions to exercise control over society by means of planning and science. Evidently, on this as well as other points in his view of science, Watson followed Comte.

Prediction and control are important aspects of scientific activity, but by stressing these without making clear how scientific theories are constructed, Watson seems to have taken a step towards wiping out the difference between science and technology and thus towards seeing psychology as a human technology. As we shall see, this view of psychology had a tremendous appeal to many psychologists and, as shown by Leonard Krasner (1996), was elaborated by Skinner. Samuelson (1981) believed this was the part of Watson's program that made him central to the behaviorist movement.

Watson on Thinking and Language

Watson's wish to base scientific psychology exclusively on physicalist descriptions – that is, on descriptions of the impact of physical energy on the sense organs – and on observations of the organism's movements, naturally gave rise to a host of questions about how psychologists should approach the human activities of thinking, remembering, and imagining. For his approach to replace psychology as the study of conscious life, Watson had to find an observable basis for these cognitive activities. He saw an opportunity to solve this problem by assuming language to be the basis for thinking, memory and imagery.

To make his view on thinking more plausible, it was crucial for him to reduce the importance of human thinking. He did this in his introduction to comparative psychology by arguing that the ratio of the weight of the brain to body weight in human beings does not differ from that of other animals. This view is wrong. Even if structural changes are important for understanding intellectual growth in primates, human beings do differ from other primates in this regard (cf. Richard Passingham, 1982). Apparently, Watson treated this important point superficially.

What makes human beings superior in intelligence to all other species is, according to Watson, their use of language. Human beings possess the ability to speak, which forms the basis of human thought. Thinking is speaking to oneself, and, Watson insisted, it is activated and guided by the muscles in the larynx and the other muscles involved in the production of speech. Over time, muscular movements in speech to oneself were eventually reduced so that speech became inaudible and also, in time, without visible signs of muscular activity. Thinking became subvocal speech, implicit speech.

Thus, speech had a central place in Watson's psychological thinking, and he evolved a theory about how speech, which he referred to as language habits, had developed ontogenetically. Speech developed as a special habit from a repertoire of unlearned vocal sounds which the child emits at birth and immediately after. These sounds are then conditioned to objects in the environment. Arguing for this view, Watson claimed at first that imitation is of great importance. Later, however, he attributed less importance to imitation. As the child acquires a few words, it begins to learn more comprehensive expressions and sentences with the help of conditioning. Watson did *not* explain how the child learns that words are symbols of aspects of its environment and of events in its life – that is, how words acquire their meaning. Nor did he discuss how the child is able to apprehend that one given sequence of sounds comprises a distinct unit in the flow of speech. All in all, he seems to have left out the fact that speech as communication requires not only a speaker but also a listener. Speaker and listener must attribute the same meaning to verbal statements. Behind Watson's – and most behaviorists' – account of speech development lurks the question of how meaning is established.

At the beginning of the twentieth century, philosophers began increasingly to emphasize the importance of language in thinking and logic. Watsonian behaviorism therefore corresponded with a philosophical orientation that was to become dominant in the Anglo-American philosophical tradition of empiricism.

Watson on Emotions

Towards the end of his academic career, Watson began his empirical investigations of how our feelings become associated with certain situations. He explained this phenomenon by assuming that when strong emotions are evoked, they become associated with the situation or with aspects of the situation the person is in at the time. The association comes into being, he claimed, as a result of conditioning.

After having studied emotions in children, Watson (1919) concluded that the infant manifests three types of unlearned emotional reactions: fear, anger, and love. Fear is evoked by loud noises or a sudden loss of the child's support; anger by the inhibition of physical movement; and love by light touches on the skin, tickling, quiet rocking, and patting – it was especially important to stimulate the erogenous zones. Subsequent research has shown that it is difficult to place emotional expressions in specific categories. Nor have researchers been able to identify Watson's three categories of unlearned emotional reactions in infants.

As a result of conditioning, Watson claimed, the original three emotional reactions are modified in various ways. He tried to demonstrate how this happens in an experiment in which a child acquires a fear reaction in a conditioning procedure. In this experiment, which Watson conducted with his wife (Watson and Rayner Watson, 1920), it was first established that a child about eight months old, known as Albert in the literature, did not show fear reactions at the sight of a white rat. It was then demonstrated that the child showed a fear reaction at the introduction of a loud noise produced by Watson striking an iron bar located behind the child. In the conditioning procedure, the child was placed on a mattress next to a white rat. When the child touched the rat, Watson struck the iron bar behind the child's head. At the sound of the blow, the child startled, toppling forward to hide his face in the mattress. In a subsequent experiment, the child began to whine. After a week the procedure was repeated seven times more, and when the rat was then presented on its own without the audible stimulus, the child began to cry and tried to crawl away from it. The experimenters were subsequently able to demonstrate that the fear reaction could be evoked when the child was presented with soft and furry objects. Watson and his wife claimed to have found that the fear reaction was present for more than one year afterwards.

It has turned out to be difficult to replicate the results from this experiment. Nor is it easy to interpret Watson's finding, as Hilgard (1987) has noted. If it had been the child's mother who made the loud noise, would the child have avoided her? We may also wonder whether the child would have shown fear of the rat had he been safely cradled in his mother's lap when he was playing with the rat and the sudden loud noise was introduced. The treatment of the infant was also of such a brutal nature as to be unsuitable for an experimental procedure. Naturally, however, these objections do not make it unlikely that evoked fear reactions can be associated with specific situations or with aspects of a situation, and that, for example, *phobias* can originate in this way.

Inspired by Watson's attempt to establish fear by conditioning, Mary Cover Jones (1924) began to investigate the possibility of removing fear expressed by children in different situations. She found that an effective procedure is to condition the fear-evoking stimulus to a positive reaction. In order to achieve this, she would, for example, present a rat while the child was eating, having previously evoked fear in the child. She found the method was effective. Further, she found that fear could also be removed when the child could observe other children who showed no fear at the introduction of the rat. The fear could thus also be removed by social imitation. This form of conditioning was further developed by Albert Bandura and Richard Walters, as we shall see in Chapter 19.

It has subsequently been documented that it is possible to remove fear by the methods devised by Cover Jones. She was inspired by Watson's thinking concerning conditioning of emotions and collaborated with him in planning her investigations. By focusing attention on the fact that fear reactions may originate as a consequence of conditioning to a specific type of situation, Watson contributed to the investigation of an important clinical problem.

Evaluation

Apart from his experiments on the conditioning of fear in infants, Watson's contributions seem to have been mainly of a methodological nature. By insisting that theoretical statements must be publicly verifiable, he probably helped highlight the need for objectivity. However, by insisting, as I think he did, that behavior must be directly observable, he narrowed the range of phenomena studied.

Ironically, Titchener, the chief target of Watson's criticism, may have inspired him to set as a requirement for psychological research that the phenomena to be studied should be directly observable. This requirement led Titchener to insist that observations could be made only by the person in whom the postulated mental processes takes place. Most psychologists today would probably regard this as an extreme position, but they would probably also regard Watson's position as extreme.

Watson's main contribution to psychology is that he forcefully argued for behaviorism as an alternative to psychology as the study of consciousness. Even if the majority of psychologists at the beginning of the twenty-first century seem to concentrate on the study of mental phenomena, most probably include the study of behavior in their definition of psychology, seeing it as the study of *consciousness and behavior*. There may be several reasons for this change, but Watson's efforts to show that psychology could be seen as the study of behavior was probably one.

Operationalism

In the empirical sciences we compile information in order to substantiate assertions and clarify concepts. To procure information, we must employ different procedures, such as making particular forms of observations with the help of specific techniques, and conduct experiments of different kinds. Thus, there is a close relationship between the procedures we use, the *operations* we perform, and the meaning of the concepts we employ to create coherence in knowledge. This implies that in order to clarify the meaning of a concept, we should analyze it in relationship to the procedures we are using.

In 1927, a distinguished US physicist, Percy Bridgman, wrote a book in which he argued that the meaning of concepts could and must be *completely* definable with reference to the operations the researchers had used to give them empirical content. In other words, he attempted to raise an important form of scientific practice to the level of a general principle. His approach was called *operationalism*.

Some of his colleagues immediately objected that if Bridgman's contention were correct, it was difficult to understand how we could decide one procedure is better than another, a decision researchers often make. Examinations of theoretical concepts by philosophers of science also showed that these were incorporated into contexts that could not be described only with reference to research procedures. Thus, it was not possible, as Bridgman had thought, to define theoretical concepts *exclusively* by reference to the operations scientists performed. (See, for example, G. Schlesinger, Jr., 1967). Later on, Bridgman modified the views of his earlier presentation.

At Harvard, where Bridgman was professor, Boring and his former student S. S. Stevens were taken by the ideas behind operationalism. They perceived an opportunity to clarify the use of concepts in psychology by requiring that they be defined operationally. In the mid-1940s, Boring arranged a symposium on operationalism (Boring et al., 1945), and there followed an extensive practice in psychological research to try to define concepts in this way.

As Hilgard (1987) has pointed out, it is no simple matter to decide whether the demand for operational definitions represented anything new in relation to the attempts to make psychology an experimental science and to give it an orientation towards the study of behavior. We may also ask whether operationalism in the modified form it eventually acquired added significantly to what Peirce and the pragmatists had already said about the meaning of concepts.

I believe operationalism made psychologists more aware that their research would often be imprecise as long as they could not refer to specific procedures. The language of daily life often obscures the fact that we have little knowledge about our more concrete use of psychological concepts. For example, we all know what it is to direct our attention towards something, but we do not realize that we do not know *how* we do it. I think it is helpful to ask which concrete operations are performed when we do this. The question reveals our ignorance, and it would give us a greater incentive to find concrete procedures to clarify the phenomenon "attention." What I have said here about "attention' has been said for many other psychological concepts as well.

However, we should not be content to clarify the meaning of a theoretical concept merely by reference to a procedure. To clarify the meaning of a concept, we must compare its use with other concepts that have a similar meaning, and thereby make the meaning clearer. For example, to clarify the meaning of "intelligence," we must compare the use of this concept with the use of concepts such as "perception," "motivation," "emotion," "thinking," and "mastery.' A reference to procedure is helpful in this analysis but cannot replace it.

Koch (1959–1963) claimed psychologists had not noted the limitations philosophers of science had shown to be associated with the use of operational definitions. As we shall see in this chapter and the next, many researchers were content to base their use of concepts on a simple reference to one or more of the experimental situations they had used, leaving it to the imaginations of their colleagues to provide a more general meaning.

B. F. Skinner (1904–1990)

B. F. Skinner began his university studies at Harvard in 1928. Watson's ideas were at this time viewed with great interest, as were Pavlov's ideas on conditioning. These two psychological thinkers were to have a crucial influence on Skinner. However, the main inspiration of his thinking and research probably stemmed from the US pragmatic philosophers, who concerned themselves with the importance of consequences to our thinking and actions. Peirce had emphasized that the meaning of a concept must be established on the basis of the consequences of its use, and James pointed to the consequences for our lives of our opinions and outlook on life. Skinner developed the pragmatic philosophers' idea of the meaning of consequences and attempted to apply it to a general approach to psychology.

With his focus on the meaning of consequences, Skinner earned a central position in US cultural life, and to many of his compatriots he came to incarnate the American outlook on life. He became the United States's answer to Freud, and in his biography of

Skinner, Daniel Bjork (1993) has placed him in a hall of fame for US intellectual and cultural celebrities.

Like Freud, Skinner was convinced that all human endeavor is predetermined. Skinner felt our cultural and philosophical traditions prevent us from recognizing that we do *not* have the freedom to act. There have been no advances in the study of psychology because we are unable to relinquish the belief in an inner force, an inner human being, that can decide the course of our actions. Skinner conducted a campaign for his view, which gave him the status of a prophet among thousands of enthusiastic followers, but that may have appeared as repugnant fanaticism to a similar number of others.

A Short Biography

Burrhus Frederick Skinner was born in Susquehanna Depot, a small town in Pennsylvania, in 1904. His father was a lawyer, and his parents appear to have held the middle-class American values typical at the beginning of the twentieth century. On completing high school in his hometown, Skinner studied for four years at Hamilton College, where he took his exams in 1926. His major subject was English literature. He planned to become an author and worked on different literary projects during the first year after his graduation. He gave these up after about a year's time, however, deciding instead to study psychology. In 1928 he began studying for his PhD at Harvard. He completed his degree in 1931, after which he worked as a fellow at this university for five years. In 1936, he began to teach at the University of Minnesota. In 1945, he moved to the University of Indiana, returning to Harvard as a professor in 1948. Skinner's association with Harvard continued after his retirement in 1974 until the end of his life.

Skinner wanted to provide a new foundation for psychology as a science and gathered around him supporters who, while he was at the University of Indiana, began to arrange conferences for discussions of research based on his ideas. These conferences grew to become the Society for the Experimental Analysis of Behavior, and its members later made up a separate division in the APA. In 1958, Skinner's followers founded *The Journal of the Experimental Analysis of Behavior*, and ten years later *The Journal of Applied Behavioral Analysis*. Skinner's thoughts received a great deal of attention from the 1950s through 1970s. Bjork's biography of him will no doubt result in more attention. Skinner has supplied eventual biographers with extremely comprehensive, if somewhat one-sided, material. In addition to numerous remarks he made about himself in his works, as well as two autobiographical sketches, he wrote three volumes about his life, in 1976, 1979, and 1983.

Besides a large body of scientific works, Skinner wrote moral, philosophical, and political texts as well. His first major scientific work was *The Behavior of Organisms* (1938). In 1953, he published *Science and Human Behavior*, which. I think. gives the most systematic and consistent presentation of his approach. In 1957, he published *Verbal Behavior*; in 1969, *The Contingencies of Reinforcement*; and in 1974, *About Behaviorism*. In 1948, Skinner wrote a novel about how we should create a future society. Its title, *Walden Two*, was taken from Henry David Thoreau's autobiographical *Walden; or, Life in the Woods* (1854).

In 1971, Skinner challenged intellectuals in the democratic nations of the West by asking whether there really is any reason to view freedom as the cornerstone of these nations, and whether on the whole it is possible to base a society on freedom. This was in a book called *Beyond Freedom and Dignity*, its title echoing that of Nietzsche's *Jenseits von Gut und Böse*. Like the book about language, this and *Walden Two* were based on the same fundamental ideas as those he pursued in his scientific works. Robert Bolles (1993) thought Skinner had already published his most important ideas in the book that came out in 1938, *The Behavior of Organisms*. Others believe his later works were important also. I hold that what he wrote after 1960 were mere afterthoughts.

View of Science

Skinner adopted a positivist view of science, as it was usually understood at the end of the 1800s. This view was close to the one advanced by Mach. In *Science and Human Behavior*, Skinner (1953, p. 13) claimed that science begins with the observation of single episodes, advancing from there to formulations of general rules and laws. At a later stage, it then moves from a collection of rules or laws to a more comprehensive, systematic arrangement. Like Mach and the early positivists, he made no claim to know how we progress from the single episodes to the laws, or how we get from a compilation of laws to a unified theory. Nor did he ask whether researchers' observations are determined by their theoretical assumptions from the start. He appears to have believed it is possible to make observations without simultaneously conceptualizing their context. This was a major point in the positivistic philosophy of science.

For some time, Skinner worked with Loeb's former student, the physiologist W. J. Crozier, who, like Loeb, emphasized the necessity for establishing laws with the help of an experiment in which we could demonstrate the relationship between the changes in dependent and independent variables. The goal of the scientist should be to establish functional relationships between different types of observations.

In the attempt to establish associations between different observations, the researcher should, according to Skinner and in correspondence with Mach's view, refrain from speculation as far as possible. Skinner emphasized that in the study of behavior it is unnecessary – and often an obscuring factor – to look for processes within the organism in order to explain the connections between specific forms of stimulation and specific movements, specific responses. As Watson had also said, the researcher should focus on what could be observed directly, and *this* in turn could only be the response and the external conditions on which the response depends. The organism must be seen as "empty," as a "black box." Skinner termed his view *radical behaviorism*. In his account of the phenomena under investigation, the scientist should adopt a physicalistic and mechanistic approach.

The goal of scientific investigation is primarily to achieve prediction and control. In the manipulation of different experimental conditions, we should obtain a given, predicted result. When we have analyzed a phenomenon down to its individual components and can manipulate these components in an experiment, we have also acquired the technology for the treatment of that phenomenon. Skinner demonstrated a unique ability both to analyze psychological phenomena and to create experimental settings in which the proposed components of the phenomena could be manipulated, but he neglected to say how we can arrive at laws and theories with the help of prediction and control.

When Skinner began his psychological studies, Bridgman's (1927) book about operationalism was published. Skinner appears to have had an immediate understanding of the importance of Bridgman's ideas, but not to have grasped that although operational definitions are important, it is not possible to define scientific concepts solely with reference to procedures in the experiments we conduct.

In most of his empirical studies, Skinner used rats and pigeons and generalized his findings to other species, including human beings. In the 1930s and 1940s, there could be no doubt that these generalizations posed a host of problems. Until the 1970s, however, Skinner (1953, 1957, 1969, 1974) did not undertake any thorough discussion of this complex problem, being content instead to claim that even if two different organisms vary with regard to complexity, they are nevertheless governed by the same underlying principles. The problem with his approach became clear when, on the basis of his experiments with pigeons and rats, Skinner attempted to account for the use of language in human beings. I will return to this issue later.

Behind Skinner's approach lies the assumption that all forms of behavior are established and sustained by their consequences for the organism. The task of the psychologist is therefore to undertake an analysis of the behavior with a view to clarifying these consequences, and, as far as possible, this analysis should be experimentally carried out. From a behaviorist and mechanistic perspective, the consequences should be sought in the organism's physical environment. Skinner insisted that it is always be possible to find the consequences, the reinforcing conditions in the environment. In this, he assumed a philosophical, a metaphysical, standpoint, in that it is hardly possible to demonstrate with the help of empirical research whether this is correct or erroneous. We can indeed define *physical environment* so that the point of departure is always correct. In order to render this perspective something more than a metaphysical principle, we must specify the concept of "physical environment" in relationship to the concept of "organism." In the empirical sciences, environment and heredity must be specified relative to one another. Skinner appears not to have understood this.

The idea that human beings' and animals' behavior is determined by the consequences of their behavior is perhaps as old as humans themselves. In Chapters 6 and 7, we saw that Bain, Spencer, and Morgan all concerned themselves with this issue. In his famous thesis from 1898, Thorndike too made the effect of consequences on behavior as his point of departure when he formulated his famous law of effect. Could anything then be added to the view of the impact of consequences on behavior? The important aspect of Skinner's efforts was that he attempted to elevate the meaning of consequences to an all-regulating principle of behavior. With this effort, he directed attention to new aspects of many psychological issues. He also developed an experimental technique for investigating the effect of consequences on behavior, based on Thorndike's experiments.

The Skinner Box

Thorndike had shown that the time it took for the cat to get out of the cage could be interpreted as a function of the number of attempts it made. Skinner believed Thorndike had made a discovery, but he pointed out that the time it took for the animal to get out was dependent on what the animal could stumble upon by coincidence. The time was also dependent on which type of behavior the experimenter or the apparatus defined as successful. Thus, according to Skinner, the learning curve Thorndike had drawn up did not give an adequate picture of the learning processes involved.

To attain better control of the processes Thorndike called "stamping in," Skinner altered the cage so the consequences could be interpreted as direct consequences of the animal's actions. He constructed a cage for the study of rats in which one wall was equipped with a lever and a food receptacle. These were connected so that pressure on the lever released a morsel of food or a drop of water into the cup from a reservoir. The reservoir could also be manipulated independently of the lever.

With the help of this simple apparatus, which became known as a *Skinner box* (Figure 12.1), Skinner could arrange the setting so the rat obtained food or water only by performing a given type of behavior, as, for example, by depressing the lever. Skinner also constructed a similar apparatus for use with pigeons. In this, he replaced the lever with a plate that could be connected to a reservoir holding food or water. When the pigeon pecked on the plate, a bit of food or a drop of water would fall into the receptacle.

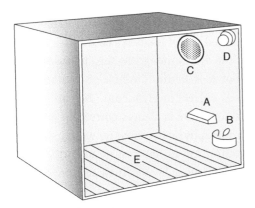

Figure 12.1 Skinner box.

Skinner was interested in investigating the relationship between a given type of behavior – for example, the lever press by the rat – and a particular consequence – for example, the appearance of food in the cup. Given that the presence of food or water in the receptacle could be apprehended as a consequence, he could then manipulate consequences in such a way as to make them depend on the actions of the animal. As

Skinner (1953, p. 64) expressed it, "we make a given consequence contingent upon certain physical characteristics of the behavior." In order to control the animal's behavior, he also had to control its nutritional state by depriving it of food or water for a certain number of hours, or by starving it down to a given weight. I will return later to this important point, which concerns the animal's motivation.

To measure the effects of changes made in the experimental conditions, Skinner registered, over relatively long periods of time, such as an hour, how often what he assumed was a specific form of behavior occurred per time unit. This rate of occurrence per time unit, which he called *rate of responding*, he used as the measure of the effect of the conditions he imposed. His goal was to find a functional relationship, which could be specified, between the rate of responding, or his dependent experimental variable, and the manipulated conditions, or his independent experimental variable.

Operant Conditioning

Skinner (1953, p. 63) also compared his procedure with the one developed by Pavlov and borrowed some terms from him. Like Pavlov, he called all events that enhance a given type of behavior *reinforcement*. In Pavlov's procedure, the conditioned stimulus was presented simultaneously with the reinforcement, while in Skinner's procedure it depended on the response being given first. Both types of reinforcement, Skinner claimed, could be termed *conditioning*. But to distinguish between the two types of conditioning, he called the one occurring in his own procedure *operant conditioning*. The other type of conditioning is often called *classical conditioning*.

Events that proved to be reinforcing Skinner called *reinforcers*. *Positive* reinforcers added something to the situation, such as food, water, or sexual contact. *Negative* reinforcers were the removal of something, such as a loud noise, a strong light, extreme cold or heat, or an electric shock.

At the initial stage of the procedure, Skinner did not relate the behavior he studied to specific stimuli. However, this did not prevent him, having been able to produce a given type of behavior, from introducing a particular stimulus when the animal exhibited this behavior. He could also find out whether this stimulus, which did not originally evoke the behavior, could have an effect on it. He called this stimulus a *discriminative stimulus*. He could produce such a stimulus by, for example, covering a hole in one of the walls of the cage with glass and then projecting light sources of different descriptions through it. To make sure the animal perceived the presence of the light, he would place the hole near the lever or the plate in the two types of cages I have described. He could also introduce a discriminative stimulus by presenting a sound of a given kind while the animal was performing the behavior he was interested in studying.

Skinner showed that after he had presented a discriminative stimulus a certain number of times simultaneously with the animal's conditioned response, the animal would give the conditioned response when the discriminative stimulus was presented. Like Pavlov, Skinner could establish a connection between a given stimulus and a given response. He also demonstrated that when such a conditioning of a discriminative stimulus was established, the animal would also give the conditioned response to similar stimuli. Thus, there existed a *generalization* here also. Further, Skinner showed that the animal could be taught to *differentiate* between different discriminative stimuli, and also that responses obtained by operant conditioning would gradually be extinguished when they were not followed by a reinforcer.

In daily life we talk about behavior that is determined by reward and punishment. In a very astute analysis, Skinner showed that punishment is not necessarily a means of achieving the removal of undesirable behavior. In many cases it merely suppresses it. If, for example, we gave a rat an electric shock on pressing a lever after lever-pressing had become conditioned, we could make the rat stop pressing the lever. After a while, however, it would begin to press the lever again at approximately the same rate as it did before the punishment was introduced. Skinner pointed out that all societies attempt to regulate behavior by different forms of punishment. He claimed that this was a major reason for maladjustment and behavioral disturbance. It is beyond our scope here to detail all the interesting but complex issues that arise from this proposal about the effects of punishment.

Skinner showed that he could very effectively sustain a particular type of behavior with his procedure, and that he could also modify or shape a type of behavior by successively reinforcing components of it. For example, he showed how to get a pigeon to peck on the plate in the cage. First he gave it food when it turned in the direction of the plate, regardless of where in the cage it was standing. Then he withheld food until the bird moved towards the plate. The next time, the bird was fed only when it moved nearer the plate. After that, the pigeon received food when it stretched its neck towards the plate, and finally, only after it actually pecked on the plate.

By manipulating the conditions that lead to reinforcement, Skinner found certain regularities of behavior in animals, and this finding received a great deal of attention. The regularities were the result of specific reinforcement procedures, or *schedules of reinforcement*. We will take a closer look at these.

In his experiments with reinforcement routines, Skinner used animals that had been deprived of food or water for a given amount of time. After having introduced this form of control over the animal's motivation, he varied the number of times the animal had to manifest a particular type of behavior before it received reinforcement. For example, whether using a rat and lever presses, or a pigeon and plate pecking, he could give the reinforcer every time the animal performed the response, or he could give the reinforcer for every other response, every third, tenth, or every ten-thousandth response. This form of reinforcement schedule is called *intermittent reinforcement*. Skinner found that the curve of the response rate became steeper the more responses the animal had to give in order to receive reinforcement.

Skinner could also vary the reinforcement schedule by giving the reinforcer at specific time intervals: every 5, 10, or 15 seconds, or every 5 minutes or 3 hours. Under these conditions, the curves also showed regularity. The shorter the time interval, the steeper the curves. After the animal had received reinforcement, however, the intervals between lever depressions became longer for a time, gradually decreasing with the approaching time for a new reinforcer. Skinner also showed that he obtained different types of curves when he combined intermittent and *interval reinforcement*.

View of Behavior

Skinner had as his point of departure that stimuli and responses can be viewed as independent of each other. In *Science and Human Behavior*, he began his account with a description of the physiological reflexes. In a physiological reflex the response, which Skinner called *respondent* behavior, is evoked by a known, specific stimulus. Skinner claimed, however, that there are many different types of behaviors for which we cannot demonstrate that the response is evoked by the given stimulus. Since he was convinced that all behavior is strictly predetermined, he did not claim this behavior is *not* determined by specific stimuli. His point was that we do not have the knowledge to make it possible to demonstrate such stimuli. As he pointed out, however, if we are not able to deal with this type of behavior, it would represent a serious obstacle to the immediate advancement of a scientific psychology. So he created a program for the treatment of such behavior.

Skinner discussed the difference between the two types of behavior by pointing out that physiological reflexes have an effect on physiological processes. Conversely, the other type of behavior has an effect on the organism's environment and could be said to operate on the external world. Thus, he called it *operant behavior*. Many contemporary psychologists at the time felt Skinner had made an important point, but the distinction between respondent and operant behavior is by no means as clear as Skinner assumed. First, many physiological reflexes are incorporated in our movements. It seems contrived to say these affect only our inner physiological processes. However, as I shall indicate, there are other and more weighty objections to the distinction he claimed.

Like Watson, Skinner insisted that the study of behavior must be founded on directly observable events. We must not attribute characteristics to the organism that we could not clearly base on objective observation. Therefore, Skinner was unwilling to describe behavior as purposeful or goal-directed, arguing that there is no room for these qualities in the account of biological evolution. The last point is, of course, correct. But this does not mean we cannot attribute goal-oriented behavior to the *individual* in a fruitful and scientific discussion of the individual's behavior. Individuals within a species, according to the theory of evolution, are adapted to a given environment, and their behavior is a means by which to achieve this adaptation. Therefore, if we do not include goal-oriented behavior in our account, we overlook that behavior is also genetically determined.

To understand Skinner, we need a closer look at his view that behavior is not goal-directed. Let us look at a form of behavior he used as an example in his approach to the study of psychology – namely, pecking behavior in pigeons. As you may recall from Chapter 7, Morgan had very astutely analyzed pecking behavior in chickens in great detail. He pointed out that it was genetically determined, but that it required a certain amount of learning to be perfected. In studying pecking in a species of birds, we must therefore clarify that a genetically determined form of motor movement is the response. As we progress in the study of this movement, we can see, as Morgan also pointed out, that it is determined by specific stimuli. Thus, we cannot describe pecking adequately without viewing it as a sensory-motor action or activity.

Let us take another example. For birds, movement of the wings is a factor in the adaptation that results in flying skills. Therefore, we can hardly understand the wing strokes of a pigeon as anything other than a factor in a complex adaptation pattern. To achieve flying skills, the bird must coordinate a pattern of complex stimuli with a series of complex muscle movements. Viewing the movement that culminates in the stroke of a wing as a response isolated from the total adaptation process is therefore an oversimplification. Skinner's research enterprise is based on the assumption that operant behavior can be understood as mechanistic movements and not as complex, genetically determined sensory-motor connections.

On the assumption that it is possible to isolate specific movements made by a biological organism and to describe these in purely physical terms, Skinner introduced the concept of the operant. He defined an operant as a class of responses determined by the same contingencies, as in the depression of a lever by a rat in a Skinner box. Whether the rat presses the lever with one forepaw or the other, or both, or with its snout, the movement, according to Skinner, represents the same operant when it is determined by the same condition. He did not specify what he meant by "the same condition," however, seriously limiting the usefulness of the definition.

Since it is often claimed that operant conditioning is a branch of biology, there is hardly any doubt that in his publications in 1953 and 1957, and probably in all the publications that followed, Skinner assumed certain movements by the organism to be completely describable in physical terms. Therefore, it would be unnecessary to specify the meaning of a movement in relationship to the organism executing it. For example, it would be unnecessary to specify the rat's lever-press in relationship to the rat as an organism manipulating objects with its forepaws, or to specify the pecking of the pigeon in relationship to the pigeon as an organism that takes its nourishment by pecking, or to specify the wing movements of the pigeon in relationship to the pigeon as an organism adapted to a life of movement in the air. In my view, Skinner overlooked the considerable problems in his use of the concept of "behavior." This difficulty became obvious when ethology, with its emphasis on species-specific traits, was introduced into the United States in the 1950s.

Interpretation of Skinner's Experimental Findings

We can interpret Skinner's experiments in a completely different way than he did. Skinner claimed that the introduction of food or water, for instance, would reinforce a response. But instead of viewing food or water as reinforcers of a response, we can see them as incentives to motivation, to a hunger motivation and a thirst motivation. Is this interpretation different from Skinner's? Yes, in that it binds the definition of the stimuli to an inner state in the animal. According to this view, the rat operates the lever (or the pigeon pecks the plate) because it is hungry, it is thirsty, or it wants to avoid pain. Skinner had to produce a certain motivational state in the animal to make it operate on the environment. If the motivation is not present, the animal will not display the behavior. Apparently, inner states and incentives are not easily separable, however. As we shall see, Lashley was already aware of this possibility in 1938.

To accommodate this objection, Skinner argued that we cannot observe an inner motivational state directly. This is indeed the case, but if we do not adopt his version of the positivist philosophy of science, there is no reason at all to believe that we must directly observe what we study. We have considerable knowledge that clearly points to processes in biological organisms that direct them towards objects such as food, water, and sexual partners, and this knowledge has been obtained by recognized scientific methods.

When food is used as reinforcement, the behavior is obviously a means to obtain nourishment; it can be viewed as a form of eating behavior. George Collier, who started as one of Skinner's laboratory assistants in the 1940s, has shown in extensive investigations that eating behavior in animals is determined by a very complicated interaction of different contingencies. As Collier and his collaborators (1990, 1997) have shown, eating behavior varies across species, and it is dependent on access to food and the nutritional value of the food, in addition to other contingencies directly involved in eating. It is also determined by the other types of behavior we find in individuals within a species, such as sexual activity and nurture of progeny. The animal must obtain nourishment in such a way as to allow it time and energy for these other forms of behavior. Based on this more holistic view of eating behavior, Collier and his collaborators have been able to demonstrate that animals appear to have the ability to adopt certain strategies for obtaining the energy they need, the food they require. We must therefore view their eating behavior as an interaction between the physiological states within them and a complex environment. It is impossible to understand this interaction if our observations of the animal are limited to simple experimental situations.

Collier's studies thus show that behavior in an animal when it is eating depends on a whole range of contingencies. We can control the lever pressing of a rat in a Skinner box by giving it food because the experimental conditions are arranged in a particular way, not because the rat's behavior follows a certain principle.

The same view can apply to all environmental conditions Skinner postulated as reinforcing contingencies. On the basis of an extensive analysis of situations in which the animal learns to avoid a damaging or unpleasant stimulus, *avoidance learning*, Bolles (1993) has concluded that in these cases it is difficult to understand learning in terms of a simple form of reinforcement. He has asked whether it is necessary to assume the presence of a reinforcement mechanism in order to explain learning at all. This raises doubt that learning takes place according to what Thorndike formulated as the law of effect.

We can interpret Skinner's results from the study of rats by assuming cognitive processes in the rat. Based on experiences from daily life, we would expect that a rat needing to obtain a meal by pressing a lever will continue to do this until it has eaten its fill, and further that it will press more rapidly the less often it gets food in this way. Likewise, it seems reasonable to expect the animal to press the lever more rapidly the shorter the time interval is for getting food with one depression of the lever. Skinner would object that this interpretation assumes an expectation in the animal, which we cannot observe. His objection in turn raises the issue of the status of observations in substantiating specific contentions. If we believe we can justify a claim by drawing conclusions from demonstrable contingencies, there can be nothing to legitimately prevent us from attributing an expectation to a mammal such as the rat. From the perspective of the theory of evolution, we must even consider it rather peculiar if the animal should not have been phylogenetically provided with the opportunity to develop this capacity. As we shall see in the next chapter, Tolman consistently attempted to interpret results from experiments on learning by assuming the presence of expectation.

From the perspective outlined here, it is difficult to see that the regularities Skinner discovered can be elevated to the status of scientific laws. They are not sufficient for the prediction and control of animal behavior.

Skinner on Language

In *Verbal Behavior*, Skinner attempted, like Watson thirty years earlier, to account for language – not only speech and reading but also thinking – as behavior. His account was not based on experimental investigations of language he had performed, and was based only to a limited extent on the empirical knowledge already available about language. The object of his effort appears to have been to account for language and thinking on the basis of his thoughts about operant conditioning.

Like Watson, Skinner thought he could account for human use of language on the basis of studies of animal behavior, and he did not ask whether the acquisition of language required a brain of a given size and structure. The principles on which he based his discussion were the same as those in his account of operant conditioning – that is, his description of lever-pressing of rats and pecking of pigeons. Skinner (1957, p. 3) justified his view by claiming the results he had obtained with his approach had all proven to be surprisingly free of species constraints. As we noted above, this claim was not justified.

The difference between what Skinner called *verbal behavior* and other behavior is that verbal behavior is reinforced by other people's reactions. In other words, the behavior of the speaker is reinforced by the listener's reactions to it. With this point of departure, Skinner suggested that the vocal sounds of infants are modified by the reactions of their parents and other listeners. Being reacted to in this way, the vocal sounds acquire the form of words and sentences. This would be a process of "shaping," just as when an experimenter got the pigeons to peck at the plate in the cage.

Skinner did not explain how a child acquires the ability to differentiate words from sentences in the flow of speech. Such an explanation would raise complex issues about auditory perception. Nor did he explain how children acquire the ability to perceive certain differentiated aspects in situations that give rise to the *discriminative stimuli* he assumed to underlie the meaning of words and sentences. An explanation of this phenomenon raises equally complex issues about visual perception. Thus, I believe Skinner was unable to formulate his views about language in such a way as to render it accessible to an empirical, scientific psychology.

Although in my opinion (Saugstad, 1989b) Skinner's ideas about language are so vague and diffuse that they are of limited use, they did draw attention to the fact that we must understand language not only as perception and thinking but also as social behavior. The same applies to Skinner's treatment of thinking. He insisted that we can understand the development of thinking as the development of a form of behavior. We then must ask what response could give rise to an operant in this instance. In his presentation, Skinner appears to have landed on a play on words.

A major problem with behavioristic psychology as it was launched by Watson is the issue of how to account for thinking and cognition without having to resort to assumptions about mental phenomena. In the 1950s, many behaviorists believed they were on the verge of fulfilling Watson's original program. By accounting for speech, they thought they had established the foundation of a behaviorist study of thinking and cognition. Thus, the accounts of language presented by behaviorists in the 1950s were met with great expectations, as was Skinner's *Verbal Behavior*. But instead of strengthening the behaviorist position, Skinner's book undermined it. Many psychologists realized that his treatment of linguistic issues was highly incomplete, and this in turn led to a more critical view of other aspects of the behaviorist thought constructs. The young linguist Noam Chomsky (1959) was particularly critical. In a review of *Verbal Behavior*, he pointed out its many shortcomings, suggesting that these reflected an obscurity in the behaviorists' way of thinking. This criticism was one of the events leading to a reorientation within psychology around 1960. I will return to this issue in Chapter 18.

Evaluation

In his evaluation of Skinner, Hilgard (1987) emphasized the great impact of his views on applied psychology; Skinner fashioned a powerful conceptual tool for the treatment of problems related to learning. Robert Bolles (1993, p. 331) has characterized Skinner as a behavioral engineer. In giving so much emphasis to the technological aspects of his work, however, I think we may risk overlooking that Skinner gave us a much better understanding of the importance of consequences in human thinking and behavior. In doing this, he illuminated important aspects of human life, and this was indeed a theoretical contribution. But to clarify his position so we could more concretely understand its point, he would have had to develop a comprehensive theory. In view of his Mach-inspired philosophy of science, Skinner appears to have thought it possible to understand his position without a theory.

Skinner had a unique ability to elucidate his thinking by devising experiments. He also made masterful use of operational definitions. But because he contented himself with defining concepts operationally, they became very open to interpretation, and this was both an asset and a liability.

Behavior Therapy

Both Pavlov and Bekhterev concerned themselves with applying conditioning procedures to problems in practical life. Watson's study of the conditioning of fear was, as we have seen, followed up by Cover Jones's studies of the removal of fear. Between 1920 and 1950, other psychologists also attempted to apply principles of learning in therapeutic treatment. The progress of the effort was slow, however.

As Carol Glass and Diane Arnkoff (1992) have proposed in their account of the growth of behavior therapy, the slowness of this effort was due to the fact that psychologists did not have the opportunity to work as psychotherapists until after World War II. Another important point may have been the dominance of psychoanalysis in American psychiatry; the therapeutic environment at the time thus had no room for explanations of mental disturbance from the perspective of learning principles. In the 1950s, however, several groups of researchers in psychology could refer to the positive results of the treatment of maladjustment and mental disturbance with the help of principles of learning.

Skinner and his students were central figures in the effort to create a form of therapy based on the principles of learning. In accordance with Skinner's view of behavior and behavior modification, they proposed that maladjustment and mental disturbance are the result of unfavorable reinforcement contingencies, and they began the systematic search for these contingencies in the client's life story. When they thought they were able to demonstrate that the client's behavior was the result of unfavorable reinforcement contingencies, they attempted either to remove these contingencies or to reinforce other forms of behavior that could replace the dysfunctional ones. They also believed mental disturbances could arise because adequate reactions to specific stimuli had not been developed for one reason or another. With the help of *shaping techniques*, they attempted to promote the development of new, adequate forms of reactions.

In time, *behavior modification therapy* was employed to treat a wide range of maladjustment and mental disturbances. Particularly impressive were the results obtained with the use of the operant technique in the training of children who suffered different types of handicaps. Useful new techniques were evolved for language training of children with various handicaps and for controlling self-destructive behavior.

While Skinner and his colleagues were making their important advances in the utilization of operant conditioning, Joseph Wolpe (1958) in South Africa attempted to create a theory based on ideas from classical conditioning. In the 1950s, he devised a technique that proved to be effective in the treatment of phobias and intense anxiety. What he called his *desensitivation method* involved first teaching his clients to relax. Wolpe would then ask them, while they were in this relaxed state, to imagine situations that would provoke anxiety. The idea behind the therapy was that the client could not be relaxed and anxious at the same time. In the relaxed state, they would therefore not be sensitive to the situations that otherwise evoked fear.

Also at the same time, Hans Eysenck and his colleagues in London began to use classical conditioning as well as other forms of learning theory in the treatment of people suffering from mental disturbance. Throughout the 1960s, psychotherapy based on learning theory gained solid support, and in time it became as widespread as the psychodynamic forms of therapy. I shall discuss Eysenck further in Chapter 15. I will mention here, however, that in 1952 he received a great deal of attention for a study in which he concluded that psychoanalytic and other existing forms of therapy were all ineffective. According to his study of a sample of persons suffering from mental disturbances, the number who experienced improvement in therapy equaled the number who improved without any intervention at all. His study had statistical shortcomings, but it helped step up investigations of the effect of therapy.

Techniques of behavior therapy were extended to encompass a broad range of different types of problems, and as Daniel Fishman and Cyril Franks (1992) have described, these came to represent rather dissimilar approaches to clinical problems. When the behavior therapy orientation came into being, the behaviorists had a strong position in psychological thinking, and its supporters emphasized the behavioral aspect of the therapeutic treatment. But with the reorienting of attitudes within psychology towards cognitive and mental processes in the 1960s, many therapists began to combine behavioral and mentalistic perspectives. Skinner's followers tended to uphold radical behaviorism, however, and a distinction arose between the Skinnerian orientation based on principles of behavior modification and a cognitively oriented behavior therapy. In the 1960s and 1970s, the psychoanalysts and the behavior therapists stood in militant opposition to each other. Yet the two orientations had in common an emphasis on the learning history of the client.

In the 1950s and 1960s, a period of heavy criticism of all learning theory began. Among other things, it became difficult to believe there is only one form of learning, or only a few forms. This lowered enthusiasm for behavioral therapies and contributed to more differentiated stances. In Chapter 19, I will return to some important events in the study of learning. The history of behavior therapy shows us how theoretical research, the needs of society, social institutions, and ideological trends all contribute to the development of psychology.

13

. . . .

Neobehaviorism

Scientific psychology was sustained by the idea that the natural sciences could be expanded to encompass the study of human beings and society. As I emphasized in Chapter 2, the natural sciences, and physics in particular, represented an ideal for many psychologists. When Watson and other behaviorists claimed that the field could be based on objective observations of behavior and not on mental processes, it led some to expect a closer approximation to the ideal the natural sciences represented. In the 1920s and 1930s, many US psychologists thought behaviorism had taken psychology an important step towards its establishment as a natural science. But it was also obvious to many that although the behaviorist approach was adopted as the point of departure, the procedures used in this field were vastly inferior to those employed in physics.

One compelling difference was, of course, the extensive use of measurements and mathematics in physics. This difference had already been noted in the time of Fechner and Galton. In the 1920s and 1930s, there was an extensive effort to develop better methods to measure intelligence. As we shall see in the next two chapters, advances were made in the use of statistical and mathematical models in social and personality psychology. But progress in measurement and mathematical treatment had been slow.

There were other ways in which the scientific activity of psychology and physics differed. Physicists had developed theoretical systems from which to deduce consequences they could compare to observations. Researchers in psychology, however, most often restricted themselves to describing the phenomena they studied and making inductive inferences from observations. In their influential accounts of the nature of science, Mill and Mach had emphasized inductive procedures. In the 1930s and 1940s, behaviorists as well as psychologists with a cognitive orientation began to concentrate more on issues related to the construction of theory.

In his attempt to build a comprehensive theory of personality, Freud had postulated the existence of inner states and forces in the organism. The behaviorists turned against all accounts of psychological events that were based on assumptions about mental states. There was a dilemma here. On the one hand, to provide psychology with a solid scientific foundation, researchers must not make claims for the existence of any inner states or forces, yet, on the other hand, to construct theories of the same kind as in physics, scientists apparently had to advance precisely such postulations. Two psychologists, Clark Hull and Edward Tolman, became famous for their efforts to lead psychology out of this dilemma.

Clark Leonard Hull (1884–1952)

After having worked within several of the main areas of psychology, Clark Hull, with Newton's *Principia* (1687) on his bedside table, began the work of developing a theory of behavior that would encompass perception, learning, motivation, personality, and, in time, social psychology as well. A main product of this ambitious endeavor, *Principles of Behavior*, was published in 1943. We can think of its title as a reference both to Newton's great work on the theory of gravitation and to James's *Principles of Psychology*. The book was received with great acclaim. According to Hergenhahn (2009), 40 percent of the articles in two of the most prestigious journals contained references to Hull's theory for a full ten-year period following its publication. Yet, as Hergenhahn also informs us, the consensus today is that the book is of historical value only. How can it be that a person is first acclaimed as the Newton of psychology, only to end in obscurity a few decades later? Hull's contemporaries, Skinner and Tolman, are not forgotten. To understand the history of psychology, let us understand both why so many admired Hull and why he was so quickly forgotten.

A Biographical Sketch

Clark Hull grew up in humble surroundings on a small farm near Akron in the state of New York. He received his early education in a one-room school, but despite poor financial circumstances and much illness, he obtained an excellent education. When he was seventeen, he qualified as a teacher and worked as such for a year. Hull showed promise in mathematics and technical subjects and trained to become a mining engineer. Shortly after beginning his first job, he contracted polio, which left him with a paralyzed leg so that he was obliged to wear a brace and walk with a cane. After recovering, he began to study psychology, receiving his PhD at the University of Wisconsin in 1918. He was also employed there in his first university position. From 1929 until his death, he was professor at Yale University.

Hull conducted research in several of psychology's main areas. His doctoral thesis in 1920 was an account of experimental studies of the formation of concepts. This and a monograph by Solomon Asch (1921) were the first empirical works on the subject. Hull also wrote a book about the testing of aptitudes and published an influential book on hypnosis in 1933.

In 1927, Pavlov's work was translated into English. Hull was impressed by the Russian, and in the 1930s he began to concentrate on issues in the study of conditioning and learning, and a theory of learning formed an important part of his *Principles of Behavior*. A revised edition of his famous book was published in 1952 under the title *A Behavior System*. In 1954, Koch presented a comprehensive and very critical evaluation of Hull's research. Lawrence Smith (1986) has accounted for Hull's philosophy and his relationship to logical positivism.

Hull's View of Science

Hull was a man with strong philosophical convictions, just like Watson. Also like Watson, he took a firm stand in favor of a consistent behaviorist view and wanted to study behavior without reference to mental conceptions. Unlike Watson and Skinner, however, he claimed that in building psychological theories, the researcher could use constructs that – even if they are not directly observable – could be identified by reference to definite sets of observations. Adhering to the stimulus–response paradigm, he believed the constructs could be interposed between stimuli and responses. Tolman, who introduced the procedure of identifying intervening variables by reference to specific sets of observations, had called the constructs *intervening variables*. Admitting his debt to Tolman, Hull also referred to his constructs as intervening variables. When the intervening variables are related to each other logically so that they comprise a chain from stimuli to responses, they could, according to Hull, have a place in empirical science despite not being directly observable. Just like researchers in physics, he felt, psychologists should utilize mathematics to specify the relationship between the different units of the chain.

Like so many other intellectuals in the history of the West, Hull was fascinated in his youth by Euclid's geometry. He became convinced that scientific theories have important similarities with mathematical systems, claiming that scientific theories must be developed with the help of the *hypothetico-deductive method*. Thus, we should begin with a set of hypotheses; Hull called them postulates. From the postulates, we should derive consequences or theorems, to be compared with observation and facts. If there is a satisfactory correspondence between a theorem and facts, we could adopt it; if not, we revise or reject the theorem. In the formulation of the postulates, we must proceed by trial and error.

Hull claimed the hypothetico-deductive method would guarantee scientific progress. Its use was a hallmark of scientific activity, he contended; without it, there was no science.

In accordance with his mechanistic orientation, Hull claimed that animals and human beings must be viewed as machines, and periodically during his life he devoted much of his time to devising models of a machine that was the perfect analog of a human being. In his speculations about the human organism, he upheld a tradition within Western culture, as well as anticipating viewpoints that were fully brought to bear in the 1950s along with the invention of powerful calculators and computers.

Some Central Features in Hull's System

Concentrating primarily on problems of learning, motivation, and sensory perception, Hull formulated a number of principles that he used as postulates in his theory. The system he constructed eventually became very complex, and I will only review some of its main ideas. In his *Principles of Behavior*, he started with the idea of a drive, which he associated with ideas about the survival of an individual. For survival, some basic conditions must be met – the intake of nourishment, fluid, and air, and the avoidance of injury – and to reproduce, the individual must have sexual contact. When these conditions are not optimal, various needs develop within the organism. Moreover, Hull thought that when such a need is present it results in an internal stimulation of the organism, such as abdominal contractions accompanying hunger, or dryness of the throat with thirst. He thought this stimulation results in activity of the nerves that stimulate contractions in different muscles of the body via the brain. Thus, he assumed physiological needs result in internal stimulation, in a *drive*, and that this drive in turn results in muscle movements. The idea of an internal stimulation he had from Cannon, to whom I will return in Chapter 17.

Hull categorized the drives as primary and secondary. The primary drives, such as hunger, thirst, sex, and the avoidance of pain, have a close association with physiological needs. The secondary drives are understood as deriving from the primary drives.

With a basis in Pavlov's views on conditioning, Hull envisioned reinforcement as the reduction of a physical need. Pavlov had shown that an association could be formed between a conditioned stimulus and a conditioned response when the conditioned stimulus is presented simultaneously with the unconditioned stimulus. Hull thought conditioning need not necessarily involve a physiological reflex and simply assumed that when a stimulus appears concurrently with a response by the organism and the reduction of a need occurs, a connection is formed between this stimulus and this response. The connection is strengthened each time it is repeated under the reduction of a need or drive.

Hull referred to the connection as a *habit*, and to the way the habit is formed as the *law of primary reinforcement*. According to this law, the strength of the habit is a function of the number of times the association is repeated under drive-reduction. Hull thought that not only Pavlovian conditioning but also all instances of learning may be accounted for by his law of primary reinforcement.

For Hull, habit strength and drive exist in a multiplicative relationship. The strength of a response thus depends on the product of drive and habit strength. He called this product a *reaction potential*. With the help of this concept, Hull claimed to have the means to account for motivation.

The Concepts of Stimulus, Response, and Drive

Hull introduced his concepts in what he referred to as demonstration experiments and gave more formal definitions of them in a glossary of symbols. In his first demonstration experiment, he presented his view of learning, basing it on his concepts of stimulus, response, and drive. The three concepts have a central place in his theory.

In the first demonstration experiment, a rat was placed in a cage partitioned into two sections, with a dividing wall low enough for the rat to be able to jump from one section of the cage to the other. The floor of the cage was made of iron bars that could be electrified, so the animal could be exposed to an electric shock in one section and avoid pain by jumping from that section of the cage to the other. Hull claimed by a simple experiment to demonstrate how the rat learned to jump away from the section of the cage in which the electric current was switched on, to the half that was safe. Here is part of his account (Hull, 1943):

After some minutes the technician throws the switch which charges both the partition and the grid upon which the rat is standing. The animal's behavior changes at once; in place of the deliberate exploratory movements it now displays an exaggeratedly mincing mode of locomotion about the compartment interspersed with occasional slight squeaks, biting of the bars which are shocking its feet, defecation, urination, and leaps up the walls. These reactions are repeated in various orders and in various parts of the compartment; sometimes the same act occurs several times in succession, sometimes not. After five or six minutes of this variable behavior one of the leaps carries the animal over the barrier upon the uncharged grid of the second compartment. Here after an interval of quiescence and heavy breathing the animal cautiously resumes exploratory behavior, much as in the first compartment. Ten minutes after the first leap of the barrier the second grid is charged and the animal goes through substantially the same type of variable behavior as before. This finally results in a second leaping of the barrier and ten minutes more of safety, after which this grid is again charged, and so on. In this way the animal is given fifteen trials, each terminated by a leap over the barrier.

In the animal's behavior after the grid had been electrified, Hull singled out diverse segments he referred to as reactions or responses. One reaction was leaping the barrier; others were leaping against the walls, squeaking, and biting the bars of the floor of the cage. The segments of the animal's behavior Hull singled out can, of course, be regarded as reactions or responses to the situation. They can be objectively described, but, as Koch (1954) made clear, they are not descriptions of the type physicists undertake of the events they study. They are simply descriptions of the animal's behavior as experienced by the experimenter. This naturally opens the reporting to arbitrariness and subjectivity, which Hull did not note.

A more serious problem is probably that it is difficult to understand more concretely and precisely what is the physical stimulation, what are the stimuli, leading to the diverse responses in the rat. Apart from squeaking, which may be a reflexive or instinctive reaction to the electric shock, it is not easy to see what the stimulus is for the other forms of behavior – leaping the barrier, leaping against the walls, and biting the bars. Clearly, these reactions are forms of behavior the animal has acquired in the course of its ontogenetic development. This means Hull was not in a position to determine the nature of the physical stimulation leading to what he called the responses.

When we look in Hull's glossary of terms, we find that R designates a reaction or response in general, and more specifically the reaction that occurs as the result of previous conditioning. This is not a definition that will help other researchers determine what a response means in other types of situations than those Hull dealt with, however; in other words, as Koch also pointed out, Hull's definition of response was severely lacking in generality.

When we turn to the concept of stimulus, matters are even more complicated because Hull operated with two different types of stimuli that we must clearly distinguish for the sake of his argument. In the first demonstration experiment, Hull referred to the effect of the electric shock as a drive and stated that the responses mentioned were evoked by the drive in conjunction with the other stimulation the rat received from the apparatus. Of course, it is quite reasonable to regard the responses as evoked by the combination of the drive and the other stimulation received from the apparatus, but how can we distinguish between the effects of the two types of stimulation? Hull did not provide his readers with the means for doing this. Thus, his definition of stimulus is also severely lacking in generality.

Hull's concept of drive has also been severely criticized. It is doubtful that he made a contribution to the study of motivation. As Dalbir Bindra (1985) has pointed out, when Hull commenced his speculations about drives, several studies already existed showing that an organism would sustain a goal-direction without the internal stimulation of the kind Hull envisioned. As we shall see in Chapter 17, Lashley in 1938 had already argued, on the basis of his own and other empirical investigations, against the idea of drives being independent of incentives. Around 1950, several other researchers also pointed out that many forms of reaction in animals appear to occur without being the result of a need-reduction. Thus, Hull's concept of drive found little support in research.

It also had the important shortcoming of not addressing how an internal stimulation could activate and direct specific responses. Hull's concept of drive was therefore hardly a contribution to psychology. A more careful study of Lashley's article from 1938 could have given his thinking a more fruitful direction.

Evaluation

Hull's fame rested on the belief that he had succeeded in constructing a theory that, like the advanced theories of physics, allowed for rigorous deductions. Actually, as I hope to have shown – and as I think Koch showed almost fifty years ago – his central concepts are so loosely defined that we may question whether it is possible to make rigorous deductions from his theory. Hull's main variables – stimulus, response, and drive – could be identified only in very simple experimental situations. This made the definition of his concepts dependent upon specific experimental designs; as emphasized by Melvin Marx and William Hillix (1979), the approach became particularistic.

The study of learning was the central area of psychology in the United States, and many regarded Hull as the leader in the field. However, his principles of learning gradually came under heavy attack. Tolman, as we shall see, performed experiments suggesting that the belief in drive-reduction is not tenable, and that cognition plays a role in animal learning. The Gestalt psychologists pointed out that the ideas underlying Hull's concept of stimulus are too simple, and Lashley criticized his concept of drive. Although his student Spence succeeded in keeping up interest in the Hullian approach to the study of learning until the mid- 1960s, attention gradually declined, beginning in the 1950s.

Hull's use of the hypothetico-deductive method was an innovation in psychology, and he was probably right in insisting that it is difficult to envision the creation of sound theoretical constructions in science without also basing the work on deductions. He may have obtained this insight from the logical positivists, but most likely he arrived at his viewpoints through his own thinking, as Smith has suggested. Nonetheless, even if we accept that the construction of scientific theory must also be based on deduction, it does not naturally follow that we cannot base our thinking on inductive reasoning as well. There must be an interplay of induction and deduction. Hull became almost monomaniacal with regard to the hypothetico-deductive method, and he thereby contributed to what Stephen Toulmin and David Leary (1985) called the worship of method in psychology. We might also have expected him to have understood that in scientific research, as Frederick Suppe (1989) has emphasized, it is difficult to clearly differentiate inductive and deductive thinking.

Hull's Students

Although Hull could not live up to his aspirations, we must not overlook the fact that he wrote useful books on psychological testing and hypnosis, as well as contributing to the study of the formation of concepts. He was also a teacher with the ability to inspire and to draw capable researchers into his sphere.

In the 1930s, Hull began a seminar with the aim of investigating psychoanalysis. Several of the participants conducted empirical investigations, attracting a great deal of attention. A group of his students (John Dollard et al., 1939) published results of empirical investigations on the *frustration-aggression hypothesis*. Although the hypothesis emphasizes the drive-aspect of aggression too strongly, it still has validity in modern research on aggression. Some of Hull's students were trained as psychoanalysts, and two of them, John Dollard and Neal Miller (1950), wrote a widely read book, *Personality and Psychotherapy*, in which they attempted to merge a Hullian and a psychoanalytic approach. Miller later performed interesting empirical research of the reinforcement concept, and Robert Sears (1985) conducted innovative studies in child psychology and social psychology. Sears has discussed the work that came out of Hull's laboratory at Yale during the 1930s. O. H. Mowrer became known for his research on anxiety and avoidance behavior. In Chapter 14, we will meet a fifth student of Hull's, Carl Hovland, who conducted extensive studies on attitudes. Here, I will conclude with an account of Hull's most famous student from the 1930s, who was later to become his coworker of many years and who continued Hull's approach in the 1950s and 1960s, after Hull's death.

Kenneth Spence (1907–1967)

Kenneth Spence contributed so significantly to the development of Hull's theory that it is often referred to as the Hull–Spence theory. Spence was a first-rate experimenter who, among other things, criticized Tolman, Lashley, and the Gestalt psychologists. I will discuss two experiments that are important for the issues they explore and that demonstrate the importance to psychology of advancing alternative explanations for the same phenomena.

The circle around Hull approached the study of psychological phenomena from the standpoint of learning and the Gestalt psychologists from the standpoint of perception. In time this led to a fruitful discussion, as well as intense experimental activity. As we shall see in Chapter 17, Lashley modified his behaviorist approach under the influence of Gestalt psychology and became the leader of a group of researchers who can be regarded neither as behaviorists nor as mentalists.

Recognition of Relationships, or Learning?

In his book on problem solving in chimpanzees from 1917, Köhler, as mentioned in Chapter 5, had also reported on experiments with hens that he claimed demonstrated a relational context between stimuli that is crucial to perceptual discrimination. For example, Köhler showed that when he had taught a hen to peck at grains located on a gray, as opposed to a white, piece of paper, and he then replaced the white paper with a gray one darker than the gray piece of paper he had used before, the bird would peck at grains from the darker of these pieces of paper. Köhler claimed this showed that the bird responded not to absolute values in the lightness of the paper, but rather to their relative values.

Spence made these experiments the object of an interpretation corresponding to principles of conditioning. He argued that during the period in which the birds were taught to peck on the gray paper, a positive association had been established with paper of this lightness, and a negative association with the white paper. When the birds were presented with the two pieces of paper of different gray values, generalization would occur with regard to both the earlier positive attachment and the earlier negative attachment. Spence demonstrated that when the relationship between earlier positive and negative associations was taken into consideration, and on the basis of an assumption about differential learning, he could explain the results without Köhler's assumption that the animal responded to a relationship between stimuli. On the basis of his own model, Spence could also predict situations in which the animal would not choose the darker of the pieces of paper. With his experiments, Spence managed to demonstrate that a stimulus–response position was just as plausible as, and perhaps even more plausible than, the Gestalt position. Nevertheless, it may be that neither the Gestalt position nor Spence's gives a comprehensive description of what occurs in the experiment. Perhaps a relational context of the type Köhler envisioned *and* learning may *both* be determinants of the animals' behavior.

The Role of Attention in Learning

A disagreement between Hull and Spence on the one side and Lashley on the other about whether learning should be viewed as a continuous or a discontinuous process raised another issue: the role of attention in learning.

Hull and Spence claimed that when a relationship between a stimulus and a response has been established, this relationship pertains to all aspects of the stimulus. To clarify, if a relationship has been established between a stimulus consisting of, for example, a figure of a given size, shape, and color, the relationship will pertain to all these attributes; that is, to size, shape, and color. Lashley opposed this view, claiming that a relationship would be established only between the attribute of the stimulus towards which the animal's attention was directed. For example, if we were to give the animal a reward when, given the choice between a large white circle and a small white circle, it chose the large circle, an association would be formed only between the size of the stimulus and the response, and not between the form and color of the stimulus and the response.

A consequence of this view is that if an animal has consistently chosen the large stimulus after having been rewarded for this response, when placed in a new situation of choice it will not show any preference for a figure having the same color but a different form. Lashley found that his rats appeared to have no such preference, and from this he concluded that during the learning sequence an association had not been established between the color and the response, and that learning of this kind occurred as a discontinuous process.

Spence and his collaborators investigated discrimination learning in different situations, however, and found that the animals showed preferences corresponding to what we might expect from the Hull–Spence theory. Several other researchers have reached this conclusion. But no one has been able to provide a convincing explanation of why Lashley did not find a preference. It may be that in certain conditions, animals' reactions are determined by a single attribute in a stimulus object, whereas in other situations they are determined by several attributes or alternate between two or more attributes.

This and a number of other controversies taught psychologists of a Gestalt and phenomenological orientation to consider more carefully the role played by learning in perceptual processes, and, conversely, psychologists of learning to take perceptual problems into account in their studies.

Edward Chase Tolman (1886–1959)

In a critical review of his own research, which he completed the year before he died, Edward Tolman wrote that the introspective psychology he became familiar with when he began to study psychology at Harvard in 1911 seemed to him to be unscientific. When he learned about Watson's book *Behavior* in a course given by Yerkes, he was fascinated by the behaviorist approach, and he subsequently referred to himself as a behaviorist. However, as he said, the only categories at his disposal for the classification of psychology were mentalistic. Consequently, in order to develop his own system, he had to attempt to transform his common-sense mentalistic concepts into operational behaviorist terms. Thus, his point of departure was an everyday understanding of conscious life. However, Tolman held that the understanding of mental life attained by introspection could not form the basis for a scientific study; we had to find a way of expressing this understanding in order to study it by objective methods. This approach to psychology has been called *methodological behaviorism*. It lacks a certain clarity. The study of thinking and cognition, indeed of cognition on the whole, does not become behaviorist because we attempt to establish it as such with the help of behavioral indications.

Unlike Watson, Skinner, and Hull, Tolman thought the study of psychology should also include conscious life. In his efforts to find a place for the study of cognition, he was to be an inspiration to the *new* cognitive psychology that came into being around 1960.

Tolman was very critical of Hull's behaviorism and his way of pursuing science. Tolman thought it important to try to view psychology as a unified field in which the different types of events and phenomena are studied in a comprehensive context. To achieve this, we need a comprehensive theory, but, unlike Hull, Tolman thought we should not attempt to develop psychological theory as a firm logical construction. In the 1940s and 1950s, Tolman and Hull were considered to be opposites in US psychology. Although they disagreed on important points, it is nevertheless obvious that their positions had fundamental points in common. They both attempted to base their theories on the stimulus–response paradigm and the idea of intervening variables. Both also understood behavior as goal-directed and incited by drives of an inner nature.

E. C. Tolman

A Short Biography

Edward Tolman was born and grew up in Newton, Massachusetts. His mother was a Quaker, and although Tolman enlisted in the armed forces and worked with Henry Murray in the Office of Strategic Services in World War II, he adhered to the pacifist ideals of the Quakers all his life. He was involved in civil rights issues, and during Senator Joseph McCarthy's campaign against communism in the early 1950s, he refused to sign an affidavit of loyalty to the State of California. This resulted in his dismissal from his position at the University of California, Berkeley, despite his conspicuous lack of communist sympathies. Together with a few other university lecturers who had also been dismissed, Tolman pressed charges against the state of California. He won his case and was reinstated as professor immediately before his retirement in 1953.

Tolman's father was trained as an engineer at the Massachusetts Institute of Technology and ran his own company. Like his older brother Richard, Edward had his first formal education in engineering, but after reading William James's *Principles of Psychology* (1890/1950), he decided to study psychology. Richard became one of the leading theoreticians in physics in the United States and was a friend of Niels Bohr and Albert Einstein. I myself studied with him in 1951, and some years later I met his wife Ruth, who was a psychologist. She told me Edward was constantly trying to understand how his brother Richard and his physicist friends understood issues within the philosophy of science. His conversations with theoretical physicists may have convinced Edward that he could not pursue a fruitful science without theory. His associations with physicists may also have given him a more relaxed attitude towards experimentation than many of his fellow behaviorists had. He limited the use of experiment to demonstrating a point that could provide material for further thinking.

After completing his PhD in 1915, Edward Tolman was employed as a teacher in psychology at Northwestern University in Evanston, Illinois, and, in 1918, he became professor at the University of California, Berkeley. He remained there for the rest of his life, except for his military service during World War II and the period of his dismissal, which lasted for about two years from 1950.

It was during the planning of a course in comparative psychology when he came to Berkeley that Tolman began to develop his own version of behaviorism. His animal studies were mostly confined to the behavior of white rats in mazes. He loved this work and dedicated his first book to his laboratory animals. In 1932, he presented a comprehensive work on his psychological system, *Purposive Behavior in Animals and Men*. In 1959, a revised version of the system was published. The book *Drives Toward War* (1942) reflects his concern for the creation of lasting peace.

Tolman was open to different tendencies within psychology. I have already mentioned his interest in James, enriched by two of his philosophy teachers at Harvard who had been James's students. He was influenced by McDougall and also by Gestalt psychology, not least by Köhler's studies in problem solving. Later he was also inspired by Lewin's field theory; by psychoanalysis; and, from the mid-1930s following a stay in Vienna, by logical positivism. Tolman was revered by his students. Among these, I will mention only the Chinese psychologist Zing Yang Kuo, who worked with Tolman in the 1920s; David Krech, who was also Lashley's student; Donald Campbell, who became known for his methodological work; and John Garcia, also a student of Krech and whom I will discuss in Chapter 19.

Purposive Behavior

James and after him McDougall had emphasized that behavior was purposive, directed towards a goal. Tolman adopted this approach, contrasting it with Watson's concentration on behavior as movements in the form of muscle contractions. Tolman thought the description of movements must be viewed in relationship to the organism's purpose. A characteristic of purposive behavior was that the organism had recourse to several ways of reaching the same goal. Tolman's term for purposive behavior was *molar* behavior. He termed Watson's view of behavior as segments of muscular movements *molecular*.

As I emphasized in Chapter 6, there is no room for goal-directed behavior in the account of biological evolution. It is meaningful, however, to describe the behavior of *an individual* within a species as being purposive or goal-directed. After all, goal-direction is a consequence of a particular adaptation to an environment, and it may even be impossible to describe behavior without including its purpose. In *Purposive Behavior in Animals and Men*, however, Tolman claimed it was possible to *observe* the purpose of the animal's behavior. This is a problematic viewpoint. It often seems obvious to us that a form of behavior has a purpose. When we see a rat running towards a piece of cheese, we would perhaps say that it is running to get to the cheese; or when we see a person with a letter in his hand walk towards a mailbox, we assume we are observing someone on his way to post a letter. However, both these cases require us to make inferences, and to claim we have observed purposive behavior is therefore dubious.

If we describe mental life as goal-directed, problems with specifying the purpose of the activity also arise. First, the activity can be guided by several objectives. Second, we must accept that, in one sense or another, our actions are sometimes determined by goals we are unable to register consciously. Third, some activities appear to be more or less without purpose. Consider a person hiking in the woods. He or she might stop to look at a tree, flower, or strange bird, or listen to the birds singing, and in many cases, it is would be difficult to specify the purpose of this behavior.

In *Purposive Behavior in Animals and Men*, Tolman also claimed we could observe cognition in behavior. "Behavior," he said, "reeks with purpose and cognition." Just as it is dubious to claim we can observe the object of behavior, to claim we can observe perception and cognition in the behavior of human beings or animals puts us in the same predicament. Do we observe the thinking in a dog when we see it running around a fence to get to the other side? Do we observe that a person sees something when she or he sidesteps a rock lying in the path? I think we shall have to say that we do not observe perception, but from their behavior we *infer* perception, thinking, and memory in other people and in animals.

Operational Definitions of Mentalistic Concepts

Tolman did in time give up the idea that we can observe goal-direction and cognition. Inspired by the idea that scientific concepts must be defined in operational terms, he envisioned that cognitive, and indeed mentalistic concepts, on the whole, could be defined operationally. After having defined them, we may interpose them as variables between, on the one hand, concepts originating, from events preceding and causing specific responses, and, on the other hand, concepts originating from observation of responses. Thus, he used independent, dependent, and intervening variables. As an example of how to define intervening variables operationally, he addressed the concept of "hunger," which he claimed to be describable from, on the one hand, the number of hours an animal had been deprived of food and, on the other hand, from different types of behavior accompanying hunger as an inner state.

Without intending to place his concepts within a firm logical structure, Tolman attempted to discover the concepts required of his theory in order to confirm its

legitimacy as a general theory of behavior. I will not discuss suggestions for such concepts but confine myself to the criticisms he himself advanced against his own procedure.
First, Tolman pointed out that the process of defining all the forms of purpose and cognition making up behavior in operational terms would be an extremely time-consuming
undertaking. Thus, Hull's system became increasingly complex with the addition of more
intervening variables. One important objective of the construction of a theory is precisely that it should provide a better overview of an area of research. Second, Tolman
pointed out that, should associations between the different types of variables exist to
any degree, so that a change in one variable occasions a change in another, the utility
of providing an operational definition of intervening variables is much reduced. Let us
illustrate this by reflecting a little on hunger. The effect of food deprivation for a given
number of hours will, as we know, depend on our nutritional state prior to the deprivation, on our expectation of getting food, and on the sight and smell of food as well
as on what we are doing during the period of deprivation. Thus, it would be difficult
indeed to specify any intervening variable in such a way as to utilize it in a system of
many variables.

Tolman on Learning

When Tolman began his course in comparative psychology at Berkeley, he became interested in Thorndike's views on learning. He agreed with Thorndike that we cannot account
for learning by only the principles of association by repetition and recency, as Watson
tried to do. Motivation would in some way or another have to be included. Tolman
felt there is something external in the law of effect, however; the effect of motivation
does not enter the process when the task is completed. Tolman thought the effect, as
Thorndike envisioned it, is irrelevant to learning. The motive must be understood as a
force in relationship to the goal.

   In accordance with this idea, Tolman claimed that as the animal becomes familiar
with the task, it gradually acquires an expectation that a certain type of behavior will
lead to the reaching of a goal. Its behavior would be guided both by inner motivation
and by an understanding of aspects of the environment. Applied to maze learning, this
would lead to the following view. As the rat moves around in the maze, an expectation
of receiving food when it reaches the goal box develops. The rat also learns that some
of the paths in the maze lead to food, while others do not. In this way, the paths will in
time be understood as means or signs that become associated with the goal. In *Purposive
Behavior in Animals and Men*, Tolman expressed this idea by stating that knowledge
of characteristics of the maze and expectations about the goal gradually form a *sign-
Gestalt*. The expectation would contribute to chaining together the different elements of
the task. When the rat moves in the maze, the start box is related to the first point of
choice in the maze; this point is related to the next; and so on. In other words, the rat
would learn what led to what. Tolman emphasized that this view of learning covers also
Pavlovian conditioning, as well as the kind of learning that took place in Thorndike's
puzzle box.

Cognitive Maps

In a famous article from 1948, Tolman formulated his view on maze learning by stating that the rat gradually accumulates a *representation* of the maze. That the organism forms a representation of the task to be carried out is something the next generation of psychologists took note of.

Hull thought attributing cognitive abilities to animals would lead to imprecise thinking, and that in order to avoid a temptation to such thinking, researchers should view the animal as if it were a robot. Tolman felt this attitude was contrived and that it was more fruitful to ask what we would have done in the rat's place as it moved in the maze. Köhler's chimpanzee studies had made an indelible impression on Tolman. He claimed there was no reason *not to* attribute cognitive abilities to the rat. Together with his students, he conducted a series of experiments suggesting that the behavior of the rats appeared to be guided by diverse types of cognition. This view was, of course, criticized by behaviorists of various brands, and Spence and his students showed, as they had done with Köhler's and Lashley's experiments, that the results could be interpreted in a different way. This led to intense research activity. I will briefly describe the experiments Tolman believed supported his position.

One type of experiment concerned *latent learning* (Figure 13.1). In cooperation with his student C. H. Honzik in 1930, Tolman divided hungry rats into three groups. One group never found food in the maze (HNR), one group found food on every trial (HR), and the third group found food on every trial after the eleventh day. In Group 1, a reduction in the number of errors occurred during the first nine days. After that, however, no change in the number of errors occurred. Group 2 also showed a regular decrease in error rates. Group 3 had approximately the same number of errors as Group 1, until the eleventh day. After this the number of errors drastically decreased; the rats even made slightly fewer errors than the rats in Group 2 (Figure 13.1). Tolman interpreted the results as an indication that learning had taken place without reinforcement. The results could thus be said to refute Thorndike's contention; they were later interpreted as indications that Hull's view of reinforcement is untenable.

Tolman drew another important conclusion from this experiment. It showed, he affirmed, that in the discussion of learning we must distinguish between learning as a process within the animal and its behavior, its performance. In the two decades that followed, the question of *latent learning* was the subject of intense debate. Latent learning is a form of learning that is not immediately expressed in an overt response. Some questioned whether such learning exists. In time, however, researchers came to understand the difficulty of defining "motivation" and "learning" in a way that made the two positions clearly different from each other.

Another type of experiment concerned spatial orientation. The rats were confronted with a type of maze learning that appeared to require them to understand very complex spatial relationships. In one experiment, the rats learned to find their way in a maze constructed as shown in Figure 13.2. When they had mastered this maze, it was altered in the way shown in Figure 13.3. The results showed that the rats had a tendency to choose paths pointing in the direction in which they had previously found food.

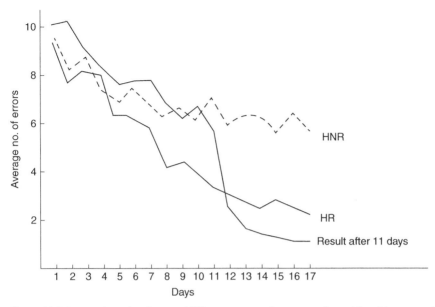

Figure 13.1 Latent learning in rats. HNR: rat group that never found food in maze; HR: rat group that always found food.

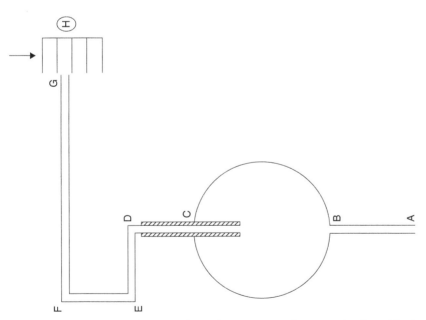

Figure 13.2 Rat maze I: "The animals ran from A across the open circular table through CD (which had alley walls) and finally to G, the food box. H was a light which shone directly down the path from G to F. After four nights, three trials per night, in which the rats learned to run directly and without hesitation from A to G, the apparatus was changed to the sun-burst shown in [Figure 13.3]" (Tolman, 1948).

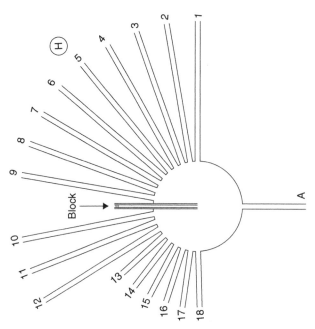

Figure 13.3 Rat maze II: "The animals were again started at A ... and ran across the circular table into the alley and found themselves blocked. They then returned onto the table and began exploring practically all the radiating paths. After going out a few inches only on any one path, each rat finally chose to run all the way out on one" (Tolman, 1948).

Finally, I will mention an experiment conducted by Tolman's student Krech (formerly Krechevsky) (1932). He demonstrated, for example, that in its attempts to find the target box of a maze, a rat would, in the first trial, run to the right at the point of choice; in the next trial, it would run to the right every other time; in the third trial, it would run once to the right and twice to the left. According to Krech, the rats' behavior could be described as a process of hypothesis testing.

Evaluation of Tolman

Tolman's interpretation of his own experiments was rough and exploratory, and, as his critics showed, the results could be interpreted in alternate ways. In order to do that, however, critics had to introduce new assumptions that were based on inner processes in the animals and yielded complex explanations. But behaviorism had come into being precisely with the objective of bringing research into closer association with the observable. In time, however, the majority of psychologists came to understand that the experiments of Tolman and his students ran counter to a behaviorism that excluded all assumptions about cognitive processes. It also became clear that psychological issues would be settled not by a few relatively simple experiments or studies but rather through the more or less gradual accumulation of knowledge and evidence.

Tolman understood that the concept of response is more complex than his behaviorist colleagues envisioned, and he pointed out that a response must be understood as something an animal did *in order to achieve something*. A response involves a performance. It contains a reaction to aspects of the environment. What he may not have been sufficiently aware of, however, is that animals of different species have a tendency to give characteristic forms of responses; in other words, responses are genetically determined. As I have already mentioned, Tolman's thinking was oriented towards Gestalt psychology, and he also understood that the concept of "stimulus" is precarious. Towards the end of his career, he remarked with regret that he had not been able to do anything constructive with the concept. Although he was critical of the concepts of "stimulus' and "response," he was unable to find an alternate framework for his reasoning about behavior.

With regard to the concept of "drive," Tolman was less critical. He tended to view drive as an inner source of energy, and he appears not to have understood that the concept of drive becomes empty of meaning unless it is related to specific physiological processes within the organism, and it is shown how the drive becomes associated with specific motor reactions and responses. As we shall see in Chapter 17, Woodworth and Lashley were ahead of Tolman on problems of motivation. Nor did Tolman show how his postulated cognitions were connected to motor reactions. As another prominent learning theorist, Edwin Guthrie, remarked, Tolman left the rat deeply submerged in thought.

In passing, I will mention that Guthrie (1896–1949) thought learning takes place in such a way that even in the very first attempt, an association forms between the execution of a particular movement and a particular stimulus. In this, Guthrie's interpretation appears to run into all the problems of the stimulus–response approach, in addition to which modern researchers have pointed out that the findings on which Guthrie based his thinking seem to be a reflection of genetically determined response tendencies in the animal. Therefore, there may not be enough to learn from Guthrie's view of learning to allot him a place in the history of psychology, even though he received the APA's highest honor for his research.

Köhler called Tolman a cryptomentalist, and some readers may perhaps ask why Tolman did not simply take as his point of departure the assumption of processes of an inner nature and then try to find support for his view by various experiments. The reason is probably that he was a devout positivist, in the sense that he thought researchers must build their theory or their system on the basis of objective observations. Concepts having no basis in such observations must be related to concepts that do. This line of thought was the origin of his idea of intervening variables. Thus, Tolman appears to have confined himself to the same restrictions as Watson, Skinner, Hull, Spence, and the other behaviorists. It was this restriction many psychologists of the next generation opposed. From our present perspective, we may say that Tolman's thinking pointed to the future, but also that he was a product of his times.

Logical Positivism

Logical positivism exerted considerable influence on US philosophy. It was the subject of a lively debate among psychologists, and Koch thought its influence had been equally important for behaviorism, and not least for Hull and Tolman. But as Lawrence Smith (1986) has documented in depth, this can hardly be the case. Behaviorism was formed by early positivism as well as by pragmatism and operationalism, but probably only to a small degree by logical positivism. Hilgard (1987) has followed up the viewpoints of Smith and emphasized the effect of the early positivism, at the same time toning down logical positivism. It is true too that ideas passed not only from philosophers to psychology, but also from psychologists to philosophy. Still, even if the direct influence of logical positivism was not so great, it accentuated and strengthened certain tendencies in US psychology and helps explain why the work of Hull and his students appealed so strongly to psychologists in the 1930s and 1940s.

Logical Analysis of the Language of Science

The logical positivists wanted to understand how advanced theories in physics, such as the theory of relativity, are structured. They attempted to account for the logical structure of theory, the role of mathematics, and the relationship between theoretical concepts and observations.

In Vienna, as mentioned in Chapter 2, Mach held a professorship in physics that also included the philosophy of science. At the beginning of the twentieth century, a group of physicists and mathematicians with an interest in the philosophy of science gathered around him. Brentano had also lectured for many years in Vienna and, as Barry Smith (1994) has emphasized, helped raise interest in the philosophy of science. From the beginning of the 1920s, Vienna became the center of endeavors to clarify the nature of science, and the logical positivists often referred to themselves as the *Vienna circle*. As we shall see, they deviated from Mach's views in one important regard, and some preferred to call themselves logical *empiricists* rather than logical positivists.

As did Mach and the early positivists, the group wished to rid scientific and philosophical thinking of speculation. They differed from Mach and Mill, however, in that they attributed a great role to formal logic in science. Inspired by the efforts of Gottlob Frege, and Bertrand Russell to demonstrate that mathematics has its foundation in logic, they settled on the idea that science has a logical basis. They attempted to understand the role of the construction of theory in scientific thinking by undertaking a formal, logical analysis of advanced theories of physics. The object of philosophy was, for them, the analysis of the thinking on which science is built.

Frege had become the spokesman for the contention that we must not look for the basis of logic in consciousness or in assumptions of a psychological nature. The point of departure for an account of logic must be its linguistic expression. The logical positivists pursued this idea, envisioning that researchers employ a particular language in the formulation of their theories. The task of the philosopher would therefore be to analyze what they called the language of science. In the 1950s, this thought came to hold a central position in the new cognitive psychology that came into being with the development of artificial intelligence. Logic, mathematics, language, and the philosophy of science were combined, and the great names in psychology came to be those who mastered the particular form of thinking arising from this combination, such as Noam Chomsky and Herbert Simon.

From the Axiomatic System to the Hypothetico-Deductive Method

Influenced by the ideas mathematicians developed on the role of axioms, the logical positivists held that advanced physical theories could be assumed to contain a calculus in the form of a set of axioms from which theorems could be deduced. For such a calculus to be used in empirical research, it must relate to scientific laws established on the basis of specific observations. The logical positivists claimed that the relationship between the calculus, on the one hand, and the laws and observation, on the other hand, could be established with the help of special interpretations of the calculus, the *coordinating definitions*.

The idea that part of a scientific theory could be considered an axiomatic system was in time modified into an assumption that researchers develop their theories by first setting up certain hypotheses, and then testing their tenability by making logical deductions that could be juxtaposed with specific observations. In this way, the hypothetico-deductive method was brought to bear on the research process. Throughout history, and long before the logical positivists appeared, researchers had utilized a procedure in which consequences are derived from hypotheses, to be compared with observations. What the logical positivists did was to make the hypothetico-deductive method a central feature of the research process. One important person in this context was Carl Hempel (1966).

The logical positivists, like the early positivists, wanted to remove all speculation from science and philosophy. In the 1920s, they formulated the principle that the cognitive meaning of a sentence is grounded in the method by which the proposition is verified to be true. Even though the different members of the Vienna circle presented different formulations of the *principle of verifiability*, they all appear to have been oriented towards the idea that meaning in some way or another must either have been or be related to statements having reference to comparatively simple perceptual impressions. The principle of verifiability was under intense debate by philosophers, and it was subject to many reformulations. The thinking behind the principle of verifiability is in important ways similar to the thinking expressed in pragmatism and operationalism.

While the logical positivists emphasized the need to develop hypotheses to guide research, they seem to have been less concerned with the need for adequate description of the phenomena to be studied. Whether or not it was the result of influence from the logical positivists, the behaviorists, as I see it, tended to neglect this important aspect of the scientific procedure. In contrast to the European ethologists, US behaviorists were little concerned with field studies in which efforts are made to describe animals in their natural habitat. Further, while the German students of perception, such as Purkinje, Helmholtz, Mach, Hering, Rubin, and the Gestalt psychologists, emphasized the need for careful descriptions, the behaviorists tended to overlook this aspect of perceptual research. As we shall see, this frequently meant they failed to specify the nature of the physical stimuli eliciting the response.

At the end of the 1950s and beginning of the 1960s, both logical positivism and the early forms of positivism were subjected to severe criticism. I will discuss this criticism in in a later chapter.

James J. Gibson (1904–1979)

James Gibson (1950, 1966, 1979) was, like Tolman, open to the influence of different orientations within psychology. He accepted the idea that psychology could be advanced by engaging in phenomenological description. At the same time, he did not reject behaviorism. During his entire career as a researcher, he collaborated closely with his wife Eleanor Gibson, who was one of Hull's former students. His importance to psychology lies perhaps primarily in his attempts to study perception in a way that was not based upon mental experience. In this lies the strength and probably also the weakness of his approach.

Our Mental Experience

The psychology of perception remained closely associated with phenomenological descriptions throughout the nineteenth century and up to the 1930s. It was considered part of the study of conscious life. The attempt to break away from this tradition in the study of perception makes Gibson an important figure in the history of psychology.

Gibson (1979) declared that he wished to avoid the notion of a division between body and soul, attempting instead to base his thinking on an ecological perspective that studies the organism in relation to its environment. His last book was entitled *The Ecological Approach to Visual Perception* (1979). In it, he endeavored to imagine perception as the result of a physical environment, but he did not specify which of the human organism's attributes makes it suitable for adaptation to its physical environment.

Gibson used the term "ecology" more or less synonymously with "environment." In his emphasis on environmental factors, his thinking showed a compelling similarity to Skinner's, as Hilgard (1987) has noted. The two were the same age, and both received their education in the 1920s, when US psychology emphasized environmental influence at the expense of heredity, as I discussed in the preceding chapter.

In emphasizing the need to describe the environment, Gibson contributed significantly to the psychology of perception. Specifically, he made it clear that the physical energy affecting our sense organs may contain information that makes redundant the assumption that perception is a construction and results from learning, as Helmholtz and many researchers before him had proposed. Gibson claimed that perception occurs directly, in the sense that it is not based on a type of learning by which sensory elements are associated with each other. I will attempt to explain what he could have implied in saying that *perception is direct*.

One major point in Gibson's thinking is that perception must be studied in a natural context. One of his tasks as a psychologist during World War II was to discover how pilots took advantage of the visual stimulation accessible to them as they were landing their aircraft. His investigations convinced him there was little to be gained from studies in which the stimulus material is simplified to, say, simple configurations such as dots and lines presented for only a brief time. Perception, he claimed, must be studied in *normal conditions*. Gibson was particularly interested in the visual sense, and by normal conditions he meant a well-lit ground containing many variations in surface structure. The objects in our environment are placed on this ground, and when we use our vision, we normally move our eyes, head, or body in relation to the ground and the objects on it. The light reflected to our eyes from the ground and the objects, and the oscillations occurring in the reflected light as we move, are sufficient material, said Gibson, to provide the information we need about our surroundings without our having to draw conclusions or build constructions of any kind.

Gradients

The reason that we receive information from our surroundings without having to resort to any processing of our sense impressions is the presence of regularities in the light that results in our sense impressions. Gibson called these regularities *gradients*. There were several, and particularly well known is the *texture gradient*. I will give a brief account of this.

Gibson thought that we always orient ourselves in relationship to the ground on which we are situated. The ground nearly always presents considerable variations in its surface structure, and this yields variation in the light that reaches the eyes. As Gibson proposed, however, in these variations there are regularities, or invariants, and specific patterns. For example, on a beach covered by stones of approximately the same size, the stones constitute the elements of a texture. When we see them in perspective, they appear to gradually get smaller the farther away they are. If we think of the size of the stones as elements along one dimension, they will constitute a texture gradient.

We can think of our visual system as having evolved in such a way as to have adapted to this gradient, implying that when our eyes are stimulated such that the stimulation forms a gradient, the space will appear to us as an expanse ahead and to the sides. This stimulation, Gibson claimed, automatically activates the visual system so that we see the surroundings as extending in all directions. He thought it unnecessary to assume our perception is the result of any kind of learning involving the association of simple sense impressions. It is *direct*.

Gibson thought there were several types of gradients, an important one being the *motion gradient*, which refers to the phenomenon that when we move in space, the objects in it appear to move in the opposite direction. The closer the object is to us, the faster it appears to move. This apparent velocity decreases gradually as the object gets farther away from our eyes and thus constitutes a gradient. A third important gradient is the *magnitude of binocular disparity*. The further away one object is from another object on which we are fixating, the greater will be the binocular disparity (the difference in image location of an object seen by the left and right eyes, resulting from the eyes' horizontal separation), and the perceived difference in size between the remote object and the near one constitutes a gradient.

With the help of the assumption that the eye registers different types of gradients, Gibson could also present simple explanations of the perceptual constancies the Gestalt psychologists had discussed. The size constancy of an object *relative to* the size of the elements constituting the ground, for example, could be accounted for in terms of the texture gradient.

An Evaluation of Gibson's Theory

During the last two decades of the twentieth century, neurophysiologists have found that Gibson's ideas of a texture gradient and a motion gradient are of prime importance in understanding visual perception. Thus, in a more recent appreciation, Ken Nakayama (1994) wrote: "In fact, for sheer breadth, incisiveness, originality, and influence, I cannot imagine anyone more qualified to be recognized as the most important perceptual psychologist of the last 100 years."

Yet, as Nakayama was well aware, Gibson's approach was weakened by his failure to specify the mechanisms by which the organism used the information in the gradients he suggested. Even if we can show the existence of gradients in the physical stimulation of the eyes, it is another thing altogether to show that our visual system is based on them. Gibson thought it would be the task of future psychologists to find which physiological mechanisms determine the ability of the visual system to exploit gradients, and he did not attempt to explain how this could occur. This means the claim that visual perception is based on his postulated gradients lacks empirical support.

In my opinion, his theory is also precarious in that in order to construct it, he had to assume we can identify objects. For example, how is it possible to register that an object far away from us appears to move more slowly than objects that are closer, unless we are able to identify the object? To identify the object, however, we must be able to perceive it as the object that it is, but this very act of perception is precisely what Gibson sought to explain in the first place.

We may also ask whether the ground on which we move is ordinarily structured in such a way that we can register a texture. A texture gradient may thus be of relatively little use to us.

Ralph Haber (1985) claimed that with the advent of Gibson's ideas came the first fruitful alternative to Helmholtz's theory of spatial perception, and it may be enlightening to compare the two theories. As you may recall, Helmholtz assumed we have only limited direct contact with the external world through our visual sense. He thought direct contact is established in the way that light stimulating points on the retina gives us information in the form of sensations. Our perception of direction in the visual field, the form and placement of objects in space, is the result of a complicated learning process. Thus, it is to a large degree the result of a construction. For Gibson, however, space perception involves no such construction through learning, and it is unnecessary to assume anything at all about mental or cognitive processes.

To understand Gibson, it is important to view him in relation to the Gestalt psychologists, whom he recognized and towards whom he felt an obligation. Having received his PhD in psychology at Princeton in 1928, Gibson began to work with Koffka and was familiar with his colleague's book on Gestalt psychology (Koffka, 1935). From this, he primarily learned to look for relationships. It was no doubt also important that the Gestalt psychologists had attempted to explain perceptual constancies by showing that the relationship between the attributes of an object and its environment remains invariant across variations in illumination, the distance of the object, and visual angle. Invariant conditions are indeed basic to Gibson's theory. He rejected the idea that the activity of the visual system represents a field that spontaneously organizes the stimulation of the retina. According to Gibson (1950, 1960), to understand what the stimulus is in a given situation, we would have to conduct an analysis of the gradients he assumed the organism employed in perception. Such an analysis would be a complex affair, and Gibson strongly criticized the contemporary behaviorists' use of the concept of stimulus. Together with the Gestalt psychologists, he thus undermined stimulus–response psychology.

Some years after Gibson's presentation of his theory in 1950, a new approach to psychology came into being called *information processing*. The pioneers of this approach were interested in perception as a construction we must understand on the basis of cognitive elements. I will discuss some aspects of the new approach in Chapter 18. Here, I shall just mention that its adherents criticized Gibson for not having said how the organism is able to utilize the information as he suggested. David Marr (1982, p. 30), an influential representative of information processing, described the weakness of Gibson's argument this way: "First the detection of physical invariants, like image-surfaces, is exactly and precisely an information-processing problem, in modern terminology. And second, he vastly underrated the sheer difficulty of such detection." A heated debate arose between the adherents of Gibson and those of Marr after the publication of Marr's book in 1982.

Much has happened in the study of perception since Helmholtz's time. Today's researchers have a better understanding of how the issues must be formulated, but there has hardly been progress in the sense that we may say, for example, that Gibson's theory is better than Helmholtz's.

14

· ·

Social Psychology

We saw in Chapter 7 that William McDougall attempted to base a social psychology on his ideas of human instincts, but that this attempt did not lead to a more lasting research tradition. George Mead, in contrast, succeeded in establishing a research tradition for the study of social phenomena, as shown in Chapter 11. But this tradition developed within sociology, not within psychology. Not until the 1920s–1930s did psychologists begin to organize a study of social psychology, or that branch of psychology dealing with social interactions, particularly regarding their origins and effects on individual behavior. However, it was not until the 1950s in the United States that they succeeded in establishing social psychology as a formal subdiscipline of psychology.

One important motive for extending psychology to include the study of social phenomena was a desire among psychologists to contribute to the solution of political and social issues by means of empirical research. In a historical introduction to the study of social psychology, Gordon Allport (1954) elaborated this motive by pointing out that there was a tradition in the United States of solving practical problems through empirical research and new technology. Following World War I, race riots; the Great Depression; the high rate of unemployment; the establishment of communist, Nazi, and fascist regimes in Europe; the outbreak of World War II; and the genocide of the Jews created numerous pressing political and social issues. According to Allport, these inspired US social scientists to contribute to solutions. The result, as he showed, was a flowering in the social sciences.

Social psychology as the study of our social nature has close ties to sociology, political science, and cultural anthropology. The division of labor among the four disciplines raises intricate questions that tend to be answered differently by the researchers in each. The disagreement between sociologists and psychologists about their respective roles has been clearly manifested in the existence, from the beginning of the 1920s to the present, of two social psychologies, one forming part of psychology and one forming part of sociology. To achieve a deeper understanding of what social psychology is about, it is useful to reflect a little on this fact, and I shall begin the chapter by commenting on the relationship between the two social psychologies.

What perhaps most strongly characterizes the social psychology established by psychologists is that it centers on the psychology of the individual. In 1924, Floyd Allport contributed to this development by publishing an influential textbook of social psychology. His younger brother, Gordon, was also important in organizing the study of social psychology as a subdiscipline of psychology and elaborated his older brother's ideas. We begin with a review of the ideas of the Allport brothers.

An important characteristic of social psychology as a subdiscipline of psychology is that, to an increasing degree, it has become an experimental science. This development has profoundly affected psychologists' thinking about social phenomena, and we must review it in some detail, even if some of the experiments we will discuss are frequently reviewed in introductory textbooks of psychology.

Since the 1920s, the study of attitudes and, somewhat later, the study of attitude change have been central in the psychologists' as well as the sociologists' social psychology. I shall review some of the very extensive research literature on these two closely related topics. Besides attitude and attitude change, two other topics, personal perception and attribution, have been extensively studied, and we will review them in this chapter as well.

Here we have an opportunity to trace some important lines through the history of psychology. We have already noted that social psychology as a subdiscipline of psychology was developed in the United States. However, from 1940 to 1960, it was dominated by Stumpf's students Lewin, Wertheimer, and Fritz Heider, and in the 1960s and part of the 1970s by their students. Thus, the phenomenology taught by Stumpf had a great impact on social psychology from 1940 to 1970/80. To complete the list of immigrants playing a role in US social psychology, we note that one of the pioneers in experimental social psychology, Muzafer Sherif, was an immigrant from Turkey.

In spite of progress, many social psychologists in the beginning of the 1970s thought the subdiscipline was in a crisis. I shall finish the chapter by reviewing some of the criticism raised against it. In the last chapter of this book, I shall return to the subdiscipline and relate how social psychologists regained their optimism.

The Two Social Psychologies

In Chapter 9, I reported on the great interest taken in the power of suggestion as a psychological phenomenon in France. I further mentioned that Le Bon made this idea central in his book on the behavior of crowds. In the 1880s and 1890s, Gabriel Tarde (1843–1904), another French pioneer in sociology, carried out extensive studies of a variety of social phenomena, which he explained by invoking psychological ideas such as *belief, desire, innovative capacity*, and *imitation*. Thus, by the end of the 1800s, French social researchers had already studied a number of social phenomena which they explained by recourse to psychological ideas. This work formed the basis of a study of social psychology carried out within sociology. A more detailed account of the early study in social psychology is given by Albert Pepitone (1981) and Robert Farr (1996). As early as 1908, the same year McDougall's *An Introduction to Social Psychology* appeared, the US sociologist Edward Ross published a comprehensive textbook of social psychology. As Sheldon Stryker (1996) notes, the two social psychologies remained separate all through the 1900s. During World War II, psychologists cooperated with sociologists and other social scientists, but, as remarked by Hilgard (1987), who participated in the cooperative efforts, sociologists tended to work with sociologists and psychologists with psychologists.

Evidently, we can view social life from two somewhat different perspectives: from conceptions of how social life is structured and from conceptions of how human individuals function as social beings. As emphasized by the sociologists Anthony Giddens (2006), and John Macionis and Ken Plummer (2005), we need both perspectives to make a complete study.

The Organization of Social Psychology as a Subdiscipline of Psychology: The Ideas of Floyd and Gordon Allport

In the historical chapter he contributed to the *Handbook of Social Psychology*, which became a standard reference book, Gordon Allport (1954) formulated a definition of the field that, as he remarked, was accepted by social psychologists with few exceptions. Allport's chapter was reprinted with some minor modifications in the second and third revisions of the handbook, appearing in 1968 and 1985. For the fourth edition, Edward Jones (1998) wrote a historical chapter in which he pointed out that Allport's definition was still accepted. Jones further noted the great influence of the book, *Textbook on Social Psychology*, written by Floyd Allport in 1924. In this book, Floyd concentrated on the study of the human individual, conceiving of social psychology as the study of the way human individuals stimulate each other. We can see Gordon's definition as an elaboration of Floyd's, and I believe it is reasonable to assume the two brothers' ideas are highly representative of US social psychology from the 1920s to the end of the century. I shall begin this chapter with a discussion of them.

Floyd Allport (1890–1978) received his PhD in psychology from Harvard in 1919. After having taught psychology at the University of North Carolina, from 1924 to his retirement, he was professor of social and political science in the Maxwell Graduate School of Citizenship and Public Affairs at Syracuse University. His most important work was his *Textbook on Social Psychology*, published in 1924, which contributed decisively to the organization of the study. Prior to writing his textbook, he had performed a series of experiments that stimulated interest in developing social psychology as an experimental discipline. Before I discuss his ideas of how the study of social psychology ought to be organized, I shall report on some of his experimental work.

As early as 1898, Norman Triplett had carried out experiments to determine the effect of the presence of others on the performance of simple tasks, such as spinning the reel of a fishing rod as fast as possible. In a series of experiments reported in his textbook but already performed in 1916–1919, Allport gave students a number of simple tasks when they were alone, when other persons were present, and when they were competing with others. One of these represents the beginning of the study of social norms and social conformity. Allport (1924, p. 278) claimed to have found support for the view that, without being aware of it, members of a group are influenced by the standards of other members. He referred to this effect as an attitude of conformity.

Allport (1924, p. 11) insisted that social psychology is a branch of psychology rather than of sociology. Although he held that psychology is a foundation science for sociology, he believed the two ought to be carried out as separate inquiries. The psychologist studied the individual in the group, whereas the sociologist studied the group as a whole, its "*formation, solidarity, continuity, and change*" (Allport, 1924, p. 10). Thus, the study of the formation of society, its structure, and its political order belong to sociology. Subsequent generations of psychologists seem in the main to have followed Allport's view.

Central to Allport's view of the study of social psychology is the belief that the individual is the unit of social life and that society can be studied as interactions between individuals. Thus, Allport conceived of social psychology as the study of the way human individuals stimulate other individuals and how they in turn are affected by stimulation from other individuals.

Distinguishing between a study of the individual in the group and a study of the group as a whole, Allport apparently thought a distinction could be made between social psychology as a subdiscipline of psychology *and*, separately, as a subdiscipline of sociology. Some twenty-five years earlier, the influential French sociologist Émile Durkheim had championed the view that sociology may be carried out as a study independent of psychology. He claimed that consciousness in human beings depends to only a modest degree on workings of the brain, and, further, that a collective consciousness exists independently of the consciousness of the individual. Thus, Durkheim claimed, culture and society may be regarded as external to the individual.

As pointed out by Anthony Giddens (2006) among others, the view that we can regard culture and society as external to the individual is not valid. Durkheim did, however, make the important point that we are born into a society that, independently of us, has been structured so that our actions are constrained in many ways. Thus, to use some of his examples, being a brother, a husband, a citizen; practicing a religion; and communicating by signs are constrained by social conventions, rules, norms, and laws. However, as emphasized by Giddens, Durkheim's argument raises the question of whether we can draw a clear dividing line between the individual and society. If we cannot draw this line clearly, it is difficult to draw a division of labor between social psychology as a subdiscipline of psychology and of sociology. In textbooks of the two disciplines, there is considerable overlap of topics.

Durkheim drew attention to the fact that the social life of each human generation is constrained by traditions created throughout history. In most conceptions of culture, the historical development of social life has a central place. Thus, Durkheim gave a forceful argument for the role culture plays in social life.

From Durkheim's point of view, Floyd Allport's view of social psychology can be criticized for leaving out the effect social structure and culture have on the thinking and behavior of human individuals.

Gordon Allport (1897–1964) is better known as a personality psychologist, and we will deal with him in this capacity in the next chapter. Gordon had a lifelong interest in the study of ethics and social work. During the year between his undergraduate and graduate studies, he taught English and sociology at a college in Istanbul. Then, like his brother, he received a PhD in psychology from Harvard. After graduation, he spent two years traveling in Europe as a Fellow. In 1930, he was appointed professor at Harvard and stayed there for the rest of his career. He wrote an influential chapter on the study of attitudes for a handbook of psychology edited by Carl Murchinson in 1935, and, as already mentioned, another influential chapter on the history of social psychology for the first edition of the handbook edited by Gardner Lindzey in 1954. He did also important research on racial prejudice and discrimination, which have been central topics in social psychology.

In the handbook chapter on the history of social psychology written thirty years after the publication of Floyd Allport's book on social psychology, Gordon Allport (1954) elaborated, as I have mentioned, his brother's definition of social psychology. To him, as to his brother, social psychology is the study of the way human individuals influence each other. He contrasted the study to political science, sociology, and cultural anthropology, holding that in these disciplines the starting points are taken in the political, social, or cultural systems. Sociology, anthropology, and political science represent higher levels of the study of social phenomena.

Making clear that the effect on the individual included thoughts and feelings in addition to behavior, Gordon Allport (1954, p. 5), defined social psychology as

an attempt to understand and explain how the thought, feeling, and behavior of individuals are influenced by the actual, imagined, or implied presence of other human beings.

As we will see later in this chapter, numerous studies of theoretical interest as well as of practical utility have been conducted in line with this definition. On closer inspection, however, it is difficult to understand how studies of the effect of social structure and culture on human individuals can be undertaken according to the definition. As mentioned above, leaving this aspect out was a weakness in Floyd Allport's conceptions. Gordon understood that the study of social psychology would be inadequate unless studies of this effect was included. In a comment on the definition, he explained that the term "the implied presence of others" was intended to refer to this aspect of social life, though it is not easy to see how.

The structure of a human society is the result of a diversity of factors: the geography of the territory inhabited, the nature of the economic resources available, and trade, political, military, and cultural activities. Without human initiatives and efforts, there would naturally have been no societies. But this does not mean we can understand the creation of the social structure only in terms of the efforts of identifiable individuals. Cultural activities, such as use of language, religious practice, and expressions of art, are the result of conventions, rules, and norms worked out for the needs of human beings. The effect of culture on a person cannot adequately be traced back to identifiable individuals. To be useful, a scientific definition must contain a clear reference to the phenomena to be studied. Gordon Allport's reference to social structure and culture does not, in my opinion, meet this requirement.

As claimed by Ivan Steiner (1979), Albert Pepitone (1981), and Robert Farr (1996), the study of collective entities tends to be neglected in American social psychology. In her historical chapter for the fourth edition of the *Handbook of Social Psychology* (1998), Taylor noted that the study of culture was almost entirely left out of the discipline in the years 1950 to 1990, and that interest in social roles had strongly declined. These tendencies reflect, in my opinion, inadequate conceptions of what the discipline ought to cover.

The Study of Attitudes

In their widely read book *The Polish Peasant in Europe and America*, William Thomas and Florian Znaniecky (1918/1927) made an interesting attempt to combine sociology and psychology, in which they introduced the concept of *attitude*. On the one hand, they argued, there are objects of various sorts that are valued by the members of a group, such as money, an instrument, an item, or a poem. On the other hand, there are human individuals having needs, desires, thoughts, and abilities. The individuals direct their activities towards the valued objects, and this activity is the attitude. Thus, the attitude represents both the values of a social group and the psychological processes in an individual.

The concept of attitude was widely used in the 1920s by sociologists and psychologists. In 1935, as we saw, Gordon Allport wrote an important chapter on attitudes for the handbook edited by Carl Murchinson. Allport reviewed the literature on the study of attitude and also the way the concept was used by Thomas and Znaniecky, but he seems to have forgotten that Thomas and Znaniecky specified that attitudes are tied to socially valued objects. Allport conceived of attitudes as sets of responses and argued that the concept is rooted in the work of the Würzburg school. The concept of set used by these psychologists to account for thinking paved the way, as Allport thought, for the concept of attitude. "As a result of the Würzburg work all psychologists came to accept the attitudes" (1935, p. 790). In line with his idea that an attitude is a set that prepares the organism for a certain type of reaction to a stimulation, Allport defined it as follows: "A mental and neural state of readiness, organized through experience, exerting a directive or dynamic influence upon the individual's response to all objects and situations with which it is related." In his discussion of the concept, Allport pointed out that the evaluation of the object as positive or negative is an important aspect of the concept of attitude, but it was left out of the definition.

Allport (1935, 1954) claimed that the concept of attitude is indispensable in social psychology. This belief is shared by a large number of modern social psychologists. As emphasized by Richard Petty and Duane Wegener (1998, p. 323), "from purchase decisions provoked by liking for a product to wars spurred by ethnic prejudices, attitudes help to determine a wide variety of potentially consequential outcomes."

Apparently, the concept is indispensable because psychology needs a way to account for the fact that our reactions to social objects are *evaluative*. We have knowledge about social objects – for example, abortion, capital punishment, and taxes – but we also evaluate as positive or negative activities relevant to the objects of our knowledge. In the *Handbook of Social Psychology*, Alice Eagly and Shelly Chaiken (1998) also emphasize that "an attitude is a psychological tendency that is expressed by evaluating an entity with some degree of favor or disfavor."

Allport (1935, 1954) pointed out that attitudes not only have a perceptual/cognitive and an affective aspect, but they also direct the responses of the individual, and it became customary to include a behavioral aspect in the concept of attitude. Thus, attitudes came to be seen as having a cognitive, an affective, and a behavioral aspect.

A wide variety of objects became the subjects of attitude research: items of consumer goods, individual persons, specific groups of people, social issues and policies, and behaviors of various sorts. The concept of attitude is thus very broad and abstract. Since it includes a cognitive, an affective, and a behavioral aspect, a classification of it raises nearly all the fundamental issues of psychology.

Between the two world wars, sociologists and psychologists had mapped out and described people's attitudes to many political, economic, social, and moral issues, to social institutions and laws, and to other groups, such as the attitudes of whites towards blacks and the attitudes of members of religious groups to other religious groups. The research was of practical interest, but it did not contribute much to the development of more rigorous accounts of the nature of attitudes. Ivan Steiner (1979) has pointed out that the advances in these years were mainly of a methodological nature. Progress was made in the construction of questionnaires that have proved useful in descriptions of attitudes, and the growing interest in the development of tests and measurements after the end of World War I, mentioned in Chapter 11, spread to the study of attitudes. At the end of the 1920s, Thurstone developed an ingenious method to construct a scale to measure attitudes. Rensis Lickert elaborated his procedure and constructed a scale of considerable applicability. The construction of these two scales, along with intelligence testing, represented a major advance in the measurement and quantitative treatment of psychological issues. By the 1930s, social scientists had also found effective techniques to obtain representative samples of subjects for opinion polls, which were readily incorporated in attitude research.

The Study of Attitude Change and Persuasion

During World War II, a shift in the study of attitudes took place. Until then, the primary concern had been the description and measurement of different types of attitudes. Now the focus moved to the study of the conditions leading to the formation of and change in attitudes. The participation of the United States in the war had made considerable changes in the social machinery and necessitated efforts to distribute information, enlist commitment, and change attitudes. Social researchers came to play a role in this work. After the war, interest in the study of attitude change continued, and it was to become the focal point in social psychology. The central figure in this research during and after the war was Carl Iver Hovland (1912–1962) at Yale University, a student and coworker of Hull.

In line with a famous question asked by H. S. Lasswell (1948), "Who says what to whom with what effect?", it had been customary to categorize these conditions or variables as source, message, recipient, and context (see Richard Petty and Duane Wegener, 1998). Concerning the source of the message, researchers studied the effect of the person's being an expert, being disinterested in the outcome or not, having the opportunity to issue rewards or punishments, and having attractive characteristics. With regard to the message itself, researchers studied the effect of appealing to fear in the recipient, of giving advice and recommendations, of disproving or ignoring conflicting arguments, of presenting ideas in different sequences, of conveying a message that conflicted with the recipient's opinion, and of presenting the message orally or in writing, face to face. or through the mass media. When it came to the recipient, researchers asked the following questions: what state was this person in, how much attention did he or she pay to the message, did the person understand the experiment, was he or she willing to be persuaded, and did the person remember the message? We can see from this brief overview that the research spanned an extensive range of issues relating to nearly all the main areas of psychology. As I mentioned, Hovland was Hull's student, and his theory of drive reduction functioned as a framework for the different types of studies. The research provided much useful information.

The Introduction of the Experimental Method into Social Psychology

To perform controlled experiments, we need considerable knowledge about the phenomenon we want to study. Given the complexity of most social phenomena, it might seem unlikely that the experimental method is applicable. Yet, experiments had been used with some success in other areas of psychology. Several social psychology researchers therefore thought to start with relatively simple situations and gradually increase the complexity, while others began with exploratory experiments, and then, as they understood more of the phenomenon they studied, gradually obtained more control over the conditions on which it was assumed to depend.

There were several pioneers in the experimental study of social phenomena. I have already mentioned Triplett and Floyd Allport. Around 1930, the British psychologist Frederick Bartlett, whom we will meet in Chapter 16, conducted exploratory studies of the effect of culture on memory processes. In the United States, Kurt Lewin, who had emigrated from Germany in 1933, was a leader. Muzafer Sherif also did influential experimental work in the 1930s. Somewhat younger than Lewin and Sherif was Solomon Asch, a student of Wertheimer and Woodworth. By the 1960s, the experimental method seems to have been fairly well established. Of the many experiments performed in this decade, that on the problem of obedience by Stanley Milgram (1963) has become famous and must also be described in this brief review of the introduction of the experimental method into social psychology.

Kurt Lewin and His Students

When Kurt Lewin immigrated to the United States from Germany, he was well received, and he engaged in a great deal of research as well as being a consultant to the US government, to industrial firms, and to welfare organizations. He was also a university lecturer, first at the University of Iowa from 1935 to 1944, and then at the Massachusetts Institute of Technology. Lewin immediately felt at home in his new country. He was a man of action with a pragmatic attitude to science, and he behaved in an easy-going and democratic way compatible with the American manner. Alfred Marrow (1969) has written a fascinating book emphasizing Lewin's years in the United States. Lewin was a charismatic person who came to dominate American social psychology from the end of the 1930s until his death in 1947.

We may wonder how Lewin, with his Social democratic views, could function so well in American capitalist society. To understand this, we must realize that he was not dogmatic but had a pragmatic attitude to social issues. Further, as pointed out by Steiner, the Great Depression at the end of the 1920s had made it clear to many that human beings often have little control over their destinies. This led to an increased incentive to understand economic and social institutions. Sociological investigations of immigrants' adaptation to society, youth gangs, the economic situation, and the effects of unemployment undermined the trust in laissez-faire individualism and directed attention to social dependence. Lewin, who in his previous career had conducted employment studies, was therefore in his element in the social psychological climate that evolved in the 1930s.

In the studies on motivation Lewin performed in Berlin, he had emphasized that behavior is a result at once of the person and the situation; $B = f(P, E)$, as expressed in his formula. His view of the close relationship between the person and the situation was taken as a guideline for research by the succeeding generations of US social psychologists.

In his studies of motivation, Lewin had not been primarily concerned with the influence individuals exert upon each other, but, in his social psychology, he, like the Allport brothers, made this influence central. He believed it was best studied in the context of small groups and that members of a group have a dynamic relationship to each other. His studies thus gave rise to what became known in social psychology as the study of *group dynamics*. From 1944 until his death, Lewin led a center for the study of group dynamics at the Massachusetts Institute of Technology.

Lewin strongly believed that social issues could be clarified by experiments. Together with his American students, he conducted experiments that convinced many that it is possible to devise experimental situations in real life. Two in particular have become famous.

An Experimental Study of Leadership Style

With Ronald Lippitt and Ralph White, Lewin (Lewin et al., 1939) conducted an experiment to investigate the influence of democratic and authoritarian leadership styles on a group of subjects. These were eleven-year-old boys who gathered after school for a club activity of making theatrical masks. The boys were put into two groups of five. Each group was assigned a leader and met eleven times. One group was led in an authoritarian and one in a democratic manner. In the first group, the leader made all the important decisions, gave orders and messages, and decided what should be considered successful results. In the other group, the decisions were made by the group members, and they were encouraged to carry out the plans they had made. A third group was added later in which the leader assumed a laissez-faire leadership style; that is, his role was quite passive. The behavior of the leaders and the group members was registered by five observers. The results indicated that cooperation was better in the democratically led group than in the authoritarian group, in which there was dissatisfaction and arguments, or in the laissez-faire group, in which there was little planning and scant interest in completing the project.

The studies conducted by Floyd Allport and later researchers on the effect of the presence of others on the individual's performance undoubtedly provide information about human social relationships. Nevertheless, it is not easy to see how this knowledge can help us understand the society we live in. The experiments Lewin and his collaborators conducted, on the other hand, appear to explain more directly central aspects of social life. At the time Lewin and his collaborators did their experiment on leadership, socially aware people throughout the democratic part of the Western world were worried about the effects of dictatorial governments, and about possible differences between people belonging to totalitarian and democratic states. This experiment therefore dealt with immediate issues and strengthened the belief that social problems could be studied in the laboratory.

However, it was clearly lacking in control. As Taylor (1998, p. 61) concluded, "The findings emerged as predicted, although a close examination of the methodology of the studies suggests that, given the guidelines offered to the democratic and autocratic leaders, one could not have expected other results."

An Experimental Study of Frustration and Regression

Lewin, who also influenced contemporary child psychology, conducted a realistic experiment on frustration and regression in children with Roger Barker and Tamara Dembo (Barker et al., 1941). The experiment was a continuation of the study Dembo had conducted in Berlin on anger. She had observed that the subjects in her study reacted differently to their own inability to satisfy the experimenter's requests for the resolution of a problem. While some gave up, others tried to get around the demands confronting them. In the new experiment, children between two and six years of age served as subjects. The effect of frustration was measured in the children's play. In the first part of the experiment, the children were observed in situations in which they had the opportunity to play with some uninteresting, simple toys. In the other part, they were first given access to toys that were much more attractive to them. They were interrupted while playing with the new toys, however, and the toys were placed behind a transparent screen so that the children could not reach them. After some time, the toys from the first part of the experiment were returned to the children to play with.

In order to determine the effect of frustration assumed to follow from the interruption, the experimenters used a scale devised to show how constructive the children's games with the uninteresting, simple toys were. This scale corresponded well with the children's ages. The results showed that after the children were interrupted while playing with the attractive toys, the quality of their play with the simple toys was reduced. In other words, in the second part of the experiment, the constructivity showed levels corresponding to lower age levels, and in this sense the results could be said to demonstrate regression as a function of frustration.

Evaluation

Lewin's formula that behavior is a function of the person's characteristics as well as those of the environment was a useful reminder. In the 1930s and 1940s, psychoanalytically oriented psychologists tended to overlook the environment, and behaviorists the characteristics of the person. Still, as his student Edward Jones (1998, p. 21) pointed out, Lewin's field theory was more like a language or point of view than a theory from which empirical hypotheses could be deduced. And, although his experiments suggested that even complicated social issues could be studied by the use of the experimental method, the experiments he performed suffered from the lack of a control group. His concentration on the study of small groups was innovative, but he provided this study with little useful theory for empirical research. Moreover, as emphasized by John Levine and Richard Moreland (1998) in their review of research on small groups, several social psychologists had commenced research on small groups independently of Lewin. A charismatic person, Lewin attracted and inspired a large number of gifted students, but in my opinion his theoretical contributions have perhaps been overrated, and, although he gave important inspiration to experimental work in social psychology, he must share the credit for introducing the experimental method with other researchers, such as Bartlett, Floyd Allport, and, as we shall see below, Sherif and Asch.

Muzafer Sherif (1906–1988)

From the years of his earliest studies in Ankara, Turkey, Muzafer Sherif was concerned with how membership in groups influences the members' views and behavior. After receiving his master's degree from the University of Ankara, he continued his studies at Harvard and Columbia, receiving his PhD in psychology at the latter. In the United States he began his investigation of the formation of groups. He focused on how opinions and behavior in members of a group are determined by norms, and he conducted experiments that examined the way norms are established when people are together in groups.

All societies have norms governing different types of behavior. Some norms are legally sanctioned, but social psychologists tend to use the concept to refer to norms *not* governed by law. Norms vary from society to society and from one social group to another. They regulate a variety of forms of behavior, such as greeting, eating, dressing, communicating, associating with those of the same and the opposite sex, and designating people of different age-groups and rank. Sherif (1936) conducted an early experiment on how norms are affected and established as a result of interaction between people. The phenomenon to which his subjects were to react was a visual illusion called *the autokinetic effect*. This effect is observed when we sit in a dark room looking at a stationary point of light. When a frame of reference is absent, after some time the light will appear to move, but neither in a definite direction nor over a definite range. Sherif told his subjects, who were ignorant of the illusion, that he would move the light a certain distance, and their task was to estimate how far it appeared to move. Subjects were tested under two conditions: one group was first tested individually and then in a group with one or two others; another group was tested first in a group and then individually.

Sherif's results showed that when the subjects were individually tested, the estimates they reported of the distance the light moved tended towards a specific value that established a standard or norm. When these subjects were subsequently tested in groups, their estimates converged towards a common norm. The subjects first tested in groups also established a common norm, and when tested individually, they tended to conform to this norm.

Sherif thought his experiment demonstrated that in an unstable situation a norm would emerge in a group of individuals as a result of their interactions in the situation. It is not unreasonable to think the tendency in Sherif's subjects to converge on a common standard is representative of the formation of various norms found in social life, and thus that the establishment and functioning of norms can be studied in laboratory experiments. Later researchers have followed up Sherif's early experiment, and considerable light has been shed on the formation and functioning of norms (see Robert Cialdini and Melanie Trost, 1998).

Sherif's choice of experimental situation allowed him to study the formation of a norm that had not been established and that quickly showed it could be studied in a laboratory setting. His choice of phenomenon, however, has the disadvantage that so little is known about the autokinetic effect. For example, we should like to know why the estimates the subjects made when they were tested individually also tended towards a specific norm. Further, we should like to know what was altered when the subjects' estimates tended towards a specific value. Was it the perceptual experience of the length of the movement, or was it the subjective measure used by the subject? In other words, did the norm evolve in relationship to how far the light appeared to move, or in relationship to which measure was used?

Solomon Asch (1907–1996): On Conformity

Solomon Asch was born in Warsaw and grew up in Poland until his parents emigrated to New York in 1920. He completed his higher education at Columbia University, where Woodworth, among others, was his supervisor. In a biographical sketch (*The Legacy of Solomon Asch*, edited by Irvin Rock, 1990), his students emphasized his extensive intellectual interests, his broad psychological experience, and his strong social commitment. The crucial event of his research career was his acquaintance with Gestalt psychology and Wertheimer, with whom he collaborated until Wertheimer's death. He was also Köhler's colleague at Swarthmore College for some time.

Asch's Experiment on Conformity

In Chapter 9, we noted the use Le Bon and Taine had made of the idea of suggestibility in exploring the behavior of crowds and mobs. In the emerging social psychology, suggestibility had been accorded a central place in the accounts given of social behavior. Emphasis was frequently placed on human tendencies to act irrationally and immorally as a result of suggestibility. Asch (1956) reacted to what he believed were excessive claims about the force of suggestion and group pressure. He wanted to show that in a situation in which stimulation is unambiguous – unlike Sherif's experiment – subjects would not be affected by group pressure.

In his experiment, subjects were to determine whether a line was shorter or longer than two other lines presented alongside. The difference was so obvious that members of a control group estimated the true dimensions nearly 100 percent of the time. The subjects were male students between seventeen and twenty-five years of age. They were each placed in a group of seven to nine other students who were said to be subjects but who in reality were confederates of the experimenter, instructed in advance to give estimates that went against their own and the subjects' perceptual impressions.

The results were surprising. Although some subjects were not influenced by the rest of the group, three-fourths of them gave one or more estimates that deviated from the objective conditions. In the hope of finding out something about the psychological processes underlying these results, Asch conducted systematic and comprehensive interviews with the subjects after they had completed the experiment. He naturally assumed those who remained uninfluenced by the majority confronting them would have other personality traits and different histories than the subjects who were influenced, but his material did not permit any conclusions about this.

Asch realized that many conditions needed to be investigated before a general conclusion could be drawn. He conducted studies himself showing that the number of confederates and the unanimity of their responses affected the results. Other researchers have shown the effect of other conditions. Still, as Cialdini and Trost (1998) concluded, the conformity effect has turned out to be fairly robust.

These findings were surprising even to Asch himself. Since the effect is robust, the experiment has formed a fruitful starting point for exploring conditions under which a minority will conform to a majority. Subsequent research, either using Asch's situation or inspired by his findings, has shed considerable light on the question of how people conform to a majority (see Cialdini and Trost, 1998).

Asch's experiment also allows us to explore the effect a minority can exert on a majority. In a series of experiments, the French social psychologist Serge Moscovici (1985) has revealed ways in which a minority can change the majority's judgment.

In many instances, of course, it is most appropriate that we conform to a majority. A characteristic of human beings is that we can cooperate, and cooperation would hardly be possible unless we conformed. Asch's experimental design does not allow us to answer questions about the desirability of conforming. Thus, it has limited use. On the other hand, it allows for variations and controls, providing information we otherwise would not be able to obtain.

Stanley Milgram (1933–1984): Experiment on Obedience to Authority

Inspired by Asch's experiment, Stanley Milgram (1963) conducted an experiment to investigate the degree to which human beings are willing to inflict pain and suffering on others when ordered to do so by people having power. The subjects, who were tested individually, were told they were to function as teachers for another person. Their task was to administer an electric shock to the person each time he made a mistake in the learning of some material. In the learning situation, which the experimenter had arranged beforehand without the subject's knowledge, the "student" was strapped to a chair and hooked up to an apparatus that appeared to deliver shocks of varying intensity. The person who was to learn the material cooperated with the experimenter, having been instructed to pretend to be receiving shocks of different strengths. The subjects, who could read on a scale the intensity of the shocks they were told to administer, were to increase the intensity each time the other person made a mistake. Thus, they were continuously aware of the voltage they were administering, and although they were seated in another room, they could hear the "student's" reactions when he was receiving the shocks. The person would, for instance, be screaming to be taken out of the situation when the shocks were of a certain strength.

Milgram found that the majority of the subjects were willing to administer shocks that would have been extremely painful, or even fatal, had they been real. Experiments conducted under similar circumstances have confirmed Milgram's findings. Based on his experimental paradigm, researchers have investigated a range of conditions under which human beings are willing to follow orders even when this can cause severe harm to others. (See Cialdini and Trost, 1998.) Yet, as in the study of the problem Asch investigated in his experiment, we have not reached conclusions of a general nature.

An Evaluation of the Experimental Method in Social Psychology

The social psychological studies I have described demonstrate the usefulness of the experimental method in the investigation of complex social phenomena. The experiments have helped clarify relationships we find in these social phenomena and disclosed conditions of which we were not previously aware. There are surprise elements in both Asch's experiment on how group pressure can lead to conformity and in Milgram's experiment on obedience to authorities. Beyond doubt, these experiments provided new knowledge, as have several others. Still, they rest on assumptions that are not adequately understood, and this prevents researchers from formulating significant general theoretical statements. At present, it seems unlikely that any of the problems investigated can be adequately examined by the experimental method alone, and there seems to be widespread agreement among modern social psychologists that the experimental method must be combined with other procedures.

In the experiments by Asch and Milgram, the subjects were led to believe the researchers' confederates were subjects like themselves, raising the question of whether it is ethical to base experiments on deceptions. Most people will probably accept that situations may arise in which it is more ethical to lie than to tell the truth, but do they believe the performance of a social psychological experiment can justify the telling of lies? For a discussion of ethical problems in social psychological research, see Elliot Aronson, Timothy Wilson, and Marilyn Brewer (1998).

The Influence on Social Psychology from Phenomenology and Gestalt Psychology

As I emphasized in Chapter 5, Brentano's student Stumpf was the teacher of Wertheimer, Koffka, Köhler, and Lewin. Stumpf convinced his students that an experimental investigation must be based on a description of the mental experiences constituting the events under investigation. He also instructed them to start from the simple experiences of daily life. Not until they had described the experiences, Stumpf claimed, could they begin to look for situations that could form the basis for an experiment. This view of procedure in psychological research contrasted with the perspective of behaviorists and psychoanalysts, and frequently also of physiologically oriented psychologists.

Unlike the Gestalt triumvirate, Lewin was concerned not with the question of what makes up a Gestalt, but more with motivation (acts of will) and the relationship between motivation and cognition. But in line with his theoretical orientation, he felt the field should be described not in objective physicalist terms, but according to the manner in which the field exists for people at the time their behavior is registered. In other words, the starting point should be the situation as the subjects perceive it and not as it is objectively described.

In the years following World War II, Lewin's students had a strong influence on social psychology. However, there were other important influences from phenomenology and Gestalt psychology. Asch (1952), who collaborated with Wertheimer, wrote a textbook, *Social Psychology*, that was to become as influential as Floyd Allport's had been twenty-eight years earlier. In contrast to his predecessor, Asch claimed that it could be more fruitful to base social psychology on a phenomenological rather than a behavioristic approach.

Neither Lewin nor Asch was a phenomenologist who studied the meaning of experiences as revealed in the flow of consciousness. The difference between them and the behaviorists was that they did not feel obliged to restrict themselves to describing behavior in objective terms but were willing to include their own experiences, and those of their subjects when they considered it appropriate.

Asch's book helped bring ideas about the self back into social psychology. Asch thought that without recognizing the self we would not be able to establish social relationships, and he attempted to understand social motivation based on conceptions of the self. In his account of the self, he also outlined how he imagined it evolves during ontogenesis, as Baldwin had done fifty years earlier.

In addition to Lewin and Asch, Fritz Heider (1896–1988) was a third highly influential psychologist, oriented towards phenomenology and Gestalt psychology. Heider grew up in Graz, Austria, where he received his education. Early in his career, he was influenced by Brentano's phenomenology. In the 1920s, he worked with Lewin at the Institute of Psychology in Berlin for a time. Like the Gestalt psychologists and Lewin, he came to represent an approach to psychology very similar to the one Stumpf had attempted to formulate. In 1930, Heider emigrated to the United States, and after having held positions at several universities and research institutions, he settled at the University of Kansas as a professor, studying the way he thought ordinary (naive) persons experienced their social environments. In his autobiography, Heider (1983) characterized his studies as an attempt to clarify the concepts of daily life. His most important publication was

The Psychology of Interpersonal Relations (1958). His ideas were an inspiration to research on questions about the consistency of our cognitions and attitudes, and to the study of attribution.

Stumpf would most likely have commended Heider's approach. It is perhaps not unreasonable to say that Stumpfian phenomenology, as represented by Lewin, Asch, Heider, and their students, dominated US social psychology in the thirty years after the end of World War II.

Cognitive processes had a central place in phenomenologically oriented social psychology, though, despite an increased interest in the cognitive aspect of social psychology in the 1970s and 1980s, there was no cognitive revolution.

Inconsistency and Cognitive Dissonance

An attitude to a social object contains a number of different beliefs related to the object. Thus, a single attitude organizes several beliefs. There is also consistency in the way we group together attitudes that belong to specific spheres of life. For example, our attitudes to food and eating make up one group, and our attitudes to sports another. Some of the groups of attitudes we form can be very comprehensive, such as attitudes contained in political and other ideologies and in religions.

In the 1940s and 1950s, social psychologists began concentrating their research on problems having to do with the way our beliefs and attitudes are related to each other. An idea underlying much of this work was that we must have some sort of need to organize our beliefs and attitudes in a consistent manner.

At this time, the idea of homeostasis developed by Cannon inspired several psychologists to assume that various kinds of imbalance or equilibrium would create needs affecting our thinking and behavior. We met this belief in Hull's thinking in the preceding chapter, and we shall meet it in Jean Piaget's thinking in Chapter 16. As we shall see, it was very popular around 1950. Thus, in postulating a need for consistency, social psychologists, in my opinion, followed a trend in psychological thinking prominent at this time. The way they approached the problem also followed another strong trend in the psychological thinking of that time, which was that as interest in behaviorism waned, there was an increasing tendency to account for psychological phenomena in terms of cognitive processes, as we will see in Chapter 18.

If we have a need for consistency, it is natural to believe we should feel some sort of discomfort when inconsistencies arise in our beliefs and attitudes. Starting with speculations of this nature, several social psychologists developed theories of how inconsistency could lead to attitude change.

Wertheimer, as we noted in Chapter 5, had speculated that our perceptions tend to be as simple, complete, regular, symmetrical, and balanced as possible – the principle of *Pragnanz*. As Taylor (1998, p. 69) recounts, several social psychologists thought the speculations underlying the principle of *Pragnanz* could also be extended to our beliefs and attitudes, and they attempted to explain attitude change as a tendency to restore balance. Based on similar assumptions, Heider (1946, 1958) worked out an approach known as *balance theory*.

Whereas Wertheimer thought our perceptions and thoughts tend to be as balanced and complete as possible, Heider believed there also tends to be harmony between our thoughts and feelings, and in his balance theory, he attempted to account for changes in attitudes as the result of an imbalance in the cognitions and feelings in various types of attitudes. Balance theory was elaborated by some contemporary psychologists and still attracts researchers. (See Alice Eagly and Shelly Chaiken, 1998.)

An even more widely discussed theory of attitude change as a result of inconsistency in our belief systems, called the theory of *cognitive dissonance*, was presented by Leon Festinger (1957). According to Taylor (1998), more than 1,200 investigations have been generated by this theory.

Jones (1998, p. 22) calls Festinger (1919–1989) the dominant figure in social psychology during the 1950s and 1960s. Festinger received his PhD from the University of Iowa, where he worked with Lewin on problems of motivation; his PhD thesis studied a problem in the level of aspiration. He joined Lewin at the Research Center for Group Dynamics at the Massachusetts Institute of Technology and was one of the leaders of the Center after it moved to the University of Michigan.

The Theory of Cognitive Dissonance

Study of the theory of cognitive dissonance will help us understand the thinking of social psychologists in the 1950s and 1960s, and illuminate some problems in social psychological research.

Festinger argued that in a cognitive system, two cognitive elements can be either related or not related. If they are related to each other, they can either be consonant or dissonant. They are consonant if one follows from the other, and dissonant if one implies the opposite of the other. Dissonance could arise between a belief and an attitude, or between an attitude and a behavior. Further, Festinger held that dissonance would create an aversive state that the person would try to reduce by changing one or both of the elements. An example he gave is a person who knows smoking is harmful yet justifies his smoking by finding reasons to do it, such as that it is so pleasurable it is worth the risk, that it is not as dangerous as doctors say, or that we cannot always live without risk of danger. By justifying smoking in this way, the person is assumed to be creating greater consonance between his ideas about smoking.

To the hypothesis that inconsistency between cognitive elements creates an aversive arousal acting as a motive, Festinger added the idea that various types of conditions might increase or decrease the strength of the dissonance. For example, threatening or rewarding a person for acting in a certain way would reduce dissonance. The more serious the threat or the greater the reward, the more reduced the dissonance would be.

Of the numerous experiments performed in attempts to confirm or falsify Festinger's theory, one he carried out in cooperation with James Carlsmith (Festinger and Carlsmith,

1959) has become a classic. The subjects, male university students, were asked to participate in an experiment said to be dealing with measures of performance. They were tested individually. In the first part, the subjects had to perform two rather monotonous tasks. In the second part, they were asked to tell another subject the tasks were enjoyable. The other subject was actually a confederate of the experimenters but was introduced as a subject who was to participate in the first part of the experiment under somewhat different conditions. The subjects of one experimental group were offered $1 and the subjects of another $20 to tell the subject the tasks were enjoyable. After this procedure, called *forced compliance*, the subjects were asked how interesting they had found the two tasks they performed in the first part of the experiment.

It turned out that the subjects paid $1 rated the tasks as significantly more interesting than the subjects of a control group who had participated only in the first part of the experiment, whereas the subjects paid $20 did not rate the tasks as significantly more interesting than did the subjects of the control group. The experimenters claimed to have predicted the results by deriving consequences from Festinger's theory and asserted that the results strongly corroborated the theory.

The finding that the subjects paid the small reward – and not those paid the larger amount – showed the effect of dissonance as apparently predicted by the theory was surprising. Similar findings have been found in other experiments. Yet, when the experimental procedure is more carefully examined, it becomes clear that the results allow for several alternate interpretations that do not support Festinger's theory. I shall review three of them.

Starting from attempts made by Skinner to account for self-descriptive statements, Daryl Bem (1967) suggested that the subjects simply inferred their attitudes from the circumstances accompanying their act of telling others the tasks were enjoyable. He argued that in situations in which we are uncertain of our opinions, we employ the same procedure as when we make judgments about other people – that is, we draw conclusions from behavior. In Festinger and Carlsmith's experiment, said Bem, the students reacted in the following manner. Those who had been well paid concluded that the payment must be the reason they said the experiment was interesting, whereas those who had been paid a small amount concluded they must really have found the experiment interesting.

Bem (1972) conducted well-designed experiments to demonstrate that his interpretation, which he later referred to as *self-perception theory*, could explain Festinger and Carlsmith's results as well as results from other studies. Subsequent research has, however, shown that neither Bem's nor Festinger's view can explain all the results.

Another way of explaining the results of the Festinger–Carlsmith experiment is to assume that the subjects telling the other students the tasks were enjoyable thought this act might have aversive consequences for the student or for themselves. This might explain the arousal of a sense of cognitive dissonance without invoking the idea of cognitive dissonance. The fact that the subjects paid $20 did not show the effect might be explained by assuming they were more inclined to think that telling what may be regarded as a lie was the responsibility of the experimenters. Like Bem's person-perception theory, the assumption of aversive consequences cannot account for all the experimental results.

A third way of explaining the results is to assume that the act of lying to another conflicts with some aspect of the subjects' self-image. Assuming they are motivated to maintain a positive self-image, the act may have led to a way of reducing the conflict by modifying the attitude they had to the tasks. This explanation is similar to the one Freud gave of what he referred to as rationalization.

However, we might also explain the results by assuming the act was inconsistent with the beliefs the subjects had about their usual way of acting. We need not assume they were trying to maintain a positive self-image. Moreover, this interpretation is more or less in agreement with Festinger's theory.

The diverse interpretations given of the findings in the Festinger and Carlsmith experiment, as well as in a number of other experiments on cognitive dissonance, have been reviewed by Richard Petty and Duane Wegener (1998) and by Thane Pittman (1998). I shall not go further into the diverse interpretations but just note that Petty and Wegener (1998, p. 337) arrived at conclusions similar to Pittman's when they stated:

In sum, it is not clear whether dissonance results from cognitive dissonance per se, the production of aversive consequences, inconsistency in specific aspects of the self concept, threats to general self integrity, all of the above, or some other process.

Some Methodological Remarks on Dissonance Research

Jones (1998, pp. 23–24) thought the theory of cognitive dissonance was a substantive contribution to our understanding of human nature, and further that it could serve as an example of the power of theory-based experimental research in social psychology. He did admit, however, that the major terms of the theory were defined in only the sketchiest way. The concept of inconsistency (dissonance) has turned out to be particularly difficult to understand. It is not of a logical nature but may perhaps better be described as a conflict of an emotional nature. Thus, in the example of smoking given by Festinger, the inconsistency between the smoker's belief that smoking can be injurious and his smoking is not of a logical but of an emotional nature.

Serious difficulties also attach to Festinger's use of the concept of cognition. The situations attracting almost all attention in the research involve a discrepancy of some sort between an act, a behavior, and an attitude. Whereas the mental representation of an act can be seen as a cognition (a cognitive element), the act has complex motor, motivational, and emotional aspects, as in the act of smoking.

Difficulties also attach to the concept of consonance. In the study of learning, as we saw, controversy arose over the role played by reward and punishment. Festinger claimed that rewards and threats should be seen as consonant elements, as elements reducing inconsistency. Unfortunately, he did not explain why this was so. In the Festinger–Carlsmith experiment, it is hardly possible to understand the effect of the payment given the subjects as a reward unless we know how they understood the experimenters' intentions in giving it. The subjects of the two experimental groups may have understood the intentions differently. Festinger and Carlsmith do not seem to have controlled adequately for this possibility.

Festinger and Carlsmith claimed the results of their experiments were predicted by Festinger's theory. Actually, as they reported, another researcher had earlier performed an experiment in which the forced-compliance procedure was used and in which results similar to their own had been obtained. Thus, perhaps the results should not be seen as a prediction from Festinger's theory. Festinger's starting point may have been the results of the earlier experiment, and he may simply have added the hypothesis of cognitive dissonance to his account.

The psychologists of the 1940s and 1950s were attracted to the idea that we have a need to order our beliefs and attitudes in a consistent manner. However, as Taylor (1998, p. 69) has pointed out, considerable evidence suggests that many people can live comfortably with what appears to be a high degree of inconsistency in their belief systems. Moreover, as Pittman (1998, p. 561) notes, more recent research suggests that "a preferred, and perhaps, the preferred mode of dissonance reduction may be to ignore inconsistency until it fades away."

One way to clarify whether we need consistency is, as Pittman suggested, to study the origins of our tendency to order our beliefs and attitudes in a consistent manner. It might be particularly helpful to know whether the need is a more fundamental motivation concerning our evolutionary orientation to our physical and social environment, or whether it is acquired as a result of norms and expectations.

Person Perception (Ordinary Personology)

The study of perception was particularly pursued in the German-speaking countries, and from the 1930s until the 1970s, person perception – the study of the way we form impressions of others – was dominated by European ideas of perception. A major influence in the 1940s was Egon Brunswick (1903–1955), who, after having been a professor in Vienna, was appointed professor at the University of California at Berkeley. In the 1950s and 1960s, Asch was a major influence, as was Heider in the 1970s and 1980s.

Brunswick developed *probabilistic functionalism*, a modification of Helmholtz's theory of visual perception. As a Helmholtzian, he was opposed to Gestalt psychology. In contrast, Asch had close links to Wertheimer and Gestalt psychology. A close friend of Brunswick, Heider was influenced by Lewin, but he could hardly be considered a Gestalt psychologist. Even if Brunswick, Asch, and Heider differed in major respects, they shared one important belief: that cognitive processes have great similarities to the visual perception of material objects. In line with this belief, they thought it appropriate to regard the processes by which we form impressions of the emotions, intelligence, traits, and personalities of other persons as highly similar to those by which we perceive material objects. This belief had a profound impact on the study of person perception.

In studies of object constancy, Brunswick (1934, 1947) proceeded in a straightforward manner by having subjects estimate attributes of material objects under different conditions. Comparing physical measures of the attributes with subjective ones, Brunswick worked out indices for the accuracy of the estimates. He tried to extend this procedure to the study of our ability to recognize feelings and to judge intelligence, character traits, and personality. The obvious weakness of the method is that, in contrast to the way we assess attributes of physical objects, we have no good procedures for assessing the characteristics of others. As shown by Gilbert (1998) in his critical and careful examination of person perception, other weaknesses are also attached to the procedure.

Asch's Studies of Impression Formation

The Gestalt psychologists had concentrated their research on problems in sensory perception, but they had also attempted to extend the principles of this research to problems of memory and personality. Believing in the Gestalt principles of perception and in the possibility of extending these to the study of personality, Asch (1946) developed a simple technique to study the forming of impressions of personality. He presented his subjects with lists of traits and asked them to write a story of an imagined person having the traits.

Asch systematically varied the number and order of the traits in the list. A particularly striking result was obtained when he substituted the word "cold" for the word "warm" in the following list: "intelligent – skillful – industrious – warm – determined – practical – cautious" – the words "warm" and "cold" were shown to be more important in forming participants' impressions than other characteristics. Another striking result was obtained when he reversed the order of the traits (A: intelligent, industrious, impulsive, critical, stubborn, envious *versus* B: envious, stubborn, critical, impulsive, industrious, intelligent). Even though the list of traits is the same, participants saw series A as more positive than series A due to the words that started the list. Asch (1946) concluded: "Qualities are seen to stand in a relation of harmony or contradiction to others within the system."

Asch's procedure was simple and allowed him to control several conditions. Yet, it leaves unanswered the question of how closely the organization of a list of traits represents the way we organize our impressions of real persons. For one thing, the organization of the impressions we form of a real person may be the result of a long and complicated learning process. Asch apparently assumed it was the result of spontaneous and immediate organization. The opening sentence of his article read: "We look at a person and immediately a certain impression of his character forms itself in us." Thus, Asch assumed we form impressions of personality in the same way that we form impressions of material objects in our physical environment. We cannot rule out that this is so, but to demonstrate that it is, we probably need detailed accounts of how our ability to form impressions of a person develops in ontogeny.

The results of Asch's experiments showed that the order of the traits affects the descriptions given by the subjects, and, probably more importantly, that the meaning of a particular trait affects the meaning of the other traits in the list. When we consider that trait names refer to highly abstract and rather diffuse entities, it is not at all surprising that they should affect each other. For example, the meaning of the word "intelligent" is, as intelligence testing has made clear, abstract and diffuse. To give a more precise meaning to expressions he used in his conclusion, such as "organized process," "dynamic relations," and "peripheral quality," Asch would have had to subject the trait names on his list to a detailed semantic examination. As Gilbert (1998, p. 104) concluded, "Asch was uncharacteristically silent when it came to describing the events that took place inside the black box."

Heider's Study of Attribution

Even if Heider spent most of his life in the United States, he worked within the Brentano–Stumpf tradition during his entire career. Thus, he represents an important link between this tradition and modern American social psychology. Like the researchers within the tradition, he started out by describing and reflecting on psychological phenomena met with in everyday life. Further, like Brentano, he made problems of intentionality a major aspect of his psychology. Still further, in line with the teaching of Brentano and Stumpf, he tried to provide accurate descriptions of his own mental experiences. But he was not a phenomenologist in the sense that he limited his attention to only what went on in his own mind. Thus, in *The Psychology of Interpersonal Relations* (1958), he discussed situations he imagined, presented intuitions concerning causes of behavior, and reflected upon behavior.

An important part of Heider's book is devoted to the problem of developing a conceptual framework for the study of how we ascribe or attribute causes to behavior. He called this *the study of attribution*. In modern textbooks, Heider is usually referred to only as an important inspiration in the study of attribution. Actually, a review of his ideas is probably the simplest way to understand the problems that confronted – and still confront – this study.

Heider's starting point was the everyday knowledge that the causes of behavior are found in properties in the person (personal dispositions) as well as in conditions of the environment or situation. The distinction between the two types of causes is essential for an understanding of his work. He illustrated the distinction by numerous examples. Here is one (Heider, 1958, p. 88). The speeches given by a politician have been poorly received. He might ascribe the failure to his own efforts, as being "too rough, too highbrow, too emotional, too general, or too factual." He might also ascribe the causes to "his appearance, or to the fact that he was not enough of a regular guy, or that he had stage fright." On the other hand, he might place the failure outside himself, on the fact that the audience was too unsophisticated, that it fell for slogans, or that it was too prejudiced. He might also find the causes of the failure in the physical setting, in the acoustics, the temperature, the quality of the seating. The reception of the speeches could thus be attributed to dispositions in himself (to properties of his person) or to properties of the situation.

Distinguishing between personal dispositions and properties of the situation as causes of behavior was no discovery. Heider, however, carried his examination a little further. He noted that we frequently tend to locate the cause (or causes) *primarily* in the person or *primarily* in the situation. This point he stated as follows (Heider, 1958, p. 88):

In the events of everyday life, we are interested not only in what people can do. We want to know whether what a person can do is primarily due to his own characteristics, his abilities for example, or primarily due to favorable environmental conditions.

Thus, if we take the study of attribution to mean just studying the causes of behavior, there is hardly anything new in Heider. What was new, and what started a new research tradition in social psychology, was his recognition that we not only attribute causes of behavior, but we also frequently emphasize either personal dispositions or the properties of the situation. As Jones (1998, p. 40) pointed out, this new perspective started attribution research:

Unravelling the determinants of internal versus external causal attribution was the central challenge for the research. Armed with such information, one could better predict the circumstances of anger and aggression, of information seeking, of social influence, of various mood shifts, of task perseverance, and of many other crucial human states and activities.

Heider believed attributing the causes of behavior helps give structure and stability to our social environment. This structure and stability in turn allow us to predict and control behavior. Further, he believed that in making attributions we follow specific rules. The aim of the study of attribution was to discover these rules.

We have seen that Heider thought there is a great similarity between our perception of material objects and our attribution of causes of behavior, and he tried to account for attribution through an analogy with object perception. Just as we have the capacity to perceive the color of an object as constant under varying degrees of illumination, we are endowed, Heider held, with the capacity to attribute enduring dispositions to a person in spite of variations in his or her behavior as a result of changes to the situation or the environment. As Gilbert (1998, p. 94) notes: "Heider pushed the analogy between person perception and object perception as far as it would go, and then some."

By describing instances of attribution, Heider was able to draw the attention of psychologists to problems of attributions. But his account hardly invited empirical research. As I see it, he was severely hampered in understanding the phenomenon he discussed because of his fascination with the analogy between object perception and what he and Brunswick called person perception. This may have made him underestimate the complexity of the problems he tried to formulate. Whereas it was natural to think – and as it actually has turned out – that object constancies are mediated by relatively simple mechanisms, it is, as I see it, implausible to believe that simple mechanisms are at work when we emphasize primarily personal dispositions or primarily properties of the situation. In contrast to the development of fundamental perceptual skills, the development of our understanding of motivation does probably involve complex learning processes.

Let me illustrate this point by considering a problem as simple as attributing the causes of eating behavior (a problem discussed by Bem). Suppose that after a meal I notice that I have eaten unusually much and wonder whether this was due primarily to hunger or to the tastiness of the food. What may have led me to raise the question in the first place was a feeling of having eaten more than usual. This feeling may have a basis in *relatively* simple mechanisms. But to ask whether my eating was primarily due to hunger or to the tastiness of the food must require me at least to know how much I ordinarily eat and how the food tasted relative to other kinds of food. I must then balance the probability of hunger against the tastiness of the food as the primary cause. I think it is implausible to believe we have mechanisms for balancing the two types of causes against each other. In general, I think this represents an extremely complicated problem.

There is also the problem, given scant attention by Heider, that it is frequently difficult to distinguish between the two types of causes. Motivation, as we shall see in Chapter 17, is probably always a joint effect of an internal disposition or state and properties of the situation.

If my reasoning is sound, it seems fair to conclude that Heider, like Brunswick and Asch, was led astray by insisting that the way we conceive of another person has great similarities to the way we perceive material objects. In the fourth edition of the *Handbook of Social Psychology*, Gilbert (1998), in my opinion, rightly objected to calling the study of the thoughts, judgments, beliefs, and opinions that people form of each other *perception*. He suggested that the term *person perception* ought to be replaced by the term *ordinary personology*.

It is not easy to follow Heider's account of attribution in *The Psychology of Interpersonal Relations*, and it contains few – if any – formulations that invite empirical investigations. Not until Jones and Keith Davis (1965), and a few years later Harold Kelley (1967), had elaborated his ideas did they attract the interest of a greater number of researchers. In Chapter 19, I shall review some of the ideas in the work of Jones and Davis and of Kelley. I shall also discuss some tendencies in the later work on attribution.

Doubt and Self-Criticism

At the end of the 1960s and the beginning of the 1970s, social psychologists began increasingly to express dissatisfaction with the way their discipline was developing. One complaint was that social psychology, originally directed towards the solution of social problems, had lost its way and developed into an abstract theoretical discipline. Another complaint concerned the extensive use of the experimental method. The preceding generation had viewed the use of the experimental method as a breakthrough in methodology and had tended to overlook its limitations. As research on cognitive dissonance and person perception progressed, it became increasingly clear that studies in the laboratory could only rarely be regarded as representative of the phenomena found in real life. The studies lacked what has become known as *ecological validity* and had to be supplemented by field studies. However, there were also some critics who thought the experimental method was inappropriate for social psychological research. Others, like Steiner (1979), complained that attention had been placed on the individual to the detriment of work on interaction and group processes.

In attitude research, there was a growing concern at the end of the 1960s that attitudes could not predict behavior, as indicated by Robert LaPiere (1934). To study prejudice against minority groups, LaPiere had traveled across the United States accompanied by a Chinese couple. In spite of the fact that this was a time of strong prejudice against Asians, they were denied service in only one of 250 establishments. While service arrangements were being made, LaPiere would make sure he was not present with the couple. Six months after the trip, LaPiere sent questionnaires to the proprietors of the establishments visited asking whether they would serve Asians. Of the 50 percent responding, 90 percent said they would not. This apparent discrepancy between attitude and behavior was also found in other studies.

Researchers of attitude change and persuasion were perturbed because the findings were frequently conflicting and lacking in coherence. (On this point, see Petty and Wegener, 1998, p. 325.) Thus, within social psychology's central area as well as in the field at general, some spoke of a crisis. In Chapter 19, as already mentioned, I shall review some of the efforts to overcome the difficulties leading to the crisis.

15

The Psychology of Personality in the United States

The study of personality arising in the United States in the 1920s and 1930s was an attempt to fuse together a number of diverse traditions, chief among which were the study of individual differences originating with Galton and the clinical study of personality begun by Freud, Jung, Adler, and their students. The European clinical psychologists had aimed to account for personality as a whole and had made it a central concept in explaining motivation. Thus, the US study, as Dan McAdams (1997) recounts, attempted to understand: 1. personality as a whole, 2. motivation, and 3. individual differences.

Wundt and the early German experimental psychologists were interested in characteristics human beings have in common; as Boring (1929/1950) noted, they studied the average adult human being. Galton had understood the role differences between individuals play in evolution, and this was his primary reason to begin the study of individual differences. The pioneers in the US study of personality were not particularly interested in the theory of evolution but were keenly interested in individuality. This focus helps explain why the study of personality became a major focus of inquiry of psychology in the United States (David Winter and Nicole Barenbaum,1999).

The emphasis on individual differences also made the US study different from earlier European work based on clinical psychology. Further, US psychologists were interested in applying the study to the selection of applicants for particular jobs in business, industry, and the military, and came to base their studies on tests and psychometric measurement. Those interested in characteristics of personality were inspired by Galton's measurements and Binet's intelligence test, and by the 1920s they had developed questionnaires and rating scales into useful instruments. When more extensive approaches were presented at the end of the 1930s, the ground had been prepared for more than a decade. This gave the study an orientation towards objective methods from the start.

Naturally, a concept covering such disparate phenomena as personality as a whole, motivation, and individual differences is not easily defined, and the editors of two comprehensive handbooks of personality (Robert Hogan et al., 1997; Lawrence Pervin and Oliver John, 1999) did not give their contributors a definition that could serve as a guideline for them or for readers. In his broad and systematic treatment of personality psychology, Pervin (2003, preface) postponed the problem of defining personality to a final chapter, noting that "over the years personality has been treated in a variety of ways, allowing each researcher to investigate the phenomena viewed as particularly important, without the field itself accepting a definition." As he also noted, since the 1960s, presentations of personality psychology have usually started by reviewing the theories of the pioneers in the field. I shall follow this procedure.

There seems to be consensus that the study of personality psychology was decisively advanced by Gordon Allport and Henry Murray, and we begin with the chapter with them. Later it was closely associated with the development of clinical psychology in the United States, on which I shall briefly report. Then we turn to the work of two theorists, Carl Rogers and George Kelly, who were important in clinical as well as personality psychology. Finally, I shall discuss a famous study of the relationship between culture and personality.

Personality psychologists attempted to explain human thinking and action by concentrating on characteristics of the person. In contrast, US behaviorists tended to explain human thinking and action in terms of environmental influences and learning. From the 1920s, the two conflicting views developed in parallel, but at the end of the 1960s, they clashed in the *person–situation debate*. Criticism of personality psychology by researchers oriented towards learning theory led to a crisis in personality psychology in the 1970s. I shall end the chapter by reporting on the crisis.

Gordon Allport (1897–1967)

Gordon Allport agreed that the European psychology of personality had yielded important viewpoints and findings, but he urged that these findings be interpreted within the framework of general scientific psychological knowledge. By drawing the study of personality into the field of psychology, he and other US psychologists helped give the psychology of personality a better foundation.

In contrast to Freud and his colleagues in neurology, who claimed to be able to base their psychological studies of personality on experiences from their clinical practice, Allport insisted that the point of departure for the study of personality must be the thinking of daily life, with an emphasis on everyday language. There was something practical and down to earth in his approach, and, in contrast to his European colleagues, he had nothing remarkable to report. In many ways, he followed in the footsteps of James, despite being independent and critical of him. As noted in Chapter 14, Allport

Gordon Allport

received his PhD at Harvard and was associated with the university from 1930 until his death. He started lecturing on personality in 1924, and in 1937 he finished a book entitled *Personality* that helped inspire and direct studies of the psychology of personality. The book was published in a revised and expanded edition called *Pattern and Growth in Personality* in 1961. In 1931, Allport and Philip Vernon published a widely used test for the description and measurement of people's values and interests.

Allport's Ideas of the Study of Personality

In a historical introduction to the study of personality, Allport emphasized the importance of Galton's investigations of individual differences. However, he insisted that the study of the human personality is not identical to the study of individual differences. Personality, he claimed, must be understood as the *organization* of several different aspects of the human mind. Human beings display different patterns of characteristics, and personality should be considered as a whole in which the patterns are integrated.

Thus, the psychology of personality differs from the study of individual differences. It also differs from general psychology. Allport held that animal psychology, physiological psychology, the study of perception, developmental psychology, social psychology, psychometrics, and problems in applied psychology do not belong within the framework of the psychology of personality.

Allport had another reason for not wanting to view personality psychology as identical to psychology in general. He held the human personality to be unique, in the sense that no two exemplars are fully the same. There was therefore something in the human personality that could never be expressed in the traditional scientific approach. While he accepted that the goal of science is to reach general, universally valid principles, he nevertheless believed we cannot fully account for the unique with the help of universal principles; an important remainder would always be present.

Most researchers in psychology would probably disagree with Allport's view on this point. They would of course concede that we are unable to describe certain aspects of personality in terms of universal principles at this time, but they would claim that, in principle, it is not impossible to do so. I believe Allport's thoughts on this point were the result of his failure to thoroughly work out how the particular could be understood. I have discussed this question earlier and shall not discuss it here (Saugstad, 1989b).

Personality Described by Traits

Allport believed personality could be most fruitfully accounted for in terms of traits described in everyday language. Hence, the researcher should begin by describing personality in the same way we characterize people we encounter– that is, by using words such as "friendly," "sociable," "reliable," "irritable," and so on. By 1921, Allport had already published an article on personality and trait-names with his elder brother Floyd, and he worked for decades to make this approach as systematic and objective as possible.

Allport divided traits into three groups. First were the *cardinal traits*, which encompass most of an individual's personality. We might, for example, describe a person inclined to having power and manipulating others as Machiavellian, or a person with a tendency to seek satisfaction through inflicting pain on others as sadistic. There were few broad traits of this type, however; most covered only a part of personality. Allport termed this second type *central traits*; they covered an important aspect of personality, such as sociability, reliability, irritability, and so on. The third type, *secondary traits*, accounted for an even smaller part of the individual's thinking and behavior.

A *trait*, according to Allport, is an underlying disposition we can infer from observation of behavior. To draw reliable conclusions about trait descriptions, we need to employ different methods, such as comparing reports from several observers and using questionnaires and tests. Careful investigation of the consistency of the traits is also necessary. Traits are *not* to be understood merely as useful terms for somewhat accidental similarities in behavior; rather, they are consistently occurring tendencies to behave in the same way in similar types of situations. According to Allport, traits originate in specific physiological processes. He also discussed the similarity between traits and attitudes, concluding that some attitudes can be viewed as traits but not all, and not all traits can be seen as attitudes. Further, he discussed the relationship between traits and motivation, arguing that some traits can initiate behavior, some can direct it, and yet others can both initiate and direct it.

Allport did not believe researchers could ever agree on a given number of traits to employ in the description of personality. Nor did he believe the number could be reduced by the use of factor analysis, as later researchers attempted to do. He claimed, however, that this limitation would not interfere with the listing of traits to make descriptions more appropriate, and, in collaboration with Henry Odbert, he took a small but consequential step in this direction (Allport and Odbert, 1936). The two went through a dictionary of 550,000 entries to obtain an index of words to describe personality in the English language. Using as their criterion that the words should distinguish the behavior of one individual from another, they compiled close to 18,000 terms, which they divided into four groups. In their judgment, only one of the groups could be said to contain trait-names in the strict sense (Allport, 1937, p. 308). This group included about 4,500 words, primarily adjectives.

Allport (1937) emphasized that the relationship between trait-names and underlying personality characteristics is a complex one. He thought that, due to prevailing standards and interests, each social epoch would tend to characterize personality in a particular way. Thus, there would be a certain arbitrariness in the lexicon of trait-names available to the persons living in a certain epoch. Yet he claimed that, because descriptions of the personalities of others are so important for social life, it was natural to believe that language would contain a vocabulary of trait-names designating "true psychic structures." Hence, descriptions of personality by means of words and expressions taken from ordinary language would not be entirely arbitrary. Allport was fully aware that ordinary language has serious shortcomings as a means of making scientific descriptions, but he believed we could gradually remedy this by making systematically controlled studies of different types.

To explain how some traits could be motivating, Allport formulated a principle of some theoretical interest. Inspired by Woodworth's view of motivation (to be presented in Chapter 17), he suggested that once an activity has been established, the performance of it will often provide satisfaction at a later time, even though the original motivation is no longer present. For example, an ex-sailor may long for the sea even if it is no longer necessary for him to earn a living as a sailor. According to Allport, a transformation of the motive from the previously desired object to the newly desired object has taken place. He called his principle *functional autonomy* and provided numerous examples. Although he did not give a satisfactory account of his principle, he called attention to the fact that some activities seem to be intrinsically motivated.

The Importance to Personality of Self

Allport thought that although no person with a fully integrated (healthy, normal, well-adjusted) personality exists, personality nevertheless comprises a whole. From this idea of unity, he claimed that what makes a person unique, what causes different people to have different personalities, is that the traits are organized in specific ways and form different patterns in different people. He also attempted to outline how personality acquires its holistic character, pointing out that learning leads to comprehensive structures of concepts and actions. Further, the fact that human beings must participate in different forms of more comprehensive activities at different times in their lives, such as attending school, working, and raising a family, also leads to an organization of personality.

The primary factor in the integration of personality is the development of self as an object of consciousness. Allport's book was published at a time when behaviorism was rapidly gaining ground. He nevertheless had no hesitation in giving the concept of *self* a central place in the psychology of personality and discussing it thoroughly. Among other things, he treated his disagreement with William James in this context. He gave a broad role to self-esteem, adopted Adler's ideas about feelings of inferiority, and presented his own interpretation of the concept of defense mechanism.

Between the publication of James's *Principles* and of Allport's book in 1937, the idea of the *self* had been virtually banned from the field of psychology. The introspective psychologists held that they could discover no self in the mental processes they attempted to describe, and the behaviorists rejected the concept of self as mentalistic. Baldwin and Mead had presented interesting ideas on the development of the self. Allport did not discuss their ideas, referring instead to Mary Calkins, of whom I shall give a brief account.

Mary Whiton Calkins (1863–1930) was one of the first women to achieve a prominent position in American psychology. She studied at Harvard with James, but despite having completed her PhD dissertation, she was never permitted to defend it because she was a woman. In 1905 she was elected president of the APA.

In line with James's thinking, Calkins thought psychology must include a study of the self. James had claimed that any form of consciousness tends to become part of a personal consciousness. Calkins (1908) insisted that we can register the presence of the self in all introspective actions. Titchener and his students opposed her views on this point, and when behaviorism gained increasing support, Calkins was left standing alone with her view.

Mary Whiton Calkins

Further Development of Trait Theory

Before Allport and Odbert's lexical approach to the study of personality, Thurstone (1947) had performed an investigation in which a number of subjects each rated a person they knew well by means of sixty adjectives in common use for describing people. The correlations for the sixty traits were then factor-analyzed, and five factors were extracted. The study was not performed so systematically that it was plausible to believe the five factors could account for the use of all trait-names. But the results suggested the number of factors might be far more limited than expected.

Raymond Cattell (1905–1998)

Raymond Cattell was an Englishman educated at the University of London and a former assistant to Spearman. He emigrated to the United States in 1937 and was for many years attached to the University of Illinois.

Allport was critical of attempts to reduce the number of traits by means of factor-analysis, and he and Odbert did not attempt to reduce the 4,500 adjectives they had found most appropriate to represent traits. However, inspired by Allport and Odbert as well as by Thurstone, Cattell (1943) set out to search for a structure of dimensions that would allow him to describe the human personality simply and consistently in terms of trait-names. To undertake a factor-analysis of the use of trait-names, he had to considerably reduce the Allport and Odbert list. This he did by first having two judges classify the words into groups of synonyms. To these groups of synonyms, he added eleven groups of synonyms for traits found in the work of earlier researchers. To reduce the resulting 171 groups to a smaller number, he used a specific statistical technique and was left with thirty-five variables. He then selected 100 persons and instructed people acquainted with any one of them to undertake a rating of the person on the basis of the thirty-five variables. The ratings were factor-analyzed and twelve factors extracted.

In subsequent investigations, Cattell (1956, 1965) used the twelve factors to construct questionnaires given to a large number of subjects. A factor-analysis of the results now gave sixteen factors. Cattell reported that twelve of these were very similar to the twelve found in the earlier study. He also worked out personality tests based on laboratory work, made an extensive factor-analysis study of motives, and by the use of factor-analysis studied the development of traits in ontogenesis.

Cattell claimed his diverse studies of traits showed excellent correspondence. According to John and Srivastava (1999), however, later researchers questioned this claim. Further, the reliability of the original classification of 4,500 words was low, and in reanalyzing Cattell's data, later researchers have not been able to confirm his conclusions about the number and nature of the factors he extracted. Still, as we shall see, his work helped give a new and fruitful direction to the study of traits.

Hans Eysenck (1916–1997)

Hans Eysenck was another Spearman student and pioneer in the factor-analysis study of traits. He emigrated from Germany to Great Britain, where he was active in research on clinical psychology and personality for more than fifty years, doing most of his work at Maudsley Hospital in London. His inspiration derived from Spearman and work on heredity by British researchers, but also from a European psychiatric tradition aimed at categorizing people on the basis of biological characteristics. This tradition can be traced back to ancient Greece. Hippocrates (460–377 BC) speculated that four different fluids in the body give rise to different temperaments. Our vocabulary still carries this 2,000-year-old legacy; to this day, we speak of people as being choleric, phlegmatic, sanguine, and melancholy. The idea that human beings can be classed according to biological characteristics lived on in Western culture, and for a time it attracted researchers after the German psychiatrist Ernst Kretschmer (1921) suggested a classification according to differences in body build.

In a comprehensive account, *The Structure of Human Personality* (1953), Eysenck presented a constructive criticism of Kretschmer and the research that followed. He claimed that, in accordance with the ideas of Jung and Kretschmer, we could classify people into types, but also that personality could be described in terms of traits. In Eysenck's (1990) opinion, there is no contradiction between these two ways of describing personality. We may understand them as two different levels in a hierarchical model.

After extensive and thorough long-term studies, Eysenck concluded that the human personality could with reasonable adequacy be described along three dimensions. In addition to the dimension *extrovert/introvert*, he had found a dimension pertaining to emotional stability, which he called *neuroticism*, and a third dimension he termed *psychoticism*. The last dimension concerns the degree to which persons are aggressive, egocentric, and nonsocialized.

Like Allport and Cattell before him, Eysenck thought traits and types have a basis in genetic and physiological conditions. The importance of his efforts to justify this view was little understood at first. But as genetic and evolutionary viewpoints gained ground in psychology from the 1960s and 1970s, the approach drew increased attention. I shall return to this point in Chapter 19, where I shall deal further with the trait approach to the study of personality.

Henry A. Murray (1893–1988)

In 1929, Morton Prince (1854–1924) founded a psychological clinic at Harvard. Prince, trained as a medical doctor, insisted the clinic should be associated with the department of psychology at Harvard. In this way, as Hilgard (1987) points out, he established that the scientific study of clinical psychology and the psychology of personality belong within the field of psychology. Prince had already visited Charcot's clinic in La Salpêtrière in 1880 and had acquired an interest in French psychiatry and clinical psychology. He was interested in hypnosis and Janet's thoughts about dissociation, but he was also open to ideas from psychoanalysis from an early stage. In 1906, he founded the *Journal of Abnormal Psychology*. He described cases of multiple personality in two books, which acquired new relevancy when this syndrome drew renewed interest in the 1950s.

Henry Murray succeeded Prince as the head of the Harvard Psychological Clinic in 1929. Murray had a wide range of interests and had studied several different subjects, beginning with history, continuing with medicine and – after receiving his MD – biochemistry, which he studied for five years. He was analyzed by Jung but was primarily influenced by McDougall and Freud; he thought, as they did, that motivation is the most important aspect of personality. While he was aware of the problems confronting the psychology of personality to a much greater degree than these two predecessors, Murray, in his theoretical reasoning, did not go much beyond what he had learned from them.

His importance lies primarily in his attempt to find an empirical basis for the study of personality.

Murray focused on the development of tests and experimental techniques, helping to give US personality psychology a more scientific empirical orientation. In the 1930s, he supervised a broadly planned research project on motivation in which several personality psychologists, who subsequently became well known, participated as his coworkers. The project was described in a comprehensive book called *Explorations in Personality* (1938). In it, intensive investigations of the personalities of fifty young men were undertaken. The men were interviewed, given extensive questionnaires, and tested in a variety of different ways. Murray presented his theory of personality as an introduction to the study and repeatedly revised it, one important version appearing in 1959.

Murray approached the study of personality and motivation in essentially the same way as McDougall. His central concept of *need* does not deviate much from McDougall's concept of *motive*, which the latter used in his later writings instead of "instinct." Need is a concept that provided energy and direction to behavior. Like McDougall and Freud, Murray made no attempt to explain how a need might instigate behavior. He did, however, suggest that aspects of the environment, which he called *press*, might also give direction to behavior. Admitting that the idea of press came late in his theorizing and therefore was not appropriately incorporated in his approach, Murray made no serious attempt to explain how needs are related to incentives. Thus, his treatment of motivation is subject to the same criticism as that raised of McDougall and Freud. Murray referred to Woodworth, but he does not seem to have understood that Woodworth had raised important points of criticism of the idea of need or drive as an internal source of energy.

In line with McDougall, Murray presented a list of motives (needs) that he classified into groups. He noted that not all needs seem to have a specifiable bodily origin, however, and he distinguished between *primary* (*viscerogenetic*) *needs* and *secondary* (*psychogenetic*) *needs*. The first group has to do with physical satisfaction, and the latter with mental and emotional satisfaction. Like Hull some years later, Murray believed the psychogenetic needs are in some way derived from the viscerogenetic needs.

Murray's list contained twenty-eight needs, eight viscerogenetic and twenty psychogenetic. Apart from Cattell (1956), who undertook a factor-analytic study of motives some years after *Explorations in Personality* had appeared, few researchers had been interested in working out a complete classification system of motives. In the years following the publication of Murray's classic work, psychologists were mainly interested in some of the psychogenetic needs proposed by Murray, particularly his proposals of a need for *achievement*, introduced as a will to exert power over things, people, and ideas; a need for *affiliation*, an inclination to form friendships and associations; and a need for *dominance*, a need to influence and control others. In some modified form, these can be regarded as the *Big Three Motives*, as Robert Emmons (1997) suggests.

As shown by Donald Hebb (1949), all motives, including the primary physiological needs, are influenced by learning. This naturally makes it difficult to work out a classification system. It is also difficult to assess the degree to which a tendency that might be a need can be influenced by learning. Freud and Lorenz regarded aggression as a need or drive, and Murray classified it as a psychogenetic need.

As Murray said repeatedly, the needs used to describe personality had to be inferred from thoughts, fantasies, and behavior. Murray and his coworkers tried to make the basis for their inferences broad and varied. The subjects were interviewed, asked to write an autobiography and fill out an extensive questionnaire, and given a number of tests. One of the tests, the *Thematic Apperception Test* (*TAT*), constructed by Murray and Christine Morgan, has become one of the most widely used personality tests

TAT and Projective Tests

Strongly influenced by Freud, Murray, and Morgan believed our thinking and behavior are determined by unconscious processes that could be disclosed if a person were engaged in an imaginative activity unobserved by others. Murray and Morgan selected twenty pictures deemed appropriate for disclosing unconscious fantasies and impulses. In each, there was at least one person with whom the subject could identify. The task was to produce a story to account for the content of the picture. Murray used the term *theme* for the need that was activated by a given type of pressure. The intuitive, empathic apprehension we have of other people's behavior and inner lives he termed *apperception*, and he called his test the Thematic Apperception Test, in accordance with these terms.

Another frequently used test was Erik Erikson's *Dramatic Picture Test*, in which dolls are used to represent imagined events. In addition to these two tests, Murray's coworkers constructed special tests of repression, reaction to frustration, ability to be hypnotized, and level of aspiration, in accordance with the studies conducted in Lewin's laboratory in Berlin.

In the TAT, the subject is thought to project his or her feelings, motives, and fantasies into the description of the pictures. In another projective test, the Rorschach Test introduced in 1921 by Hermann Rorschach, the subject is asked to recount ideas brought to mind by inkblots that do not represent any particular objects or situations. Projective tests are based on the assumption that we have unconscious thoughts of the kind Freud hypothesized, which we can express through some form of inner dynamic that is independent of any specific stimulus. As I pointed out in the discussion of Freud's concept of the unconscious, there are no empirical studies that clearly demonstrate the validity of this belief. Although many clinical psychologists claim to find projective tests useful, they do not have a high degree of validity, and reliability is also often low. The reason may simply be that the underlying assumption is not tenable.

Clinical Psychology

Until World War II, clinical psychological treatment was provided almost exclusively by medical doctors, particularly neurologists and psychiatrists. Psychologists who did clinical work by and large only administered tests to patients and assisted in the diagnostic work. The few who practiced therapy did so under the supervision of doctors. During

World War II, psychologists began to work alongside psychiatrists in the US Army, and when a serious shortage of staff to treat soldiers suffering from mental disturbance occurred after the war (today these would be seen as symptoms of post-traumatic stress disorder), psychologists were employed as responsible therapists in military hospitals.

To remedy the lack of trained staff, the education of clinical psychologists began in 1946. This training, of three years' duration, was led by the US organization for the treatment of wounded war veterans, the Veterans Administration (VA), and was combined with an education program in clinical psychology at selected universities. The enterprise of the VA came to have a great impact on American clinical psychology, since this new and comprehensive education program raised fresh interest in the discipline. This part of the history of US psychology, which demonstrates Americans' organizing abilities, is comprehensively discussed by Dana Moore (1992).

At about the same time as formal training of clinical psychologists was established in hospitals under the VA, the National Institute of Mental Health was founded. This institute conducted clinical psychological research and distributed funds to universities and other institutions conducting clinical research. Considerable sums were also awarded as scholarships for students wishing to specialize in clinical psychology. Thus, in the years following World War II, opportunities were created in clinical psychology as well as in clinical research.

US psychologists were also developing original forms of psychotherapy at this time. I will discuss two of them, Carl Rogers and George Kelly.

Carl Rogers (1902–1987)

Freud, Jung, and Adler all had adherents in the United States who were supervising clinics according to the respective guidelines of the three. There were also psychoanalysts who deviated from Freud in different ways and who had settled in the United States. Thus, several different forms of psychodynamic therapy were practiced that all originated from the German-speaking part of Europe. The only influential form of therapy developed by a US psychologist was that of Carl Rogers. This gives it a special position in the history of psychology.

Rogers's view of life was imbued with the values of the democratic and capitalistic United States, and, as Philip Cushman (1992) has pointed out, there is a close association between these values and Rogers's theory of personality. In accordance with capitalistic thinking, he emphasized the development of individuality in human beings, and from the vision of the United States as the land of opportunity, he believed people could develop their innate abilities when allowed to do so without obstructions. According to Cushman and other historians, the idea that people can realize their potential as thinking, feeling, and acting human beings independently of the economic, political, and social conditions in which they mature is deeply embedded in the American way of thinking. In his account of the reasons for inadequate psychological functioning, Rogers discussed upbringing, but not economic, social, or political conditions. In this, he stands as a typical representative of tendencies that were strongly prevalent from the 1930s until well into the 1960s and are likely to be present still.

Personal Life Experience and View on Psychology: A Biographical Outline

Rogers's psychotherapy and theory of personality reflect experiences that appear to have influenced his life. It lends perspective to his professional psychological approach when we view it in the context of these experiences as recounted in his biography. In two autobiographical sketches, Rogers (1980) described how he viewed his own intellectual development. As a child, he was immersed in a fundamentalist Protestant sect. According to his account, his parents accentuated the evil nature of human beings and emphatically rejected any way of living that did not conform to their puritan morals. Rogers responded adversely to this upbringing, and in time he came to think children would display their positive characteristics if treated with understanding, warmth, and respect. He viewed the asocial and destructive traits he found in people not as innate tendencies in human nature, but instead as the result of upbringing.

Rogers grew up in a wealthy home in one of Chicago's suburbs. When he was twelve years old, the family moved to a farm, and he soon became interested in agricultural science, and indeed in science in general. After a couple of years of study, his interests shifted to theology, and he enrolled at the Union Theological Seminary, a well-known liberal Protestant seminary in New York where Hall had also been a student. Two years later, however, he turned to psychology and began to study at Columbia University, which lay directly across the street from the seminary. Here, he encountered the strong empirical orientation to psychology of Cattell and Thorndike. Rogers received his PhD in 1931 and was then already working in a counseling clinic for children, supervised by psychoanalytically oriented psychologists. After completing his studies, he practiced for twelve years in a counseling clinic in Rochester, after which he held professorships at Ohio State University and the University of Chicago. During his years as a university lecturer, he developed his psychology of personality and began systematic studies of the effects of his therapy.

While his view of life moved away from the religiosity of his childhood home, Rogers could perhaps be said to have given a worldly rendering to some central Protestant ideas in his therapy. His requirement that the therapist should be absolutely accepting of his clients and meet them with deep and genuine understanding is reminiscent of the promise given in Protestantism that believers will meet a God unwavering in His love and understanding of all human qualities. Like most pioneers in clinical psychology, Rogers emphasized that his form of therapy was the result of his clinical experience. I nevertheless think his childhood experience and the Union Theological Seminary may have been a primary source of inspiration as well.

In 1942, Rogers published a book about counseling and psychotherapy that earned him a central place in US clinical psychology. In the fifteen years after its publication, he reworked his viewpoints into a more consistent theory that was expressed first in the very influential work *Client-Centered Therapy* (1951), and later in a more coherent and systematic form in the extensive work Koch edited in 1959, *Psychology: A Study of a Science* (see Chapter 1).

In the hope of demonstrating that his form of therapy was suitable not only for milder mental disturbances but also for psychotic disorders, Rogers conducted a comprehensive therapy and research program as professor of psychiatry and psychology at the University of Wisconsin. In his later years, he wished to demonstrate how people cooperating in small groups could realize what he saw as their innate qualities. With time, however, he appears to have lost interest in finding a scientific basis for his viewpoints, and in scientific psychology on the whole.

Influence of Phenomenology and Existential Philosophy

Although Rogers was a product of his times, he fought against certain contemporary tendencies as well, and he achieved originality in a battle to free himself from traditional conceptualizations of God, human nature, and the purpose and methods of psychology. During his years of studying and establishing his practice as a psychologist, behaviorism was becoming a dominant trend in US psychology. Rogers repudiated behaviorism, claiming that the basis for the study of psychology must be the description of the world as we perceive and understand it. The task of the psychologist was to attempt to empathize with the way other people experienced the world.

In his therapy, Rogers consistently tried to implement his phenomenological approach; for instance, clients were asked to talk about their problems and describe their feelings while the therapist adopted a listening stance, interrupting the narration as little as possible. Rogers disapproved of diagnoses, and consequently he did not seek to construct the client's life history from accessible information. The therapist was instead to form an image of the client based on the client's own description of his or her problems and feelings.

In time, but perhaps already from the beginning of his career, Rogers came to doubt that we could encompass all aspects of human thought and activity in a scientific psychology. In his view, scientific psychologists tend to forget that it is our nature as human beings to seek meaning in life, that we must make choices, and that we feel responsible for our actions. In this, Rogers's views corresponded closely with existential philosophy, which I described in the account of the phenomenological movement in Chapter 5 and which I shall discuss further in Chapter 18.

View of Psychology as a Science

In his clinical practice, Rogers had found it unsatisfactory not to try to systematize and structure the observations he made as a therapist. Theory construction and observation of clients had to proceed hand in hand. He rejected the central assumption of the early positivist philosophy that the empirical researcher must begin by acquiring a solid foundation in observation, claiming that at an initial stage of research observations would have little precision, the hypotheses would be speculative, and the reasoning would be full of errors. The crucial task in science, Rogers held, was to obtain increasingly precise measurements, clearer and more consistent theoretical formulations, and greater generalizability in the formulation of theoretical statements.

Although we may agree with Rogers on this point, I believe it is also important to remember that not all issues lead to a productive development of empirical research. For a field of study to evolve in a profitable way, researchers must be able to formulate essential questions. As Rogers did not discuss this point in scientific procedure, it may be that, like many of his contemporaries, he did not perceive that once we begin to work through what appear to be consequential issues by way of scientific methods, the advances will turn up more or less by themselves.

There was no room for the perspective of the theory of evolution in Rogers's psychological thinking. Nor did he attempt to disclose a physiological basis for psychological processes. In this he was at variance with James, but in accord with influential contemporaries such as Tolman and Skinner.

View of Psychotherapy and Personality

Rogers received his first introduction to therapeutic practice at an institution governed by psychoanalytic thinking, but in time he came to oppose several of Freud's central ideas, and his treatment of clients is, at least *apparently*, very different from Freud's. We may therefore easily lose sight of the great similarities between the two. Modern therapy research indicates that the two approaches have approximately the same effect. (See Michael Lambert, 2004.) We should thus concentrate on disclosing not only differences between the two forms of therapies, but similarities as well.

Rogers and Freud: Similarities and Differences

According to Rogers, sexuality has a central place in human life, but he did not view the sexual drive as an all-pervasive force in human thought and action. He did not reject the idea of unconscious processes and realized that human beings could behave irrationally, but he did not place the same emphasis on unconscious and irrational processes as had Freud. He also thought that in order to achieve a more objective psychology, to the extent this was possible, we must confine ourselves to the study of conscious processes. Rogers also had a more optimistic view of human beings than Freud did, believing we have resources for solving our problems when the right conditions prevail. Nor did Rogers view the client as a person suffering from any specific form of illness to be treated with a specific technique. To him, the relationship between therapist and client represented a cooperation in which the client was active and the therapist merely contributed by providing the setting for recovery. The difference in perspective between Freud and Rogers may reflect a difference between the social structures of the Austro-Hungarian Empire and the democratic United States.

With regard to similarities, we find these in Freud's and Rogers's views of motivation. Like Freud, Rogers assumed that human motivation could be explained in terms of a single, ubiquitous force. This pervasive force is not the libido, however, but a force that is effective in all human beings, serving not only to sustain life but also to lead the individual to achieve his or her potential. Rogers called this force *the tendency to self-actualization*. This force was central in his approach, just as the libido was central to Freud's. Rogers emphasized that this force is present in what we call our *self* in everyday speech. He postulated that the tendency to self-actualization manifests itself in the individual's development of an increasingly richer self, in which the different concepts and emotions do not conflict with each other. The individual with a healthy mind is characterized by harmony and unity of thoughts and feelings. I will return to this point in the work of Rogers.

Freud had attempted to explain neuroses on the basis of inferences about a process of psychosexual development in the child. Rogers was less concerned with uncovering his clients' childhood experiences. Nevertheless, he also thought the origins of human psychological problems are to be found in childhood experiences. He believed the child has a strong wish for recognition and respect from its parents and others close to it. Should the caregivers reject the thoughts and emotions the child expresses, these thoughts and emotions would not gain a place in the child's self-image. Because the thoughts and feelings are expressions of the tendency to self-actualization, they would still be effective in the mind, but now as a dividing force. Thus, Rogers, like Freud, imagined that inadequate psychological functioning arises as the consequence of an obstacle to the expression of a drive. Neither of the two placed much emphasis on how poor childhood development could be due to a lack of stimulation and care. Like Freud, Rogers believed defense mechanisms operate to distort or repress conceptions and emotions incompatible with the child's self-image.

According to Rogers, *all* forms of psychological problems originate from disturbances due to the incompatibility between thoughts and emotions and the person's self-image. In his view, this explanation accounts for both mild forms of maladjustment, such as shyness in social situations, and disabling disorders, such as psychoses.

Self-Actualization as a Therapeutic Goal

The therapeutic goal is to create conditions allowing the self-actualizing tendency in the individual to work so that disturbing thoughts and emotions can be encompassed in the self-image instead of being repressed or disavowed. Rogers began therapy by quite simply asking the client to tell about her or his problems and feelings. The therapist must pay attention to the client's account without undue interruption and not guide it by asking questions. He or she is to sustain the momentum of the client's account by intermittently recapitulating the account, and ask questions only when the client's account becomes unclear. Thus, the client is at the center of this communicative situation, and Rogers called this *client-centered therapy*. He later altered this term to *person-centered therapy*.

The therapist is to try to fulfill three requirements in his or her cooperation with the patient. First of all, the therapist must be true to his or her own nature and not attempt to adapt to the situation or pretend to any attitudes or meanings other than those he or she actually stands for. As Rogers said, the therapist must be *genuine*. Second, the therapist must meet the client with unconditional tolerance, with goodwill and involvement. Third, the therapist must be able to empathize with the client's situation.

In this type of setting, when the client is given the opportunity to account for her or his problems and state, the self-actualizing tendency is set free so that the self-image can change in a positive direction. Clearly, the central feature of Rogers's therapy is his concept of the self. In a presentation by Rogers (1959) for the work edited by Koch (1959– 1963), he accounted for his initial hesitation over this policy. He claimed that expressions like the following from his clients had made him emphasize the self in his therapy and theory of personality: "I feel that I am not myself," "I wonder who I really am," "I would not like anyone to know my real self," and "I have never had the chance to be myself."

Rogers on the Self

I shall now elaborate Rogers's thoughts and studies of the self. As I have said, he based his view on a phenomenological description – that is, the description he thought the individual could produce of his or her own conscious experience of a self. He described what he called the *self*, or *self-structure*, as an organized, consistent, conceptual Gestalt made up of ideas of an *I* or *me* and associations between this *I* and other aspects of life. Values were also associated with these ideas or images of the self or the *I*. Following these and a few other equally cryptic comments about the self, Rogers claimed that his concept could be defined in operational terms; that is, with reference to specific procedures.

The procedure he primarily employed was the *Q-sort*. This was based on a compilation of expressions Rogers and his coworkers had collected from their clients' remarks about themselves. These remarks were written on cards, and the clients were to place them in categories ranging from least to most descriptive of their self-image. The cards were to be placed so that there was a predetermined number in each category. The clients were also asked to describe the self they would like to have, their *ideal self*.

We might reasonably think we could obtain a certain impression of a person's self-image and ideal self with this procedure. But in order to interpret the results of this test, we must make several assumptions: that people do not misrepresent themselves, that they do not repress or distort their expressions, that their self-image is accessible to them at the time of reporting, and that it does not fluctuate strongly over time or across situations.

In the 1950s, Rogers and his coworkers began investigating the relationship between the clients' self-image and their ideal self. They obtained tape recordings of the therapeutic sessions and claimed that on the basis of these they could identify actual alterations in this relationship. As we could expect from Rogers's theoretical inferences, the differences between the ideal self and the self-image decreased as the therapy progressed.

Evaluation of Rogers's Contribution

There appears to be widespread agreement among experts in therapy research that the form of therapy Rogers developed has beneficial effects. Nevertheless, much remains to be done if we are to obtain more concrete knowledge about how effective the therapy is, and whether it is effective for *all* forms of psychological problems and suffering. Many would perhaps express doubt about its impact on more severe mental disturbance. For the time being, we know little about what a definitive effect would be.

The investigation of the effect of client-centered therapy that Rogers and his coworkers initiated was a pioneering enterprise of great importance to subsequent research in therapy. Rogers probably also contributed to the psychology of personality by highlighting, by the Q-sort method, the difference between our understanding of the self and of an ideal self. One shortcoming of Rogers's approach to the study of personality is that it is difficult to understand what he meant by "the tendency to self-actualization." He had little concrete to say about it.

While Rogers, along with Gordon Allport, must be credited for reviving interest in the study of the self, he apparently held that the self can be described phenomenologically as some consciousness entity. This is a dubious belief. As Baumeister (1998) said, we cannot directly perceive the self, but we can infer it from some of our activities. Rogers seems to have been confused on this point.

George Kelly (1905–1967)

George Kelly's *The Psychology of Personal Constructs* (1955) soon came to be considered a major work in the psychology of personality. As noted by his biographer, Fay Fransella (1995), Kelly was regarded by many as a genius who revolutionized clinical psychology and the study of personality. An organization was even founded with a view to working with clinical problems and personality psychology on the basis of the guidelines he presented. Kelly drew the study of clinical psychology and personality closer to the study of cognition and seems to have been an inspiration to humanistic psychology and to cognitive therapy (see Chapter 16).

Biographical Outline

George Kelly grew up on a small farm near Perth, Kansas; his family was poor. His father had been educated as a Presbyterian clergyman, but he lived as a farmer. At first, Kelly's major interest lay in the natural sciences, but he eventually turned his attention to sociology, pedagogy, and psychology. He received his PhD in 1931 at the University of Iowa, after which he taught psychology at a small college in Kansas. Here, he became involved with clinical psychology and school psychology. During World War II, he worked in the armed forces on the selection and training of pilots. For twenty years, beginning in 1945, he was employed as a professor at Ohio State University, and, from

1946, he was head of clinical psychology there. In 1965, he was appointed professor of theoretical psychology at Brandeis University.

Cultural Influences on Kelly's Thinking

In accordance with American liberalism and individualism, the individual, for Kelly, was always at the center. As Fransella (1995) notes, Kelly grew up in poverty and was aware of the limitations that economic and social relationships impose on the individual's opportunities for self-expression. But in his famous work, he did not discuss social structures as a factor in the formation of personality. The central thought was that we are in charge of our lives. In this, Kelly's psychological thinking corresponded with the American liberal tradition. Naturally, Kelly acknowledged that human attitudes and lifestyles are the result of a learning process. It was important to him, however, to emphasize that this learning process does not deprive us of the opportunity for choice. Kelly (1955, p. 15) put this view into words by saying, "No one needs to be a victim of his biography."

Whereas Rogers was interested in how people may attain a deeper sense of the meaning of life and a richer emotional life by learning to accept their own inclinations, Kelly was more concerned that the will enabling us to master the challenges of life must not be undermined. To him, human beings primarily appear to be creatures of will and action. This difference between the two may at least partially be explained by the fact that Kelly grew up in poverty and had to learn early how to support himself by hard labor, while Rogers belonged to an affluent family, giving him greater freedom to choose his own lifestyle and education.

Kelly's thinking had two main sources. The first was Dewey's philosophy, which Kelly had an enthusiasm for (as Fransella noted). Dewey emphasized that human knowledge is constantly undergoing change. He believed the procedures of natural science have a place in philosophy, focusing on the role the testing of hypotheses plays in thinking. Kelley appropriated the idea that knowledge is in constant change, as well as the idea that we gain knowledge about ourselves by hypothesis testing.

The second important source, as noted by Hergenhahn (2009), was existential philosophy, in which the core ideas are that our outlook on the world is subjective, and that we have the freedom to make choices. Kelly combined the ideas of subjectivity and free choice with Dewey's ideas of change and hypothesis testing into a psychology of personality. He tried to account for subjectivity by general, scientific principles, and it would have been a tremendous achievement if he had succeeded.

A System of Personal Constructs

From Dewey's philosophy and existential philosophy, Kelly developed a theory of personality and psychotherapy in which he postulated that we form constructs enabling us to anticipate future events. The way we test these constructs against reality is analogous to the way scientists test their constructs. Depending upon the outcome of the test, we keep or change the constructs. We also relate the constructs to each other so that they form a system, which we again test against reality.

Because each human being views the world in her or his own way, each of us will have specific, particular constructs. To express this point, Kelly called the constructs *personal constructs* and the system each of us has, a *system of personal constructs.*

To account for the way the individual's system of personal constructs is formed, Kelly worked out a theory that starts from a single fundamental postulate. The meaning of this postulate he specified in eleven corollaries, which we will not examine here. I shall, however, note that the theory aimed to cover a wide variety of psychological events.

Kelly's View of Psychotherapy

To function in a constantly changing world, we must constantly alter our personal constructs. In certain circumstances, a person's constructs or system of constructs do not undergo the necessary changes. The individual then does not function satisfactorily, and, according to Kelly, this is the origin of psychological maladjustment. His therapy therefore aimed to bring about changes in the system of personal constructs in order to render it more appropriate.

It was important for the therapist to set the person on a course that would bring about change. Unlike Rogers, Kelly thought the therapist should suggest changes for the client to make. However, the therapist must not prescribe which changes are necessary but instead attempt to empathize with clients, so as to cooperate with them in creating the changes that would align their system of constructs to their life situation. The therapist does not have the key to understanding the client's problems (as assumed in psychoanalysis) but can only contribute advice. In this view, Kelly agreed with Jung, who also viewed therapy as a cooperation between therapist and client.

To repeat, a fundamental point in Kelly's thinking is that each individual views the world in his or her own way, and that the basis for psychotherapy therefore must proceed according to the way the world appears to the client. In this, Kelly was in accord with Rogers, although they held different opinions about the manner in which the client's experiences should be described and altered.

One way to understand the client's system of personal constructs is the *Role Construct Repertory (REP) Test.* In this test, the client is presented with a list of designations or categories that can be selected in different ways. The list may, for example, contain categories such as mother, father, sister, brother, admired teacher, and disliked neighbor. The client's first task is to name a person to represent each category. The next step is to conduct successive comparisons of three persons with a view to identifying characteristics that are common to two of them while the third person has the opposite characteristic. For example, two people may be characterized as friendly while a third is characterized as hostile. On the basis of these characterizations, the therapist attempts to form an impression of the client's personal constructs.

To get a person suffering from psychological problems to function more satisfactorily, we must bring about a change in the client's system of personal constructs. Kelly tried to achieve this in various ways. He talked to the client, often offering advice. Or he asked the client to provide a self-characterization. A more drastic procedure was role-playing. After forming an impression of the client, Kelly would give him or her the task of role-playing a person with opposite personal constructs. The client was then to attempt, over a time period that could span several weeks, to play the role of the person he or she had imagined.

Discussion and Evaluation

Kelly's view of the person as a scientist testing hypotheses and his emphasis on rational choice makes him a *cognitively oriented personality psychologist*. By emphasizing the role of cognitive processes in human adjustment, he contributed to a more balanced view of personality, although his own personality theory can be criticized for neglecting motivational and emotional aspects.

To judge from some handbooks (Hogan et al., 1997; Gilbert et al., 1998; Pervin and John, 1999), Kelly's theory does not play an important role in present-day research. I shall give some reasons why this may be so.

Kelly was a revolutionary, and in the preface to *The Psychology of Personal Constructs*, he declared that he thought he could dispense with central psychological concepts, such as learning, emotion, motivation, and ego (self). When we more carefully analyze his system, it becomes clear that it fails to cover many of the phenomena subsumed under these traditional concepts. This is perhaps most noticeable in his treatment of motivation.

Most researchers hold that a theory of personality must be able to account for motivation. Kelly claimed that he could give this account without invoking traditional ideas of motivation. Because human beings as living organisms are constantly moving, it is not necessary to explain how behavior is instigated. The fact that human beings are constantly moving does not mean, however, that the same motives are always at work. As we noted in Chapter 7, basic physiological needs have a cyclical nature, and the fact that we seem to engage in a wide variety of activities suggests that we need a theory explaining how motivation is instigated. The direction of behavior, Kelly argued, could be taken care of by building the theory so that it becomes clear what choices a person would make. In his discussion of choices, Kelly seems to have left out of account genetic disposition and physiological states. He rightly pointed to the inadequacies of accounts of motivation in terms of stimuli and responses, as well as of accounts in terms of needs, but he seems to have overlooked the possibility of explaining motivation as a joint effect of an internal state and an external incentive. (I shall return to this problem in Chapter 17.)

Kelly gave little attention to emotions in his theory and tried to define fear and anxiety in terms of a person's personal constructs. Like Freud, Kelly (1955) distinguished between fear and anxiety and defined *fear* as "the awareness of an imminent comprehensive change in one's core structures." Even if it is reasonable to assume fear may arise as the result of a change in constructs that helps a person anticipate future events, it is a stretch to assume that most instances of fear originate in this way. It is highly plausible, however, that fear in many instances is a result of Pavlovian conditioning with a minimum of cognitive appraisal. In his treatment of emotions, Kelly seems to have overlooked that emotions frequently serve as motives.

Towards the end of the twentieth century, there was a strong reorientation of psychology towards biology, and genetics was shown to affect psychological processes far more than psychologists had earlier assumed. Kelly's lack of orientation towards biology may be an important reason his theory attracts so few psychologists today.

Culture and Personality

Freud, like Wundt, was deeply absorbed in problems of history and culture, and, again like Wundt, he tried to provide the study of culture with a psychological basis. When North American anthropologists at the beginning of the twentieth century focused on problems of culture, they tried to explore Freud's ideas by studying people of different cultures. One outcome of these attempts was the study of culture and personality.

The ideas underlying these studies were that the child-rearing practices of a society are shaped by the culture of that society, and that these practices in turn shape the personality of the society's people. Therefore, by studying the effects of child-rearing practices on the developing child, researchers could determine the effect of culture on personality. The studies aroused great interest in the 1940s and 1950s but were severely criticized in the 1950s, particularly by Alex Inkeles and Daniel Levinson (1954). In a chapter in the *Handbook of Social Psychology*, they pointed out that in all societies there are so many differences in personality that it is difficult to choose any one personality as representative of the culture, and further that cultures are not as homogeneous as researchers assume.

Although the investigations of culture and personality were mainly carried out by anthropologists, many psychologists took an interest in them as well. Thus, Erikson's book *Childhood and Society* (1950) was received with enthusiasm. In the first edition of the *Handbook of Social Psychology*, there were two chapters on culture and psychology, the one by Inkeles and Levinson and the other by one of the leading representatives of US cultural anthropology, Clyde Kluckhuhn (1954). But then, as David Winter and Nicole Barenbaum (1999) noted, interest declined after 1960, and not until the 1980s did it return. One of the researchers who has been faithful to this research tradition from the beginning of the 1960s, Harry Triandis (1997), has discussed the difficulty of defining culture and suggested how it might be overcome. The fourth edition of the *Handbook of Social Psychology* (1998) has a chapter reviewing modern studies of culture and psychology.

The Authoritarian Personality

One study of the relationship between culture and personality, *The Authoritarian Personality* by Theodor Adorno et al. (1950) became a classic. The researchers, a group of immigrants to the United States working at the University of California, Berkeley, carried out extensive investigations of prejudice and authoritarianism. The researchers represented the ideas of the Frankfurt school of philosophy, which aimed to fuse psychoanalysis and Marxism.

The underlying idea is that specific socialization practices create a personality type, the authoritarian personality, which is prone to accept a dictatorial system such as Nazism. The authoritarian personality is characterized by a syndrome of traits, chief among which are obedience to authority, conventionality, rigidity in thinking, and hostility to minority groups and people manifesting deviant behavior. The authoritarian syndrome is the result of child-rearing practiced by status-driven, dominant, strict, and punitive parents who suppress sexual and aggressive impulses in children and expect them to be obedient and respectful. The Berkeley group considered hostility to minority groups low in personal power to be the result of an ego-defensive mechanism as well as a substitute for a reaction to a more powerful oppressor (the *scapegoat theory of prejudice*).

A major problem for the Berkeley group was to find support for the belief that people vary with regard to characteristics contained in the authoritarian syndrome. To demonstrate this, the group first worked out a scale to measure the degree of anti-Semitism, and a scale to measure ethnocentricism as a general attitude. Having constructed these scales, the group selected for interview forty persons scoring high and forty scoring low on the ethnocentrism scale. On the basis of these interviews and psychoanalytic theory, the researchers constructed a third scale, the so-called F-(fascism) Scale. They then correlated the performance of a group of subjects on the F-Scale with the group's performance on the Anti-Semitism Scale. They found a high positive correlation, suggesting that there is an authoritarian syndrome related to prejudice against minority groups.

Despite these findings, the belief that an authoritarian personality type is produced by specific child-rearing practices was merely postulated on the basis of the interviews and psychoanalytic theory. As we shall see in Chapter 19, it is difficult to maintain adequate control of studies of the effects of child rearing on personality, and it is particularly difficult to control for genetic differences. An alternative to the psychoanalytic view adopted by the Berkeley group is that some children have genetic dispositions that attract them to values adhered to by authoritarian persons.

The theory of the authoritarian personality could explain how the Nazi Party could seize power, but this historical event could also be explained by several other factors. Germany had been through a long, brutalizing war, had been forced to accept a humiliating peace treaty, was in deep economic depression, and had a new democratic constitution with little support in the population. Further, the Nazi leaders represented a tightly knit group of unscrupulous people with an extraordinary gift for political tactics. The theory of the authoritarian personality could at best form part of a complex explanation of Nazism.

As noted by Susan Fiske (1998, pp. 358–359), research on the authoritarian personality fell into disfavor after a decade, but it resurfaced in the construction of a new scale of authoritarianism relating to prejudice and stereotyping. Further, as Alice Eagley and Shelly Chaiken (1998, p. 303) point out, the belief that the authoritarian attitude functions as an ego-defensive mechanism has been investigated but with mixed results.

The Crisis in the Study of Personality

In the 1950s, there was considerable interest in the personality theories of Gordon Allport, Rogers, and Kelly, and in psychodynamic theories as well. Substantial progress was also made in the trait descriptions of personality, as we shall see in Chapter 18. Nevertheless, at the end of the 1960s, interest in personality psychology declined. Social psychologists studied many of the same problems as personality psychologists, but they tended to view them as the result of the influence exerted by the situation, not personality characteristics. In the 1960s, social psychologists seemed to have had great success in their use of the experimental method, and social psychology gained in popularity, to the detriment of personality psychology, which seemed to work with more primitive methods. Skinner and other learning theorists regarded the concept of personality as unnecessary.

Thus, strong tendencies in the 1960s led many psychologists to doubt that the study of personality should be a specific area of psychology. At the end of the 1960s and the beginning of the 1970s, personality psychology was attacked from various quarters. Particularly effective was the criticism raised by Walter Mischel (1968), a student of Kelly, in a book titled *Personality and Assessment*. A main point Mischel made was that there is little consistency in behavior from situation to situation. Behavior is much more specific to situations than personality psychologists assumed. Mischel drew particular attention to the low correlations – usually not higher than .3 – between actual behavior in single situations and measures obtained on personality scales based on traits. His criticism revived the person–situation debate, which had started earlier in the century. Mischel also reminded psychologists of the study undertaken by Hartshorne and May in 1928 on the moral behavior of children. The results of this study could be interpreted to show that the behavior of the children was not consistent. For example, a child might lie, cheat, or steal in one situation but not in another. Mischel cited a number of other studies showing a lack of consistency from situation to situation.

The criticism by Mischel and others led to a crisis in the study of personality. However, personality psychologists slowly found answers to some of the most pressing questions about their research, and the area regained its vigor in the late 1970s. To this development I shall return in Chapter 18.

16

The Study of Cognition in Europe and the United States (1920–1960)

Three Influential European Cognitive Psychologists: Piaget, Vygotsky, and Bartlett

Extensive research in cognition took place in the United States and Europe throughout the first half of the twentieth century. In Europe, where American behaviorism had little influence, some of the most creative and influential cognitive psychologists did most of their work.

Jean Piaget, a dominant figure not only in child psychology but also in cognitive psychology, began his research in the 1920s. His early work was known in Europe and the United States, but it was not until the 1950s that he was recognized as a central figure in psychology. His Russian contemporary, Lev Vygotsky, exerted a profound influence on Soviet psychology from the 1930s, but his work first became influential in Western psychology in the 1960s. The Gestalt psychologists carried out extensive studies in cognition throughout the period 1920–60. The British psychologist Frederick Bartlett of Cambridge University began to have an impact on US cognitive psychology only in the 1960s, but his main work was already published in 1932, and so he belongs in this chapter.

The study of animal learning attracted the greatest interest among US experimental psychologists, but a number of researchers also pursued the study of memory in the Ebbinghaus–Müller tradition. Their work, as well as that of other US cognitive psychologists outside this tradition, has a place in the history of psychology and shall be reviewed in this chapter.

Jean Piaget (1896–1980)

Jean Piaget was interested and active in research in biology, logic, philosophy, and psychology. A book on language and egocentricity in children made him famous as early as 1924. His reputation as a central figure in child psychology rests mainly on his idea that philosophical problems, particularly logical problems, can be elucidated by a study of ontogenetic development. When his book *La psychologie de l'intelligence* (*The Psychology of Intelligence*) was translated into English in 1950, it aroused enormous interest, and in the 1950s and 1960s, this interest spread like wildfire. I shall concentrate on Piaget's ideas of language and egocentricity, and the development of intelligence and logical thinking.

To obtain a perspective on his work, it is useful to view Piaget against a background of European and particularly French intellectual life in the early decades of the 1900s. During an early stay in Paris in 1919, he worked for some time with Henri Simon, Binet's coworker. Piaget's ideas of intelligence are frequently contrasted with those of Binet. While Binet regarded intelligence as developing more or less continuously through childhood, Piaget believed it developed in stages, each of which is characterized by the child's mastery of new logical relationships. Thus, according to Piaget, the child's thinking is qualitatively different from that of the adult. Actually, Binet had discussed this idea in one of his last papers. Therefore, even if Binet tended to regard the development of intelligence as continuous, he had realized that thinking in the child and in the adult might be qualitatively different.

A central idea of Piaget is that cognition is closely related to the organism's movements. Kant had emphasized the dependence of thought on action, and Jackson had introduced this idea into his neurology. Throughout his career, Janet was concerned with the idea of the close relationship between cognition and action. Piaget was acquainted with Janet during his first stay in Paris, and the French psychologist may have helped draw Piaget's attention to this relationship.

Even more important to Piaget than the ideas of Binet and Janet were the ideas of the American psychologist James Baldwin, who had left the United States after a scandal and settled in Paris. As mentioned in Chapter 11, in a number of books Baldwin had accounted for the way he thought philosophical problems could be elucidated by a study of human ontogenesis. In a massive work, he had also argued that intelligence develops through a number of logical stages. Moreover, he had made efforts to find a substitute for the concept of stimulus, and he had introduced the concept of assimilation, which is very similar to Piaget's concept of assimilation to be discussed later in this chapter. Baldwin was a friend of Janet, and although Piaget does not appear to have met Baldwin, the similarities in their work are so conspicuous that it is highly probable, as Robert Cairns (1992) maintained, that Piaget drew some of his main ideas from Baldwin. The similarities are further corroborated in the collection of studies on developmental psychology by Baldwin, edited by John Broughton and D. G. Freeman-Moir (1982).

A Brief Biography

Piaget had no formal training in psychology. Like his Russian contemporary Lev Vygotsky, he approached psychological problems from an interest kindled by his work in other areas of study. Piaget, who was born and raised in Neuchâtel, Switzerland, developed an early interest in biology, and even before he entered university, he had written several scientific articles in this field. He received his doctorate in biology at the university in his home town in 1918. He was also interested in abnormal psychology, and after completing studies for his doctorate, he spent a year in Zürich studying psychiatry with Eugen Bleuler among others. During this year, Piaget became acquainted with Jung and read Freud.

In 1919, Piaget went to Paris, where he continued his studies at La Salpêtrière and, as already mentioned, became acquainted with Janet and worked with Simon. He also studied the philosophy of science and logic at the Sorbonne. He continued these studies throughout his life and participated in international debates on problems in these areas of philosophy. In 1921, Édouard Claparède (1873–1940) brought Piaget to the Institut de J.-J. Rousseau, a center for studies in child psychology and education established on Claparède's initiative in 1912. Piaget remained at this institute until 1955, when he became the director of the Centre international d'épistémologie génétique. Early on, he was attached to the University of Geneva, where he held a professorial position for most of his career. Further, he held a several positions at the Sorbonne from 1952 to 1963.

As his biography makes clear, Piaget not only grew up in the French-speaking part of Switzerland but was also closely linked to French culture and science. For this reason, it is natural to see him as a representative of French thinking and psychology, even if he was born and lived in Switzerland for the greater part of his life. Piaget wrote a large number of books, including *The Language and Thought of the Child* (1924/1926); *The Moral Judgment of the Child* (1932/1965); *The Psychology of Intelligence* (1947/1950), which contains lectures Piaget gave in Paris in 1942; and *The Psychology of the Child* (1969), with Bärbel Inhelder.

The Genetic–Epistemological Approach

Before Piaget's work, Binet and Simon had studied the development of intelligence in children, and Binet had studied thinking in his two daughters. Back in 1877, Darwin had published his report on one of his children, and, inspired by him, Preyer had described in detail the development of one of his sons, with an emphasis on the development of the sensory processes and of language. Shortly after Preyer began his work, Hall carried out extensive investigations of the way children's knowledge increases with age. At the beginning of the century, Thorndike had also begun to study learning in children. Both Hall and Thorndike had numerous students. Child psychology was thus an active field of research at the time Piaget began his work.

Piaget's revival of Baldwin's genetic-epistemological approach – an approach relating to the genesis or origin of knowledge and thinking – did, however, bring something important and new. Piaget was interested in the way central concepts in science develop in ontogenesis, and, together with coworkers, he carefully studied children's conceptions of space, time, quantity, velocity, reality, number, and causality. Moreover, like Baldwin before him, he was interested in the development of children's understanding of logical relationships. To Piaget, intelligence was primarily the mastery of problems of a logical nature. Of all his work, his study of the development of the ability to understand logical relationships has received the most attention. Piaget also undertook studies of the development of morality in children that were later continued by Lawrence Kohlberg (1982). (For a review of the genetic studies of philosophical problems in Baldwin and Piaget, see Broughton and Freeman-Moir, 1982.).

Egocentricity in Children

Piaget attracted the attention of child psychologists when, in his book on language and thought published in 1924, he claimed that children, even after reaching six or seven years of age, still have a poorly developed ability to understand that others could have a different perspective on certain aspects of the environment. Children, he said, are egocentric. He had noticed that children as old as seven said many things that did not appear to be directed to another person, and that also did not appear to be spoken with the purpose of giving information to another person. He referred to this type of speech as *egocentric language* and contrasted it to *socialized language*, speech directed to another person as a means of communicating something. By comparing the number of utterances of the two types, he worked out a measure he thought would indicate the degree to which the child was egocentric. Based on this measure, he concluded that until about age seven the child seems to talk to itself, and to have a highly limited understanding of how other people perceive their environment.

As John Macnamara (1982) suggested, a more careful examination of the relationship between language and thinking would have convinced Piaget that his view of egocentricity was probably wrong. According to MacNamara, to be able to acquire the use of language, a child must have a highly developed ability of logical thinking. Consider, for example, the difference between definite and indefinite articles. We use the indefinite article when we introduce some person or object unknown to the person to whom we speak, and the definite article when we refer to some person or object known to the person. In other words, in order to use the indefinite and the definite articles correctly, we must adopt the perspective of the other person. Investigations have shown that the child masters this logical problem as early as the age of four.

Before I leave Piaget's early study of language and thought, I shall mention that even if his view of the egocentricity of the child was inadequate, he recognized that many utterances of young children do not seem to be clearly directed to other persons. Inspired by Piaget, Vygotsky, as we shall see, used this finding to show how he thought language became a means of thinking. Moreover, Piaget's study of egocentricity in children highlighted for child psychologists the problem of finding out when and how children learn to adopt the perspective of others.

Stages in Logical Thinking

Elaborating the idea of a qualitative difference in the thinking of children and adults, and the idea of separate stages of development, Piaget constructed a theory of cognitive development according to which the child passes through four main stages, at each of which the child is able to solve tasks he or she could not solve before. Individual children pass through the stages at different ages, so the age at which children generally master a certain type of task could be indicated only approximately. Piaget first presented his *cognitive stage theory* in a series of lectures given in Paris in 1942. The four stages are still described and discussed in most modern textbooks; I shall give a brief description of them.

The Sensorimotor Stage

Piaget called the first stage the *sensorimotor* stage. It extends from birth to about eighteen months to two years. The designation "sensorimotor" was chosen to underline that perception and movement are closely connected, and also that the connection does not contain a cognitive element. At this stage, the child gradually acquires an understanding of the consequences of its acts: objects can be moved, glasses of milk can be overturned, and plates can fall from the table and break.

At this stage, it is also of particular importance that the child gradually achieves an awareness that objects continue to exist even when they are no longer perceptually present; that is, when the child does not receive a direct stimulation from the objects. Piaget's procedure for determining whether objects had achieved *object permanence* was simply to cover or remove an object, such as a toy to which the child was attentive. If the child did not reveal any sign that he had registered a change in respect to the presence of the object, Piaget concluded that the child had not yet achieved object permanence. He found that children as old as eight months do not seem to have developed object permanence. Not until approximately the age of ten months does the child develop this ability.

The Preoperational Stage

The second stage extends roughly from two to seven years. Piaget held that during the sensorimotor stage the child acquires the ability to understand and use symbols. Children display this ability in their play, as when a stick may represent a car or a person. Still, on reaching the second stage, the child is not able to use what Piaget called *logical operations* or mental transformations, such as changing the form of an object and then making new changes that restore the original. Piaget referred to the ability to carry out these transformations as *reversibility*. He called the ability to understand that logical operations are reversible *conservation* and claimed that conservation does not occur until the end of the second stage. Because children are unable to perform logical operations at this stage, he designated it the *preoperational* stage.

In support of the belief that children do not have the ability to understand conservation until the end of the second stage, Piaget presented them with tasks that require an understanding that changes have taken place. In one task, he presented the child with two ball-shaped lumps of clay and asked whether the child agreed the lumps were equally large. Then he would shape one of the lumps into a cylinder and ask whether the lumps were still equally large. If the child did not agree, Piaget concluded the child did not have an understanding of conservation.

In another procedure, he began by presenting the child with two glasses of the same shape, filled with water to the same level, and asked whether the quantity was the same in both glasses. He then poured the water from one of the glasses into a thinner and taller glass and asked whether the quantity was still the same. To examine the understanding of conservation in respect to number, he placed glass beads or other objects in two rows in such a way that it was evident each row contained the same number. He then changed the form of one of the rows by bringing the beads or objects closer together and asked whether the number was the same in the two groups. The results of all three types of tasks were the same. Not until the end of the second stage did the child show that he or she could solve the tasks.

The Concrete–Operational Stage

The third stage, extending from about seven to eleven years, is the *concrete-operational* stage. Here the child has acquired the ability to perform logical operations but only if they are performed with material to which the child can immediately react. For example, the child can recognize that if we have equal amounts of water in two identical glasses, but then pour the water from one of the glasses into a taller, thinner glass, the amount of water in the new glass is still the same as before. But presented in the abstract, the child is not capable of making the same conclusion. The child's thinking could be characterized as dependent on the here and now.

The Formal–Operational Stage

The *formal-operational* stage is fourth and extends from about eleven to –fourteen years of age. I shall only mention about this stage that Piaget believed the child does not attain it until he or she has mastered the logical operations that characterize the thinking of the mature, adult human being.

Cognition and Bodily Movements

A central point in Piaget's theory was that cognition is closely tied to bodily movements. To account for the relationship between cognition and bodily movements, Piaget introduced the concepts of schema and assimilation. A *schema* is a sensorimotor connection that has been modified by being connected to new sensory aspects. A schema is formed, for instance, when a child begins to suck objects other than the mother's breast, like a rattle or a thumb. By means of the schema, the organism makes contact with the environment. Aspects of the environment that the organism experiences by following or employing a schema are, according to Piaget, assimilated. Hence, to explain how the organism is oriented to the environment, Piaget did not start with the concept of a stimulus. Instead, he based his account on the idea of a sensorimotor reaction that occurs through processes he called *assimilation*.

Existing schemas are not always sufficient to keep the organism in equilibrium with its environment. To achieve equilibrium, the schemas must be changed. This, Piaget said, takes place by a process of *accommodation*. The process or processes maintaining equilibrium he called *equilibration*. Piaget took the concept of the physiological reflex as his starting point.

As I see it, it is difficult to understand what Piaget meant by the four terms he introduced here. What characterizes the physiological reflex is simply the fact that it is elicited by a definite stimulus. For example, an object placed in the mouth of a mammal elicits a salivary reaction, and touching the lips of a newborn mammal elicits a sucking reflex. Further, Piaget apparently held that schemas are transformed gradually into logical operations. On this point, his thinking seems to lack coherence. Nor did he refer to any concrete biological knowledge enabling him to move from the idea of reflexes to logical operations. I believe, therefore, that Piaget did not show that movements are necessary for the development of cognition. Of course, to do him justice, we must remember that psychologists still do not have a reasonable explanation of the way an external physical stimulation becomes connected to an organism's movements and responses.

Evaluation of the Stage Theory

An enormous number of studies have been conducted to confirm or refute Piaget's stage theory. I shall review some salient points in the research literature and begin by examining his idea that cognition (intelligence) originates in ontogenesis in sensorimotor reactions. Piaget wanted to develop an alternative to Pavlov's theory, but, as I have already mentioned, it is difficult to understand how the movement involved in a physiological reflex can be connected to stimuli other than those eliciting the reflexive movement, unless this takes place by Pavlovian conditioning. This, in my opinion, makes Piaget's concepts of schema and assimilation virtually useless.

An infant manifesting object permanence is evidently in possession of cognitive processes of some sort. Therefore, Piaget attached great importance to his finding that the infant does not know object permanence until the age of about eight months. However, experiments by Renée Baillargeon (1987) suggest that the infant grasps object permanence as early as four and a half months. In all, there seems to be no evidence that cognition originates in ontogenesis at the sensorimotor stage as postulated by Piaget.

Still, even if the idea of a sensorimotor stage is not an apt one, Piaget must be credited with having shown that understanding that objects have permanence is of central importance in our cognition, and that it is of interest to find out when and how this ability is attained.

With regard to the second and third stages, researchers have shown that the ability to remember past events may influence the answers children give in the conservation tasks. Apparently, motivation must also be taken into account. Further, results of research make clear that the child's ability to understand language and use it for communication are important factors affecting the solutions of the conservation tasks. Still further, it has been shown that children may master the same type of tasks at different chronological ages. This, of course, also raises a difficulty for the stage theory. Altogether, it seems reasonable to conclude that empirical research has given scant – if any – support to Piaget's stages.

In her evaluation of Piaget's work, Margareth Boden (1979, p. 153) noted, as an important drawback, "his general failure to appreciate alternative explanations." Like Freud and Skinner, Piaget was reluctant to relate his studies to the work of other researchers. In particular, Binet and Simon's alternative view of intelligence as a gradual increase in knowledge might have helped him to formulate his problems more productively.

If the stage theory had been formulated in a consistent and coherent manner and supported by empirical evidence, Piaget would have revolutionized child psychology. However, if it is correct, as I have maintained, that the theory is incoherent and lacking empirical support, his contributions mainly consist of having raised some important problems, such as how we learn to adopt the perspective of other persons, and when and how we attain object permanence. Piaget must also be credited with having shown that an increase in intelligence is the result not only of an increase in knowledge, but also of an improvement in the ability to handle logical problems.

Lev Vygotsky (1896–1934)

The communist revolution in Russia in 1917 was followed by civil wars, political unrest, famine, and economic depression. Still, until the communist regime under Stalin gained control over political, social, and cultural life, innovative ideas were produced in art, poetry, the study of language, and psychology. Of the work done in psychology, only that of Lev Vygotsky still interests not only Russian but also many Western psychologists.

Notes About Vygotsky's Life

Like his contemporary Piaget, Lev Vygotsky had wide interests in philosophy and science, and, also like him, he seems to have begun a study of psychology with a view to clarifying other areas of academic research. While Piaget was mainly interested in epistemology, Vygotsky seems to have been drawn to the history of culture and art. For both men, the study of the intellectual development of the child was a means of clarifying problems traditionally considered outside psychology.

Vygotsky graduated from the University of Moscow in 1917 with a degree in law, but he had also studied history, language, and philosophy. After graduation, he settled in the town of Gomel in Belarus, lecturing on literature and psychology at a teachers' college. While in Gomel, he finished a treatise on the psychology of art, which he presented as a PhD thesis at the Institute of Psychology of the University of Moscow in 1925. The year before, he had presented a paper on the methodology of psychological studies at a psychoneurological congress held in St Petersburg. His paper aroused the interest of Alexander Luria, who was secretary of the Institute of Psychology at the University of Moscow, and he was able to bring Vygotsky to the Institute as a research fellow. Vygotsky stayed in Moscow until his death in 1934, first attached to the Institute of Psychology and then to the Institute of Defectology. The latter institute was founded by Vygotsky for the study and treatment of children with physical and psychological handicaps.

When Stalin tightened party control at the beginning of the 1930s, Vygotsky's work was condemned as heresy. After Stalin's death in 1953, it was again considered legitimate to be interested in his ideas, and, as Alex Kozulin (1986) remarked in the introduction to his translation into English of Vygotsky's *Thought and Language* (1934/1986), Vygotsky's theory "has broken the linguistic, cultural, and ideological barriers and is about to become a topic of international interest and study." In the years following, interest in Vygotsky's work does not seem to have abated. Vygotsky had contracted tuberculosis during his early years in Gomol and eventually died from this disease.

Vygotsky, Marx, and Wundt

The ideas of dialectical and historical materialism played a central role in Vygotsky's thinking. Marx and Engels had argued that not only society but also human consciousness is determined by economic and technological factors. They had called attention to the role tools play in the development of society and human beings, and, as Michael Cole et al. (1978) note, Vygotsky extended the idea of the role of tools to include all kinds of signs, claiming that the use of signs had led to the development of society as well as to the development of human consciousness.

Vygotsky combined the idea of the role of signs in the development of consciousness with Wundt's idea that the higher mental processes must be studied as they were manifested in our cultural history, in language, ritual, and myth. Like Wundt, Vygotsky distinguished between psychological processes of an elementary nature and higher mental processes. To account for the latter, he proposed they are the result of the use of signs. Signs originated in culture. Hence, by learning to master the use of signs, human beings become members of the culture in which they grow up, and because the use of signs also results in the development of mind, the human mind could be seen as a product of culture. Thus, by extending the Marxist idea of the role played by tools in the development of society and humans to signs of a cultural nature, Vygotsky thought he could bridge the gap between Marxist philosophy and Wundtian psychology. Vygotsky's and George Herbert Mead's thinking have important points in common. They do not seem to have known each other; the similarity is probably due to the fact that they both were inspired by Marx and Wundt.

I shall here deal primarily with Vygotsky's theory of how thinking and language develop in the child, although his studies went beyond that.

Vygotsky on the Development of Language

Vygotsky (1934/1986, ch. 1) began his examination of thought and language by insisting that a word is a union between sound and meaning, not a mechanical association between the two. Yet he held (ch. 4) that an examination of the behavior of chimpanzees shows they have thought but not speech, and from this he concluded that thought and speech have different phylogenetic roots. In human ontogenesis, the two roots are not so easily discernible as they are in human phylogenesis, but here it is also possible, he said, to discern them. Thus, according to Vygotsky, we find in the infant's speech development a prelinguistic cognitive stage. However, at about the age of two, thought and language (speech) fuse together, forming verbal thought.

Inner Speech

What Vygotsky called *inner speech*, or speech to oneself, originates in the further development of thought and language. Vygotsky attributed great importance to inner speech and gave an interesting and detailed account of its development, of which I shall review some points.

His starting point was Piaget's study of egocentric speech, speech that does not seem to be directed to another person. Piaget had explained egocentric speech by assuming that at the earliest developmental stages, the child's thinking is autistic. Vygotsky, in contrast, held that the child is social from birth and that speech too is social from the onset. However, from the age of three, the child increasingly directs speech to himself or herself as a means of thinking. As language develops into inner speech, vocalization is gradually eliminated until inner speech becomes inaudible. So, whereas Piaget assumed that at the age of seven language ceases to be egocentric, Vygotsky held that at this time inner speech has become inaudible.

Vygotsky (1934/1986) supported his hypothesis of inner speech by observing the language development of children as well as by experimenting. His observations agreed with those of Piaget with regard to the frequency of egocentric speech; the frequency dropped with increasing age from three to seven. However, with increasing age the child's speech becomes more inscrutable, more difficult to understand, and the changes egocentric speech undergoes are in line with what is to be expected if it were a means of thinking.

To demonstrate that egocentric speech is actually used as a means of thinking, Vygotsky performed experiments in which he manipulated the conditions under which the child produces it. If egocentric speech is a means of thinking, we would expect it to increase if the child has difficulty in performing a task. To test this hypothesis, Vygotsky placed the child in a situation in which he or she suddenly found there was no pencil or crayon to use for drawing. As expected, egocentric speech increased.

Further, to demonstrate that egocentric speech is social in nature, Vygotsky performed experiments in which the immediate social relationships of the child were weakened by placing the child alone or with children who did not understand the child's language. In these situations, the frequency dropped, as was to be expected from his hypothesis.

Concluding Remarks

To understand Vygotsky's view of language and thinking, let us compare it to the views of Watson and Piaget.

As noted in Chapter 12, Watson believed the development of language in the child could be accounted for without any assumptions about thought processes. In contrast, Piaget and Vygotsky believed language development presupposes the ability to think. The two disagreed, however, on the role attributed to language in thinking. Whereas Piaget paid little attention to language in the development of thinking in the child, Vygotsky made it central in the form of inner speech.

Vygotsky assumed a study of egocentric speech would help him settle the disagreement between Piaget and himself. This may be disputed. Even if he was right in believing egocentric speech to be directed to the child, this does not mean it has a function in the child's thinking. Thus, the experiments performed by Vygotsky may be taken as evidence against Piaget's view of egocentric speech, but not as evidence for Vygotsky's hypothesis about the role played by language – in the form of inner speech – in thinking. A study of child development along the lines suggested by Vygotsky does not seem to produce evidence for his hypothesis.

Related to the belief that higher forms of thinking occur as a form of inner speech is the belief that words serve as tools. To make the analogy between words and tools useful in empirical research, I believe we must explain how words obtain their status as tools and symbols. Thus, Vygotsky would have had to give an account of how human beings learn to speak during their ontogenetic development. To my knowledge, he gave no satisfactory account of language development. This may seriously limit the usefulness of his analogy.

Vygotsky's ideas about thinking, language, child development, and culture appealed strongly to intellectuals of the first decade of the Soviet state. He attracted a number of gifted students, and throughout the communist era, Russian psychologists produced original ideas. However, psychological thinking in this era became so entangled with Marxist philosophy that it is difficult to assess its value independently of an assessment of Soviet Marxist philosophy. Many Russian intellectuals, including Vygotsky, were fascinated by this philosophy and took a stand relating to it. From the mid-1930s, as Kozulin (1986) reported, the communist regime expected that psychologists would derive their concepts directly from the works of Marx, Engels, and Lenin. This naturally restricted their freedom.

One of Vygotsky's students, Alexei Leontiev (1903–1979), criticized him for conceiving of culture and society too narrowly. Based on Marxist philosophy, Leontiev worked out a complex theory explaining how human beings become members of society and culture through their mental and social activity. By 1936, this theory of the activity of the mind had achieved the status of official Soviet psychological doctrine. For reasons stated above, I shall not go into this theory.

Alexander Luria, who brought Vygotsky to Moscow, turned his own interests to neuropsychology, probably to avoid being entangled in questions of official Marxist doctrine. Luria (1973) became a distinguished neuropsychologist, respected in the Soviet Union as well as in the West. With the cooperation of US colleagues, his ideas about assessing the effects of neurological damage have been worked into the Luria–Nebraska Neuropsychological Battery.

British Psychology and Frederic Bartlett (1886–1979)

As shown in Chapters 6 and 7, British researchers made substantial contributions to comparative psychology and to the study of individual differences by means of tests. However, Great Britain had no researchers doing productive experimental work in psychology during the latter half of the nineteenth century. Titchener helped create interest in experimental psychology in the United States, but in his native country, there was no one who effectively promoted experimental psychology.

Towards the end of the 1800s, as Hearnshaw (1964) showed, a rather abrupt change occurred in the intellectual climate in Britain. British empirical philosophy was supplanted by versions of Hegelianism and idealist philosophies, and views of human nature more in line with conventional morality and religion were predominant. This was an intellectual climate unfriendly to a scientific empirical psychology, and there was a scarcity of positions and laboratories for psychologists. As late as 1920, even a psychologist of the caliber of McDougall left the country in the hope of finding more favorable conditions for psychological research in the United States.

When experimental psychology finally evolved in Great Britain, it was, according to Boring (1929/1950), in close contact with the philosophy of mind predominate at British universities. The man who must be given a good deal of credit for establishing this branch of psychology is Frederic Bartlett. Bartlett was appointed reader of experimental psychology at Cambridge in 1922 and professor of the subject in 1931. Prior to his appointment, he had done work in anthropology and social psychology, and his first book in psychology was entitled *Psychology and Primitive Culture* (1923). In 1932, he published his most influential book, *Remembering*, and after retirement, in 1958, a book on thinking. Through his book on memory, Bartlett influenced the new cognitive psychology emerging in Great Britain and the United States in the 1950s and 1960s.

Bartlett also influenced psychology through his work in applied psychology. The Unit of Applied Psychology at Cambridge, which he directed, became particularly known for research on psychological problems arising in connection with the use of instruments for navigation and communication devised during and after World War II. The Unit of Applied Psychology became a center for the new *information-processing approach* to the study of cognition. Bartlett trained a number of experimental psychologists who obtained leading positions in British psychology. He was knighted in 1948.

Bartlett's Ambivalence About Experimental Psychology

Strange as it may sound, Bartlett was rather ambivalent about experimental psychology. Alan Costall (1995) suggested this ambivalence may have arisen because Bartlett's prime interest was in social and not experimental psychology. Another reason may have been that, like James Ward (1843–1925), the philosopher dominating psychological thinking at Cambridge, Bartlett may have doubted that the more fundamental questions of psychology could be answered by experiments.

Ward, who also influenced William James, was an original thinker who could present complex psychological problems in a clear and systematic manner. An extensive article of his in the *Encyclopaedia Britannica* in 1886 was much admired. Having studied in Germany and become familiar with German physiology and experimental psychology, Ward was not opposed to experimental psychology but allotted it only a minor place in his philosophy of mind. Highly dependent on Ward's ideas of psychology, Bartlett was thus understandably ambivalent. The experiments he performed were exploratory in nature and the results were reported without the use of statistics.

Bartlett's Study of Remembering

A central idea in Ward's (1886) philosophy of mind is that mental representations never appear as separate, discrete entities; they always form part of other representations. Thus, no representation can be regarded as entirely new because it always must be seen as closely connected to other mental representations. Ward therefore held that learning and remembering cannot be accounted for as associations between discrete elements.

We can see Bartlett's experimental work as an elaboration and exploration of Ward's idea. Bartlett insisted that remembering is always affected by previous experience, motivational and emotional states, and values and culture. This view of remembering was extended to other mental functions, to perceiving, imagining, and thinking. Hence, these functions have fundamental points in common with remembering. In *Remembering*, Bartlett (1932) presented experiments on perceiving and imagining and discussed thinking. His book might therefore appropriately have been entitled *A Study of Cognition*.

Bartlett is mainly known for his studies of recall, but since he insisted that the results of his research on perception illustrated the processes taking place in remembering, I shall briefly review some of this research. In the experiments on visual perception, he used material of varying degrees of complexity. I shall only report on the studies where he used simple designs.

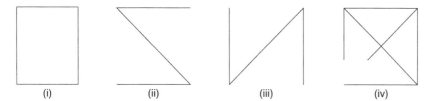

Figure 16.1 Figures used in Bartlett's experiments on perception.

The simple designs (Figure 16.1) were presented for a brief time interval (0.067–0.25 second). After the presentation, the subjects were asked to draw what they had seen. If they experienced difficulty with the drawings, they were asked to describe what they had seen. The subjects would also frequently make spontaneous comments on their drawings.

On the basis of the drawings and comments, Bartlett concluded the following: 1. perception is dominated by specific details; 2. the perceiver provides a frame, a setting for what is perceived; 3. temperament, attitude, and values often direct the course and determine the content of perceiving; 4. perception is the result of an inferential process.

The subjects' responses were not rigorously classified according to specific criteria, nor were they subjected to statistical tests. Further, no controls were introduced to rule out interpretations other than those advanced by Bartlett. The most serious objection is probably that the responses were given *after* and not simultaneously with the presentation of the material. This raises the question of whether the experiments should count as experiments in perception. I think the German researchers in perception, from Helmholtz and Hering to the Gestalt psychologists, would have objected to this procedure. They would have pointed out that the sensory organs react extremely quickly to changes in stimulation. Recall after presentation would therefore *not* reflect the processes involved in perception. Bartlett had no data that could convincingly overcome this objection. Later in this chapter, we shall meet this problem in the debate over the so-called New Look in perception. The debate is still going on in the twenty-first century. Yet, even if Bartlett's conclusions had only scant support in the experimental results, they contained some ideas that were new in experimental psychology.

Ward's and Bartlett's ideas of learning and remembering deviated strongly from those of Ebbinghaus. Believing firmly in the principles of association, Ebbinghaus had tried to rule out the effects of previous experience in the subjects by constructing his lists of meaningless syllables. In contrast, Bartlett (1932) naturally wanted to allow the previous experience of his subjects to enter maximally into the memory processes. He used various types of material, including short stories. His subjects read each story twice and then reproduced it repeatedly at different time intervals, giving Ebbinghaus a number of reproductions from each subject that could be ordered serially.

One story was "The War of the Ghosts," from the folklore of a Native American tribe. Ghosts are very important to the story, but to a person unfamiliar with the folklore, the plot would appear to run approximately as follows. Two young Native Americans hunting seals are invited by a war party in canoes to attack a group living further up the river. One of the two excuses himself while the other one joins the war party. This second youth is wounded, and when he is brought home, he lives through the night but dies at sunrise.

Reproducing the story, the subjects tended to omit telling about the ghosts and reacted to the story in their own way, adding and omitting details and making their accounts more consistent. Bartlett found that the reproductions varied somewhat with the lengths of the time intervals, but for all intervals there was a tendency to construct a setting that provided a frame for the reproduction of the stories. Further, there was a tendency to find explanations for the events reported in the stories. On the basis of these and other results, Bartlett concluded that we seek meaning in remembering, and that remembering must be seen as a constructive process and not as an exact, literal rendering of the material to be remembered.

In accounting for his theoretical position, Bartlett introduced the concept of the schema. By *schema*, he had in mind an organization of previous experience relevant to the event to be remembered – thus a mental structure of some sort. However, as I understand him, schemas are not static structures but vary with the motivational and emotional states of the person as well as with the object of cognition. Bartlett likened an instance of recall to a stroke in a game of tennis: "How I make the stroke depends on the relating of certain new experiences, most of them visual, to other immediately preceding visual experiences and to my postures, or balance of postures, at the moment."

The analogy may give us a notion of what he had in mind, but a scientific discussion would require a far more detailed specification. Bartlett's experiments on remembering were of the same exploratory nature as those on perceiving, and they are perhaps more appropriately regarded as illustrations of a point of view than as experiments to support a hypothesis.

While he was well aware of the difficulty of giving a clear definition of remembering, Bartlett failed to discuss the problems in finding procedures that would allow him to assess what his subjects had learned or understood after being presented with the material. Their understanding of the material, particularly the stories, might have been different from Bartlett's. Hence, what he regarded as transformations of the material in memory may simply have been transformations the material underwent in the subjects' attempts to understand it, to learn it. Perhaps, too, they were not always able to report their memories adequately. Thus, we may fault Bartlett for not being sufficiently aware of the difficulty in inferring from the subjects' behavior what they remembered.

Bartlett made an important point when he claimed that remembering is governed by previous experience, motivational and emotional states, and values and culture. But he overstated his point, overlooking that, as Woodworth (1938) insisted, memory is frequently a very exact rendering of some previous experience. In many instances, it does not seem to be the result of a search for meaning or of a new way of assembling items in previously presented material.

Ebbinghaus apparently took an extreme position when he tried to rule out the role played by meaning in remembering. But Bartlett may have taken an equally extreme position in attempting to rule out the ability human beings have for accurate retention.

When Bartlett started his work in cognition, the field was dominated by Ebbinghaus, but other psychologists used procedures similar to Bartlett's, as we can see from Woodworth's (1938) review of the study of memory. The Gestalt psychologists looked at perception and cognition from a different perspective than Bartlett, but they disagreed strongly with Ebbinghaus and emphasized that our mental experiences are structured. Koffka and one of his students had studied changes undergone by memory traces. This and Bartlett's study had important points in common. Further, as noted in Chapter 4, G. E. Müller had reported that his subjects seemed to strive to conceive of the material to be remembered in a way that made it appear meaningful to them. Bartlett neither discussed research based on procedures similar to his own nor related his position to that of the Gestalt psychologists. The quality of his work would have been improved if he had undertaken a scholarly examination of previous and contemporary research on memory.

The Study of Cognition in the United States (1920–1960)

In the twentieth century, extensive research on cognition took place in the United States. Inspired by Harvey Carr (1925) at the University of Chicago, Woodworth (1938) at Columbia, John McGeoch (1942) at the University of Iowa, and others, US psychologists continued the study of learning and memory that Ebbinghaus and G. E. Müller had begun. This study emphasized objective processes but not behavior. (Reviews of this research have been presented by Hovland, 1951; Cofer, 1979; and Hilgard, 1987.)

In the US study of verbal learning and memory, the point of departure was the idea that learning occurs by association, as Ebbinghaus and Müller had proposed. Like the two German psychologists, the US researchers primarily employed material consisting of lists of meaningless syllables, but also various forms of meaningful verbal material. The work focused on finding the most beneficial conditions for learning these types of materials and asked, for example, whether the learning process was most effective when the list was learned in one consecutive session, or whether it was better to learn a list as a whole or divide it into sections and then assemble the sections afterwards. The US researchers also continued the important studies initiated by Müller on retroactive and proactive inhibition as causes of forgetting.

Müller's laboratory team had begun to investigate how the learning of new material is influenced by previous learning. The problem, referred to as *transfer of learning*, was extensively studied by American psychologists in the first half of the 1900s. The reason interest appeared to lose momentum after the 1940s was probably, as Hovland (1951) pointed out, that it is difficult to formulate the problem in clear terms. This does not imply the issue is not important, however; we may even ask whether it is possible to provide an adequate account of learning without demonstrating how previous learning influences what is to be learned afterwards.

Research on Thinking

In addition to the extensive work they carried out on human learning and memory, US psychologists established the study of thinking in the form of *concept formation*. Asch and, Hull were the first to study concept formation. As material, Hull used Chinese characters with the root character in red and the differentiating strokes in black. He assigned nonsense syllables as names for each of the root characters and instructed the subjects to learn the names in the series. Hull thus performed the study without attempting to clarify the cognitive processes involved in the task. However, later researchers, such as Eugenia Hanfmann (1941), investigated the *strategies* subjects employed in a task requiring the classification of items. Hanfmann used a test originated by Vygotsky and, with Jacob Kasanin, developed the *Hanfmann–Kasanin Test*. The materials of the test are wooden blocks varying in color, shape, and size, and the task is to find blocks of the same kind as a block chosen by the experimenter. Using a similar type of material and procedure, Jerome Bruner et al. (1956) examined the role played by strategies in thinking.

A main difficulty in the study of strategies in thinking is to design tasks that can be regarded as representative of concept formation and thinking. The studies of Hanfmann and Bruner et al. have been criticized for being based on arbitrary, artificially constructed concepts and thus for lack of representativeness, and for being trivial.

In a chapter in the *Handbook of Experimental Psychology* (edited by Stanley Stevens), Robert Leeper (1951) made clear that the study of cognition had been carried out more or less continuously all through the first half of the twentieth century. Moreover, he pointed out that a more adequate idea of cognition would be formed if psychologists saw it not solely in terms of conscious experiences but also in terms of function. After a careful review of investigations performed since the days of the Würzburg psychologists, Leeper (1951, p. 736) concluded that we should see cognitive processes as including "all the means whereby the individual represents anything to himself or uses these representations as a means of guiding his behavior." This view of the study of cognition, based on the accumulation of knowledge through the first half of the twentieth century, was, as I see it, more or less identical to the one adopted by the cognitive psychologists of the latter half of the century.

The New Look in Perception

In his article on the reflex arc concept, Dewey had argued that whether an event is perceived or not depends not only on its physical characteristics but also on the state of the perceiver, and Bartlett had said perception and recognition are dependent not only upon the physical characteristics of the stimulation but also on the psychological orientation, the attitude, and the motivation of the perceiver.

At the end of the 1940s, an intense debate arose about whether perceptual processes are influenced by the previous experience, the motivational and emotional states, and the values of the perceiver. The debate was started by Jerome Bruner and Leo Postman (1947a, b), who presented experiments in support of this way of looking at perception. David Krech, who participated in the debate, jokingly called their view the "New Look in Perception," referring to a change in fashion, and the name has stuck. One reason the debate was so intense was that the belief that perception is affected by motivational and emotional states agreed with psychoanalytic ideas of defense mechanisms.

A number of experiments were performed in support of and against the New Look. It was then widely agreed that the experiments had been too poorly controlled to allow the conclusion that perception is affected by factors of the type suggested by proponents of the view. However, the issue was revived by Matthew Erdelyi (1974), who pointed out that the New Look agreed well with the way adherents of the information-processing approach conceived of perception. He also showed that many of the questions asked by the critics could be answered. Still, he could not refer to experiments that convincingly showed perception is affected by the factors suggested by the adherents of the New Look.

To my knowledge, the question of whether motivational and emotional factors affect perception has never been systematically discussed from a biological perspective. To adapt properly to their environments, our ancestors needed keen senses that could accurately detect food, including animal prey, and register danger. From an evolutionary point of view, it would probably have been highly detrimental to the species if the sensitivity and accuracy of perception had been reduced when our ancestors were hungry, frightened, or otherwise brought into a strong motivational or emotional state. Consequently, under normal external conditions, such as daylight illumination and an acoustic environment relatively free of noise, we should not expect an effect from motivational and emotional states. Since it seems to be a widespread experience, however, that imagining, remembering, and thinking frequently *are* affected by such states, we might expect effects to occur under less favorable external conditions. If this reasoning is sound, we need a more precise definition of perception than is now available to have a fruitful discussion of the role of motivation in perception.

As this chapter shows, all through the period in which behaviorist influence was at its height, the study of cognition was carried out by a number of productive and able psychologists. In the next chapter, I shall review the research of the neuropsychologists, which also reveals that cognitive problems held an important place in psychology in 1920–60.

17

Physiological Psychology

In the introductory chapter to this book, I emphasized the great role played by physiology, particularly the study of the brain, in early empirical psychology. German experimental psychology began as physiological psychology, and Russian psychology, originating in the study of reflexes, had a physiological basis. French and Austrian clinical psychology grew out of neurology and psychiatry. However, as we have seen in the preceding chapters, as empirical psychology developed, it tended to lose contact with physiology. This was apparent in experimental as well as clinical psychology, and in European as well as American psychology.

One possible reason that psychology and physiology did not become better integrated was that the two studies had not advanced far enough for researchers to visualize how to integrate them in a productive manner. At the beginning of the 1900s, empirical psychology had little to offer physiologists interested in extending their work to include the psychological studies of perceiving, remembering, learning, thinking, emotions, and motivation. Even as late as the mid-1900s, psychology still had little more for physiologists than intelligence tests.

Physiology, in contrast, had made considerable progress at the beginning of the 1900s, though little of it helped register activity going on in the nervous system. That had to be inferred from brain damage in human beings and lesions made in the brains of animals. Although most psychologists probably believed the phenomena they studied had a foundation in physiology, they were not able to see how they could use physiological knowledge productively to advance their study. When techniques for registering brain activity were finally developed in the mid-1900s, there was an explosion of interest in physiological psychology.

In this chapter, I shall begin by reporting on some of the main advances in the study of the brain in the latter half of the 1800s and the beginning of the 1900s. While these advances by and large were the result of European research, the development of the modern study of physiological psychology was mainly due to the efforts of psychologists of the United States. Then I shall report on two American researchers, Robert Woodworth and Walter Cannon, who both helped clarify the concept of motivation. Cannon also made substantial contributions to the study of emotions and stress. Along with Woodworth and Cannon, Karl Lashley contributed to the study of motivation. His main research, however, was directed towards localizing the psychological functions of the brain, and he promoted the study of *neuropsychology*. Having reviewed the work of Lashley and of some of the researchers working in his laboratories, I shall report on the progress made in registering activity in the brain, and some of the findings made by means of the new techniques introduced in neuropsychology.

Advances in Neurophysiology

In the study of the brain, researchers faced two somewhat different kinds of problems. On the one hand, they had to describe *the brain as a physical object*; they had to determine its shape, size, structure, and chemical composition. In the latter half of the 1700s, it had been discovered that the brain had electrostatic properties, and these had to be explored. On the other hand, researchers had to uncover the brain's role in the preservation and reproduction of the individual; they had to study *the brain as an organ of the organism*.

A breakthrough in the first problem came at the end of the 1800s and the beginning of the 1900s. Anatomists, headed by the Spaniard Santiago Ramon y Cajal, were able to demonstrate that nervous tissue, like the other types of bodily tissue, consists of discrete cells, later to be called *neurons*.

The view of the nervous tissue as composed of discrete cells raised the question of how the neurons are connected to each other and to muscle and gland cells. By the early twentieth century, we had gained considerable knowledge to answer this question. A leading researcher in that work was the Briton Charles Sherrington, who also gave the name *synapse* to the juncture where a neuron is connected to another neuron or to a muscle or gland cell. It took some time before most brain researchers accepted that the nervous system represents a network of discrete cells connected to each other by synapses. But gradually this view became the framework in terms of which the nervous system was studied.

By the beginning of the 1900s, researchers had also learned a great deal about the functions of the nervous system and how it regulates bodily activities such as respiration, blood circulation, digestion, and reproduction. At the same time, physiologists were making steady progress in the study of the senses. They had described the sensory organs and traced the nerve paths connecting them to the cerebral cortex. They had found that the paths from the sensory organs for smell, vision, hearing, and touch end in fairly well circumscribed areas of the cerebral cortex. These areas were referred to as *sensory cortical areas*. It was widely believed that the remaining areas of the cerebral cortex serve to relate the sensory areas to each other and to the motor area (already discovered). These were therefore called *association areas*.

In the early 1900s, as Stanley Singer (1994) recounts, there was fairly good agreement that the sensory and motor areas exist, but great disagreement about how to interpret these findings. While some held that sensory and psychological functions could be localized to specific parts of the cortex, others argued that the brain functions as a totality in such a way that no function is localizable to any specific part. Thus, the debate started by Gall and Flourens a century earlier was carried on and kept alive by Broca in the 1860s.

When psychology was established as an empirical science, physiologists and neurologists had already begun the study of a number of problems that were later included in empirical psychology. Researchers within the medical specialties mentioned continued to extend their study to new types of problems, independently of the development within psychology. At the beginning of the 1900s, not only sensory perception, hypnosis, learning by conditioning, and aphasia but also pain, emotions, sleep, and sexual reproduction were studied by physiologists and neurologists. Thus, just as there were two social psychologies, one within sociology and one within psychology, there were at the beginning of the twentieth century two physiological psychologies, one within neurophysiology and one within psychology.

To integrate physiology and psychology in a productive manner, researchers had to develop concepts that allowed them to deal with knowledge and problems in the two fields. In line with the plan of the book, I shall focus on this aspect of the history of physiological psychology.

Robert Sessions Woodworth (1869–1962)

Born in Belchertown, Massachusetts, the son of a Protestant minister, Robert Woodworth had a background similar to Thorndike's. He obtained a BA at Amherst College in 1891 and studied for an MA at Harvard from 1895 to 1897. At Harvard, he studied with William James and formed a lifelong friendship with Thorndike. After having been assistant in a course in physiology at Harvard Medical School, he joined Thorndike at Columbia as a student of Cattell. Here Woodworth received his PhD in 1899. He then taught physiology at various hospitals in New York and studied with Sherrington in Great Britain in 1902–1903. Working with Sherrington, Woodworth performed a neurophysiological study on pain and affect in cats. The next year he was employed at Columbia, first as an instructor and then from 1909 as a professor. He taught psychology at Columbia until the age of eighty-nine.

Regarding himself as a follower of James, Woodworth (1918, pp. 18–19) wanted to develop psychology as a broad field of research in which both an introspective and a behaviorist approach had a place. Still, even if psychology was broadly conceived of as including the study of consciousness as well as of behavior, it would still lack coherence. To make psychology a coherent study, Woodworth thought, brain physiology had to be included.

The breadth of Woodworth's interests in psychology is reflected in four widely used textbooks. In 1911, he undertook a revision of the textbook on physiological psychology written by Ladd. It became the standard textbook in the area for twenty-five years. In 1921, he published an introductory textbook: *Psychology: A Study of Mental Life*, which dominated the field until Ernest Hilgard's *Introduction to Psychology* appeared in 1953. In 1933, Woodworth presented a history of psychology that reviewed the main

Robert Woodworth

schools in a balanced way. Five years later came *Experimental Psychology*, in which Woodworth reported on the work done in experimental psychology up to about 1930. The book contained accurate and balanced critical reviews of a large number of experiments. To the student interested in the older literature of experimental psychology, it is the main source of information.

Behaviorism, psychoanalysis, and Gestalt psychology were heatedly debated in the period from 1920 to 1950, and this debate has tended to overshadow the fact that a great number of psychologists took a middle-of-the-road position, regarding psychology as a broad field taking in the study of mental processes as well as behavior. The popularity of Woodworth's textbooks is a testimony to the strength of his position in US psychology in the first half of the twentieth century.

Woodworth on Motivation

Pointing out that by a *motive* we mean something internal, Woodworth (1918, p. 38) wanted to account for motivation by starting out in external stimulation. To achieve this, he began by drawing a distinction between what he called the problem of *mechanism* and the problem of *drive*. The problem of mechanism concerned *how* we do things, and the problem of drive *why* we do things. Having drawn this distinction, Woodworth proceeded to suggest that this mechanism might provide the drive for other mechanisms. He illustrated his two points with the example of a predator searching for, hunting, catching, and consuming prey. Searching for, hunting, catching, and consuming were the mechanisms in the act of feeding. The drive was what motivated the act. In this example, as I understand him, Woodworth suggested that the mechanism of eating would uphold the behavior of searching, hunting, and catching.

Woodworth emphasized that motivation has a basis in inherited dispositions to react, but did not, as I read him, consider that basic motives like sleep, hunger, thirst, and sex are instigated and motivated by internal stimuli. Thus, he did not consider the possibility that in the example he used to illustrate his point, the animal's behavior was instigated and motivated not only by external stimuli, but also by internal stimuli. We know that hunger and thirst are instigated and upheld by internal stimuli arising from the metabolism of the organism. This is in line with everyday thinking, and would, as I see it, have represented a natural belief also when Woodworth wrote his book in 1918.

Thus, while Woodworth must be given credit for identifying the role played by external stimulation, he overlooked the importance of internal stimulation in basic motivation. The view of basic motivation presented by McDougall and Freud was one-sided, but so, apparently, was Woodworth's. Not until the 1960s was a balanced view worked out. Woodworth (1958) returned to the problem of motivation, but he does not seem to have drawn a distinction between a mechanism and a drive, or explained how a mechanism is a drive for other mechanisms.

In his treatment of motivation, Woodworth also contributed by reviving James's idea that humans have more instincts than other animal species. He objected strongly to the idea advanced by McDougall and Freud that humans have a small number of motives from which all other motives can be derived. Instead humans are endowed with a variety of genetically determined capacities that form the basis for numerous types of motives. Here Woodworth emphasized human perceptual capacities as the basis for our many interests and claimed that "the field of human motivation is as broad as the world that man can deal with and understand." He also believed that when we are absorbed in an interesting activity, the drive is *inherent* in the activity.

Before I leave Woodworth, I shall make a few remarks on his use of the concepts of stimulus and response. Like Thorndike, Woodworth advocated an approach in line with the stimulus–response paradigm, but influenced by Dewey's examination of the reflex arc, he realized that what constitutes a stimulus depends on the state of the organism at the moment the stimulation acts upon the sensory organ. Therefore, the S–R formula had to be modified to S–O–R, where O refers to the organism's variables such as drives and current state of the organism. Hence, Woodworth can be said to have contributed to the introduction of the stimulus–response paradigm as well as to the criticism of it that eventually led most psychologists to reject it.

Walter Cannon (1871–1945)

Walter Cannon was born and grew up in Minnesota. He obtained his medical degree at Harvard and was appointed professor of physiology there in 1906. In discussing James's theory of emotions, I mentioned that Cannon was a critic of it. Cannon's most important contribution to physiological psychology, however, was probably his *emergency theory of emotion*, which combined physiological knowledge with an evolutionary biological perspective.

As Singer (1994) relates, British physiologists had clarified important aspects of the autonomous nervous system. Cannon (1915) became interested in the problem of how the autonomic system is regulated by the central nervous system. He observed that during excitement the heart rate, blood pressure, and level of blood sugar increase; that blood flows to the skeletal muscles; and that the activity of the digestive system is reduced. He interpreted these observations through the perspective of evolution, proposing that physiological reactions prepare the organism for fighting or fleeing. Thus, he gave us a functional interpretation of the emotions, one in which anger and fear seem to involve the same basic physiological processes. What makes the two emotions different is that the object arousing them has different meanings for the organism. In his discussion of anger and fear, James (1950, p. 415) had earlier made this point. Thus, Cannon's research supported the idea that we must take account of the subject's *appraisal* of the situation in attempting to account for emotions. This idea is an important one. Magda Arnold (1960) gave an extensive treatment of it, and since then it has been central in the study of emotions.

Cannon demonstrated that the physiological reactions accompanying anger and fear originate in the sympathetic branch of the autonomic nervous system and in the body's production of adrenaline. In his further studies, he helped describe the role of neurotransmitters in the formation of synaptic connections in the nervous system. Sherrington had postulated that such substances are present when the nerve impulse is transmitted from one cell to another through the synapse.

Early in the 1900s, Cannon conducted studies demonstrating the existence of internal stimulation for hunger and thirst. With his coworkers, he showed that abdominal contractions are present during hunger by having a subject swallow a rubber balloon that was inflated inside the stomach. The rubber balloon was attached to a mechanism that registered abdominal contractions, making it possible to see that when the need for nourishment occurs, these contractions are triggered. We might think of the contractions as stimuli for the registration of a state of hunger, and thus for the experience of hunger. Cannon also pointed out that thirst is accompanied by a feeling of dryness in the mouth and throat, and from this line of thought, we could assume specific stimuli underlie different physiological drives.

In the further development of his view, Cannon revived Claude Bernard's ideas about the internal environment. As mentioned in Chapter 9, these included the notion that there must be a certain constancy in the internal environment. For example, the organism must maintain a certain temperature and a constant volume of fluid, and the blood must have a given content of sugar, salt, and oxygen. Thus, fundamental physiological processes are regulated so that they are maintained at specific levels. Cannon called this set of levels the condition of *homeostasis*. It follows, then, that when deviations from the optimal balance occur, the body would in some way have information about the imbalance. Physiological needs would arise, which in turn would lead to different forms of stimulation.

Cannon's model conveyed something important about bodily functions. Subsequent research has shown that the mechanisms regulating the intake of nourishment and fluid are extremely complex, but some time elapsed before psychologists became aware of this complexity. What was perhaps more serious was that in employing the model, they neglected to ask how the drive activates the different types of behavior necessary to satisfy it, and, further, how the drive directs the behavior. The idea of drive occurring as the result of a homeostatic imbalance took on monumental proportions in psychology, and throughout the 1940s and 1950s, it was more or less the height of fashion to postulate needs and drives in accounts of behavior. The fact that it became popular to interpret motivation in terms of homeostasis should not, however, lead us to overlook that Cannon's idea is an important one.

Stress and Psychosomatic Disease

The emergency theory of emotions was an important contribution to psychology. By relating emotional reactions of anger and fear to the autonomic nervous system, Cannon also laid the foundation of an important approach to the study of *psychosomatic disorders*. He referred to the effects on the body of anger and fear as *stress*.

The idea of stress was elaborated a few decades later by the physician Hans Selye (1956), who argued that in many situations in which a person's resources are overtaxed and the person is thus the object of stress, the bodily reactions are of the same nature:

rise in blood pressure, increased secretion of norepinephrine, change in heartbeat, and slowed digestion. When the stress is frequent or prolonged, it may lead to damage in the body – among other things to cardiovascular illness. More recently, researchers have argued that stress can affect the immune system.

The concept of stress has proven useful in attempts to clarify the causes of cardiovascular and other diseases believed to be affected by emotional states. As is so frequently the case in psychology, however, its use has been limited by the difficulty of giving it a relatively simple and precise meaning. One difficulty is that a certain amount of stress seems to be necessary for a healthy life. Another is that there are great individual differences in people's capacities for tolerating stress, as well as in the type of stress they can tolerate.

Karl Lashley (1890–1958)

Karl Lashley (1923) declared himself a behaviorist in the early years of his career, but he later developed into a stern critic of behaviorism. Like the contemporary behaviorist theorists, he concentrated on the study of learning in the rat. Unlike his contemporaries, however, he sought a basis for psychology in neurophysiology. Further, he became a persistent critic of the stimulus–response approach as well as of the use of the concept of drive in contemporary psychology.

Lashley became famous for his criticism of the view that learning, remembering, and intelligence could be localized to specific areas of the cortex. However, serious defects in his experimental studies of localization have been revealed at the same time as evidence for localization has accumulated. Thus, Lashley did not make a very positive contribution to the problem to which he devoted most of his work. In my opinion, however, he did further the study of basic motivation, on which I shall report after discussing his work on localization.

Even if Lashley did not help the study of brain localization, he promoted interest in physiological psychology by showing that the study of the brain is relevant to the current discussion of psychological problems. He was also a remarkably efficient director of the psychological laboratories he led, and many of the students and fellows he attracted to his laboratories became prominent in psychological research. In previous chapters, mention has been made of David Krech, Harry Harlow, and Robert Leeper. In the present chapter, I shall report on the studies of Frank Beach and discuss in some detail the work of Donald Hebb and Roger Sperry, and in Chapter 19, I shall review some of the ideas of Theodore Scheirla.

Lashley (1923, p. 244) apparently held a reductionist view of psychology, believing that behavior as well as mental experience could be accounted for in terms of physiology and that the study of humans is "adequately desirable in concepts of mechanics and chemistry." Because he does not seem to have gone more deeply into how we can account for biological evolution in terms only of mechanical and chemical principles, nor into how to account for behavior and mental experience in terms of physiology, I shall not discuss these aspects of his work.

Karl Lashley

Some Biographical Notes

Lashley was born in Davis, West Virginia. His interest in biological science being aroused in early youth, he took a BA in zoology at the University of West Virginia. After having taken a master's degree at the University of Pittsburgh, he enrolled at Johns Hopkins University in 1911. He received his PhD in zoology with Jennings, but during his graduate years he also worked with Adolph Meyer, who, as mentioned in Chapter 12, was the director of the Phipps Clinic. At this time Lashley also did extensive work with Watson, assisting him in his early studies of conditioning and his fieldwork on terns in Florida.

After having received his PhD, Lashley began extensive studies with Shepherd Franz (1879–1933) at St Elizabeth Hospital in Washington. Franz, who was a student of James McKeen Cattell, was known for his work on restoring function after brain damage and for his ablation studies of the prefrontal cortex. As Finger (1994) recounts, he was critical of the idea of a strict localization of functions in the cortex.

Lashley had had good and versatile training as a researcher in psychology and biology when he began directing a laboratory at the University of Minnesota in 1917, a post he held until 1926. He was a professor at the University of Chicago from 1929 to 1935, and after that at Harvard. In 1942, he moved to Florida as director of the Yerkes Laboratories of Primate Biology while keeping his professorship at Harvard.

As we shall see, Lashley could be opinionated, but he left the students and fellows working in his laboratories with great freedom even when they were opposed to his own views in their research. As a result, the work in his laboratories was not clustered around his specific ideas but covered a wide range of problems.

Lashley on Brain Localization

After Lashley had left Johns Hopkins, he continued the work on brain localization he had carried out with Franz. In 1929, he published the results of his research in *Brain Mechanisms and Intelligence*, a book that gave him a name in brain research.

In a series of technically well done experiments, the performance of rats was assessed before and after different portions were surgically removed from different areas of their cortices. The tasks used to assess performance consisted mainly of learning diverse types of mazes, but a brightness discrimination task and a problem-solving task were also included. Lashley summed up the results of his experiments in two main points: 1. reduction in performance is proportional to the amount of destroyed brain tissue (the principle of mass action); 2. equal amounts of destroyed brain tissue in an area of the cortex result in the same reduction in performance (the principle of equipotentiality). Lashley (1929/1963, p. 176) drew several inferences from his findings. I shall quote the first one:

The learning process and the retention of habits are not dependent upon any finely localized structural changes within the cerebral cortex. The results *are* incompatible with theories of learning by changes in synaptic structure, or with any theories which assume that particular neural integrations are dependent upon definite anatomical paths specialized for them. Integration cannot be expressed in terms of connections between specific neurons.

Instead of explaining the findings in terms of structural differentiation in brain tissue, Lashley explained them as a result of dynamic integration among parts of the nervous system.

At first glance, the results of his experiments seem to give solid evidence against the view that intellectual functions are localized in the brain. Actually, however, before Lashley began his research, experiments had already been carried out that made his conclusions doubtful. It had been shown that after rats are deprived of various senses as well as of motor responses, they could still learn to run mazes. As contemporary critics including Clifford Morgan (1968) pointed out, this strongly suggests that even if a large portion of cortex were removed, it might be expected that rats would be able to learn the mazes. These early findings could explain mass action as well as equipotentiality.

Lashley continued his work on brain localization for many years after the publication of *Brain Mechanisms and Behavior*. In particular, he studied discrimination learning in rats and some monkeys after having removed the motor cortex or cut what he believed to be the connections between cortical areas necessary for perceiving, learning, and remembering. One of Lashley's (1950/1960) conclusions was that it was "not possible to demonstrate the isolated localization of a memory trace anywhere within the nervous system."

Evidence of localization had accumulated by the second half of the twentieth century, however. The reason Lashley did not find it in his own studies was probably that the anatomical knowledge of his day was too incomplete to allow him to remove the tissue or cut the paths mediating the psychological functions he studied. Semir Zeki (1993), one of the pioneers in the new research on brain localization, felt that Lashley's viewpoints and research contributed to a misdirection of research development. He further claimed that Lashley overlooked clinical discoveries.

While Lashley seems to have been too critical of the idea of brain localization, many of the critical points he made about contemporary theories of learning seem to have been well taken. In the discussion of Spence in Chapter 13, I mentioned his view that attention plays a role in learning. Another criticism of the stimulus–response psychology was that it overlooked how complex behavior is governed by central nervous mechanisms. In a famous article entitled *The Problem of Serial Order in Behavior*, Lashley (1951) pointed out that the diverse movements in many types of behavior follow each other in a definite temporal order. For example, to use language, we must master complicated temporal sequences; phonemes, syllables, words, and sentences are joined to each other in a serial order. This order, he convincingly argued, presupposes a central mechanism governing the activity. Learning of such activities could not, he concluded, be a result simply of the fact that associations were established between the individual links in a sequence representing a serial order. This idea paved the way for the view that use of language is genetically determined, as argued a few years later by Chomsky when he criticized Skinner's account of language as a form of behavior. In his article on the reflex arc, Dewey had pointed to the influence of the state of the organism in perception, and Woodworth, as already mentioned, had pointed to the role played by organismic factors in perception and reaction to stimuli. We can see Lashley's article as a continuation of their thinking.

Lashley on the Nature of Motivation

Lashley parted company with Watson not only in his views of associative learning and conditioning, but also on the question of the role genetics plays in behavior. In a period in which psychologists tended to reject the idea of instincts, Lashley, along with Woodworth, argued for retaining it. He had done field studies of birds and extensive laboratory work on the reproductive behavior of the rat. A study of instincts revealed, he thought, important aspects of motivation. In 1938, he presented his view of instincts and motivation in an article entitled "Experimental Analysis of Instinctive Behavior." Personality and clinical psychologists were intensely interested in Freud's and Murray's ideas but seem to have overlooked those of Lashley.

Lashley complained that in banishing the concept of instinct, psychologists had lost sight of the fact that the anti-instinct movement was primarily directed against the hypothesis that imaginary forces explain behavior. Instead, psychologists had made heredity the scapegoat and had continued to postulate psychic energies of different sources, such as "desires and aversions, field forces and dynamic tensions, needs and vectors, libidos and means-end-readinesses." So not only Freud's and McDougall's postulations of inner sources of energy, but also Lewin's and Tolman's views of motivation were included in the criticism. When Hull launched his idea of drive, the group around Lashley became its chief critics.

Lashley followed up Woodworth's idea that we must undertake an analysis of instincts and motivation in terms of stimuli and responses. However, Lashley argued, we must understand stimulation as *patterns of stimuli*. In his view of stimuli, he now took a position close to that of the Gestalt psychologists, even if he rejected their idea of a brain field. Due to genetic endowment, specific patterns of stimulation result in definite types of perceptual organization as well as, if I understand him, definite types of reactions. The perceptual-motor relationships thus arising, Lashley (1938/1960, p. 386) held, were totally integrated as a unity given by the activity of the cortex. As I interpret him, this integrated unity of the perceptual-motor relations corresponds more or less to what Woodworth had called a mechanism.

Referring to his own experiments on reproductive behavior, Lashley argued that the mechanisms, the genetically determined perceptual-motor connections, were elicited by specific stimuli; it was unnecessary, he said, to call upon "some source of energy apart from that of the specific sensory-motor pattern." A mechanism would act as a drive, and it was not necessary to assume, as Woodworth proposed, that a mechanism *could* act as a drive; "physiologically all drives are no more than expressions of the activity of specific mechanisms," he said.

Although Lashley gave a plausible account of how instincts and physiological motives are directed towards specific goals, he did not satisfactorily explain the periodic nature of physiological motives. He mentioned that instincts have a periodic nature and extensively discussed the role of hormones in sexual behavior, but he did not clarify why it is only in certain periods that stimuli arouse the instinctive reactions. Hence, if I have understood him correctly, he did *not* show that the idea of a drive is unnecessary.

In his research on reproductive behavior in the rat, Lashley demonstrated the fundamental importance of external objects for the motivation underlying this behavior. The perception of a female rat in heat motivates the male rat to sexual activity, and the perception of a younger litter arouses the waning retrieving activity of the female rat. Lashley realized that it was a characteristic of the physiological motives that they are aroused by incentives in the form of external objects. This view implies that olfactory, visual, and auditory perceptions play a fundamental role in motivation, an aspect in the study of motivation that, in my judgment, is rarely treated in personality and clinical psychology. (See, for example, Lawrence Pervin and Oliver John, 1999; Robert Hogan et al., 1997.)

By emphasizing the role played by the perception of external objects in motivation, Lashley corrected Freud's and McDougall's one-sided picture of motivation as originating in an internal source of energy. However, his emphasis on the perception of external objects apparently led him to neglect that motivation has a hedonistic aspect. Pleasure forms part of the explanation for why we eat, drink, and mate. Freud had emphasized this by attributing a fundamental importance to erogenous zones in sexual behavior.

Before I leave Lashley and turn to his students and the researchers working in his laboratory, I want to mention that he started out as a behaviorist, presenting a version of behaviorism in two articles in 1923, but, by 1933, he had made clear, in opposition to Pavlov, that many facts about behavior can be expressed only in psychological terms. In formulating his problems in neuropsychology, Lashley drew upon concepts such as *perception*, *attention*, *memory*, and *thought*. He insisted that psychological studies should be made objective, but he was not a behaviorist. Most of his students and coworkers held the same attitude to the subject matter of psychology.

Lashley's Students and Coworkers on Motivation

Lashley's student Frank Beach (1942, 1951) made extensive comparative studies of sexual behavior. He showed in great detail how the sexual behavior of animals is governed by a number of diverse types of perceptual stimuli. Donald Hebb (1949), another of Lashley's students, pointed out that sexual motivation is the result of interaction between internal states and sexual objects. Without going into the history of motivation, we note the same view has been established for thirst and hunger. Hence, we cannot view the basic motives – thirst, hunger, and sex – as determined only by either internal states or external stimulation.

Hebb (1946) also demonstrated that chimpanzees respond with fear to objects they could never have seen before. This showed there are types of behavior that seem not to derive from any of the basic motives that Freud and Hull proposed. Another demonstration of this point was made by Harry Harlow, who for some time worked in the Yerkes Laboratories along with Hebb. Harlow showed that chimpanzees engage in tasks like the solving of mechanical puzzles without extrinsic rewards. This demonstration was in line with Woodworth's view that many types of behaviors contain their own motivation. They were *intrinsically motivating*.

As emphasized by Hebb's student Dalbir Bindra (1985), the fact that motives are closely dependent on external stimulation makes it difficult to draw a hard and fast line between motives and emotions. Not only emotions such as anger, fear, and disgust but *all* feelings and emotions must be considered motivating. Apparently, what determines the difference is the degree to which the internal state and the external stimulation each play a role in eliciting the reaction. The difficulty in making the distinction may be illustrated by a comparison of sex and aggression. Modern researchers tend to regard sex as a basic motive and aggression as an emotion, whereas Freud – and as we shall see in Chapter 19, Konrad Lorenz – regarded aggression as a basic motive.

Donald Hebb (1904–1985)

Donald Hebb worked with Lashley for several years as his graduate student, first at the University of Chicago and then at Harvard. When Lashley became director of the Yerkes Laboratories in 1942, Hebb was invited to work there as a fellow and stayed for five years. Though he was heavily influenced by Lashley, his views differed on important points.

Before joining Lashley, Hebb had participated, in 1934, in research on conditioning led by one of Pavlov's students working at McGill University in Canada. As Hebb (1980) remarked in his autobiography, he became critical of conditioning but retained a belief in associative learning and regarded himself as representing a form of neoconnectionism.

After his first stay with Lashley, Hebb obtained an assistantship with Wilder Penfield at McGill University (Hebb was a Canadian, born in Nova Scotia). Penfield was a neuro-surgeon, famous for successfully operating on persons suffering from epilepsy, and he contributed to the mapping of the functions of human cortical areas by electrical stimu-lation. As his assistant, Hebb described the effects of the brain operations on the patients' subsequent behavior.

Hebb made some findings that greatly surprised him: some of the patients obtained high scores on the Stanford–Binet intelligence test even if large parts of their cortex had been removed. One had a measured IQ of 160 after removal of a prefrontal lobe, and another an IQ of 115 after losing the entire right half of the cortex. Hebb set out to explain these findings by constructing a model of the nervous system, presented in 1949 in a book entitled *The Organization of Behavior*. After his years as a fellow at Yerkes Laboratories, Hebb was appointed professor at McGill, where he stayed until retirement.

Hebb's Theory

While Lashley had ended up a severe critic of associative learning theories, some of the researchers working in the laboratories he directed took a more positive attitude to the prevailing tendency in American psychology to explain psychological phenomena in terms of learning. Harlow and Hebb, for example, tried to reconcile Gestalt psychological ideas with ideas of learning. They elaborated the view that learning in the early phases of ontogenetic development proceeds as a slow building up of associations. When a number of associations have been built up, thinking and the use of concepts become possible. This view became central in Hebb's neuropsychological theory. Hebb proposed that in the early phases of learning in mammals, networks of neurons corresponding to concepts of diverse types are formed in the cortex by associative learning. This learning is slow in contrast to later learning involving concepts.

The networks are established in the way that neurons firing in close temporal contigu-ity make synaptic connections with each other. Hebb called the networks *cell assemblies*. Further, he assumed that cell assemblies are connected into a series he called a *phase sequence*. The two concepts were introduced in the following way (Hebb, 1949, p. xix). Any frequently repeated, particular stimulation leads to the slow development of a cell assembly, a diffuse structure made up of cells in the cortex and diencephalon (and also, perhaps, in the ganglia of the cerebrum), capable of acting briefly as a closed system, delivering facilitation to other such systems, and usually having a specific motor facilitation. A series of such events constitutes a phase sequence – the thought process.

To explain the performance of his brain-damaged patients, Hebb proposed that the building of a network underlying a concept requires connections between a much larger number of neurons than the subsequent use of the concept once this has been acquired. By assuming that performance, as assessed by the Binet test, is based on the use of concepts, Hebb suggested that adult human beings could lose large portions of their cortex and still perform well on intelligence tests.

Evaluation of Hebb's Theory

It is definitely plausible that the building of associative networks underlying the use of concepts is a slow process. However, it seems equally plausible that many of the skills mammals learn to master are highly dependent upon the maturation of the nervous system. Even relatively simple perceptual skills, such as distinguishing the different shapes of objects, require the mastery of subfunctions, such as localizing the object and fixating it. The subfunctions must be coordinated, and this coordination may require maturation of the nervous system. Moreover, mammals, including human beings, seem to acquire a number of skills surprisingly fast.

Hebb distinguished between two types of learning: early associative learning and later conceptual learning. Apparently, he thought all types of early learning were associative. This view was challenged at the end of the century, as we shall see in Chapter 19.

There is probably no single explanation of the neurological findings underlying Hebb's theory. Before we can accept his interpretation of the findings, we must ensure that in the cases where one hemisphere of the cortex has been removed, function has not transferred to the other hemisphere. (I shall return to this problem when discussing the work of Sperry.) With regard to Hebb's finding that intelligence as measured by the Stanford–Binet test is retained after extensive damage to the prefrontal cortex, there is a problem of localization of function involved. Extensive research on the role of the prefrontal cortex has revealed that patients with damage to this area tend to score within the normal range when assessed by conventional intelligence tests. However, when more sensitive and specific tests are used, damage to the prefrontal cortex has been found to produce a number of problems in cognition and memory and to be involved in other functions, such as planning and judgment. Hence, the reason Hebb found no effect of the removal of tissue of the prefrontal cortex was probably that he used too crude a measure of function. (On the role played by the prefrontal cortex, see Michael Gazzaniga et al., 2009.)

Hebb's concepts of cell assembly and phase sequence were highly general, and he presented no concrete evidence of the existence of the neurophysiological connections he proposed. Further, his use of the psychological concepts of perception, attention, learning, remembering, and thinking (concepts) was not clear enough to help in defining the neurophysiological constructs. In his discussion of the idea of a cell assembly, Hebb (1949, p. 62) did, however, suggest what might happen at the synapse during learning. His suggestion, which attracted many later researchers, is known as *Hebb's law*:

When an axon of cell A is near enough to excite a cell B repeatedly or persistently takes part in firing it, some growth process or metabolic change takes place in one or both cells such that A's efficiency, as one of the cells firing B, is increased.

As readers may have noted, Hebb's law conforms to what we would expect if the law of association by temporal contiguity is valid. As we shall see in Chapter 19, the view that learning takes place by the building up of associations came under renewed attack in the later twentieth century. However, even if associations should play a minor role in learning and remembering, considerable evidence has been produced in support of Hebb's view of the changes taking place in the synapse during learning, as documented by Neil Carlson (2007) and Gazzaniga et al. (2009).

The Organization of Behavior was a very stimulating book because it showed that with certain modifications, association theory could meet the challenges of Gestalt psychology and also explain some surprising findings in neurology. Hebb paved the way for neoassociationism, resulting in *network models* and the later *connectionism*. Reviews of network models and connectionism have been made by Michael Eysenck and Mark Keane (2005) and Daniel Reisberg (2001).

Roger Sperry (1913–1994)

Roger Sperry received his PhD in zoology from the University of Chicago in 1941. The following year, he joined Lashley and his group at the Yerkes Laboratories and worked there as a fellow until 1946. He then returned to the University of Chicago, first as a professor of anatomy and then as a professor of psychology. From 1952 until his retirement, he was professor of neuropsychology at the California Institute of Technology. Sperry contributed to the solution of a number of problems in neuropsychology, but he is mainly known for his work on the anatomical and functional relationship between the two cerebral hemispheres. I shall report on some of this work.

To prevent the spread of epileptic seizures from one cerebral hemisphere to the other, neurosurgeons in the 1930s had begun to cut the corpus callosum, an extensive fiber tract connecting the two. Examinations of patients after the operation did not reveal a noticeable loss of function. Some case studies of persons suffering brain damage gave hints as to what the function of the corpus callosum might be, but no clear picture emerged. In the early 1950s, Sperry and his students set out to identify it.

With Robert Meyers, Sperry performed initial experiments on cats and monkeys that have become classic. They first studied the role of the corpus callosum in vision. Since half the nerve fibers from the retina cross at the optic chiasm, they had to cut the optic nerve at the optic chiasm. When this operation is performed, each eye feeds information to only one cerebral hemisphere. Therefore, if one eye is covered by a patch, information will be fed to only one hemisphere. The experimenters subsequently trained an animal to perform a visual discrimination task, such as discriminating between a square and a circle. After the animal had learned to perform this task, the patch was removed from the covered eye and placed on the other eye. It now turned out that the animal did not transfer the solution when the problem was presented to the uncovered eye. In contrast, when the corpus callosum was not cut, the solution was readily transferred.

Splitting the brain of the animal allowed Sperry (1961, 1964) to study how the two hemispheres interact and also what role is played by subcortical parts of the brain. I shall not report on these studies but turn to the research he began with his student Michael Gazzaniga around 1960.

In cats and monkeys in which the brains had been split, the two hemispheres seemed to be equivalent in function. In human beings, however, it had been known since Broca's day that the use of language is usually localized in the left hemisphere. Hence, it was reasonable to believe the two hemispheres do not function equivalently in human beings in all respects. Sperry and Gazzaniga began a systematic study to reveal differences in function between the two hemispheres.

This research led to an enormous interest in the problem of differences in function between the two hemispheres. However, it has not turned out to be easy to control all necessary conditions and arrive at clear-cut conclusions. I shall just note that, according to Gazzaniga et al. (2009), there are marked differences in the functions of the two hemispheres. Although, as we might expect, the left hemisphere has been found to be superior in enabling the use of language, when more specific tests have been used, the right hemisphere has been found to have some capacity for language as well, and to be superior in certain visual-spatial tasks. As Gazzaniga et al. noted, it is important not only to clarify how the two hemispheres differ in function but also to realize that, to understand the differences, we must understand how they work together.

The Revival of Wernicke's Theory of Aphasia

The research of Sperry and his coworkers greatly heightened interest in the study of the neural basis of cognition and language. In the mid-1960s, another event also increased interest in neuropsychological studies of language. The Harvard neurologist Norman Geschwind (1974) revived the old Wernicke theory of the localization of the capacity for language. In agreement with Wernicke, Geschwind demonstrated cases of damage to Broca's area in which speech was labored and slow, with faulty grammar and inadequate articulation, and cases of damage to Wernicke's area in which speech was fluent but semantically defective. Geschwind also supplemented the old theory to make it more coherent.

The revised Wernicke theory of localization identified structures of the brain that are important in the production of language, but several findings have made clear that, at least in its present formulation, the theory is not adequate. Cases have been described in which damage to Broca's area does not have the effect attributed to it; similarly, damage to Wernicke's area does not always result in the effects ascribed to this area. Moreover, damage to areas other than these two has been found to produce the defects ascribed to both.

A Case of Anterograde Amnesia

At the end of the nineteenth century, neurologists had very limited means of diagnosing the location and extent of brain damage in their patients. To verify conjectures, they could in some rare cases perform a postmortem examination. And even in these cases, the information they could obtain from a single case was highly restricted because so little was known about the anatomy and physiology of the brain. However, as brain surgery advanced, neurologists could carefully study persons in whom specific parts of the brain had been removed or nerve paths had been cut. The patient initially studied by Sperry and Gazzanica was such a case. Because a wealth of knowledge about the brain had accumulated, a single case could be very informative.

In many instances, the researcher could rule out with high probability that individual differences in brain structure or specific experiences could not explain the findings. In other words, it was possible on the basis of a single case to arrive at highly general conclusions concerning the importance of specific areas for the functioning of the brain. In the later twentieth century, a number of carefully described cases have contributed to advance the study of neuropsychology. I shall here mention only one case that – as in the Sperry and Gazzaniga study – has been important for raising interest in neuropsychology and has led to numerous investigations to amplify and clarify the early conclusions.

In 1954, the neurosurgeon William Scoville at the Montreal Institute of Neurology reported the case of H.M., which continued to be studied for the next forty years. In his later research on the case, Scoville was joined by the psychologist Brenda Milner at McGill University. They issued a report in 1957 covering H.M. and a number of similar cases. Gazzaniga et al. (2009) have summarized and analyzed the research to clarify the findings that have accumulated over the years.

H.M. suffered from epileptic seizures from the age of ten and had to stop working at the end of his twenties because the seizures had worsened. His physicians decided to perform bilateral medial temporal lobectomy. After the operation, the seizures became less frequent and less severe, but the patient's memory was severely damaged. Psychological examinations after the operation revealed that his intelligence was above normal as measured on a widely used intelligence scale. He could remember his personal past and general knowledge acquired up to three years before the operation. However, he seemed to have almost completely lost the ability to remember events taking place in the immediate present; for example, he appeared unable to learn the names of the doctors examining him or the way to the toilet.

The results of the study of H.M. were of great importance for neurology as well as for psychology. Scoville and Milner also had a patient in their sample on whom the resection had been performed only on one hemisphere (unilaterally), and in this case it did not cause lasting memory deficits. So it was natural to conclude that the memory effect was due to the fact that the removal of brain tissue was made *bilaterally*.

Since the performance of H.M. showed that somehow his capacity for storing memory of the immediate present had been damaged by the operation, it seemed logical that the medial temporal area, the hippocampus, and the surrounding cortical areas had to be implicated in some way in the storing of memories over longer time intervals. Other evidence from neurology further suggested that this area must take part in the consolidation of long-term memories. As readers may remember, Müller and Pilzecker by 1900 had already argued, on the basis of their studies of interference between memory processes, that there is a stage at which new memory traces must be consolidated.

The results are important since they indicate that a specific lesion to the brain can affect memory mainly for events occurring after the operation, but not events prior to it. This suggested that there might be two different types of memory, memory of immediate events, later called *short-term memory*, and memory of events that occurred in a more distant past, *long-term memory*.

Thus, the investigation of the case of H.M. led to questions that seemed central to an understanding of the processes involved in memory. Other, similar cases were carefully studied and compared to the case of H.M., and extensive investigations were subsequently undertaken of individual primates as well as other species of mammals. I shall return to these studies in the next chapter.

New Techniques in Neurology

The studies I have reviewed so far were undertaken with relatively simple procedures. The performance of brain-damaged persons was compared to the performance of normal persons, and in animals, performances before and after a lesion were compared. Since the early twentieth century, a number of new techniques have made the study of brain functions considerably more effective. Since knowledge of these techniques is necessary for an understanding of the progress made in studying the relationship between the brain and the mind, I shall give a brief historical account of the main ones introduced in the 1900s.

In animal studies, the site and extent of the lesions could be determined after the animals had been killed. In studies of brain-damaged persons, the neurologist could perform a postmortem examination after the patient had died only if the person had given consent. Moreover, the techniques for performing this examination were rather crude. Thus, the task of achieving a reliable correlation between brain structure and performance was fraught with many difficulties.

The electrical properties of nerve tissue had been known since the days of Galvani and Volta. DuBois Reymond, Helmholtz's friend and colleague, had made the study of these properties his specialty in physiology, and Helmholtz had performed his epoch-making measurement of the speed of conduction in a nerve in 1848. Fritz and Hitzig had demonstrated the existence of a motor cortical area in dogs by applying an electrical current to the brain tissue of the cortex. And, as we have seen, Penfield and Jaspers had used this technique to make functional maps of the human cortex. In the 1920s, an entirely new technique, *electroencephalography* (EEG), was developed.

It had long been known that the brain produces electrical potentials of varying magnitude that can be registered by placing a sensitive electrode on the outside of the scalp. By recording changes in brain potentials over time, *brain waves* were obtained. The pattern of brain waves was found to change with varying states of consciousness and with diverse types of malfunctioning of the brain, and researchers gradually realized that descriptions of these patterns would be a useful means of studying the activity of the brain in normal as well as abnormal persons. EEG was found to be a particularly valuable means of diagnosing epilepsy.

Around 1950, EEG also led to important discoveries about the functioning of the brain. In 1949, two Californian neurologists, Giuseppe Moruzzi and Horace Magoun, discovered that electrical stimulation of the reticular formation of the brainstem excites sensory areas in the cortex and thus alerts the organism to diverse types of stimulation.

Another important discovery was made by Nathaniel Kleitman and his student Eugene Aserinsky of the University of Chicago (Aserinsky and Kleitman, 1953). They found that during sleep, rapid eye movements (REM) can be registered, and that these movements are accompanied by specific patterns of brain waves as recorded by EEG. By means of this technique, researchers had already found that during the night the activity of the brain went through five different stages that follow each other in a definite order. REM sleep is the fifth stage, and when persons are awakened during this stage, they usually have been dreaming. This knowledge made it possible to relate dreaming to the activity of the brain, made it easier to study dreaming, and resulted in a revival of the study of dreams.

By 1950, it was clear to neurophysiologists that the brain is continuously active during the whole day and night. The findings of Aserinsky and Kleitman, along with those of Moruzzi and Magoun, raised interest in the study of attention and different states of consciousness.

An ordinary electroencephalogram does not reveal the onset of activity as being due to a specific stimulus event. However, by averaging a number of individual recordings, researchers have found that effects from irrelevant sources can be canceled out, so that only the change in action potential resulting from a given signal can be registered. Such *evoked potentials*, or *event-related potentials* (ERP), have been sensitive and reliable measures of activity in the brain. At the end of the twentieth century, this was one of the best techniques to measure activity in the brain. The ERP does not allow the researcher directly to localize the source of the stimulus. This is possible, however, if we record and average the small magnetic changes accompanying synaptic activity. This technique, developed towards the end of the twentieth century, is known as *magnetoencephalography* (MEG).

From the beginning of the twentieth century, damage to the brain had been diagnosed by means of X-ray. At the end of the 1960s, the technique of using X-rays to make an image of sections of the brain was greatly improved, and *computed tomography* (CT or CAT) became widely used in hospitals to scan the brain. Some years later, another and even more precise technique to image the brain was introduced. This technique, *magnetic resonance imaging* (MRI), is based on the magnetic properties of brain tissue, which can also be used to measure changes in blood flow in the brain due to neuronal activity. This technique, called *functional MRI* (fMRI), allows researchers to obtain a picture of the activity of a region of the brain.

Measurements of the activity of the brain have also been made possible by the injection of radioactive elements as tracers in the bloodstream. This technique, *positron emission tomography* (PET), exploits the fact that the decay of radioactive elements can be measured, thus providing a means of registering which regions of the brain receive the greatest blood flow. Assuming the greatest neural activity is accompanied by the greatest blood flow, we can take increased blood flow as an indication of the level of neural activity.

Both fMRI and PET have good resolution and allow precise measurements. However, after the onset of an activity, it takes a relatively long time before registration of it can be made. For PET, the time interval is no less than 40 seconds, and even if the time interval for fMRI is far less, a couple of seconds, this is a long time relative to the speed at which impulses can be transmitted in the nervous system.

As shown by this very brief sketch, scientists have an increasing number of instruments at their disposal for diagnosis and research. The invention of the electron microscope and new techniques to stain neural tissue have also greatly advanced the anatomical study of the brain, and we can now measure the chemical changes taking place in the brain. These techniques may prove essential for progress.

Knowledge of the Visual System as a Guide to Understanding the Functioning of the Brain

The most sensational – and probably also the most important – progress in neurophysiological techniques in the mid-twentieth century was the recording of the changes in electrical potentials occurring in individual neurons as a response to stimulation.

From the beginning of the century, research workers had been able to record changes in potential from single neurons in invertebrates. The squid was an important subject because some of its axons have a very large diameter compared to other animals. A breakthrough in the study of the brains of mammals was made when Stephen Kuffler (1953) succeeded in making reliable recordings of the activity of ganglion cells in the cat's retina. (For a more recent and complete account, see Kuffler and John Nicholls, 1976.) The retina of mammals forms part of the brain, and Kuffler's study was thus a study of how the brain processes information contained in physical energy in the form of light waves. Subsequent research showed that study of the visual system reveals much about the function of the brain, and this is one reason the study of visual perception is so central in neuropsychology.

The anatomy of the retina had been described in detail before Kuffler began his physiological research. It was known that there are more than 100 million photoreceptors in each retina and that these converge on about 500,000 ganglion cells. This meant there would be many ganglion cells that would each be excited by a number of photoreceptors. It was also known that the neurons, the bipolar cells connecting the ganglion cells to the photoreceptors, are connected by transversal neurons, and that this is probably also the case for the photoreceptors. Hence, it was known that the ganglion cells must be connected to the photoreceptors by a complicated retinal circuitry.

To his surprise, Kuffler found that a uniform illumination of the eye by flashes of light is not the best way to obtain a discharge of the ganglion cells. It is far more effective to stimulate the retina with small spots of light. By systematically exploring the sensitivity of the cells by this type of stimulation, Kuffler detected that each ganglion cell is sensitive only to a restricted area of the retina. He called these areas *receptive fields*. They were approximately circular and varied in size, being small in the fovea and getting larger towards the periphery.

However, when he explored the receptive fields further, Kuffler made the unexpected finding that some ganglion cells are maximally sensitive when their receptive fields are stimulated by light covering only an area of the center of the field. When the receptive field is stimulated by light falling on its outer part, the activity of the cell is inhibited. What determines the excitation of the ganglion cell is the relationship between the intensity of the stimulation of the two parts of the receptive fields. Hence, the cell is not sensitive to differences in absolute intensity. Kuffler also found cells in which the two parts of the receptive field give the opposite result. He called the two types of ganglion cells "*on*" *center cells* and "*off*" *center cells*.

Most of the ganglion cells have been found to be either the "on" center or the "off" center types. This means that most primarily react to differences in stimulation between the center and the surround of the receptive field. This reaction contrasts to the reaction in the photoreceptors, which primarily respond to the absolute intensity of the light stimulating them. Hence, in an important respect, the signals transmitted from the receptor cells are changed in the retina.

The fact that the receptive fields are smallest in the fovea and increase towards the periphery is in line with the known anatomical structure of the retina. It explains why visual acuity is best in the fovea and decreases towards the periphery. This finding is important – but not surprising in view of what we know of the anatomy of the retina. What was surprising is that the ganglion cells are maximally sensitive to differences in intensity within small areas of the retina and not to absolute intensity differences. It can be shown that this enhances contours and thus is favorable for our perception of shape.

When Kuffler had accounted for the transformation of the signal transmitted from the receptor cells to the ganglion cells of the retina, a next step was naturally to try to figure out what happened higher up in the system, particularly in the neurons of the primary visual cortex, the striate cortex. Kuffler's findings were surprising. Would there also be surprises at the cortical level? Two of his students, David Hubel and Torsten Wiesel, devised procedures to find out.

Indeed, there were surprises. The two researchers were unable to find cortical neurons responding to receptive fields of the kind discovered by their teacher. As so often happens in science, after repeated failures they accidentally detected something unexpected – that some neurons respond maximally to edges in a particular orientation.

Systematically studying the reactions in the neurons of the striate cortex, Hubel and Wiesel (1979) found that the cells responded not to spots of light but to line segments in specific orientations. Some cells referred to as *simple cells* responded "to an optimally oriented line in a narrowly defined orientation." Another major group of cells referred to as *complex cells* differed from simple cells by "being less particular about the exact position of the line." The orientation to which the cells responded optimally varied from cell to cell. There were also cells sensitive to the movement across the field in a specific orientation.

Kuffler had shown that the ganglion cells react to light stimulating the receptive fields of cells in a definite manner. Still, it was surprising that some neurons in the striate cortex do not react to light as such but only to light conforming to certain patterns of stimulation. The findings of Hubel and Wiesel are also significant because they suggest that it is possible to give a coherent account of the processes taking place in the visual system.

The research of Hubel and Wiesel seemed to help bridge the gap between physiological and psychological processes. Edges, contours, and lines are features of the world as we visually perceive it, and so are orientation and movements. We might therefore wonder whether the two researchers had found nerve mechanisms for perceiving definite perceptual features. Hubel and Wiesel (1979, p. 89) cautiously avoided jumping to this conclusion:

Although there is no direct evidence that orientation-sensitive cells have anything to do with visual perception, it is certainly tempting to think they represent some early stage in the brain's analysis of visual forms.

Reflecting a little on our perceptual experience, we can see that they may have had good reason for being so cautious. Visual form is always perceived in a context where objects form part of space, and orientation in our visual field is always experienced as relative to ourselves as observers. Yet, it was not at all implausible to believe their findings pointed to definite mechanisms underlying visual perception of direction, shape, and movement. Later researchers have been intensely occupied with finding these mechanisms. (For accounts of progress in this work, see Carlson, 2007; Gazzaniga et al., 2009.) Hubel and Wiesel received the Nobel Prize for Medicine in 1981.

Even if Hubel and Wiesel's findings allow no definite conclusions as to how our visual perceptions are formed, they strongly suggest that the neurons involved are arranged in specific anatomical structures containing specific chains for the transmission of signals.

This makes it implausible that the primary visual cortex acts as a field, as the Gestalt psychologists believed.

However, the findings do not support the Helmholtzian view of visual perception. Helmholtz thought the retina contains a number of nerve fibers, each of which sends a signal to the brain and there gives rise to sensations that are combined into perceptions by means of associative learning. If perception is the result of associative learning, important parts of the associative work must take place before the signals reach our consciousness. However, if there are associations between line segments of diverse lengths and orientations, we can account for shape in terms of associations between elements. Some psychologists seized eagerly upon this opportunity, and towards the end of the twentieth century the approach called *connectionism* arose. In my judgment, present knowledge about the nerve processes underlying the perception of shape is too fragmentary for us to evaluate this approach.

The Role Played by the Primary Visual Cortex

Before I proceed, I want to draw some long historical lines. A great step forward in the understanding of vision was taken when researchers in the 1600s discovered that the light entering the eye forms an inverted image of the outside world on the retina. When they realized this, it was natural to believe the image formed upon the retina is somehow transmitted to the brain. When neurologists later discovered that a specific area of the cortex is excited by stimulation of the eyes, they believed that somehow the image impressed on the retina is transmitted to this area and referred to it as the *primary visual cortex*. (A more neutral name for it is *area striata*.) The information transmitted to the primary visual cortex was then thought to be transmitted to other parts of the cortex, the *association areas*.

However, according to Zeki (1993), at the end of the 1800s researchers were already claiming that there is an area for chromatic color perception outside the striate cortex. In the 1970s, Zeki supported this claim with anatomical studies, recordings from individual neurons in animals, the results of PET scanning in human beings, and the description of a case of failure to perceive color as a result of damage to a restricted extrastriatal area. Zeki also helped identify a specific area for the perception of movements. Subsequently, several different extrastriate areas involved in visual perception have been found.

In line with the thinking of the British empiricist philosophers, Helmholtz, Wundt, and Titchener held that our perceptual impressions are made up of diverse types of elements. The discovery of the receptive fields of the cells of the striate cortex and of the extrastriate areas supported the idea that sensory impressions are composed of various elements, now referred to as *features*. Inspired by the neurophysiological findings, psychological researchers engaged in intense activity to account for our visual impressions by hypothesizing the existence of diverse types of features. Support has been found for some of the hypotheses about features, but, as shown by Michael Eysenck and Mark Keane (2005), Carlson (2007), and Gazzaniga et al. (2009), all the hypotheses have met with difficulties.

Before I leave the problem of accounting for our perceptual mental experience by means of features, I want to point out that the neurological findings seem to agree with Stumpf's view of our sensory impressions as representing wholes in which quite specific components, features, are discernible. The wholes do not seem to determine the parts in the way the Gestalt psychologists believed.

Hubel and Wiesel were very systematic in their work, basing their physiological study on extensive and, as I understand them, solid anatomical studies of the striate cortex. They refused to hypothesize about what happens to the neuronal signals when they are transmitted to levels higher than the striate cortex. Nor were they willing to speculate broadly about how the brain works. In contrast to them, Zeki (1993) apparently agreed with Helmholtz that a poor theory is better than none and attempted to explain how a visual mental experience is produced and how this explanation might help us understand how the brain works.

Speculations about the transformations undergone by the neuronal signals when they leave the striate area and the extrastriate area raise the intricate question of whether there is a center in the brain that integrates signals. Because our visual mental impressions have the character of being wholes, it is natural to think an integration of features – such as color, shape, size, and location – must take place. However, the idea of a center raises the question of how the brain could monitor it. Zeki (1993) did not find the idea of an integrating center appealing, and he also noted that no center in the cortex has been found that does not have connections leading from it to other centers.

Instead of assuming a center of integration, Zeki speculated that integration is accomplished when the striate and extrastriate areas connected to each other are activated synchronously. Conscious experience could arise when this synchronous activity takes place. This view of visual experience can, according to Zeki, serve as a model for the way the brain works to produce our integrated conscious experience. I shall not discuss Zeki's view of consciousness but just note that towards the end of the twentieth century, neuroscientists as well as philosophers were intensely studying problems of consciousness.

As this historical sketch shows, by 1970, researchers working on the border between physiology and psychology had found a physiological basis for a number of concepts that promised to be useful in integrating the two fields of study.

Neuropsychology has already contributed to a better understanding of a number of psychological processes. The results are of great practical importance, and towards the end of the twentieth century they opened up the possibility of investigating fundamental problems of consciousness. Further progress in the field is highly dependent upon the development of techniques for the anatomical and physiological investigation of the brain, but, as I hope to have made clear, it is equally dependent upon the ability of researchers to formulate meaningful psychological questions.

Physiology and Psychology

In their successful study of the relationship between the brain and bodily functions, physiologists have apparently regarded the brain as an organ and have investigated how it regulates bodily functions, such as breathing, blood circulation, digestion, sleep, wakefulness, sensory perceiving, and sexual reproduction. In these studies, they were able to give an anatomical and physiological description of the bodily functions. For example, in the study of breathing, they provided an anatomical description of the lungs as well as a physiological description of the role the lungs play in metabolism. Given these descriptions, they could then study how the brain regulates breathing through the peripheral nervous system.

The role of the brain as an organ is to regulate the bodily functions. It does not *produce* the functions; for example, the brain does not produce breathing. When we turn to functions we designate as psychological, such as attending, remembering, thinking, feeling, and willing, we will see that it is not easy to apply what I have regarded as a general physiological model for the study of the relationships between the brain and bodily functions.

The reason may be that the model of the brain as an organ regulating bodily functions is inappropriate because psychological functions are different from bodily functions. However, the reason may also be that it is more difficult to give an adequate description of psychological functions. When we consider that the physiologists' model has been very successful, we must have strong reasons for abandoning it. Moreover, it is natural to believe the same molecules are involved in all functions of the body. This makes it inappropriate to begin by postulating functions of fundamentally different natures.

On the other hand, it is not easy to understand how to describe the psychological functions without first making assumptions about brain processes. However, we may think of the psychological functions as the result of various types of interactions between the organism and its environment. This is the model followed by the sensory physiologists from Helmholtz to Hubel and Wiesel in which sensory perception is an interaction between the organism and its environment, regulated by the brain. Attention as well as the other psychological functions can also be accounted for in this way.

If we take the position that psychological functions are the result of interactions between an organism and its environment, we seem, as N. H. Pronko (1996) notes, to avoid running into the mind–body problem, as well as problems raised by a reductionist position. I shall not go further into the question of relating the psychological functions to the brain but just note that if we take the position just outlined above, it seems to follow that psychology is necessary for a complete study of the brain, and that psychological processes are not explicable only in terms of processes in the brain.

The brain is necessary for psychological functions, and we cannot properly understand relationships *between* psychological functions of the brain without understanding their relationship *to* the brain. Yet, whether psychology can be studied independently of physiology and the study of the brain seems to be an empirical question. As we saw above, during the last fifty or more years physiologists have accumulated considerable knowledge that helps formulate problems for psychological research in a more productive manner. This suggests that the study of psychology will benefit from close contact with physiology. While psychology is not ultimately biology, the biological correlates of psychological life must be understood and studied.

18

Revolt Against Traditions

After World War II, the United States and the Soviet Union became the leading nations of the world. The two superpowers stood in uncompromising opposition to each other as leaders of two separate political blocs, but with the exception of the Korean and Vietnam Wars, the Cold War did not lead to armed conflict.

Social development in the United States was stable for a time, accompanied by prodigious growth in technology, science, and the economy. Tensions increased at the beginning of the 1960s, however. The United States deepened its involvement in the war in Vietnam, and differing viewpoints on this war effort came to divide the nation in two. The assassination of President John F. Kennedy in 1963 came as a shock, while the Civil Rights movement acquired a large following. The women's movement and, towards the end of the decade, the environmental movement gained momentum as well. Many young Americans turned against what they considered a materialistic and self-satisfied society and sought a more spontaneous and less conventional lifestyle.

As we have seen in the preceding chapters, psychology in the United States was under-going rapid development during the time between World War I and World War II. After the Nazis seized power and Germany then lost World War II, psychology stagnated in both Germany and Austria. In the first half of the 1900s, the British took little interest in psychology, but in the 1950s, British psychologists again began to make contributions to the study, as did Canadian. Still, in the latter half of the twentieth century, empirical psychology was dominated by the United States, and in this chapter, I shall for the most part discuss the history of psychology in the United States.

Expansion in US Psychology

Psychology had proved to be important in preparing for and waging war. This increased interest in it, and psychological research enjoyed substantial funding from the US government after the war. The opportunity to study at universities was also considerably broadened when the government gave war veterans the right to three years of higher education. Students flocked to the field of psychology. The number of members of the American Psychological Association (APA), which gives a realistic impression of the number of psychologists educated in the United States, increased from 1,000 in 1929 to 7,000 in 1950. (At the beginning of the twenty-first century, the APA had approximately 150,000 members. In Europe and South America, too, the number of psychologists has increased sharply.)

Along with the increase in the number of psychologists, a further development has also taken place. Since the founding of the APA in 1892, both theoretical and applied psychology has branched out. In 1946, the body of members consisted of so many groupings with such specialized interests that it was decided to organize the association in separate divisions, numbering a total of nineteen. The number of divisions has increased steadily and today there are fifty-six.

The organization into separate divisions indicates that a great deal of specialization has taken place, and it raises the question of the degree to which we can view psychology as one study. It also is a consequence of the issues within the field being so complex, and its body of knowledge being so little integrated by theory. But it is also undoubtedly a result of conflicts in psychologists' understanding of the field. There have always been controversies between applied and academic psychologists. In the 1930s, a group of the former broke away from the APA and formed their own association, but they joined the APA again after some years. In 1988, a group of the latter in turn broke away to form the American Psychological Society (APS). At the beginning of the twenty-first century it had about 16,000 members.

In the years following World War II, conditions for doing empirical work in psychology were considerably improved; progress was made in all the main areas of empirical research. But no radical new programs like those of psychoanalysis, Gestalt psychology, and behaviorism were launched until the late 1950s and early 1960s. In these years, two new approaches were worked out. Within clinical and personality psychology, the so-called *humanistic psychology* arose as an alternative to psychodynamic and behavioral approaches. Within core areas of experimental psychology, *information processing* became a strong influence. Like the pioneers in psychoanalysis, Gestalt psychology, and behaviorism before them, the pioneers in these two new approaches found little of value in the psychology developed until the mid-century, and their reactions to the then-prevalent views took the form of revolt.

Before I turn to an examination of the advent of these two approaches, I shall discuss a change taking place in the more general intellectual and philosophical climate of the United States in the 1950s and 1960s.

New Thoughts on Science

A constantly recurring question in the philosophy of science is how we should understand the relationship between theoretical postulates and observations. In their account of scientific theories as axiomatic systems, the logical positivists had differentiated between the concepts contained in the postulates about regularities and explanation, and those contained in descriptions of observations. Throughout the 1950s and the beginning of the 1960s, philosophers of science became increasingly critical of logical positivism, pointing out that in the choice of observations supporting a theory, the theorist is also led by theory. Observations could therefore not, as the logical positivists as well as the early positivists had assumed, be considered neutral in relation to theory. Although the observations comprise the basis for theory, they must be viewed as dependent on theory as well. A thorough and comprehensive review of the criticism of logical positivism has been presented by Frederick Suppe (1977).

The change in the view of the role of observations in scientific research caused many psychologists to become more aware of how much more they must emphasize that hypotheses are parts of a larger context. Issues must not only be clarified in relationship to procedures and experimental findings; they must also be placed within contexts that often include philosophical inferences as well as social and cultural backgrounds. It was understood that the tenability of psychological beliefs could not be determined by simple tests. Hypotheses had to be examined with a view to accumulating evidence for or against them. Hypothesis testing, therefore, had to be viewed as a far more complex process than it had been before.

Instead of beginning by reasoning on the basis of concrete experimental findings, many found it more appropriate to clarify the issue by placing it in a larger context. Researchers therefore adopted a freer stance in formulating hypotheses and choosing procedures. They also came to understand that speculation often plays a greater role in science than the positivists had envisioned. With the increased inclination to view psychological issues within broader contexts, the differences between the study of physics and of psychology became clearer. Physics, and mechanics in particular, had been the ideal for psychology. At this time, however, some began to look for ways in which to conduct psychological research within disciplines other than the natural sciences. Linguistics, history, and other humanistic subjects, as well as the social sciences, were drawn into the philosophy of science debate. As we can see in the collection of essays edited by Carl Graumann and Kenneth Gergen (1996), there is still a tendency to orient psychology towards these disciplines.

Thomas Kuhn's View of Paradigms

Several of the critics of positivism presented alternatives to the positivist view of science. One viewpoint influencing many psychologists at the time was advanced by Thomas Kuhn (1962/1970). Whereas the logical positivists had attempted to analyze scientific theories, primarily Newton's theory of gravity and Einstein's theory of relativity, Kuhn attempted to understand science as a historical study, as Whewell, Mach, and others had done before him. He claimed that the interests of scientists, their understanding of the phenomena they studied, the demands they made on theories, and the criteria they posed for what is to be considered acceptable science, were all determined by a higher-order perspective, a comprehensive view of the world. This higher-order perspective, determining the interests and the formulation of issues and procedures of researchers, he called a *paradigm*.

A primary concern of Kuhn was to demonstrate how scientists' views of their fields and their practices change over the course of time. To explain this, he pointed out that when a specific paradigm has been established, researchers engage in what he called *normal science*. As long as the paradigm is acceptable, they solve the problems associated with it. Eventually, however, unresolved issues accumulate and create doubts about the paradigm. Alternate theories then come into being, and these eventually lead to new paradigms. These changes of paradigm are considered to be revolutions in science; a new conception of the world is adopted.

An important point in Kuhn's thinking is that the change of paradigm by and large arises as a consequence of changes in the scientists' system of values. The change is therefore of a social nature. According to Kuhn, theories are not rejected as a consequence of having been subjected to specific testing.

Evaluation of Kuhn's View

Kuhn pointed to new aspects of scientific activity and contributed to a greater understanding of the social and sociological aspect of the scientific endeavor. His account of the confusion existing in an area of research before the arrival of a specific paradigm was instructive. Critics rapidly pointed out that Kuhn's definition of *paradigm* is imprecise, however, and in part also self-contradictory.

In Kuhn's view of science, what we understand as *facts* within a branch of science depends on the perspective, the paradigm, we adopt at a given period of time. This point has been strongly criticized. Although no forms of scientific knowledge can be considered absolutely incontestable, certain forms of knowledge as facts are nearly independent of change, and many will consider them the appropriate basis for scientific theory. For example, when we study the theory of evolution, we may ascertain that it rests on knowledge of the anatomy, physiology, and embryology of animals as well as on meticulous descriptions of their environment and way of living in the past and present.

We have also been able to establish the time span of the existence of different animal species. Biology thus gives us knowledge of a factual nature, and this is the basis for the theory of evolution. A major part of this knowledge was available before Darwin presented his theory and will continue to represent knowledge should the theory of evolution be replaced by another theory. Thus, in my judgment, theory determines which kind of knowledge is important, but hardly what are to be considered facts.

Kuhn and Psychology

Most researchers in psychology today probably agree that psychology must be provided with a basis in factual knowledge, and I believe they would agree that this body of knowledge has increased considerably since the inception of psychology as an empirical science in the latter half of the 1800s. They hold that this factual knowledge should determine their thinking about psychological events to an increasing degree. All scientific theory contains an element of construction, but, as Frederick Suppe (1977) and many others have pointed out, it is too extreme to view science as primarily an effort to achieve social consensus. Kuhn's concept of *scientific paradigm* is highly obscure. His thoughts about revolutions in science have an intuitive appeal, but a methodical study of history might reveal that the development of knowledge is better characterized as a gradual accumulation. Although Kuhn's view of science was soon strongly criticized (see Suppe, 1977), it still exerted considerable influence on psychology.

When positivism broke down, it does not seem to have been succeeded by any widely accepted system of philosophy of science. This does not imply that we do not know what constitutes scientific thinking, however. There can be no doubt it is important to systematize knowledge; to formulate and find support for hypotheses; to make observations more reliable; to devise methods of measurement; to employ mathematics; to make causal analysis by means of experiments; to construct theories allowing explanation, deduction, and prediction; and to eliminate alternate approaches and explanations.

New Views on Human Beings: Humanistic Psychology

Positivism had as its object not only the expansion of science to encompass new problem areas. It also aimed to create a perspective on human beings and society to correspond to the progress made in science. Although perhaps the majority of psychologists in the early twentieth century felt that psychology had not provided results that could form the basis for a new outlook on life, they would probably have emphasized perspectives and factual knowledge that could be investigated by empirical methods. They would therefore have tended to ignore viewpoints that lay beyond the reach of natural science. Towards the end of the 1950s, a movement arose to criticize psychology on precisely this basis. Its adherents gave it the name *humanistic psychology*.

The Roots of Humanistic Psychology

The humanist movement comprised psychologists who felt, based on their view of life, their life experience, or their psychological practice, that psychology as it had been developed so far disregarded important aspects of human life. This reaction appears to have been inspired by *existential philosophy*, which took a critical view of positivism and the view of human beings it represented. In Germany, the prominent critic Wilhelm Dilthey (1833–1911) claimed that the methods of the natural sciences are inappropriate for the study of human beings. Through the humanistic sciences – the study of history, religion, poetry, the arts, and language – we could acquire a more profound understanding of human thinking and activity. We must differentiate between the methods of the natural and the humanistic sciences, and between what Dilthey called explanatory and descriptive psychology. Explanatory psychology, like the natural sciences, seeks to break wholes into less complex parts. Descriptive psychology, on the other hand, tries to understand human beings through the study of history. We may recall that Wundt's *Völkerpsychologie* was an expression of similar thoughts.

Criticism of the positivists' view of the human being, already quite clearly articulated at the end of the 1800s, continued in existential philosophy. The existential philosophers claimed to base their ideas on the phenomenological description of how life is experienced by the individual. The point of departure for several of them was the later philosophy of Edmund Husserl. Martin Heidegger (1889–1976) was a central figure in the endeavor to develop a philosophy with the objective of understanding the unique features of human life. According to what he considered to be a phenomenological approach, Heidegger argued that an essential feature of the human outlook on life is that it is *subjective*. This implied that it is particular to each individual. Other characteristics are that human beings have the freedom to choose within the framework of their abilities and the conditions in which they have grown up. Further, he claimed that the execution of freedom of choice gives rise to an anxiety that human beings must live with. To become a genuine human being, to acquire *authenticity*, we need the courage to choose according to our own nature as a human individual. When we do not dare to make these choices, the result is guilt.

The idea of freedom of choice for human beings is central to both Christianity and other religions. At the beginning of the 1800s, Søren Kierkegaard (1813–1855) had advanced his thoughts about the consequence of choice for human beings, which many found convincing. Towards the end of the century, Nietzsche had pointed out that neither religion nor science could inform people of the perspective they should adopt for their way of life. This perspective must be determined by the person's own choices. The viewpoints of these two thinkers gained a renewed relevance with the advent of existential philosophy. Existential philosophy was formed within Christian theology as well as within an atheist view of life.

The Growth of Humanistic Psychology

In the United States, existential philosophy gained a representative in Rollo May (1909–1994). Like Rogers, May first studied theology at the Union Theological Seminary and later psychology at Columbia University. He was strongly influenced by Kierkegaard and further developed Kierkegaard's and Heidegger's ideas about anxiety. May claimed we must differentiate between anxiety that is the natural result of choice leading us into unfamiliar situations, and anxiety that results from fear of freedom of choice. He also formulated thoughts about how love and will function in the lives of human beings.

May worked as a clinical psychologist in private practice, and in the 1950s he was one of the pioneers in the effort to establish the right of clinical psychologists to have a clinical practice. He presented his thoughts about human beings, mental health, and psychotherapy in several widely read books and commanded a great deal of respect from his contemporary US clinical psychologists. As an expression of their esteem, he was asked to write the preface to a major work, *History of Psychotherapy: A Century of Change* (1992), published as a jubilee edition for the hundredth anniversary of the founding of the APA.

Rogers and Kelly, as I recounted in Chapter 15, had views on human beings that corresponded with existential philosophy in important ways. At a symposium arranged by the APA, Rollo May, Abraham Maslow, and others expressed their commitment to, as well as criticism of, central ideas in existential philosophy. Along with other psychologists, they evolved viewpoints that they believed to comprise a new direction in psychology. They called this orientation *humanistic psychology*. In 1961, adherents of the new orientation founded their own journal, and, in 1972, a separate division for its adherents was founded in the APA.

As Hergenhahn (2009) and other historians have emphasized, the adherents of humanistic psychology were not opposed to scientific psychology; their contention was that it neglects important aspects of human thinking and activity. They criticized psychoanalysis and behaviorism for not allowing for the prospect of human beings making choices and planning their lives. A major point among the humanistic psychologists was that human beings have an innate potential for developing a rich cognitive and emotional life and for working constructively with others. They were particularly opposed to the mechanistic and deterministic view of life characteristic of psychoanalysis and behaviorism. Conversely, they emphasized the subjective and the unique in human beings' outlook on life, and they claimed that psychology must take a phenomenological description of human experience and meaning as lived as its point of departure. In order to emphasize their opposition to psychoanalysis and behaviorism, they termed their orientation *the third force of psychology*.

Along with Rogers, Kelly, and May, other humanistic psychologists were developing their own forms of therapy on the basis of the general underlying guidelines of the movement. According to Richard Farson (1978), who held a central position in the movement, innumerable versions of humanistic forms of therapy had evolved. But in the jubilee edition of the book mentioned above, Laura Rice and Leslie Greenberg (1992) accentuated the following four trends in the humanistic forms of therapy: a phenomenological approach, emphasis on the individual's own resources for the growth of personality, belief in human beings' ability to make their own choices, and respect for the personality of the client.

Abraham Maslow (1908–1970)

Abraham Maslow (1908–1970) was considered the leader of the humanistic movement. He was born in Brooklyn, New York, the eldest of seven children in a Jewish family. Upon completing his psychological studies in New York and studying for a term with Titchener at Cornell, he received his PhD under Harry Harlow in 1934. After finishing his studies in Wisconsin, he became a research assistant to Thorndike at Columbia University, followed by work as a teacher at Brooklyn College, and from 1951 he was head of the department of psychology at Brandeis University in Massachusetts. From 1968 to his death in 1970, he had a paid fellowship as researcher in a private institution.

During the time Maslow taught psychology in New York, he became acquainted with Alfred Adler and the German brain physiologist Kurt Goldstein (1878–1965), who had been forced to leave Germany in 1933 because he was a Jew. These two thinkers appear to have had a great influence on him. Adler may have helped draw his attention to the role played by the need in human beings to belong to and act within a social community. Goldstein may have imparted to him his idea that the need to use our resources and abilities is a compelling force in human beings.

After World War I, Goldstein had led a major project for the rehabilitation of soldiers with brain injuries from the war. He worked with Köhler's brother-in-law, Adamar Gelb, who joined the Gestalt psychologists in Berlin. Goldstein was opposed to some aspects of Gestalt psychology, but he did reject the idea that human responses could be understood as chains of reflexes. The reactions of the organism must be viewed as a whole. Together with a coworker, Goldstein devised a test for brain damage that was widely used at the time. I shall here point out only that, while treating his brain-damaged patients, he was struck by the degree to which they were able to mobilize energy to meet the challenges their disability entailed. Goldstein came to think that human beings possess a force that motivates them for development. He called this innate force, which he viewed as a motive, *self-actualization*, and it came to hold a central position in the humanistic movement.

The greatest influence on Maslow's thinking probably stemmed from Henry Murray, and we can see his main contribution to psychology as an elaboration of Murray's classification of human needs. In his book *Motivation and Personality* (1954), Maslow presented a theory in which he organized human motives in a hierarchic structure. At the bottom of the hierarchy are physiological needs such as hunger, thirst, and sex, and needs pertaining to the organism's health. At the next level of the hierarchy are needs pertaining to the organism's safety – protection from rain, cold, pain, and sudden danger. Then follow needs to belong with other people and to love and be loved. Above this level are needs that have to do with the individual's wish to work for the human community and be acknowledged by others.

The needs stand in relationship to each other such that they must be satisfied in a given order; before a need can be satisfied, the preceding one must be accommodated. When all the needs have been satisfied, the individual would develop self-actualization. One condition for self-actualization is that nothing has disturbed the fulfillment of needs at lower levels in the hierarchy. Only a very few are in this situation, according to Maslow.

Maslow conducted a study of persons he considered to be *self-actualizing*. Among them were Albert Einstein, Albert Schweitzer, Sigmund Freud, Jane Adams, William James, and Abraham Lincoln, whom, according to Maslow, had important traits in common, such as spontaneity, high need for privacy, deep social interest and sense of responsibility to mankind, and acceptance of self, others, and nature. The idea that there are individuals who, after having all their fundamental needs satisfied, function from their need for *self-actualization* suited affluent members of US society, who perceived the benefit of acquiring knowledge and understanding, of cultivating the arts, and of seeking greater creativity. As John Benjafield (1996) has remarked, Maslow's book became part of the syllabus in many US high schools.

Maslow drew attention to an important point in the study of motivation by emphasizing that, whereas physiological needs are characterized by regular recurrence and orientation towards specific goals, the need for *self-actualization* does not have this characteristic. It is not what Maslow termed a *deficiency need*, but rather a *need of being*. As he noted, this characteristic is an important aspect of several forms of human motivation – they do not appear to be subject to temporal regularity like the physiological needs, and they do not always seem to be unequivocally directed towards specific objectives.

Maslow's work had a great appeal to many of his contemporaries, but at the end of the twentieth century, psychological researchers seemed to take little interest in them. He is not even mentioned in the two handbooks of personality edited by Hogan et al. (1997) and Pervin and John (1999).

An Evaluation of Humanistic Psychology

The humanistic direction within psychology gained ground throughout the 1960s and helped expand the field. It also pointed out the role of states such as hope, happiness, despair, and apathy in the lives of human beings and clarified that regardless of how we think about the issue of free will, human beings make choices and feel responsible for their actions, and we try to build relationships with each other based on trust and love. Questions about freedom, will, and responsibility must therefore have a place in psychology, even though we have limited means to answer them by scientific methods. The humanistic psychologists, and particularly Rogers, must also be credited for emphasizing the importance for psychotherapists of meeting their clients with empathy and understanding, of being genuine, and of showing respect for the client's worth as a human being.

Interest in humanistic psychology declined sharply in the 1970s when the difficulty of shaping its fundamental concepts into a systematic, scientific psychology became clear. Concepts such as subjectivity, the human mind as a whole and the individual as a unique being may perhaps acquire meaning only within an extensive analysis of the cultural traditions we hold.

The central idea of humanistic psychology, self-actualization, must be viewed in the context of the ideals that evolved during the Enlightenment and the Romantic period at the end of the 1700s and beginning of the 1800s. That the idea of self-actualization has long roots in Western cultural tradition naturally does not exclude the possibility that it has a basis in genetically determined dispositions. However, if the relationship between genetic dispositions and cultural influence is not clarified, the concept can be of little use in a systematic psychological argument. Michael Wertheimer (1978) has also commented that the term *humanistic psychology* is unsatisfactory, claiming that the movement's program was obscure. Farson, in the article I referred to above, emphasized that humanistic clinical psychologists helped create expectations about life enhancement in the US population that might not be beneficial for the development of society in the long run. There are limits, he contended, to how much people can and should unburden themselves of social expectations and norms in the pursuit of self-realization. Some of the ideas of humanistic psychology, such as the role played by hope and happiness in human life, have been further elaborated in *positive psychology* (Seligman et al., 2005).

Tendencies in Clinical Psychology from the 1960s

Humanistic psychology gave rise to a wide variety of therapy forms. At the same time, as Michael Lambert et al. (2004) remarked in the fifth edition of Bergin and Garfield's *Handbook of Psychotherapy and Behavior Change*, there has been an increasing move towards eclecticism in the selection of therapeutic approach. Some have termed this tendency integrative, while others see it as the expression of a somewhat ill-considered eclectic attitude.

While the number of different forms of therapy has increased, the requirement for the individual therapist to follow procedures that have a clearly documented beneficial effect has been reinforced. Interest in *therapy research* has increased considerably since its rather feeble beginning in the 1950s. While the differences between various forms of therapy help motivate us to investigate their effects, public opinion and the authorities are also putting pressure on clinical psychologists to document the effect of their practices. As Lambert and Benjamin Ogles (2004) and many other contributors to the above handbook claim, therapy research has provided a reasonably solid basis for the assumption that all the most widespread forms of psychotherapy appear to have beneficial effects.

This is an encouraging result. Nevertheless, it raises a critical question with regard to the effect of psychotherapy. As Lambert et al. (2004) report, the most widely used forms of therapy all seem to yield the same degree of beneficial results. When we consider how different these forms are, we may wonder whether the effects are due to the specific techniques employed, or to general factors such as the therapist's effort to create an atmosphere of kindliness and hope, and the clients' opportunity to express their emotions; get support, advice, and explanations for their problems; and try out other forms of behavior.

Decline in Interest in Behaviorism

As research had disclosed important shortcomings in behaviorism, it began to lose its attraction during the 1950s. The Gestalt psychologists, as well as Lashley and Koch, had criticized the concept of stimulus, and the difficulty of accounting for behavior in terms of chains of stimulus–response connections was now understood. It was also becoming clear that the behaviorist view of learning as a unitary process was untenable. Finally, as I mentioned in Chapter 12, Chomsky's criticism of Skinner's attempt to apply behaviorist principles to the study of language further contributed to disenchantment with behaviorism.

Behaviorism had been formed within the framework of the positivist philosophy of science, with its demand that we must forego all speculation and that the events and phenomena under investigation must be directly observable. When positivism was subjected to criticism, this also contributed to the undermining of the behaviorist approach.

One factor that may have been a primary cause of the increasing disenchantment with behaviorism was that it imposed severe restrictions on psychological thinking and research. As long as it was considered unacceptable to employ inferences about human consciousness and cognition, many believed that too many important questions were rendered inaccessible. However, although many felt the time was ripe for innovation, behaviorism continued to exert an influence.

As I showed in Chapter 16, the study of cognition grew from 1920 to 1960. In Chapter 14, I also pointed out that from the 1940s, a phenomenological and cognitive orientation was strongly prevalent in US social psychology. Behaviorism had an impact on personality and clinical psychology, but I believe it is correct to state that in this area of psychology, the phenomenological and cognitive approaches held stronger positions than behaviorism. Finally, as noted in Chapter 17, the trend-setting researchers in physiological psychology who gathered around Lashley hardly considered themselves behaviorists. And with the exception of Russian reflexology, European psychology has never been behaviorist.

Increased Interest in the Study of Cognition

In the beginning of the 1950s, two influential books on experimental psychology appeared. One was the *Handbook of Experimental Psychology*, edited by Stanley Stevens (1951b). The other was a radically revised second edition (1954) of *Experimental Psychology*, written by Woodworth in cooperation with Harold Schlosberg. Neither book tried to draw a boundary between psychology studied as mental experience and psychology studied as behavior. I suspect this reflected a general tendency among US experimental psychologists at the beginning of the 1950s to conceive of psychology as the study of mental experience and behavior, or, as Hilgard (1953) did, as behavior and mental experience.

Both books treated problems of cognition extensively. In Stevens's *Handbook* we find, in addition to chapters on perception, a chapter by Hovland on human learning and retention and the chapter on cognitive processes by Leeper mentioned in Chapter 16. Cognition is also treated in a chapter on comparative psychology. In Woodworth's book, there are chapters on perception, attention, verbal learning, and problem-solving thought. I believe it is fairly safe to conclude that a majority of experimental psychologists at the beginning of the 1950s believed the study of cognition had a central place in psychology, even if they may have thought the study of sensory perception, motivation, learning, or emotions was a more important area of research, at least for the time being.

In the 1950s and 1960s, an important change in research interests seems to have taken place among experimental psychologists. Interest in the behaviorist position declined, as I have already noted, and interest in the study of cognition increased. The change is frequently referred to as the *cognitive revolution in psychology*. It was important because it seems to have given the study of cognition the central place in empirical psychology. But the term is unfortunate because it may lead to the belief that there was no scientific cognitive psychology prior to the 1950s. Empirical psychology began in the study of perception and cognition, and, as I hope to have documented in Chapters 16 and 17, there was steady progress in the study all through the first half of the twentieth century.

Several reasons are probably needed to explain the shift of interest. First, all through the early twentieth century, psychology as the study of mind and psychology as the study of behavior had been vying for supremacy. When interest in behaviorism declined, it was natural for interest in the study of mind to increase. Psychologists may simply have realized they had neglected the study of cognitive functions.

Second, as Bruner (1983, p. 274) notes in his autobiography, awareness of the role played by knowledge rose among his generation of psychologists, philosophers, and anthropologists. Knowledge had been highly valued from the early years of the United States, and schools and universities were rapidly built after the Civil War. As science and technology advanced in the early twentieth century, it became even more apparent that knowledge plays a great role in the development of US society. As Bruner pointed out, industrial life depends on well-informed citizens.

It is not easy to see why Bruner's generation of psychologists should have been more interested in the promotion of knowledge than was Dewey's generation. But if we recall that behaviorism as well as psychodynamic psychology had discouraged the study of cognition for some years, it is perhaps not unreasonable to believe Bruner's peers were more interested in developing it. The competition for international leadership with the Soviet Union may also have increased the quest for knowledge. When the Russians were the first to send up a satellite, the United States renewed efforts to stimulate the growth of knowledge and creativity in children.

Third, as I reported in the preceding chapter, new techniques in neurology and neuropsychology had led to an increased interest in the study of cognition, and neuropsychologists as well as neurophysiologists became important contributors to it. Thus, by the mid-1950s, studies of cognition were being carried out in neuropsychology and neurophysiology along with studies of cognition in general experimental psychology.

At the end of the 1950s, a new approach to the study of cognition, called *information processing*, emerged.

In the course of ten years, information processing grew into a school of psychology with an important place in its history. Before I turn to reviewing it, I want to emphasize that the study of cognition was also carried out within the other three research traditions, as is well documented in Michael Eysenck and Mark Keane's (2005) student handbook of cognitive psychology. The study of cognition, as an undertaking within the psychology of the twenty-first century, is thus the result of contributions from all four research traditions.

Information Processing

Information processing emerged as an attempt to base a study of cognition on ideas taken from communication theory, cybernetics, and computer technology. Often referred to as *cognitive science*, it began in the latter half of the 1950s as an interdisciplinary endeavor in which logicians, mathematicians, engineers, neuroscientists, philosophers, linguists, and psychologists participated. I shall limit my review to information processing as a research tradition within the psychological study of cognition.

The promoters of information processing revolted against the then-current psychology, behaviorism, because most behaviorists excluded cognitive problems, and against psychology as the study of the mind because they regarded it as based on introspection. The pioneers seem to have looked upon themselves as having carried out a scientific revolution and to have given the study of cognition an entirely new foundation. The latter belief, which has become widely accepted, fostered the view that the study of cognition originated in the late 1950s and 1960s. Two books on the history of information processing contributed to this view. One was by Roy Lachman, Janet Lachman, and Earl Butterfield, *Cognitive Psychology and Information Processing* (1979). The authors based their presentation on Kuhn's ideas of scientific paradigms. In line with these ideas, information processing represented a scientific paradigm that, by a scientific revolution, had overthrown the earlier behaviorist paradigm. The other book, *The Mind's New Science: A History of the Cognitive Revolution*, by Howard Gardner (1987), was a broad history of cognitive science. Even if he reviewed a large portion of the earlier history of the study of cognition, Gardner held that it took the advent of the modern computer and information theory to grant legitimacy to cognitive studies.

These two books account in detail for the origin of the ideas underlying information processing and present research in a clear, systematic, and critical manner. In my opinion, however, they greatly overestimate the role played by behaviorism in the mid-twentieth century, underestimate the progress made in the study of cognition in the early twentieth century, and create the impression that information processing led to a revolution in psychology overthrowing behaviorism. As I hope to have made clear, most mid-twentieth-century psychologists probably conceived of psychology as the study of mind and behavior. The scientific study of cognition had made steady progress throughout the first half of the century; behaviorism had been undermined by a trenchant critique before the advent of information processing; and in the later twentieth century, the study of cognition was carried on in general experimental psychology, neuropsychology, and neurophysiology, more or less independently of information processing.

The tendency of the pioneers of information processing to accept uncritically the Kuhnian ideas of science prevented them from searching for inspiration in the earlier work on cognition. In my attempt to identify what was new in information processing, I shall point to the ideas of prominent historical figures that were relevant to the new research endeavor.

What most plainly characterized information processing was the introduction of ideas taken from computer technology, communication theory, and cybernetics. I shall, therefore, begin my review by giving an outline of this development. Then I shall discuss the meaning of the term *information processing* within empirical psychology.

For the empirical psychologist, the most interesting aspect of information processing is naturally how its promoters attempted to adjust to psychology the ideas taken from technology. This adjustment met with several intricate questions, to which I shall devote some time. I shall discuss some of the work of pioneers such as George Miller, Donald Broadbent, Herbert Simon, and Allen Newell. The linguist Noam Chomsky also played an important role in the early information-processing work on cognition, and I shall discuss some of his ideas as well.

Adherents of information processing worked within all subareas of the study of cognition: perception, attention, learning, imagining, remembering, thinking, decision making, intelligence, and use of language. I shall also review some of the studies of memory, since it is probably in this study that the approach has proved most successful.

Background in Advances in Technology

Artificial Communication Systems and Cybernetics

Throughout the years, human beings have attempted to construct signal systems of different descriptions. These efforts underwent a dramatically rapid development from the end of the 1800s. In the course of one hundred years, inventors and engineers devised the telegraph, telephone, radio, and television. A research discipline was also formed to deal with issues common to all these means of transmitting information, such as the fact that transmission of information must occur over time. Conservation of temporal differences in a system therefore became a focal problem in all forms of communication. Another important common problem was the way the transmission of information is influenced by disturbing elements, called noise. A third problem was the quantity of information that can be transmitted per time unit by way of a given medium; that is, the system's information capacity.

The media we employ in artificial communication systems differ from one system to another, but they do have similarities, including *channels* and *channel capacity*. Around 1950, a sophisticated *communication theory* was constructed to calculate the efficiency of the various systems for transmitting information. Claude Shannon was a central figure in the development of this theory. Researchers believed the way human beings handle many types of cognitive tasks could be compared to the handling of information in an artificial channel, and that, like artificial channels, these human skills have *capacity limitations*. As in the transfer of a message via a channel, information must be *encoded* by the sender. For the information to be of use, the recipient then must *decode* it.

A second important source of inspiration for the formation of information processing was *cybernetics*, developed by the mathematician Norbert Wiener. Cybernetics is the study of processes that sustain balance in machines and organisms, thus controlling these processes. An important concept in this context is *feedback*, information from a mechanism that rebounds on the system and regulates it, like the thermostat in a heating system. By means of the thermostat, a heating element is turned on when the temperature falls below a given value, and off when it reaches a specific upper value. By using such self-regulating mechanisms, we can construct extremely complex systems that can be adapted to oscillations of different kinds. Wiener, who claimed that his cybernetics model could be adapted to all areas of science, contended that machines having self-regulating mechanisms could be said to strive towards a goal, to function according to a purpose.

Modern Computers

While these influential models of communication and self-regulating mechanisms were being developed, major advances were also taking place in the development of fast computers; modern computers were invented that have proved applicable to an astounding array of practical problems. This may lead us to forget that they were the outcome of the extremely abstract thinking of mathematicians and logicians.

One source of ideas came from the attempts of Gottlob Frege and later of Bertrand Russell and Alfred North Whitehead to find a logical basis for mathematics. One result of their efforts was the construction of systems of logic in which expressions from everyday language were replaced by more precisely defined symbols, and the rules for deciding the truth and falsity of sentences were made more explicit. This formalization expanded the study of logic and, as a theory of formal systems, also found use in the development of computers.

Independently of the endeavors of Frege, Russell, and Whitehead, David Hilbert began a systematic examination of the foundations of mathematics. Questions about the nature of mathematical proofs and the closely related problem of what we mean by *computability* were clarified by Hilbert and later mathematicians.

The discussion of the nature of proofs and computability led Alan Turing in 1936 to develop the idea of a system, or what he called a *universal machine* (now referred to as the *Turing machine*) for the computation of mathematical problems. Turing proved that his system was so constructed that it solved any mathematical or logical problem that could be expressed in binary code. The way his system was constructed also suggested that it is possible to construct a machine that can execute any type of mathematical calculation.

Hence, if we could write a program in binary code containing the necessary steps and an *algorithm* for the solution of a problem, the machine could perform the computations. Thus, by writing a program meeting the requirements of the Turing machine, a person was guaranteed that his or her reasoning met the requirements for being computable. This, of course, can be an enormous advantage in tasks requiring reasoning. Turing also grappled with the question of whether a machine could be so programed that it could be said to be thinking. He suggested a specific procedure, called the Turing test, for answering this question, in which the machine is said to think if an interlocutor is unable to distinguish between the answers given by the machine and by a human being.

The study of logic and the foundation of mathematics has made it clear that these studies are primarily concerned with relationships between objects, and not with the contents of these objects. In a chapter entitled "The Greatness of Mathematics and Human Experience," the French mathematician and physicist Henri Poincaré (1902/1952, p. 20) expressed the point in the following way:

Mathematicians do not study objects but relations between objects; to them it is a matter of indifference if these objects are replaced by others, provided that the relations do not change. Matter does not engage their attention, they are interested by form alone.

Clearly, unless mathematical concepts are somehow anchored in the environment to which humans are biologically adapted, it is impossible to understand what mathematics is about. Mathematics is therefore somehow directed towards objects, but Poincaré was right in emphasizing that mathematicians and logicians are primarily concerned with *relationships* between objects.

The idea that logic and mathematics primarily deal with relationships, with syntax, and not with content, not with semantics, came to greatly influence information processing. This may be its strongest, but also its weakest, point. Information

Information Processing: A Study of Knowledge

Modern computers were constructed to help mathematicians carry out complex and time-consuming computations. But the machines were soon found to be useful in the solution of a great variety of tasks. Some researchers realized there is an apparent similarity between the way computers process information and the processes taking place in human beings when they solve tasks of a cognitive nature. In other words, they realized that human beings may be regarded as processors of information. This is the core idea in information processing.

In computer technology, the term "information processing" means the processes going on in the computer when it is set to solve some problem. To understand more concretely the use of the term in *psychology*, we must examine the meaning given to the term "information" as well as to the term "processing."

The term "information," as explained by Lachman et al. (1979, p. 75), is taken from communication theory, where its meaning has a basis in a mathematical argument. After a few years, it was found that, defined in this way, the term has limited usefulness, and its meaning was changed to *knowledge*. The account given by Lachman et al. seems to be in good agreement with that given by Arthur Reber and Emily Reber (2001, p. 352) in their widely read *Dictionary of Psychology*: "Any attended input, any idea, image, fact, knowledge, etc. counts as information." Thus, the term "information" as ordinarily used in psychological research in information processing has no technical meaning. It is used in the broad everyday meaning of knowledge.

The term "processing" in computer technology refers to the series of interdependent and progressive stages in the solution of a task: input, coding, storage, retrieval, decoding, and output. By analogy, the human being is assumed to possess a system that treats cognitive tasks such as perceiving, remembering, and thinking as a series of interdependent stages. The meaning of the term "processing" is thus highly abstract and must be inferred from the nature of the cognitive task and the subjects' performance of it.

Putting the two terms together gives the following definition: information processing is a study of the stages cognitive processes are assumed to go through when knowledge of some kind is produced in the human being. Clearly, the subject matter of information processing is abstract and not easily referred to in a clear and precise manner. Thus, Reber and Reber (2001, p. 352) end their explanation of the term as follows: "Hence, when one says that information is processed one means that knowledge of some kind is dealt with in some cognitive fashion."

Ulric Neisser (1967, p. 4), who wrote the first textbook on the new approach to the study of cognition, did not discuss the meaning of the terms "information" and "processing." He expressed the main point in the approach in the following way: "As used here, the term *cognition* refers to all the processes by which the sensory input is transformed, reduced, elaborated, stored, recovered, and used." Neisser did not define the term "sensory input."

As we shall see later in this chapter, it proved difficult to identify definite stages in cognitive performance, and information processing developed into a broad study of knowledge. According to Daniel Reisberg (2001), the following three questions became the main topics of the study: "How is knowledge acquired? How is knowledge retained, so that it's available when needed? How is knowledge used, as a basis for action, or as a basis for generating further knowledge?"

As Lachman et al. (1979, pp. 99–100) pointed out, researchers have interpreted the computer metaphor differently. Some attempted to simulate human cognitive processes in the computer, writing out their accounts of the subjects' serial performance as programs to be run by the computer. This allowed them to achieve great coherence and consistency in the accounts. By this procedure, they hoped to approach the natural science ideal of expressing the relationship between two stages by means of an algorithm. Others did not draw upon the computer as an example of a Turing machine but rather studied the succession of stages in cognitive acts by traditional experimental methods.

Early Attempts to Apply the New Perspectives in Psychological Research

George Miller (1920–2012)

George Miller received his PhD from Harvard in 1946 and was research fellow at the Psychoacoustics Laboratory there from 1944 to 1948. He returned to Harvard as a professor in 1955, having spent five years at MIT, where he worked closely with Noam Chomsky. From 1962 to 1972, he directed Harvard's Center for Cognitive Studies with Jerome Bruner. Miller left Harvard in 1972. After a few years at Rockefeller University, he went to Princeton, where he remained until his retirement and continued his research as emeritus professor.

World War II had brought to the fore problems of speech perception and communication, and the study of these problem areas became Miller's lifelong research interest. He was a pioneer in these studies, and as early as 1951 he published a textbook on speech and communication. He also had a broad interest in psychology, as is evidenced by the history of psychology he published in 1962. Along with Eugene Galanter and Karl Pribram (1960), he wrote a book on cybernetics, *Plans and the Structure of Behavior*, which demonstrated how ideas from cybernetics could be utilized in psychology. An article published in *Psychological Review* in 1956 was, however, probably his main contribution to the development of information processing. One of the goals of the article was to demonstrate that scientific psychology could be advanced by ideas taken from communication theory. The article convinced many psychologists and also gave a new perspective on some old questions in empirical psychology. The study of the problems Miller treated became central in information processing.

Miller's name has thus been closely associated with the introduction into psychology of ideas from communication theory. This may overshadow the fact that he was deeply influenced by the experimental psychology at Harvard in the 1940s. A line can be drawn from Titchener to Miller via Miller's teacher Boring. I think it is difficult to understand Miller's contributions to information processing unless we view it against the background of psychology at Harvard.

Miller and Experimental Psychology at Harvard

In a contribution to the volume Koch and Leary (1985) edited for the centenary of the establishment of Wundt's laboratory, Miller reported on his training as follows: "I grew up in the tradition of experimental psychology that was begun by Wilhelm Wundt and traced its way down to me through E.B. Titchener, E.G. Boring, and S.S. Stevens."

In Chapter 1, I mentioned Boring's influential history of psychology and the experimental work he carried out in the tradition of Wundt and Titchener. In contrast to his teacher, Titchener, he did not believe psychological research ought to be limited to the study of sensations and their combinations; instead he took a broad view of the subject matter of psychology. He did, however, agree with Titchener that scientific psychology could be decisively advanced by improvements in its methods. In Chapter 11, we noted Titchener's concern to improve the introspective method. When the Harvard physicist

Percy Bridgeman launched his ideas of operationalism, Boring and his student Stanley Stevens became champions of Bridgeman's ideas.

Titchener's influence was evident not only in Boring's belief in method, but also in his choice of problems to be studied in the laboratory he led. Boring realized that the concept of sensation was an abstraction, but he believed Titchener's work could be continued as a study of what he called the attributes of sensations. By refining measurements, he and his coworkers attempted to lay bare the dimensions of sensations. As Hilgard (1987) noted, some progress was made in this direction in the study of tones.

Work on measuring the dimensions of sensations was carried on by Stanley Stevens, who along with Boring became a leader of experimental psychology at Harvard. Stevens became known for contributing to the development of new procedures in psychophysics. As noted in Chapter 3, Fechner had introduced the concept of threshold in his attempt to determine how our sensory impressions are related to physical stimulation. Stevens cut out threshold determinations and simply asked his subjects to denote by a number the degree to which they experienced a sensory attribute, say, pitch, in a stimulus. For example, the subject was told the pitch of a given tone is represented by the number 100 and then was asked to denote with appropriate numbers the relative pitches of subsequent tones. The procedure was called *direct magnitude estimation* or *absolute judgment*. It turns out that subjects are able to give reliable and consistent responses in experiments by this method.

Like the Fechner procedure, the method of absolute judgment has weaknesses. One is that it is difficult to know whether the subjects use numbers according to mathematical definitions. Further, it is difficult to know the effect of the fact that the subjects have to anchor their judgments to the impression of the stimulus used as a reference (in the example above, the pitch denoted as 100).

From the Harvard laboratory, Miller brought with him a strong belief in the importance of improving and working out new methods. Boring and Stevens had been inspired by communication theory and cybernetics. Like them, Miller was interested in measuring the attributes of sensations. The data on which he based his reasoning in his famous article (Miller, 1956) were primarily taken from psychophysical experiments in which a version of the method of absolute judgment was used.

That there was a close relationship between Miller's work in psychophysics and his attempts to develop information processing is seen from the following remark: "In the experiments on absolute judgment the observer is considered to be a communication channel." In information processing, the human being as a thinker is considered to be a communication channel.

The Magical Number Seven

In his article, "The Magical Number Seven, Plus or Minus Two: Some Limits on Our Capacity for Processing Information," Miller (1956) discussed two well-known problems in empirical psychology: our limited capacity to simultaneously attend to several stimuli (span of attention), and our limited capacity to retain in immediate memory several items successively presented (span of immediate memory). Miller claimed that, in both instances, our capacity is about seven items. Although warned that the two capacities might not be expressions of the same underlying mechanism, he believed they were somehow related to each other and suggested that we function as communication channels having *a limited capacity.*

To describe more adequately the nature of capacity limits, Miller examined psychophysical data obtained by a specific version of the method of absolute judgment in which the subjects were to tag a sensory impression with a number and also identify the stimuli presented. Thus, as I understand it, they had to use the same number for the same stimuli when these were repeatedly and randomly presented to them. The purpose of the experiment was to determine the number of stimuli the subjects could identify without making an appreciable number of errors.

Using this specific version of absolute judgment, researchers could express the subjects' performance by means of the measure used in communication theory, the *binary unit* (bit). This is a measure based on the idea that information can be expressed as a reduction of uncertainty. Thus, in the present case, to identify one stimulus of two represents one bit of information; one of four, two bits, one of eight, three bits, and so on. Using this measure, Miller found that for one-dimensional stimuli, the subjects could receive 2.5 bits of information (or 6.5 different sensory impressions). However, when the stimuli differed in more than one dimension, as in pitch as well as loudness, the capacity wasoften considerably greater.

The capacity to identify sensory impressions apparently depends on a number of conditions. This raises the question of under what conditions we obtain the best measure of capacity. The sensory impressions we receive always contain more than one attribute. Thus, a one-dimensional attribute is an abstraction. If we assume, as Miller seems to have done, that the measure obtained on stimuli differs only in one dimension, we face a problem similar to the one in Titchener's psychology when it was claimed that our sensory experience is made up of sensations. It seems fair to say that Miller worked in a Titchenerian tradition.

It proved difficult to find ways of using the binary unit in psychological research, and it was abandoned. Thus, so far, the use of this measure does not seem to have led to progress in scientific psychology. This raises the question of whether it is productive to compare the human being to a communication channel, as Miller did. Miller deserves credit for noting that span of attention and immediate memory must somehow be related to each other. But there is no strong reason to believe this relationship occurred to him as a result of his attempt to introduce ideas from communication theory into psychology.

Having argued that our limited capacity may form part of a general problem of great significance, Miller recognized that we can compensate for its limits in various ways. Although we may not be able to attend to or remember more than seven units, we can organize them so they contain more items. Miller called such units *chunks* and referred to the process of organizing items into chunks as *chunking.* He reported on two experiments illustrating the idea of chunking and argued that mnemonic tricks are based upon this way of handling information.

Miller proposed that chunking is a form of recording the items to be remembered, but he did not say what rules people might use for it. It is probably a general human experience that we retain better material organized into some form of whole than a loose collection of items. G. E. Müller, as noted in Chapter 4, had reported that his subjects seemed to try to find meaning in the list of nonsense syllables he gave them, and he regarded the search for meaning as a central factor in remembering. Inspired by Gestalt psychology, George Katona (1940) reported, in a book entitled *Organizing and Memorizing*, on a series of experiments demonstrating the positive effect on memory of organizing the material according to the principles of Gestalt psychology. To conduct productive empirical research, Miller would, in my opinion, have had to discuss the relationship of parts to wholes that Brentano and his students had described. On the whole, I believe it is difficult to give a psychological meaning to the term "code" and the derivatives "encoding," "recoding," and "decoding," which were introduced into psychology by information processing.

Donald Broadbent (1926–1993) on Perception and Attention

During World War II, British psychologists had worked on psychological problems arising from the use of modern instruments for navigation and communication. This work, which made them familiar with communication theory, continued after the war. The study of attention was the main area of interest of the British pioneers in information theory, and, as Jon Driver (2001) showed, a research tradition in the study of attention developed in Great Britain in the second half of the twentieth century.

Neurology was a strong tradition in Great Britain, dating back to John Hughlings Jackson, and after World War II British psychologists began contributing substantially to neuropsychology. It was the specialty of Oliver Zangwill, who succeeded Frederick Bartlett as the leader of the psychological laboratory at the University of Cambridge. However, there was no great interest in experimental psychology in Great Britain until the mid-twentieth century and Donald Broadbent's studies of attention. Broadbent is therefore an important figure not only in the history of information processing but also in British experimental psychology.

Broadbent trained as a pilot during World War II and at that time became interested in psychological problems arising from the use of new technological equipment. After having studied psychology at Cambridge, he joined the Medical Research Council's Applied Psychology Research Unit in Cambridge. He was director of this unit from 1958 to 1974 and later member of the Medical Research Council's external staff, working in the Department of Experimental Psychology at Oxford. In 1968, he was elected a fellow of the Royal Society. In 1958, he published *Perception and Communication*, an influential book in information processing, on which I shall concentrate my presentation of him.

The "Cocktail Party" Problem

Like Miller, Broadbent had a primary interest in speech and hearing, and in his early studies he was influenced by Colin Cherry, professor of telecommunication at the Imperial College of Science and Technology. Cherry (1953), a champion of information processing, is known in psychology for his investigations of the so-called *cocktail party problem*. This effect refers to the fact that in a crowd of people speaking to each other, we are still able to carry on a conversation with one or more persons. Cherry simulated listening at a cocktail party by using earphones so that he could send two different messages at the same time, one to each ear, creating the effect called *dichotic listening*. He found that physical differences, such as male versus female voice, intensity of voice, and location of speaker, served as cues for the speakers carrying on the conversation.

Cherry was also interested in a somewhat different question: what would a listener attentive to the stimulation to one ear register of stimulation to the other ear? Cherry usually presented stories to the attended ear. To ascertain that the subject did not shift attention between the two ears, he had his subject carefully report the message presented to the attended ear, a process called *shadowing*. He found that subjects could report very little of the material presented to the unattended ear. Thus, they would not register that the language was changed from English to German, or that the speech was reversed. They would, however, register that the voice changed from male to female, that the story ended, and that the voice was replaced by a pure tone.

Of Broadbent's experiments on attention, one on dichotic listening has become well known. In this experiment, Broadbent simultaneously presented one series of three digits, say, 7, 2, 3, to one ear, and another series of three digits, say, 9, 4, 5, to the other ear, and asked the subjects to report all six digits in the order they chose. He found that they frequently could do so, but in most instances they would report first the series from one ear, and then the series from the other. Thus, they would reproduce the digits in order as either 7, 2, 3, 9, 4, 5, or 9, 4, 5, 7, 2, 3. Broadbent found it was virtually impossible for subjects to alternate digits received by one ear with digits received by the other – for example, to reproduce the figures in the order 7, 9, 2, 4, 3, 5.

Broadbent's Model of Cognition

In *Perception and Communication*, Broadbent reported on his own experiments as well as those of other researchers on dichotic listening skills, the effects of noise and fatigue on attention, and immediate memory. To account for the results of this research, he developed a model that compared the human being to a communication channel. Communication theorists had used flowcharts to depict the way information is transmitted through a telecommunication channel, and Broadbent adopted this way of representing the way he thought cognitive tasks are performed. His flowchart, according to Lachman et al. (1979), was the first to be developed in psychology.

In the first stage, information is transmitted through the senses. This is assumed to occur in parallel and results in the extraction (the perception) of simple sensory features, such as pitch, loudness, and direction of sound. Information coming in from the senses is kept for a few seconds in a short-term store, a buffer, before it is transmitted to a single channel in the next stage. This channel has limited capacity, and the processing taking place in it is serial. From the limited-capacity channel, information is transmitted either to a long-term memory store or to response systems of diverse kinds. To protect the limited-capacity channel from overload, a *filter* is placed between the first and second stage. The filter may be modulated, or tuned, to let through only information having certain physical characteristics. The filtering of information is a chief characteristic of Broadbent's model, and the model has often been referred to as his *filter theory of attention.*

The model could explain Cherry's results as well as those of other researchers on dichotic listening and shadowing. The results of the experiment in which Broadbent presented digits in pairs, one digit in each ear, could be explained by assuming that information is tuned to one ear, and that information from the other ear is held in the buffer and not sent through the filter until information from the attended ear has passed through.

As Eysenck and Keane (2005) note, research on the model has shown that it is difficult to identify a preattentive state. Inspired by Broadbent, later researchers have developed new approaches to the question of whether focused attention is a two-stage process. As Driver (2001) and Eysenck and Keane (2005) concluded, so far there is no clear evidence of two-stage processing. In my judgment, the new attempts, like that of Broadbent, suffer from the weakness that their underlying conceptions of attention are unclear.

Four years before Broadbent published his book, Woodworth and Schlosberg (1954) had reviewed the research carried out on attention in the early twentieth century (*Experimental Psychology*). They had made clear that it is difficult to define attention in a way useful for scientific psychology. Emphasizing that a person always does more than one thing at a time, Woodworth and Schlosberg (1954, p. 88) pointed to the difficulty of defining attention: "Aside from the psychological processes of breathing, heart action, and digestion, he is standing or walking while seeing or hearing or in some way engaged in more than one line of activity." When we hear, see, smell, talk, or touch something, or we make a movement, we react selectively to the stimulation impinging upon our sensory organs. In other words, we are always in some way attending to something. Thus, it seems difficult to find a state we can call preattentive, as Broadbent and before him Wundt had assumed.

Neglect of Previous Studies of Attention

Broadbent undoubtedly contributed to increased interest in attention in the later twentieth century. But as we can see from Woodworth and Schlosberg's (1954) textbook, the subject was studied throughout the early century as well. Moreover, as noted in the preceding chapter, at the mid-century, Lashley (1942, 1950/1960), Hebb (1949), and Maruzzi and Magoun (1949) had studied attention, and Gazzaniga et al. (2009) note an important inspiration in Helmholtz's observation that attention could be voluntarily directed to definite parts of the visual field without accommodating the eyes to the stimulation.

Psychologists studying attention at the mid-century overlooked William James's explanation, which differed from Cherry's and Broadbent's, of the "cocktail party" problem. James's view was in line with Helmholtz's and his own idea of voluntary attention as a preperception, or an attempt to anticipate events that may immediately happen. James (1950, p. 450), thus explained our ability to carry on a conversation in noisy surroundings, as in a party, by pointing out that the first words spoken by our companion suggest what she or he is about to talk about. From an idea of what the topic is, we anticipate what our companion will say. This explanation of the "cocktail party" problem seems to represent an important supplement to Cherry's and Broadbent's physicalist explanation.

Before we leave James, I will point out that he thought there is a close relationship between attention and imagination. This may be a point to consider in the study of attention as well as of imagination. I shall not discuss the study of imagination here, but what in many instances makes imagining different from perceiving is that the latter requires a voluntary effort.

I noted above that Woodworth and Schlosberg pointed to the difficulty of defining attention. They elaborated this further in their chapter by showing that attention is not a single function: "It must be obvious to the reader that the problems we have covered in this chapter will never be understood in terms of some single faculty or function called 'attention.'" Nearly fifty years after Woodworth and Schlosberg (1954) made their point, Driver (2001, p. 73) concluded his review of selective attention as follows: "While attention is here to stay as a topic, it has become increasingly clear that it is just that: a general topic, not a single psychological process."

Problems of attention are extremely complicated. They are closely related to perception but also, as Wundt and James believed, to motivation. If Helmholtz and James are correct in conceiving of voluntary attention as the anticipation of events that may happen, this must have a basis in remembering. Finally, as emphasized by Woodworth and Schlosberg (1954, p. 106), attention has a motor aspect. It is not easy to formulate problems of attention in a scientific and productive manner, and the British psychologist D. A. [Alan] Allport (1993) may have raised an important point when he asked whether researchers in attention have asked the right questions.

The Influence of Allen Newell and Herbert Simon

In the mid-twentieth century, a number of outstanding mathematicians and engineers attempted to construct machines that could be said to think and display intelligent behavior. The construction of programs for such machines has been called the study of *artificial intelligence*. In particular, Allen Newell (1927–1992) and Herbert Simon (1916–2000) have been instrumental in advancing this field.

Newell and Simon also influenced computational work directed towards understanding problem solving and thinking. They insisted that both the human mind and the computer manipulate symbols and that the mind could be regarded as a computer. In line with this way of looking at mental processes, they held that the study of human thinking could be advanced by devising programs for thinking that computers could execute. Simon and Newell (1964) thought, however, that too little is known about the nervous system to construct computer programs simulating the functioning of the brain. They discouraged this type of effort, insisting that what must be simulated is the mind.

Along with Clifford Shaw, Newell and Simon started their work at the Rand Corporation and continued it at the Carnegie Institute of Technology, later Carnegie–Mellon University in Pittsburgh. In the mid-1950s, the three succeeded in constructing a program, the Logical Theorist, for simulating one of the theorems of Russell and Whitehead. Gradually, they extended the program to include a number of logical theorems, chess, and even puzzles studied in human problem solving. Simon and Newell (1964) called their extended program the General Problem Solver. An extensive account of it was published in 1972. Both researchers continued their work on cognition for the remaining years of their scientific careers, and both received the Distinguished Scientific Contribution Award of the APA. Simon also received the Nobel Prize in Economics in 1974. I shall return to Newell's and Simon's work on thinking later in the chapter.

What of their assertion that the computer may be seen as a manipulator of symbols? To manipulate symbols, the computer must be able to handle relationships between processes going on in the machine. To justify this way of expressing matters, the relationships between the processes must in some way be inherent in the machine. John Searle (1992), who has raised this point, argued that the relationship is produced by us as perceivers. Even if we concede that relationships may exist in the physical world and thus also in the machine, to make their point relevant to empirical research Newell and Simon would, in my opinion, have had to show how human beings have acquired the ability to perceive relationships. This seems to be a fundamental question in evolutionary biology, to which we at present have no good answer. The definition of a symbol as something that stands for something else is merely a crude dictionary definition.

Newell and Simon's Work on Thinking

Newell and Simon conceived of problem solving as a number of knowledge states that problem solvers must pass through successively. There are an initial state and a goal state (the solution to the problem), and between these two states intervening knowledge states. To pass from one state to the next, the problem solver has to apply one or more mental operators. Thus, one task of the researcher is to determine the states the problem solver has to pass through and the operators applied at each state. Since Newell and Simon assumed that there are conceivably many states that do not lead to the goal state, the subjects would use various hypotheses, strategies, or heuristics, as a help in solving the problem. A main task of the researcher is thus to find the heuristics used by problem solvers.

To make Newell and Simon's idea more concrete, I shall consider their studies of one problem representative of their work. I shall examine this problem with a view to finding out whether the heuristics they invented to explain problem solving are related to the empirical data on which they based their theory. Human problem solving involves extremely subtle processes, and to have a hope of understanding them, we must, I think, describe the tasks studied in great detail.

An Examination of the "Tower of Hanoi" Problem

The "Tower of Hanoi" is a problem in the form of a game, simpler than but similar to chess. It consists of moving disks of varying sizes, usually three, from one peg to another. The subjects are introduced to the problem by being shown the three vertical pegs, on one of which (peg 1) the three disks have been placed in decreasing size order, the large disk at the bottom (see Figure 18.1). They are then instructed to place the three disks on peg 3, making as few moves as possible, in such a way that they remain in the same order as on peg 1. The subjects are given two additional instructions: 1. only one disk can be moved at a time; 2. a larger disk cannot be placed on a smaller one.

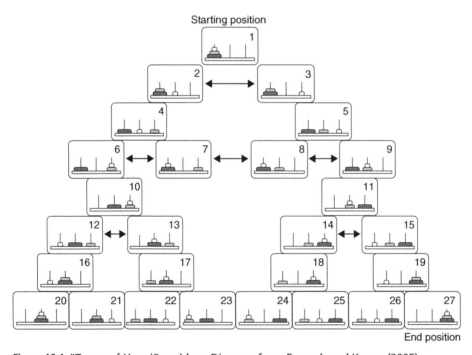

Figure 18.1 "Tower of Hanoi" problem. Diagram from Eysenck and Keane (2005).

To obtain an overview of possible moves that can be made, it is useful to draw diagrams of possible moves. Eysenck and Keane (2005, p. 401) have drawn such a diagram (Figure 18.1), which I shall refer to by the numbers of the positions they used.

A main point in Newell and Simon's problem-space theory is the claim that subjects use strategies or *heuristics* of a general nature, heuristics that can be used for all types of problems, or at least for a large number of problems. One such heuristic is the *means–ends analysis*, which Eysenck and Keane characterize in the following way: "Note the difference between the current state [and the desired state], create a subgoal to reduce this difference, and select an operator that will solve the subgoal." To illustrate, they consider position 15 in Eysenck and Keane's diagram. They hold that three moves can be taken at this position.

According to the means–ends analysis, the subject notices that the medium disk is at peg 2, not peg 3; establishes the subgoal of reducing this difference; and selects an operator that solves the subgoal and applies it. As a result of this analysis, the subject moves the medium disk to peg 3. Applying this heuristic once again solves the problem. It is possible, as Eysenck and Keane noted, to apply the means–ends heuristic at the initial position too, although this is not a safe method.

Newell and Simon (1972) thought they could show that the problem–space theory allowed them to structure the Tower of Hanoi problem, and that their study of their subjects' performance gave empirical support to their belief that the problem is solved by the use of definite types of heuristics. I think it can be shown that a person can find the correct solution with a minimum of moves simply by following the instructions. If my claim should be substantiated, it will be reasonable to believe the problem is structured not by the problem–space theory but simply by the instructions, and that Newell and Simon's assertions about the use of heuristics are in doubt.

The instructions tell the subject to build a tower at peg 3. This means the large disk must be placed at the bottom of peg 3, information that can be regarded as a subgoal. Next, the medium disk must be placed on the large disk, the second subgoal. Third, the small disk must be placed on the medium disk, the third subgoal.

To achieve the first subgoal, the subject must remove the two disks placed on top of the large disk. Because both pegs 2 and 3 are free, this can be done, but peg 3 must then be made free if the large disk is to be placed on it. At the initial position, the subject thus has the choice of moving the small disk to either peg 2 or peg 3.

If it is moved to peg 2, the medium disk must be moved to peg 3. Now, if the latter disk is moved to peg 3, it must be moved back to peg 1 to make peg 3 free. Moving a disk first to one position and then back to the same position would clearly represent two unnecessary moves, and this should naturally be avoided. In contrast, if the small disk is moved to peg 3, it can be placed on disk 2 after the medium disk has been moved to peg 2. Hence, by undertaking these three moves, we can move the large disk to peg 3 and reach the first subgoal in four moves. The subject is now at position 11.

By simply placing the medium disk on the large disk on peg 3, we reach the second subgoal. Having reached position 15, we achieve the third subgoal simply by moving the small disk to peg 3. Hence, by following instructions, we can solve the Tower of Hanoi problem in a minimum of moves with a minimum of errors.

If this is correct, it means the problem is structured by the instructions. This is not surprising when we consider that the problem is constructed to serve as a game. Further, there is no need for heuristics. Of course, this does not exclude the possibility that some subjects apply the procedure in Newell and Simon's descriptions of their heuristics, but this would be unnecessary, and if it is unnecessary, it is difficult to see that the procedure represents a heuristic.

Against my argument, someone might perhaps object that I have used a heuristic to find the subgoals. To this I shall answer that I have simply followed instructions. Another possible objection is that in order to reach the first subgoal, the subject must anticipate three moves. I am unable to see why a normal adult subject should not be able to do so. The instructions do not confine the subject to *mentally* performing one move at a time even if the problem is physically divided into a series of discrete moves. The reason Newell and Simon may have failed to see that the problem can be solved without their proposed heuristic could be that they overlooked this distinction.

Issues Arising in Extending the Problem–Space Theory to Problems Other Than Puzzles

Learning and doing mathematics involve thinking. At first we might therefore believe that a study of the way human beings solve mathematical problems could be a path to understanding thinking. On reflection, however, we can see that it is not easy to understand the thinking involved in doing mathematics. Mathematical systems have been developed through the centuries by a number of people with exceptional ability for abstract, coherent, and consistent thinking. When we do mathematics, we follow the rules they have formulated and we have learned but not *ourselves invented*. This means that in order to understand thinking as manifested in the solving of mathematical problems, we must distinguish between what the persons solving mathematical problems have learned and remembered, and what they add to the process by their own thinking. Clearly, it is difficult to make this distinction.

Puzzles like the Tower of Hanoi and chess are similar to mathematical problems; like mathematics, they are constructions based upon rules figured out by their constructor. To understand the thinking involved in the solving of puzzles, we must distinguish between the structure imposed upon the problem by the instructions and the structure created by the problem solver. I suspect Newell and Simon confused these two conceptions of structure.

Problem–Space Theory and Earlier Approaches

In Chapter 5, I reviewed Wertheimer's ideas of how he believed our thinking is structured and noted that Duncker developed a view of problem solving as hypotheses testing via trial and error. Newell and Simon's problem–space theory can be seen as an elaboration of Duncker's view. One of the differences between the two approaches is that Newell and Simon's view conceives of problem solving as proceeding through definite segregated states. This naturally is an advantage if it is possible to conceive of the process as the passage from one definite state to another.

The Tower of Hanoi problem allows us to conceive of definite states, but this may be the result of the fact that the puzzle is constructed in this way. In their attempt to find support for their theory, Newell and Simon may have selected a problem to fit it. Hence, a study of this problem can give no strong support to their theory. As we saw, it is difficult to know whether the subject mentally moves though the steps successively or considers more than one move at a time. As Eysenck and Keane (2005, p. 443) noted, the problems we meet in everyday life are rarely so well structured as puzzles. This normally makes it difficult to extend the theory to other types of problems, and if this is difficult, the theory may have no advantage over Duncker's view.

A main challenge in studying problem solving is that we can hardly conceive of a problem without considering the subject's previous experience. A problem for one person may be a routine performance for another. Further, unless we have an understanding that something is a problem, it does not represent a problem to us. For example, if asked to solve a third-grade equation, many adults will not see it as a problem. In their reproduction of Köhler's insight problems, Birch demonstrated, as noted in Chapter 5, that insight solutions are not found unless the animal has extensive experience with the material to be used for the solution. In my judgment, Newell and Simon did not devote sufficient attention to the role of previous experience in problem solving. Difficulty in defining problem situations may also arise because emotional blocking or temporary distractions may prevent us from solving the problem, and we have restricted knowledge of how emotions and distractions affect previous experience.

Since the 1970s, research on the problems formulated by Köhler, Duncker, Krech, and Luchins has been carried out, and progress seems to have been achieved. (On this point, see Eysenck and Keane, 2005.) However, because it is so difficult to extend the problem–space theory to the problems originally studied by the pioneers in problem solving, it is naturally also difficult to attribute the progress to the theory.

Another part of Newell and Simon's work that has become well known is their studies of differences between expert and novice problem solvers in chess playing and programming. Here again, we have problems with clearly demarcated steps or states. Newell and Simon also studied experts in physics. In this case, we can believe the superiority of the experts is due to the simple fact that they are highly familiar with the laws and general procedures of physics. Before another interpretation is accepted, I think this alternative must be ruled out.

Noam Chomsky's Ideas of Language

As noted in the preceding chapter, Lashley (1942, 1951) had argued that behavior forming temporal sequences, such as language, could not easily be explained as being made up of stimulus--response connections. Noam Chomsky (1959) pursued this point and gave detailed, convincing arguments against the behaviorist account of language.

To explain mature speakers' use of language, Chomsky postulated that they possess a set of internalized rules that allow them to produce well-formed sentences. The task of the linguist is to reveal these rules by an examination of language. Chomsky thought that the linguistic rules reflect underlying cognitive abilities.

We can see information processing as simulated by the computer as following fixed rules. To compare human thinking to this process, we need to see that it can be described according to a set of rules. Chomsky's account of language did this well, as we shall see, and that made his ideas of language central in the information-processing approach.

In line with the thinking of Humboldt and Wundt as well as of earlier students of language, Chomsky (1959, 1972, 1980) claimed that since speakers of a language are able to construct and understand sentences they had never heard before, language has a creative aspect. The ability to form sentences, he further claimed, is *innate* and based upon specific nervous mechanisms. The idea that the ability to form sentences is innate agrees with the European ethologists' view of instincts.

An Evaluation of Chomsky's Ideas of Language

The title of one of Chomsky's books, *Cartesian Linguistics* (1966), signaled a return to a Cartesian conception of mind. Chomsky had no place for a behavioral component in his account of language. Thus, in *Language and the Mind* (1972, p. 114), he argued that the study of language is a branch of human theoretical psychology, and that the goal of this study "is to exhibit and clarify the mental capacities that make it possible to learn and use language."

Although Chomsky insisted that language has a basis in mental capacities, he undertook no systematic examination of the role played by language in thinking. He seems to share the view of analytic philosophers and behaviorists that language is a main determiner of human thinking. Thus, he emphasized that language has a creative aspect, but he did not discuss the possibility that the vast number of verbal utterances we can make may simply reflect the fact that our mental capacities are so well developed.

US comparative psychologists had reacted strongly to the ethologists' view of instincts as innate. Chomsky did not explain how we might demonstrate that the acquisition of language is innate in the sense that no learning or experience is necessary for the child's mastery of it. While it is highly probable that use of language has an important genetic component, the idea of innateness is not easily upheld.

In *The Descent of Man*, Darwin (1871/1981) had argued that language evolved as a result of natural selection and in many steps. He had further pointed out that language has homologies in the mental capacities as well as in the communication of other animal species. Without going more deeply into the issue, Chomsky (1972, p. 114) said the mental capacities that made the use of language possible are unique to humans and "have no significant analogue to any other species." Thus, on the issue of the origin of use of language, he took an anti-Darwinian position.

In a book entitled *Rules and Representations*, Chomsky (1980) discussed the purpose and function of language. He pointed out that language has many functions, and he maintained that it is difficult to understand what it means to say that language's main function is communication. It is easy to find innumerable cases in which communication is the main function. Moreover, it is possible, as I have argued elsewhere (Saugstad, 1989b), to regard functions other than communications as derived from the function of communication. Thus, it is difficult to see that Chomsky presented any good arguments for his insistence that communication is not the main function of language.

If we assume language originated in human phylogenesis as a means of communication, we can readily imagine that it may have evolved in many steps. As proposed by

S. L. Washburn and Shirley Strum (1972) in a chapter on the evolution of language, a first step may have been that mental capacities evolved that allowed our ancestors to connect definite meanings to specific sounds they could produce. While Washburn and Strum stressed the importance of the evolution of a sound code for producing linguistic signs, they also pointed to the enormous advantage a small community of our ancestors would have in possessing a few signs for communication. As the capacity for reasoning increased, the sound code would allow our ancestors to increase their vocabulary. Further steps might then have been a development from single signs to simple sentences, and then by still further steps to more complex grammatical sentences.

Chomsky's revival of the old ideas that all existing languages have common features and that language has a genetic basis represented important contributions. But his return to a Cartesian conception of mind and his rejection of the idea that language has evolved as a result of natural selection may have been obstacles to progress in the study of cognition.

As a grammarian, Chomsky took the *sentence* to be the unit of language and failed to see that his view of language might have changed in essential respects if the *word* were taken as the unit instead. Then we would have to explain what is meant by a sentence. In their later criticism of Chomsky, Stephen Pinker and Paul Bloom (1992) also failed to see this point. A discussion of this essential point is given by Saugstad (1989b) and more recently by Peter MacNeilage and Barbara Davis (2005).

The confrontation between Chomsky and the behaviorists inspired researchers to investigate the possibility of teaching chimpanzees language. Although these investigations so far have not shown that chimpanzees can learn to use symbols in the way humans do, they have revealed that chimpanzees, particularly the bonobo (*Pan paniscus*), have a remarkable ability to understand verbal communication when familiar with it from infancy (see Michael Tomasello and Joseph Call, 1997). This finding may turn out to be of great significance for understanding the biological processes underlying language.

The Study of Remembering

The new ideas of cognitive processes led to an outburst of experimental activity, and some well-controlled experiments were performed that gave direction to the study of remembering. I shall begin this section by presenting some of the early experiments. Then I shall report on an early influential model of remembering and the criticism of this model that led to the present-day working memory models. I shall end the chapter with some concluding remarks on the information-processing work on remembering.

Some Early Experiments

The Sperling Experiment
Miller's new interpretation of the span of apprehension revived psychologists' interest in the problem of how many items we are able to perceive in a brief interval of time.

Some researchers wondered whether we can actually perceive more in a short time than we are able to report. To test this hypothesis, some well-controlled experiments were performed, and one by George Sperling (1960) was particularly informative.

Sperling used a technique called the *partial report*. In one part of an experiment, he first tested the span of apprehension under the conditions ordinarily used in this type of measurement. Twelve different letters were presented in an array containing four letters in each of three rows. The subjects were instructed to recall the letters immediately after the presentation, and they reported 4–5 letters. Next, Sperling changed the conditions to the partial report. The subjects were now told that tones of three different pitches would be sounded immediately after the presentation of the letters, and they were to report on the first row when the highest tone was sounded, and on the middle and third rows when the intermediate and lowest tones were sounded, respectively. Under these conditions, the subjects almost always correctly reported all the letters in a row. Evidently, they could see more than they could report.

Sperling interpreted the findings to mean that the image of the letters would decay so rapidly after presentation that by the time the subjects had reported 4–5 of them, the image had faded. He tested this hypothesis by varying the interval between the presentation of the array and the tones and found that lengthening the interval led to a decrease in the number of letters reported. Apparently the decay occurred very fast, because after 1 second the subjects reported only 4–5 letters. Results similar to those obtained for the visual modality have been found for the auditory modality, but here the image seems to fade more slowly.

A great deal of work has been devoted to determining the nature of the rapid decay of the image and the possible function of its persistence. It is reasonable to believe the persistence of the image after the end of the physical stimulation has a function, particularly for auditory perception when it is essential to keep information present for a longer period of time. According to Eysenck and Keane (2005), however, recent research suggests that persistence may play a great role in visual perception as well. Adherents of the information-processing approach have tended to regard the phenomenon of persistence as belonging to the study of memory, but it seems far from clear that the processes are of the same nature as those in the phenomena we ordinarily refer to as memory processes.

The Sternberg Experiment on Recognition

Another experiment that created enthusiasm for information processing was undertaken by Saul Sternberg (1966, 1969). Among other researchers, Sternberg revived the idea of mental chronometry that had been launched by Donders and explored in Wundt's laboratory (see Chapter 4).

The idea that a more complex cognitive task can be divided into components occurring independently of each other in time is central to information processing, as it had been in the early work in mental chronometry. Oswald Külpe had criticized the idea. His main argument was that the time taken by each component depends upon the subject's conception of the task as a totality. Sternberg wanted to show that when conditions are better controlled than in Wundt's and Külpe's laboratories, the idea of a mental chronometry is a productive one.

Working with the recognition of items such as digits and letters, Sternberg assumed that this type of task could be divided into four stages: 1. encoding (learning the items to be recognized); 2. searching through memory to find the item presented earlier; 3. selecting the item thought to be correct; 4. giving the response. I shall look only at the second stage, which Sternberg thought required a comparison of the item to be recognized with items stored in memory. In a typical experiment, Sternberg proceeded as follows. From a set of 10 digits: 0, 1, 2, 3, 4, 5, 6, 7, 8, 9, a subset of 1–6 digits was presented to the subjects serially, at a rate of 1.2 seconds per digit. Two seconds after the set had been presented, a target digit drawn arbitrarily from the original set of 10 was presented. The subject's task was to pull one lever if he or she recognized the target digit (a yes response), and another (a no response) if not. Reaction times were recorded.

Sternberg could show that reaction time increased linearly for each digit added to the subset, and that each digit added about 40 milliseconds. Moreover, by analyzing his data, he made the surprising discovery that the subjects did not seem to stop comparing the target to the items of the remembered subset when they had hit the digit corresponding to the digit target. The basis for this conclusion was that the curve of the plot of the yes responses was parallel to that of the plot of the no responses. (We would not expect this if the subjects stopped their search when they had hit the right digit of the remembered subset.) Sternberg's experiments were well controlled, but, as noted by Lachman et al. (1979) and Gardner (1987), his findings turned out not to be robust (the effects do not seem to be present when changes are introduced that should not affect the results). A more serious criticism, as Gardner stated, is that Sternberg's model has proved to be of little help in understanding real-life situations.

Two Experiments on Short-Term Memory

In his treatment of memory, James had distinguished between what he referred to as primary and secondary memory. Primary memory explained the fact that impressions seemed to be present in consciousness for just a short time, only a few seconds, while secondary memory was what we ordinarily refer to as memory.

Miller's interpretation of the span of apprehension as the result of a limited capacity for remembering revived interest in the question of whether we could distinguish between primary and secondary memory. In his model of how information is transmitted through a number of stages, Broadbent had distinguished between a stage where information is stored for a very brief interval of time and a stage where it is more permanently stored. As the idea that a human being may be regarded as a channel for the transmission of information gained acceptance, the distinction between short-term and long-term memory was brought to the fore. A number of experiments were performed to clarify the difference.

An elegant early experiment was performed by M. A. Peterson and M. J. Peterson (1959). They had their subjects learn three consonants, say, *PQX*. At different time intervals after the presentation of the three consonants, the subjects were to count backward by three before they gave their reports. It turned out that the subjects' ability to recall the letters declined rapidly after a few seconds. After 20 seconds, there was practically no recall. These results were explained by assuming that counting backward prevented the subjects from rehearsing, and that the rapid drop in retention was the result of the decay in short-term memory.

Another, now-classic experiment was carried out by Murray Glanzer and his coworker A. R. Cunitz (Glanzer and Cunitz, 1966). US researchers working in the Ebbinghaus–Müller tradition had repeatedly found that when a list of items is to be remembered, the first and last items are better retained than those in the middle of the list. In other words there is a *primacy* and *recency effect*. Glanzer and Cunitz interpreted the recency effect by assuming that the last items of the list were still in short-term memory when the subjects began recalling the list. The researchers believed the recall of words at the beginning and middle is the result of long-term memory.

In accordance with this interpretation, Glanzer and Cunitz hypothesized that if subjects were given another task of a different nature immediately after the list had been presented, this task would eliminate the recency effect. They proceeded as follows. They presented a list of 15 words and then asked the subjects to count backward from an arbitrary number 0, 10, or 30 seconds after the presentation of the list. The results confirmed their expectations. At 10 seconds, the recency effect was reduced, and at 30 seconds it was eliminated. In contrast to the last part of the list, the first and middle parts were not affected by counting backward. Although there are other explanations of the recency effect, the Glanzer and Cunitz experiment supported the working of short-term memory.

The Atkinson and Shiffrin Model

While Broadbent developed his model mainly to assist him in describing attention, Richard Atkinson and Richard Shiffrin (1968) developed their model in an attempt to account for memory. Still, the two models have much in common.

Atkinson and Shiffrin conceived of memory as having a permanent structure consisting of three components: a sensory register, a short-term store, and a long-term store. Stimulation of the sensory organs was thought to result in information being stored in a sensory register, one register for each sensory modality. Information is stored in the sensory register for a very brief time (less than a second).

While some information is lost in the register (decayed), some is transmitted to the short-term memory store, where it could be retained for up to 30 seconds. The short-term store also receives information from the long-term store. From the short-term store, information is transmitted to long-term memory, where it is stored more or less permanently. Also in the short-term store, some information is lost.

Atkinson and Shiffrin saw the three stores as permanent structures reflecting properties of the nervous system. In addition to these permanent structures, the system contains control processes under the subject's command. One control process to which Atkinson and Shiffrin ascribed a significant role is rehearsal. By rehearsal, the subject is thought to be able to keep information in short-term memory for a longer interval than the hypothesized 30 seconds.

Evidence for the sensory register was found in Sperling's experiments. In support of the existence of a short-term memory, the two model-builders referred to the types of memory loss found in the patient reported upon by Scoville (1954) and more thoroughly studied by Scoville and Milner (1957). Support for this distinction was also found in experiments by Peterson and Peterson. Atkinson and Shiffrin were mainly concerned with the distinction between the three stores and with short-term memory, and they gave little attention to the long-term store.

The Atkinson and Shiffrin model received considerable attention. Much work was devoted to exploring it, and many attempts were made to improve it. But as Eysenck and Keane (2005) noted, as research has progressed, the model has lost its attraction. Studies of long-term memory have made it clear that the idea of only one kind of long-term memory gives all too simple a picture of remembering. Further, it has been shown that subjects hardly use rehearsal as extensively as Atkinson and Shiffrin assumed. Neurological evidence also suggests that short-term memory is not a unitary process; memory loss may be limited to verbal but not other types of material. More importantly, some brain-damaged persons have been found to have greatly reduced short-term memory without losing the ability to form long-term memory. (On these points, see Eysenck and Keane, 2005; Gazzaniga et al., 2009.)

An attempt to improve the Atkinson and Shiffrin model that attracted much attention was made by Alan Baddeley. His model of *working memory* has been elaborated by him and his coworkers for more than twenty-five years. Baddeley and C. J. Hitch (1974) divided short-term memory into three parts: *a central executive*, *a phonological loop*, and a *visuospatial sketch pad*. More recently, Baddeley and B. Wilson (2002) added a fourth component, *an episodic buffer*. Thus, the concept of working memory represents a complex system. The central executive is assigned the role of coordinating memory in tasks putting strains on immediate memory. The phonological loop is supposed to hold information in a speech-like state of memory by rehearsal, and the visuospatial sketchpad to hold memory in a visual or spatial state. The episodic buffer coordinates memory held in the two other states into a single episode.

The model is fascinating because it helps us envision how we deal with tasks requiring what we refer to as awareness or consciousness. Tests that help define the components have given the model a certain concreteness. It seems to be of use in locating difficulty in cognitive tasks, for brain-damaged as well as for normally functioning individuals. An apparent weakness in the model, however, is that it is difficult to understand more precisely how the diverse components are related to each other, and particularly how the chief executive is supposed to carry out its integrative functions. Attempts to account for its role seem invariably to entangle us in subtle problems of introspection. In my judgment, it is difficult to understand how it is possible, within the present framework of psychological research, to conceive of the chief executive without assuming a homunculus.

Another apparent weakness of the working-memory model of Baddeley and coworkers is that the role of long-term memory is not clear. We know that mastery of tasks that may tax working memory, such as speaking, reading, writing, and doing mathematics, is not attained unless an individual has gone through complex training. This suggests that when we engage in these activities, we draw heavily upon long-term memory. The model does not explain how this is done.

Some Concluding Comments

Everyday experience teaches us that we remember many of the perceptual impressions we have received, and that in our thinking we employ knowledge stored in memory. Thus, we derive from experience the idea that cognition is built up hierarchically, in that remembering is preceded by perceiving, and thinking by perceiving and remembering. Helmholtz and Wundt elaborated this idea. Helmholtz conceived of perception as taking place in two stages. Wundt speculated that mental contents in the forms of elements are integrated into mental structures by an associative process, and that the mental structures are then integrated into more complex entities by a process of apperception. Thus, the idea of cognition as a sequence of stages in which processes are successively transformed was not new with information processing.

What *was* new was the development and testing of models of the successive transformations. Information processing must be credited with recognizing the importance of accounting for cognition as a sequence of stages, and its researchers with elaborating the old ideas of a span of attention and a span of memory into the distinction between short-term and long-term memory. They also introduced the concept of a *sensory register*, which may be important in explaining not only auditory but also visual perception.

Earlier in this review of information processing, I mentioned that the concept of *information* seems to be used in its everyday meaning. Gibson (1960/1979) criticized this use of the term in the study of perception. From the point of view of the adult human being, it appears self-evident that perception gives us information about our physical environment. The reason it appears this way may be, as Helmholtz said, that during ontogeny perception is built up such that we can anticipate what we will perceive. But this does not necessarily mean, as Marr (1982) and many information-processing researchers seem to have assumed, that perception is best understood as a means of obtaining information. Perception may perhaps better be understood as a construction made up by the organism to allow it to react to the stable and predictable aspects of a changing environment. The view of perception as a means of obtaining information about the physical environment may be too narrow.

In this brief review of information processing, I have dealt only with research that resulted in generally accepted conclusions. Therefore, I have not discussed attempts to support what many adherents of information processing regard as central – namely, that the mind functions as a modern, high-speed digital computer. The idea raises questions

I believe must be discussed in terms of modern theories of the origin of life. After all, the debate is about whether properties traditionally ascribed to biological phenomena can be ascribed to a physical object, the computer.

So far, researchers studying the brain and psychology do not seem to agree that consciousness performs computations like a Turing machine, nor that the brain does. Thus, in the extensive presentation of research on physiological psychology by Neil Carlson (*Physiology of Behavior*, 2007), we find no reference to research carried out within the information-processing tradition, although in the ninth edition of his book Carlson treated perception, learning, memory, and communication in detail and also discussed attention and thinking. In contrast, in *Cognitive Neuroscience: The Biology of the Mind*, Gazzaniga et al. (2009, p. 117) held that "the computer is a powerful metaphor for cognitive neuroscience."

Carlson (2007) insisted that evolution works on behavior and treated cognitive problems in terms of a moderate behaviorist perspective. According to this perspective, it is difficult to find an observational basis for the concept of *internal representation*, which is a key concept in information processing and in the book by Gazzaniga et al. In my opinion, it is not unreasonable to ask, as Searle (1992) did, whether we can define this concept without assuming a homunculus. In this chapter, I pointed out difficulties in the use of the concepts of *information* and *symbol*. Thus, the use made of the central concepts in information processing seems to be far from clear and precise. It may also turn out that it was a backward step to define psychology as the study of the mind and not as the study of the mind and behavior.

Information processing is primarily an experimental study of cognition in the adult human being. The roles played by motivation and emotions have been left out of consideration and attempts are usually not made to clarify phenomena by applying a developmental perspective. A few years before information processing was established as an approach to the study of cognition, Henry Nissen's (1951) chapter "Phylogenetic Comparison" in Stevens's *Handbook of Experimental Psychology* had reviewed a large amount of research demonstrating how an evolutionary, phylogenetic perspective could illuminate cognitive problems.

Nissen also emphasized that psychological phenomena must be studied in the ontogenetic and the cultural developmental perspective. When we consider the material used in most of the experiments performed in information processing, we note that it mainly consists of written material, words, letters, and digits, and that the tasks used in the study of thinking are highly abstract. In other words, the material is based upon cultural products with which young children and tribal people having no written language are unfamiliar. The lack of both an evolutionary, phylogenetic perspective and an ontogenetic and cultural developmental perspective may represent a serious limitation in information processing. In fairness, it must be added that developmental perspectives are also missing in the other approaches to the study of cognition.

19

· ·

Important Trends in the Psychology of the Twenty-First Century

In Chapters 16 and 18, I reported on progress in the study of cognition, and in Chapter 17 on progress in physiological psychology. In the present chapter, I shall review some events that led to continuity and progress in social, personality, and evolutionary biological psychology. In Chapters 14 and 15, I reported that the study of social psychology and personality in the 1970s had ended in what many regarded as a crisis. In the present chapter, I shall also account for some of the progress in these two areas that contributed to keeping the interest in them alive.

In social psychology, progress was made in the study of attitudes, the oldest – and regarded by many as the central study – of social psychology. In the 1970s, attribution research attracted enormous interest, and some of this research must be reviewed. Around 1970, health psychology emerged as an important new area in which the knowledge and techniques of social psychology proved useful. Other new areas have attracted the interest of psychologists. Of these, in my opinion, attraction and close relationships are of particular interest because they may help integrate a number of problem areas in psychology, as well as integrate psychology with the other social sciences.

In personality psychology, there seems to have been progress, particularly in attempts to describe personality in terms of traits, an undertaking begun by Gordon Allport and Odbert in 1933. Advances have also been made in the study of the self. Made central in psychology by James, Baldwin, and Mead in the late 1800s, this area is again a main concern of psychologists.

Social psychology and personality psychology developed more or less in parallel, and there is considerable overlap between the two. Since the debate in the 1960s and 1970s, the relationship between them does not seem to have been a question of major concern to psychologists. I shall therefore not go into it but merely point out that, if the study of personality is the study of the human being as some sort of psychological totality, it seems problematic to regard a social being as a separate part of this being. There is also considerable overlap between these two areas and developmental psychology. A new area of study in developmental psychology, the *life-span study*, appeared in the 1960s and 1970s. This study draws heavily upon social and personality psychology and is important because it helps to integrate the three areas. Rather than a separate chapter on developmental psychology, I have treated this new area after the section on progress in personality psychology.

In the 1970s, a breakthrough occurred in finding a basis for psychology in genetics. Advances in the study of *behavioral genetics* will continue in the twenty-first century, and I shall briefly account for findings that seem to justify the belief that a breakthrough has occurred.

As I reported in Chapter 11, there was considerable interest in biological evolution in the psychology practiced in the United States at the beginning of the 1900s, and it seems fair to say that comparative psychology became part of mainstream American psychology. Interest in comparative psychology was kept alive through the first half of the twentieth century but then seemed to decline. A revival took place when the European study of ethology became known in the United States. Its influence seems to have been strongest in the study of development and learning, and I shall focus on its impact in these areas.

In the mid-twentieth century, a breakthrough in evolutionary biology was revealed when researchers succeeded in formulating a reasonably coherent and consistent theory of evolution called the *evolutionary synthesis*. This was followed by a number of new insights that strengthened the theory, and evolutionary biologists began applying these insights to problems of human sexual and social life, and basing psychology more firmly on evolutionary biology. A new school of psychology, *evolutionary psychology*, emerged towards the end of the twentieth century.

All through the history of psychology, we have seen that psychologists grappled with the question, what is the subject matter of our science? Evolutionary psychologists made the question topical by treating psychology as a branch of evolutionary biology. They did, however, also raise the question of psychology's relationship to culture. In a final section of this chapter, I shall discuss ideas about the relationship between psychology and culture in evolutionary as well as in comparative psychology.

Progress in Social Psychology

Overcoming the Crisis in the Study of Attitudes

As noted in Chapter 14, examination of the literature on the relationship between attitudes and behavior revealed that attitudes do not seem to predict behavior. Since a main reason for studying attitudes was that they were assumed to be closely related to behavior, this finding created a crisis in the study of attitudes. Some researchers reacted by more carefully examining the relationship. The work of Martin Fishbein and Icek Ajzen (1974) and Ajzen and Fishbein (1977) was particularly clarifying.

Fishbein and Ajzen began by noting that most researchers who examined the relationship between attitudes and behavior had blamed the procedures for measuring attitudes for lacking consistency. Instead of concentrating on this measurement, they suggested that the nature of the behavior that is to be predicted should be more carefully considered, especially whether we should use a single act or several different acts as an index of behavior.

In most studies, single acts had been used as the measure of behavior. The two researchers pointed out that in many instances this measure is justified. For example, voting for a political candidate or a political issue could be taken as a measure of behavior because this act reflects the voter's evaluation of the candidate or issue and thus might be expected to be related to the voter's attitude. However, in many other instances, we should not expect single acts to be closely related to attitudes. To substantiate their claim that multiple acts might be more appropriate, Fishbein and Ajzen undertook extensive research on the relationship between attitudes to religion and acts considered as religious, such as praying before and after meals, taking a religious course for college credit, and donating money to religious institutions. Altogether, they collected a hundred behaviors to make up a multiple-act index. The correlation between measurements of attitudes to religion and the multiple-act index was high, whereas no systematic relationship was found between the single-act index and the attitude measurements.

As Alice Eagly and Shelly Chaiken (1998, I, p. 296) explained in their account of how the crisis in attitude research was overcome, an attitude in many instances will only partially determine a single act because this act may be determined by other causes as well. For example, the behavior of donating money to the election campaign of a senator is only partially determined by a favorable attitude towards the senator. The voter's finances also influence behavior: can she afford to give the money? When an attitude only partly determines a single behavior, that behavior is an unreliable indicator of an attitude. From a psychometric point of view, we find a more reliable indicator of attitude when the responses of each individual are aggregated across a number of different behaviors or situations. This was what Fishbein and Ajzen (1974) proposed. When this procedure has been followed, many investigations have found significant correlations between attitudes and behavior.

After having shown that attitudes are related to behavior, Ajzen and Fishbein (1977) went on to examine more carefully under what conditions we might expect measurements of attitudes to correlate significantly with behavior. This helped to explain why some earlier researchers had found a relationship and others had not. Examining LaPiere's (1934) frequently cited finding, mentioned in Chapter 14, Ajzen and Fishbein pointed out that the questions addressed to the directors of the establishments visited referred to Chinese people in general, whereas the behavior examined was directed towards a specific Chinese couple accompanied by a European–American. Re-examinations such as this one made clear that when the nature of the attitude and the nature of the behavior were appropriately specified and measured, significant correlations between the two were found.

From the end of the 1970s, researchers have been creating models that can account for the relationship between attitudes and behavior. I shall note only that, as Gerd Bohner and Norbert Schwarz (2001) made clear, although there is a relationship between attitudes and behavior, it seems to be more complex than social-psychological researchers have expected so far.

Before I end this brief account of the study of attitudes, I want to mention that advances have also been made in the study of attitude change. Researchers have been able to develop models which allow them to explain why studies in the 1950s and 1960s obtained conflicting results. (A review of this research is given by Richard Petty and Duane Wegener, 1998.)

The Study of Attribution After Heider

Fritz Heider (1958) had suggested that we follow rules when we make attributions. He had also suggested that we follow Mill's methods of experimental inference (see Chapter 2). Jones and Davis (1965) and Kelley (1967) began with these suggestions by Heider. Their two approaches complement each other, but I shall report only on Kelley's, which seems to have been the more influential.

Kelley (1967, p. 194) made the method of difference his basic analytic tool, stating that "the effect is attributed to that condition which is present when the effect is present and absent when the effect is absent." In other words, he proposed that we examine attribution in terms of a covariation of cause and effect. He illustrated his approach with the following example. He had enjoyed a movie and wondered whether his enjoyment was due to the properties of the movie or to dispositions in himself. To find out, he applied Mill's method of difference and determined: 1. whether the effect of the movie on him was specific to that movie or was present also in other movies; 2. whether other persons enjoyed the movie; 3. whether the enjoyment was invariant over time. He concluded that if he enjoyed only that movie, enjoyed it consistently over time, and other people also enjoyed it, the enjoyment would most naturally be attributable to the movie. On the other hand, if these conditions were not met, the attribution would probably be related to himself (to personal dispositions).

Kelley argued that a number of studies regarded as central in social psychology could be seen as instances of attribution, and psychologists began increasingly to view social psychological phenomena as problems of attribution. The study of cognitive dissonance had been the favorite theme in the 1960s, and when the interest declined in the early 1970s, the study of attribution replaced it. By the end of the twentieth century, interest in attribution had resulted in about 4,000 investigations and does not seem to have abated in the twenty-first century (Gilbert, 1998, p. 108).

Clearly, we can make logical errors in our reasoning about problems in attribution. Heider; Jones and Davis; and Kelley attempted to account for such errors, and in the 1970s and 1980s numerous other investigations sought to reveal what were believed to be errors of attribution. Several interesting hypotheses resulted. One is that our attributions represent a *self-serving bias*; that is, we defend ourselves by blaming circumstances when we fail and enhance ourselves by taking credit when we succeed. Another hypothesis is that in many instances we unjustifiably assume that other people will think or act as we do (*egoistic bias*). The deviation that has received most attention is the *fundamental attribution error*.

The Fundamental Attribution Error

Heider (1958, p. 53) discussed various conditions that might lead to error, particularly when we separate behavior from the circumstances under which it occurs. Lee Ross (1977, p. 183) formulated this tendency as "the tendency for attributers to underestimate the impact of situational factors and to overestimate the role of dispositional factors (personal factors) in controlling behavior," and termed it the *fundamental attribution error*. Treating problems from a somewhat different angle, the Polish psychologist and refugee to the United States, Gustav Ichheiser (1943, 1949) had pointed out before Heider that we tend to give insufficient weight to the properties of the situation, but his ideas had not attracted psychologists' attention.

A number of experiments indicate that under certain conditions the fundamental attribution error is a rather robust phenomenon. An elegant and particularly striking demonstration was given in an experiment by Ross (1977). Students at Stanford University were arbitrarily divided into two groups; one was assigned to make up a number of difficult general knowledge questions, and the other to answer the questions. After this session, the students of both groups were asked to rate themselves and each other on their general knowledge.

The subjects who made up the questions rated themselves as slightly more knowledgeable than the subjects answering them, whereas the subjects of the latter group tended to rate themselves as significantly inferior to the subjects of the former group and slightly inferior to the average Stanford student. A group of students shown a videotape of a session rated the students asking the questions as particularly knowledgeable but did not rate the subjects answering them as particularly ignorant. The results are surprising. Yet, when we recognize that in many familiar situations those who ask the questions are usually the most knowledgeable, perhaps it is not surprising that subjects overlooked the great advantage the students asking the questions had.

Even if the tendency to make the fundamental attribution error is found in several experiments, it may have different sources, as Gilbert (1998) has convincingly argued. If a tendency to behave in the same way has different sources, the behavior may be of different kinds. In other words, the term "fundamental attribution error" may refer to disparate phenomena.

Moreover, the fact that the fundamental attribution error seems to be a robust finding in experimental situations does not necessarily mean human beings have *a general* tendency to make the error. Critics have pointed out that it may be a product of the type of situations used in the experiments. Research has also suggested the tendency is less pronounced in and may even be absent from other cultures (again, see Gilbert, 1998). Even if the fundamental attribution error can be produced in experimental situations, we apparently do not yet know whether the study of it represents a fruitful theoretical endeavor.

Before I leave the study of attribution, I want to mention that, independently of the research of the social psychologists, personality psychologists have carried out extensive work on individual differences in attribution (Bernard Weiner and Sandra Graham, 1999).

Health Psychology

One of the complaints of social psychologists during the years of crisis was that the discipline was no longer oriented towards current problems of society. The field of health psychology, which emerged in the 1970s, gave psychologists an opportunity to apply their techniques and knowledge to a wide range of problems. As Peter Salovey, Alexander Rothman, and Judith Rodin (1998) emphasized, this study was a response to the increasing understanding in the latter half of the twentieth century that change in people's behavior is the most efficient way of reducing early death and death from disease.

For medical authorities, it became imperative to encourage behaviors promoting health, such as choosing an appropriate diet and getting physical exercise, and discouraging habits that damage health, such as smoking, excessive consumption of alcohol, use of narcotics, and failure to take precautions against sexually transmitted diseases. Lifestyle studies were carried out by medical doctors, physiologists, pharmacologists, biologists, geneticists, sociologists, anthropologists, social workers, administrators, and psychologists. Central to their study was behavior as it is relevant to health and disease; accordingly, it became known as *behavioral medicine* or *health psychology*. The two areas overlap so much that the terms are used more or less interchangeably. The study of health psychology, however, also encompasses the study of how disease is affected by psychological processes. Thus, it includes the earlier study of psychosomatic disorders discussed in Chapter 17.

Psychology had developed techniques and theories that could further the study of health psychology; the social psychological study of attitudes, attitude change, and attribution was particularly relevant. Other social psychological approaches, such as Bandura's theory of personality, also formed the basis for many investigations. For a further discussion of the development of health psychology, see Salovey et al. (1998).

The Study of Attraction and Close Relationships

Attraction between human beings and the formation of close relationships between them, such as friendship, love, and more enduring sexual relationships, as well as relationships between family members, forms part of the basis for all human communities and societies. It is therefore surprising that a systematic study of these phenomena was not undertaken by psychologists until the 1960s. It began as an interest in initial encounters between strangers, developed as a study of attraction in ongoing relationships, and continued further into a study of more long-lasting relationships, such as those mentioned above. As Ellen Berscheid and Harry Reis (1998) pointed out, the concept of *close relationships* is not easily defined for more exact measurements. I shall take it in its common-sense interpretation, meaning two or more people frequently interacting over some time, as in friendship, love, sexual partnership, and families.

Richard Bell (1968) gave important impetus to this study. In an epoch-making review of the literature on the effect of upbringing on personality development, he pointed out that personality characteristics of children may profoundly affect the way they are treated by their parents. Thus, the effect of upbringing could not be seen only as the effect the parents produced on the child, as earlier researchers had believed, but had to be regarded also as the result of interaction between the child and the parents.

Another important new perspective on the development of the child opened when psychologists began investigating the influence exerted on children by their peers. A third was the practice of relationship therapy, or *family therapy*, in which the focus is on the relationship between members of the couple or the family, not on the individual as in psychoanalysis and most other therapies developed prior to the 1960s. The dissolution of traditional family life as a result of the great increase in the divorce rate in Western society has spurred the study of close relationships, as has greater awareness of violence within the family and abuse of children by parents.

By systematizing knowledge, introducing new measurement and statistical techniques, and studying the development of relationships over time, researchers have found uniformities that make it easier to understand the conditions affecting close relationships. Research has also suggested important relationships between people's mental and physical health and the nature of their close relationships. On the whole, as shown in the handbook chapter by Berscheid and Reis (1998), the research on attraction and close relationships has produced a wealth of information on a large variety of psychological topics.

This study of attraction and close relationships links psychology to evolutionary biology, on the one hand, and to sociology and anthropology, on the other hand. It is thus an interdisciplinary endeavor that also links social psychology to developmental psychology. Its connection to so many other disciplines gives this study great potential for growth.

Evaluation of Progress in Social Psychology

The fifth edition (Fiske et al., 2010) of Gilbert et al.'s (1998) *Handbook of Social Psychology* presents a wealth of well-documented knowledge in a systematic and scholarly manner. The authors of the various chapters also carefully point out what is new. In my judgment, there can be no doubt that many of the problems dealt with in each of the chapters are better formulated than they were thirty years ago. Moreover, the knowledge accumulated is clearly relevant to a number of current social issues.

Some thirty chapters of the handbook are devoted to specific problem areas. Efforts are made to integrate the material within each chapter, but not so much across them. This reflects the fact that social psychology as a field remains fragmented, containing few, if any, general principles stating how human beings interact and influence each other. In this sense, no breakthrough seems to have been made. Further, apart from the study of attraction and close relationships, no great progress has been made in relating social psychology to the other social sciences.

While the great majority of social psychologists apparently believe the crisis of the 1970s has been overcome, one group maintains that the field has not fulfilled its promise and that greater progress could have been made if study had been directed otherwise. Some dissenters presented their objections to mainstream social psychology in a book entitled *Critical Social Psychology* (edited by Tomás Ibáñez and Lupicinio Íñiguez, 1997). One theme is that mainstream social psychologists overlook that the concepts used to study social problems are basically constructions based on linguistic practice and communication. Another is that traditional scientific, empirical procedures are inappropriate for the study of social problems. This view of social psychology and its procedures has repeatedly been presented by Kenneth Gergen (1996). However, no alternative to mainstream social psychology has so far been worked out. Until the critics present a better approach, there is no basis for believing they have new creative ideas.

Progress in Personality Psychology

The Revival of Trait Theory

Here, I shall continue the story of personality psychology by accounting for the way trait theorists answer the questions raised about their study. Later in the chapter, I shall review some of the studies of the self that illustrate how other aspects of the study of personality regained their strength.

In an article entitled "In Defense of Traits," Jerry Wiggins (1997) made clear that the concept of trait may have various different meanings. If a trait were understood as a category summarizing the behavior of an individual in a number of situations, we could measure behavior over a range of situations. If a measure of this type were correlated with measures of trait scales, Wiggins could show the correlations were quite high. Seymour Epstein (1979, 1980) performed extensive studies showing that if composite or aggregated measures are used, correlations increase when the range of situations and their duration over time are increased. Trait theorists apparently had to conceive of traits as Wiggins suggested. In fact, Gordon Allport (1937) had explicitly argued for this way of looking at traits. Gradually, it became accepted that in many instances it is more reasonable to use aggregate rather than single measures.

Whereas the concept of trait had been discussed at least since the publication of Allport's book on personality, the concept of situation seems to have been taken for granted until recently. It is now more widely understood that the concept of situation may be no less difficult to define than the concept of trait. William Ickes, Mark Snyder, and Stella Garcia (1997) have discussed the difficulty met with in attempts to define the concept of situation. The reason that criticism of the trait approach was so widely accepted is probably that psychologists tended to conceive rather naively of the use of the concept of situation.

The Five-Factor Model

Cattell's work inspired several researchers to undertake extensive investigations with a view to finding a structure in the use of trait names. At the beginning of the 1960s, there was converging evidence from factor-analytic studies that five broad dimensions could describe personality. According to Oliver John and Sanjay Srivastava (1999, p. 105), the factors were typically labeled as follows:

1. Extraversion or Surgency (talkative, assertive, energetic)
2. Agreeableness (good-natured, cooperative, trustful)
3. Conscientiousness (orderly, responsible, dependable)
4. Emotional Stability versus Neuroticism (calm, not neurotic, not easily upset)
5. Intellect or Openness (intellectual, imaginative, independent-minded).

Neuroticism and Openness are today the names used for items 4 and 5, respectively.

These eventually became known as the "Big Five" (Lewis Goldberg, 1981). The title is chosen to reflect that each of these factors is broad, not that personality differences can be reduced to only five traits. Rather, the factors represent five dimensions describing personality at a broad, abstract level, and each summarizes a large number of distinct, more specific characteristics.

A number of psychologists working independently of each other, studying different samples of English-speaking subjects, and using somewhat different procedures ended up with what appeared to be the same five factors. Although some researchers do not agree with five as the exact number, and there is still disagreement about how to label them, there has been broad consensus on the five-factor structure. Not only are the five factors a robust finding, but the five-factor model can also integrate results obtained on a variety of personality tests, as Robert Costa, Jr., and R. R. McCrae (Costa and McCrae, 1997; McCrae and Costa, 1999) have shown in an extensive research program. (On this point, see Wiggins and Trapnell, 1997; John and Srivastava, 1999.)

When we consider that the English language contains a large number of words descriptive of personality and thus allows for numerous ways of describing personality, it is surprising that the same five factors are consistently found in so many studies. As Goldberg (1993) pointed out, the leading proponents of the five-factor model started out as critics arguing for alternatives but became supporters as their research proceeded.

The trait structure described in the five-factor model was extracted from data produced by English-speaking persons. For the model to apply to all human beings, the same structure must also be found in subjects speaking different languages and belonging to different cultures. Naturally, many difficulties attach to performing investigations on such samples of subjects. Much cross-language and cross-cultural research has been carried out. John and Srivastava (1999, p. 107) finished their review of this research by stating that while strong conclusions are premature, the best working hypothesis is to assume the Big Five represent a universal structure. Support for this belief is also found in the fact that all five factors have a basis in genetics.

The five-factor model allows us to classify descriptions of personality in a relatively well-defined system of dimensions. Although this apparently represents great progress in communication among researchers, it is just a way of describing a set of complex phenomena; it does not provide an explanation of them. In this sense, as leading researchers have emphasized, the five-factor model is *not* a theory.

The model is based on individual differences in traits and does not tell us how traits function in the individual. To obtain this account, we need a more extensive description of personality. A comparison of the trait model with descriptions in anatomy will make this clear. We have not described the human body by describing size differences between its parts, such as the head and limbs. Similarly, we have not described personality by describing differences between psychological traits. To change the model into a theory of personality, we must show how traits function in the social lives of human individuals. The model provides only scant information on this point. As Pervin (2003, p. 65) argued, we would like to know more precisely whether traits should be taken as a predisposition to respond or as actual behavior. Further, if traits are taken to relate to overt behavior, do they then also relate to feelings, thoughts, and values? Still further, without a theory of how traits function, our reasoning may easily become circular. We infer trait concepts from behavior and may easily come to use the inferred concepts in an explanation. Only a theory can help us ensure that we are not falling into this type of circularity.

Psychologists doing research on the five-factor model disagree about how their findings should be interpreted. Some, such as McCrae and Costa (1999), claim this model "summarizes much of what psychologists mean by the term *personality*" and that it has been of "great utility to the field by integrating and systematizing diverse conceptions and measures." Accepting this as the state of the art, they urge that the time is ripe for changing the model into a theory of traits and suggested how this might be done. This and similar proposals, as well as the question of the universality of the big-five factors, will surely be intensively debated during the coming decades.

The Modern Study of the Self

In the 1940s and 1950s, Rogers, Asch, and others insisted, as Calkins and Gordon Allport had done before them, that the concept of self is needed in psychology. However, Rogers was virtually alone in conducting empirical investigations of the self. The overwhelming majority of psychologists seem to have believed that the study of the self is beyond the reach of empirical psychology. Then, in the mid-1970s, there was an abrupt change in thinking (see Richard Robins et al., 1999). In a comprehensive review of the modern empirical study of the self, Roy Baumeister (1998) noted that 31,550 articles on the self had been registered between 1974 and 1993. There are a number of reasons why interest increased so strongly.

Some reasons come from the social changes that have taken place in Western societies during recent centuries. As Baumeister (1998, p. 726) points out, "the burgeoning psychology of self is itself partly a reflection that self confronts the Western individual as a problem and a puzzle." Perhaps as the influence of traditional religion and morality has waned, Western individuals have been forced to find guides for their thinking and conduct in their personal experiences, feelings, and judgments, and this can lead to an increased concentration on their inner lives. Cultivating our own thinking and inclinations can be a way of marking our uniqueness as an individual. Thus, we can see the great interest in the self as forming part of the individualism that has been increasing since the Renaissance in the West, and perhaps particularly in the United States. Finally, technological development has given Westerners more time to reflect on their nature.

These reasons may help explain increased curiosity about the self in the general population, but to explain the great interest among psychological researchers in the 1970s, we must turn to changes that have taken place in psychology. These include the decrease in interest in behaviorism in the 1960s and the development of new techniques for studying aspects of the self.

The comprehensive review of the research literature on the self undertaken by Baumeister (1998) in the fourth edition of the *Handbook of Social Psychology* demonstrates that much useful knowledge has been produced. Psychologists have accumulated knowledge about the effects of self-awareness on our thinking and behavior; the role played by self-esteem; the way our conceptions of ourselves are influenced by the way others look at us; the way we exercise self-control; and many other problems related to ideas of the self. I think most readers of the chapter written by Baumeister will concur with him that progress has been made in the study of the self. Yet, as he admitted and Robins et al. (1999) report, the study of the self as an area of research has resisted attempts at a broader integration; there is a plethora of theories and models. Baumeister begins his review by stating that, in some ways, the thousands of journal articles have tended to make an answer to the question "What is the self?" more elusive rather than clearer.

Still, as I see it, Baumeister removes two important obstacles to clear thinking about the self. First, he points out that the self is not available to introspection. As Chapter 16 showed, Titchener criticized Calkins for holding that view. We are able to conceive of some activity of the self, but not of a self. The self must be inferred from the activities of the self. Second, the self is hardly phenomenally present to us; that is, we can scarcely know the self by means of the senses. At a given moment, only a small part of self-knowledge can be present to us. Rogers seems to have missed this point.

Instead of making a formal definition of the concept of self, Baumeister points to three important roots of selfhood. The first is *reflexive consciousness*. Our attention is somehow turned towards our own activities, as when we lie awake late at night thinking of our failures and inadequacies or glorying in our triumphs. The second root is the *interpersonal aspect of selfhood*. This is the knowledge we have acquired about ourselves from the way other people look at us. One of Baumeister's examples is occasions when we try to make a good impression on someone or try to live up to that person's expectations. The third root is the *executing function*, as when we decide what we want to buy, work on, or become.

Most research has been done on the first two roots. This seems reasonable as the greatest difficulties seem to arise when we try to conceive of ourselves as agents, as originators and directors of our thinking and behavior. Here, it is all too easy to come to assume there is a homunculus inside us who originates and directs our acts. Unless we are able to suggest in a plausible way how our thinking and behavior originates and is directed, we may easily either engage in circular, empty reasoning or state trivialities.

The abrupt increase in research on the self among psychologists must be explained, at least in part, as a result of the fact that procedures have been developed to make this work possible. A study by Hazel Markus (1977) is reckoned as groundbreaking, and a review of it is a convenient way of introducing some of the problems in this area of research. E. Tory Higgins (1987) made a frequently cited study that sheds light on the organization of our knowledge of our selves, as well as on emotions and motivations accompanying our conceptions of our selves. One of the best-known researchers of personality as well of clinical psychology is Albert Bandura (1986, 1999). He consistently attempted to develop a comprehensive theory of psychology by starting out with a view of the person as an agent initiating actions and exercising self-control. He began his career influenced by behaviorist theories of learning, and thus illustrates the change the thinking of many psychologists underwent from 1950 to 1980, from emphasis on behavior to emphasis on cognition and mentalism.

Markus's Self-Schema

Markus wanted to demonstrate that our conceptions of ourselves determine our thinking and behavior. To make her demonstration, she first selected three groups of subjects differing in how independent they saw themselves in relationship to others. On the basis of different types of tests, she selected a group of subjects rating themselves as high in independence, another group rating themselves as high in dependence, and a third group rating themselves in the middle range. Next, she had the three groups perform several tasks meant to reveal their conceptions of themselves as to independence and dependence. The tasks consisted of selecting trait adjectives descriptive of themselves, and judging how likely it was that they would behave in accordance with descriptions given of independent and of dependent behavior. In a second part of the investigation, Markus explored the degree to which the subjects were willing to accept information that contradicted the beliefs they had of themselves. The results of both parts of the investigation consistently showed that the subjects' performances agreed with their ratings of themselves on the initial tests.

Markus called the type of knowledge she ascribed to her subjects *self-schema*, meaning a cognitive generalization about the self derived from experience. Her study demonstrates that a facet of the self can be illuminated by empirical research. However, further progress seems to depend on how well researchers are able to describe the organization of the knowledge we have of ourselves. Selz, Piaget, and Bartlett used the concept of schema, and researchers on the study of memory have tried to make the concept useful for research (see Elliot Smith, 1998), but it is too early to decide to what extent they have succeeded. Therefore, Markus's "schema" is not a refined technical concept that can give her findings explanatory power.

Higgins's Self-Discrepancy Theory

James, who inspired much of the research in the 1970s, had played with the idea that we have a number of selves and possible selves. He had also noted that a variety of feelings could be understood as related to the self, such as pride, conceit, vanity, self-esteem, arrogance, and vainglory, on the one hand, and modesty, humility, confusion, diffidence, shame, mortification, contrition, the sense of obloquy, and despair, on the other hand.

James suggested that our different selves frequently conflict with each other. Freud made the conflict between the ego and superego central in his theory of personality, and Rogers concentrated his theorizing on the idea that certain ideas are incompatible with our conception of our self. Higgins (1987) combined the idea of a conflict between different aspects of our self with the idea that such conflicts are accompanied by various types of discomfort, and he developed hypotheses of the emotions that might be expected to result from specific types of conflicts.

To Rogers's ideas of an *actual (real) self* and an *ideal self*, Higgins added the idea of an *ought self* (the representation of the attributes persons believe they should or ought to possess). Further, he viewed each of the three types of selves from the standpoint of the person possessing them, as well as from the standpoint of significant others. This gave him six categories of selves and a number of relationships between them, though he concentrated on four: 1. actual own versus ideal own; 2. actual own versus ideal other; 3. actual own versus ought own; 4. actual own versus ought other.

Higgins worked out a theory to account for the effects of discrepancies between the selves. I shall review only some of his hypotheses concerning the effects of the four discrepancies listed above. He predicted that the first discrepancy would tend to be accompanied by dejection-related emotions and more specifically by disappointment and dissatisfaction; the second would also be accompanied by dejection-related emotions but more specifically by shame, embarrassment, and feeling downcast; the third would be accompanied by agitation-related emotions but more specifically by fear and feeling threatened; and the fourth would also be accompanied by agitation-related emotions but more specifically by guilt, self-contempt, and un-easiness.

To investigate his hypotheses, Higgins developed a questionnaire consisting of two sections, one in which the subjects responded according to their own standpoint and one according to what they thought would be the standpoint of their fathers, mothers, and closest friends. To measure the degree of discomfort and the emotional symptoms, Higgins used a variety of questionnaires taken from other researchers. The results of his investigation supported his hypotheses. If further explorations of the hypotheses confirm the results, Higgins would seem to have shown the following: 1. that the self has a certain organization; 2. that specific feelings and emotions are associated with diverse organizations of the self.

At about the same time as Higgins did his study of self-discrepancies, Markus and Paula Nurius (1986) made a similar type of investigation. They studied the idea that we have conceptions of the selves that we could possibly possess and would want to have, such as the self of an artist, or selves we would dread to have, like the self of a lonely old woman. The idea of possible selves is important because they seem frequently to act as motives; they instigate as well as direct behavior. By studying the nature of possible selves, we may thus have a means of shedding light on psychogenetic needs as these were conceived of by Murray.

Albert Bandura (1923–)

Together with Mischel, Bandura developed an approach to the study of personality and clinical psychology called *social learning theory*. Bandura is also interesting to historians because his work reflects the change in dominant trends in the latter half of the twentieth century. He started out in learning theory in the 1950s, a time when it was believed a study of learning would help solve psychological problems; then, during the 1960s, he became increasingly oriented towards cognitive psychology and changed the name of his approach to *social cognitive theory*. Finally, he concentrated his research on problems of the self.

Bandura grew up in northern Alberta, Canada, studied at the University of British Columbia, and received his PhD from the University of Iowa. From 1952 to the present, he has been attached to Stanford University. In 1974, he was elected president of the APA, and in 1980 he received the association's Distinguished Scientific Contribution Award. I shall consider three of his main contributions to psychology: his study of aggression, his study of modeling, and his concept of self-efficacy.

Aggression. Bandura and his coworker Richard Walters (1963) opposed Freud's and Lorenz's view of aggression as a drive needing an outlet, and the view of Dollard et al. (1939) of aggression as a drive evoked by frustration, the frustration–aggression hypothesis. Although there seems to be an important relationship between frustration and aggression, the hypothesis fails to recognize that aggression is only one of several reactions to frustration, and aggressive acts may be carried out without frustration. Bandura and Walters showed that learning affects the view of the situation in which aggression is evoked, the form it takes, the frequency of its occurrence, and the target at which it aims. The two researchers did not deny that aggression has a biological basis, but this basis only forms the potential for aggression. Aggressive behavior has aspects Bandura and Walters did not deal with, but, by calling attention to the important role played by learning, they contributed to a more balanced view and pointed out important directions for future research. (See Russell Geen, 1998.)

Observational Learning. Bandura took an independent stand on problems of learning. Although he was trained at the University of Iowa, which in the 1950s was the center of the Hull–Spence approach to learning, he was at first more influenced by Skinner and later more by Tolman. Although he agreed with Skinner that behavior is modified by its consequences, Bandura (1986, 1999) insisted that there is also another basic form of learning in humans, *observational learning*. He thought this mode of learning had largely been overlooked.

As he noted, some researchers had emphasized the role of imitation in human learning. The early French sociologist Gabriel Tarde had argued that changes in social life are the results of imitation, and Baldwin attributed a great role to imitation in the development of the child. Thorndike, however, argued that imitation plays no significant role in learning, and the behaviorists had been little concerned with learning as a result of imitation. In contrast, Piaget studied imitation, and C. W. Valentine (1930) had claimed that infants in the first months of life imitate acts they have not performed beforehand. The problem of imitation in neonates arose again at the end of the 1970s, and now it was also argued that this ability is genetically determined. Further, as mentioned in Chapter 12, Watson's student Mary Cover Jones had shown that children's anxiety about an object could be removed by social imitation. Finally, Freud argued that children acquire ideas of morality through identification with their parents.

Bandura (1986, 1999) pointed to certain general conditions under which observational learning takes place and applied the idea of observational learning to the study of aggression, phobias, and a number of other clinical phenomena. By calling attention to the role played by imitation in the formation of human behavior, he contributed to the study of learning. His descriptions, however, lack precision, and there are probably several forms of observational learning, not just *one*. Further, like previous theorists of learning, Bandura neglected the perceptual processes in his descriptions of observational learning. Finally, although he noted that infants at a very early stage seem to be able to imitate the facial expressions of adults, he seems to have ignored the likelihood that observational learning has a basis in genetically determined response tendencies. Without giving any compelling reasons (as I see it), Bandura changed the name "learning by imitation" to "modeling."

Self-Efficacy. Central in Bandura's (1999) social cognitive theory is the idea that human beings have cognitive capabilities of different kinds, the main ones being capabilities of symbolization, observational learning, forethought, self-regulation, and self-reflection. The last of these allows us to make judgments of our own ability to perform various activities and to achieve various goals.

Bandura (1999, p. 181) used the concept of *perceived self-efficacy* to refer to "people's belief in their capabilities to perform in ways that give them control over events that affect their lives." These beliefs, he claimed, form the foundation of human agency. "Unless people believe that they can produce desired results by their actions, they had," he held, "little incentive to act or to persevere in the face of difficulties." The belief a person has in his or her self-efficacy determines (in Bandura's term "regulates') his or her performance on a given task.

Bandura drew attention to a variety of activities and tasks affected by our beliefs in our self-efficacy. For example, we abstain from or are reluctant to engage in activities when we judge our self-efficacy to be poor, expand little effort in tasks we believe we master poorly, and feel we perform more smoothly and adequately when we believe we are up to a task. Bandura extended his idea of self-efficacy to clinical problems, holding that the development of a low belief in self-efficacy with regard to social activities or tasks might make a person dysfunctional. He thought that this sort of dysfunction is at the root of many types of clinical disorders. To change inadequate beliefs concerning self-efficacy, he had his clients observe models demonstrating desired activities and assisted them in performing the activities by instructing them. He thought that improvement with respect to beliefs in self-efficacy is at the core of all psychotherapy.

Bandura and his coworkers have done extensive research to clarify the nature of self-efficacy beliefs. They have also applied their therapeutic procedure to a variety of clinical disorders and have reported many positive results. However, because an evaluation of psychotherapy is a slow process, it is too early to draw more definitive conclusions.

The social cognitive theory constructed by Bandura (1986, 1999) is comprehensive and contains several highly abstract and rather loosely related concepts. It is, therefore, frequently difficult to interpret his statements in a precise manner. Although he took great pains to explain how he thought human beings interact with their social environment, he failed, in my view, to specify how behavior is motivated. Unless this specification is made, it is difficult to understand more precisely what he means by his core concepts of "self-regulatory capability" and "self-reflective capability," and unless their meaning has been made clear, it is difficult to obtain a more precise understanding of the concept of self-efficacy.

Not only Bandura but also Mischel and coworkers and a number of other psychological researchers have taken a great interest in the study of conditions regulating motivation, affect, and action since the 1970s (Baumeister, 1998; Mischel and Shoda, 1999). This focus seems to represent a return to the study of the will that figured so prominently in the psychologies of Wundt and James and in the psychology of the nineteenth century generally. Actually, Brian Little (1999) notes, there is a growing interest in the study of "what people are trying to do in their daily pursuits, their engagement in personal projects and life tasks, and commitments with which they struggle in their lives." According to Little, we can designate these studies as conative, concerned with phenomena involving the exercise of the will. Thus, whereas Wundt attempted to study volition as a process observable in introspection, modern researchers try to study it as it manifests itself in our daily strivings. Still, the study of the will has evidently returned to psychology.

Cognitive Behavioral Therapy

While Bandura started out in behaviorism and increasingly focused on cognitive processes, Aaron Beck started out in psychoanalysis and increasingly focused on cognitive processes. Beck, who had training as a psychiatrist and a psychoanalyst, believed, like Adler, that mental disorders develop as a result of the unrealistic or false beliefs persons have about themselves or their social environments He and a number of other therapists have developed techniques for changing such beliefs. Because it is not easy to decide whether the interventions these therapists undertake should be designated as cognitive or behavioral, their therapy is frequently referred to as cognitive behavioral therapy.

As Steven Hollon and Aaron Beck (2004) have shown, cognitive behavioral therapists have invented techniques for treating a wide range of mental disorders. A very large number of studies have been made to assess the effect of this form of therapy. It seems fairly safe to conclude that it is effective in treatment of depression and a number of anxiety disorders.

A New Perspective on Development: The Life-Span Study

Until the mid-twentieth century, the study of human ontogenetic development was usually limited to childhood and adolescence. Jung, however, was concerned with development over the entire life course, and Erikson extended his account of development to old age. Thus, these two psychologists paved the way for the study of the entire life span.

Another impetus to the life-span study came from the longitudinal studies begun in the 1920s. As D. C. Charles (1970) recounts, testing the subjects participating in these studies made researchers aware that important developmental changes take place in adulthood and old age. Extensive research on developmental changes in adulthood was undertaken by Robert Havighurst (1957) in the 1950s. In the 1960s, the dramatic increase in the number of people reaching old age had become apparent, and research on problems relating to old age, including psychological problems, intensified.

As more was known about adulthood and old age, it became clear that changes taking place in different periods of life have elements in common. This made a comparative study of the diverse periods more productive and gave the study a new perspective, as noted by one of the pioneers, P. B. Baltes (1987).

Another important perspective on the life-span study was given by John Elder, Jr. (1974). Throughout our entire history, human lives have probably been significantly influenced by events such as famines, epidemic diseases, natural catastrophes, wars, and the political and economic structure of society. Elder undertook an extensive study of the psychological effects of the Great Depression on American families in the 1930s. By this study, he showed that it was possible to obtain knowledge of the psychological effects of changes taking place in society at large.

Of course, the life course of a human being is also determined by events significant for each person alone, such as winning a lottery or being persuaded to choose a certain career. Still, most people choose a career, and many perform military service, become parents, divorce, lose a spouse or close friend, suffer chronic disease, and face old age and loneliness when children leave home. A study of events like these can contributed much to our understanding of human development, as Leo Hendry and Marion Kloep (2002) have shown.

A central problem in the study of development is, of course, what causes the changes. Elder, Baltes, Hendry and Kloep, and others have suggested that challenges, small as well as great, are a main cause of development. This is apparently an old idea deriving from folk wisdom, but that need not make it less important. The new perspective given by life-span research has produced results that throw doubt on the idea that development takes place in stages, as postulated by Freud, Erikson, and Piaget. Life-span research has the potential of integrating psychology with sociology, anthropology, and the biological sciences. It may also help integrate the diverse areas of psychology; they are all needed to understand the development taking place over the entire life-span.

Behavioral Genetics

During the twentieth century, US psychologists' view of heredity was twice radically changed. In the first two decades, many of the most influential psychologists were adherents of the eugenics movement and of the belief that heredity is a major factor in behavior. The behaviorists rejected this belief, probably under the influence of anthropology and sociology, and a strong environmentalism dominated psychology until the 1970s.

According to Robert Plomin et al. (1997), an important reason environmentalism was discarded was the result of a study undertaken by the psychiatrist Leonard Heston (1966) on schizophrenia. When Heston started his training as a psychiatrist, the predominant view of schizophrenia was that it is caused by poor interaction between the child and its parents, especially inadequate mothering. (Compare Bowlby's starting point.) One of Heston's schizophrenic patients had a schizophrenic father and three schizophrenic brothers. The mother was a decent, caring woman. Heston was interested in genetics and began a study of the family relations of schizophrenics, studying a number of persons who were the children of mothers hospitalized as schizophrenics and who had been adopted at birth. The study revealed a high incidence of schizophrenia in this group compared to a control group of adoptees. This strongly indicated that the mental disorder has a genetic basis. Heston also made another surprising finding: the incidence of schizophrenia in the group of adoptees was similar to that of persons growing up with their schizophrenic mothers. This suggested that the environment of shared rearing had little effect.

Another important study that helped challenge environmentalism was undertaken by John Lochlin and R. C. Nichols (1976), who made an extensive study of twins and found that in almost all personality traits, as assessed by self-report questionnaires, identical twins correlated higher than fraternal twins. This suggested a genetic influence even if the differences between the two groups of twins were not high. Lochlin and Nichols also reported another surprising result: They found that almost all the effects of the environment contributed to making children growing up in the same family *different*. Until then, psychologists had tended to believe the opposite was true. This finding has been repeated a number of times in research using different procedures for assessing the effects of the environment. Research has consistently shown that what makes siblings similar is heredity, whereas the environment tends to make them dissimilar. Moreover, Lochlin and Nichols's research showed that the environment siblings share contributes little to making them similar.

The discovery that it is not the environment but genetics that makes siblings similar led genetic psychologists to examine more carefully the relationship between genetic disposition and environmental influence. They have been able to demonstrate that many measures of environmental effects are influenced by genetics. For example, the way children are treated by their parents is an environmental effect that can be heavily influenced by the genetic dispositions of the parents.

The genetic psychological research reported here, called *quantitative genetics*, was not dependent upon the great progress achieved in molecular genetics by the mid-twentieth century when the structure of the DNA molecule, responsible for heredity, was discovered. Quantitative genetics of the type dealt with here was based upon simple methods such as comparing siblings growing up with their biological parents with siblings adopted away, siblings growing up in the same family with adopted children growing up in the same family, identical twins with fraternal twins, and identical twins growing up together with identical twins reared apart. The study of psychology by means of quantitative genetics will keep psychologists busy in the coming decades even if the greatest progress will probably come with the use of techniques and knowledge from molecular genetics. The results of this approach are already becoming known, but we will not pursue them here.

In a history of psychology, it is natural to ask why the breakthrough in genetic psychology come so late, close to one hundred years after Galton conducted his first twin study. Several reasons come to mind. American ideology traditionally accentuated the environment over heredity, and behaviorism had emphasized the role of environment and learning. Another reason may be found in the fact that the Nazis based their regime on ideas of genetic differences between ethnic groups. This may have kept later researchers from studying differences between people that originate in genetics.

Whether child psychologists around 1950 were influenced by psychoanalysis or by learning theory, they believed the way children are brought up has a decisive effect upon their personality. After World War II, a vast amount of empirical research was undertaken to determine the role played by upbringing in the development of the child. In Chapter 16, we noted the studies aimed to show how child-rearing practices contribute to forming personalities. The results of the genetic psychological investigations led researchers to question whether the methods employed to assess the role played by child rearing were adequate. If the shared environment had little effect on the formation of personality, it was difficult to understand how child-rearing practices could be as important as most psychologists believed. However, genetic research revealed that the environment also contributes substantially to personality formation. This was a dilemma.

But if the effect of upbringing could not be determined independently of the assessment of the genetic capacity of the child, the dilemma would be resolved. We might then assume that aspects of the environment regarded as objectively the same could affect children differently because they react differently to them as a result of having different genetic capacities. For example, divorce or a lenient or harsh upbringing might affect children differently. According to this view, developmental psychologists had until then based their research on inadequate ideas of what constitutes the environment of children. Although siblings have half their genetic endowment in common, they are sufficiently different genetically to react to the same objectively described situation in different ways. Hence, the environment can make them different.

In line with this way of thinking, genetic psychologists began exploring the question, *why are siblings so different?* Three good reasons were pointed out:

1. They react differently to what may objectively be regarded as the same environment.
2. Parents treat children with different heredity differently.
3. Children expose themselves to different environments and also create different environments because they have different genetically determined inclinations.

According to Charles Halverson and Karen Wampler (1997), the findings of genetic psychologists mean studies of family influences on the child must take into consideration similarities between sibling and parent and differences in personality between the members of the families studied. In their opinion, few of the studies previously conducted meet the requirements for adequate study of family influences.

The Revival of Interest in Comparative Psychology

Behaviorist Learning Psychology Meets Ethology

The behaviorist learning theorists were largely unconcerned with comparative animal psychological studies and concentrated on studies of only a few species. Nor did they conduct field studies to describe animal behavior in natural environments, confining themselves instead to experimental laboratory studies, for which they mainly used rats. During the 1920s, they placed little emphasis on genetic factors, as I reported in Chapters 12 and 13. The concentration on a limited number of species, and the lack of acknowledgment that behavior is genetically determined, led to their overlooking the importance of species-specific characteristics of learning. Like Thorndike, they tended to think learning occurs in the same way in all species and at all levels of ontogenetic development.

Unlike the behaviorists, the European ethologists placed much emphasis on genetic factors but hardly any on learning. When the ethological approach was introduced in the United States around the 1950s, it led to a dramatic confrontation that, like the one between the behaviorists and the Gestalt psychologists, proved fruitful for psychology.

In 1947, Tinbergen lectured at the American Museum of Natural History and at Columbia University. An expanded version of these lectures was published in a book in 1951. The lectures and the book received a great deal of attention, and ethology slowly became incorporated into American psychology. In 1950, Lorenz claimed that comparative psychology should cover the study of many animal species, and not, like US behaviorism, concentrate on only a few species. Theodore Schneirla and Frank Beach, two US researchers among the few who had conducted comparative studies, advanced the same criticism. As ethology gained recognition, it was exposed to strong criticism from the American learning-oriented biological psychologists. Before I turn to the discussion between them and the ethologists, I shall briefly introduce Schneirla.

Theodore Schneirla (1902–1968)

Theodore Schneirla's work covered a wide range of issues in the field of comparative psychology. A primary concern of his was that in the study of both phylogenesis and ontogenesis, researchers must differentiate between the various levels of development. In this, he followed up the idea of *emergent evolution*, of which Lloyd Morgan, among others, had been an advocate. When new components are added to development, this leads to a reorganization that gives the system new characteristics. This was an anti-reductionist approach. Moreover, Schneirla emphasized that in ontogenesis there is a subtle interaction between physical and psychological forms of influence. Physical influences contribute to the development of different organs that in turn influence behavior. Instead of the concept of learning, he claimed, we should use the concept of experience, allowing this to include a wide range of influences.

Schneirla called attention to important aspects of development. His work suffers, however, from the tendency to underrate genetic factors, and, as Stephen Glickman (1985) has remarked, he placed too little emphasis on the fact that animals acquire species-specific characteristics through ontogenetic development.

Instinct, Maturation, and Learning

Schneirla's student Daniel Lehrman perhaps did most to lift the ethological debate to a high professional standard. In an article first published in 1953, as well as in a subsequent article published in 1970, Lehrman presented a thorough and astute account of the reasons the behavior Tinbergen and Lorenz had termed *instincts* cannot be considered innate. Studies of ontogenetic development had demonstrated that the behavior previously termed instinctive is also the result of different types of environmental influence. One instance is nest building in rats. Although female rats build nests without prior experience or practice even when they have grown to maturity in isolation, they will not do so if prevented from manipulating and carrying objects while maturing. A body of research conducted later has shown that many different forms of behavior considered to be innate are affected by environmental influence. This was the same understanding of instincts Morgan had promoted in the 1890s.

Knowing that behavior once considered instinctive cannot be considered innate made it more difficult to determine stable characteristics to use in defining *instinct*, and few comparative psychologists today appear to use the concept. However, Rejecting the concept of instinct does not mean we cannot view behavior as genetically determined. It may at times be beneficial to speak of *instinctive behavior.*

Lorentz and Tinbergen were, of course, aware that the behavior they termed instinctive often requires time to develop. What occurs during this time they claimed to be the result of *maturation.* Lehrman's demonstration of the impact of environmental influence revealed that this concept could not be used in such a straightforward and simple way as the two Europeans had thought. Of course, Lehrman did not oppose the contention that maturation occurs in a growing organism. What he said was that we cannot consider maturation independently of environmental influences. As I mentioned in Chapter 11, American child psychologists headed by Hall and Gesell had emphasized the importance of maturation in children's development. Thus, Lehrman's criticism also applied to the use many child psychologists had made of the concept of maturation. Actually, it is difficult – if not impossible – to separate maturation from learning. This also demonstrates the difficulty of using the concept of "learning" in an adequate way.

The ethologists emphasized the importance of understanding behavior as a result of biological adaptation. In this, they appear to have been more strongly inclined towards the modern theory of evolution than was Schneirla. However, they often reasoned that similar behavior in different animal species is the same, without considering the function of the behavior for the different species. They often generalized from the species they had studied to human beings. Lehrman pointed out that this is contrary to the idea of biological evolution, and that there is an inconsistency between Lorenz's concern with comparative studies and his interpretation of the comparative material. As discussed in Chapter 7, Lorenz's view on motivation was caught in the crossfire.

The debate between ethologists and the US comparative psychologists helped clarify important aspects of behavior and their development. The productivity of the debate was in part due to Lehrman's unique willingness to understand his opponents' points of view. In the article from 1970, he apologized for the sharp tone he had used in the earlier article, emphasizing that the ethologists had formulated issues of great importance to the understanding of evolution. He also acknowledged the importance of the ethologists' efforts in giving scope to the species-specific aspects of behavior. Emphasis on species-specific factors was to be of great consequence for the study of learning and child development. It was also vital to these two areas that, in accordance with Schneirla's and Lehrman's viewpoints, researchers began to look for environmental factors that were early influences in human development. I shall briefly discuss the new thinking that emerged in the study of learning and child development.

A New Orientation in the Study of Learning

In the 1960s and 1970s, among experiments demonstrating the role of species-specific characteristics, John Garcia's work was significant. In cooperation with Robert Koelling (Garcia and Koelling, 1966), Garcia performed an experiment in avoidance learning under two different reinforcement conditions. Rats were trained to receive water by licking at the tube. The water was flavored, and licking was accompanied by a bright light and the sound of a buzzer. After they were accustomed to the situation, one group of rats was nauseated by exposure to X-rays, and another group was exposed to an electric shock while drinking. Post-tests showed that the nauseated rats tended to avoid the flavored water, whereas the shocked rats tended to avoid licking when this was accompanied by the bright light and noise.

It is reasonable to associate these results with certain species-specific characteristics. Rats appear to choose their food mainly on the basis of taste and smell, and not on visual and auditory perception. This in turn makes it reasonable to assume they are disposed to learn connections between reactions in the digestive system and taste and olfactory impressions. The results of other experiments support this conclusion. Birds, on the other hand, appear to base their choice of food on visual input, and in birds it has been demonstrated that it is much simpler to establish conditioning to visual stimuli than to taste stimuli. In operant conditioning, it has been shown that when food is used as a reinforcement, it is easier to teach a pigeon to peck at a plate than to flap its wings. Conversely, it is simpler to establish wing flapping than pecking when the reinforcement is shock.

These studies demonstrated that in accounting for learning we must consider species-specific characteristics. When we do, learning no longer appears to be a simple unitary process. As Robert Bolles (1993) has noted, it took a long time before American learning theorists were willing to accept the ethological claim that species-specific characteristics must be included in the study of learning. A thoughtful review of this incident in the history of the US study of learning is given by Glickman (1985).

Further Attacks on Conditioning and Associationism

Garcia's work also questioned the view that the principle of temporal contiguity is adequate to account for the learning taking place in Pavlovian conditioning. A few years later, Robert Rescorla (1967, 1988) and Leon Kamin (1969) performed experiments revealing that this principle is not sufficient to explain conditioning.

In this series of experiments, Rescorla demonstrated that in order for us to establish a connection between a conditioned and an unconditioned stimulus, the conditioned stimulus must *regularly* accompany the unconditioned. His conclusion was that contiguity between presentation of the unconditioned and the conditioned stimuli is insufficient to establish a conditioned reflex; the conditioned stimulus must also have a predictive value for the animal.

Kamin followed a somewhat different procedure in that he first established a connection between a sound, which functioned as a conditioned stimulus, and shock as an unconditioned stimulus. He then repeated the procedure, but with the addition of another stimulus (light). The result was that no connection was established between the last introduced stimulus (light) and the unconditioned stimulus. Kamin concluded that the formation of the first connection blocked the formation of a connection between the new stimulus and the unconditioned stimulus. The stimulus that had been introduced last had no informative value for the animal.

The experiments of Garcia, Rescorla, and Kamin showed that the principle of temporal contiguity is not sufficient to explain conditioning. They did not, however, question the belief that learning is a result of the formation of associative bonds. The Gestalt psychologists and Bartlett had opposed associationism, but they had not performed experiments that directly attack the view that learning is the result of the formation of associations. In the 1990s, Randy Gallistel (1995) made a frontal attack on the associative learning tradition. Based on a variety of experiments he and other researchers had performed, he argued that learning must be viewed as *domain specific*. That is, animals of diverse species have, through adaptation, acquired mechanisms for solving specific problems; there can be no such thing as a general learning mechanism.

I shall briefly report on an experiment cited in Gallistel (1995) on a species of ant (*Cataglyphis bicolor*) living in the Tunisian desert. The ant lives in a small nest in the sand and forages for dead arthropods. When it is searching for food, it makes a twistedrun, but when it has taken a bite from a dead arthropod, it returns in an *almost straight* line to its nest. If it is picked up when it returns to its nest and transported to a point some distance away from its nest, it will run in a straight line in a direction closely corresponding to the direction in which it would have run if it had not been picked up; it also runs for a distance corresponding to the one between the site where it was picked up and its nest. Having run this distance, it starts searching for its nest. To perform this marvelous feat, the ant must possess a mechanism that allows it to register the distance from its nest as well as the direction of the run.

In addition to reviewing a number of investigations supporting his view of learning as domain-specific, Gallistel performed a series of experiments suggesting that Pavlovian conditioning is also based upon a domain-specific mechanism. Thus, he appears to have provided substantial support to his view of learning as domain-specific and not as dependent upon a general principle of association. His idea has not gone unchallenged, and I shall return to the question of domain specificity later in the chapter.

Influence from Ethology on Developmental Psychology

As pointed out in Chapter 11, the study of development and learning was central in American psychology. Gesell as well as other researchers had made systematic investigations of the sensory and motor development of infants and children, and the role of maturation and learning had been heatedly debated. Around 1950, there was also considerable interest in the age-old problem of empiricism versus nativism in perception. The ethologists held that animals have preferences for specific aspects of the stimulation, and they showed that behavior we could regard as having adaptive significance is elicited by definite types of stimuli. The ethologists had further drawn attention to important relationships of a social nature in the animal kingdom. This emphasis led to increased interest in the study of the perception of the human face, voices, smells, and reactions, such as smiling and weeping in infants. Tinbergen's demonstrations based on simple experiments with animals probably also inspired researchers to develop simple techniques for experimental studies of infants.

These studies combined field observations and experiments, and looked at problems in terms of both learning theory and evolutionary biology. Beginning in the 1950s, a number of surprising results were obtained, and the study of infants has continued since. Here I shall mention only the pioneer research of Robert Fantz (1961) on visual perception in infants, beginning in the 1950s. By means of a simple technique, Fantz first demonstrated that newborn babies have a preference for certain types of visual stimulation. For example, they favor patterns such as stripes over homogeneously illuminated surfaces. In agreement with ethological thinking, Fantz also investigated the perception of faces and showed that infants as young as three months have a preference for drawings of faces over other types of stimuli, although it was later shown that babies first pass through a period in which they prefer curved to more regular figures and are probably unable to recognize faces.

Another simple, elegant design to demonstrate that visual perception develops much earlier in infants than previously assumed was the visual cliff constructed by Eleanor Gibson and R. D. Walk (1960). Here the infant is placed on a solid glass plate through which a floor forming a cliff can be seen. When infants as young as six to seven months are placed opposite their mothers and encouraged to crawl towards them, they will stop before the cliff, demonstrating that they are able to perceive space.

Ethologists had wondered how specific forms of stimuli from parents cause a bond to form between them and their young. Examples of such bonds are imprinting in birds and following behavior in many animals. Freud had asked how the bond is established between mother and child. One widely adopted view was that the infant is bonded to its mother primarily by way of nursing. At the end of the 1950s, Harry Harlow, in cooperation with his wife Mary Harlow, demonstrated that this view is not correct. The Harlows allowed rhesus monkeys that had been taken from their mothers at an early age to grow up with two different surrogate "mothers." One of these was made of steel wire and the other of wire covered with a soft material. The young monkeys preferred to stay around the soft surrogate mother, even when they were receiving milk only from the steel wire mother. Harlow also showed that monkeys growing up in isolation had difficulty with social interaction later in life when allowed to be with others of their kind. For example, they had problems in mating, and females lacked the ability to care for their offspring.

Attachment Theory

Ethology also exerted an influence on psychoanalytically oriented child psychology. The British psychoanalyst John Bowlby (1907–1990), working within the object-relations tradition, tried to fuse ideas from psychoanalysis and ethology. His attempt is known as *attachment theory.*

During World War II, British children from the cities were sent away from their families into the countryside to keep them safe from the bombing. Systematic investigations were made of the effects on them of the temporary loss of their mothers, in which Bowlby took a great interest. In 1950, he became a consultant to the World Health Organization to advise on the mental health of homeless children. From his study of the literature and his own experience with children separated from their mothers, Bowlby (1969/1971, pp. 49–57) concluded that the behavior of infants after such separation could be divided into three phases: a phase of protest against the separation manifested by reactions such as crying, expressions of anger, and clinging to the mother when she was leaving; a phase of depression manifested by reactions such as monotonous crying, withdrawal, and inactivity; and a phase of detachment manifested by decreased interest in other people, heightened interest in material objects, and a turning away from the mother when she returned. Bowlby believed the phase of detachment was the result of repression.

Based on his own as well as other psychologists' experience, Bowlby (1969/1971, p. 14) claimed that the same types of reactions found in infants are manifested in adults believed to have suffered separation in early life. They would make excessive demands on others, be anxious and angry when demands are not met, and be unable to form deep relationships. Bowlby set himself the task of explaining how earlier experiences of separation from mother or primary caregiver would affect the development of personality.

Inspired by the thinking of ethology, Bowlby suggested that infants become attached to their mothers by a class of instinctive reactions. Crying, smiling, and babbling in the infants would tie mother and child together. A tie to the mother would also keep infants in proximity to her and result in their following her closely and being alert to her movements. Close proximity to the mother was believed to have had survival value because it had protected infants from predators in our ancestors' more primitive environment. As soon as the child had developed enough to be able to make plans, he or she would begin forming working models of the mother's behavior and his or her own behavior and relationship with the mother. In these models, cognitive representations would interact with emotions of different sorts. The working models built at early stages in the child's life would determine the expectations the child would have of other persons later in life.

A central point in Bowlby's theory was that the mother's sensitivity to the child's needs is a main determinant of the quality of the child's attachment to her. Lack of sensitivity might easily result in mental malfunctioning in the child, and inadequate attachment was believed to be a main reason for the development of mental disorders in the child.

Before I discuss the theory, I should also like to call attention to the fact that since hardly anybody would deny that somehow infants are tied to their mothers, the question is not *whether* they are, but *how* the tie is established. Similarly, we want to know not whether the infant's relationship to its mother or primary caretaker determines the infant's later relationships with other people, but *how* these relationships are affected.

Bowlby discussed the role learning may play in the development of the infant's bonds to the mother. However, his work was carried out within the narrow confines of the most popular learning theories of the 1950s. In my judgment, he did not systematically try to rule out the role experience may play in the establishment of the child's bonds to his or her mother. Nor, I think, did he gave sufficient weight to the infant's cognitive abilities; the child's cognitive appraisal of the mother's role in satisfying his or her needs may have developed far earlier than Bowlby assumed. On the whole, his account of how the child becomes attached to its mother leaves a number of questions unanswered.

Cooperating with Bowlby, Mary Ainsworth (Ainsworth and Bowlby, 1991) developed a specific procedure to assess the nature of a child's attachment to the mother, known as the *strange situation procedure*. The child is placed in an unfamiliar setting and observed when with its mother and a stranger, later when alone with the stranger, and still later during the reunion with the mother. By means of a scoring system, the child is assessed as securely or insecurely attached, and, if insecurely attached, is placed in one of two different groups. Using this or a similar procedure, an enormous amount of research has been performed to study the degree to which attachment is stable, whether attachment affects the later development of personality, and whether it can be regarded as a cause of mental disturbance.

Reviews by Rebecca Eder and Sarah Mangelsdorf (1997) of the studies on attachment show that when the sample of mothers represents a normal range of personalities, no clear relationship is found between their personality and the child's attachment classification. However, mothers diagnosed as suffering from affective disorders will frequently have children who are insecurely attached. Similarly, children of neglecting and abusing parents will frequently be insecurely attached. When the personalities of the mothers are assessed as outside the normal range, it is reasonable to expect that the effect is indirect and not the result of ties to the mother as Bowlby suggested.

Clearly, the child's relationship to his or her mother is determined by a variety of factors. Michael Lewis (1999) has pointed to context as a decisive factor and shown how the way the family functions for its members, the way it is integrated in society, and its economic status may all affect the mother–child relationship.

Lewis undertook a longitudinal study in which he measured attachment in a group of children at one year and their reports of attachment at eighteen years. He found no continuity in attachment. To explore whether changes in context, such as family relationships, affect the nature of children's attachment, he studied the effects divorce had had on attachment in a subgroup of children in his sample who had experienced it during the eighteen years. He found that these children tended to be classified as insecure at eighteen, whereas those classified as secure at this age tended to come from intact families. This indicates that to understand the nature of attachment, we must take contextual factors into account.

Lewis's research demonstrates that the question of how early childhood experiences influence later personality development is a very complex one. Other critics of the attachment theory have drawn attention to the temperament of the child as a factor decisively affecting the relationship, and Judith Harris (1995) has argued that the mother's role in child upbringing may have been overestimated in modern Western countries. So far, the evidence may perhaps best be interpreted as suggesting that Freud and Bowlby overrated the role played by early experience *and* the mother in the development of personality.

Psychology and Evolution

Progress in Evolutionary Biology

Not until a great deal of work had been done in several biological specialties was the theory of evolution satisfactorily formulated. This happened, as I mentioned above, in the evolutionary synthesis finished at the end of the 1940s (modern synthesis). Simpson (1949/1967), Theodosius Dobzhansky et al. (1977), and Mayr (2002) have explained the importance of this event in the study of evolution. It provided an account of evolution consistent with existing knowledge in all relevant biological disciplines. Thus, it was a decisive event in biology and provided a secure basis for the principle of natural selection by integrating it with Mendelian genetics. Natural selection then became the cornerstone of the biologists' account of evolution. Progress in molecular biology and genetics in the 1940s and 1950s greatly strengthened the theory. It became clear to biologists that an increased understanding of genetics would help increase the precision and rigor of evolutionary biology.

There were, however, still unanswered questions in evolutionary biology. One was as follows. What is the object, the unit, of evolution? Is it the species, the population, the individual, or the gene? Another question was the following. How do we weigh the significance of random, stochastic factors relative to natural selection? Studies of genetics had made clear that evolution can take place without natural selection. For example, in *genetic drift*, changes in gene frequency can be brought about by chance, raising the question of the role played by chance relative to natural selection. Dobzhansky (1977, ch. 5, p. 164), an important contributor to the evolutionary synthesis, regarded assessing the importance of natural selection relative to genetic drift as the most important unsolved problem in the study of the mechanisms of evolution.

The evolutionary synthesis led to a reorientation of the study of organisms' adaptation to their environments. Through the ages, observers of nature have noted how well organisms and their parts are adapted to the environment in which they live: fish to water, birds to the air, hands for grasping, eyes for seeing. In so-called natural theology, structures of living beings and their adaptations were seen as designed by a creator. A number of acute observations were made by theologians of this school. Around 1800, as Browne (1995) and others have reported, the British theologian William Paley was particularly famous for his acute observations of design in organisms. He was one of the few authors Darwin enjoyed studying at Cambridge.

Darwin radically changed our ideas about adaptation by explaining it as the result of natural selection. According to this principle, individuals having a specific favorable character or trait over time avoid being eliminated. To clarify our thinking about adaptation, we need three terms, respectively, for the following: 1. the process; 2. the state of being adapted; 3. the trait that results from adaptation. According to Mayr (2002), it is convenient to use "adaptation" for the process as well as for the trait, and "adaptedness" for the state of being adapted. When we use the term *adaptation*, we must remember that, according to the principle of natural selection, the process is one of elimination over time. It is thus a passive, mechanical process and not one of striving for perfection or the achievement of some final end. Nor is it affected by the organism's use or disuse of a trait, as Lamarck believed. Having noted these points, Mayr (2002, p. 166) presented the following definition of an adaptation:

The legitimate use of the term adaptation is for a property of an organism, whether a structure, a psychological trait, a behavior, or anything else that the organism possesses, that is favored by selection over alternate traits.

As already noted, evolution may also take place without natural selection, as the result of random events. Evolutionary changes may also be byproducts of traits acquired through natural selection. Darwin (1871/1981) had discussed the latter types of traits in *The Descent of Man*. Therefore, to clarify the causal relationship in the study of a biological trait, we must ascertain that the trait is an adaptation; that is, the result of natural selection.

Biologists disagreed, as I have reported, on the role played by natural selection in evolution. Stephen Gould and Richard Lewontin (1978) thought that too much importance had been attached to the principle and that other aspects of the evolutionary process had been neglected. In a famous article, they named the study of adaptations the *adaptationist program*. Mayr (2002) agreed with Gould and Lewontin that random, stochastic factors play a great role in evolution, but he maintained that most traits are acquired through natural selection and that the study of adaptations is central in evolutionary biology. As I understand it, most present-day evolutionary biologists agree with him that the adaptationist study is of central importance.

Progress in the study of genetics led to attempts to tie the study of evolution more closely to it. Prominent researchers in these attempts were George Williams, William Hamilton, and Robert Trivers. Inspired by these three researchers, Edward Wilson proposed a comprehensive theory called *sociobiology* to account of all forms of social life, animal as well as human. Wilson was an important figure in evolutionary biology as well as in psychology. Sociobiology drew upon knowledge produced in the study of our hominid ancestors. I shall give a brief account of some ideas of these four researchers as well as of the progress in the study of human ancestry.

In their attempts to show how Mendelian genetics may be integrated with the principle of evolution, Ronald Fisher and other mathematical geneticists had, as Mayr (1982, p. 588) reported, chosen the gene as the unit of evolution. In his book *Adaptation and Natural Selection*, Williams (1966) took inspiration from them and drew the study of adaptation closer to the study of genetics. In his final chapter he wrote:

The preceding discussions have portrayed a certain view of natural selection and have advocated this view as the only acceptable theory of the genesis of adaptation. Natural selection arises from a reproductive competition among individuals, and ultimately among the genes, in a Mendelian population. A gene is selected on one basis only, its average effectiveness in producing individuals able to maximize the gene's representation in future generations.

Ten years after the publication of Williams's book, Richard Dawkins (1976) argued that all evolutionary phenomena should be examined at the level of the gene, and he made the gene the unit of evolution in a book provocatively titled *The Selfish Gene*. Williams's and Dawkins's views on the role played by the gene in evolution are controversial. Most present-day evolutionary biologists, to my understanding, take the view that to account adequately for evolution we must use all three concepts: gene, individual, and population.

Dawkins's book was primarily a criticism of the view that selection cannot work on a level above individuals (on a population or a species). Dawkins concluded that *group selection* only rarely occurs. His view seems at first to have been widely accepted, but more recently it has been opposed. Elliot Sober and David Sloan Wilson (1998) in particular have become known for their defense of the view that group selection plays a role in evolution. Mayr (2002, pp. 145–146), who apparently disagreed with Williams on several points, insisted that group selection plays a role in social groups where the members cooperate by "warning of enemies, sharing newly discovered sources of food, and joint defense against enemies." According to Mayr, the human species, at least during the hunter-gatherer stage, may have benefited from group selection.

In his discussion of adaptation, Williams revived the idea of design that had been developed in Aristotelian thinking of biology and in natural theology. Evolutionary psychology has made the idea of design central, as in *The Handbook of Evolutionary Psychology* edited by David Buss (2005). I shall, therefore, go into the idea in some detail in my presentation.

In the final chapter of his book, Williams (1966, p. 258) explained that he wanted to relate his position formally to the Aristotelian conception of teleology (from the Greek *telos*, meaning end). To achieve this reconciliation, he suggested that he would replace Aristotle's idea of a final cause with the principle of natural selection. This way of reconciling a modern view of evolution with an Aristotelian view would allow him, he thought, to account for adaptation as a means–end relationship. In the introduction to his book, he made his view explicit, stating:

Thus I have stressed the importance of the use of such concepts as biological means and ends because I want it clearly understood that I think that such a framework is the essence of the science of biology.

Basing his examination on a means–end analysis, Williams argued that biological phenomena could be ascribed goals, functions, or purposes. Thus, an apple could be ascribed the goal or function of seed dispersal and the eye the goal or function of vision. He then went on to explain the idea of design. Taking the apple as an example, he held that as a biological object the apple possesses a number of properties or traits. These traits could be seen, he said, as elements of a design for an efficient role in the propagation of the tree from which it came. The design had originated in evolutionary time and had been perfected over a long period of time. The evolutionary story that could be told of the design of the apple could be told of any species in the biota of the Earth.

Williams did not explain how he thought his idea of a design could be expressed in the traditional natural science explanation of cause and effect. Not until that has been done will it be possible, I believe, to see how concretely the concept of design is anchored to observations. Williams pointed out that we can find numerous analogies between the design of human contrivances or implements and the design found in biological structures. Thus, there is a striking analogy between, for example, bird wings and airplane wings and between bridge suspensions and skeletal suspensions. Williams proposed using such analogies as a rule or criterion for deciding whether some biological structure is an adaptation acquired through natural selection. If there is a clear analogy, we could be fairly certain the structure is an adaptation. The rule is not infallible, however, as Williams noted. He suggested as an additional criterion that a biological trait is an adaptation when it serves a biological function precisely, economically, and reliably.

Not all biologists agree that Williams arrived at adequate criteria for deciding whether a trait is an adaptation. Francisco Ayala (1977), in a chapter on philosophical issues in evolution, referred to Williams but was critical of his ideas of function. In his rather detailed discussion of adaptation Mayr (2002) does not even mention Williams's idea of design. More important, Ayala and Mayr both seem to insist that in every case where an adaptation is postulated, we can reach a decision about it only by detailed testing; that is, they seem to believe no general rules or criterion have so far been found.

Hamilton (1963, 1964) made topical an idea that, according to Mayr (1982, p. 598), had been presented thirty-two years earlier by the British biologist John B. Haldane. The idea is that an individual can spread his or her own genes equally effectively by taking care of the young of siblings or by taking care of his or her own young. This hypothesis could explain the existence of infertile castes in social insects, a problem that had puzzled Darwin. For example, in the beehive, worker bees care for the descendants of their sisters but do not themselves reproduce. If, as Darwin reasoned, the hereditary material is transferred to succeeding generations through the individual, the existence of infertile castes raises a problem. Having an inadequate idea of hereditary mechanisms, Darwin was unable to present a satisfactory solution.

Hamilton (1963, 1964) made clear that because the fertile sisters of the sterile workers share 50 percent of their genes with them, it would be just as advantageous to the latter to take care of their sisters' descendants as of their own. According to this view, from an evolutionary perspective, we should not see reproduction only as the direct reproduction of an individual; we must also consider it as the reproduction of kin. This way of looking at reproduction, called *kin selection* or *inclusive fitness*, made it possible to understand altruistic behavior towards a wider range of relatives than the individual's children. It explained important social relationships in the animal world.

Inspired by Hamilton and Williams, Robert Trivers (1971) speculated that altruism might also originate in social relationships *not* involving kinship. Membership in groups in which individuals reciprocated favors such as sharing food or other forms of help would benefit the individuals. Trivers further pointed out that collective endeavors, such as hunting and defending a territory, might favor individuals' being trustful and con-scientious. Thus, altruism might also originate in the beneficial effect on a population that came from individuals' reciprocating favors and duties. Trivers called this *reciprocal altruism.*

Another influential idea presented by Trivers (1972) was *parental investment.* Biol-ogists had noted that males and females of some species invested different amounts of energy in reproduction. Trivers examined reproductive behavior in many different species, showing that investment in the production and care of the young differed from species to species and determined the reproductive behavior of the female and male. These findings, he thought, also included human sexual and parental behavior.

A third hypothesis presented by Trivers (1972) was *parent–child conflict.* As we all know, parents and children have numerous conflicts, some even ending in murder. Trivers's point was that these conflicts should be examined rigorously in terms of genetic differences between parent and child, who share only 50 percent of their genes.

In 1975, Edward Wilson published a book – based on the ideas of Hamilton, Williams, and Trivers and his own extensive studies of social life in animals – in which he proposed that all studies of social life, animal as well as human, should be organized as one field of study, as a branch of evolutionary biology. His proposal, which, as I already mentioned, he called sociobiology, stirred up an intense debate. The study, which was to include the social sciences as well as psychology, was to be based on the theory of evolution as it had been formulated in the evolutionary synthesis and later developments in genetics. Although he was reluctant to abandon entirely the idea of group selection, Wilson made the ideas of kin selection and altruism central in his proposal.

Wilson was extremely erudite and supported his proposal with detailed studies of social interactions in numerous species of animals; he concentrated on colonial inverte-brates, social insects, nonhuman mammals, and humans. To bridge the gap between the nonhuman primate species and humans, he drew upon knowledge of hominid evolution accumulated since the publication of Darwin's *Descent of Man* in 1871.

According to Wilson, evolution has led to strong ties between human parents and children, altruism towards relatives, male dominance, division of labor between the two sexes, dominance hierarchy within the group, hostility to strangers, and competition for resources. He did not discuss how learning and culture could modify this picture of human nature and social life, and many social scientists and psychologists reacted negatively to his book.

Wilson attributed a great role to Trivers's theory of parental investment, and feminists reacted strongly to this part of his picture of human nature. Biologists with a Marxist orientation, such as Stephen Gould and Richard Lewontin, accused Wilson of having a hidden political agenda. The debate over sociobiology became acrimonious. Although many biologists, anthropologists, and psychologists still support Wilson's proposal, the term *sociobiology* has been dropped, and the study of behavior in terms of evolutionary biology is usually referred to now as *behavioral ecology*. It includes ideas from ethology.

Progress in the Study of Hominid Evolution

When Darwin wrote *The Descent of Man*, there were no fossil and paleoanthropolog-ical finds to allow him to describe human evolution from the time our ancestors sep-arated from the ape-like line to the present. Since the publication of that book, biolo-gists, anthropologists, and archeologists have invested an enormous amount of work in attempts to reconstruct the evolution of our hominid ancestors. They have succeeded in establishing a fairly coherent fossil record of our hominid ancestors, and by correlating this record with archeological knowledge, knowledge of climatic changes, and observa-tion of present tribal people, they have been able to construct meaningful scenarios of our ancestors' lives.

Although considerable progress has been made in this study, the material is still too incomplete to allow us to understand why our ancestors began walking on two legs, or why their brains tripled in size from about 450 to about 1,350 cc. Further, so far, we apparently do not know when our ancestors acquired language and the use of fire.

A collection of essays on the important questions in the study of hominid evolution was edited by Frans de Waal (2001). These essays show how relevant the study of our hominid ancestors is to the study of many of the problems treated in traditional empirical psychology. They also show how uncertain are many of the main points in the hominid record, however. That behavior is not recorded in fossil form is a serious handicap, as noted by Dobzhansky (1977) in a chapter on hominid evolution and by Tinbergen (1951) in *The Study of Instinct*. To this problem we can probably add that only the cavities of the skull remain in fossil form and not the structure of the brain and its fibers, transmitter substances, and hormones. A small change in these anatomical and physiological aspects can lead to dramatic changes in thinking and social life.

Evolutionary Psychology

Inspired by the progress in evolutionary biology, a group of psychologists in the late 1980s began to formulate a new program for integrating evolutionary biology, psychology, and the social sciences into a broad view of human nature. The program, like that of information processing thirty years earlier, rapidly attracted a large number of psychologists, and a new school called *evolutionary psychology* was established.

An early version of the program was presented in a collection of essays entitled *The Adapted Mind: Evolutionary Psychology and the Generation of Culture* (1992), edited by Jerome Barkow, Leda Cosmides, and John Tooby (1992). In the years following this publication, numerous studies inspired by the program were undertaken. In 1999, David Buss, one of the psychologists taking the initiative in working out the program, published *Evolutionary Psychology: The New Science of Mind* (2nd edition, 2004), a textbook reviewing the new research. As the subtitle indicates, the program had by now led to a school of psychology. Buss edited a comprehensive handbook of evolutionary psychology in 2005.

The psychologists developing the program were strongly influenced by Wilson's (1975) sociobiology. Like him, they aimed to integrate the social sciences by means of evolutionary biology. But, in contrast to him, they wanted to give psychology a central place. A considerable part of the research performed by evolutionary psychologists was inspired by Hamilton's view of kin selection and Trivers's three theories. An even greater influence than Hamilton and Trivers was Williams (1966). He was credited with, among other things, having provided "the first fully modern statement of the relationship between selection and adaptive design" and with having developed rigorous criteria for determining traits that are adaptations.

The pioneers of evolutionary psychology took a great interest in reconstructing the lives of our hominid ancestors. Indeed, we can see evolutionary psychology as an attempt to relate the study of our hominid ancestors to the study of psychology by means of the theory of evolution. The study of our hominid ancestors was further related to the study of present-day tribal people living as hunter-gatherers. On the whole, the pioneers of evolutionary psychology took a strong interest in social anthropology. (Barkow and Tooby were trained as social anthropologists.)

But they took little interest in earlier and contemporary psychology, with the exception of information processing. Along with evolutionary biology, they regarded information processing as one of the foundations of evolutionary psychology. In the introductory chapter of *The Handbook of Evolutionary Psychology*, Tooby and Cosmides (2005, p. 14) accounted for ideas in science they thought had particularly influenced the new school. Like many of their contemporaries, they believed there had been a cognitive revolution and that information processing had provided psychology with precise terminology for describing psychological events. This was believed to be one of the advances in science on which they could base their approach: "*Advance 1*: the cognitive revolution was producing, for the first time in human history, a precise language for describing mental mechanisms as programs that process information." As a result, "the mental world was no longer a mysterious, indefinable realm, but locatable in the physical world in terms of precisely, describable, highly organized causal relations" (p. 10). Evolutionary psychology was seen as the inevitable intersection of the computationalism of the cognitive revolution and the adaptationism of Williams's evolutionary biology. Tooby and Cosmides (2005) did not discuss the terms "mind" and "information," and they did not present empirical evidence in support of the claims made on behalf of information processing and Williams.

Evolutionary psychology was the study of mind, and not of behavior or of mind and behavior. Evolutionary psychologists thought that mind as found in human beings, what they referred to as *the human mind*, was built up around mechanisms for solving *domain-specific problems*. The mechanisms had been acquired through natural selection by our evolutionary ancestors as solutions to adaptive problems they had encountered. Thus, the aim of evolutionary psychologists was not only to demonstrate that some postulated trait is an adaptation but also to demonstrate that it is a *mechanism*.

Like the pioneers of the schools of psychology I have reviewed in earlier chapters, the pioneers of evolutionary psychology claimed to base their research on radically new ideas. Darwin, along with Romanes, started a comparative study of animals in which he naturally included humans. This study continues today. The claim made by evolutionary psychologists to have new ideas in a field based upon the theory of evolution must be evaluated by comparing the two fields to each other. This I shall do in the next subsection below.

There is also another aspect of evolutionary psychologists' claim to have new ideas. Evolutionary biologists in the 1960s and 1970s had, as we have seen, raised central questions concerning human psychology. The evolutionary psychologists' claim to new ideas must, therefore, also be evaluated relative to the studies of psychology made in evolutionary biology. To this evaluation I shall turn in the last section of this chapter.

An important part of the studies carried out by evolutionary psychologists aims to detect what are believed to be evolved mechanisms in human sexual life. A leader in these studies was Donald Symons. I shall illustrate the reasoning in this research by reviewing two examples given by Symons (1992) in a chapter of *The Adapted Mind*.

Symons (1992, p. 141) characterized evolutionary psychology as the application of the adaptationist program to the study of the human brain/mind. Evolutionary psychology aimed to identify adaptations in human mental life, and in this sense it is adaptationist psychology. However, evolutionary psychologists took a specific approach to the study of adaptations because they were searching for mechanisms in human mental life. To understand this approach, we must be familiar with their concept of an *adaptive problem*. In my judgment this is the key concept in evolutionary psychological thinking. It is a difficult one, and I shall devote a subsection to it below. In a final subsection, I shall review the use of the concept *mind* in evolutionary psychology.

What Was New in Evolutionary Psychology?

In Chapters 6, 7, and 10, as well as in the present chapter, I have reported on the study of comparative psychology that was started by Darwin and Romanes and incorporated in empirical psychology by James and his American contemporaries. Comparative psychology is based on the belief that all biological species are related to each other through biological evolution. It is thus an evolutionary psychology. Evolutionary psychologists did, however, not discuss the relationship between their form of evolutionary psychology and comparative psychology. In Buss's handbook, comparative psychology is not even listed in the index. Evolutionary psychology has, in my judgment, added some important new ideas to empirical psychology. But it is not possible to understand what is new in it, nor what is true in it, unless we consider it relative to comparative psychology. I shall, therefore, begin my discussion with a summary of the historical development of comparative psychology.

Prior to Darwin, there was a field of comparative anatomy and physiology. As noted in Chapter 3, Johannes Müller was a prominent representative. The comparative study of human and animal anatomy and physiology was a sound scientific endeavor producing much useful knowledge. With the acceptance of evolution as a fact, the study was revitalized. Instead of simply noting similarities and dissimilarities between different animals, researchers began to search for continuities between animals in the same phyletic lines. One important outcome was an increased understanding of several different anatomical/physiological systems in humans, such as the locomotory, digestive, circulatory, reproductive, visual, auditory, and olfactory systems. A study of fish and creatures even lower in the chordate phylum can give information about human anatomical/physiological systems.

Comparative psychology dating back to Darwin's *The Descent of Man* and his book on the expression of emotions (1872/1965) can be seen as an extension of the evolutionary study of anatomy and physiology, including psychological questions. Comparative psychology included all the main areas of psychology: perception, learning, remembering, thinking, intelligence, emotions, and motivation, as reported in Chapters 7 and 11. Work carried out by evolutionary biologists, physiologists, and psychologists formed part of mainstream psychology. Thus, as noted in Chapter 18, Stevens's (1951b) *Handbook of Experimental Psychology* contained a chapter on phylogenetic comparison, and comparative studies were included in general textbooks of psychology, just as they are in textbooks today.

In a chapter on phylogenetic comparison, Nissen (1951) made the following important points:

1. In all animals there are innate predispositions for particular motor coordinations, perceptions, and sensory or perceptual motor sequences (p. 360).

2. The most important axis in the evolution of behavior in the vertebrate series from fish to anthropoid apes is the increasing role of experience in the ontogenetic development of perception (p. 364).
3. It is in the cognitive rather than in the motivational aspects of behavior that we find the significant axes of behavioral evolution (p. 380).
4. The accomplishments of ontogeny and culture depend, in the first place, on phylogenetic heritage (p. 360).

These four points, which have been supported by a considerable amount of evidence, are of great help in understanding the relationship between psychology and evolutionary biology.

Nissen reviewed research carried out by the ethologists, but the influence from ethology was more strongly felt within psychology in the 1960s and 1970s, as noted above. The study of the evolution of the hominids is a comparative evolutionary study, as we can see from the collection of essays edited by de Waal (2001).

Comparative psychology was, as noted, based on the belief that all forms of life are related to each other. However, whereas the principle of common descent plays a role in comparative psychology, no systematic attempts were made to apply the principle of natural selection to the study. Evolutionary psychology aimed to make the principle of natural selection and the related study of adaptation central in the study of psychology. Tooby and Cosmides (2005, p. 16) emphasized this point when they explained what was new in evolutionary psychology:

The primary tool which allows evolutionary psychologists to go beyond traditional psychologists in studying the mind is that they take full advantage in their research of an overlooked reality: The programs comprising the human mind were designed by natural selection to solve the adaptive problems regularly faced by our hunter-gatherer ancestors – problems such as finding a mate, cooperating with others, hunting, gathering, protecting children, navigating, avoiding predators, avoiding exploitation, and so on.

Tooby and Cosmides were right, I believe, that traditional psychology had not taken advantage of making adaptive problems part of the study. The pioneers of evolutionary psychology understood that, since Darwin wrote *The Descent of Man*, considerable progress had been made in reconstructing the lives of our hominid ancestors. They believed a study of what we know in this area could be used to generate hypotheses of the origin of human mentality.

Some Early Influential Studies

Symons (1992, p. 141) believed that thinking inspired by what he referred to as Darwin's theory "leads one to expect that an array of specialized (specifically 'sexual') psychological mechanisms underpins human sexual behavior." Elaborating this belief, he declared that selection "produced brain/mind adaptations specialized to detect conspecifics of the opposite sex who evidence high 'mate value.'" In line with this view, Symons hypothesized that human males universally are maximally attracted to certain physical correlates of female nubility. By "physical correlates," he had in mind physical characteristics "indicative of a human female who has recently begun fertile menstrual cycles and who has not yet borne a child." Believing that almost all human evolution occurred in the Pleistocene Epoch, he suggested that such a woman would probably have been 15–18 years of age. Symons did think, however, that, due to the use of contraception, women in modern industrialized societies retain their youthful appearance longer. Yet, he claimed that in no society would men tend to be more attracted to women of thirty-eight than to women of eighteen. Concerning women's attraction to men, Symons hypothesized that women are attracted to men showing signs of high status.

Buss (2005) has reviewed investigations in which men were asked about the age of the women they would prefer to date. The results show that after the age of twenty, men have a preference for women younger than themselves. But the data do not seem to reveal a tendency in men 40–50 years of age to prefer women of eighteen to women of thirty-eight. Thus, they do not seem to give clear support to Symons's hypothesis of men's attraction to nubile women. Further, some data seem to run counter to his hypothesis. Men of eighteen do not seem to prefer women their own age, but women some years older than themselves.

Symons's claim that women are attracted to men showing signs of high status can be seen as forming part of Trivers's parental investment theory. According to this theory, women tend to prefer men who have resources and status and are willing to take care of the child. Research undertaken in various cultures seems to confirm the hypothesis. It has also been found that women are more discriminating than men in their choice of sexual partners, prefer men some years older than themselves, and give less weight than men to physical appearance in their choice of mate.

There is, however, another way of interpreting the results of the differences between women and men with regard to mate preference. In most societies, women tend to have fewer material resources, less political power, and lower status than men. They learn a gender role in which they take care of the household and play little part in political and public life, whereas the man is the breadwinner, makes more decisions, and is active in political life. It is not unreasonable to believe that this gender role contributes decisively to shape women's choice of mates. Alice Eagly and Wendy Wood (1999) have made a systematic examination of the results of research on women's and men's mate preferences in terms of a *theory of social structure*. Their examination shows that an explanation of the results in terms of social structure and gender roles is hardly less convincing than Symons's hypothesis. The two explanations are clearly not incompatible, however. It seems possible that genetically determined propensities interact with the environment.

According to the definition given by Mayr, which I quoted above, an adaptation is a trait an organism possesses that is favored by selection over alternate traits. With this in mind, I shall examine Symons's claim. Symons (1992, p. 144) held that his hypothesis entails the following four assumptions:

(a) During the evolutionary past, heritable variation existed among ancestral males in tendencies to be sexually attracted to certain physical characteristics of female nubility; (b) males who preferred nubile females outreproduced, on the average, males with different sexual preferences, specifically for the former's preference for nubility; (c) selection designed at least one mechanism for nubility-preferring; and (d) genes for nubility-preferring thus became established in human gene pools.

I shall discuss the first two assumptions.

A premise of Darwin's reasoning was that there is variation in all biological traits. It is thus to be expected that there is variation in sexual attraction when this is regarded as a trait. This means that before our ancestors were sexually attracted to nubile females, there must have been variation in their sexual attraction to conspecific females. In addition to this variation, Symons proposed that there also was variation in the sexual attraction of the ancestral males to nubile females. But why should there be variation of the latter type? In the chapter in which Symons presented his study, he did not attempt to answer this question. One possible answer I can think of is that nubile females have more pronounced sexual characteristics, such as more protruding breasts, a more pronounced waist/hip ratio, softer and clearer skin, and more shining hair. If there was competition among the females for the males, males' perception of these physical characteristics might have varied. It is, to my judgment, not at all improbable that there might have been variation in the males' attraction to nubile females. But it is not easy to find evidence that can make this a safe conclusion.

A scrutiny of the second assumption reveals that it may not be tenable. For a number of reasons nubile females might not have been younger than other females. For our ancestral females, bearing young may have been very risky. The death rate among females bearing a child for the first time may have been greater than among females bearing for a second or later time. Further, the death rate among firstborns may have been higher than among children born later. Older and experienced females may also have been better at taking care of the young.

It is possible to formulate a simpler and perhaps equally probable explanation of men's preference for younger women than that proposed by Symons. If we simply assume that the trait determining the ancestral males' mate preferences was the females' willingness to mate, it is natural to expect that the older females became less willing to mate after some years, and, further, that poorly fed or ill females would also be less willing to mate. Over time this would lead to a preference in the males for the younger females having the perceived characteristics of willingness and health. Admittedly, this explanation cannot explain Symons's hypothesis of a maximal attraction of ancestral males to nubile females. However, as I pointed out in the presentation of Symons's hypothesis, there is no clear empirical evidence for his claim of a maximal attraction in men for nubile females.

The examination of Symons's hypothesis reveals two difficulties met with in research aimed to demonstrate that a psychological trait is an adaptation. First, it is difficult to identify traits in human thinking and behavior, as exemplified by Symons's assertion that men are maximally attracted to nubile women. Second, because our knowledge of hominid life is so fragmentary, it is difficult to rule out alternate explanations of the origin of a psychological trait.

The Concept of an Adaptive Problem

Symons characterized evolutionary psychology as an adaptationist psychology. However, evolutionary psychologists give a somewhat unconventional meaning to the concept of adaptation. To explain this meaning, I shall go back to Mayr's definition of an adaptation as an inheritable trait that has been favored by selection over alternate traits. In line with this definition, the researcher studying adaptations starts out by identifying some trait and attempts to demonstrate that it is an adaptation. This was the straightforward procedure followed by Symons in the two examples discussed above.

Tooby and Cosmides (2005) did not follow this procedure. Whereas Symons was primarily interested in questions about human sexual life, they wanted to develop a general study that allowed them to identify mechanisms in what they referred to as the human mind. To take an example they gave, they wanted to find the mechanisms underlying avoidance of incest in human beings. To reach this goal, they started with the idea that avoidance of incest in human beings is an adaptation acquired in our evolutionary past. Then they asked under what conditions the adaptation could have evolved. The conditions represented what they called an *adaptive problem*. The solution was obviously to avoid having sexual intercourse with close relatives. Our ancestors would have had to acquire specific mechanisms that prevented them from engaging in this behavior. The researcher's final task was to specify what these mechanisms could be. As this example shows, Tooby and Cosmides (2005) made the concept of an adaptive problem central in their approach. I shall comment on their use of the concept.

In the introductory chapter to *The Adapted Mind*, Cosmides, Tooby, and Barkow (1992, p. 6) stated that the collection of essays focuses on adaptive problems faced by our hunter-gatherer ancestors. The idea of an adaptive problem was here introduced as

a problem that affected reproduction, however distantly, such as finding mates, parenting, choosing an appropriate habitat, cooperating, communicating, foraging, or recovering information through vision.

In the introductory chapter to *The Handbook of Evolutionary Psychology*, Tooby and Cosmides (2005, p. 21) characterized *adaptive problems* as "enduring conditions in the world that create reproductive opportunities or obstacles." Having defined an adaptive problem, Tooby and Cosmides (2005, p. 22) defined an adaptation as "an integrated structure or device that is well engineered to solve its adaptive problem." Later in the text, they claimed that Williams (1966) had provided rigorous criteria for deciding whether some trait is an adaptation. In line with this claim, I shall assume that they believed a structure or device is well engineered when it meets Williams's criteria.

It may be noted that Tooby and Cosmides's procedure is based on the belief that it is possible to give two different definitions of an adaptation. One is straightforward: an adaptation is the solution to an adaptive problem. The other defines an adaptation as a trait that functions according to the criteria developed by Williams (1966). Not all evolutionary psychologists agree that Williams had developed rigorous criteria for deciding whether a trait is an adaptation. Nor did he claim that his criteria are infallible. To decide whether a trait functions in a reliable, precise, and economical manner, we need a standard for deciding when a trait functions in this way. Take, for example, the human male genitals. Does it make sense to say they function reliably, precisely, and economically without having developed standards for evaluating their function?

In *The Adaptive Mind*, evolutionary psychologists assumed the traits they studied were formed in the Pleistocene Epoch about one million years ago. In *The Handbook of Evolutionary Psychology*, Tooby and Cosmides (2005) seem to have extended the time interval to the time when our ancestors lived as hunter-gatherers. We do not know how far back in time they did so. But we know that during this age, their brains may have doubled or even tripled in size, though we do not know why. Other events of great importance in hominid evolution were the beginning of bipedal locomotion, the mastery of fire, and the use of language. Again, we do not know when and how these traits were acquired. Recent research has made it seem highly probable that incidental factors have played a decisive role in human evolution. A reconstruction of adaptive problems that led to an increase in mental capacities must obviously be based on many conjectures.

In discussing what is new in evolutionary psychology, I asserted that evolutionary psychology cannot dispense with the traditional comparative psychological study. The definition of an adaptive problem contains no reference to the fact that, according to the principle of natural selection, an adaptation is a trait that has shown itself to be favorable for reproduction *relative to alternate traits*. Thus, to determine that a situation represented an adaptive problem to specific ancestors – say, an ancestor living in the Pleistocene Epoch – we must know how the *ancestor of this ancestor* behaved in the situation. In the passage in which Tooby and Cosmides (2005, p. 16) explained what was new in their approach and introduced the concept of an adaptive problem, they failed to specify how the ancestor of the ancestor studied solved the problem said to represent the adaptive problem. I shall illustrate my point by the first example Tooby and Cosmides gave of an adaptive problem: finding a mate. Evidently, if our ancestor could solve the problem in the same way as *his* ancestor, he would be faced with no adaptive problem. From this it seems to follow that unless we are able to compare the behavior of our ancestors at two different stages in their evolutionary development, we cannot adequately specify what is meant by an adaptive problem. To make this specification, we need a phylogenetic comparison.

Reflecting a little more on the need for a phylogenetic comparison, we note that the way human beings find mates has great similarities not only to the way apes find mates, but also to the way mammals, reptiles, amphibians, and even fish do. This naturally raises the question of whether some of the mechanisms in finding mates are the same down the vertebrate or even down the whole chordate phyletic line. Limiting the comparison to our hunter-gatherer ancestors may give us too little information to understand how human beings find mates. Further, the theory of sexual attraction must also account for attraction to members of the same sex.

The Concept of Mind in Evolutionary Biology

Evolutionary psychology wanted, on the one hand, to integrate psychology closely with evolutionary biology and, on the other hand, to found a new science of mind. So how did researchers think the study of psychology differs from the study of evolutionary biology? Buss (2004, pp. 49–50) answered the question in this way:

Whereas the broader field of evolutionary biology is concerned with the evolutionary analysis of all the integrated parts of an organism, evolutionary psychology focuses more narrowly on those parts that are psychological – the analysis of the human mind as a collection of evolved mechanisms, the contexts that activate those mechanisms, and the behaviors generated by those mechanisms.

Buss apparently thought he could draw a distinction between psychological and other biological processes by referring to the fact that evolutionary psychology studies mind. But this way of solving the problem raises the question of how we are to conceive of mind in a way that makes the study of it different from a study of evolutionary biology. Buss did not go into this problem. Nor did Tooby and Cosmides (2005) in their introductory chapter to *The Handbook of Evolutionary Psychology*. Evolutionary psychology seems to be caught in the mind–body problem.

If I am correct in asserting that the pioneers of evolutionary psychology have not presented cogent arguments for the claim that the parts of the organism they study are different from the parts studied by evolutionary biologists, it is difficult to see that their study differs from that of evolutionary biology. It would then just represent an extension of evolutionary biology.

After having equated the psychological with the mental, Buss, as we see from the passage just quoted, went on to conceive of mind as a collection of evolved mechanisms. As we have noted, evolutionary psychologists conceive of the mind as made up of numerous mechanisms to solve domain-specific problems. Our sensory systems can be seen as containing a series of evolved mechanisms, making the idea that mind is a series of evolved mechanisms plausible. In an afterword to *The Handbook of Evolutionary Psychology*, Dawkins (2005, p. 978) wondered whether there is an alternative to this view, which he referred to modularity. I think Nissen (1951) had developed a view that we can see as an alternative.

In his chapter on phylogenetic comparison, Nissen (1951, p. 360) had claimed that "in all animals there are predispositions for particular motor coordinations, perceptions, and sensory or perceptual motor sequences." He thought most of the predispositions are modified by experience and learning. The importance of learning is greater the higher the animal is on the phylogenetic scale. Nissen supported his view with considerable empirical evidence, and I believe it was widely accepted among contemporary and later comparative and physiological psychologists. Carlson (2007, p. 21), in apparent agreement with Nissen, argued that, due to the long period in which children are dependent upon their parents, "the evolutionary process did not have to produce a brain with specialized circuits that performed specialized tasks. Instead, it could simply produce a large brain with an abundance of neural circuits that could be modified by experience." Nissen's and Carlson's way of explaining that the brain enables human beings to solve a great number of specific problems is compatible with the idea that we find a great deal of modularity in the brain. Further, I believe it is simpler to identify predispositions in the infant than a number of ready-made mechanisms in the infant's brain.

In my judgment, there are two reasons that we need a study of psychology to supplement the study of evolutionary biology. First, culture affects human thinking and behavior in a way that at present cannot be accounted for in evolutionary biology. Second, because *Homo sapiens* is the only extant species of the hominid family, the use we can make of the comparative biological method is greatly limited. The functions underlying the myriad different behaviors manifested by human beings must be extricated by extensive experimentation combined with ontogenetic studies of human development, genetic studies of individual differences, and studies of the functions of the brain.

Some Concluding Comments

Symons characterized evolutionary psychology as the application of the adaptationist program to the study of brain/mind. Another way of characterizing it is to say that it calls attention to the need for ultimate explanations in psychology. In the review of the early German experimental physiology in Chapter 3, I reported on the distinction between proximate and ultimate explanations of biological phenomena and noted that both types are necessary. The main contribution of evolutionary psychology is, in my opinion, that it has made clear that ultimate explanations are needed if psychology is to be closely integrated with evolutionary biology. Although I believe it doubtful that evolutionary psychologists have developed procedures adequate for this task, they have shown that a search for ultimate explanations can give a new perspective to many psychological phenomena.

While evolutionary psychologists must be credited with demonstrating the need to search for ultimate explanations, they have paid too little attention to proximate explanations. When physiologists realized they needed ultimate as well as proximate explanations, physiology was so well structured that a productive search for historical evolutionary explanations could be made. I do not think psychology has been sufficiently structured yet to allow an effective application of the adaptationist program.

Moreover, as I have emphasized, psychology also lacks knowledge of how mental and social human life has evolved in human phylogenesis. As Nissen (1951) pointed out, we need accounts of how culture has come to have an influence on human mental and social life.

Psychology and Culture

To understand the relationship between the study of empirical psychology and the study of culture, the study of social anthropology, we must consider the history of the two disciplines. As Adam Kuper (1999) notes in his critical review of present as well as past use of the concept of culture in social anthropology, the discipline of the study of culture arose partly as a historical study of earlier ways of life in the European nations and partly as an attempt to systematize observations of the way of life of people of non-Western cultures. However, the discipline of empirical psychology arose from the attempts of physiologists, evolutionary biologists, and psychiatrists to extend their studies to psychological phenomena. Thus, the two disciplines had little in common at their early stages of development.

As reported in Chapter 4, Wundt took an interest in the historical study of the ways of life of different nations (*Volk*) and attempted to unite this study with his experimental psychological study. Social anthropologists of the first half of the twentieth century studied psychoanalysis, and psychologists of the same period studied the reports of social anthropologists such as Margaret Mead and Ruth Benedict. But by the mid-century, the interest of researchers in the other discipline had declined. Not until the last decade of the century did they began to understand the close relationship between their disciplines.

As the twentieth century ended, many psychologists had begun to doubt that the results of studies undertaken in social psychology in North America are reproducible in other cultures (as reported by Alan Fiske et al., 1998). A considerable amount of work has been invested to find out whether the results of US studies can be generalized to individuals of other cultures.

Evolutionary psychologists took a somewhat different approach to the problem of relating psychology to the study of culture. I shall report on their approach and discuss it with a view to shedding light on the relationship between psychology, evolutionary biology, and culture. Further, I shall report on the attempt of comparative psychologists to explain how culture originated in our hominid ancestors.

As Kuper (1999) showed, *culture* is a concept used in a great variety of ways. In my review of psychologists' attempts to relate psychology to culture, I shall focus on the view of culture as the way of thinking or behaving that individuals in a group learn and that is transmitted from one generation to another.

Durkheim's view of society and the individual is a convenient starting point. Durkheim held that culture and society exert a constraint on the individual, and that we could regard them as existing independently of the individual; society was said to be external to the individual.

Having discussed some of the criticisms that can be raised of Durkheim's view of society and the individual, Giddens (2006, p. 668) concluded that Durkheim's view is clearly valid in some respects: "Social institutions do precede the existence of any given individual; it is also evident that they exert constraint over us." Durkheim had a profound influence not only on sociology, but also on the social anthropologists' study of culture. A number of ethnographic studies of tribal people support Durkheim's view that culture has a profound influence on the thinking and behavior of the members of the communities studied. The ethnographer Roger Keesing (1981, p. 7) did, however, think the ethnographers' view "exaggerates the diversity of cultures; it exaggerates their integration as coherent and unchanging 'total systems' and minimizes individual diversity, conflict, and change." Kuper (1999, p. 244) agreed with Keesing.

But even if social anthropologists have tended to exaggerate the cultural conformity in local communities and the differences between the world's cultures, it is still reasonable to believe culture exerts considerable influence on human thinking and behavior. This raises the question of whether human individuals can be said to have a universal nature. If we cannot answer yes, it will be clearly difficult to find individuals for a study who are representative of human beings in general. Further, if we cannot conceive of human thinking and behavior as independent of culture, it is difficult to understand how psychology can be a study separable from social anthropology. Therefore, our conception of the relationship between human thinking and behavior, on the one hand, and culture, on the other hand, affects our idea of empirical psychology.

The pioneers of evolutionary psychology opposed Durkheim's view that society could be regarded as external to the individual and thus could be studied without concern for psychology. This view had led, they contended, to the widespread belief that the content of the mind derives from culture. A further consequence was the belief that human beings do not have a universal nature.

These pioneers presented their initial view of the relationships between psychology and culture in *The Adapted Mind*. The main idea was that through evolution humans had acquired psychological mechanisms for the generation of culture. What I believe is primarily important in this idea is that it centers the study of culture on the human individual as the generator of culture. In an evolutionary perspective, it is natural to believe that culture is produced by individuals who have acquired properties for generating it. Therefore, to understand what culture is about, we must understand how it has been – and is – generated.

If we think of cultural expressions as having evolved in close relationship to fundamental biological functions, such as eating, hunting, foraging, fighting, and mating, it is perhaps a little awkward to refer to properties in the individual that generate culture as mechanisms, as evolutionary psychologists did. The use of the concept of *psychological mechanisms* in evolutionary psychology meets with more serious difficulty, however. It is not easy to understand what the justification is for calling them psychological. They are said to generate cultural expressions. Barkow (1992) expressed the view in a slogan-like statement: "Beneath new culture is old psychology." What we can observe are only the cultural expressions. From these observations we can infer that some biological mechanisms are involved. But it is difficult to understand how we are justified in inferring that the mechanisms are psychological in nature.

In the introductory chapter to *The Adapted Mind*, Cosmides, Tooby, and Barkow (1992) do not, as far as I can see, attempt to justify why they refer to the mechanisms as psychological. Nor have I found an explanation in their lengthy essay in *The Adapted Mind* entitled "The Foundation of Culture." In other words, I cannot see why they believe we need psychology in addition to biology to explain culture. To answer this question, in my judgment, we need an account of what we mean when we refer to some events as psychological as opposed to biological and cultural. I note that Buss's *The Handbook of Evolutionary Psychology* has no chapter on culture and no systematic discussion of it.

In his attempt to establish social psychology as a study of social phenomena, Gordon Allport (1954) was aware of the difficulty of finding a place for social psychology along with social anthropology. He discussed Durkheim's view in detail in his historical chapter in the *Handbook of Social Psychology*. In this discussion he replied to a social anthropologist claiming that psychology could not explain social phenomena, just as Durkheim had claimed. Allport (1954, pp. 38–39) admitted that cultural models prescribe what individuals must learn to conform to society. Further, he noted that "over long periods of time language and other cultural forms seem to go through cycles of change independently of what any particular individual may do or think." He did, however, insist that "within this cultural matrix certain psychological factors are presupposed." He listed the following factors: "motivation, learning, the processes of perception, concept formation, and the organization of attitudes and sentiments."

The factors Allport claimed to be psychological can be seen as representing characteristics all human individuals have in common and thus to represent a universal human nature. Allport did not take a great interest in evolutionary biology. When we take this perspective on his factors, we see that all of them seem to be present in the anthropoid apes. It is thus natural to believe they are common to human beings as descendants of some common ancestor of both mankind and anthropoid apes. In my judgment, this view gives strong support to the idea of a universal human nature. I shall elaborate this point.

We know that human sensory processes have fundamental traits in common with the sensory processes in the apes; that the basic motivational systems – hunger, thirst, and sex – have much in common; and, as argued by Darwin and supported with additional evidence by Paul Ekman (1992) and Joseph LeDoux (1996), that the emotional systems also have much in common. What we seem to need is a more cogent argument that human intellectual capacities have fundamental features in common with the intellectual capacities of the anthropoid apes. Below I shall report on empirical research in primatology which supports the claim that human cognitive capacities have fundamental features in common with those of anthropoid apes. Before I turn to this comparison, I want to point out that the great similarities we find between humans and the anthropoid apes strongly suggest that human beings have a universal nature.

When we conceive of human beings not as apes having incidentally acquired language and culture, but as individuals having acquired the ability to develop culture, it is not too difficult to understand how human beings can be similar to the apes and still lead lives entirely different from theirs. The point I am making can be illustrated by the systematic studies of primate cognition undertaken by Michael Tomasello and Joseph Call (1997).

After systematically comparing and examining cognitive functions in a great number of primate species, Tomasello and Call undertook a comparison of human cognitive functioning with that found in other primate species. The comparison substantiated the conclusion arrived at by earlier researchers that human beings share with the other primate species "their cognitive adaptations for space, objects, tools, categorization, quantification, understanding of social relationships, intentional communication, social learning, and social cognition." However, their comparison also revealed that human beings have unique adaptations for social life, and it is the latter types of adaptations that make possible social and cultural activities, such as language, use of tools and symbols, and social learning.

According to Tomasello and Call, the key to understanding the difference between humans and nonhuman primates is a change in cognition "from a basically individual enterprise to a basically social-collective enterprise." Looking at the basis of culture in this way, Tomasello and Call were able to account for the great similarity between humans and the nonhuman primates as well as for the great dissimilarity in their social life.

Tomasello and Call supported their view of human evolutionary development with research on child development showing that, at an early age, human infants seem to a greater extent than the young of anthropoid apes to share emotions with and be more attentive to their parents, to have joint attention with the parents, to imitate and mimic them, and to have a greater understanding of their intentions. The great ability of the human child to interact socially may then be seen as making possible socially shared symbols, language, and social learning, which are essential for culture. (On this point, see also Saugstad, 1989b.) Thus, by means of an evolutionary comparative study, it is possible to better understand the development of the child as well as the nature of culture.

Human beings share most of their genetic material with the chimpanzee. It is therefore surprising that the human way of life differs so greatly from that of our close relatives. However, if we assume the difference is mainly in sociability and that it makes culture possible, we can understand, as Tomasello and Call argued, that a small difference in genetic material can make a great difference in the way of life.

If to our social nature we add the idea that at the initial stages of cultural development we lived in relatively small groups, we can begin, roughly, to understand how culture evolved. Thus, by combining comparative psychology, child psychology, genetics, and social anthropology, we can try, as modern researchers do, to piece together a picture of how culture evolved.

Bibliography

Abbagnano, N. (1967). Positivism. In P. Edwards (ed.), *The encyclopedia of philosophy*, vol. V, pp. 414–419.

Ach, N. (1905). *Über die Willenstätigkeit und das Denken.* Göttingen: Vandenhoeck und Ruprecht.

Ach, N. (1921). *Über die Begriffsbildung.* Bamberg: Buchners.

Adams, D.K. (1929). Experimental study of adaptive behavior in cats. *Comparative Psychology Monographs, 6.*

Adler, A. (1907). *Studien über Minderwertigkeit von Organen.* Wien: Urban und Schwarzenberg. (English trans., 1917: *Study of organ inferiority and its psychical compensation.* New York: Nervous and Mental Disease Publishing.)

Adler, A. (1912/1917). *Über den nervösen Character: Grundzüge einer vergleichenden Individual-Psychologie und Psychotherapie.* Wiesbaden: Bergmann. (English trans., 1912: *The neurotic constitution.* New York: Moffat, Yard.)

Adler, A. (1920/1925). *Praxis und Theorie der Individual psychologie.* (English trans., 1924: *The practice and theory of individual psychology.* New York: Harcourt Brace.)

Adler, A. (1927). *Menschenkenntnis.* Leipzig: Hirzel. (English trans., 1927: *Understanding human nature.* New York: Greenberg.)

Adorno, T.W., Prenkel-Brunswick, E., Lewinson, D.J., and Sanford, R.N. (1950). *The authoritarian personality.* New York: Harper.

Ainsworth, M.D.S. and Bowlby, J. (1991). An ethological approach to personality development. *American Psychologist, 46,* 333–341.

Ajzen, I. and Fishbein, M. (1977). Attitude–behavior relations: A theoretical analysis and review of empirical research. *Psychological Bulletin, 84,* 888–918.

Allport, D.A. (1993). Attention and control: Have we been asking the wrong questions? A critical review of twenty-five years. In D.E. Meyer and S.M. Kornblum (eds.), *Attention and performance*, vol. XIV, pp. 183–219. London: MIT Press.

Allport, F.H. (1924). *Textbook on social psychology.* Boston, MA: Houghton Mifflin.

Allport, G.W. (1935). Attitudes. In C. Murchison (ed.), *A handbook of social psychology*, pp. 798–844. Worcester, MA: Clark University Press.

Allport, G.W. (1937). *Personality: A psychological interpretation.* New York: Holt.

Allport, G.W. (1943). The productive paradoxes of William James. *Psychological Review, 50,* 95–120.

Allport, G.W. (1954). The historical background of modern social psychology. In Lindzey, *Handbook of social psychology*, vol. I, pp. 3–56

Allport, G.W. (1961). *Pattern and growth in personality.* New York: Holt, Rinehart and Winston.

Allport, G.W. and Odbert, H.S. (1936). Trait-names: A psycholexical study. *Psychological Monographs, 47,* no. 1.

Allport, G.W. and Vernon, P.E. (1931). *A study of values.* Boston, MA: Houghton, Mifflin.

American Psychiatric Association (2000). *Diagnostic and statistical manual of mental disorders* (4th edn.). Washington, DC: American Psychiatric Association.

Angell, J.R. (1904). *Psychology: An introduction to the study of the structure and function of consciousness*. New York: Holt & Co.

Angell, J.R. (1907). The province of functional psychology. *Psychological Review, 14,* 61–91.

Arnold, M (1960). *Emotion and personality*. New York: Columbia University Press.

Aronson, E., Wilson, T.D., and Brewer, M.B. (1998). Experimentation in social psychology. In Gilbert et al., *Handbook of social psychology*, pp. 99–142.

Asch, S.E. (1946). Forming impressions of personality. *Journal of Abnormal and Social Psychology, 41,* 258–290.

Asch, S.E. (1952). *Social psychology*. Englewood Cliffs, NJ: Prentice-Hall.

Asch, S.E. (1956). Studies of independence and conformity. I. A minority of one against unanimous majority. *Psychological Monographs, 70,* 1–70.

Aserinsky, E. and Kleitman, N. (1953). Regularly occurring periods of eye mobility and concomitant phenomena during sleep. *Science, 118,* 273–274.

Ash, M.G. (1983). The self-presentation of a discipline: History of psychology in the United States between pedagogy and scholarship. In L. Graham, W. Lepenis, and P. Weingart (eds.), *Functions and uses of disciplinary histories*, pp. 143–189. Dordrecht: Reidel.

Ash, M.G. (1995). *Gestalt psychology in German culture: Holism and the quest for objectivity*. Cambridge, UK: Cambridge University Press.

Atkinson, R.C. and Shiffrin, R.M. (1968). Human memory: A proposed system and its control processes. In K.W. Spence and J.T Spence (eds.), *The psychology of learning and motivation*, vol. II, pp. 89–195. London: Academic Press.

Ayala, E.J. (1977). Philosophical issues. In T. Dobzhansky, F.J. Ayala, G.L. Stebbins, and J.W. Valentine (eds.), *Evolution*, ch. 16. San Francisco: W.H. Freeman.

Baddeley, A.D. and Hitch, G. (1974). Working memory. In G.H. Bower (ed.), *The psychology of learning and motivation*, vol. VIII, pp. 47–90. London: Academic Press.

Baddeley, A.D. and Wilson, B. (2002). Prose recall and amnesia: Implications for the structure of working memory. *Neuropsychologia, 40,* 1737–1743.

Baillargeon, R. (1987). Object permanence in 3½- and 4½-month-old infants. *Developmental Psychology, 23,* 655–664.

Bain, A. (1855). *The senses and the intellect*. London: Parker.

Bain, A. (1859). *The emotions and the will*. London: Parker.

Baldwin, J.M. (1889–1891). *Handbook of psychology*. Vol. I. *Senses and intellect*; vol. II. *Feeling and will*. New York: Holt.

Baldwin, J.M. (1895). *Mental development in the child and the race*. New York: Macmillan.

Baldwin, J.M. (1896). A new factor in evolution. *American Naturalist, 30,* 441–451.

Baldwin, J.M. (1897). *Social and ethical interpretations in mental development: A study in social psychology*, 4th edn. New York: Macmillan.

Baldwin, J.M. (1906–1911). *Thoughts and things, or genetic logic*, vols. I–III. New York: Macmillan.

Baltes, P.B. (1987). Theoretical propositions of life-span developmental psychology: On the dynamics between growth and decline. *Developmental Psychology, 23,* 611–626.

Bandura, A.L. (1977). *Social learning theory*. Englewood Cliffs, NJ: Prentice-Hall.

Bandura, A.L. (1986). *Social foundations of thought and action: A social cognitive theory*. Englewood Cliffs, NJ: Prentice-Hall.

Bandura, A.L. (1999). Social cognitive theory of personality. In Pervin and John, *Handbook of personality*, pp. 154–196.

Bandura, A.L. and Walters, R.H. (1963). *Social learning and personality development.* New York: Holt, Rinehart and Winston.

Barker, R., Dembo, T., and Lewin, K. (1941). Frustration and regression. *University of Iowa Studies in Child Welfare, 18*(1), 195–293.

Barkow, J.H. (1992). Beneath new culture is old psychology: Gossip and social stratification. In Barkow et al., *The adapted mind*, pp. 627–637.

Barkow, J.H., Cosmides, L., and Tooby, J. (eds.) (1992). *The adapted mind: Evolutionary psychology and the generation of culture.* New York: Oxford University Press.

Bartlett, F.C. (1923). *Psychology and primitive culture.* Cambridge, UK: Cambridge University Press.

Bartlett, F.C. (1932). *Remembering.* Cambridge, UK: Cambridge University Press.

Bartlett, F.C. (1958). *Thinking: An experimental and social study.* London: Allen and Unwin.

Batson, C.D. (1998). Altruism and prosocial behavior. In Gilbert et al., *Handbook of social psychology*, vol. II, pp. 282–316.

Baumeister, R.F. (1997). Identity, self-concept, and self-esteem: The self lost and found. In Hogan et al., *Handbook of personality*, pp. 681–710.

Baumeister, R.F. (1998). The self. In Gilbert et al., *Handbook of social psychology*, pp. 680–740.

Baumeister, R.F. (1999). On the interface between personality and social psychology. In Pervin and John, *Handbook of personality*, pp. 367–377.

Beach, F.A. (1942). Analysis of the stimuli adequate to elicit mating behavior in the sexually inexperienced male rat. *Journal of Comparative Psychology, 33*, 163–207.

Beach, F.A. (1951). Instinctive behavior: Reproductive activities. In Stevens, *Handbook of experimental psychology*, pp. 387–434.

Beck, A.T. (1976). *Cognitive therapy and the emotional disorders.* New York: New American Library.

Bekhterev, V.M. (1913). *La psychologie objective.* Paris: Alcan. (Russian edition 1907–12.)

Bekhterev, V.M. (1932). *General principles of human reflexology: An introduction to the objective study of personality.* Norwich, UK: Jarrold. (Russian edition 1918.)

Bell, R.Q. (1968). A reinterpretation of the direction of effects in studies of socialization. *Psychological Review, 75*, 81–95.

Bem, D.J. (1967). Self-perception: An alternative interpretation of cognitive dissonance phenomena. *Psychological Review, 74*, 183–200.

Bem, D.J. (1972). Self-perception theory. In L. Berkowitz (ed.), *Advances in experimental social psychology*, vol. VI, pp. 1–62. New York: Academic Press.

Bem, D.J. (1996). Exotic becomes erotic: A developmental theory of sexual orientation. *Psychological Review, 103*, 320–335.

Benjafield, J.G. (1996). *A history of psychology.* Boston, MA: Allyn and Bacon.

Benussi, V. (1914). Gesetze der inadäquaten Gestaltauffassung. *Archiv für die gesamte Psychologie, 32*, 396–419.

Bernard, C. (1865). *Introduction à l'étude de la médecine expérimentale.* Paris: Baillièr. (English trans., 1927: *An introduction to the study of experimental medicine.* New York: Macmillan.)

Berscheid, E. and Reis, H.T. (1998). Attraction and close relationships. In Gilbert et al., *Handbook of social psychology*, vol. II, pp. 193–281.

Bindra, D. (1985). Motivation, the brain, and psychological theory. In S. Koch and D.E. Leary (eds.), *A century of psychology as science*, pp. 338–363. New York: McGraw-Hill.

Binet, A. (1903). *L'étude expérimentale de l'intelligence*. Paris: Schleicher.

Binet, A. (1911). La mesure du développement de l'intelligence chez les jeunes enfants. *Bulletin de la Société libre pour l'étude psychologique de l'enfant*, *70*, 241–248.

Binet, A. and Henri, V. (1896). La psychologie individuelle. *L'Année Psychologique*, *2*, 411–465.

Binet, A. and Simon, T. (1908). Le développement de l'intelligence chez les enfants. *L'Année Psychologique*, *14*, 1–94.

Birch, H.G. (1945). The relation of previous experience to insightful problem-solving. *Journal of Comparative Psychology*, *38*, 295–317.

Bjork, D.W. (1993). *B. F Skinner*. New York: Basic Books.

Blumenthal, A.L. (1975). A reappraisal of Wilhelm Wundt. *American Psychologist*, *30*, 1081–1088.

Blumenthal, A.L. (1980). Wilhelm Wundt and early American psychology: A clash of cultures. In R.W. Rieber (ed.), *Wilhelm Wundt and the making of a scientific psychology*. New York: Plenum Press.

Blumenthal, A.L. (1985). Psychology and linguistics: The first half-century. In S. Koch and D.E. Leary (eds.), *A century of psychology as science*, pp. 804–824. New York: McGraw-Hill.

Boakes, R. (1984). *From Darwin to behaviourism: Psychology and the minds of animals*. Cambridge, UK: Cambridge University Press.

Boden, M.A. (1979). *Piaget*. Glasgow: Fontana.

Bohner, G. and Schwarz, N. (2001). Attitudes, persuasion, and behavior. In A. Tesser and N. Schwarz (eds.), *Blackwell handbook of social psychology: Intraindividual processes*, pp. 413–435. Oxford, UK: Blackwell.

Bolles, R.C. (1993). *The story of psychology: A thematic history*. Pacific Grove, CA: Brooks/Cole.

Boorstin, D.J. (1974). *The Americans: The democratic experience*. New York: Random House.

Boring, E.G. (1929/1950). *A history of experimental psychology*. New York: Appleton-Century-Crofts.

Boring, E.G., Bridgman, P.W., Feigl, H., Israel, H., Pratt, C.C., and Skinner, B.F. (1945). Symposium on operationism. *Psychological Review*, *52*, 241–294.

Bowlby, J. (1969/1971). *Attachment and loss*, vol. I. *Attachment*. London: Hogarth Press.

Bowlby, J. (1973). *Attachment and loss*, vol. II. *Separation*. New York: Basic Books.

Bowlby, J. (1980). *Attachment and loss*, vol. III. *Loss*. New York: Basic Books.

Brentano, F. (1874/1924). *Psychologie vom empirischen Standpunkt*, vols. I–III. Leipzig: Dunker und Humblot. (Reprinted Hamburg: Meiner, 1955, 1959, 1968. English trans. 1973: *Psychology from an empirical standpoint*. London: Routledge.)

Breuer, J. and Freud, S. (1895). *Studien über Hysterie*. Wien: Deuticke. (Standard Edition of Freud's works, vol. II.)

Bridgman, P.W. (1927). *The logic of modern physics*. New York: Macmillan.

Bringmann, W.G. and Tweney, R.D. (ed.) (1980). *Wundt studies: A centennial collection*. Toronto: Hogrefe.

Broadbent, D.E. (1958). *Perception and communication*. London: Pergamon Press.

Broughton, J.M. and Freeman-Moir, D.J. (eds.) (1982). *The cognitive-developmental psychology of James Mark Baldwin: Current theory and the research in genetic epistemology*. Norwood, NJ: Ablex.

Browne, J. (1995). *Charles Darwin: Voyaging*, vol. I. London: Jonathan Cape.

Browne, J. (2002). *Charles Darwin: The power of place*, vol. II. London: Jonathan Cape.

Bruce, D. (2000). Introduction to the Transaction edition. In Edward L. Thorndike, *Animal intelligence*. New Brunswick, NJ: Transaction.

Bruner, J.S. (1983). *In search of mind: Essays in autobiography*. New York: Harper and Row.

Bruner, J.S., Goodnow, J.J., and Austin, G.A. (1956). *A study of thinking*. New York: John Wiley & Sons.

Bruner, J.S. and Postman, L. (1947a). Emotional selectivity in perception and reaction. *Journal of Personality, 16*, 69–77.

Bruner, J.S. and Postman, L. (1947b). Tension and tension-release as organizing factors in perception. *Journal of Personality, 15*, 300–308.

Brunswick, E. (1934). *Wahrnehmung Gegenstandswelt*. Vienna: Deuticke.

Brunswick, E. (1947). *Systematic and representative design of psychological experiments*. Berkeley, CA: University of California Press.

Bryan, W.L. and Harter, N. (1899). Studies of telegraphic language. The acquisition of a hierarchy of habits. *Psychological Review, 6*, 345–375.

Buckley, K.W. (1989). *Mechanical man: John Broadus Watson and the beginnings of behaviorism*. New York: Guilford Press.

Buss, A. (1997a). Evolutionary perspectives on personality traits. In Hogan et al., *Handbook of personality psychology*, pp. 346–366.

Buss, D.M. (1997b). Evolutionary foundations of personality. In Hogan et al., *Handbook of personality psychology*, pp. 318–344.

Buss, D.M. (2004). *Evolutionary psychology: The new science of mind*. Boston, MA: Pearson.

Buss, D.M. (ed.) (2005). *The handbook of evolutionary psychology*. Hoboken, NJ: John Wiley & Sons.

Buss, D.M. and Kenrick, D.T. (1998). Evolutionary social psychology. In Gilbert et al., *Handbook of social psychology*, vol. II, pp. 992–1026.

Cairns, R.B. (1992). The making of a developmental science: The contributions and intellectual heritage of James Mark Baldwin. *Developmental Psychology, 28*,17–24.

Calkins, M.W. (1900). Psychology as a science of selves. *Philosophical Review, 9*, 490–501.

Calkins, M.W. (1908). Psychology as the science of the self. *Journal of Philosophy, Psychology, and Scientific Method, 5*, 12–19, 64–68, 113–121.

Cannon, W.B. (1915). *Bodily changes in pain, hunger, fear and rage*. New York: Appleton-Century-Crofts.

Carlson, N.R. (2007). *Physiology of behavior*, 9th edn. Boston, MA: Allyn and Bacon.

Carr, H.A. (1925). *Psychology: A study of mental activity*. New York: Longmans, Green.

Carr, H.A. (1930). Functionalism. In C. Murchison (ed.), *Psychologies of 1930*. Worcester, MA: Clark University Press.

Carroll, J.B. (1985). Psychology and linguistics: Detachment and affiliation in the second half-century. In Koch and Leary, *A century of psychology as science*, pp. 825–854.

Carroy, J. and Plas, R. (1993). La méthode pathologique et les origines de la psychologie française au XIXe siècle. *Revue Internationale de psychopathologie, 12*, 603–612.

Cartwright, D. (1959). Lewinian theory as a contemporary systematic framework. In Koch, *Psychology: A study of a science*, vol. II, pp. 7–91.

Cattell, J.McK. (1890). Mental tests and measurements. *Mind, 15*, 373–381.

Cattell, R.B. (1943). The description of personality: Basic traits resolved into clusters. *Journal of Abnormal and Social Psychology, 38*, 476–506.

Cattell, R.B. (1956). Validation and interpretation of the 16PF questionnaire. *Journal of Clinical Psychology, 12*, 205–214.

Cattell, R.B. (1965). *The scientific analysis of personality.* Baltimore, MD: Penguin.

Chalmers, A.F. (1982). *What is this thing called science?*, 2nd edn. St Lucia, Queensland: University of Queensland Press.

Charles, D.C. (1970). Historical antecedents of life-span developmental psychology. In L.R. Goulet and P.B. Baltes (eds.), *Life-span developmental psychology: Research and theory.* New York: Academic Press.

Cherry, E.C. (1953). Some experiments on the recognition of speech, with one and with two ears. *Journal of the Acoustical Society of America, 25*, 975–979.

Chomsky, N. (1957). *Syntactic structures.* The Hague: Mouton.

Chomsky, N. (1959). Review of Skinner's *Verbal behavior. Language, 35*, 26–58.

Chomsky, N. (1966). *Cartesian linguistics: A chapter in the history of rational thought.* New York: Harper & Row.

Chomsky, N. (1968/1972). *Language and the mind*, enlarged edn. New York: Harcourt Brace Jovanovich.

Chomsky, N. (1980). *Rules and representations.* Oxford, UK: Basel Blackwell.

Cialdini, R.B. and Trost, M.R. (1998). Social influence: Social norms, conformity, and compliance. In Gilbert et al., *Handbook of social psychology*, vol. II, pp. 151–192. Boston, MA: McGraw-Hill.

Cofer, C.N. (1979). Human learning and memory. In E. Hearst (ed.), The first century of experimental psychology, pp. 323–370. Hillsdale, NJ: Erlbaum.

Cole, M., John-Steiner, V., Scribner, S., and Souberman, E. (1978). *L. S. Vygotsky: Mind in society.* Cambridge, MA: Harvard University Press.

Collier, G. and Johnson, D.F. (1990). The time window of feeding. *Physiology and Behavior, 48*, 771–777.

Collier, G. and Johnson, D.F. (1997). Who is in charge? Animal vs experimenter control. *Appetite, 29*, 159–180.

Comte, A. (1830–1842). *Cours de philosophie positive.* Paris: Baillière.

Conant, J. (1947/1951). *On understanding science.* New York: Yale University Press.

Cooper, L.A. and Shepard, R.N. (1973). Chronometric studies of the rotation of mental images. In W.G. Chase (ed.), *Visual information processing*, pp. 75–176. New York: Academic Press.

Corsini, R.J. and Auerbach, A.J. (eds.) (1996). *Concise encyclopedia of psychology*, 2nd edn. New York: John Wiley & Sons.

Cosmides, L., Tooby, J., and Barkow, J.H. (1992). Introduction: Evolutionary psychology and conceptual integration. In Barkow et al., *The adapted mind*, pp. 3–15.

Costa, P.T., Jr. and McCrae, R.R. (1997). Longitudinal stability of adult personality. In Hogan et al., *Handbook of personality*, pp. 269–386.

Costall, A. (1995). Sir Fredrick Bartlett. *The Psychologist, 8*, 307–308.

Cross, S.E. and Markus, H.R. (1999). The cultural constitution of personality. In Pervin and John, *Handbook of personality*, pp. 378–396.

Cushman, P. (1992). Psychotherapy to 1992: A historically situated interpretation. In D.K. Freedheim (ed.), *History of psychotherapy. A century of change*, pp. 21–64. Washington, DC: American Psychological Association.

Damasio, A. (2004). *Looking for Spinoza: Joy, sorrow, and the feeling brain.* London: Vintage.

Danziger, K. (1980a). Wundt and the two traditions in psychology. In R.W. Rieber (ed.), *Wilhelm Wundt and the making of a scientific psychology*, pp. 73–84. New York: Plenum Press.

Danziger, K. (1980b). Wundt's theory of behavior and volition. In R.W. Rieber (ed.), *Wilhelm Wundt and the making of a scientific psychology*, pp. 89–115. New York: Plenum Press.

Danziger, K. (1980c). On the threshold of the new psychology: Situating Wundt and James. In W.B. Bringham and R.D. Tweney (eds.), *Wundt studies: A centennial collection.* Toronto: Hogrefe.

Danziger, K. (1990). *Constructing the subject.* Cambridge, UK: Cambridge University Press.

Darwin, C. (1859/1979). *On the origin of species by natural selection or the presentation of favoured races in the struggle for life.* London: Murray.

Darwin, C. (1871/1981). *The descent of man and selection in relation to sex.* London: Murray.

Darwin, C. (1872/1965). *The expression of the emotions in man and animals.* London: Murray.

Darwin, C. (1877). A biographical sketch of an infant. *Mind, 2,* 286–294.

Darwin, C. (1881). *The formation of vegetable mould, through the action of worms, with observation of their habits.* London: Murray.

Dawkins, R. (1976). *The selfish gene.* Oxford, UK: Oxford University Press.

Dawkins, R. (2005). Afterword. In Buss, *The handbook of evolutionary psychology*, pp. 975–977.

Dawkins, M.S., Halliday, T.R., and Dawkins, R. (ed.) (1991). *The Tinbergen legacy.* London: Chapman and Hall.

Deese, J. (1990). James on the will. In M.G. Johnson and T.B. Henley (ed.), *Reflections on 'The principles of psychology': William James after a century*, pp. 295–310. Hillsdale, NJ: Erlbaum.

Dembo, T. (1931). Der Ärger als dynamsisches Problem. *Psychologische Forschung, 15,* 1–144.

Desmond, A. and Moore, J. (1991). *Darwin.* London: Michael Joseph.

de Waal, F.B.M. (2001). *Tree of origin: What primate behavior can tell us about human social evolution.* Cambridge, MA: Harvard University Press.

Dewey, J. (1896). The reflex arc concept in psychology. *Psychological Review, 3,* 357–370.

Dewey, J. (1910a). *How we think: A restatement of the relation of relative thinking to the educative process.* Boston, MA: Heath.

Dewey, J. (1910b). The need for social psychology. *Psychological Review, 24,* 266–277.

Diamond, S. (1980). Wundt before Leipzig. In Rieber, *Wilhelm Wundt and the making of a scientific psychology*, pp. 3–70.

Dobzhansky, T. (1977). Evolution of mankind. In Dobzhansky et al., *Evolution*, ch. 14.

Dobzhansky, T., Ayala, F.J., Stebbins, G.L., and Valentine, J.W. (eds.) (1977). *Evolution.* San Francisco: Freeman.

Dollard, J., Doob, L.W., Miller, N.E., Mowrer, O.H., and Sears, R.R. (1939). *Frustration and aggression.* New Haven, CT: Yale University Press.

Dollard, J. and Miller, N.E. (1950). *Personality and psychotherapy: An analysis in terms of learning, thinking, and culture.* New York: McGraw-Hill.

Donders, F.C. (1868/1969). On the speed of mental processes. *Acta Psychologica, 30,* 412–431. (German and French trans., 1869; Dutch, 1870).

Donnelly, M.E. (ed.) (1992). *Reinterpreting the legacy of William James.* Washington, DC: American Psychological Association.

Driver, J. (2001). A selective review of selective attention research from the past century. *British Journal of Psychology, 92,* 53–78.

Duncker, K. (1935/1945). *Zur Psychologie des produktiven Denkens.* Berlin: Springer. (English trans., 1945: *On problem solving. Psychological Monographs, 58,* 1–113; (whole no. 270).

Eagly, A.H. and Chaiken, S. (1998). Attitude structure and function. In Gilbert et al., *Handbook of social psychology*, vol. I, pp. 269–322.

Eagly, A.H. and Wood, W. (1999). The origins of sex differences in psychology: Evolved dispositions versus social roles. *American Psychologist, 54*, 408–423.

Ebbinghaus, H. (1885). *Über das Gedächtnis*. Leipzig: Veit. (English trans., 1913: *On Memory: A contribution to experimental psychology*, New York: Teachers College.)

Ebbinghaus, H. (1897). Über eine neue Methode zur Prüfung der geistigen Fähigkeiten und ihre Anwendung bei Schulkindern. *Zeitschrift für Psychologie, 13*, 401–459.

Ebbinghaus, H. (1897–1908). *Grundzüge der Psychologie*, vol. II. Leipzig: Veit. (English trans., M.S, Gazzaniga, 1973: *Fundamentals of psychology*. New York: Elsevier.)

Ebbinghaus, H. (1908). *Abriss der Psychologie*. Leipzig: Veit.

Eder, R.A. and Mangelsdorf, S.C. (1997). The emotional basis of early personality development: Implications for the emergent self-concept. In Hogan et al., *Handbook of personality*, pp. 209–240.

Ehrenfels, C.V. (1890). Über 'Gestaltqualitäten'. *Vierteljahrsschrift für wissenschaftliche Philosophie, 14*, 242–292. (English trans., 1988: B. Smith (ed.), *Foundations of Gestalt theory*. Munich: Philosophia.)

Ekman, P. (1992). An argument for basic emotions. *Cognition and Emotions, 6*, 169–200.

Elder, G.H., Jr. (1974). *Children of the great depression: Social change in life experience*. Chicago: University of Chicago Press.

Ellenberger, H.F. (1970). *The discovery of the unconscious: The history and evolution of dynamic psychiatry*. New York: Basic Books.

Emmons, R.A. (1997). Motives and goals. In Hogan et al., *Handbook of personality*, pp. 486–512.

Epstein, S. (1979). The stability of behavior. I. On predicting most of people much of the time. *Journal of Personality and Social Psychology, 77*, 1097–1126.

Epstein, S. (1980). The stability of behavior. II. Implications for psychological research. *American Psychologist, 35*, 790–806.

Erdelyi, M.H. (1974). A new look at the new look: Perceptual defence and vigilance. *Psychological Review, 81*, 1–25.

Erikson, E.H. (1950). *Childhood and society*. New York: Norton.

Estes, W.K. (1954). Kurt Lewin. In W.K. Estes, S. Koch, K. MacCorquodale, P.E. Meehl, C.G. Mueller, Jr., W.N. Schoenfeld, and W.S. Verplanck (eds.), *Modern learning theory*, pp. 317–344. New York: Appleton-Century-Crofts.

Eysenck, H.J. (1952). The effects of psychotherapy: An evaluation. *Journal of Consulting Psychology, 16*, 319–324.

Eysenck, H.J. (1953). *The structure of human personality*. London: Methuen.

Eysenck, H.J. (1990). Biological dimensions of personality. In L.A. Pervin (ed.), *Handbook of personality: Theory and research*, pp. 244–276. London: Guilford Press.

Eysenck, M.W. and Keane, M.T. (2000). *Cognitive psychology: A student's handbook*. Hove, UK: Psychology Press.

Eysenck, M.W. and Keane, M.T. (2005). *Cognitive psychology: A student's handbook*, 5th edn. Hove, UK: Psychology Press.

Fantz, R.L. (1961). The origin of form perception. *Science, 204*, 66–72.

Farah, M.J. (1988). Is visual imagery really visual? Overlooked evidence from neuropsychology. *Psychological Review, 95*, 307–317.

Farr, R.M. (1996). *The roots of modern social psychology 1872–1954.* Cambridge, MA: Blackwell.

Farson, R. (1978). The technology of humanism. *Journal of Humanistic Psychology, 18,* 5–35.

Fechner, G.T. (1860). *Elemente der Psychophysik,* vols. I–II. Leipzig: Breitkopf and Härtel. (English trans., 1966: *Elements of psychophysics.* New York: Holt, Rinehart and Winston.)

Ferster C.S. and Skinner, B.F. (1957). *Schedules of reinforcement.* New York: Appleton-Century-Crofts.

Festinger, L. (1957). *A theory of cognitive dissonance.* Evanston, IL: Row, Peterson.

Festinger, L. and Carlsmith, J.M. (1959). Cognitive consequences of forced compliance. *Journal of Abnormal and Social Psychology, 68,* 359–366.

Finger, S. (1994). *Origins of neuroscience: A history of explorations into brain functions.* Oxford, UK: Oxford University Press.

Fishbein, M. and Ajzen, I. (1974). Attitudes toward objects as predictors of single and multiple behavior criteria. *Psychological Review, 81,* 59–74.

Fishman, D.B. and Franks, C.M. (1992). Evolution and differentiation within behavior therapy: A theoretical and epistemological review. In D.K. Freedheim (ed.), *History of psychotherapy: A century of change,* pp. 159–196, Washington, DC: American Psychological Association.

Fiske, A.P., Kitayama, S., Marcus, H.R., and Nisbett, R.E. (1998). The cultural matrix of social psychology. In Gilbert et al., *Handbook of social psychology,* vol. II, pp. 915–981.

Fiske, S.T., Gilbert, D.T., and Lindzey, G. (ed.) (2010). *The handbook of social psychology,* 5th edn. New York: Wiley.

Fiske, S.T. (1998). Stereotyping, prejudice, and discrimination. In Gilbert et al., *Handbook of social psychology,* vol. II, pp. 357–411.

Foucalt, M. (1961/1966). *Folie et déraison: histoire de la folie à l'âge classique.* Paris: Librairie Plon. (English trans., 1965: *Madness and civilization: A history of insanity in the age of reason.* London: Tavistock.)

Fransella, F. (1995). *George Kelly.* London: Sage.

Freud, A. (1936). *Das Ich und die Abwehrmechanismen.* Wien: Internationaler Psychoanalytischer Verlag. (English trans., 1937: *The ego and the mechanisms of defence.* New York: International Universities Press.)

Freud, S. (1900). *Die Traumdeutung.* Wien: Deuticke. (English trans., 1913: *The interpretation of dreams.*) (Standard Edition, vols. IV–V.)

Freud, S. (1904). *Zur Psychopathologie des Alltagslebens.* Berlin: Karger. (English trans., 2002: *The psychopathology of everyday life.*) (Standard Edition, vol. VI.)

Freud, S. (1905). *Drei Abhandlungen zur Sexualtheorie.* Wien: Deuticke. (English trans., 1910: *Three essays on the theory of sexuality.*) (Standard Edition, vol. VII, pp. 130–243.)

Freud, S. (1912). A note on the unconscious in psychoanalysis. *Proceedings of the Society for Psychical Research, 26,* 312–318. (German trans. 1913; Standard Edition, vol. XII.)

Freud, S. (1912–1913). *Totem und Tabu.* Über einige Übereinstimmungen im Seelenleben der Wilden und der Neurotiker. *Imago, 1,* 17–33, 213–227, 301–333; *2,* 1–21, 357–409. (Standard Edition, vol. XIII.)

Freud, S. (1915a). Triebe und Triebschicksale. *Internationale Zeitschrift für Psychoanalyse, 3,* 84–100. (English trans., 1957: *Insects and their vicissitudes.*) (Standard Edition, vol. XIV, pp. 117–140.)

Freud, S. (1915b). Das Unbewusste. *Internationale Zeitschrift für Psychoanalyse, 3,* 189–203, 257–269. (Standard Edition, vol. XIV, pp. 166–204.)

Freud, S. (1916–1917). *Vorlesungen zur Einführung in die Psychoanalyse.* Wien: Hugo Heller. (English trans., 1989: *Introductory lectures on psycho-analysis.*) (Standard Edition, vols. XV–XVI.)

Freud, S. (1920). *Jenseits des Lustprinzips.* Wien: Internationaler Psychoanalytischer Verlag. (English trans., 1989: *Beyond the pleasure principle.*) (Standard Edition, vol. XIV, pp. 7–64.)

Freud, S. (1923). *Das Ich und das Es.* Wien: Internationaler Psychoanalytischer Verlag. (English trans., 1962: *The ego and the id.*) (Standard Edition, vol. XIX, pp. 12–66.)

Freud, S. (1927). *Die Zukunft einer Illusion.* Wien: Internationaler Psychoanalytischer Verlag. (English trans., 1976: *The future of an illusion.*) (Standard Edition, vol. XXI.)

Freud, S. (1930). *Das Unbehagen in der Kultur.* Wien: Internationaler Psychoanalytischer Verlag. (English trans., 1961: *Civilisation and its discontents.*) (Standard Edition, vol. XXI, pp. 64–145.)

Freud, S. (1932). *Neue Folge der Vorlesungen zur Einführung in die Psychoanalyse.* Wien: Internationaler Psychoanalytischer Verlag. (English trans., 1990: *New introductory lectures on psycho-analysis.*) (Standard Edition, vol. XX.)

Freud, S. (1939). *Moses und Monotheism.* New York: Knopf.

Freud, S. (1895/1950). *Project for a scientific psychology* [*Entwurf einer Psychologie*, a paper written in 1895]. (Standard Edition, vol. I, pp. 283–397.)

Freud, S. (1953–74). *The Standard [English] Edition of the complete psychological works of Sigmund Freud,* ed. James Strachey. London: Hogarth Press, 24 vols.

Frisch, K.V. (1955). *The dancing bees.* New York: Harcourt, Brace.

Gallistel, C.R. (1995). The replacement of general-purpose theories with adaptive specializations. In M.S. Gazzaniga (ed.), *The cognitive neurosciences,* pp. 1255–1267. Cambridge, MA: MIT Press.

Galton, F. (1869). *Hereditary genius: An inquiry into its laws and consequences.* London: Macmillan.

Galton, F. (1874). *English men of science: Their nature and nurture.* London: Macmillan.

Galton, F. (1876). The history of twins, as a criterion of the relative powers of nature and nurture. *Journal of the Anthropological Institute,* 5, 391–406.

Galton, F. (1883). *Inquiries into human faculty and its development.* London: Macmillan.

Galton, F. (1889). *Natural inheritance.* London: Macmillan.

Garcia, J. and Koelling, R.A. (1966). Relation of cue to consequence in avoidance learning. *Psychonomic Science,* 4, 123–124.

Gardner, H. (1987). *The mind's new science: A history of the cognitive revolution.* New York: Basic Books.

Garfield, S.L. and Bergin, A.E. (1994). Introduction and historical overview. In A.E. Bergin and S.L. Garfield (eds.), *Handbook of psychotherapy and behavior change,* 4th edn., pp. 3–18. New York: John Wiley & Sons.

Gazzaniga, M.S., Ivry, R.B., and Mangun, G.R. (2009). *Cognitive neuroscience: The biology of the mind,* 3rd edn. New York: Norton.

Geen, R.G. (1997). Psychophysiological approaches to personality. In Hogan et al., *Handbook of personality,* pp. 387–414.

Geen, R.G. (1998). Aggression and antisocial behavior. In Gilbert et al., *Handbook of social psychology,* vol. II, pp. 317–356.

Gergen, K.J. (1996). Social constructionism. In Corsini and Auerbach, *Concise encyclopedia of psychology,* pp. 849–851.

Gergen, K.J. and Graumann, C.F. (1996). Psychological discourse in historical context: An introduction. In C.F. Graumann and K.J. Gergen (eds.), Historical dimensions of psychological discourse, pp. 1–16. Cambridge, UK: Cambridge University Press.

Geschwind, N. (1974). *Selected papers on language and the brain*. New York: Reidel.

Gesell, A. (1943). *Infant and child in the culture of today: The guidance of development in home and nursery school*. New York: Harper.

Ghiselin, M.T. (1969). *The triumph of the Darwinian method*. Berkeley, CA: University of California Press.

Gibson, E.J. and Walk, R.D. (1960). The "visual cliff." *Scientific American, 202*, 64–71.

Gibson, J.J. (1941). A critical review of the concept of set in contemporary experimental psychology. *Psychological Bulletin, 38*, 781–817.

Gibson, J.J. (1950). *The perception of the visual world*. Boston, MA: Houghton Mifflin.

Gibson, J.J. (1960). The concept of the stimulus in psychology. *American Psychologist, 15*, 694–703.

Gibson, J.J. (1966). *The senses considered as perceptual systems*. Boston, MA: Houghton Mifflin.

Gibson, J.J. (1979). *The ecological approach to visual perception*. Boston, MA: Houghton Mifflin.

Giddens, A. (2006). *Introduction to sociology*, 5th edn. New York: Norton.

Gilbert, D.T. (1998). Ordinary psychology. In Gilbert et al., *Handbook of social psychology*, vol. II, pp. 89–150.

Gilbert, D.T., Fiske, S.T., and Lindzey, G. (ed.) (1998). *The handbook of social psychology*, 4th edn. Boston, MA: McGraw-Hill.

Glanzer, M. and Cunitz, A.R. (1966). Two storage mechanisms in free recall. *Journal of Verbal Learning and Verbal Behavior, 5*, 351–360.

Glass, A.C. and Holyoak, K.J. (1986). *Cognition*. New York: Random House.

Glass, C.R. and Arnkoff, D.B. (1992). Behavior therapy. In D.K. Freedheim (ed.), *History of psychotherapy: A century of change*, pp. 587–628. Washington, DC: American Psychological Association.

Glickman, S.E. (1985). Some thoughts on the evolution of comparative psychology. In S. Koch and D.E. Leary (ed.), *A century of psychology as science*, pp. 738–782. New York: McGraw-Hill.

Goethe, J.W. (1810). *Zur Farbenlehre*, vols. I–III. Tübingen: Cotta. (English trans., 1970: *Theory of colors*. Cambridge, MA: MIT Press.)

Goldberg, L.R. (1981). Language and individual differences: The search for universals in personality lexicons. In L. Wheeler (ed.), *Review of personality and social psychology*, vol. II, 141–165. Beverly Hills, CA: Sage.

Goldberg, L.R. (1993). The structure of phenotypic personality traits. *American Psychologist, 48*, 26–34.

Goldstein, K. (1939). *The organism: A holistic approach derived from pathological data in man*. New York: American Book Company.

Gorfein, D.S. and Hoffman, R.R. (ed.) (1987). *Memory and learning*. Ebbinghaus Centennial Conference. Hillsdale, NJ: Erlbaum.

Gould, S.J. and Lewontin, R.C. (1978). The spandrels of San Marco and the Panglossian paradigm: A critique of the adaptationist programme. *Proceedings of the Royal Society of London, Series B, 205*, 581–598.

Gundlach, H. (1987). Anfänge der experimentellen Willenspsychologie. In H. Heckhausen, P.M. Gollwitzer, and F.E. Weinert (ed.), *Jenseits des Rubikon: Der Wille in den Humanwissenschaften*, pp. 67–85. Berlin: Springer.

Guthrie, E.R. (1935). *The psychology of learning.* New York: Harper.

Haber, R.N. (1985). Perception: A one-hundred-year perspective. In S. Koch and D.E. Leary (ed.), *A century of psychology as science*, pp. 250–281. New York: McGraw-Hill.

Haeckel, E. (1866). *Generelle Morphologie der Organismen: Allgemeine Grundzüge der organischen Formen – Wissenschaft, mechanisch begründet durch die von Charles Darwin reformierte Descendenz-Theorie*, 2 vols. Berlin: Reimer.

Hall, G.S. (1883). The contents of children's minds. *Princeton Review, 11*, 249–272.

Hall, G.S. (1904). *Adolescence: Its psychology and its relations to physiology, anthropology, sociology, sex, crime, religion, and education*, vols. I–II. New York: Appleton.

Hall, G.S. (1922). *Senescence: The last half of life.* New York: Appleton.

Halverson, C.F. and Wampler, K.S. (1997). Family influences on personality development. In Hogan et al., *Handbook of personality psychology*, pp. 241–267.

Hamilton, W.D. (1963). The evolution of altruistic behavior. *American Naturalist, 97*, 354–356.

Hamilton, W.D. (1964). The genetical evolution of social behaviour. I, II. *Journal of Theoretical Biology, 7*, 1–52.

Hanfmann, E. (1941). A study of personal patterns in an intellectual performance. *Character and Personality, 9*, 315–325.

Harlow, H.F. and Harlow, M.K. (1965). The affectional systems. In A.M. Schrier, H.F. Harlow, and F. Stollnitz (ed.), *Behavior of non-human primates*, vol. II, pp. 287–334. New York: Academic Press.

Harris, J.R. (1995). Where is the child's environment? A group socialization theory of development. *Psychological Review, 102*, 458–489.

Hartmann, H. (1939). Ich-Psychologie und Anpassungsproblem. *Internationale Zeitschrift für Psychoanalyse, 24*, 62–135. (English trans., 1958: *Ego psychology and the problem of adaptation.* New York: International Universities Press.)

Hartshorne, H. and May, M.A. (1928). *Studies in the nature of character*: vol. I. *Studies in deceit.* New York: Macmillan.

Havinghurst, R.J. (1957). The social competence of middle-aged people. *Genetic Psychology Monographs, 56*, 297–375.

Hearnshaw, L.S. (1964). *A short history of British psychology, 1840–1940.* London: Methuen.

Hearst, E. (1979). One hundred years: Themes and perspectives. In E. Hearst (ed.), *The first century of experimental psychology*, pp. 1–38. Hillsdale, NJ: Erlbaum.

Hebb, D.O. (1946). On the nature of fear. *Psychological Review, 53*, 259–276.

Hebb, D.O. (1949). *The organization of behavior.* New York: John Wiley & Sons.

Hebb, D.O. (1980). In G. Lindzey (ed.), *A history of psychology in autobiography*, vol. VII. San Francisco: Freeman.

Heider, F. (1946). Attitudes and cognitive organization. *Journal of Psychology, 21*, 107–112.

Heider, F. (1958). *The psychology of interpersonal relations.* New York: John Wiley & Sons.

Heider, F. (1983). *The life of a psychologist: An autobiography.* Lawrence, KA: University Press of Kansas.

Helmholtz, H.V. (1850). Messungen über den zeitlichen Verlauf der Zuckungen animalischer Muskeln und die Fortpflanzungsgeschwindigkeit der Reizung in den Nerven. *Archiv der Anatomie und Physiologie*, 1850, 276–364. (English part trans., 1948: On the rate of transmission of the nerve impulse. In W. Dennis (ed.), *Readings in the history of psychology.* New York: Appleton-Century-Crofts.)

Helmholtz, H.V. (1856–1866). *Handbuch der physiologischen Optik*. Hamburg: Voss. (English trans., 1924–1925: *Treatise on physiological optics*, vols. I–III. Rochester, NY: Optical Society of America.)

Helmholtz, H.V. (1863). *Die Lehre von den Tonempfindungen als physiologischer Grundlage für die Theorie der Musik*. Braunschweig: Vieweg. (English trans., 1975: *On the sensations of tone as a physiological basis for the theory of music*. New York: Dover.)

Hempel, C.G. (1966). *Philosophy of natural science*. Englewood Cliffs, NJ: Prentice-Hall.

Hendry, L. and Kloep, M. (2002). *Lifespan development*. London: Thomson.

Herbart, J.F. (1816). *Lehrbuch zur Psychologie*. Königsberg: Unzer. (English trans., 1891: *A textbook in psychology: An attempt to found the science of psychology on experience, metaphysics, and mathematics*. New York: Appleton.)

Herbart, J.F. (1824–1825). *Psychologie als Wissenschaft*, vols. I–II. Königsberg: Unzer. (English trans., 1906: *Psychology as a science*. Leipzig: Voss.)

Hergenhahn, B.R. (2009). *An introduction to the history of psychology*, 6th edn. Pacific Grove, CA: Brooks/Cole.

Hering, E. (1905–1920). *Grundzüge der Lehre vom Lichtsinne*. Leipzig: Engelmann. (English trans., 1964: *Outlines of a theory of the light sense*. Cambridge, MA: Harvard University Press.)

Heston, L.L. (1966). Psychiatric disorders in foster home reared children of schizophrenic mothers. *British Journal of Psychiatry*, *112*, 819–825.

Hewstone, M., Stroebe, W., Codol, J.-P., and Stephenson, G.M. (eds.) (1988). *Introduction to social psychology: A European perspective*. Oxford, UK: Blackwell.

Higgins, E.T. (1987). Self-discrepancy: A theory relating self and affect. *Psychological Review*, *94*, 319–340.

Hilgard, E.R. (1953). *Introduction to psychology*. New York: Harcourt, Brace and Company.

Hilgard, E.R. (1977). *Divided consciousness: Multiple controls in human thought and action*. New York: John Wiley & Sons.

Hilgard, E.R. (1987). *Psychology in America: A historical survey*. New York: Harcourt Brace Jovanovich.

Hinde, R.A. (1991). From animals to humans. In Dawkins et al., *The Tinbergen legacy*, pp. 31–39.

Hinde, R.A. (1995). Konrad Lorenz (1903–89) and Nickolas Tinbergen (1907–88). In R. Fuller (ed.), *Seven pioneers of psychology: Behaviour and mind*, pp. 75–105. London: Routledge.

Hobhouse, L.T. (1901). *Mind in evolution*. London: Macmillan.

Hochberg, J.E. (1979). Sensation and perception. In E. Hearst (ed.), *The first century of experimental psychology*, pp. 89–142. Hillsdale, NJ: Erlbaum.

Hogan, R., Johnson, J., and Briggs, S. (ed.) (1997). *Handbook of personality psychology*. San Diego, CA: Academic Press.

Hollon, S.D. and Beck, A.T. (2004). Cognitive and cognitive behavioral therapies. In M.J. Lambert (ed.), *Bergin and Garfield's handbook of psychotherapy and behavior change*, 5th edn., pp. 447–492. New York: John Wiley & Sons.

Hovland, C.I. (1951). Human learning and retention. In S.S. Stevens (ed.), *Handbook of experimental psychology*, pp. 613–689. New York: John Wiley & Sons.

Hubel, D.H. and Wiesel, T.N. (1979). Brain mechanisms of vision. *Scientific American*, *241*, 150–162.

Hull, C.L. (1943). *Principles of behavior*. New York: Appleton-Century-Crofts.

Hull, C.L. (1952a). *A behavior system*. New Haven, CT: Yale University Press.

Hull, C.L. (1952b). Clark L. Hull. In E.G. Boring, H.S. Langfeld, H. Werner, and R.M. Yerkes (eds.), *A history of psychology in autobiography*, vol. IV. Worcester, MA: Clark University Press.

Humphrey, G. (1951). *Thinking: An introduction to its experimental psychology*. New York: John Wiley & Sons.

Huntingford, F. (1991). 'War and peace' revisited. In Dawkins et al., *The Tinbergen legacy*, pp. 40–59.

Hurwich, L.M. and Jameson, D. (1964). Introduction. In Hering, *Grundzüge der Lehre vom Lichtsinne*.

Ibáñez, T. and Íñiguez, L. (ed.) (1997). *Critical social psychology*. London: Sage.

Ichheiser, G. (1943). Misinterpretations of personality in everyday life and the psychologist's frame of reference. *Character and Personality*, *12*, 145–160.

Ichheiser, G. (1949). *Misunderstandings in human relations: A study in false social perception*. *American Journal of Sociology*, Supplement, *55*(2), part 2.

Ickes, W., Snyder, M., and Garcia, S. (1997). Personality influences on the choice of situations. In Hogan et al., *Handbook of personality*, pp. 166–195.

Inkeles, A. and Levinson, D.J. (1954). National character: The study of modal personality and sociocultural systems. In Lindzey, *Handbook of social psychology*, vol. II, pp. 977–1020.

Jaeger, S. (1982). Origins of child psychology: Wilhelm Preyer. In W.R. Woodword and G. Ash (eds.), *The problematic science: Psychology in nineteenth-century thought*, pp. 300–321. New York: Praeger.

James, W. (1884). What is an emotion? *Mind*, 9, 188–205.

James, W. (1887). What is an instinct? *Scribner's Magazine*, 1, 355–365.

James, W. (1892). *Psychology – briefer course*. New York: Holt.

James, W. (1899). *Talks to teachers on psychology: And to students on some of life's ideals*. New York: Holt.

James, W. (1902). *The varieties of religious experience: A study of human nature*. New York: Longmans, Green.

James, W. (1890/1950). *Principles of psychology*, 2 vols. in one (reprint of 1890 edn). New York: Dover.

Janet, P. (1889). *L'automatisme psychologique: Essai de psychologie expérimentale sur les formes intérieures de l'activité humaine*. Paris: Alcan.

Janet, P. (1909). *Les névroses*. Paris: Flammarion.

Janet, P. (1919). *Les médications psychologiques*. Paris: Alcan.

Janet, P. (1926). *De l'angoisse à l'extase*. Paris: Alcan.

Janet, P. (1930). Pierre Janet. In C. Murchinson (ed.), *A history of psychology in autobiography*. Worcester, MA: Clark University Press.

Janet, P. (1938). *La psychologie de la conduite*. *Encyclopédie Française*, vol. VII.

Janik, A. and Toulmin, S. (1973). *Wittgenstein's Vienna*. New York: Simon and Schuster.

Jennings, H.S. (1906). *Behavior of the lower organisms*. New York: Macmillan.

John, O.P. and Srivastava, S. (1999). The Big Five trait taxonomy: History, measurement, and theoretical perspectives. In L.A. Pervin (ed.), *Handbook of personality: Theory and research*, pp. 102–138. New York: Guilford Press.

Joncich, G. (1968). *The sane positivist: A biography of Edward L. Thorndike*. Middletown, CT: Wesleyan University Press.

Jones, E. (1953–1957). *The life and work of Sigmund Freud*, vols. I–III. New York: Basic Books.

Jones, E.E. (1998). Major developments in five decades of social psychology. In Gilbert et al., *Handbook of social psychology*, vol. I, pp. 3–57.

Jones, E.E. and Davis, K.E. (1965). From acts to dispositions: The attribution process in person perception. In L. Berkowitz (ed.), *Advances in experimental social psychology*, vol. II, pp. 219–266. New York: Academic Press.

Jones, M.C. (1924). A laboratory study of fear: The case of Peter. *Journal of Genetic Psychology*, *31*, 308–315.

Jones, W., Couch, L., and Scott, S. (1997). Trust and betrayal: The psychology of getting along and getting ahead. In Hogan et al., *Handbook of personality*, pp. 465–482.

Jung, C.G. (1953–1978). *The collected works of C.G. Jung*, 24 vols, at vols. II, VI, and IX. London: Routledge and Kegan Paul.

Jung, C.G. (1961). *Erinnerungen, Träume, Gedanken von C.G. Jung.* Freiburg, Breisgau: Wolter Verlag, Olten. (English trans., 1961: *Memories, dreams, reflections.* New York: Random House.)

Kamin, L.J. (1969). Predictability, surprise, attention, and conditioning. In B.A. Campbell and R.M. Church (eds.), *Punishment and aversive behavior.* New York: Appleton.

Kanizsa, G. (1994). Gestalt theory has been misinterpreted, but has also had some real conceptual difficulties. *Philosophical Psychology*, *7*(2), 149–162.

Katona, G. (1940). *Organizing and memorizing.* New York: Columbia University Press.

Katz, D. (1911). *Die Erscheinungsweisen der Farben und ihre Beeinflussung durch die Individuelle Erfahrung. Zeitschrift für Psychologie*, Supplement, vol. VII. (English trans., 1935: *The world of colour.* London: Routledge and Kegan Paul.)

Keesing, R.M. (1981). *Cultural anthropology: A contemporary perspective.* New York: Holt, Rinehart, and Winston.

Kelley, H.H. (1967). Attribution theory in social psychology. In D. Levine (ed.), *Nebraska Symposium on Motivation*, vol. XV, pp. 192–238. Lincoln, NB: University of Nebraska Press.

Kelly, G.A. (1955). *The psychology of personal constructs*, vols. I–II. New York: Norton.

Kent, G.H. and Rosanoff, A.J. (1910). A study of association in insanity. *American Journal of Insanity*, *67*, 37–96.

Kihlstrom, J.F. (1999). The psychological unconscious. In Pervin and John, *Handbook of personality*, pp. 424–442.

Kimble, G.A. and Schlesinger, K. (ed.) (1985). *Topics in the history of psychology*, vols. I–II. Hillsdale, NJ: Erlbaum.

Kluckhohn, C. (1954). Culture and behavior. In Lindzey, *Handbook of social psychology*, vol. II, pp. 921–976.

Koch, S. (1954). Clark L. Hull. In W.K. Estes, S. Koch, K. MacCorquodale, P.E. Meehl, C.G. Müller, Jr., W.N. Schoenfeld, et al. (eds.), *Modern learning theory.* New York: Appleton-Century-Crofts.

Koch, S. (1959). Epilogue. In Koch, *Psychology: A study of a science*, vol. III.

Koch, S. (ed.) (1959–1963). *Psychology: A study of a science*, vols. I–VI. New York: McGraw-Hill.

Koch, S. (1969). Psychology cannot be a coherent science. *Psychology Today*, *14*, 64–68.

Koch, S. (1985a). Foreword: Wundt's creature at age zero – and as centenarian. In Koch and Leary, *A century of psychology as science*, pp. 7–45.

Koch, S. (1985b). The nature and limits of psychological knowledge. *Lessons of a century qua "science."* In Koch and Leary, *A century of psychology as science*, pp. 75–97.

Koch, S. (1985c). Afterword. In Koch and Leary, *A century of psychology as science*, pp. 928–950.

Koch, S. (1993). "Psychology" or "the psychological studies"? *American Psychologist, 48*, 902–904.

Koch, S. and Leary, D.E. (ed.) (1985). *A century of psychology as science.* New York: McGraw-Hill.

Koffka, K. (1924). *The growth of the Mind. An Introduction to Child Psychology.* New York: Harcourt, Brace.

Koffka, K. (1935). *Principles of Gestalt psychology.* Oxford: Harcourt, Brace.

Kohlberg, L. (1982). Moral development. In Broughton and Freeman-Moir, *The cognitive-developmental psychology of James Mark Baldwin*, pp. 277–325.

Köhler, W. (1915). Optische Untersuchungen am Schimpansen und am Haushuhn. *Abhandlungen der Königlich Preussischen Akademie der Wissenschaften, phys.-math.* Kl. Nr. 3.

Köhler, W. (1917). Die Farbe der Sehdinge beim Schimpansen und beim Haushuhn. *Zeitschrift für Psychologie, 77*, 248–255.

Köhler, W. (1917). Intelligenzprüfungen an Anthropoiden. In *Abhandlungen der Königlich Preussischen Akademie der Wissenschaften, phys.-math.* Kl. Nr. 1. (English trans., 1925: *The Mentality of Apes.* New York: Harcourt, Brace.)

Köhler, W. (1928/1947). *Gestalt psychology: An introduction to new concepts in modern psychology.* New York: Liveright.

Köhler, W. (1971). *The selected papers of Wolfgang Köhler.* New York: Liveright.

Kosslyn, S.M., Ball, T.M., and Reiser, B.J. (1978). Visual images preserve metric spatial information: Evidence from studies of image scanning. *Journal of Experimental Psychology: Human Perception and Performance, 4*, 47–60.

Kozulin, A. (1986). Vygotsky in context. In L. Vygotsky, *Thought and language.* Cambridge, MA: MIT Press.

Krasner, L. (1996). Behaviorism: History. In Corsini and Auerbach, *Concise encyclopedia of psychology*, p. 101.

Krechevsky, I. (1932). "Hypotheses" in rats. *Psychological Review, 39*, 516–532.

Kretschmer, E. (1921). *Körperbau und Charakter.* Berlin: Springer. (English trans., 1925: *Physique and character.* New York: Harcourt, Brace.)

Kuffler. S.W. (1953). Discharge pattern and functional organization of the mammalian retina. *Journal of Neurophysiology, 16*, 37–68.

Kuffler, S.W. and Nicholls, J.G. (1976). *From neuron to brain.* Sunderland, MA: Sinauer Associates.

Kuhn, T.S. (1962/1970). *The structure of scientific revolutions*, 2nd edn. Chicago: University of Chicago Press.

Külpe, O. (1893). *Grundriss der Psychologie: Auf experimentelle Grundlage dargestellt.* Leipzig: Engelmann. (English trans., 1895: *Outlines of psychology.* New York: Macmillan.)

Külpe, O. (1920). *Vorlesungen über Psychologie.* Leipzig: Hirzel. (English trans., 1920: *Lectures on psychology.* Leipzig: Hirzel.)

Kuper, A. (1999). *Culture: The anthropologists' account.* Cambridge, MA: Harvard University Press.

Lachman, R., Lachman, J.L., and Butterfield, E.G. (1979). *Cognitive psychology and information processing: An introduction.* Hillsdale, NJ: Erlbaum.

Ladd, G.T. (1887). *Elements of physiological psychology.* New York: Scribners.

Ladd, G.T. and Woodworth, R.S. (1911). *Elements of physiological psychology*, rev. edn. New York: Scribners.

Lambert, M.J. (2004). *Bergin and Garfield's handbook of psychotherapy and behavior change*, 5th edn. New York: John Wiley & Sons.

Lambert, M.J., Garfield, S.L., and Bergin, A.E. (2004). Overview, trends, and future issues. In Lambert, *Bergin and Garfield's handbook of psychotherapy and behavior change*, pp. 805–821.

Lambert, M.J. and Ogles, B.M. (2004). The efficacy and effectiveness of psychotherapy. In Lambert, *Bergin and Garfield's handbook of psychotherapy and behavior change*, pp. 139–193.

LaPiere, R.T. (1934). Attitudes versus actions. *Social Forces, 13*, 230–237.

Laplanche, J. and Pontalis, J.-B. (1967). *Vocabulaire de la psychoanalyse.* Paris: Presses Universitaires de France. (English trans., 1973: *The language of psychoanalysis.* London: Hogarth Press.)

Lashley, K.S. (1923). Behavioristic interpretation of consciousness. *Psychological Review, 30*, vol. I, 237–272; vol. II, 329–353.

Lashley, K.S. (1929/1963). *Brain mechanisms and intelligence.* Chicago: University of Chicago Press.

Lashley, K.S. (1938/1960). Experimental analysis of instinctive behavior. *Psychological Review, 45*, 445–471.

Lashley, K.S. (1942). An examination of the "continuity theory" as applied to discriminative learning. *Journal of General Psychology, 26*, 241–265.

Lashley, K.S. (1950/1960). In search of the engram. *Symposia of the Society for Experimental Biology*, vol. IV, pp. 454–482. New York: Cambridge University Press. (Reprinted in S.A. Beach et al. (1960), *The neuropsychology of Lashley. Selected papers of K.S. Lashley.* New York: McGraw-Hill.)

Lashley, K.S. (1951). The problem of serial order in behavior. In L. Jeffress (ed.), *Cerebral mechanisms in behavior*, pp. 112–136. New York: John Wiley & Sons.

Lashley, K.S. (1958). Cerebral organization and behavior. In *The brain and human behavior, Proceedings of the Association for Research in Nervous and Mental Disease, 36*, 1–18.

Lasswell, H.D. (1948). The structure and function of communication in society. In L. Bryson (ed.), *The communication of ideas*, pp. 37–51. Religion and Civilization Series. New York: Harper and Row.

Leahey, T.H. (2004). *A history of psychology: Main currents in psychological thought*, Upper Saddle River, NJ: Prentice-Hall.

Leary, D.E. (1982). Immanuel Kant and the development of modern psychology. In W.R. Woodword and M.G. Ash (eds.), *The problematic science: Psychology in nineteenth-century thought*, pp. 17–42. New York: Praeger.

Le Bon, G. (1895). *Psychologie des foules.* Paris: Olean. (English trans., 1896: *The crowd.* London: Unwin.)

LeDoux, J.E. (1996). *The emotional brain.* New York: Touchstone.

Leeper, R. (1951). Cognitive processes. In S.S. Stevens (ed.), *Handbook of experimental psychology*, pp. 730–767. New York: John Wiley & Sons.

Lehrman, D.S. (1953). A critique of Konrad Lorenz's theory of instinctive behavior. *Quarterly Review of Biology, 28*, 337–363.

Lehrman, D.S. (1970). Semantic and conceptual issues in the nature–nurture problem. In L.S. Aronson, E. Tobach, D.S. Lehrman, and J.S. Rosenblatt (eds.), *Development and evolution of behavior: Essays in memory of T.C. Schneirla*, pp. 17–52. San Francisco, CA: Freeman.

Levine, J.M. and Moreland, R.L. (1998). Small groups. In Gilbert et al., *Handbook of social psychology*, vol. II, pp. 415–469.

Lewin, K. (1931). The conflict between Aristotelian and Galileian modes of thought in contemporary psychology. *Journal of General Psychology, 5*, 141–177.

Lewin, K. (1935). *A dynamic theory of personality: Selected papers.* New York: McGraw-Hill.

Lewin, K. (1936). *Principles of topological psychology.* New York: McGraw-Hill.

Lewin, K. (1951). *Field theory in social science.* New York: Harper.

Lewin, K., Lippitt, R., and White, R.K. (1939). Patterns of aggressive behavior in experimentally
created "social climates." *Journal of Social Psychology, 10*, 271–299.

Lewis, M. (1999). On the development of personality. In Pervin and John, *Handbook of personality*,
pp. 327–346.

Lindzey, G. (ed.) (1954). *A handbook of social psychology*, vols. I–II. Cambridge, MA: Addison-
Wesley.

Lindzey, G. and Aronson, E. (ed.) (1968–1970). *A handbook of social psychology*, 2nd edn., vols.
I–V. Reading, MA: Addison-Wesley.

Lindzey, G. and Aronson, E. (ed.) (1985). *A handbook of social psychology*, 3rd edn., vols. I–III.
New York: Random House.

Little, B.R. (1999). Personality and motivation: Personal action as the conative evolution. In Pervin
and John, *Handbook of personality*, pp. 501–524.

Lochlin, J.C. and Nichols, R.C. (1976). *Heredity, environment, and personality.* Austin, TX: University of Texas Press.

Loeb, J. (1889). *Der Heliotropismus der Tiere und seine Übereinstimmung mit dem Heliotropismus
der Pflanzen.* Würzburg: Georg Hertz.

Loeb, J. (1918). *Forced movements, tropisms, and animal conduct.* Philadelphia: Lippincott.

Lorenz, K. (1935). Der Kumpan in der Umwelt des Vogels. *Journal für Ornithologie, 63*, 137–213,
289–413.

Lorenz, K. (1950). The comparative method in studying innate behaviour patterns. In *Physiological
mechanisms in animal behavior. Symposia of the Society of Experimental Biology, 4*, 221–
268. Cambridge, UK: Cambridge University Press.

Lorenz, K. (1966). *On aggression.* London: Methuen.

Losee, J. (1980). *A historical introduction to the philosophy of science*, 2nd edn. Oxford, UK:
Oxford University Press.

Luchins, A.S. (1942). Mechanization in problem solving: The effect of *einstellung. Psychological
Monographs, 54*, no. 248.

Luria, A.R. (1973). *The working brain.* London: Penguin.

Mach, E. (1886/1903). *Analyse der Empfindungen und das Verhältnis des Physischen zum Psy-
chischen*, 4th edn. Jena: Fischer. (English trans., 1897: *The analysis of sensations, and the
relation of the physical to the psychical.* Chicago: Open Court.)

Macionis, J.J. and Plummer, K. (2005). *Sociology: A global introduction*, 3rd edn. Harlow, UK:
Pearson Education.

Macmillan, M. (1991). *Freud evaluated: The completed arc.* Amsterdam: North-Holland.

Macnamara, J. (1982). *Names for things: A study of human learning.* Cambridge, MA: MIT Press.

MacNeilage, P.F. and Davis, B.L. (2005). The evolution of language. In Buss, *Handbook of evolutionary psychology*, pp. 698–723.

Magnusson, D. (1999). Holistic interactionism: A perspective for research on personality development. In Pervin and John, *Handbook of personality*, pp. 219–247.

Maher, B.A. and Maher, W.B. (1985a). Psychopathology. II. From the eighteenth century to modern times. In Kimble and Schlesinger, *Topics in the history of psychology*, vol. II, pp. 295–330.

Maher, W.B. and Maher, B.A. (1985b). Psychopathology. I. From ancient times to the eighteenth century. In Kimble and Schlesinger, *Topics in the history of psychology*, vol. II, pp. 251–294.

Mandler, J.M. and Mandler, G. (1964). *Thinking: From association to Gestalt*. New York: John Wiley & Sons.

Marbe, K. (1901). *Experimentell-psychologische Untersuchungen über das Urteil*. Leipzig: Engelmann.

Markus, H.R. (1977). Self-schemata and processing information about the self. *Journal of Personality and Social Psychology*, *35*, 63–78.

Markus, H.R. and Nurius, P.S. (1986). Possible selves. *American Psychologist*, *41*, 954–969.

Marr, D. (1982). *Vision*. New York: Freeman.

Marrow, A.J. (1969). *The practical theorist: The life and work of Kurt Lewin*. New York: Basic Books.

Maruzzi, G. and Magoun, H.W. (1949). Brainstem reticular formation and activation of the EEG. *Electroencephalography and Clinical Neurophysiology*, *1*, 455–473.

Marx, K. (1867). *Das Kapital*. Hamburg: Verlag Otto Meissner.

Marx, M.H. and Hillix, W.A. (1979). *Systems and theories in psychology*, 3rd edn. New York: McGraw-Hill.

Maslow, A.H. (1954). *Motivation and personality*. New York: Harper and Row.

Masson, J.M. (1984). *The assault on truth: Freud's suppression of the seduction theory*. New York: Farrar, Straus and Giroux.

May, R. (1950). *The meaning of anxiety*. New York: Ronald Press.

May, R. (ed.) (1961). *Existential psychology*. New York: Random House.

May, R. (1992). Foreword. In D.K. Freedheim (ed.), *History of psychotherapy: A century of change*. Washington, DC: American Psychological Association.

May, R., Angel, E., and Ellenberger, H.F. (eds.) (1958). *Existence: A new dimension in psychiatry and psychology*. New York: Basic Books.

Mayr, E. (1982). *The growth of biological knowledge*. Cambridge, MA: Harvard University Press.

Mayr, E. (2002). *What evolution is*. London: Phoenix.

Mazlish, B. (1967). Comte, Auguste. In P. Edwards (ed.), *The encyclopedia of philosophy*, vol. I, pp. 173–177. New York: Macmillan.

McAdams, D.P. (1997). A conceptual history of personality psychology. In Hogan et al., *Handbook of personality*, pp. 3–39.

McAdams, D.P. (1999). Personal narratives and the life story. In Pervin and John, *Handbook of personality*, pp. 478–500.

McCrae, R.R. and Costa, P.T., Jr. (1999). A five factor theory of personality. In Pervin and John, *Handbook of personality*, pp. 139–153.

McDougall, W. (1905). *Physiological psychology*. London: Dent.

McDougall, W. (1931). *An introduction to social psychology*, 22nd edn. London: Methuen.

McDougall, W. (1912). *Psychology: The study of behavior*. London: Williams and Norgate.

McDougall, W. (1923). *Outline of psychology*. New York: Scribners.

McDougall, W. (1926). *Outline of abnormal psychology*. New York: Scribners.

McGeoch, J. (1942). *The psychology of human learning: An introduction.* London: Longmans, Green.

McGrew, W. (2001). The nature of culture: prospects and pitfalls of cultural primatology. In F.B.M. de Waal (ed.), *Tree of origin: what primate behavior can tell us about human social evolution,* pp. 229–254. Cambridge, MA: Harvard University Press.

Mead, G.H. (1934). *Mind, self, and society from the standpoint of a social behaviorist* (C.W. Morris, ed.). Chicago: University of Chicago Press.

Meyers, G. (1986). *William James: His life and thought.* New Haven, CT: Yale University Press.

Milgram, S. (1963). Behavioral study of obedience. *Journal of Abnormal and Social Psychology, 69,* 137–143.

Mill, J.S. (1843/1956). *A system of logic.* London: Longmans, Green.

Miller, G.A. (1956). The magical number seven plus or minus two: Some limits on our capacity for processing information. *Psychological Review, 63,* 81–97.

Miller, G.A. (1985). The constitutive problem of psychology. In S. Koch and D.E. Leary (eds.) *A century of psychology as science.* New York: McGraw-Hill.

Miller, G.A., Galanter, E., and Pribram, K.H. (1960). *Plans and the structure of behavior.* New York: Holt.

Milner, B. (1962). Les troubles de la mémoire accompagnant des lésions hippocampiques bilatérales. In P. Passouant (ed.), *Physiologie de l'hippocampe,* pp. 257–272. Paris: Centre Nationale de la Recherche Scientifique.

Mischel, W. (1968). *Personality and assessment.* New York: John Wiley & Sons.

Mischel, W. and Shoda, Y. (1999). Integrating dispositions and processing dynamics within a unified theory of personality: The cognitive affective personality system. In Pervin and John, *Handbook of personality,* pp. 194–218. New York: Guilford Press.

Moore, D.L. (1992). The Veterans Administration and its training program in psychology. In D.K. Freedheim (ed.), *History of psychotherapy: A century of change,* pp. 776–800. Washington, DC: American Psychological Association.

Morgan, C.L. (1890). *Animal life and intelligence.* London: Arnold.

Morgan, C.L. (1894). *An introduction to comparative psychology.* London: Scott.

Morgan, C.L. (1896). *Habit and instinct.* London: Arnold.

Morgan, C.T (1943). *Physiological psychology.* New York: McGraw-Hill.

Morgan, C.T. (1968). Karl S. Lashley. *International encyclopedia of the social sciences,* vol. 99, pp. 27–30. New York: Macmillan.

Moscovici, S. (1985). Social influence and conformity. In Lindzey and Aronsen, *Handbook of social psychology,* vol. II, pp. 349–412.

Moustgaard, J.K. (1990). *Psychological observation and description.* Bergen: Sigma.

Müller, G.E. (1873). *Zur Theorie der sinnlichen Aufmerksamkeit.* Leipzig: Edelman.

Müller, G.E. (1878). *Grundlegung der Psychophysik.* Berlin: Hoffman.

Müller, G.E. (1923). *Komplextheorie und Gestalttheorie: Ein Beitrag zur Wahrnehmungspsychologie.* Göttingen: Vandenhoek and Ruprecht.

Müller, G.E. and Pilzecker, A. (1900). *Experimentelle Beträge zur Lehre vom Gedächtnis. Zeitschrift für Psychologie,* Supplement, vol. I.

Müller, J. (1833–1840). *Handbuch der Physiologie des Menschen.* Coblenz: Hölscher.

Müller, R.A. (1990). *Geschichte der Universität: Von der mittelalterlichen Universitas zur deutschen Hochschule.* Munich: Callwey.

Münsterberg, H. (1909a). *On the witness stand.* New York: McClure.

Münsterberg, H. (1909b). *Psychotherapy.* New York: Moffat Yard.

Münsterberg, H. (1913). *Psychology and industrial efficiency.* Boston, MA: Houghton Mifflin.

Murchison, C. (ed.) (1935). *Handbook of social psychology.* Worcester, MA: Clark University Press.

Murray, H.A. (1938). *Explorations in personality.* New York: Oxford University Press.

Murray, H.A. (1959). Preparations for the scaffold of a comprehensive system. In Koch, *Psychology: A study of a science,* vol. III, pp. 7–54.

Mysterud, I. (2003). *Mennesket og moderne evolusjonsteori.* Oslo: Gyldendal Akademisk.

Nagel, E. (1961). *The structure of science: Problems in the logic of scientific explanation.* London: Routledge and Kegan Paul.

Nakayama, K. (1994). James Gibson – an appreciation. *Psychological Review, 101,* 329–335.

Neisser, U. (1967). *Cognitive psychology.* New York: Appleton-Century-Crofts.

Newell, A., Shaw, J.C., and Simon, H.C. (1958). Elements of a theory of human problem solving. *Psychological Review, 65,* 151–166.

Newell, A. and Simon, H.A. (1972). *Human problem-solving.* Englewood Cliffs, NJ: Prentice-Hall.

Newton, I. (1687). *Philosophiae Naturalis Principia Mathematica.* London.

Nietzsche, F. (1878). *Menschliches, Allzumenschliches.* (English trans., 1996: *Human, all too human.* Cambridge, UK: Cambridge University Press.) In *Friedrich Nietzsche. Werke in zwei Bänden,* vol. I. Munich: Hanser.

Nietzsche, F. (1886, 1967). *Jenseits von Gut und Böse.* (English trans., 1973: *Beyond good and evil.* New York: Vintage.) In *Friedrich Nietzsche. Werke in zwei Bänden,* vol. II. Munich: Hanser.

Nietzsche, F. (1891). *Also sprach Zarathustra.* Chemnitz: Verlag. Ernst Schmelzer.

Nissen, H.W. (1951). Phylogenetic comparison. In S.S. Stevens (ed.), *Handbook of experimental psychology,* pp. 347–386. New York: John Wiley & Sons.

O'Donnell, J.M. (1979). The crisis of experimentalism in the 1920s: E. G. Boring and his use of history. *American Psychologist, 34,* 289–295.

O'Donnell, J.M. (1985). *The origins of behaviorism: American psychology 1870–1920.* New York: New York University Press.

Owens, D.A. and Wagner, M. (ed.) (1992). *Progress in modern psychology: The legacy of American functionalism.* Westport, CT: Praeger.

Paivio, A. (1971). *Imagery and verbal processes.* New York: Holt, Rinehart and Winston.

Passingham, R. (1982). *The human primate.* Oxford, UK: Freeman.

Paulhus, D.L., Friedhandler, B., and Hayes, S. (1997). Psychological defense: Contemporary theory and research. In Hogan et al., *Handbook of personality,* pp. 543–579.

Pavlov, I.P. (1927). *Conditioned reflexes: An investigation of the physiological activity of the cerebral cortex.* London: Oxford University Press.

Pavlov, I.P. (1928, 1932). *Lectures on conditioned reflexes,* vols. I–II. New York: International Publishers.

Pavlov, I.P. (1955). *Selected works.* Moscow: Foreign Publishing House.

Peirce, C.S. (1878). How to make our ideas clear. *Popular Science Monthly, 12,* 286–302.

Pepitone A. (1981). Lessons from the history of social psychology. *American Psychologist, 36,* 972–985.

Perky, C.W. (1910). An experimental study of imagination. *American Journal of Psychology, 21,* 422–452.

Perry, R.B. (1935). *The thought and character of William James,* 2 vols. Boston, MA: Little, Brown.

Pervin, L.A. (2003). *The science of personality*, 2nd edn. New York: Oxford University Press.

Pervin, L.A. and John, O.P. (ed.) (1999). *Handbook of personality: Theory and research*, 2nd edn. New York: Guilford Press.

Peterson, C. and Seligman, M.E.P. (2004). *Character strengths and virtues: A handbook and classification*. Washington, DC: American Psychological Association.

Peterson, L.R. and Peterson, M.J. (1959). Short-term retention of individual verbal items. *Journal of Experimental Psychology*, *58*, 193–198.

Petty, R.E. and Wegener, D.T. (1998). Attitude change: Multiple roles for persuasion variables. In Gilbert et al., *Handbook of social psychology*, 4th edn., vol. I, pp. 323–390.

Piaget, J. (1924/1926). *Le langage et la pensée chez l'enfant*. Neuchâtel: Delachaud and Niestlé. (English trans., 1926: *The language and thought of the child*. London: Routledge and Kegan Paul.)

Piaget, J. (1932/1965). *The moral judgement of the child*. London: Kegan Paul.

Piaget, J. (1947/1950). *La psychologie de l'intelligence*. Paris: Colin. (English trans., 1950: *The psychology of intelligence*. London: Routledge and Kegan Paul.)

Piaget, J. (1970). Piaget's theory. In P.H. Mussen (ed.), *Carmichael's manual of child psychology*, vol. I, pp. 703–732.

Piaget, J. and Inhelder, B. (1966/1969). *The psychology of the child*. London: Routledge and Kegan Paul.

Pinker, S. and Bloom, P. (1992). Natural language and natural selection. In Barkow et al., *The adapted mind*, pp. 451–493.

Pittman, T.S. (1998). Motivation. In Gilbert et al., *Handbook of social psychology*, vol. I, pp. 549–590.

Plas, R. (1994). La psychologie pathologique d'Alfred Binet. In P. Fraisse and J. Segui (eds.), *Les origines de la psychologie scientifique: Centième anniversaire de L'Année Psychologique (1894–1994)*. Paris: Presses Universitaires de France.

Plomin, R., DeFries, J.C., McClearn, G.E., and Rutter, M. (eds.) (1997). *Behavioural genetics*, 3rd edn. New York: Freeman.

Poincaré, H. (1902/1943). *La science et l'hypothèse*. Paris: Flammarion.

Popper, K.R. (1934, 1959). *The logic of scientific discovery*. New York: Harper Row.

Preuss, T.M. (1995). The argument from animals to humans in cognitive neuroscience. In M.S. Gazzaniga (ed.), *The cognitive neurosciences*, pp. 1227–1241. Cambridge, MA: MIT Press.

Preyer, W.T. (1882/1923). *Die Seele des Kindes*, 9th edn. Leipzig: Griebens. (English trans., 1888–89: *The mind of the child*. New York: Appleton.)

Prince, M. (1906). *The dissociation of a personality; A biographical study in abnormal psychology*. New York: Longmans, Green.

Pronko, N.H. (1996). Physiological psychology (nonreductionism). In Corsini and Auerbach, *Concise encyclopedia of psychology*, pp. 686–688.

Purkinje, J.E. (1819–1825). *Beobachtungen und Versuche zur Physiologie der Sinne*, vols. I–II. Berlin: Reimer.

Rapaport, D. (1959). The structure of psychoanalytic theory: A systematizing attempt. In Koch, *Psychology: A study of a science*, vol. III, pp. 55–183.

Reber, A.S. and Reber, E.S. (2001). Information processing. In A.S. Reber and E.S. Reber, *Dictionary of psychology*. London: Penguin.

Reisberg, D. (2001). *Cognition: Exploring the science of the mind*, 2nd edn. New York: Norton.

Rescorla, R.A. (1967). Pavlovian conditioning and its proper control procedures. *Psychological Review*, *74*(1), 71–80.

Rescorla, R.A. (1988). Pavlovian conditioning: It's not what you think it is. *American Psychologist*, *43*, 151–160.

Rescorla, R.A. (1990). Associative learning in animals: Asch's influence. In Rock, *The legacy of Solomon Asch*.

Ribot, Th.-A. (1870). *La psychologie anglaise contemporaine: l'école expérimentale*. Paris: Alcan.

Ribot, Th.-A. (1881). *Les maladies de la mémoire*. Paris: Alcan.

Ribot, Th.-A. (1883). *Les maladies de la volonté*. Paris: Alcan.

Ribot, Th.-A. (1889). *Les maladies de la personalité*. Paris: Alcan.

Rice, L.N. and Greenberg, L.S. (1992). Humanistic approaches to psychotherapy. In D.K. Freedheim (ed.), *History of psychotherapy: A century of change*, pp. 197–224. Washington, DC: American Psychological Association.

Rieber, R.W. (ed.) (1980). *Wilhelm Wundt and the making of a scientific psychology*. New York: Plenum Press.

Ringer, F.K. (1969). *The decline of German mandarins: The German academic community 1890–1933*. Cambridge, MA: Harvard University Press.

Robins, R.W., Norem, J.K., and Cheek, J.M. (1999). Naturalizing the self. In Pervin and John, *Handbook of personality*, pp. 443–477. New York: Guilford Press.

Robinson, D.N. (1995). *An intellectual history of psychology*, 3rd edn. London: Arnold.

Robinson, D.N. (1998). Two views of *Psychology: A study of a science*. *Contemporary Psychology*, *43*, 1, 10–12.

Rock, J. (ed.) (1990). *The legacy of Solomon Asch: Essays in cognition and social psychology*, pp. 159–174. Hillsdale, NJ: Erlbaum.

Rogers, C.R. (1942). *Counselling and psychotherapy*. Boston, MA: Houghton Mifflin.

Rogers, C.R. (1951). *Client-Centered therapy*. Boston, MA: Houghton Mifflin.

Rogers, C.R. (1959). A theory of therapy, personality, and interpersonal relationships, as developed in the client-centered framework. In Koch, *Psychology: A study of a science*, vol. III, pp. 184–256.

Rogers, C.R. (1980). *A way of being*. Boston, MA: Houghton Mifflin.

Romanes, G.J. (1882). *Animal intelligence*. London: Kegan Paul.

Romanes, G.J. (1883). *Mental evolution in animals*. London: Kegan Paul.

Romanes, G.J. (1888). *Mental evolution in man*. London: Kegan Paul.

Ross, B. (1991). William James: Spoiled child of American psychology. In G.A. Kimble, M. Wertheimer, and C. White (eds.), *Portraits of pioneers in psychology*, vol. I, pp. 13–26. Washington DC: American Psychological Association.

Ross, D.K. (1972). *G. Stanley Hall: The psychologist as a prophet*. Chicago: University of Chicago Press.

Ross, E. (1908). *Social psychology: An outline and source book*. London: Macmillan.

Ross, L. (1977). The intuitive psychologist and his shortcomings. In L. Berkowitz, *Advances in experimental social psychology*, vol. X, pp. 173–220. New York: Academic Press.

Ross, L., Amabile, T.M., and Steinmetz, J.L. (1977). Social roles, social control, and biases in social perception processes. *Journal of Personality and Social Psychology*, *35*, 485–494.

Rothschuh, K.E. (1953). *Geschichte der Physiologie*. Berlin: Springer.

Rubin, E. (1915/1921). *Synsopplevede Figurer*. Copenhagen: Gyldendal. (German trans., 1921: *Visuell wahrgenommene Figuren*. Copenhagen: Gyldendal.)

Rubin, E. (1920). Vorteile der Zweckbetrachtung für Erkenntnis. *Zeitschrift für Psychologie*, 85, 210–223. (Reprinted 1949 in E. Rubin, *Experimenta Psychologica*. Copenhagen: Munksgaard.)

Rubin, E. (1926). Die Nichtexistenz der Aufmerksamkeit. *Kongressbericht der IX Kongress für experimentelle Psychologie, Munich*.

Sabini, J. (1995). *Social psychology*, 2nd edn. New York: Norton.

Sadock, B.J. and Sadock, V.A. (2007). *Kaplan and Sadock's synopsis of psychiatry: Behavioral sciences/clinical psychiatry*, 10th edn. Philadelphia: Lippincott, Williams and Wilkins.

Salovey, P., Rothman, A.J., and Rodin, J. (1998). Health behavior. In Gilbert et al., *Handbook of social psychology*, vol. II, pp. 633–683.

Samuelson, F. (1981). Struggle for scientific authority: The reception of Watson's behaviorism, 1913–1920. *Journal of the History of the Behavioral Sciences, 17*, 397–425.

Saugstad, P. (1955). Problem-solving as dependent on availability of functions. *British Journal of Psychology, 46*, 191–198.

Saugstad, P. (1958). Problem-solving and availability of functions: A discussion of some theoretical aspects. *Acta Psychologica, 13*, 384–400.

Saugstad, P. (1965). *An inquiry into the foundations of psychology*. Oslo: Universitetsforlaget.

Saugstad, P. (1989a). Towards a methodology for the study of psychology. In J.A. Bjørgen (ed.), *Basic issues in psychology: A Scandinavian contribution*, pp. 221–241. Bergen: Sigma.

Saugstad, P. (1989b). *Language: A theory of its structure and use*. Oslo: Solum.

Schlesinger, G.J. (1967). Operationalism. In P. Edwards (eds.), *The encyclopedia of philosophy*, vol. V, pp. 543–544.

Schlesinger, K. (1985). Behavioral genetics and the nature/nurture question. In G.A. Kimble and K. Schlesinger (ed.), *Topics in the history of psychology*, vol. I, pp. 19–57. Hillsdale, NJ: Erlbaum.

Schneiria, T.C. (1949). Levels in the psychological capacities of animals. In R.W. Seilars, V.J. McGill, and M. Faber (eds.), *Philosophy for the future*, pp. 243–286. New York: Macmillan.

Schopenhauer, A. (1819). *Die Welt als Wille und Vorstellung*. Leipzig: F.A. Brockhaus. (English trans., 1883: *The world as will and idea*. Leipzig: Brockhaus.)

Scott, W.D. (1903). *The theory of advertising*. Boston, MA: Small, Maynard.

Scoville, W.B. (1954). The limbic lobe in man. *Journal of Neurosurgery. Psychiatry, 11*, 64–66.

Scoville, W.B. and Milner, B. (1957). Loss of recent memory after bilateral hippocampal lesions. *Journal of Neurology, Neuroscience, and Psychiatry, 20*, 11–21.

Searle, J.R. (1992). *The rediscovery of the mind*. Cambridge, MA: MIT Press.

Sears, R.R. (1985). Psychoanalysis and behavior theory: 1907 to 1965. In Koch and Leary, *A century of psychology as science*, pp. 208–220.

Sechenov, J.M. (1863/1965). *Reflexes of the brain*. Cambridge, MA: MIT Press.

Seligman, M.E.P. and Hager, J.L. (1972). *Biological boundaries of learning*. New York: Appleton-Century-Crofts.

Seligman, M.E., Steen, T.A., Park, N., and Peterson, C. (2005). Positive psychology progress: Empirical validation of interventions. *American Psychologist, 60*, 410–421.

Selye, H. (1956). *The stress of life*. New York: McGraw-Hill.

Selz, O. (1913). *Über die Gesetze des geordneten Denkverlaufs*. Stuttgart: Speman.

Selz, O. (1922). *Zur Psychologie des geordneten Denkverlaufs und des Irrtums*. Bonn: Cohen.

Selz, O. (1927, 1964). The revision of the fundamental conceptions of intellectual processes. In J.M. Mandler and G. Mandler (eds.), *Thinking: From association to Gestalt*, pp. 225–228. New York: John Wiley & Sons. (English trans., 1927: *Kantstudien*, 243–280.)

Shannon, C.E. and Weaver, W. (1949). *The mathematical theory of communication.* Urbana, IL: University of Illinois Press.

Sherif, M. (1936). *The psychology of social norms.* New York: Harper and Row.

Sherif, M. (1948). *An outline of social psychology.* New York: Harper and Brothers.

Sherrington, C.S. (1906). *The integrative action of the nervous system.* New Haven, CT: Yale University Press.

Shorter, E. (1997). *A history of psychiatry: From the era of the asylum to the age of Prozac.* New York: John Wiley & Sons.

Simon, H.A. and Newell, A. (1964). Information processing in computer and man. *American Scientist, 53*, 281–300.

Simpson, G.G. (1949/1967). *The meaning of evolution: A study of the history of life and of its significance for man.* Clinton, MA: Yale University Press.

Simpson, G.G. (1983). *Fossils and the history of life.* New York: Scientific American Library.

Singer, S. (1994). *Origins of neural science: A history of explorations into brain functions.* New York: Oxford University Press.

Skinner, B.F. (1938). *The behavior of organisms: An experimental analysis.* New York: Appleton-Century.

Skinner, B.F. (1948). *Walden two.* London: Macmillan.

Skinner, B.F. (1953). *Science and human behavior.* New York: Macmillan.

Skinner, B.F. (1957). *Verbal behavior.* New York: Appleton-Century-Crofts.

Skinner, B.F. (1969). *The contingencies of reinforcement: A theoretical analysis.* New York: Appleton-Century-Crofts.

Skinner, B.F. (1971). *Beyond freedom and dignity.* New York: Knopf.

Skinner, B.F. (1974). *About behaviorism.* New York: Knopf.

Skinner, B.F. (1976). *Particulars of my life.* New York: Knopf.

Skinner, B.F. (1979). *The shaping of a behaviorist.* New York: Knopf.

Skinner, B.F. (1983). *A matter of consequences.* New York: Knopf.

Smith, B. (1994). *Austrian philosophy: The legacy of Franz Brentano.* Peru, IL: Open Court.

Smith, E.R. (1998). Mental representation and memory. In Gilbert et al., *Handbook of social psychology*, vol. I, pp. 391–445.

Smith, L.D. (1986). *Behaviorism and logical positivism: A reassessment of the alliance.* Stanford, CA: Stanford University Press.

Smith, M.B. (1992). James and the psychology of self. In M.E. Donnelly (ed.), *Reinterpreting the legacy of William James*, pp. 173–187. Washington, DC: American Psychological Association.

Sober, E. and Wilson, D.S. (1998). *Unto others: The evolution and psychology of unselfish behavior.* Cambridge, MA: Harvard University Press.

Sokal, M.M. (1982). James McKeen Cattell and the failure of anthropometric mental testing, 1890–1901. In W.R. Woodward and M.G. Ash (eds.), *The problematic science: Psychology in nineteenth-century thought*, pp. 322–346. New York: Praeger.

Sokal, M.M. (1984). James McKeen Cattell and American psychology in the 1920s. In J. Brozek (ed.), *Explorations in the history of psychology in the United States*, pp. 273–323. Lewisburg, PA: Bucknell University Press.

Spearman, C.E. (1904). General intelligence objectively determined and measured. *American Journal of Psychology, 15,* 201–293.

Spence, K.W. (1936). The nature of discrimination learning in animals. *Psychological Review, 43,* 427–449.

Spence, K.W. (1940). Continuous versus non-continuous interpretations of discrimination learning. *Psychological Review, 47,* 271–288.

Spencer, H. (1855). *The principles of psychology,* London: Longman, Brown, Green, 2nd edn., 1870–1872.

Spencer, H. (1870–1872). *The Synthetic psychology,* London: Longman.

Sperling, G. (1960). The information that is available in brief visual presentations. *Psychological Monographs, 74*(11) (whole no. 498), 1–29.

Sperry, R.W. (1961). Cerebral organization and behavior. *Science, 133,* 1749–1757.

Sperry, R.W. (1964). The great cerebral commissure. *Science, 210,* 42–52.

Spillmann, J. and Spillmann, L. (1993). The rise and fall of Hugo Münsterberg. *Journal of the History of the Behavioral Sciences, 29,* 322–338.

Squire, L.R. (1992). Memory and the hippocampus: A synthesis from findings with rats, monkeys, and humans. *Psychological Review, 99*(2), 195–231.

Steiner, I.D. (1979). Social psychology. In E. Hearst (ed.), *The first century of experimental psychology,* pp. 513–558. Hillsdale, NJ: Erlbaum.

Sternberg, S. (1966). High-speed scanning in human memory. *Science, 153,* 652–654.

Sternberg, S. (1969). Memory-scanning: Mental processes revealed by reaction-time experiments. *American Scientist, 57,* 421–457.

Stevens, S.S. (1935). The operational definition of concepts. *Psychological Review, 42,* 517–527.

Stevens, S.S. (1951a). Mathematics, measurement, and psychophysics. In Stevens, *Handbook of experimental psychology,* pp. 1–49.

Stevens, S.S. (ed.) (1951b). *Handbook of experimental psychology.* New York: John Wiley & Sons.

Stryker, S. (1996). "In the beginning there is society": Lessons from a sociological social psychology. In C. McCarty and S.A. Haslam (eds.), *The message of social psychology: Perspectives on mind and society,* pp. 315–327. Cambridge, MA: Blackwell.

Stumpf, C. (1883, 1890). *Tonpsychologie,* 2 vols. Leipzig: Hirzel.

Stumpf, C. (1939–1940). *Erkenntnistheorie,* 2 vols. Leipzig: Barth.

Sulloway, F.J. (1979/1983). *Freud: Biologist of the mind: Beyond the psychoanalytic legend.* New York: Basic Books.

Suppe, F. (ed.) (1977). *The structure of scientific theories.* Urbana, IL: University of Illinois Press.

Suppe, F. (1989). *The semantic conception of theories and scientific realism.* Urbana, IL: University of Illinois Press.

Symons, D. (1992). On the use and misuse of Darwinism in the study of human behavior. In Barkow et al., *The adapted mind,* pp. 157–159.

Taine, H. (1870). *De l'intelligence.* Paris: Hachette.

Taine, H. (1875–1893). *Origines de la France contemporaine.* Paris: Hachette.

Taylor, S.E. (1992). The case for a uniquely American Jamesian tradition in psychology. In M.E. Donnelly (ed.), *Reinterpreting the legacy of William James,* pp. 3–28. Washington, DC: American Psychological Association.

Taylor, S.E. (1998). The social being in social psychology. In Gilbert et al., *Handbook of social psychology*, vol. I, pp. 58–95.

Teigen, K.H. (2004). *En psykologihistorie*. Bergen: Fagbokforlaget.

Terman, L.M. (1916). *The measurement of intelligence*. Boston, MA: Houghton Mifflin.

Thomas, W.I. and Znaniecky, F. (1918/1927). *The Polish peasant in Europe and America*, 3 vols. Boston, MA: Badger.

Thorndike, E.L. (1898). *Animal intelligence: An experimental study of the associative processes in animals. Psychological Review*, Monograph Supplement 2.

Thorndike, E.L. (1898/2000). *Animal intelligence: Experimental studies*. New Brunswick, NJ: Transaction. (First published in *Psychological Review*, 1898, Supplement 2.)

Thorndike, E.L. (1911). *Animal intelligence*. New York: Macmillan.

Thorndike, E.L. (1913–1914). *Educational psychology*, 3 vols. New York: Teachers College.

Thoreau, D. (1854). *Walden, or, life in the woods*. Boston, MA: Ticknor and Fields.

Thurstone, L.L. (1947). *Multiple factor analysis*. Chicago: University of Chicago Press.

Tinbergen, N. (1951). *The study of instinct*. London: Oxford University Press.

Titchener, E.B. (1896). *An outline of psychology*. New York: Macmillan.

Titchener, E.B. (1898). The postulates of structural psychology. *Philosophical Review, 7*, 449–465.

Titchener, E.B. (1901–1905). *Experimental psychology: A manual of laboratory practice*, 2 vols. New York: Macmillan.

Titchener, E.B. (1909). *Lectures on the experimental psychology of thought processes*. New York: Macmillan.

Titchener, E.B. (1909–1910). *A textbook of psychology*. New York: Macmillan.

Tolman, C.W. (1993). Is there a functionalist psychology? *Contemporary Psychology, 28*(12), 1318–1319.

Tolman, E.C. (1932). *Purposive behavior in animals and men*. New York: Appleton-Century.

Tolman, E.C. (1938). The law of effect. *Psychological Review, 45*, 165–203.

Tolman, E.C. (1942). *Drives towards war*. New York: Appleton-Century.

Tolman, E.C. (1948). Cognitive maps in rats and men. *Psychological Review, 55*, 189–208.

Tomasello, M. and Call, J. (1997). *Primate cognition*. New York: Oxford University Press.

Tooby, J. and Cosmides, L. (1992). The psychological foundations of culture. In Barkow, *The adapted mind*, pp. 19–136.

Tooby, J. and Cosmides, L. (2005). Conceptual foundations of evolutionary psychology. In Buss, *The handbook of evolutionary psychology*, pp. 5–67.

Toulmin, S. and Leary, D.E. (1985). The cult of empiricism in psychology and beyond. In Koch and Leary, *A century of psychology as science*, pp. 594–617.

Traxel, W. (1986). Hermann Ebbinghaus und die experimentelle Erforschung des Gedächtnisses – Anmerkungen zu einem Jubiläum. In Traxel and Gundlach, *Ebbinghaus-Studien 1*, pp. 11–22.

Traxel, W. and Gundlach, H. (1986). *Ebbinghaus-Studien 1. Passaver Schriften zur Psychologiegeschichte*. Passau: Passavia Universitätsverlag.

Triandis, H.C. (1997). Cross-cultural perspectives on personality. In Hogan et al., *Handbook of personality*, pp. 440–464.

Triplett, N. (1898). The dynamogenic factors in pacemaking and competition. *American Journal of Psychology, 9*, 507–533.

Trivers, R.L. (1971). The evolution of reciprocal altruism. *Quarterly Review of Biology, 46*, 35–57.

Trivers, R.L. (1972). Parental investment and sexual selection. In B. Campbell (ed.), *Sexual selection and the descent of man, 1871–1971*, pp. 136–179. Chicago: Aldine.

Valentine, C.W. (1930). The psychology of imitation with special reference to early childhood. *British Journal of Psychology, 21*, 105–132.

Vucinich, A. (1963/1970). *Science in Russian culture, 1861–1917*. Stanford, CA: Stanford University Press.

Vygotsky, L.S. (1934/1986). *Thought and language*, trans. A. Kozulin. Cambridge, MA: Harvard University Press.

Ward, J. (1886). Psychology. *Encyclopaedia Britannica*, 9th edn., vol. XX. Edinburgh: Black.

Washburn, M.F. (1908). *The animal mind*. London: Macmillan.

Washburn, S.L. and Strum, S.C. (1972). Concluding comments. In S.L. Washburn and P. Dolhinow (ed.), *Perspectives on human evolution*, vol. II, pp. 469–491. New York: Holt, Rinehart, and Winston.

Watson, J.B. (1913). Psychology as the behaviorist views it. *Psychological Review, 20*, 158–177.

Watson, J.B. (1914). *Behavior: An introduction to comparative psychology*. New York: Holt.

Watson, J.B. (1919). *Psychology from the standpoint of a behaviorist*. Philadelphia: Lippincott.

Watson, J.B. (1924). *Behaviorism*. Chicago: University of Chicago Press.

Watson, J.B. (1928). *Psychological care of infant and child*. New York: Norton.

Watson, J.B. and Rayner, R. (1920). Conditioned emotional reactions. *Journal of Experimental Psychology, 3*, 1–14.

Watt, H.J. (1905). Experimentelle Beiträge zu einer Theorie des Denkens. *Archiv für die gesamte Psychologie, 4*, 289–436. (English trans., 1929: *Journal of Anatomy and Physiology, 40*, 257–266.)

Weber, E.H. (1834/1905). *Der Tastsinn und das Gemeingefühl*. Leipzig: Engelmann.

Wegener, D.M. and Bargh, J.A. (1998). Control and automaticity in social life. In Gilbert et al., *Handbook of social psychology*, vol. I, pp. 446–496.

Weiner, B. and Graham, S. (1999). Attribution in personality psychology. In Pervin and John, *Handbook of personality: Theory and research*, pp. 605–628.

Wertheimer, M. (1912). Experimentelle Studien über das Sehen von Bewegung. *Zeitschrift für Psychologie, 60*, 321–378.

Wertheimer, M. (1922). Untersuchungen zur Lehre von der Gestalt. I. Prinzipielle Bemerkungen. *Psychologische Forschung, 1*, 47–58.

Wertheimer, M. (1945). *Productive thinking*. New York: Harper.

Wertheimer, M. (1978). Humanistic psychology and the humane but tough-minded psychologist. *American Psychologist, 33*, 739–745.

Wertheimer, M. (1998). Two views of psychology: A study of a science. *Contemporary Psychology, 43*(1), 7–10.

Westen, D. and Gabbard, G.O. (1999). Psychoanalytic approaches to personality. In Pervin and John, *Handbook of personality*, pp. 57–101.

Wiebe, D.J. and Smith, T.W. (1997). Personality and health: Progress and problems in psychosomatics. In Hogan et al., *Handbook of personality*, pp. 891–918.

Wiener, N. (1948). *Cybernetics*. New York: John Wiley & Sons.

Wiggins, J.S. (1997). In defence of traits. In Hogan et al., *Handbook of personality*, pp. 97–115.

Wiggins, J.S. and Trapnell, P.D. (1997). Personality structure: The return of the Big Five. In Hogan et al., *Handbook of personality*, pp. 737–765.

Williams, G.C. (1966). *Adaptation and natural selection.* Princeton, NJ: Princeton University Press.

Wilson, E.O. (1975). *Sociobiology: The new synthesis.* Cambridge, MA: Harvard University Press, Belknap Press.

Winter, D.G. and Barenbaum, N.B. (1999). History of modern personality theory and research. In Pervin and John, *Handbook of personality*, pp. 230–250.

Wolpe, J. (1958). *Psychotherapy by reciprocal inhibitions.* Stanford, CA: Stanford University Press.

Woodworth, R.S. (1918). *Dynamic psychology.* New York: Columbia University Press.

Woodworth, R.S. (1921). *Psychology: A study of mental life.* New York: Holt.

Woodworth, R.S. (1931). *Contemporary schools of psychology.* New York: Ronald Press.

Woodworth, R.S. (1938). *Experimental psychology.* New York: Holt.

Woodworth, R.S. (1958). *Dynamics of Behavior.* New York: Holt, Rinehart & Winston.

Woodworth, R.S. and Schlosberg, H. (1954). *Experimental psychology*, rev. edn. New York: Henry Holt.

Woodworth, R.S. and Sheehan, M.R. (1965). *Experimental psychology*, rev. edn. London: Methuen.

World Health Organization (1992). *The ICD-10 international classification of mental and behavioral disorders.* Geneva: WHO.

Wundt, W. (1858–1862). *Beiträge zur Theorie der Sinneswahrnehmung* (English trans., 1987: *Contributions to the theory of sense perception.* Washington, DC: American Institute for Psychological Research.) Leipzig: Winter.

Wundt, W. (1863). *Vorlesungen über die Menschen- und Thierseele.* Leipzig: Voss. (English trans., 1894: *Lectures on human and animal psychology.* New York: Macmillan.)

Wundt, W. (1873–1874). *Grundzüge der physiologischen Psychologie.* Leipzig: Engelmann. (Further editions in 1880, 1887, 1893, 1902–03, and 1908–11; English trans., Titchener, 1904: *Principles of physiological psychology.* New York: Macmillan.)

Wundt, W. (1880–1883). *Logik: Eine Untersuchung der Principien der Erkenntnis und der Methoden Wissenschaftlicher Forschung.* Stuttgart: Enke. (English trans., 1880–1883: *Logic: An investigation into the principles of knowledge and the methods of scientific research.* New York: Macmillan.)

Wundt, W. (1896a). *Grundriss der Psychologie.* Leipzig: Engelmann. (English trans., 1907: *Outlines of psychology.* Leipzig: Engelmann.)

Wundt, W. (1896b). Über die Definition der Psychologie. *Philosophische Studien, 12,* 1–66.

Wundt, W. (1900–1920). *Völkerpsychologie*, vols. I–X. Leipzig: Engelmann.

Wundt, W. (1907). Über Ausfrageexperimente und über die Methoden zur Psychologie des Denkens. *Psychologische Studien, 3,* 301–360.

Wundt, W. (1920). *Erlebtes und Erkanntes.* Stuttgart: Kröner.

Zajonc, R.B. (1998). Emotions. In Gilbert et al., *Handbook of social psychology*, vol. I, pp. 591–632.

Zeigarnik, B. (1927). Das Behalten erledigter und unerledigter Handlungen. *Psychologische Forschung, 9,* 1–85.

Zeki, S. (1993). *A Vision of the brain.* Oxford, UK: Blackwell.

Index